Unlocking Life Satisfaction in Digital Global Markets and Segments

Theodore Tarnanidis
https://orcid.org/0000-0002-4836-3906
International Hellenic University, Greece

Vijaya Kittu Manda
https://orcid.org/0000-0002-1680-8210
PBMEIT, India

IGI Global
Scientific Publishing
Publishing Tomorrow's Research Today

Vice President of Editorial — Melissa Wagner
Director of Acquisitions — Mikaela Felty
Director of Book Development — Jocelynn Hessler
Production Manager — Mike Brehm
Cover Design — Jose Rosado

Published in the United States of America by
IGI Global Scientific Publishing
701 East Chocolate Avenue
Hershey, PA, 17033, USA
Tel: 717-533-8845 | Fax: 717-533-7115
Website: https://www.igi-global.com E-mail: cust@igi-global.com

Library of Congress Cataloging-in-Publication Data

Names: Tarnanidis, Theodore, 1977- editor | Manda, Vijaya Kittu, 1980- editor
Title: Unlocking life satisfaction in digital global markets and segments / edited by: Theodore Tarnanidis, Vijaya Kittu Manda.
Description: Hershey PA : IGI Global Scientific Publishing, [2027] | Includes bibliographical references. | Summary: "This book examines how digital transformation shapes consumer behavior, well-being, and life satisfaction across global markets. Integrating marketing, psychology, and ethics, it offers frameworks and measurement models to understand and enhance human-centered value, happiness, and community connection in digital ecosystems"-- Provided by publisher.
Identifiers: LCCN 2026003210 (print) | LCCN 2026003211 (ebook) | ISBN 9798337383576 hardcover | ISBN 9798337383583 paperback | ISBN 9798337383590 ebook
Subjects: LCSH: Technological innovations--Social aspects
Classification: LCC HM846 .U55 2026 (print) | LCC HM846 (ebook)
LC record available at https://lccn.loc.gov/2026003210
LC ebook record available at https://lccn.loc.gov/2026003211

British Cataloguing in Publication Data
A Cataloguing in Publication record for this book is available from the British Library.

Editorial Advisory Board

Table of Contents

Detailed Table of Contents

This chapter examines the impact of Artificial Intelligence (AI) on the future of marketing education, emphasizing the importance of life satisfaction and well-being outcomes for both students and faculty. Drawing on recent literature, the chapter proposes an evaluation framework that emphasizes life satisfaction and human well-being as central outcomes of AI-enabled marketing education. The chapter integrates Expectancy-Value Theory, Self-Determination Theory, and emerging AI-literacy research with evidence from marketing, education, and psychology journals to examine the impact of artificial intelligence on autonomy, competence, trust, and ethical judgment. In marketing education, assessing this impact is a priority. The chapter ends with the possibility that future research agendas may focus on curriculum design, faculty development, and related areas.

Satisfaction with digital life is a complicated result of psychological needs, ethical design preferences, and a more comprehensive economic setting that connects individuals to platforms. In this chapter, the authors discuss the experiences of autonomy, competence, and belonging to social relations as the foundation of the positive use of digital technologies and reflect on the design practices that encourage well-being instead of manipulating the attention of users. It further describes the architecture of human-centric digital markets that balance commercial interests with user prosperity via transparency, choice structure, and participative governance. It concludes that forging meaningful collaboration among designers, policymakers, educators, and communities is necessary to construct trustworthy digital futures that foster creativity, protect agency, and guarantee equitable access to the social and economic benefits of technology.

Digital markets have transformed global commerce, yet many platforms prioritize technological efficiency over human well-being and user experience. This chapter examines the theoretical foundations and practical implementations of human-centered design principles in digital market ecosystems. Through systematic analysis of consumer psychology, platform economics, and ethical frameworks, we explore how organizations can create digital marketplaces that enhance life satisfaction while maintaining commercial viability. The research synthesizes current literature on digital transformation, consumer behavior, and human-computer interaction to propose a comprehensive model for human-centered digital markets. Key findings indicate that platforms integrating user well-being metrics, transparent algorithmic decision-making, and participatory design methodologies demonstrate superior long-term customer retention and market sustainability.

The study explores how the integration of online and offline life influences subjective well-being and happiness. Positive emotions, meaning, gratitude, and pro-social digital engagement enhance long-term happiness, while materialism and social comparison diminish it. Workplace platforms like Microsoft Teams and digital health interventions can support well-being when autonomy, competence, and relatedness are fulfilled, though digital fatigue and inequality remain key challenges. Digital well-being depends on purposeful, inclusive technology use that strengthens autonomy, connection, and balance between online and offline life.

instrument with a scalable quantitative basis to support the research of human-driven digital market design and global digital well-being.

This chapter discuss the role of cultural frameworks and their effects on digital life satisfaction and happiness in general in the current globalized world. Technological change affects communications, education, health, and leisure, and there are many critical questions surrounding the effects of technological change on happiness and psychological wellness. Technologically, there is connectivity and engagement, but there are challenges faced in the matter of too much information, privacy, and stress. Based on cultural psychology, studies in technology, and the study of happiness, this chapter will explore cross-cultural variations in digital experiences, including cultural norms, economy, and global trends in cultures around the world the Middle East, North Africa, Europe, Africa, Asia, and the America.

This chapter explores the metaverse as a psychosocial ecosystem that blends technology, culture, and emotion to shape digital life satisfaction. Drawing on Self-Determination Theory and Flow Theory, it proposes and tests a conceptual model using Structural Equation Modeling (SEM) across diverse cultural contexts. Data from 600 metaverse users across North America, Europe, and Asia-Pacific reveal that psychological need fulfillment (autonomy, competence, relatedness) and flow significantly mediate the relationship between digital engagement and life satisfaction. Cultural orientation moderates these effects, showing that collectivist and individualist values shape the paths to well-being differently. The findings provide theoretical insights into digital transformation and practical guidance for user-centered design, policymaking, and ethical platform development in immersive virtual environments.

Digital tools now shape how people pick products worldwide. Not only do online stores offer endless choices, but they also track user behaviour to suggest items. From TikTok shops to streaming plans, what users see gets tailored without them noticing. Because algorithms learn preferences, decisions feel easier - yet sometimes less conscious. Even when choice seems broader, hidden patterns guide attention behind the scenes. Though more access sounds beneficial, some studies point to mental fatigue instead. With every click shaping future suggestions, control might be more illusion than reality. What looks like freedom could quietly narrow perspectives over time. Global reach means cultural differences blend into one shopping flow. Behind convenience lies a shift in who really influences each purchase.

This chapter examines how consumption practices embedded in digital ecosystems reshape consumer behavior and long-term life satisfaction. Drawing on the classical Diderot Effect, the chapter introduces the concept of the Digital Diderot Effect to explain how ecosystem dependence, algorithmic recommendation systems, and platform design intensify cascading consumption cycles in digital markets. The chapter conceptualizes digital ecosystems as structures that actively guide consumption through technical lock-in, economic dependency, and psychological habituation, transforming isolated purchase decisions into continuous consumption processes. It further discusses how these dynamics contribute to hedonic adaptation, decision fatigue, and diminished psychological autonomy, despite short-term gains in convenience and satisfaction. The chapter reframes digital consumption as a multi-criteria decision-making problem and proposes a normative evaluation framework integrating technical compatibility, cognitive load, financial sustainability, autonomy, and life satisfaction.

Preface

The modern world connects people through screens. However, true happiness often feels distant within these digital spaces. This situation is fueling scholars to examine how technology shapes our daily lives and influences the deep sense of satisfaction we seek. This book explores the complex relationship between global markets and the personal fulfillment found in online environments today. Understanding these dynamics requires a fresh perspective on how consumers interact with platforms across different cultural boundaries worldwide. This journey begins by acknowledging that digital tools should serve human needs rather than dictate the pace of existence. We aim to bridge the gap between technological advancement and the enduring global quest for meaningful human connection.

Central to our discussion is the idea that markets must prioritize human experiences over mere market shares, financial gains, or other efficiency metrics. Designing systems with people in mind ensures that technology enhances life rather than creating stress or confusion for users. This book offers a glimpse of how ethical design principles can guide the development of platforms that respect individual autonomy and dignity. It is crucial to consider how digital environments affect mental health and emotional resilience in various global communities. By focusing on human-centered approaches, we can create digital spaces that foster genuine well-being and long-term satisfaction for everyone. This shift requires collaboration between researchers, policymakers, and industry leaders to build a more compassionate digital future together.

Consumer psychology plays a vital role in understanding why people choose certain products within the vast online marketplace ecosystem. The book investigates the emotional drivers behind buying decisions and how these choices significantly impact overall life satisfaction. Impulsive behaviors often arise from targeted advertising, yet understanding these triggers helps us promote healthier consumption habits globally. The paradox of choice suggests that too many options can reduce happiness, a phenomenon prevalent in modern digital retail sectors. The analysis examines how personalization algorithms shape identity and self-perception among users navigating complex virtual shopping environments. Balancing commercial interests with psychological well-being is essential for sustainable growth in today's evolving global digital economy.

Measuring well-being in digital contexts requires new tools that go beyond traditional economic indicators, such as gross domestic product figures. The book proposes integrated models that capture the nuances of subjective happiness across hyperconnected societies and national borders. Developing a global index allows us to track progress and identify areas where digital life satisfaction urgently needs improvement. Statistical methods help us validate these measures, ensuring that our findings reflect the actual experiences of diverse populations worldwide. Data-driven insights provide a foundation for policies that support mental health and reduce digital overload in competitive market environments. Ultimately, accurate measurement is the first step toward creating meaningful change in how we value human flourishing online.

OVERVIEW OF THE BOOK

Chapter 1: Modeling Human-Centered Artificial Intelligence in Marketing Education

This chapter examines the impact of Artificial Intelligence (AI) on the future of marketing education, emphasizing the importance of life satisfaction and well-being outcomes for both students and faculty. Drawing on recent literature, the chapter proposes an evaluation framework that emphasizes life satisfaction and human well-being as central outcomes of AI-enabled marketing education. The chapter integrates Expectancy-Value Theory, Self-Determination Theory, and emerging AI-literacy research with evidence from marketing, education, and psychology journals to examine the impact of artificial intelligence on autonomy, competence, trust, and ethical judgment. In marketing education, assessing this impact is a priority. The chapter ends with the possibility that future research agendas may focus on curriculum design, faculty development, and related areas.

Chapter 2: Digital Life Satisfaction-Psychological Drivers, Ethical Design, and Global Pathways to Human-Centred Digital Markets

Satisfaction with digital life is a complicated result of psychological needs, ethical design preferences, and a more comprehensive economic setting that connects individuals to platforms. In this chapter, the authors discuss the experiences of autonomy, competence, and belonging to social relations as the foundation of the positive use of digital technologies and reflect on the design practices that encourage well-being instead of manipulating the attention of users. It further describes the architecture of human-centric digital markets that balance commercial interests with user prosperity via transparency, choice structure, and participative governance. It concludes that forging meaningful collaboration among designers, policymakers, educators, and communities is necessary to construct trustworthy digital futures that foster creativity, protect agency, and guarantee equitable access to the social and economic benefits of technology.

Chapter 3: Building Human-Centered Digital Markets

Digital markets have transformed global commerce, yet many platforms prioritize technological efficiency over human well-being and user experience. This chapter examines the theoretical foundations and practical implementations of human-centered design principles in digital market ecosystems. Through systematic analysis of consumer psychology, platform economics, and ethical frameworks, we explore how organizations can create digital marketplaces that enhance life satisfaction while maintaining commercial viability. The research synthesizes current literature on digital transformation, consumer behavior, and human-computer interaction to propose a comprehensive model for human-centered digital markets. Key findings indicate that platforms integrating user well-being metrics, transparent algorithmic decision-making, and participatory design methodologies demonstrate superior long-term customer retention and market sustainability.

Chapter 4: From Offline Happiness to Online Fulfilment: Understanding Life Satisfaction in Digital Spaces

The study explores how the integration of online and offline life influences subjective well-being and happiness. Positive emotions, meaning, gratitude, and pro-social digital engagement enhance long-term happiness, while materialism and social comparison diminish it. Workplace platforms like Microsoft Teams and digital health interventions can support well-being when autonomy, competence, and relatedness are fulfilled, though digital fatigue and inequality remain key challenges. Digital well-being depends on purposeful, inclusive technology use that strengthens autonomy, connection, and balance between online and offline life.

Chapter 5: An Integrated Model for Measuring Digital Well Being & Life Satisfaction in the Global Digital Ecosystem

The rapid expansion of digital technologies has fundamentally transformed human behavior, social interaction, and overall quality of life, making digital well-being a critical determinant of life satisfaction in the contemporary global digital ecosystem. This chapter proposes an integrated conceptual model that examines the multidimensional relationship between digital well-being and life satisfaction by incorporating psychological, social, technological, and behavioral factors. It explores how digital usage patterns, online social connectivity, mental and emotional health, privacy concerns, and digital stress collectively influence individual perceptions of well-being and satisfaction with life.

Chapter 6: Developing a Global Digital Life Satisfaction Index (DLSI) Using a Multi-Criteria Optimization and Structural Equation Modeling Framework.

This research builds a Global Digital Life Satisfaction Index (DLSI) to objectively assess the level of life satisfaction in digital international markets. The index combines multidimensional indicators of digital well-being which entail economic, psychological, technological, and institutional aspects. Multi-criteria optimization techniques are used to normalize, weight and aggregate heterogeneous indicators which have robustness and comparability across digital ecosystems. The validation of latent constructs and causal relationships between digital trust, autonomy, access, and subjective satisfaction are tested by Structural Equation Modeling. The proposed DLSI offers a cross-market evaluation, policy analysis, and strategizing analytical instrument with a scalable quantitative basis to support the research of human-driven digital market design and global digital well-being.

Chapter 7: Cross-Cultural Digital Well-Being Determinants, Frameworks, and Policy

This chapter discuss the role of cultural frameworks and their effects on digital life satisfaction and happiness in general in the current globalized world. Technological change affects communications, education, health, and leisure, and there are many critical questions surrounding the effects of technological change on happiness and psychological wellness. Technologically, there is connectivity and engagement, but there are challenges faced in the matter of too much information, privacy, and stress. Based on cultural psychology, studies in technology, and the study of happiness, this chapter will explore cross-cultural variations in digital experiences, including cultural norms, economy, and global trends in cultures around the world the Middle East, North Africa, Europe, Africa, Asia, and the America.

Chapter 8: The Metaverse as a Space of Happiness_Cross Cultural Determinants of Digital Life Satisfaction in Global Markets

This chapter explores the metaverse as a psychosocial ecosystem that blends technology, culture, and emotion to shape digital life satisfaction. Drawing on Self-Determination Theory and Flow Theory, it proposes and tests a conceptual model using Structural Equation Modeling (SEM) across diverse cultural contexts. Data from 600 metaverse users across North America, Europe, and Asia-Pacific reveal that psychological need fulfillment (autonomy, competence, relatedness) and flow significantly mediate the relationship between digital engagement and life satisfaction. Cultural orientation moderates these effects, showing that collectivist and individualist values shape the paths to well-being differently. The findings provide theoretical insights into digital transformation and practical guidance for user-centered design, policymaking, and ethical platform development in immersive virtual environments.

Chapter 9: The Paradox of Choice and Personalization in Digital Global Markets: Impacts on Consumer Life Satisfaction

Digital tools now shape how people pick products worldwide. Not only do online stores offer endless choices, but they also track user behaviour to suggest items. From TikTok shops to streaming plans, what users see gets tailored without them noticing. Because algorithms learn preferences, decisions feel easier - yet sometimes less conscious. Even when choice seems broader, hidden patterns guide attention behind the scenes. Though more access sounds beneficial, some studies point to mental fatigue instead. With every click shaping future suggestions, control might be more illusion than reality. What looks like freedom could quietly narrow perspectives over time. Global reach means cultural differences blend into one shopping flow. Behind convenience lies a shift in who really influences each purchase.

Chapter 10: The Digital Diderot Effect - Ecosystem Dependence, Consumption Cycles, and Life Satisfaction

This chapter examines how consumption practices embedded in digital ecosystems reshape consumer behavior and long-term life satisfaction. Drawing on the classical Diderot Effect, the chapter introduces the concept of the Digital Diderot

Effect to explain how ecosystem dependence, algorithmic recommendation systems, and platform design intensify cascading consumption cycles in digital markets. The chapter conceptualizes digital ecosystems as structures that actively guide consumption through technical lock-in, economic dependency, and psychological habituation, transforming isolated purchase decisions into continuous consumption processes. It further discusses how these dynamics contribute to hedonic adaptation, decision fatigue, and diminished psychological autonomy, despite short-term gains in convenience and satisfaction. The chapter reframes digital consumption as a multi-criteria decision-making problem and proposes a normative evaluation framework integrating technical compatibility, cognitive load, financial sustainability, autonomy, and life satisfaction.

Chapter 11: Digital Ethics, Data Justice, and Human Autonomy

Digital technologies pervade modern life, raising critical questions about ethics, justice, and human autonomy. This chapter examines the intersection of digital ethics, data justice, and human autonomy in the context of life satisfaction within digital global markets. Drawing on contemporary frameworks and empirical research, the chapter explores how ethical principles govern digital technology development, how data justice ensures equitable access and protection, and how human autonomy is preserved in increasingly algorithmic environments. The analysis reveals tensions between technological advancement and fundamental human rights, highlighting the need for comprehensive governance frameworks. Key findings demonstrate that digital well-being and life satisfaction depend on balanced approaches to privacy protection, algorithmic fairness, and inclusive digital participation.

Chapter 12: Life Satisfaction in Digital Retail - A Human-Centered Analysis of E-Commerce Experience, Trust, and Emotional Engagement

The soaring development of digital retail transformed the purchasing patterns of people and, to a greater extent, the daily experiences of life. In addition to convenience and efficiency, the online shopping platforms have become an important factor in the emotional state, perception of trust, and overall life satisfaction of the consumers. With the digital marketplace increasingly adopting the most innovative technologies, there is an increasing desire to learn about these platforms not as a system of transactions only, but more as an environment of human interaction that has an effect on the well-being of consumers. This paper will discuss the role of digital retail experience in improving life satisfaction through the lenses of quality of experience, emotional involvement, trust, and relationship development in the long-term. . In general, the paper highlights that to measure the success of digital retail, it is essential to consider its impact on the economic performance, as well as, its role in promoting trust, emotional well-being, and satisfaction with life.

Chapter 13: Digital Social Media Experience Perceived Digital Brand Meaning Digital Presence & Social Embeddedness and Digital Life Satisfaction: A Cross-Cultural Perspective

The frequent use of social media in everyday life has modified the communication used by marketers to communicate with one another. They now do not exchange just promotions online, but they indulge in immersive and relationship-based online interactions that have a huge impact on the health of people. This paper looks at the understanding of digital brand meaning, digital presence and social embeddedness and how they combine to create digital life satisfaction that eventually creates a long-lasting brand loyalty. The chapter reevaluates now the concept of social media marketing differently than the conventional metrics involving its performance. The prospective implications of the study, which is based on the psychological importance, digital life satisfaction, and the impact of cultural values on brand perception and brand creation, will offer fundamental details on the future research. The SDGs 4 (Quality Education), 8 (Decent Work and Economic Growth), and 9 (Industry, Innovation and Infrastructure) are supported by the literature review presented in this chapter.

Chapter 14: Augmented Self in Hyper-Personalized E-Commerce: Exploring Longitudinal Effects of AI-driven Digital Retail on Life Satisfaction and Identity Coheren

This paper explores how AI-based hyper-personalization of e-commerce has been affected over time on augmented self, identity coherence and life satisfaction among the young adults in Indian metropolitan cities. Digital platforms contribute to creating improved identities due to predictive algorithms that can empower individuals at the expense of losing autonomy and constructing discontinuous self-accounts. The research uses 12-month longitudinal research design based on self-determination theory and extended self-frameworks. The 307 participants (18-35 years) of the survey were used as data to complete quarterly surveys on the validated ASHPE scale, identity coherence, agency, emotional well-being and life satisfaction. Latent growth modeling and fsQCA show promising results with good coherence and agency but well-being going down with excessive individualization. Results are in favour of human oriented AI regulations and policy interventions.

Chapter 15: Digital Platforms and Sustainable Financial Behavior: Pathways to Financial Well-Being and Life Satisfaction

The significance of digital financial platforms in encouraging sustainable financial conduct and improving life satisfaction is examined in this chapter. It offers an integrated conceptual framework that connects responsible spending, disciplined saving, cautious borrowing, and ESG-aligned investment practices with digital platform elements including nudges, gamification, personalisation, and embedded financial education. The chapter emphasises how sustainable financial conduct mediates the relationship between platform participation and financial well-being, which in turn adds to subjective life satisfaction. It does this by drawing on frameworks for financial well-being, behavioural finance, and self-determination theory. Platform design, digital marketing strategies, consumer protection, and regulatory issues are among the ethical, managerial, and policy ramifications that are covered. Additionally, the chapter highlights issues including algorithmic bias, behavioural risks, and greenwashing and suggests directions for further empirical study.

Chapter 16: Digital Reverse Logistics and Urban Life Satisfaction in Sustainable Automobile Digital Service Markets

The rapid expansion of automobile service workshops in urban centres has intensified waste generation, environmental stress, and operational inefficiencies, particularly in emerging economies. Simultaneously, digital transformation has reshaped market ecosystems, influencing not only performance but also human well-being and life satisfaction. This work examines how digitally enabled sustainable reverse logistics practices contribute to waste minimisation, cost efficiency, and collective well-being within the urban automobile service sector. It focuses on the link between DRL and human well-being. The objective of this study is to develop a conceptual framework that illustrates this link. The findings propose a novel, human-centred DRL framework. The study highlights how digital tools for waste recovery can enhance environmental conditions and improve the perceived quality of urban life. The findings have direct implications for policymakers, researchers, and practitioners seeking to align digital transformation strategies with human-centric sustainability goals.

Chapter 17: Digital Health and Emotional Resilience in Global Markets: Attention Restoration and Cultural Integration Pathways

Digital markets transform consumer psychology, through connectivity that threatens well-being. This chapter studies the impact of digital engagement on life satisfaction through Attention Restoration Theory, Self-Determination Theory, and cross-cultural frameworks. Uninterrupted digital exposure exhausts cognitive resources via attention demands, social comparison, and information overload. Emotional resilience mediates these effects. The analysis integrates Western coping strategies with Eastern equanimity practices, recognizing how individualist-collectivist orientations shape digital behaviors. A multidimensional framework measures attention quality, emotional regulation, autonomy, resilience capacity, and satisfaction across populations. Evidence-based interventions include mindfulness practices, ethical platform design, workplace policies, and regulatory frameworks. It provides academics, practitioners, marketers, and policymakers with actionable frameworks tailored to their needs. These tools enable building ethical digital ecosystems that enhance global well-being.

Artificial intelligence brings powerful capabilities, but it also raises serious ethical questions regarding privacy and data justice for all. We must address how algorithms can perpetuate bias, affecting vulnerable groups who rely on digital services for daily needs. Building trust requires transparency into how automated systems make decisions that markedly influence consumer lives and financial security. Responsible innovation means ensuring that technology serves the public good without compromising individual rights or personal autonomy levels. The metaverse presents new governance challenges, requiring frameworks that protect users from harm in immersive virtual spaces. Ethical considerations must be embedded into the core of marketing strategies to foster inclusivity and equity in digital markets.

Cultural differences shape how individuals perceive happiness and interact with technology in their specific local contexts and regions. Chapters in the book explore cross-cultural determinants of well-being to understand what drives satisfaction across diverse societies worldwide. Policies must be adaptable, respecting local values while promoting universal standards for digital health and global emotional resilience. Emerging markets offer unique insights into how digital transformation affects life satisfaction across populations with diverse economic backgrounds. Inclusive development ensures that gender and other social factors are considered when designing digital solutions for broader communities. Recognizing these nuances helps us build a more equitable global ecosystem where everyone can thrive digitally and personally.

Sustainable practices are increasingly linked to consumer satisfaction, as people seek out brands that align with their environmental values. Green technologies and circular economies offer pathways to financial well-being that support both planetary health and human happiness levels. We examine how digital platforms can encourage responsible consumption without sacrificing the convenience that users expect from services. The future of retail depends on integrating sustainability into the core experience, fostering trust and loyalty among conscious consumers. Long-term success requires balancing profit motives with the urgent need to protect our shared environment for future generations. This book highlights strategies for achieving this balance, ensuring that digital growth contributes positively to global sustainability goals.

The book's collective goal is to unlock life satisfaction by reimagining how digital markets serve human needs in meaningful ways. We invite readers to join this conversation and help build a digital world that prioritizes well-being above all. The insights within these pages offer a roadmap for researchers and practitioners committed to positive change in society. Together, we can shape a future where technology enhances life rather than diminishing the quality of human experience globally. Let this work inspire action toward creating digital ecosystems that are safe, inclusive, and fulfilling for every individual user. The journey toward digital happiness begins now, with a shared commitment to understanding and improving our connected lives.

Theodore Tarnanidis
International Hellenic University, Greece

Vijaya Kittu Manda
PBMEIT, India

Acknowledgment

This publication is an important reference source for academics and researchers, undergraduate students, postgraduate students, consultants, technology developers and policymakers interested in exploring the challenges of unlocking life satisfaction in digital global markets and segments. We are confident that this book will be essential for readers to upgrade their current work and education.

We would like to express our gratitude to all those who contributed to this project, particularly the authors and reviewers who took part in the evaluation process. Their help was instrumental in the success of this book. We express our sincere appreciation to the chapter writers who contributed their time and knowledge to this book from all over the world. Thank you to all the peer reviewers for their valuable ideas that have improved the quality, coherence, and substance of the chapters. We are thankful to the writers who gave up their time to act as reviewers. This book would not have been possible without the production staff at IGI Global. Throughout this process, they were extremely helpful and encouraging and provided the highest level of service. The work of many individuals goes into publishing a successful book, not just those who are acknowledged as authors or editors.

Theodore Tarnanidis
International Hellenic University, Greece

Vijaya Kittu Manda
PBMEIT, India

Chapter 1
Modeling Human-Centered Artificial Intelligence in Marketing Education

Theodore Tarnanidis
http://orcid.org/0000-0002-4836-3906
International Hellenic University, Greece

Vijaya Kittu Manda
http://orcid.org/0000-0002-1680-8210
PBMEIT, India

Bruno Barbosa Sousa
http://orcid.org/0000-0002-8588-2422
Polytechnic University of Cávado and Ave, Portugal & UNIAG, Portugal

ABSTRACT

This chapter examines the impact of Artificial Intelligence (AI) on the future of marketing education, emphasizing the importance of life satisfaction and well-being outcomes for both students and faculty. Drawing on recent literature, the chapter proposes an evaluation framework that emphasizes life satisfaction and human well-being as central outcomes of AI-enabled marketing education. The chapter integrates Expectancy-Value Theory, Self-Determination Theory, and emerging AI-literacy research with evidence from marketing, education, and psychology journals to examine the impact of artificial intelligence on autonomy, competence, trust,

DOI: 10.4018/979-8-3373-8357-6.ch001

and ethical judgment. In marketing education, assessing this impact is a priority. The chapter ends with the possibility that future research agendas may focus on curriculum design, faculty development, and related areas.

1. INTRODUCTION

Scholarship on Artificial Intelligence (AI) in marketing education has increased rapidly. However, existing research remains fragmented and uneven in its focus on both conceptual and empirical aspects. Technology capability, pedagogical innovation, employability outcomes, and instructional efficiency have been the predominant focus of previous studies on AI (Al Issa & Maheshwari, 2025; Schlegelmilch & Mills, 2025; Yu et al., 2025). These contributions significantly advanced our understanding of how AI influences curricula, assessment, and faculty roles. However, to date, they have underestimated the human outcomes of AI integration. It is especially true when it comes to enhancing life satisfaction and well-being among students and educators. Specifically, the current literature exposes four crucial gaps. Although psychological outcomes, such as anxiety, trust, or motivation, are increasingly acknowledged in studies, life satisfaction and well-being are rarely considered central dependent variables. Instead, they are only peripheral or implicit concerns (Schneider & Haried, 2024; Yu et al., 2025). In marketing education, research on AI is primarily instrumental. It is focusing on its potential rather than its impact on learners and faculty in cognitive, emotional, and ethical dimensions. Researchers have widely discussed ethical challenges, including bias, academic integrity, and transparency. However, their connection to satisfaction, trust, and perceived fairness in educational contexts is significant. It is not sufficiently integrated into coherence frameworks (Schlegelmilch & Mills, 2025). Lastly, there is a lack of research that connects AI-enabled marketing education with its downstream societal implications.

The core research gap identified is as follows: What remains critically underexplored is the direct impact of integrating AI in marketing education on the life satisfaction and well-being of students and educators. This gap is especially pressing now and requires urgent attention. AI adoption is accelerating unimaginably. It raises urgent questions about the human and ethical consequences beyond efficiency and employability. Amidst this backdrop, focusing specifically on marketing education is vital. The discipline sits at the intersection of technology, consumer behavior, and ethical practice. In this context, AI's role is both transformative and contentious. Without a human-centered framework, AI integration risks undermining autonomy, competence, and long-term fulfillment. These elements are essential for both effective marketing professionals and meaningful educational experiences.

In the age of AI, this chapter presents a human-centered perspective on marketing education that focuses on human well-being, addressing these gaps. Thus, life satisfaction (LS) is the primary criterion used in this chapter. It helps assess the success and sustainability of AI integration in marketing education, rather than solely evaluating it as a technological or pedagogical innovation. As a result, our goal in this work is to expand the discussions about AI in marketing education beyond efficiency and employability. It emphasizes the impact - faculty identity, student well-being, and long-term professional fulfillment. It emphasizes the impact on faculty identity, student well-being, and long-term professional fulfillment. For instance, generative AI has been successfully used as a career coach to help students explore pathways. They align personal experiences with professional goals, building confidence in job search tasks. This demonstrates its potential to support meaningful career development and reduce anxiety related to future events (Flink et al., 2025). Moreover, it proposes future research directions and practical recommendations. These support an AI adoption approach that prioritizes human well-being, ethics, and marketing education. By focusing on the above objectives, the chapter contributes to the literature on marketing education. It reframes AI not merely as an instructional technology but as a socio-technical system in its entirety.

2. LITERATURE REVIEW: LIFE SATISFACTION, AI, AND MARKETING EDUCATION

Life satisfaction is defined as how someone evaluates their overall quality of life cognitively (Sirgy, 2012). In the context of rapid technological change, life satisfaction is now more relevant than it was previously studied in psychology and sociology(Ehrhardt et al., 2000). Several studies have demonstrated that AI has a direct impact on life satisfaction through interactions between humans and AI. AI indirectly impacts through perceptions of automation, job displacement, and societal change (Hinks, 2024; Lissitsa & Chachashvili-Bolotin, 2016). This relationship is examined empirically by Hinks (2024) using data from 39 European countries in one of the most comprehensive ways possible. According to the study, individuals who consider AI and automation as threatening or harmful have significantly lower levels of life satisfaction. Even after controlling for income, employment status, education, and health, these findings remain robust. It suggests that attitudes toward AI have a significant influence on subjective well-being. Notably, the study demonstrates that societal narratives and institutional contexts influence perceptions of AI and life satisfaction. Evidence of this exists through cross-national variations.

Life satisfaction is a comprehensive assessment of a person's quality of life, as determined by their selected criteria (Diener, 1984; Diener et al., 1985; Mrad et al., 2025). By focusing on the subjective and evaluative nature of well-being, their research provides a valuable foundational lens. Life satisfaction is influenced by a wide array of domains, including health, relationships, work, and meaning in life. However, in marketing and consumer happiness contexts, this definition is at risk of narrowing life satisfaction to evaluations related to consumption. Life satisfaction can be achieved through AI in marketing education by functioning as a congruent, empowering, and ethically embedded learning partner. Without such alignment, AI is liable to replicate adverse effects and diminish autonomy. It can weaken self-concept and ultimately undermine student well-being.

3. MODELING HUMAN-CENTERED AI IN MARKETING EDUCATION

With this backdrop, this study proposes the Human-Centered AI in Marketing Education Model. The model is a conceptual framework that links AI integration to life satisfaction through core psychological and ethical mediators. The model identifies five core constructs: AI integration, autonomy, competence, ethics, and life satisfaction. All these are central to human well-being in educational contexts. AI integration is not merely the use of AI tools, but the intentional, pedagogically aligned embedding of AI into curriculum design, assessment, and faculty practice. When AI integration supports autonomy by enabling learners to choose, control, and direct their own learning, it promotes motivation and psychological well-being. Similarly, AI systems that provide timely, actionable feedback enhance students' sense of competence, a key predictor of life satisfaction (Ryan & Deci, 2000). Ethics serves as both a moderator and mediator: ethically grounded AI use strengthens trust, perceived fairness, and the legitimacy of AI as a learning partner. The model posits directional relationships: ethically informed AI integration → enhanced autonomy and competence → higher life satisfaction among students and educators.

These relationships are not universal; critical boundary conditions, including institutional context, AI literacy, and cultural norms, shape them. For instance, in institutions with strong governance and AI literacy programs, students are more likely to perceive AI as supportive rather than threatening. So, this move amplifies positive outcomes. Conversely, in low-literacy or ethically ambiguous environments, the same AI tools may erode autonomy. It increases anxiety and diminishes life satisfaction—even if technically advanced. Figure 1 briefly describes the model. Table 1 clearly maps the proposed relationships between AI integration, psychological/ethical mediators, and outcomes (such as life satisfaction), including moderating factors.

Figure 1. Core Concepts of the Human-Centered AI in Marketing Education Model

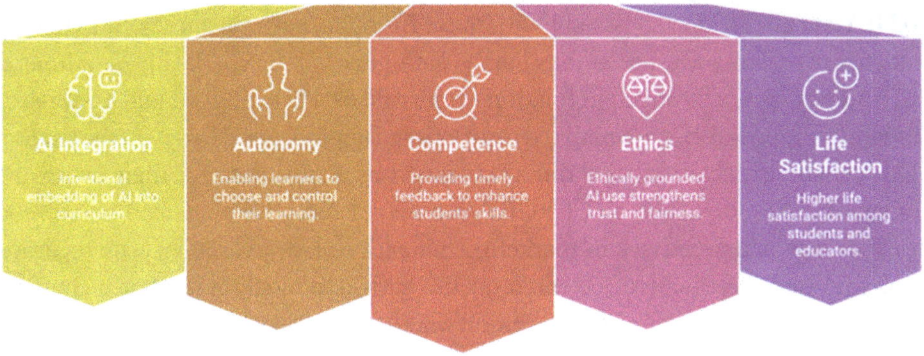

Source: Authors' creation

Table 1. Human-Centered AI in Marketing Education: Pathways to Life Satisfaction

Core Construct	Definition in Context	Proposed Relationship to Life Satisfaction	Key Moderators / Boundary Conditions
AI Integration	Intentional, pedagogically aligned embedding of AI into curriculum, assessment, and faculty practice.	Foundation for subsequent effects. The quality of integration determines whether pathways are positive or negative.	Institutional support, AI literacy programs, and pedagogical design.
Autonomy	Learners' sense of choice, control, and self-direction in AI-enhanced learning.	Positive: Supports intrinsic motivation and well-being. Negative: Eroded by opaque or controlling AI systems.	Cultural norms, instructional design, and transparency of AI tools.
Competence	Learners' perceived ability and mastery, enhanced by AI feedback and scaffolding.	Positive: Increases self-efficacy and satisfaction. Negative: Undermined by AI dependency or unfair assessment.	Quality of AI feedback, alignment with learning goals, and faculty guidance.
Ethics (Trust & Fairness)	Perceived ethical grounding of AI use (bias, transparency, accountability).	Serves as a critical mediator/ moderator. High trust amplifies the positive effects of autonomy/ competence.	Governance frameworks, ethical literacy, and algorithmic transparency.
Life Satisfaction	Cognitive evaluation of overall quality of life and well-being in the educational context.	Outcome Variable. Enhanced when AI supports autonomy, competence, and ethical trust.	Individual resilience, institutional culture, and broader societal narratives about AI.

Source: Authors' creation

The adoption of AI in education results in heterogeneous outcomes, as evidenced by recent empirical research. For example, according to relevant studies, personalization, perceived learning quality, and student motivation have improved (Manda et al., 2025), but anxiety risks have also increased (Grewal et al., 2025; Grewal et al., 2024; Yu et al., 2025). Consistent with these findings, a recent survey of marketing students revealed widespread familiarity with generative AI (Pavlov & Almanza, 2026). They have a strong appreciation for its role as a learning aid and an apparent demand for innovative, personalized instructional approaches. However, the students held realistic expectations and did not view AI as a substitute for their own work. Generative AI tools, such as ChatGPT, are associated with enhanced perceptions of efficiency and creativity in marketing education. However, concerns regarding academic integrity persist. Research on life satisfaction suggests that technology can enhance well-being only if it promotes autonomy and competence (Gaggioli et al., 2017; Huang & Rust, 2024; Steckermeier, 2021).

Additionally, researchers such as Schlegelmilch and Mills (2025) state that AI is a force that necessitates a 'full reimagining' of marketing education, rather than merely minor curriculum modifications. The importance of this framing lies in its positioning of AI as an intelligent partner that can create, analyze, and act independently, rather than just as a tool (Narang et al., 2025). Recent research further clarifies this shift by conceptualizing generative AI in marketing education as assuming three distinct roles: tutor, teammate, and tool. Each of these roles shapes cognitive, social, and teaching presence in the learning environment.

In terms of life satisfaction, there are two consequences of this shift. AI can have a positive impact on satisfaction and motivation. It is accomplished by reducing cognitive overload, automating routine tasks, and personalizing learning (Cillo & Rubera, 2025). On the other hand, AI can hurt in the form of anxiety, dependency, and loss of agency, especially when learners are displaced or monitored by algorithmic systems. We can argue that marketing education is no longer focused solely on traditional frameworks, such as segmentation, positioning, or customer journey mapping. Instead, it is increasingly about acquiring the skills to coexist, collaborate, and compete with intelligent systems while maintaining a personal and professional identity. A fundamental question for educators is raised by AI's ability to predict consumer behavior, generate content, and initiate marketing actions. Marketing graduates must cultivate unique human contributions to maintain both relevance and satisfaction in their careers (Allil, 2024).

Research in educational psychology consistently shows that autonomy, competence, and relatedness are the core components of self-determination theory (Guay, 2021; Niemiec & Ryan, 2009). These core components significantly predict life satisfaction. Complementing this perspective, Expectancy-Value Theory (EVT) provides an additional lens. EVT helps us understand student engagement with AI in marketing education. EVT states that learners' motivation is shaped by their expectation of success and the subjective value they assign to a task. For example, it discusses the utility of AI in future careers or its intrinsic interest. When AI tools are perceived as enhancing competence (with high expectancy) and aligned with personal or professional goals (with high value), they are more likely to support well-being and sustained engagement. Conversely, if students view AI as opaque, irrelevant, or threatening to their identity, both expectancy and task value may decline. It eventually undermines life satisfaction. When designed thoughtfully, experiential AI-driven learning environments can support the above three dimensions. By experimenting with AI tools, students actively shape learning outcomes through autonomy. Skill acquisition can be accelerated by receiving immediate feedback from AI systems. Social connections and a shared purpose can be fostered through collaborative projects (Wang et al., 2019).

Nevertheless, these advantages are not unavoidable. Students' ability to become active, prompt engineers or evaluators of machine output is undermined if AI-enhanced learning experiences are poorly designed. It risks their transformation into passive prompt engineers or evaluators. To that extent, critical thinking, ethical judgment, and reflection are emphasized as essential complements to the integration of AI. In these, risk is implicitly acknowledged (Schlegelmilch & Mills, 2025). To achieve life satisfaction, experiential learning must be centered on meaning, rather than merely focusing on skills. Projects need to prompt students to examine the social impact of AI-driven marketing (Raj & Sathiyan, 2024). The projects, of course, include concerns about consumer well-being.

Psychological resilience and satisfaction are directly linked to AI literacy. The students' understanding of how AI systems function decreases the likelihood of experiencing issues, such as the fear of being replaced or putting too much faith in algorithmic outputs (Kim et al., 2025). Students who are AI-literate can experience a sense of control, which can enhance their confidence and career satisfaction. Conversely, the use of AI that is not transparent can lead to stress when the automated assessments are not transparent (Biagini, 2025). Hence, the perceptions of fairness and procedural justice can be improved by AI systems that are transparently and ethically governed.

AI can mitigate certain human biases, but it can also introduce new ones, raising concerns about emotional legitimacy. Even if an algorithm is statistically fairer, students may be more inclined to accept critical feedback from a human instructor (Baker & Hawn, 2022). Therefore, marketing education should focus on teaching students how to use AI ethically. From that viewpoint, we can assert that the fundamental marketing insight can be applied to both education and service experience, as well as how ethical perceptions impact satisfaction and behavior. Furthermore, AI can be advantageous in reducing burnout, allowing more time to research and better pedagogy. The downside of this is that it could pose a threat to professional autonomy/authenticity and expertise.

AI technologies, including predictive analytics, recommendation systems, and generative content tools, are bringing about a profound transformation in the marketing discipline. To prepare graduates for an AI-driven professional environment, marketing education must adapt to the evolving practice of marketing. Scholars also emphasize experiential and project-based learning. Students can engage with AI technologies more critically by integrating AI-driven simulations, real-world datasets, and hands-on projects (George, 2023; Richter et al., 2025). These pedagogical approaches have been shown to enhance problem-solving skills and promote adaptive learning, which are crucial for navigating AI-enhanced marketing environments. Ethical considerations also influence AI in marketing education. Data privacy, algorithmic bias, consumer manipulation, and transparency are all concerns that arise when AI is used (Kumar & Suthar, 2024). Increasingly, academic literature recommends incorporating ethics and responsible AI use into marketing curricula (Schlegelmilch & Mills, 2025). Educators can mitigate technology-related anxiety and promote more positive attitudes toward AI. Students can be encouraged to engage in ethical reflection, which may also contribute to students' long-term career satisfaction.

Institutional initiatives further underscore the growing significance of AI in business and marketing education. Universities worldwide are now offering AI-centered programs, interdisciplinary institutes, and compulsory AI training components in their degree programs (Tyagi et al., 2024). These initiatives suggest a shift in perspective towards AI competence as a fundamental skill, comparable to digital literacy in earlier years (Hadi & AlShaikh-Hasan, 2025).

Based on these findings, educators are now required to develop curricula that are as dynamic and responsive to AI technologies. Ethics play a crucial role in the implementation of automation and personalization. Students need to possess creativity, data analysis, critical thinking, and decision-making abilities. Modern marketing practice can be directly engaged with by integrating project-based learning into courses, as educators provide students with opportunities to do so. In light of the growing use of AI for automating routine tasks, such as syllabus design, content generation, and administrative functions, educational tools must be practical and prioritize high-quality feedback and transparency. The importance of clear policies and ethical literacy cannot be overstated. For example, ethical ambiguity can arise from the use of AI by many students without formal guidance and oversight. As a whole, Educators can reduce anxiety and promote a more balanced understanding of technological change. This can happen by framing AI as a collaborative tool rather than a replacement for human creativity. Human-centered AI approaches that emphasize creativity, ethical judgment, and social value align with broader research on well-being. These approaches may lead to more satisfied marketing professionals in the future.

4. CONCLUDING REMARKS & FUTURE AGENDA

The downstream impact of AI-driven marketing education on consumer satisfaction with life is often overlooked. Graduates who have received training in AI-enhanced marketing can create campaigns and customer experiences that are more effective in promoting consumer happiness. AI's potential to reinforce manipulative practices that undermine consumer autonomy enhances ethical concerns. Consequently, future marketers can utilize AI to enhance transparency, inclusivity, and value creation.

Even with optimistic stories, the implementation of AI in marketing education creates conflicts between efficiency and the depth of learning. The use of unstructured AI has impacted critical thinking and intrinsic motivation, as evidenced by empirical research. On the other hand, structured reflective pedagogies minimize these dangers and boost happiness. Transparency in governance frameworks for AI is necessary for institutions to maintain trust and satisfaction. To examine causal relationships between AI use and life satisfaction, future research should utilize longitudinal and mixed-methods designs. Marketing education is especially deficient without validated well-being metrics and cross-cultural studies. AI will be a factor in the future of marketing education. However, it is human-centered design and ethical stewardship that will impact life satisfaction.

AI presents a challenge for the future of marketing education, not only in terms of technology and pedagogy, but also in terms of human challenges. This commentary advocates for a broad evaluative lens. It acknowledges education's fundamental role in personal and societal prosperity by expanding its framework to include life satisfaction and well-being. This commentary advocates for a broad evaluative lens. It acknowledges education's fundamental role in personal and societal prosperity by expanding its framework to include life satisfaction and well-being. Recent work in marketing communications education echoes this call. It warns that the uncritical adoption of generative AI may lead to "algorithmic subjugation," while intentional, reflective engagement could foster "poietic symbiosis." Therefore, AI can facilitate a co-creative partnership that preserves and enhances human agency (Karimova et al., 2025). Ultimately, AI will continue to reshape marketing education going forward. The way educators encode values into curriculum, institutions, and everyday teaching practices determines whether it enhances or diminishes life satisfaction. Adding ethical, human-centered, and experiential AI learning to marketing curricula is essential for educating students on both personal success and professional well-being in today's AI-driven world, according to educators and policymakers.

Marketing educators face a significant challenge: aligning established academic theories with rapidly evolving real-world applications. However, this challenge is not uniform across contexts or institutions. It is essential to note that this pedagogical shift is not merely the addition of AI-focused modules. Instead, we should consider how marketing education integrates technological innovation in ways that promote students' autonomy, perceived competence, and sense of purpose. If there is no alignment, rapid AI integration could result in an exacerbation of anxiety, cognitive overload, and uncertainty among both students and faculty. It can potentially undermine their well-being and long-term satisfaction. Rethinking marketing education necessitates both curricular innovation and a focus on human well-being, ethical decision-making, and sustainable outcomes. This is especially necessary in today's AI-driven business environment. A collaborative effort to create a shared vision for the future necessitates the collaboration of educators, industry practitioners, researchers, and policymakers. AI's ability to enhance human aspects of learning, such as collaboration, has the potential to be transformative. To be effective in the learning process, educators must be more proactive in fostering empathy and intellectual curiosity. AI's worth should not be solely determined by its learning performance metrics, but rather by its capacity to encourage students. Students should be able to: develop their academic and professional self-concepts. It should provide support for autonomy instead of replacing judgment. It should promote the development of competence without encouraging dependence and contribute in a meaningful way to their long-term happiness. Marketing education that overlooks these mediating mechanisms is at risk of promoting intense engagement without healthy psychological alignment. This situation can lead to a decline in well-being.

REFERENCES

Al Issa, H.-E., & Maheshwari, G. (2025). Shaping the future of education: A cluster analysis of generative AI's transformative impact. *Interactive Technology and Smart Education*. Advance online publication. DOI: 10.1108/ITSE-01-2025-0013

Allil, K. (2024). Integrating AI-driven marketing analytics techniques into the classroom: Pedagogical strategies for enhancing student engagement and future business success. *Journal of Marketing Analytics*, *12*(2), 142–168. DOI: 10.1057/s41270-023-00281-z

Baker, R. S., & Hawn, A. (2022). Algorithmic Bias in Education. *International Journal of Artificial Intelligence in Education*, *32*(4), 1052–1092. DOI: 10.1007/s40593-021-00285-9

Biagini, G. (2025). Towards an AI-Literate Future: A Systematic Literature Review Exploring Education, Ethics, and Applications. *International Journal of Artificial Intelligence in Education*, *35*(4), 2616–2666. DOI: 10.1007/s40593-025-00466-w

Cillo, P., & Rubera, G. (2025). Generative AI in innovation and marketing processes: A roadmap of research opportunities. *Journal of the Academy of Marketing Science*, *53*(3), 684–701. DOI: 10.1007/s11747-024-01044-7

Diener, E. (1984). Subjective well-being. *Psychological Bulletin*, *95*(3), 542–575. DOI: 10.1037/0033-2909.95.3.542 PMID: 6399758

Diener, E., Emmons, R. A., Larsen, R. J., & Griffin, S. (1985). The Satisfaction With Life Scale. *Journal of Personality Assessment*, *49*(1), 71–75. DOI: 10.1207/s15327752jpa4901_13 PMID: 16367493

Ehrhardt, J. J., Saris, W. E., & Veenhoven, R. (2000). Stability of Life-satisfaction over Time. *Journal of Happiness Studies*, *1*(2), 177–205. DOI: 10.1023/A:1010084410679

Flink, N. A., Black, H. G., & Dingus, R. (2025). Explore, Identify, and Align: Utilizing Generative AI as a Career Coach. *Marketing Education Review*, *35*(2), 109–119. DOI: 10.1080/10528008.2024.2430266

Gaggioli, A., Riva, G., Peters, D., & Calvo, R. A. (2017). Positive Technology, Computing, and Design: Shaping a Future in Which Technology Promotes Psychological Well-Being. In Jeon, M. (Ed.), *Emotions and Affect in Human Factors and Human-Computer Interaction* (pp. 477–502). Academic Press., https://doi.org/https://doi.org/10.1016/B978-0-12-801851-4.00018-5 DOI: 10.1016/B978-0-12-801851-4.00018-5

George, A. S. (2023). Preparing students for an AI-driven world: Rethinking curriculum and pedagogy in the age of artificial intelligence. *Partners Universal Innovative Research Publication*, *1*(2), 112–136. DOI: 10.5281/zenodo.10245675

Grewal, D., Guha, A., Beccacece Satornino, C., & Becker, M. (2024). The Future of Marketing and Marketing Education. *Journal of Marketing Education, 47*(1), 61-77. https://doi.org/ (Original work published 2025)DOI: 10.1177/02734753241269838

Grewal, D., Satornino, C. B., Davenport, T., & Guha, A. (2025). How generative AI Is shaping the future of marketing. *Journal of the Academy of Marketing Science*, *53*(3), 702–722. DOI: 10.1007/s11747-024-01064-3

Guay, F. (2021). Applying Self-Determination Theory to Education: Regulations Types, Psychological Needs, and Autonomy Supporting Behaviors. *Canadian Journal of School Psychology, 37*(1), 75-92. https://doi.org/ (Original work published 2022)DOI: 10.1177/08295735211055355

Hadi, W., & AlShaikh-Hasan, M. N. (2025). AI-Driven Curriculum Transformation and Faculty Development in Developing Universities. In Al Maqousi, A., Almomani, A., Aldweesh, A., & Alauthman, M. (Eds.), *Revolutionizing Urban Development and Governance With Emerging Technologies* (pp. 289–322). IGI Global Scientific Publishing., DOI: 10.4018/979-8-3373-1375-7.ch010

Hinks, T. (2024). Artificial Intelligence Perceptions and Life Satisfaction. *Journal of Happiness Studies*, *25*(1), 5. DOI: 10.1007/s10902-024-00727-w

Huang, M.-H., & Rust, R. T. (2024). The Caring Machine: Feeling AI for Customer Care. *Journal of Marketing, 88*(5), 1-23. https://doi.org/ (Original work published 2024)DOI: 10.1177/00222429231224748

Karimova, G. Z., Kim, Y. D., & Shirkhanbeik, A. (2025). Poietic symbiosis or algorithmic subjugation: Generative AI technology in marketing communications education. *Education and Information Technologies*, *30*(2), 2185–2209. DOI: 10.1007/s10639-024-12877-8

Kim, J. J. H., Soh, J., Kadkol, S., Solomon, I., Yeh, H., Srivatsa, A. V., Nahass, G. R., Choi, J. Y., Lee, S., Nyugen, T., & Ajilore, O. (2025). AI Anxiety: A comprehensive analysis of psychological factors and interventions. *AI and Ethics*, *5*(4), 3993–4009. DOI: 10.1007/s43681-025-00686-9

Kumar, D., & Suthar, N. (2024). Ethical and legal challenges of AI in marketing: An exploration of solutions. *Journal of Information. Communication and Ethics in Society*, *22*(1), 124–144. DOI: 10.1108/JICES-05-2023-0068

Lissitsa, S., & Chachashvili-Bolotin, S. (2016). Life satisfaction in the internet age – Changes in the past decade. *Computers in Human Behavior*, *54*, 197–206. https://doi.org/https://doi.org/10.1016/j.chb.2015.08.001. DOI: 10.1016/j.chb.2015.08.001

Manda, V. K., Bezawada, K., & Bhukya, M. (2025). Applications of Artificial Intelligence in Education: Implications for Pedagogy, Learning Outcomes, and Policy Development. In *Artificial Intelligence Implementation in Education Processes* (pp. 01–21). Deep Science Publishing. https://doi.org/DOI: 10.70593/978-81-984306-7-0_1

Mrad, M., Itani, O. S., & Cui, C. C. (2025). Unlocking life satisfaction: The impact of self-image congruence on consumers' life satisfaction through brand love and brand addiction. *European Journal of Marketing*, *59*(8), 2054–2088. DOI: 10.1108/EJM-02-2024-0103

Narang, U., Sachdev, V., & Liu, R. (2025). When AI Wears Many Hats: The Role of Generative Artificial Intelligence in Marketing Education. *Journal of Public Policy & Marketing*, *44*(3), 473–489. DOI: 10.1177/07439156251328237

Niemiec, C. P., & Ryan, R. M. (2009). Autonomy, competence, and relatedness in the classroom: Applying self-determination theory to educational practice: Applying self-determination theory to educational practice. *Theory and Research in Education, 7*(2), 133-144. https://doi.org/ (Original work published 2009)DOI: 10.1177/1477878509104318

Pavlov, N., & Almanza, L. C. M. (2026). Artificial Intelligence in the Professional Activity and Education of Marketing Specialists: A Survey of Students' Opinions. In Krastev, K. V., Rani, C., Ergunova, O., Kansra, P., & Kajla, T. (Eds.), (pp. 59–102). Advances in Computational Intelligence and Robotics. IGI Global Scientific Publishing., DOI: 10.4018/979-8-3373-8612-6.ch003

Raj, J. D., & Sathiyan, G. (2024). Enhancing Life Skill Progression and Psychological Well-being of Undergraduate Students through AI-driven Recommendation System. *Multidisciplinary Science Journal*, *7*(2), 2025054. DOI: 10.31893/multiscience.2025054

Richter, S., Giroux, M., Piven, I., Sima, H., & Dodd, P. (2025). A Constructivist Approach to Integrating AI in Marketing Education: Bridging Theory and Practice. *Journal of Marketing Education*, *47*(2), 94–111. DOI: 10.1177/02734753241288876

Schlegelmilch, B. B., & Mills, A. J. (2025). Artificial Intelligence and the Future of Marketing Education. *Journal of Marketing Education*, *47*(2), 91–93. DOI: 10.1177/02734753251336956

Schneider, S., & Haried, P. (2024). Use of artificial Intelligence in higher education with particular reference to automated content generation, trust, and anxiety. *Journal of Business and Educational Leadership*, *14*(1), 4–21.

Sirgy, M. J. (2012). *The psychology of quality of life: Hedonic well-being, life satisfaction, and eudaimonia* (Vol. 50). Springer science & business media. DOI: 10.1007/978-94-007-4405-9

Steckermeier, L. C. (2021). The Value of Autonomy for the Good Life. An Empirical Investigation of Autonomy and Life Satisfaction in Europe. *Social Indicators Research*, *154*(2), 693–723. DOI: 10.1007/s11205-020-02565-8

Tyagi, S., Gupta, V., & Mehndiratta, V. (2024). Building Smart Campuses: Integrating AI in Higher Education. In Arya, R., Sharma, S. C., Verma, A. K., & Iyer, B. (Eds.), *Recent Trends in Artificial Intelligence Towards a Smart World: Applications in Industries and Sectors* (pp. 399–431). Springer Nature Singapore., DOI: 10.1007/978-981-97-6790-8_15

Wang, C. K. J., Liu, W. C., Kee, Y. H., & Chian, L. K. (2019). Competence, autonomy, and relatedness in the classroom: Understanding students’ motivational processes using the self-determination theory. *Heliyon*, *5*(7), e01983. Advance online publication. DOI: 10.1016/j.heliyon.2019.e01983 PMID: 31372524

Yu, J. H., Chauhan, D., Iqbal, R. A., & Yeoh, E. (2025). Mapping academic perspectives on AI in education: Trends, challenges, and sentiments in educational research (2018–2024). *Educational Technology Research and Development*, *73*(1), 199–227. DOI: 10.1007/s11423-024-10425-2

ADDITIONAL READING

Becchetti, L., & Conzo, P. (2018). Preferences for Well-Being and Life Satisfaction. *Social Indicators Research*, *136*(2), 775–805. DOI: 10.1007/s11205-017-1566-8

Becker, G. S., & Murphy, K. M. (1988). A Theory of Rational Addiction. *Journal of Political Economy*, *96*(4), 675–700. DOI: 10.1086/261558

Buecker, S., Luhmann, M., Haehner, P., Bühler, J. L., Dapp, L. C., Luciano, E. C., & Orth, U. (2023). The development of subjective well-being across the life span: A meta-analytic review of longitudinal studies. *Psychological Bulletin*, *149*(7-8), 418–446. DOI: 10.1037/bul0000401

Campbell, A., Converse, P. E., & Rodgers, W. L. (1976). *Quality of American Life, The: Perceptions, Evaluations, and Satisfactions*. Russell Sage Foundation.

Choung, Y., Pak, T.-Y., & Chatterjee, S. (2021). Consumption and life satisfaction: The Korean evidence. *International Journal of Consumer Studies*, *45*(5), 1007–1019. https://doi.org/https://doi.org/10.1111/ijcs.12620. DOI: 10.1111/ijcs.12620

Cummins, R. A., & Nistico, H. (2002). Maintaining Life Satisfaction: The Role of Positive Cognitive Bias. *Journal of Happiness Studies*, *3*(1), 37–69. DOI: 10.1023/A:1015678915305

Diener, E., Oishi, S., & Lucas, R. E. (2003). Personality, Culture, and Subjective Well-Being: Emotional and Cognitive Evaluations of Life. *Annual Review of Psychology*, *54*(Volume 54, 2003), 403-425. https://doi.org/DOI: 10.1146/annurev.psych.54.101601.145056

Ekici, A., Joseph Sirgy, M., Lee, D.-J., Yu, G. B., & Bosnjak, M. (2018). The Effects of Shopping Well-Being and Shopping Ill-Being on Consumer Life Satisfaction. *Applied Research in Quality of Life*, *13*(2), 333–353. DOI: 10.1007/s11482-017-9524-9

Martin, K. D., & Paul Hill, R. (2011). Life Satisfaction, Self-Determination, and Consumption Adequacy at the Bottom of the Pyramid. *The Journal of Consumer Research*, *38*(6), 1155–1168. DOI: 10.1086/661528

Rogers, P. P., Allen, C., & Busby, A. (2024). Marketing Educators and Artificial Intelligence: A Perspective on Productivity and Innovation. *Journal of Marketing Education*, *47*(2), 156-169. https://doi.org/ (Original work published 2025)DOI: 10.1177/02734753241299095

Ruggeri, K., Garcia-Garzon, E., Maguire, Á., Matz, S., & Huppert, F. A. (2020). Well-being is more than happiness and life satisfaction: A multidimensional analysis of 21 countries. *Health and Quality of Life Outcomes*, *18*(1), 192. DOI: 10.1186/s12955-020-01423-y PMID: 32560725

Tegmark, M. (2017). *Life 3.0: Being human in the age of artificial intelligence*. Knopf.

KEY TERMS & DEFINITIONS

Artificial Intelligence (AI): AI is a set of technologies that enables computer systems to perform tasks that typically require human intelligence. The use of algorithms and data-driven models is used for activities such as learning, reasoning, pattern recognition, decision-making, and language processing.

Human Well-being: It is defined as the overall state of an individual's physical, mental, and social functioning. Assuring that individuals have life satisfaction, good mental health, meaningful engagement, autonomy, and the ability to thrive in personal, professional, and societal settings.

Life Satisfaction: This term describes an individual's overall cognitive assessment of the quality of their life, which is determined by their own values, goals, and standards. It reflects a comprehensive and steady assessment of well-being, rather than momentary emotions.

Marketing Education: Marketing Education is a term that encompasses both formal and informal means by which people acquire knowledge, skills, and ethical judgment. Learners are prepared to analyze markets, create value, and respond effectively to evolving business and social contexts through a strategic understanding of marketing principles and practices.

Chapter 2
Digital Life Satisfaction: Psychological Drivers, Ethical Design, and Global Pathways to Human-Centred Digital Markets

Muhammad Usman Tariq
http://orcid.org/0000-0002-7605-3040
Abu Dhabi University, UAE & University College Cork, Ireland

ABSTRACT

Satisfaction with digital life is a complicated result of psychological needs, ethical design preferences, and a more comprehensive economic setting that connects individuals to platforms. In this chapter, the authors discuss the experiences of autonomy, competence, and belonging to social relations as the foundation of the positive use of digital technologies and reflect on the design practices that encourage well-being instead of manipulating the attention of users. It further describes the architecture of human-centric digital markets that balance commercial interests with user prosperity via transparency, choice structure, and participative governance. It concludes that forging meaningful collaboration among designers, policymakers, educators, and communities is necessary to construct trustworthy digital futures that foster creativity, protect agency, and guarantee equitable access to the social and economic benefits of technology.

INTRODUCTION

Digital life satisfaction has emerged as a crucial concept as digital technologies weave themselves into nearly every dimension of contemporary life. It reaches beyond the convenience or entertainment value of digital tools into the realms of people's

DOI: 10.4018/979-8-3373-8357-6.ch002

sense of meaning, autonomy, connection, and security in increasingly mediatised environments (Saha, 2025). At its core, digital life satisfaction refers to the degree to which individuals feel that their digital experiences support their personal goals, emotional well-being, relationships, and quality of life in general. Its relevance has grown sharply because of the ways in which digital platforms shape social interactions, economic opportunities, political participation, and identity formation. Where it used to appear as a series of unrelated online activities, it is now a fluid experience stream that permeates daily life and thus obliterates the proposed barrier between the digital and non-digital world. The question in this augmented ecosystem is never about the usefulness of technology but whether it can help humans flourish sustainably and fairly.

Digital ecosystems are expanding in scale to unprecedented levels worldwide, generating both unmatched benefits and pressures that directly impact satisfaction perceptions. Although individuals now have access to educational content, medical databases, cultural products, and professional connections, the very platforms that enable them are usually the ones that flood them with information, introduce them to persuasion methods that are manipulative, algorithmically biased, and progressively demanding their attention (Kotler et al., 2024).The model does not favor users and instead ignores the societal costs of fatigue, polarization, misinformation, and destroyed trust on a larger scale.

Human-centric value creation involves changing the process of conceptualizing, measuring, and assessing digital products. Rather than posing the question of how to keep users engaged, the guiding question becomes how to provide an environment that favors meaningful goals and healthy experiences (Saha, 2025). It gives due weight to the fact that people are active participants rather than passive data points, with agency and vulnerabilities and diverse needs and wants. Where digital systems honor this complexity, they can help improve satisfaction by fostering clarity, reducing cognitive load, supporting informed choice, and reinforcing social bonds.

A potential future of going beyond engagement metrics is to reconsider design practices: to create interfaces that prompt more deliberate than automatic use, provide clearings as to how systems operate, and provide users with the power to manage the information, timeframes, or algorithms that shape their experience. This means designing for moments of disconnection as well as for moments of interaction. Features that allow users to set boundaries, customize notifications, or pause algorithmic personalization help cultivate a sense of autonomy that reduces feelings of being overwhelmed. The aim is not to eliminate engagement but to create engagement that aligns with personal values and well-being of the employees. When people feel safe, respected, and in control, their satisfaction naturally increases without the need for coercive or manipulative tactics.

Human-centered value creation also requires acknowledgment of the social dimension of digital life. Most digital experiences are relational by nature, shaping, creating, learning, expressing, or simply being present with others. Satisfaction is higher in interactions based on trust, empathy, and reciprocity rather than noise, interruption, or conflict. The design of platforms that encourage reflective discussion, lower the reward of outrage, endorse community censoring, or even prosocial norms can greatly improve people's digital lives. This is all the more pertinent when digital spaces are made public and influential in terms of defining political discourse, collective memory, and cultural identities. A human ecosystem appreciates that healthy digital interactions translate into healthy societies. Economies that form the foundation of digital platforms are determinants of value (Mani et al., 2025). As long as ethics-based designs are not advantageous in the sense that they encourage attention to be the greatest value in advertising-driven models, ethical design will be a mountainous battle. When companies are encouraged to contribute to satisfaction instead of taking advantage of attention, they will invest more in features that add value to people's lives. This does not discredit innovation; instead, it turns innovation into more sustainable and humanistic goals. Digital literacy and education are also significant factors in the development of satisfaction. Individuals cannot make the most of digital tools if they are unable to interact critically in online contexts, protect their privacy, or recognize manipulative techniques in the digital environment.

Digital literacy entails more than competence; it is a form of empowerment. It involves developing healthy habits in the use of devices, evaluating information, effective communication, and decision-making. When people comprehend how function-and, most importantly, how they might shape experiences-they have a more intentional and confident use of technology. This worldview also opens up inter-cultural education, interdisciplinary inquiry, and collective standards that honor the diversity of localities without obstructing the universal set of values known as dignity and fairness. This convergence is becoming increasingly necessary as digital markets become more interdependent to prevent fragmentation and ensure that technological advancement can benefit everybody. Finally, it is necessary to change the attitude towards digital life satisfaction and the adoption of human-centered value creation: the human experience should be the core of technological development. Digital systems are not objective; they embody the decisions, biases, and priorities of designers, companies, and societies. When such decisions are made with human well-being in mind, the digital world can be created in a way that promotes creativity, connection, learning, and growth. When they focus on extraction, the effects are felt by both people and society. Therefore, moving beyond engagement metrics is not only a design challenge but also a moral one. This calls for a shared commitment to building digital ecosystems that honor human complexity and nurture environments in which people can thrive (Tariq, 2026).

Table 1. Core Dimensions and Drivers of Digital Life Satisfaction

Dimension	Key Drivers	Manifestation in Digital Contexts	Risks When Poorly Designed
Emotional	Joy, anxiety, trust, validation	Social feedback, immersive content, health reassurance	Emotional overload, anxiety, fatigue, distrust
Cognitive	Attention, clarity, sense-making	Information architecture, recommendations, dashboards	Cognitive overload, confusion, misinformation
Behavioural	Habits, routines, reinforcement	Notifications, nudges, rewards, scrolling	Addiction, loss of agency, compulsive use
Autonomy	Control, choice, transparency	Customisation, privacy controls, opt-outs	Manipulation, coercive engagement
Social	Belonging, reciprocity, empathy	Online communities, social platforms, peer support	Polarisation, hostility, isolation
Cultural	Values, norms, language	Localised content, communication styles	Exclusion, cultural mismatch
Ethical & Governance	Fairness, accountability, justice	Algorithms, data use, AI decision systems	Bias, loss of trust, systemic harm

Psychology of the Digital Consumer

The psychology of the digital consumer has increasingly become central to efforts to understand why people interact with technology the way they do and how such interactions shape well-being. Digital environments do not passively reflect user behavior but actively mold it through a constant feedback loop of design cues and social norms embedded into platforms. Simultaneously, digital experiences become frictionless due to emotional, cognitive, and behavioral processes that are usually not conscious and build up habit preferences and even self-concepts. Because these psychological processes determine the degree to which individuals feel satisfied, overwhelmed, empowered, or frustrated in the online environment, it is necessary to learn their specifics of them in order to create healthier digital ecosystems. Individuals do not navigate digital spaces as rational agents who make fully informed decisions; they do so as emotional and social beings responding to cues that trigger curiosity, belonging, fear, pleasure, novelty or uncertainty. When such responses align with personal values and needs, the digital experience enhances well-being. When these needs conflict, they undermine autonomy and satisfaction.

Emotional drivers play a powerful role in digital life because online environments are designed to evoke rapid and continuous emotional reactions. Positive emotions, such as joy, inspiration, and amusement, often fuel digital engagement, particularly through social sharing, creative expression, and supportive communities. When people experience positive feedback, they feel validated, which can lead to a sense of connection and affirmation. At the same time, however, digital systems stimulate emotions like anxiety, envy, outrage, or fear, which tend to spread more rapidly and keep people hooked for longer. Emotional induction factors are particularly strong in settings that apply content personalization, where users receive an uninterrupted stream of content that is precisely adjusted to their sensitivities. Constant bombardment and exposure to emotionally charged content cause emotional overload, which spoils well-being. Over time, they may feel as though their emotional responses are being manipulated, which erodes trust and generates fatigue. Therefore, understanding emotional drivers affords insight into how digital environments may support rather than undermine mental and relational health.

Cognitive drivers shape how individuals interpret information, form judgments, and make decisions in digital spaces. Digital environments heavily tax attention because they present overwhelming amounts of information in a fragmented and fast-moving format (Singh & Chaudhary, 2025). A person can end up adopting perspectives, ways of living, or standards when they are exposed to them repetitively without being aware of the logic behind the platform.

Behavioral drivers are the results of repeated interactions that solidify into habits. The majority of digital behaviors are supported by few incentives, including likes, messages, and fresh content, which support repetitive use. The long-term effects could be that individuals do not have to look at their phones any longer, they scroll randomly, or even react to notifications immediately. These habits appear to be small, and they become everyday, the pattern of attention, emotional cycles. Behavioral psychology notes that intermittent rewards, or unpredictable feedback on variables, are particularly powerful motivators of prolonged engagement. This feature is applied to social media feeds, games, and productivity applications. Nevertheless, other intentional routines created by individuals to benefit their well-being also dictate behaviors, including the use of mindfulness apps, the creation of digital spaces, or online supportive community membership. When online spaces are in parallel with the objectives of the users, they reinforce positive habits, as opposed to spontaneous habits. Being able to see behavioral drivers helps designers and policymakers identify where damaging patterns arise and how healthier digital practices might be fostered.

Trust plays a foundational role in shaping digital well-being. Without trust, users feel anxious, skeptical, or unsafe, which affects how freely they engage and how satisfied they are. Trust impacts interpersonal relationships online and the relationships between users and platforms. People need to trust that the information they encounter is accurate, that their data are secure, and that the communities they join are supportive rather than hostile. Digital environments are weak in terms of trust, as individuals tend to have no idea who is posting what, how decisions are made, and on what principles the platform is operating. Whenever the platforms show ambiguous data behaviors or algorithms that change feeds in unusual ways, individuals can be disoriented or manipulated (Duarte, 2025). This is not about settings and options; it reflects the attitude of users since it is whether technology is restricting or facilitating their intentions. The majority of digital systems cross that boundary with the help of minor design features that appeal to cognitive biases and make users want to do some specific things: spend more time there, purchase something, or invite more people (Cooke, 2024). However, by supporting satisfying and significant digital lives, digital environments are recognized to consider emotional needs, encourage cognitive clarity, and support healthy behaviors. This needs to be consciously architected in a way that respects agency, secures identity, and builds trust. This requires social debate on the values and aspirations that inform digital ecosystems. Identity influences how people interpret information, which communities they join, and how they present themselves. When these psychological dimensions positively reinforce each other, digital life becomes a space for exploration, connection, and creativity. When at odds, users may become overwhelmed, manipulated, or disconnected from their intentions to use the app. Ultimately, understanding the psychology of digital consumers is about design, incentives, and social dynamics affecting human experience rather than a means to pathologize digital behavior. Instead, people do not fail in their use of technology "properly"; most often, technologies fail to honor the psychological realities of their users. This demands social dialogue concerning the values and objectives that define digital ecosystems. As technologies change, the psychology of the digital consumer will be of central importance to the development of environments that enhance human well-being without compromising it (Tariq, 2026; Tarnanidis and Vlachopoulou, 2025).

CROSS-CULTURAL PERSPECTIVES ON DIGITAL LIFE SATISFACTION

The satisfaction with digital life varies greatly across the world, influenced by cultural expectations, levels of digital access, political environments, and the meaning that society attaches to technology. While digital tools promise connection, opportunity, and empowerment, the way people interpret these experiences is far from universal. What is perceived as a good, satisfying online experience in one culture may be perceived as stressful, invasive, or insignificant in another. This diversity indicates deeper trends in culture: attitudes toward community and individuality, vision of privacy, anticipations of social roles, and general values attributed to work, communication, and identity. With the increase in digital ecosystems, these cultural peculiarities predetermine not only the positive values of people in technology usage but also the difficulties they face in their lives on the Internet. The overall message is that cross-cultural differences should be considered in the creation of a global digital system in which human dignity should be respected and local values should be prioritized. Nevertheless, digital satisfaction in cultures that emphasize social harmony and belonging is more likely to be evaluated in relation to experience (Saha, 2025). The worth of a digital life is related to how well technology has served family bonds, responsibilities to the community, or a shared cultural life. Such different emphases shape what people celebrate online, what they fret about, and how they handle digital boundaries within their social networks.

At the same time, these settings often combat burnout, overexposure, and the lack of boundaries between personal and professional life (Cooke, 2024). In collectivistic settings, young people are usually forced to conform their online habits to the expectations of their family, and in individualistic settings, the youth are usually pressured to be different or eccentric. Meanwhile, older generations might prefer to use digital tools to stay in touch with their family or perform some useful functions but occasionally mention that they feel uneasy about the ongoing transformations of platforms or that they think about their privacy. These generational differences define digital happiness by determining the degree of confidence or empowerment that people have in their use of digital landscapes (Tariq, 2026). In such contexts, frustrations regarding digital life are mostly about infrastructural deficiencies, such as slow connections, unstable networks, high costs, or the unavailability of content in one's own language. Socio-economic inequity also produces differentiated experiences of digital risks: more literate users may manage privacy settings, filter misinformation, and curate healthier digital environments than less literate users. In contrast, those with limited digital education are more likely to be exploited, manipulated through targeted means, or bewildered by complicated systems with which they interact (Fusco Girard, 2024). For example, modest cultures see high levels of expressiveness or self-promotion online as inappropriate, even if such practices are usual on global platforms. Conversely, cultures that believe in openness and directness consider communication styles that are more subtle than these baffling or off-putting. Individuals might fear the idea of data gathering, monitoring, or targeted advertising, and a person can measure online happiness through the extent of control they believe they possess over their digital presence.

The political environment is another aspect that determines digital life satisfaction (Yip et al., 2025). Digital access cannot be considered only a technical problem; it is also a cultural problem. There is also communal access to devices or public Internet points in certain societies. It has an impact on the way digital behaviors are framed, which leads to the possibility of group use, coordination, or family based decision-making. These contexts might have been associated with learning together and supporting collective goals, which are shared outcomes. On the other hand, personal gadgets and online accounts in societies endorse privacy, customization, and self-centered organization of web experiences. These access models determine how individuals think about ownership, accountability, and digital boundaries. Language also defines the elements of the global digital world. The availability of digital content in a first language has a drastic influence on satisfaction and inclusivity (Issac, 2024). When most of the digital world is dominated by the English language, it can give a sense of power to those who are conversant with the language at the expense of others who find it hard to maneuver the interfaces, translate information, and take part in international dialogues. In local language ecosystems where a local language is more dominant, digital satisfaction is often more prone to high levels due to the relevancy and accessibility of local language content, as well as the capabilities of local language content to connect with specific cultural audiences in learning opportunities, entertainment, and professional growth. Areas with a low density of local-language content will make people feel anomalous or out of learning, entertainment, and professional development opportunities. Digital happiness is also subject to the process of cultural narration on the role of technology in society. In other places, technology is regarded as an icon of modernity and progress; thus, individuals might be proud or hopeful about using digital technology in those areas. Elsewhere, technology can be considered with suspicion, either as a danger to local customs or a spur to undesirable social change. Such stories create expectations of how people interact with digital technology on an emotional level and what they have to do. Technology becomes more amicable to daily life when it correlates with cultural identity. When it clashes with cultural values, it can cause tension, conflict, or resistance. Cross-cultural differences also manifest in people's use of digital spaces for stress relief or seeking help. Cultures that are highly dependent on the Internet, support networks, or access to mental health support to gain emotional strength, and others that are more dependent on physical social connections and view digital coping systems as secondary or insufficient. These trends determine the degree to which digital life is supportive or isolating for various groups of people. Moreover, due to the stigma that mental health holds globally, different parts of the world will feel more or less comfortable using online assistance or digital well-being tools for mental health. Nevertheless, among these differences, there are also common international trends in digital life satisfaction (Tarnanidis, 2024).

Table 2. Digital Life Satisfaction Across Key Digital Sectors

Digital Sector	Primary Value Offered	Key Satisfaction Enablers	Typical Well-being Risks	Design & Governance Implications
Digital Retail	Convenience, identity expression	Personalisation, usability, reviews	Decision fatigue, manipulative nudges	Transparent algorithms, bounded choice
FinTech	Security, autonomy, stability	Clarity, trust, financial control	Anxiety, opaque risk, exploitation	Ethical nudging, explainability
Digital Health	Care, reassurance, resilience	Access, monitoring, support communities	Over-monitoring, data privacy fears	Human-centred design, data protection
Social Platforms	Connection, visibility	Belonging, expression, feedback	Polarisation, emotional manipulation	Prosocial norms, moderation
AI-driven Systems	Efficiency, assistance	Reduced cognitive load, prediction	Loss of autonomy, bias	Explainable, accountable AI
Metaverse & Immersive Spaces	Presence, identity exploration	Co-presence, creativity	Escapism, commodified identity	Ethical governance, cultural inclusion

Across the world, many individuals appreciate the potential for being connected to loved ones, immediate access to information, learning new skills and engaging with broader communities. Across cultures, people become frustrated when digital systems feel manipulative, overwhelming, or exclusionary. There is a universal desire to possess technology that improves rather than consumes life every day. The main global collaboration on digital well-being is based on such concerns, which provide the opportunity to make local adjustments that do not violate cultural diversity (Mishra et al., 2025). No even a single model can encompass what digital life can bring to all people, and no universal design principle can suit all needs. Rather, digital ecosystems need to maintain some degree of global connectedness and cultural responsiveness so that tools and platforms can serve communities of diverse cultures, not make them conform to homogenized patterns of behavior.

MEASURING DIGITAL WELL-BEING

It is important to note that digital well-being demands a combination of psychological insight, statistical rigor, and practical assessment tools, which can reflect the complexity of people's digital lives. Digital well-being is multi-layered and constantly changing due to changes in technology, unlike conventional well-being, which is usually measured by well-established social indicators. Digital wellbeing is multifaceted and involves emotional states, behavioral trends, cognitive load, trust, autonomy, identity expression, and the quality of social interactions (Kristiyanto et al., 2025). Owing to the interconnection between these dimensions, it is impossible to identify the particular indicator that can help reflect the way people feel about their digital experience fully. Researchers thus depend on a mix of quantitative modelling, qualitative interpretation, and multi-criteria evaluation tools, where different dimensions of digital life can be compared and synthesized. Simultaneously, measuring usage is not the issue, but interpreting meaning, context, and user agency. A proper measurement needs to include how digital systems influence satisfaction, empowerment, and health, and how individuals adjust to these settings in the long run. SEM has emerged as a key approach for measuring digital well-being, as it enables scholars to examine the relationship between latent psychological variables and digital behaviors. SEM is a powerful methodology because it reveals the generally hidden architecture of digital experiences, that is, how emotions, beliefs, and behavior interact to shape well-being. Allowing for complex relationships to be tested and compared affords a finer-grained view of what aspects of digital life most robustly contribute to happiness and what factors undermine it.

Complementing SEM, sentiment analytics maps the emotional tone of users' interactions in real time. Sentiment analytics, instead of self-report surveys, are based on text messages on social media posts, feedback messages, reviews, or discussion forums to establish how individuals feel when navigating digital spaces. Sentiment analytics can trace the mood swings of users, determine the causes of frustration or pleasure, and detect well-being concerns early on before they spiral out of control through the use of word patterns, emotional indicators, and linguistic signals. It is especially useful in situations where emotional states are affected by rapid changes in platforms or social dynamics. Sentiment analytics can be used to determine whether design decisions will improve well-being or cause stress. Although the sentiment analysis technique is not an ideal reflection of inner emotions, it does provide a dynamic large-scale perspective of collective emotional reactions that are perhaps not easily seen under the covers of statistical survey models (Tariq, 2026).

However, digital well-being cannot be measured by emotional tone or structural relationships alone. Multi-criteria decision models have become a part of digital life, as digital life implies competing priorities, which implies access, privacy, autonomy, satisfaction, safety, and efficiency. Digital wellbeing can be evaluated using techniques such as PROMEethe, AHP, and TOPSIS, which allow researchers and policy analysts to evaluate it in several dimensions that cannot be directly compared. These models are useful in helping decision-makers trade off, for example, improving personalization in favor of less privacy or more engagement at the expense of mental health. PROMETHEE is particularly suited for comparing alternatives when the criteria have different scales or weights. These comparisons enable the AHP to develop a hierarchy of priorities that represents common or personal preferences. This has the advantage of cross-cultural online research, where other societies place varying values on privacy, community membership, and the use of digital technology. The AHP assists in converting subjective priorities into measurable judgments, which can be used to inform policy and design.

TOPSIS is another model that works based on the wellbeing assessment by finding solutions that are closest to the best and farthest from the worst. This technique will assist in digital environment studies because it covers how well a platform or policy will operate concerning its optimal and undesirable states. The best digital experience involves a careful balance between autonomy, security, clarity, and emotional satisfaction in a finely tuned equilibrium. TOPSIS can be used to study how close different digital systems are to the ideal and at what points they deviate from it. Its power lies in demarcating what the "best possible" digital wellbeing will look like and how current systems fall short of it.

While these models are powerful individually, they achieve greater value when they are integrated into broader digital happiness frameworks. Survey-based SEM models may be used together with sentiment analytics to elicit emotions, AHP may be used to rank the value of the user, PROMETHEE may be used to compare policy options, and TOPSIS may be used to evaluate the results against the ideal value. This provides a stratified view of digital happiness, subjective experiences, and objective conditions. Unified frameworks are also used to adjourn conflicts in digital lives. For example, a user might appreciate convenience and be concerned about privacy at the same time; they might like social networks but are over-exercised with notifications (Firescu & Filip, 2025). These tensions can be modeled using decision models rather than being ignored. Frameworks can indicate the kind of trade-offs that users are prepared to make and the sacrifices that jeopardize their well-being. Integrated approaches can be used to determine designs that cause harmony and not friction in digital experiences by mapping the reinforcement of various dimensions on each other and how they conflict with each other (Bucci et al., 2024). The tools through which well-being is measured may influence behavior or tap into sensitive aspects of people's lives. Sentiment analytics can require personal expressions; SEMs can use large datasets about behavior; and multi-criteria models may affect resource allocation. Accordingly, measurement strategies must be accompanied by an ethical framework. There is no one discipline that can claim digital wellbeing; it is a result of human experience, technology design, and social systems interaction. This way, subtle insights that represent the diversity and complexity of digital life are offered, which also provide viable advice on how to build healthier digital futures.

Life Satisfaction Across Digital Sectors

Digital life satisfaction across these different digital sectors hinges on the rhythms, pressures, and rewards people encounter as they move between online shopping spaces, financial platforms and digital health environments. Both sectors have a significant impact on well-being, not only by the activities they allow but also by the feelings, anticipations, and actions they promote (Nasir et al., 2025). Nonetheless, when systems appear perplexing, manipulative, or unconcerned, the emotional cost may overwhelm any expediency. Residents of the country can feel the authentic pleasure of using Internet shops, negotiating prices, trying new brands, and having their products delivered to their homes without a lot of hassle.

Personalization is also a significant basis for consumer satisfaction. An effective set of tailored recommendations enables users to find relevant products quickly, especially in cases where they feel accurate rather than intrusive. Well-designed interfaces reduce cognitive effort by clearly arranging information, using layouts and options that are already well-known, and providing helpful filters. Nevertheless, online shopping may erode well-being in the case of excessive and manipulative personalization. A large portion of users can sense when algorithms are too pushy about products or when they employ scarcity indicators to make people make a decisive purchase (Szostak, 2025). End-of-time clocks, alerts with limited editions, and continuous notifications are stressful rather than enjoyable for users. There are also far too many choices, which can cause people to experience decision fatigue because they feel overwhelmed rather than empowered. When there seem to be no limits to choices, the process of shopping becomes more of an entertaining discovery than a thinking tourism. This tension makes satisfaction fragile, and people can later doubt whether their purchases were out of a real need or because of digital persuasion.

Even product reviews intended to provide information and make decisions may cause anxiety in the case of a strong divergence in opinion or an unnatural opinion. With trust compromised, there is less satisfaction, and users may turn back emotionally, although they may continue to use the platform out of necessity or habit (Cooke, 2024). In contrast to the retail sector, which is consumption- and identity-focused, make-well-being in digital financial technologies is based on security, autonomy, and long-term stability. FinTech applications, including mobile banking, investment apps, and digital wallets, provide common people with control over monetary activity, which was previously controlled by visiting the bank or employing the services of specialists. This comfort saves time and eliminates stress, which brings more happiness in day-to-day life. For individuals maintaining tight budgets or facing financial uncertainty, access to account information can be reassuring. Being able to track spending, divide savings, or make sense of patterns builds feelings of capability and decreases anxiety.

Trust is the foundation of digital financial well-being. Because financial transactions have both emotional and material value, users approach FinTech platforms with high sensitivity. Where interfaces are transparent, fees are presented clearly, and data protection is sound, people feel safe. Safety is not only technical but also emotional; it is about respect and recognition of vulnerability when one shares financial information. This level of clarity and ease of communication, the absence of extravagant costs, and reliable customer service turn the platform into an element of stability in the users' financial lives. Nevertheless, trust can be easily destroyed. In the case of platforms with confusing terms, often altering the structure with no notification, or suggesting financial products that do not have well-defined risks, users may feel exploited. The associated resentment or fear can be long-lasting. Financial mistakes, whether due to user error or complicated app design, tend to assume oversized emotional proportions, and clarity and guidance must be foregrounded in FinTech tools. A high percentage of users approach digital platforms because they feel intimidated by traditional financial systems. When digital mechanisms reproduce the same fears through jargon or opaque structures, the affective cost increases.

Behavioral design in FinTech can support positive habits only when used ethically. Soft reminders to save, notifications about bills to pay, and graphs of the progress made make a person feel more competent and lessen their financial burdens. The ability to achieve long-term stability is taught to the user in small steps. Nevertheless, high-ticket services or high-risk financial products can be promoted in the same way, which poses a threat to health. Nudges are more likely to increase satisfaction when they are used in line with the goals of users and decrease satisfaction when they are used in line with corporate profit and not the safety of the individual. In this sense, digital financial wellbeing depends on the alignment of intentions between the platform and the user (Issac, 2024). Access is another dimension of digital financial well-being. Digital financial tools around the world open opportunities for underserved people, including mobile money, easier credit systems, and less expensive remittance services. This expands their economic participation and increases their dignity and sense of independence.

Digital health brings a new form of interaction between technology and well-being, which, however, reaches vulnerability, resilience, and emotional sustainability. These may include telemedicine services, symptom checkers, wearables, mental health apps, and patient communities on the web (Boni, 2024). These tools have drastically changed the quality of life of most people by making healthcare more accessible and providing just-in-time assistance. Remote access to a doctor, access to medical records via the Internet, or monitoring of health indicators via wearable devices enables people to become more proactive regarding their health. Digital health helps people become more resilient, with a feeling of reassurance in uncertain situations. For a person living with a chronic condition, ongoing feedback from a device or being part of a community that offers support gives rise to decreases fear and increases confidence.

However, digital health can amplify anxiety if it encourages hyper-monitoring or unrealistic expectations. Wearables that monitor every step, every hour of sleep, or every heartbeat sometimes spur individuals toward self-criticism rather than motivation. Information out of context can breed anxiety, especially when minor fluctuations in readings seem to indicate impending doom. Platforms need to balance measurement with reassurance so that the user feels taken care of and not judged. In psychological cases, applications should not ignore the complexity of human emotions and cannot standardize or simplify the reactions. The problem of privacy is rare in digital health because medical data have a strong personal meaning. Mismanagement of data may expose users to stigma and discrimination and compromise their privacy. In contrast, with platforms talking with clarity and boundaries observed, a feeling of security and belongingness to the healthcare system may become more pronounced. Experiential relationships in digital health are also a basic constituent of satisfaction. \ Even minor design decisions can help create more human-friendly and supportive digital experiences through giving more time to the appointment, employing easy language, or sending follow-up messages. Online health communities present other complications. Mutually encouraging spaces, shared experiences, and learning were established. These communities cannot be substituted in isolation or in rare circumstances (Passalacqua et al., 2025). However, there are many risks: a rumor can be transmitted within a short period of time, and uncontrollable discussions may provoke fear or panic. Emotional sustainability in such spaces relies on thoughtful restraint, evidence-based leadership, and community conventions that emphasize kindness and precision. In digital retail, FinTech, and digital health, there is a trend: the higher the digital life satisfaction, the greater the support of autonomy, the establishment of trust, reduction of complexity, and provision of emotional reassurance. The digital industries that are most rewarding are those that acknowledge human needs, as opposed to subjecting people to behavioral outcomes or profitability. Retail shapes identity and convenience, FinTech shapes confidence and stability, and digital health shapes resilience and care. When these sectors prioritize human experience, they contribute not only to efficient daily routines but also to deeper forms of well-being that sustain people over time.

ETHICS, GOVERNANCE, AND HUMAN AUTONOMY

Digital ethics fundamentally raises questions about the effects of technology on human well-being and the values inherent in the systemss we operate. It involves consideration of the beneficiary and the costs incurred by digital innovation. Decisions on credit, employment, content visibility, and risk scoring are increasingly automated, with algorithms casting ethical doubts aboutout fairness and transparency. These systems seldom present logic, and their lives have a direct impact on people (Callaghan, 2025). Algorithms used in biased data spread historical disparities where the algorithms are applied; they can promote harmful content or harm human psychology, where they only optimize engagement. Ethical digital design does not just mean the mere use of laws but involves making purposeful decisions that never prioritize short-term gains at the expense of respect, inclusion, and long-term societal benefits.

Data justice goes a bit further and seeks to understand the ways in which data collection, processing, and application are indicative of larger social power frameworks. While digital ethics is concerned with the rights of individuals, data justice highlights the common good. This raises questions about whether data practices reinforce the status quo, whether the community is actively involved in decision-making on a case-by-case basis, and whether structural inequities manifest in data-driven systems. For example, a facial recognition device can incorrectly identify some population groups over others, whereas predictive policing can target disadvantaged communities more than others (Casiddu et al., 2024). These are not outcomes that occur by chance, but rather by the data that are gathered, their interpretation, and the experiences that are portrayed. Data justice calls for transparency, community consultation, and responsible stewardship to recognize the social weight of data. Data justice also requires questioning who controls the data infrastructure. Much of the world's data is owned or processed by a few dominant technology companies headquartered in a handful of regions. Such a concentration of power gives corporations the ability to shape global practices, influence public policy, and set the terms of digital participation. Ethical concerns arise when these actors operate with little oversight or accountability. People often have a limited understanding of how their data are monetized, exchanged, or used to shape their behavior. For true data justice to be realized, governance structures must be reimagined in such a way that power is distributed more equitably, users genuinely have agency, and communities can contest unjust practices.

The intersection of these ethical debates is human autonomy itself. It is not merely a case of choices but of significant, goal-congruent choices that show the values and knowledge a person has. Digital space distorts the borders of self-agency by providing hints in favor of a particular course of action (Cooke, 2024). The way messages are delivered, persuasive design, endless scrolling, and content feeds can modify behavior, and sometimes the user is hardly aware of it. While some nudges will no doubt be positive-they may remind people to do tasks or manage their health-others exploit attentional and emotional vulnerabilities. Governance should deal with the obligations of companies, the rights of individuals, and the demands of society

(Kuijer & Laschke, 2024). A human-centered digital market is one in which users understand how decisions are made, what data are used, and how they can exercise control. Governance becomes a shared responsibility involving ethical leadership within companies and oversight mechanisms that guard public interest (Tariq, 2026).

Just policies should also be established concerning international digital divides and representation. In most regions across the globe, digital platforms are important entry points into the economy, education, and governmental services. (Issac, 2024). An inclusive regulatory approach recognizes that, in the end, the meaning of digital fairness is not uniform; it must vary with the people it serves. Another critical aspect of governance is embedding accountability into algorithmic systems. Algorithm transparency does not pertain to the disclosure of proprietary code, but rather to how a decision will be made, what factors will be used to drive the results, and how the user may pursue redress in the event of errors. They also help reestablish trust by letting users know that someone is responsible for the digital decisions affecting their lives. Digital literacy should also be supported through governance structures. Autonomy and choice cannot be exercised unless users are empowered to learn about digital risks. Digital literacy concerning privacy, data rights, misinformation, persuasive design, and algorithmic influence is the foundation of a population confident in using digital environments.

Digital literacy is not only a technical aspect of life but also a kind of empowerment that makes people resilient to the digital environment and provides them with the opportunity to work within it on their conditions. Literacy is another highly enticing element of safety, along with ethical design and responsible governance, in digital settings. Finally, ethical digital governance will be collaborative in the future. Each of the players-governments, companies, civil society, academia, and communities-comes with a different perspective. No single actor can handle the complexity of digital ethics. This requires multistakeholder dialogues, public consultations, and international cooperation for the elaboration of principles that will guide technology towards humane outcomes. Showing a free online market, which operates according to human values, is not that something that occurs as a coincidence; it is an outcome of the active choice, common ideas, and efficient regulation. By basing digital systems on the respect of dignity, justice, and self-determination, societies are able to develop digital futures that not only work but also allow human flourishing.

EMERGING DIGITAL SPACES AND FUTURE WELL-BEING

New digital spaces are transforming the relationships that people have with themselves, each other, and the world around them to generate new opportunities in the meaning-making process, expressing their identity, and getting a sense of satisfaction in their daily lives (Cooke, 2024). The metaverse, artificial intelligence, and other emerging digital ecosystems are not only current trends in technology; they are also social worlds of the future that can impact emotional health, ethical conduct, and the organization of the digital existence of the future. Understanding how these spaces shape happiness requires moving beyond novelty and considering how they influence autonomy, cultural participation, and the quality of human relationships.

The metaverse is often envisioned as a shared, immersive digital environment and has emerged as a place where people seek not only entertainment but also meaning. Unlike other digital platforms, which have come before it, the metaverse enables people to inhabit embodied digital identities that shape how people present and interact with others (Issac, 2024). The sense of co-presence–being together even when physically apart-can reduce loneliness and strengthen social bonds. When access to physical community spaces is restricted, the metaverse offers alternative paths to involvement and recognition.

Nonetheless, the metaverse also raises complicated issues concerning online happiness. Immersion is a positive experience, yet it can also create a boundary between the virtual and real worlds. People may be so fond of their managed online selves or the ease of online fantasy that they experience less satisfaction in real-life relationships. It is not the peril of escapism as such; humans have always desired a creative escape in stories, art, and fantasy. Nevertheless, there is a possibility that digital worlds may cause expectations of the type of social interaction to change (Chrusciak et al., 2025). If virtual environments can be stimulated continuously, fed with great care, or offer an immediate response of emotions, real-life interactions might appear slow or strenuous. The outcome may be emotional disequilibrium, which minimizes the long-term viability of well-being. The complexities of this topography are compounded by the economic arrangements in the metaverse. (Saha, 2025). People may feel pressured to conform to commercialized standards of identity or to perform constantly for visibility. In these cases, the pursuit of digital happiness becomes entangled with economic competition, which can undermine genuine well-being.

Another dimension of future digital well-being is the integration of AI into everyday life. The boundary between support and control can be one of these challenges: AI systems learn from previous actions to predict needs but also tend to lead users in one way or another without their direct knowledge (Cooke, 2024). It can decrease cognitive load and increase convenience, but at the same time undermine autonomy, since it limits the area of options that users view as available. The impact of AI on information environments is also influential. Recommendation systems that aim to influence how individuals experience news, entertainment, and social content can increase emotional polarities, propagate falsehoods, or promote addictive media use when they focus on engagement concerns over well-being. Digital happiness does not just lie in the tools but also in the informational ecosystems that surround them. Provided that AI is somehow stimulating people against their own will or in a completely polarizing manner, it is difficult to stay emotionally balanced. Designing ethical AI requires mechanisms to assist in reflection, socialize people to different opinions, and make their results predictable instead of enhancing impulsive actions.

AI also raises complex questions regarding fairness and representation. Algorithms are only as good as the data they learn from, and if that data reflect existing biases, then AI systems might repeat or even amplify inequalities. For digital wellbeing to be fair, AI must reflect a diversity of needs, languages, cultures, and experiences. In the absence of representative training data and close attention to it, AI may exclude or misrepresent the experiences of the most marginalized groups. This may result in fewer opportunities, mistreatment of automated systems, and a lack of access to digital services. These results have physical and emotional harm, which results in material damage as well as emotional damage to dignity, belonging, and trust, the pillars of digital life satisfaction. As AI is introduced into new digital spaces, new dimensions are being questioned in terms of authenticity and emotional relationships. People are increasingly interacting with AI companions, creative assistants, and conversational agents that offer comfort, reduce loneliness, and provide non-judgmental support. For some, AI-based companionship may even be considered liberating because of its consistency without social pressure. However, such relationships also raise difficult questions regarding emotional dependency and the meaning of connecting with others as humans (Mortezapour & Vitiello, 2025). As AI systems begin to provide emotional needs with flawless functionality, there is a danger that people will establish expectations that cannot be recreated in human relationships. One of the most important ethical issues in the coming decades will be the need to balance AI-based emotional support with the creation of real human connections. The future of digital societies will be largely influenced by the fact that governance systems will undergo changes to handle AI systems. Openness in decision-making, sound supervision, and involvement of the people are some of the key requirements of AI governance. Communities are entitled to determine the manner in which AI tools are implemented, what information is gathered, and the level to which it influences their actions. Without collective responsibility, AI will only be an instrument of power concentration and not a common-good driver. Ethical governance should ensure that AI advances human abilities rather than leaving or undermining them. One of the potential questions of future digital well-being is how individuals will manage to feel agency within the world created by AI and immersive technologies. Agency is a process of making a choice and having knowledge of the consequences of these choices.

If fairness, inclusivity, and care guide the creation and design of the metaverse, it can become a place of creativity and expression. AI will be useful in improving well-being only when developed in an ethical, transparent, and respectful manner towards cultural diversity. These tools can add value to the human experience, but their application will be influenced by how societies will use them. In the next few decades, there will be no emergence of new technologies that make digital well-being, rather the richness of the human experience that the new technologies will allow. The future of digital life will be constructed by more than just engineers, communities, policymakers, designers, educators, and individuals who mediate the meaning of participation. New digital spaces allow individuals to prosper when they uphold individual autonomy and a sense of belonging and are able to help individuals fight off emotional losses. What we need In the future, imagination, wisdom, and responsibility-all elements that need to be combined to make digital technology–should be guided towards human flourishing and not its destruction.

CONCLUSION

The need to obtain digital life satisfaction is no longer a niche issue that can only be addressed by user interfaces or the number of people online. The key to understanding and enhancing digital life satisfaction requires a globally encompassing, psychologically conscious approach that incorporates the perspectives of human behavior, cultural diversity and variety, ethics, and technological design. The aim is not just to maximize engagement or consumption but rather to create ecosystems in which digital interactions support autonomy, resilience, trust, and meaningful connections. A psychologically informed framework begins with defining digital wellbeing drivers. All these emotional reactions, cognition, and behavioral patterns integrate to form the experience of users in dealing with technology. In the digital environment, satisfaction arises when the systems create a sense of better competence, clarity, and control. Digital spaces that overpower, control, or obscure decisions, on the other hand, impair well-being (Saha, 2025). Psychological evidence stresses that the elements of human motivation–autonomy, relatedness, and competence; are at the heart of user experience. People experience autonomy as a perception that they can make meaningful choices. Relatedness captures the sense of belonging and attachment to others. Competence involves being effective in negotiating tasks in a predictable and reliable manner. To the extent that digital systems support these needs, they will tend to enhance life satisfaction; to the extent that digital systems compromise these needs, they will tend to generate stress, frustration, or disengagement. Embedding these principles within the design of the platform will ensure that psychological well-being is considered integral to digital experiences, such as usability or performance.

Beyond individual psychology, digital life satisfaction is deeply influenced by cultural and socio-economic contexts. Users worldwide interact with technology in ways that reflect local norms, values, and infrastructure. Issues of access, language, and culturally specific expectations about communication or privacy impact how satisfaction is experienced by patients. A globally inclusive framework would consider such diversity into account in order to make digital environments accessible, respectful, and responsive to diverse populations (Bafadhal et al., 2025). Inclusion goes beyond technical access; it extends to ethical design, content representation and fair participation in governance. Through such considerations, digital ecosystems can become a place of empowerment instead of exclusion and positively contribute to well-being, regardless of socio-cultural boundaries.

Two pillars of digital life satisfaction are ethics and governance. Emotional stability in the digital world depends on data justice, transparency, and accountability, which enable trust. Users are more likely to be satisfied by being aware of the usage of their information, being satisfied that their interactions are safe, and having a way to get redress in case of harm. In contrast, systems of complete opaqueness, exploitative monetization approaches, and manipulative algorithmic nudges undermine trust and reduce well-being. Global inclusive governance structures ought to create standards that safeguard users while permitting innovation in a manner that does not impose regulation on innovation and creativity. The mechanisms of international cooperation, involvement of the population, and control may ensure that platforms function in a way that can guarantee the principles of fairness, equity, and human dignity. Such governance protects users and strengthens the legitimacy of digital markets, creating an environment in which life satisfaction can thrive.

Digital sectors have widely differing impacts on well-being, underlining the need for a comprehensive and sectoral understanding (Stengg, 2024). Telemedicine, mental health apps, and wearable devices can be used to strengthen the feeling of autonomy and affirm positive habits; however, they can be derailed by ethical failures, over-monitoring, or unreachable designs that erode emotional sustainability. These industry-specific dynamics are key to designing interventions that will provide people with better life satisfaction when they engage in various digital experiences.

The new digital spaces are the metaverse and AI-driven spaces, introducing new layers to the framework. These provide identity experimentation, self-expression, and socialization. Total immersive digital experiences may be used to support belonging, confidence building, and experimentation outside of traditional media. Ethically designed AI-driven systems should make the process more convenient, provide personalized support, and reduce cognitive load. However, these technologies are dangerous; AI can condition and control behavior in a subtle way, reinforce prejudice, and destroy autonomy in their improper use. New strains over digital status or economic activity can be created in the metaverse, and immersive worlds undermine the distinction between virtual and real-world engagements. Such risks are anticipated in a psychologically aware, globally accommodating framework that entrenches the protection of autonomy, transparency, and fairness.

Digital literacy and education are important factors in achieving life satisfaction. People who have the skills to use online spaces safely and guard their privacy and those who are able to think critically and critically process information are more independent and more emotionally strong. Literacy programs should not be based only on teaching skills of technical competencies, but also include moral reasoning, the capacity to discern an algorithmic impact, and approaches to juggling between online and offline life (Issac, 2024). Human experience prioritization can help designers, policymakers, and researchers develop ecosystems in which digital tools are tools of empowerment, creativity, and connectivity instead of distractions, manipulation, or exclusion. The framework also requires adaptability to changing circumstances. Digital environments are rapidly changing with new interfaces, immersive experiences, and AI capabilities that are reshaping user expectations and behaviors.

A digital life satisfaction approach cannot be fixed; it will soon become obsolete. In its place, an iterative, responsive model is needed, which monitors emergent trends, evaluates the effects of well-being, and changes governance, design, and educational policies on this basis. Feedback loops provide participatory design and intersector collaboration to ensure that the structures are relevant and efficient in supporting human needs. Through adaptation, newer psychological knowledge, technological change, and social change can be continually incorporated to achieve satisfaction in life, and adherence to old norms or beliefs can be cemented. Global inclusivity is central to this framework. Digital well-being cannot be achieved if solutions are concentrated in particular regions, cultural contexts or socio-economic groups. Equitable access to technology, ethical governance reflecting the diversity of values, culturally relevant design, and context-sensitive education are required to avoid reproducing inequalities in digital life satisfaction. Inclusion also means representation in research, governance and decision-making. Marginalized groups, which have been underrepresented in technology development, need the opportunity to shape the digital environments they live in. Inclusive models recognize that not everyone can have happiness, autonomy, and emotional resilience, but that these concepts must be learned and nurtured in the multiplicity of human existence (Saha, 2025). In conclusion, a globally welcoming, psychologically aware model of digital life satisfaction brings together many dimensions-psychology, culture, ethics, governance, sectoral practice, emerging technologies, measurement, and education–in one comprehensive approach that appreciates human flourishing. It prioritizes autonomy, competence, relatedness, trust, and emotional resilience in digital well-being. This framework will be able to prioritize diversity, incorporate ethics, create valuable interactions, and be flexible enough to lead the development of digital ecosystems that will make people and communities all over the world satisfied with their lives.

REFERENCES

Bafadhal, A. S., Hanafiah, M. H., & Anuar, F. I. (2025). Human behaviour in virtual tourism: A systematic literature review from a digital humanities perspective. *Current Issues in Tourism*, •••, 1–39. DOI: 10.1080/13683500.2025.2534460

Boni, E. K. (2024). *Exploring perceived risk and digital ethics affecting consumer experiences and decision-making in smart retailing* (Doctoral dissertation, Brunel University London).

Bucci, I., Fani, V., & Bandinelli, R. (2024). Towards human-centric manufacturing: Exploring the role of human digital twins in Industry 5.0. *Sustainability (Basel)*, *17*(1), 129. DOI: 10.3390/su17010129

Callaghan, C. (2025). *Rethinking growth and the future of work: The alignment economy as a general theory of human-centered AI*. SSRN working paper.

Casiddu, N., Burlando, F., & Chen, B. (2024). Human-de-centred design: Towards a (new) era of suffering. *Agathón | International Journal of Architecture. Art and Design*, *16*, 242–249.

Chrusciak, C. B., Szejka, A. L., & Junior, O. C. (2025). Integrating digital transformation with human-centric factors strategies to enhance organisational process performance: The HOPE model. *Journal of Industrial Information Integration*, *44*, 100785. DOI: 10.1016/j.jii.2025.100785

Cooke, F. L. (2024). Sustainability and human-centred human resource management. In *A research agenda for work and employment* (pp. 23–40). Edward Elgar Publishing. DOI: 10.4337/9781803929972.00007

Duarte, P. (2025). Beyond incentives: Rethinking internal marketing drivers of commitment in the AI-transformed banking sector. *International Journal of Bank Marketing*, •••, 1–25.

Firescu, V., & Filip, D. (2025). Human factors and ergonomics in sustainable manufacturing systems: A pathway to enhanced performance and wellbeing. *Machines (Basel)*, *13*(7), 595. DOI: 10.3390/machines13070595

Fusco Girard, L. (2024). The circular "human-centred" adaptive reuse of cultural heritage: Theoretical foundations. In *Adaptive reuse of cultural heritage: Circular business, financial and governance models* (pp. 15–69). Springer.

Issac, A. L. (2024). The human-centred workplace in Industry 4.0: Cultivating well-being and engagement. In *Smart cities and circular economy* (pp. 1–8). Emerald Publishing Limited. DOI: 10.1108/978-1-83797-957-820241001

Kotler, P., Pfoertsch, W., Ancarani, F., & Ureta, I. (Eds.). (2024). *Humanism in marketing: Responsible leadership and the human-to-human approach.* Springer Nature. DOI: 10.1007/978-3-031-67155-5

Kristiyanto, D. Y., Purnomo, H. D., Cesna, G. P., & Ani, N. (2025). The strategic role of orange technology in cultivating innovation and well-being. *IAIC Transactions on Sustainable Digital Innovation*, *7*(1), 27–37. DOI: 10.34306/itsdi.v7i1.707

Kuijer, L., & Laschke, M. (2024). Designing for a post-growth society through the eco-harmonist: A critical examination of the role of HCI and technology design. In *Proceedings of the 13th Nordic Conference on Human-Computer Interaction* (pp. 1–13). DOI: 10.1145/3679318.3685405

Mani, S., Tiwari, P., Ramchandani, S., Acharya, P. S., & Irudayaraj, V. D. (2025). From clicks to conversions: How AI shapes consumer trust, experience, and online buying behaviour. *Advances in Consumer Research. Association for Consumer Research (U. S.)*, *2*, 5028–5035.

Mishra, R., Tripathi, P., & Kumar, N. (2025). Human-centered infrastructure for sustainable smart cities in Industry 5.0. In *Building a human-centred infrastructure for sustainable Industry 5.0 in Asia* (pp. 301–319). Springer Nature Singapore. DOI: 10.1007/978-981-95-0417-6_13

Mortezapour, A., & Vitiello, G. (2025). Human-centered AI with focus on human–robot interaction. *arXiv preprint.*

Nasir, V., Hosseini, A., Binfield, L., Hasani, N., Ghotb, S., Diederichs, V., & Hansen, E. (2025). Human-centric Industry 5.0 manufacturing: A multi-level framework from design to consumption within Society 5.0. *International Journal of Sustainable Engineering*, *18*(1), 2551000. DOI: 10.1080/19397038.2025.2551000

Passalacqua, M., Pellerin, R., Magnani, F., Doyon-Poulin, P., Del-Aguila, L., Boasen, J., & Léger, P. M. (2025). Human-centred AI in Industry 5.0: A systematic review. *International Journal of Production Research*, *63*(7), 2638–2669. DOI: 10.1080/00207543.2024.2406021

Saha, A. (2025). Human-centred innovation in Society 5.0. In *Society 5.0: A transformation towards human-centered artificial intelligence* (p. 143). Springer. DOI: 10.1201/9781003643166-7

Singh, P., & Chaudhary, R. (2025). Enhancing employee wellbeing in Industry 5.0: A comprehensive literature review. In *Building a human-centred infrastructure for sustainable Industry 5.0 in Asia* (pp. 249–272). Springer Nature Singapore. DOI: 10.1007/978-981-95-0417-6_11

Stengg, W. (2024). *Digital policy in the EU: Towards a human-centred digital transformation*. Edward Elgar Publishing. DOI: 10.4337/9781035338641

Szostak, M. (2025). Aesthetic insight into humanistic management and AI: Research perspectives. In *AI and humanistic management* (pp. 13–58). Springer. DOI: 10.4324/9781003654377-3

Tariq, M. U. (2026). The Semiotics of AI-Driven Consumer Experiences: Decoding Emotional Branding and the Experience Economy. In Piccolo, R., & Boero, M. (Eds.), *Emotional and Experiential Dimensions of Modern Marketing* (pp. 245–268). IGI Global Scientific Publishing., DOI: 10.4018/979-8-3373-7615-8.ch010

Tariq, M. U. (2026). Innovation and Agility-Adapting Business Strategies for Sustainable Growth in Dynamic Markets. In Ananthan, S., Kohli, A., Manickam, T., & Dhanabalan, T. (Eds.), *New Business Development Strategies for Achieving Sustainable Growth* (pp. 113–140). IGI Global Scientific Publishing., DOI: 10.4018/979-8-3373-2048-9.ch005

Tariq, M. U. (2026). Breaking the Glass Ceiling: Strategies for Closing the Gender Gap in the Modern Workplace. In Montaudon-Tomas, C., & Pinto-López, I. (Eds.), *Reducing the Gender Gap in the Workplace* (pp. 65–88). IGI Global Scientific Publishing., DOI: 10.4018/979-8-3693-9000-9.ch003

Tarnanidis, T., & Vlachopoulou, M. (Eds.). (2025). *Cultural Sensitivity, Cross-Border Logistics, and E-Commerce in Global Marketing*. IGI Global Scientific Publishing., DOI: 10.4018/979-8-3373-0528-8

Tarnanidis, T. K. (Ed.). (2024). *Reshaping Marketing Science in Wholesaling and Retailing*. IGI Global Scientific Publishing., DOI: 10.4018/979-8-3693-6145-0

Yip, C., Dong, Z. Y., Tao, Y., & Lai, S. (2025). Towards sustainable human-centred smart cities: Design framework and case studies for Hong Kong and Riyadh. *IET Smart Cities*, *7*(1), e70010. DOI: 10.1049/smc2.70010

KEY TERMS AND DEFINITIONS

Digital Life Satisfaction: The degree to which individuals perceive their digital experiences as supporting well-being, autonomy, meaningful relationships, and overall quality of life.

Human-Centred Digital Design: An approach to technology development that prioritises human needs, values, and psychological well-being over engagement maximisation or purely commercial outcomes.

Autonomy: The individual's capacity to make informed, voluntary, and value-aligned choices within digital environments without undue manipulation or coercion.

Digital Well-Being: A multidimensional state encompassing emotional balance, cognitive clarity, healthy behaviours, trust, and social connectedness in digital contexts.

Choice Architecture: The design of digital environments that subtly shapes user decisions through interface structure, defaults, and nudges, influencing behaviour and satisfaction.

Data Justice: A normative framework concerned with fairness, accountability, and equity in the collection, use, and governance of data, particularly in relation to power asymmetries.

Digital Literacy: The ability to critically engage with digital technologies, including understanding risks, protecting privacy, recognising algorithmic influence, and exercising informed agency.

Chapter 3
Building Human-Centered Digital Markets

Deepak Gupta
http://orcid.org/0000-0003-3929-1362
Institute of Technology and Management, Gwalior, India

Rakhmatullayev Bobir
Termez University of Economics and Service, Termez, Uzbekistan

Jabbarov Umarbek
Mamun University, Khiva, Uzbekistan

Tuychieva Madina
University of Science and Technologies, Uzbekistan

Melibayeva Gulxon Nazrullayevna
Kokand University, Uzbekistan

Inomjon Madaminov
Urgench State University, Uzbekistan

Gulchekhra Nazarova
Tashkent University of Information Technologies, Uzbekistan

ABSTRACT

Digital markets have transformed global commerce, yet many platforms prioritize technological efficiency over human well-being and user experience. This chapter examines the theoretical foundations and practical implementations of human-centered design principles in digital market ecosystems. Through systematic analysis of consumer psychology, platform economics, and ethical frameworks, we explore how organizations can create digital marketplaces that enhance life satisfaction while maintaining commercial viability. The research synthesizes current literature on digital transformation, consumer behavior, and human-computer interaction to propose a comprehensive model for human-centered digital markets. Key findings indicate that platforms integrating user well-being metrics, transparent algorithmic decision-making, and participatory design methodologies demonstrate superior long-term customer retention and market sustainability.

DOI: 10.4018/979-8-3373-8357-6.ch003

1. INTRODUCTION

The digital revolution has fundamentally transformed how humans interact with markets, creating unprecedented opportunities for global commerce while simultaneously introducing complex challenges related to user experience, privacy, and well-being (Verhoef et al., 2021). As digital platforms increasingly mediate economic transactions, the imperative to design these systems with human needs at their center has become critical for sustainable market development and societal progress.

Digital markets represent complex socio-technical systems where technological capabilities, business models, and human behaviors intersect to create value for multiple stakeholders (Hanelt et al., 2021). However, traditional market design approaches often prioritize technological efficiency and profit maximization over user well-being and life satisfaction. This misalignment has led to various challenges including digital addiction, privacy concerns, algorithmic bias, and reduced user agency in digital environments.

1.1 The Emergence of Human-Centered Digital Design

The concept of human-centered design in digital markets emerges from the recognition that sustainable business success requires more than technological sophistication—it demands deep understanding of human needs, motivations, and well-being outcomes (Cutolo & Kenney, 2021). This approach shifts focus from purely transactional relationships to meaningful user experiences that enhance life satisfaction.

1.1.1 Defining Human-Centered Digital Markets

Human-centered digital markets prioritize user well-being, autonomy, and meaningful choice while maintaining commercial viability. These markets integrate psychological insights, ethical considerations, and user participation in design processes to create platforms that serve human flourishing alongside business objectives.

1.1.2 Key Characteristics and Principles

Effective human-centered digital markets exhibit several core characteristics: transparency in algorithmic decision-making, user control over personal data, inclusive design practices, and mechanisms for user feedback and participation in platform governance. These principles ensure that technological capabilities serve human needs rather than exploiting user vulnerabilities.

1.2 Market Evolution and Digital Transformation

Digital transformation has fundamentally altered market structures, creating new forms of value creation and exchange that require novel approaches to user experience design (Rietveld & Schilling, 2021). Understanding this evolution provides essential context for developing human-centered approaches to digital market design.

1.2.1 Platform Economy Dynamics

The platform economy has created new forms of market intermediation where digital platforms facilitate interactions between multiple user groups. These multi-sided markets present unique challenges and opportunities for implementing human-centered design principles across diverse stakeholder needs.

1.2.2 Technology-Mediated Relationships

Digital markets increasingly rely on algorithmic mediation of human relationships and transactions. This technological mediation creates both opportunities for personalization and risks of manipulation, highlighting the importance of ethical design frameworks that prioritize user agency and well-being.

2. THEORETICAL FOUNDATIONS

The theoretical foundation for human-centered digital markets draws from multiple disciplinary perspectives, including consumer psychology, platform economics, human-computer interaction, and digital ethics. These diverse theoretical streams converge to provide a comprehensive framework for understanding how digital markets can be designed to enhance human well-being while maintaining commercial viability.

2.1 Consumer Psychology in Digital Environments

Digital markets fundamentally alter traditional consumer behavior patterns, creating new psychological dynamics that require careful consideration in platform design. Understanding these psychological mechanisms is essential for creating markets that support rather than exploit human decision-making processes.

2.1.1 Digital Trust and Relationship Formation

Trust represents a fundamental component of successful digital market interactions, with research demonstrating that consumer trust significantly influences purchase intentions and platform loyalty. Digital environments present unique challenges for trust formation due to the absence of traditional social cues and the prevalence of algorithmic mediation.

Figure 1. Digital Trust Formation Model in Human-Centered Markets

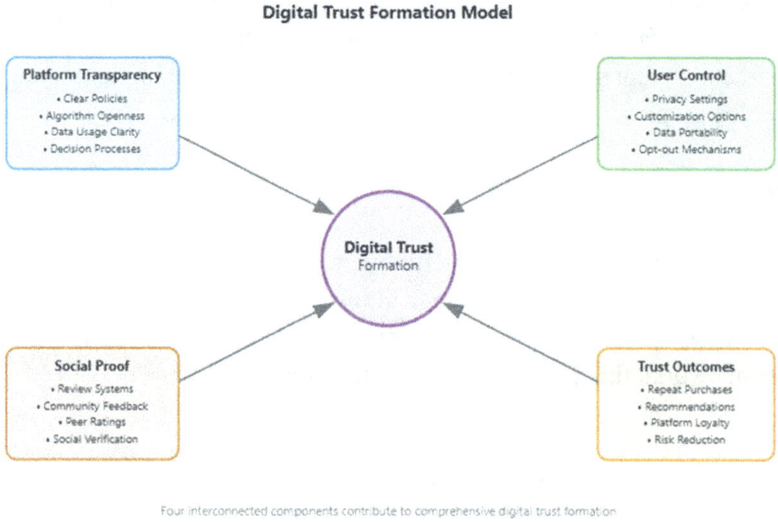

Figure 1. The multi-dimensional nature of trust formation in digital environments, showing the relationship between platform transparency, user control mechanisms, social proof systems, and resulting trust outcomes. The diagram should display four interconnected components: Platform Transparency (showing algorithmic openness and data usage clarity), User Control (depicting privacy settings and customization options), Social Proof (illustrating review systems and community feedback), and Trust Outcomes (showing behavioral indicators like repeat purchases and recommendation likelihood).

Trust formation in digital markets involves multiple dimensions including competence trust (belief in platform capabilities), benevolence trust (belief in platform good intentions), and integrity trust (belief in platform honesty and reliability). Human-centered design approaches recognize these psychological foundations and implement design features that support natural trust-building processes.

2.1.2 Psychological Impact of Digital Market Interactions

The psychological impact of digital market interactions extends beyond immediate transaction satisfaction to influence broader well-being outcomes. Research indicates that positive digital market experiences can enhance life satisfaction through increased autonomy, competence, and social connection, while negative experiences can contribute to stress, anxiety, and reduced sense of agency (Chen et al., 2022).

Digital market design significantly influences user psychological states through interface design, interaction patterns, and feedback mechanisms. Human-centered approaches prioritize design features that support psychological well-being, including clear information presentation, meaningful choice architecture, and positive feedback loops that enhance user confidence and satisfaction.

2.2 Platform Economics and Network Effects

Platform economics provides essential insights into the structural characteristics of digital markets and their implications for human-centered design. Understanding these economic dynamics is crucial for developing sustainable approaches to human-centered digital market design.

2.2.1 Multi-Sided Market Dynamics

Digital platforms often operate as multi-sided markets where different user groups interact through the platform infrastructure. Designing human-centered experiences in multi-sided markets requires balancing the needs and well-being of all participant groups while maintaining platform viability (Böttcher et al., 2022).

The challenge of multi-sided market design lies in creating value propositions that serve multiple stakeholder groups without exploiting any single group. Human-centered approaches emphasize fair value distribution, transparent governance mechanisms, and participatory design processes that include all stakeholder perspectives.

2.2.2 Network Effects and User Value Creation

Network effects represent a fundamental characteristic of digital markets, where platform value increases with user participation. Human-centered design approaches recognize that sustainable network effects must be based on genuine user value rather than artificial engagement mechanisms or addictive design patterns.

Positive network effects in human-centered digital markets emerge from authentic social connections, meaningful content sharing, and collaborative value creation. These effects are sustained through design features that support user autonomy, meaningful choice, and positive social interactions rather than exploiting psychological vulnerabilities.

2.3 Digital Ethics and Responsible Design

Ethical considerations provide essential guidance for human-centered digital market design, addressing questions of user autonomy, algorithmic fairness, and platform responsibility. These ethical frameworks help ensure that technological capabilities serve human flourishing rather than causing harm.

2.3.1 Algorithmic Transparency and User Agency

Algorithmic transparency represents a critical component of ethical digital market design, enabling users to understand how platform decisions affect their experiences and outcomes. Research demonstrates that increased algorithmic transparency can enhance user trust, perceived fairness, and overall satisfaction with digital platforms.

Implementing algorithmic transparency requires careful balance between providing meaningful information and avoiding information overload. Human-centered approaches develop transparency mechanisms that are accessible, relevant, and actionable for typical users rather than purely technical disclosures.

2.3.2 Data Privacy and User Control

Data privacy and user control over personal information represent fundamental ethical requirements for human-centered digital markets. Users must have meaningful choice over data collection, usage, and sharing practices, with clear understanding of how their data contributes to platform operations and value creation.

Effective privacy frameworks in human-centered digital markets go beyond legal compliance to implement privacy-by-design principles that embed user control into platform architecture. These approaches recognize privacy as an enabler of user autonomy and platform trust rather than merely a regulatory requirement.

3. DIGITAL CONSUMER BEHAVIOR AND MARKET PSYCHOLOGY

Understanding digital consumer behavior requires recognition of how technological mediation alters traditional psychological processes related to decision-making, social interaction, and value perception. Digital markets create new forms of consumer experiences that differ substantially from traditional retail environments in their psychological impact and behavioral implications.

3.1 Psychological Mechanisms in Digital Purchasing

Digital purchasing involves complex psychological processes that extend beyond traditional consumer decision-making models. The absence of physical products, reliance on digital representations, and algorithmic recommendation systems create unique psychological dynamics that influence consumer behavior and satisfaction outcomes.

3.1.1 Cognitive Processing in Digital Environments

Digital environments alter cognitive processing through information presentation methods, interaction designs, and attention management techniques. Research demonstrates that online reviews significantly influence consumer purchasing decisions through both cognitive and emotional processing pathways (Chen et al., 2022). Eye-tracking studies reveal that consumers process digital information differently than physical information, with implications for how markets should present product information and choice options.

Human-centered design approaches recognize these cognitive differences and implement information architecture that supports natural human information processing patterns. This includes appropriate information density, logical organization structures, and visual design that reduces cognitive load while providing necessary decision-making support.

3.1.2 Emotional Responses and Digital Satisfaction

Emotional responses to digital market interactions significantly influence both immediate purchasing decisions and long-term platform relationships. Digital environments can evoke both positive emotions (excitement, satisfaction, social connection) and negative emotions (frustration, anxiety, overwhelm) depending on design choices and interaction patterns.

The metaverse and immersive digital environments represent emerging frontiers for emotional engagement in digital markets, offering new possibilities for creating meaningful consumer experiences (Dwivedi et al., 2023). These technologies enable more embodied and emotionally rich interactions that can enhance consumer satisfaction when designed with human well-being as a priority.

3.2 Trust Dynamics in Digital Commerce

Trust formation in digital commerce involves unique challenges related to the absence of face-to-face interaction, reliance on technological mediation, and concerns about data privacy and security. Understanding these trust dynamics is essential for creating digital markets that support positive user experiences and long-term relationship development.

3.2.1 Multi-Dimensional Trust Formation

Digital trust formation involves multiple interacting dimensions including institutional trust (trust in platform organization), technological trust (trust in platform capabilities), and interpersonal trust (trust in other platform participants). Research demonstrates that effective digital platforms must address all three trust dimensions to create sustainable user relationships (Wang et al., 2022).

Figure 2. Three-Dimensional Trust Framework for Digital Markets

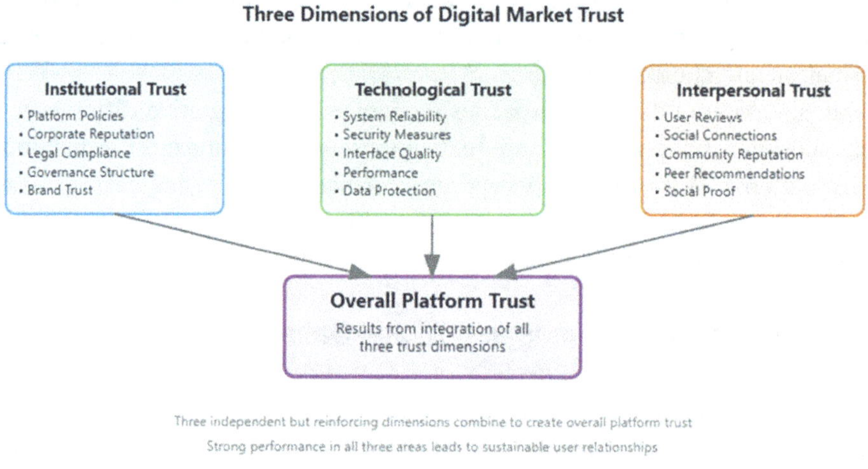

Figure 2. A comprehensive model showing how different types of trust interact in digital market environments. The diagram should illustrate three overlapping circles representing Institutional Trust (showing platform policies, reputation, and governance), Technological Trust (depicting system reliability, security measures, and user interface quality), and Interpersonal Trust (showing user reviews, social connections, and community reputation). The intersection areas should highlight how these trust types reinforce each other to create overall platform trust.

Human-centered design approaches recognize the interconnected nature of these trust dimensions and implement design features that support trust development across all three areas. This includes transparent governance systems, reliable technological infrastructure, and community features that enable positive interpersonal interactions.

3.2.2 Trust Maintenance and Recovery

Trust maintenance in digital environments requires ongoing attention to user experience quality, transparent communication, and responsive customer service. Digital platforms face unique challenges in trust recovery when negative experiences occur, as digital interactions may lack the personal relationship elements that facilitate trust repair in traditional business relationships.

Live streaming commerce represents an emerging model for trust formation that combines digital efficiency with more personal interaction elements, demonstrating how digital markets can incorporate human relationship dynamics to enhance trust and satisfaction. These hybrid approaches provide insights into how digital markets can maintain human elements while leveraging technological capabilities.

3.3 Personalization and Individual Differences

Effective human-centered digital markets must accommodate significant individual differences in user needs, preferences, and capabilities. Understanding these differences and implementing appropriate personalization approaches is essential for creating inclusive and effective digital market experiences.

3.3.1 Artificial Intelligence in Personalized Marketing

Artificial intelligence enables sophisticated personalization capabilities that can enhance user experiences when implemented with human-centered principles. Research demonstrates that AI-enabled personalization can improve customer journey experiences and satisfaction outcomes when designed to enhance rather than manipulate user decision-making (Huang & Rust, 2021).

Effective AI personalization in human-centered digital markets focuses on providing relevant choices and information rather than limiting user options or exploiting psychological vulnerabilities. This approach requires careful attention to algorithmic bias, user control over personalization settings, and transparency about how personalization systems operate.

3.3.2 Personalization Trends and User Agency

Current trends in personalization emphasize increasing sophistication in user modeling and recommendation systems, with implications for user agency and choice architecture. Research indicates that effective personalization must balance recommendation accuracy with user autonomy and choice diversity (Chandra et al., 2022).

Human-centered personalization approaches prioritize user control over personalization intensity, clear explanations of recommendation logic, and mechanisms for users to provide feedback about personalization effectiveness. These approaches recognize personalization as a tool for enhancing user agency rather than replacing user decision-making.

Figure 3. Personalization Effectiveness vs. User Control

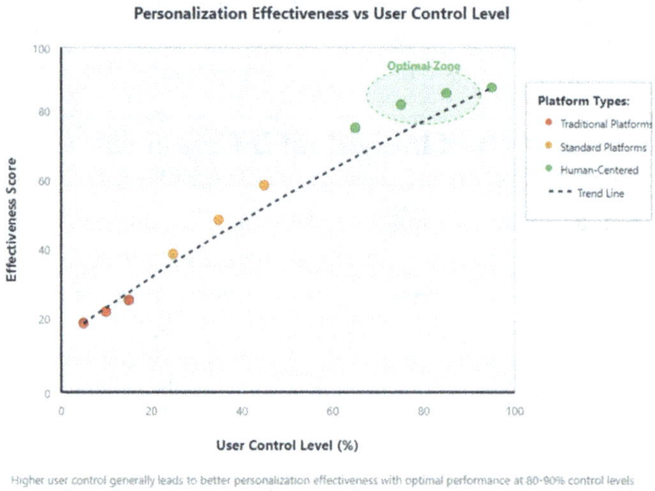

Figure 3. A scatter plot showing the relationship between personalization effectiveness (y-axis) and user control levels (x-axis) across different digital platforms. The data should demonstrate that platforms providing higher levels of user control over personalization settings achieve better long-term user satisfaction scores. Include trend lines showing optimal balance points and highlight examples of platforms that successfully combine high personalization with strong user control.

4. TECHNOLOGY INTEGRATION AND HUMAN-CENTERED DESIGN

The integration of advanced technologies in digital markets creates both opportunities and challenges for human-centered design. Successful integration requires careful consideration of how technological capabilities can enhance rather than replace human judgment, social connection, and meaningful choice.

4.1 Algorithmic Decision-Making and User Autonomy

Algorithmic decision-making systems increasingly influence user experiences in digital markets through recommendation systems, pricing algorithms, and content curation. Designing these systems to support rather than undermine user autonomy represents a critical challenge for human-centered digital markets.

4.1.1 Customer Segmentation and Algorithmic Fairness

Advanced algorithms enable sophisticated customer segmentation approaches that can provide more relevant and personalized experiences. However, algorithmic customer segmentation also raises concerns about fairness, transparency, and user autonomy. Research demonstrates that algorithmic segmentation can improve user experiences when implemented with appropriate transparency and control mechanisms (Salminen et al., 2023).

Human-centered approaches to algorithmic segmentation prioritize fairness, interpretability, and user control over how segmentation affects their experiences. This includes providing users with information about how they are categorized, mechanisms for contesting or modifying categorizations, and assurance that segmentation serves user needs rather than exploiting user characteristics.

4.1.2 Machine Learning and User Experience Enhancement

Machine learning capabilities offer significant potential for enhancing user experiences through improved personalization, predictive assistance, and automated support systems. However, implementing machine learning in human-centered digital markets requires careful attention to user understanding, control, and trust in algorithmic systems (Ngai & Wu, 2022).

Effective machine learning implementation focuses on augmenting rather than replacing human decision-making capabilities. This includes providing clear explanations of machine learning recommendations, enabling user override of algorithmic decisions, and implementing feedback mechanisms that allow users to improve algorithmic performance based on their preferences and needs.

4.2 User Experience Design Principles

User experience design in digital markets must address the unique characteristics of digital environments while maintaining focus on human needs and capabilities. Effective UX design creates interfaces and interaction patterns that feel natural, trustworthy, and empowering for users.

4.2.1 Customer Journey Optimization

Digital customer journeys involve multiple touchpoints and interaction modes that must be coordinated to create coherent and satisfying user experiences. Research demonstrates that effective customer journey optimization requires understanding of digital signals and user behavior patterns across multiple channels (Schweidel et al., 2022).

Table 1. Human-Centered Design Principles for Digital Customer Journeys

Journey Stage	Design Principle	User Need Addressed	Implementation Method	Success Metric	Example Application
Awareness	Transparent Value Communication	Clear understanding of platform value and expectations	Plain language messaging, honest benefit descriptions, educational content	Message comprehension rate >90%	Educational content marketing, clear value propositions
Consideration	Information Accessibility & Choice Support	Informed decision making with adequate information	Comparison tools, detailed specifications, user reviews, FAQ sections	Time to decision <15 minutes	Product comparison matrices, detailed product pages
Purchase	Friction Reduction & Security	Effortless, secure transaction completion	One-click checkout, transparent pricing, security indicators, multiple payment options	Cart abandonment rate <10%	Guest checkout options, saved payment methods

continued on following page

Table 1. Continued

Journey Stage	Design Principle	User Need Addressed	Implementation Method	Success Metric	Example Application
Post-Purchase	Proactive Support & Transparency	Confidence in purchase decision and support access	Order tracking, delivery updates, easy returns, responsive customer service	Customer satisfaction score >4.5/5	Real-time shipping notifications, self-service portals
Advocacy	Community Building & Recognition	Sense of belonging and valued contribution	User forums, review systems, loyalty programs, user-generated content features	Net Promoter Score (NPS) >50	Referral reward programs, community recognition systems

Table 1. A comprehensive overview of design principles organized by customer journey stage (Awareness, Consideration, Purchase, Post-Purchase, Advocacy). For each stage, include columns for: Design Principle, User Need Addressed, Implementation Method, Success Metric, and Example Application. The table should demonstrate how human-centered design principles can be systematically applied throughout the entire customer journey.

Human-centered customer journey design prioritizes user goals and contexts rather than solely focusing on business conversion objectives. This approach recognizes that supporting user success and satisfaction throughout their journey creates stronger long-term business outcomes than optimizing for short-term conversion metrics.

4.2.2 Accessibility and Inclusive Design

Accessibility and inclusive design represent essential components of human-centered digital markets, ensuring that platforms serve users with diverse capabilities, preferences, and contexts. Inclusive design approaches recognize diversity as a source of innovation rather than a compliance requirement.

Digital accessibility involves multiple dimensions including visual, auditory, motor, and cognitive accessibility considerations. Human-centered digital markets implement accessibility features that benefit all users rather than treating accessibility as specialized accommodations for specific user groups.

4.3 Omnichannel Experience Integration

Modern digital markets increasingly operate across multiple channels and touchpoints, requiring integration approaches that maintain consistency while adapting to different interaction contexts and user preferences.

4.3.1 Multi-Channel User Experience Coordination

Omnichannel experience coordination involves creating seamless transitions between different interaction channels while maintaining appropriate adaptation to each channel's characteristics and user contexts. Research demonstrates that effective omnichannel experiences significantly influence customer engagement and satisfaction outcomes (Roy et al., 2023).

Human-centered omnichannel design recognizes that different users prefer different channels for different activities and contexts. Rather than forcing standardization across channels, effective approaches optimize each channel for its unique strengths while maintaining overall experience coherence.

4.3.2 Digital-Physical Integration

The integration of digital and physical touchpoints creates new possibilities for enhanced user experiences that leverage the strengths of both digital and physical interactions. This integration is particularly important for markets serving products or services that benefit from tactile evaluation or social interaction.

Effective digital-physical integration recognizes the unique value propositions of each interaction mode and creates complementary rather than competitive relationships between digital and physical touchpoints. This approach enhances overall user choice and satisfaction by providing multiple options for achieving user goals.

5. MARKET SEGMENTATION AND PERSONALIZATION STRATEGIES

Effective market segmentation in human-centered digital markets requires approaches that recognize human diversity while avoiding discrimination or manipulation. Advanced technological capabilities enable sophisticated segmentation approaches that can enhance user experiences when implemented with appropriate ethical safeguards and user control mechanisms.

5.1 Data-Driven Consumer Understanding

Contemporary digital markets generate vast amounts of user data that can provide insights into consumer preferences, behaviors, and needs. Utilizing this data effectively while respecting user privacy and autonomy represents a critical challenge for human-centered design approaches.

5.1.1 Behavioral Analytics and User Insights

Behavioral analytics provide detailed insights into how users interact with digital platforms, enabling identification of patterns, preferences, and pain points that inform design improvements. However, behavioral analytics must be implemented with appropriate privacy protections and user understanding of data collection practices.

Human-centered approaches to behavioral analytics focus on understanding user needs and improving user experiences rather than maximizing platform metrics that may not align with user well-being. This requires careful selection of analytics metrics that reflect genuine user value rather than merely engagement or revenue indicators.

5.1.2 Predictive Modeling and User Anticipation

Predictive modeling enables platforms to anticipate user needs and provide proactive assistance or relevant recommendations. When implemented effectively, predictive capabilities can enhance user convenience and satisfaction by reducing effort required to accomplish user goals.

However, predictive modeling also raises concerns about user privacy, algorithmic bias, and manipulation. Human-centered approaches implement predictive modeling with strong user control mechanisms, clear explanations of how predictions are made, and safeguards against discriminatory or manipulative applications.

5.2 Personalization Technologies and User Control

Advanced personalization technologies enable highly customized user experiences that can significantly enhance satisfaction and effectiveness when implemented with appropriate user control and transparency mechanisms.

5.2.1 AI-Enabled Personalization Systems

Artificial intelligence enables sophisticated personalization capabilities that can adapt to user preferences, contexts, and goals in real-time. Research demonstrates that effective AI personalization can improve customer journey experiences and business outcomes when designed to enhance rather than replace user decision-making capabilities (Gao & Liu, 2023).

Human-centered AI personalization prioritizes user agency and control over algorithmic decisions. This includes providing users with understanding of how personalization works, control over personalization intensity and focus areas, and mechanisms for providing feedback to improve personalization effectiveness.

5.2.2 Dynamic Personalization and Context Awareness

Dynamic personalization approaches recognize that user preferences and needs change based on context, time, and circumstances. Effective dynamic personalization adapts to these changes while maintaining user control and preventing manipulation or unwanted behavioral modification.

Context-aware personalization considers factors such as user location, time of day, device type, and social context to provide more relevant and appropriate experiences. Human-centered approaches ensure that context awareness enhances user convenience without compromising privacy or creating uncomfortable surveillance experiences.

5.3 Segmentation Ethics and Fair Treatment

Ethical considerations in market segmentation address questions of fairness, discrimination, and user autonomy in how platforms categorize and treat different user groups. Human-centered segmentation approaches prioritize fair treatment and user well-being across all segments.

5.3.1 Avoiding Discriminatory Segmentation

Discriminatory segmentation practices can harm users by limiting opportunities, charging different prices unfairly, or providing inferior service quality based on demographic characteristics or other factors outside user control. Human-centered approaches implement segmentation practices that enhance rather than harm user opportunities and experiences.

Effective anti-discrimination measures include algorithmic auditing, diverse development teams, user feedback mechanisms, and ongoing monitoring of segmentation outcomes across different user groups. These approaches recognize that fairness requires active effort rather than neutral treatment of biased data or systems.

5.3.2 Transparency and User Control in Segmentation

Users have legitimate interests in understanding how they are categorized and treated by digital platforms. Transparency in segmentation practices enables users to make informed decisions about platform participation and provides opportunities for feedback and correction when segmentation is inaccurate or unfair.

Human-centered transparency approaches provide meaningful information about segmentation practices without overwhelming users with technical details. This includes clear explanations of how user data influences their experiences, mechanisms for users to view and modify their categorizations, and processes for addressing concerns about unfair treatment.

6. ETHICAL CONSIDERATIONS AND DIGITAL WELL-BEING

Ethical considerations in digital market design address fundamental questions about user autonomy, well-being, and fair treatment. Human-centered approaches prioritize ethical principles not merely as constraints but as enablers of sustainable business success and positive social impact.

6.1 Dark Patterns and Consumer Protection

Dark patterns represent design practices that manipulate or deceive users into making decisions that benefit platforms at user expense. Understanding and avoiding dark patterns is essential for creating digital markets that serve user interests and maintain long-term trust.

6.1.1 Identifying and Preventing Manipulative Design

Dark patterns take many forms including hidden costs, difficult cancellation processes, forced continuity, and deceptive interface elements. Research demonstrates that dark patterns particularly affect vulnerable consumers and can significantly harm user trust and satisfaction when discovered.

Human-centered design approaches actively identify and eliminate dark patterns through design review processes, user testing, and ongoing monitoring of user experiences. This requires organizational commitment to user well-being over short-term revenue optimization and implementation of design standards that prioritize user interests.

6.1.2 Positive Design Alternatives

Replacing dark patterns with positive design alternatives often improves both user experiences and long-term business outcomes. Positive alternatives include clear pricing information, easy cancellation processes, helpful reminders about subscription services, and interface designs that support rather than manipulate user decision-making.

Implementing positive design alternatives requires rethinking business models and success metrics to prioritize user satisfaction and long-term relationships over short-term conversion optimization. This shift often leads to improved user retention, positive word-of-mouth, and sustainable business growth.

6.2 Privacy and Data Ethics

Privacy and data ethics represent fundamental concerns for digital market participants, affecting user trust, platform legitimacy, and social acceptance of digital commerce. Human-centered approaches treat privacy as an enabler of user autonomy rather than merely a compliance requirement.

6.2.1 Privacy-by-Design Implementation

Privacy-by-design approaches embed privacy protections into platform architecture rather than treating privacy as an afterthought or add-on feature. This includes data minimization, user control over data collection and usage, and technical measures that protect user information throughout its lifecycle.

Effective privacy-by-design implementation requires interdisciplinary collaboration between technical teams, legal experts, and user experience designers to create solutions that are both technically robust and user-friendly. This approach recognizes privacy as a core feature rather than a burden to be minimized.

6.2.2 Data Ownership and User Rights

Questions of data ownership and user rights become increasingly important as digital platforms accumulate vast amounts of user information. Human-centered approaches recognize users as active participants in value creation rather than passive sources of data to be extracted.

User rights frameworks include rights to data portability, correction, deletion, and explanation of algorithmic decisions. Implementing these rights effectively requires technical capabilities, organizational processes, and user interface designs that make rights meaningful and accessible rather than merely theoretical.

6.3 Digital Well-Being and Life Satisfaction

Digital well-being encompasses the broader impacts of digital market participation on user psychological health, social relationships, and life satisfaction. Human-centered digital markets prioritize positive well-being outcomes as both intrinsic goods and enablers of sustainable business success.

6.3.1 Measuring and Monitoring Well-Being Impacts

Measuring digital well-being requires metrics that go beyond traditional engagement or satisfaction measures to assess impacts on user autonomy, stress levels, social connections, and overall life satisfaction. This includes both quantitative metrics and qualitative feedback mechanisms that capture user experiences holistically.

Human-centered measurement approaches recognize that well-being impacts may be delayed or indirect, requiring longitudinal assessment and careful attention to unintended consequences of design decisions. This includes monitoring for addictive usage patterns, social isolation, or financial stress resulting from platform design features.

6.3.2 Design for Positive Well-Being Outcomes

Designing for positive well-being outcomes requires understanding of psychological needs, social relationship dynamics, and factors that contribute to human flourishing. This includes supporting user autonomy, competence, and social connection through design features and interaction patterns.

Positive well-being design approaches include features such as usage time awareness, social connection facilitation, achievement and progress recognition, and tools for self-reflection and goal-setting. These features support user agency and self-determination rather than exploiting psychological vulnerabilities for platform benefit.

7. CUSTOMER EXPERIENCE AND ENGAGEMENT

Customer experience in human-centered digital markets encompasses the entire spectrum of user interactions with platforms, from initial awareness through long-term relationship development. Effective customer experience design creates positive emotional connections and practical value that enhance both user satisfaction and business outcomes.

7.1 Omnichannel Customer Experience Design

Modern customer experiences span multiple digital and physical touchpoints, requiring coordinated design approaches that maintain consistency while optimizing for each channel's unique characteristics and user contexts.

7.1.1 Cross-Channel Consistency and Adaptation

Effective omnichannel experiences balance consistency in core brand values and user experience principles with appropriate adaptation to different channel capabilities and user expectations. Research demonstrates that well-designed omnichannel experiences significantly impact customer satisfaction and loyalty (Rahman et al., 2022).

Human-centered omnichannel design recognizes that users may prefer different channels for different activities based on personal preferences, contexts, and capabilities. Rather than forcing standardization, effective approaches optimize each channel while maintaining coherent overall experiences that serve user goals.

7.1.2 Seamless Channel Integration

Seamless integration between channels enables users to move fluidly between different interaction modes based on their preferences and changing contexts. This includes technical integration that maintains user state and preferences across channels, as well as design integration that provides consistent interaction patterns and visual elements.

Effective channel integration requires understanding of user journey patterns and contexts that drive channel switching behaviors. This understanding informs design decisions about what information and capabilities should be available across channels versus optimized for specific channel strengths.

7.2 Digital Engagement and Community Building

Digital engagement extends beyond individual transactions to encompass ongoing relationships, community participation, and collaborative value creation that benefit both users and platforms through positive network effects.

7.2.1 Community-Centered Design Approaches

Community-centered design approaches recognize that many digital markets benefit from fostering connections between users rather than merely facilitating individual transactions. These approaches create spaces and mechanisms for users to share knowledge, provide mutual support, and collaborate on shared goals.

Effective community design requires understanding of social dynamics, moderation approaches, and incentive systems that encourage positive participation while preventing harmful behaviors. This includes attention to diversity, inclusion, and power dynamics that affect community health and sustainability.

7.2.2 User-Generated Content and Collaboration

User-generated content and collaborative features can enhance platform value while providing meaningful engagement opportunities for users. However, implementing these features effectively requires careful attention to content quality, user safety, and intellectual property considerations.

Human-centered approaches to user-generated content prioritize user agency, creative expression, and fair recognition of user contributions. This includes transparent content policies, user control over content visibility and usage, and mechanisms for users to benefit from their creative contributions.

7.3 Customer Journey Optimization

Customer journey optimization in human-centered digital markets focuses on supporting user goals and creating positive experiences throughout the entire relationship lifecycle rather than solely optimizing for business conversion metrics.

7.3.1 Journey Mapping and User Research

Comprehensive understanding of customer journeys requires ongoing research into user goals, pain points, emotional responses, and contextual factors that influence experience quality. This research informs design decisions and identifies opportunities for experience improvements.

Human-centered journey research emphasizes user perspectives and experiences rather than solely focusing on business process optimization. This includes understanding of user emotions, motivations, and broader life contexts that influence their interactions with digital platforms.

7.3.2 Experience Personalization and Adaptation

Experience personalization enables platforms to adapt to individual user preferences, capabilities, and contexts while maintaining respect for user autonomy and privacy. Effective personalization enhances user convenience and satisfaction without creating manipulative or addictive experiences.

Adaptive experience design recognizes that user needs and preferences change over time and across different contexts. This requires dynamic personalization capabilities that respond to changing user circumstances while maintaining user control over adaptation mechanisms and outcomes.

8. GLOBAL MARKET PERSPECTIVES AND CULTURAL CONSIDERATIONS

Human-centered digital markets must address the diverse cultural contexts, regulatory environments, and user expectations that characterize global digital commerce. Understanding these differences is essential for creating inclusive platforms that serve users effectively across different cultural and economic contexts.

8.1 Cultural Adaptation in Digital Markets

Cultural considerations significantly influence user expectations, interaction preferences, and value perceptions in digital markets. Effective cultural adaptation goes beyond language translation to address deeper cultural values, social norms, and communication styles.

8.1.1 Cross-Cultural User Experience Design

Cross-cultural user experience design requires understanding of cultural differences in information processing, decision-making styles, visual preferences, and social interaction norms. Research demonstrates that cultural adaptation can significantly improve user satisfaction and platform adoption in different geographic markets (Dwivedi et al., 2021).

Human-centered cross-cultural design avoids both cultural stereotyping and cultural imperialism by engaging with local users and communities to understand their specific needs and preferences. This includes participatory design approaches that involve local users in platform development and iteration processes.

8.1.2 Localization vs. Standardization Balance

Effective global platforms balance localization that addresses specific cultural needs with standardization that maintains platform coherence and development efficiency. This balance varies depending on the specific features, user groups, and cultural dimensions involved.

Human-centered localization prioritizes user value over development convenience, implementing cultural adaptations that meaningfully improve user experiences rather than superficial customizations that may not address real cultural differences or needs.

8.2 Regulatory Compliance and User Rights

Global digital markets must navigate diverse regulatory environments that address privacy, consumer protection, competition, and other aspects of digital commerce. Human-centered approaches treat regulatory compliance as a minimum baseline rather than a ceiling for user protection and rights.

8.2.1 Privacy Regulation and User Control

Privacy regulations such as GDPR, CCPA, and emerging frameworks worldwide establish minimum requirements for user control over personal data. Human-centered platforms often exceed these requirements by providing more granular control, clearer explanations, and easier mechanisms for exercising privacy rights.

Effective privacy implementation requires technical capabilities, organizational processes, and user interface designs that make privacy rights meaningful and accessible rather than merely theoretical. This includes considering diverse user technical literacy levels and cultural privacy expectations.

8.2.2 Accessibility Standards and Inclusive Design

Accessibility regulations and standards provide frameworks for ensuring digital platforms serve users with diverse capabilities. Human-centered approaches treat accessibility as an enabler of innovation and broader usability rather than merely a compliance requirement.

Universal design approaches often benefit all users rather than only those with specific accessibility needs. This includes clear information architecture, flexible interaction modes, and robust error handling that improves experiences for all users while particularly benefiting those with specific accessibility requirements.

8.3 Economic Development and Digital Inclusion

Digital markets can either exacerbate or help address global economic inequalities depending on their design approaches and business models. Human-centered platforms consider their broader social and economic impacts rather than focusing solely on profitable user segments.

8.3.1 Financial Inclusion and Access

Financial inclusion considerations address how digital markets can serve users with limited access to traditional financial services or lower economic resources.

This includes payment method flexibility, pricing approaches, and service designs that accommodate diverse economic circumstances.

Human-centered financial inclusion approaches recognize that serving economically diverse users often requires innovative business models and design approaches rather than simply reducing prices or features. This includes understanding of informal economies, alternative value exchange systems, and community-based financial practices.

8.3.2 Digital Literacy and Capability Building

Digital literacy differences significantly affect user ability to participate effectively in digital markets. Human-centered platforms consider their role in supporting user digital capability development rather than exploiting literacy differences for platform advantage.

Capability building approaches include intuitive interface design, progressive disclosure of advanced features, educational resources, and community support mechanisms that help users develop digital skills while accomplishing their immediate goals.

9. FUTURE DIRECTIONS AND EMERGING TECHNOLOGIES

The future of human-centered digital markets will be shaped by emerging technologies, evolving user expectations, and growing awareness of digital technology's social impacts. Understanding these trends is essential for developing sustainable approaches to human-centered design that remain effective as technology and society evolve.

9.1 Emerging Technology Integration

New technologies such as artificial intelligence, augmented reality, blockchain, and quantum computing create new possibilities for digital market design while also introducing new challenges for human-centered implementation.

9.1.1 Artificial Intelligence and Human Augmentation

Artificial intelligence technologies offer significant potential for enhancing user experiences through improved personalization, predictive assistance, and automated support. However, implementing AI in human-centered ways requires careful attention to user understanding, control, and trust in algorithmic systems.

Future AI integration in digital markets will likely emphasize human-AI collaboration rather than AI replacement of human capabilities. This includes AI systems that augment human decision-making, provide explanations for their recommendations, and enable users to easily override or modify AI decisions based on their preferences and expertise.

9.1.2 Immersive Technologies and Embodied Experiences

Immersive technologies such as virtual reality, augmented reality, and mixed reality create new possibilities for more embodied and emotionally rich digital market experiences. The metaverse represents one vision for how these technologies might create new forms of digital commerce and social interaction (Dwivedi et al., 2023).

Human-centered implementation of immersive technologies requires attention to user comfort, accessibility, privacy, and psychological well-being. This includes consideration of motion sickness, social anxiety, data collection in immersive environments, and the potential for more intense forms of manipulation or addiction in highly immersive settings.

9.2 Sustainability and Environmental Considerations

Growing awareness of digital technology's environmental impacts is driving attention to sustainability considerations in digital market design. Human-centered approaches recognize environmental sustainability as connected to human well-being and social responsibility.

9.2.1 Digital Carbon Footprint and Energy Efficiency

Digital markets consume significant energy resources through data centers, network infrastructure, and user devices. Human-centered sustainability approaches consider how to minimize environmental impact while maintaining service quality and accessibility.

Sustainable design approaches include energy-efficient algorithms, optimized data transfer, and user interface designs that reduce device energy consumption. These approaches often align with good user experience design principles such as fast loading times and efficient interactions.

9.2.2 Circular Economy and Product Lifecycle

Digital markets can support circular economy principles through features that extend product lifecycles, facilitate repair and reuse, and reduce waste generation. This includes platforms that connect users with repair services, enable product sharing, and provide information about product environmental impacts.

Human-centered circular economy approaches recognize that sustainability features must provide clear user value rather than merely creating burden or inconvenience. Effective implementations make sustainable choices easier and more attractive for users rather than relying solely on user environmental motivation.

9.3 Social Innovation and Collaborative Value Creation

Future digital markets may increasingly emphasize collaborative value creation, social innovation, and community-oriented business models that create value for broader stakeholder networks rather than solely extracting value for platform owners.

9.3.1 Platform Cooperatives and Shared Ownership

Platform cooperative models enable users to participate in platform ownership and governance, potentially aligning user interests with platform development decisions more effectively than traditional ownership structures. These models require new approaches to governance, decision-making, and value distribution.

Human-centered cooperative approaches focus on creating meaningful user participation rather than token involvement. This includes accessible governance mechanisms, transparent decision-making processes, and fair distribution of platform benefits among all stakeholders.

9.3.2 Social Impact and Community Benefit

Digital markets can create positive social impacts beyond commercial value by addressing social challenges, supporting community development, and enabling collaborative solutions to shared problems. This includes platforms that facilitate social services, enable community organizing, and support local economic development.

Effective social impact integration requires understanding of specific community needs and ongoing engagement with affected communities rather than top-down assumptions about social benefit. This includes participatory design processes, community feedback mechanisms, and measurement of social outcomes alongside business metrics.

10. CONCLUSION

The development of human-centered digital markets represents both a significant challenge and a critical opportunity for creating sustainable digital economies that enhance human well-being while maintaining commercial viability. This chapter has explored the theoretical foundations, practical approaches, and future directions for designing digital markets that prioritize human needs, autonomy, and life satisfaction.

10.1 Key Findings and Implications

The research synthesized in this chapter demonstrates that human-centered design approaches in digital markets can create competitive advantages through enhanced user trust, satisfaction, and long-term engagement. Organizations that integrate user well-being metrics, transparent algorithmic decision-making, and participatory design methodologies achieve superior customer retention and market sustainability compared to platforms focused solely on short-term revenue optimization.

10.1.1 Convergence of Business and Social Benefits

A critical finding is that human-centered design approaches often align business interests with user well-being rather than creating trade-offs between profitability and user benefit. Platforms that prioritize user agency, transparency, and positive well-being outcomes typically achieve better long-term financial performance through reduced customer acquisition costs, higher customer lifetime value, and positive brand reputation.

This convergence challenges traditional assumptions about business-user relationship tensions and suggests that sustainable digital market success requires genuine attention to user interests rather than manipulation or exploitation of user vulnerabilities.

10.1.2 Systemic Change Requirements

Implementing human-centered digital markets requires systemic changes in organizational culture, success metrics, design processes, and stakeholder relationships. These changes extend beyond individual design decisions to encompass fundamental questions about platform purpose, value creation models, and social responsibility.

Successful implementation requires leadership commitment, cross-functional collaboration, and ongoing engagement with user communities to understand evolving needs and expectations. Organizations must develop new capabilities in areas such as ethical design review, user well-being measurement, and participatory design facilitation.

10.2 Recommendations for Practice

Based on the analysis presented in this chapter, several key recommendations emerge for organizations seeking to develop human-centered digital markets:

10.2.1 Implement Comprehensive Ethical Design Frameworks

Organizations should develop and implement comprehensive ethical design frameworks that address user autonomy, transparency, fairness, and well-being throughout the design and development process. These frameworks should include specific guidelines, review processes, and accountability mechanisms that ensure ethical considerations are integrated into technical decisions rather than treated as afterthoughts.

10.2.2 Invest in User Research and Participatory Design

Deep understanding of user needs, contexts, and well-being outcomes requires ongoing investment in user research and participatory design processes. Organizations should develop capabilities for longitudinal user research, cultural sensitivity, and community engagement that inform platform development and evolution.

10.2.3 Develop Well-Being Metrics and Measurement

Traditional business metrics such as engagement time, conversion rates, and revenue per user may not align with user well-being outcomes. Organizations should develop complementary metrics that assess user autonomy, life satisfaction, and positive outcomes, using these measures to guide design decisions and evaluate platform success.

10.3 Future Research Directions

Several important areas require additional research to advance understanding and practice of human-centered digital market design:

10.3.1 Long-Term Impact Assessment

Research is needed to understand the long-term impacts of different digital market design approaches on user well-being, social relationships, and economic outcomes. Longitudinal studies can provide insights into how design decisions affect users over extended periods and inform development of more effective design approaches.

10.3.2 Cross-Cultural Design Methodologies

As digital markets become increasingly global, research into effective cross-cultural design methodologies becomes essential. This includes understanding of cultural differences in design preferences, trust formation, and value perception, as well as methods for incorporating diverse cultural perspectives into design processes.

10.3.3 Technology Ethics and Governance

Emerging technologies such as artificial intelligence, immersive reality, and blockchain create new challenges for human-centered design that require ongoing research attention. This includes development of ethical frameworks, governance mechanisms, and design practices that can address novel technological capabilities while maintaining focus on human well-being.

10.4 Final Reflections

The transition toward human-centered digital markets represents more than a design methodology—it embodies a fundamental shift in how we understand the relationship between technology and human flourishing. As digital markets become increasingly central to economic and social life, the imperative to design these systems in ways that enhance rather than exploit human capabilities becomes both a moral obligation and a practical necessity for sustainable business success.

The challenge ahead lies not in choosing between technological advancement and human well-being, but in achieving their integration through thoughtful design, ethical reflection, and ongoing commitment to user interests. The frameworks, principles, and practices outlined in this chapter provide a foundation for this integration, but their successful implementation requires sustained effort, continuous learning, and genuine commitment to placing human flourishing at the center of digital innovation.

The future of digital markets will be shaped by the design choices made today. By prioritizing human-centered approaches, organizations can contribute to creating digital economies that enhance life satisfaction, support community development, and create sustainable value for all stakeholders. This represents not just an opportunity for competitive advantage, but a responsibility to future generations who will inherit the digital systems we create today.

REFERENCES

Böttcher, T. P., Weking, J., Hein, A., Böhm, M., & Krcmar, H. (2022). Pathways to digital business models: The connection of sensing and seizing in business model innovation. *The Journal of Strategic Information Systems*, *31*(4), 101742. Advance online publication. DOI: 10.1016/j.jsis.2022.101742

Chandra, S., Verma, S., Lim, W. M., Kumar, S., & Donthu, N. (2022). Personalization in personalized marketing: Trends and ways forward. *Psychology and Marketing*, *39*(8), 1529–1562. DOI: 10.1002/mar.21670

Chen, T., Samaranayake, P., Cen, X. Y., Qi, M., & Lan, Y.-C. (2022). The impact of online reviews on consumers' purchasing decisions: Evidence from an eye-tracking study. *Frontiers in Psychology*, *13*, 865702. Advance online publication. DOI: 10.3389/fpsyg.2022.865702 PMID: 35756238

Cutolo, D., & Kenney, M. (2021). Platform-dependent entrepreneurs: Power asymmetries, risks, and strategies in the platform economy. *The Academy of Management Perspectives*, *35*(4), 584–605. DOI: 10.5465/amp.2019.0103

Dwivedi, Y. K., Hughes, L., Wang, Y., Alalwan, A. A., Ahn, S. J. G., Balakrishnan, J., Barta, S., Belk, R., Buhalis, D., Dutot, V., Felix, R., Filieri, R., Flavián, C., Gustafsson, A., Hinsch, C., Hollensen, S., Jain, V., Kim, J., Krishen, A. S., & Wirtz, J. (2023). Metaverse marketing: How the metaverse will shape the future of consumer research and practice. *Psychology and Marketing*, *40*(4), 750–776. DOI: 10.1002/mar.21767

Dwivedi, Y. K., Ismagilova, E., Hughes, D. L., Carlson, J., Filieri, R., Jacobson, J., Jain, V., Karjaluoto, H., Kefi, H., Krishen, A. S., Kumar, V., Rahman, M. M., Raman, R., Rauschnabel, P. A., Rowley, J., Salo, J., Tran, G. A., & Wang, Y. (2021). Setting the future of digital and social media marketing research: Perspectives and research propositions. *International Journal of Information Management*, *59*, 102168. Advance online publication. DOI: 10.1016/j.ijinfomgt.2020.102168

Gao, Y., & Liu, H. (2023). Artificial intelligence-enabled personalization in interactive marketing: A customer journey perspective. *Journal of Research in Interactive Marketing*, *17*(5), 663–680. DOI: 10.1108/JRIM-01-2022-0023

Hanelt, A., Bohnsack, R., Marz, D., & Marante, C. A. (2021). A systematic review of the literature on digital transformation: Insights and implications for strategy and organizational change. *Journal of Management Studies*, *58*(5), 1159–1197. DOI: 10.1111/joms.12639

Huang, M.-H., & Rust, R. T. (2021). A strategic framework for artificial intelligence in marketing. *Journal of the Academy of Marketing Science, 49*(1), 30–50. DOI: 10.1007/s11747-020-00749-9

Ngai, E. W. T., & Wu, Y. (2022). Machine learning in marketing: A literature review, conceptual framework, and research agenda. *Journal of Business Research, 145*, 35–48. DOI: 10.1016/j.jbusres.2022.02.049

Rahman, S. M., Carlson, J., Gudergan, S. P., Wetzels, M., & Grewal, D. (2022). Perceived omnichannel customer experience (OCX): Concept, measurement, and impact. *Journal of Retailing, 98*(4), 611–632. DOI: 10.1016/j.jretai.2022.03.003

Rietveld, J., & Schilling, M. A. (2021). Platform competition: A systematic and interdisciplinary review of the literature. *Journal of Management, 47*(6), 1528–1563. DOI: 10.1177/0149206320969791

Roy, S. K., Singh, G., Sadeque, S., Harrigan, P., & Coussement, K. (2023). Customer engagement with digitalized interactive platforms in retailing. *Journal of Business Research, 164*, 114001. Advance online publication. DOI: 10.1016/j.jbusres.2023.114001

Salminen, J., Mustak, M., Sufyan, M., & Jansen, B. J. (2023). How can algorithms help in segmenting users and customers? A systematic review and research agenda for algorithmic customer segmentation. *Journal of Marketing Analytics, 11*(4), 677–692. DOI: 10.1057/s41270-023-00235-5

Schweidel, D. A., Bart, Y., Inman, J. J., Stephen, A. T., Libai, B., Andrews, M., Rosario, A. B., Chae, I., Chen, Z., Kupor, D., Longoni, C., & Thomaz, F. (2022). How consumer digital signals are reshaping the customer journey. *Journal of the Academy of Marketing Science, 50*(6), 1257–1276. DOI: 10.1007/s11747-022-00839-w PMID: 35221393

Verhoef, P. C., Broekhuizen, T., Bart, Y., Bhattacharya, A., Dong, J. Q., Fabian, N., & Haenlein, M. (2021). Digital transformation: A multidisciplinary reflection and research agenda. *Journal of Business Research, 122*, 889–901. DOI: 10.1016/j.jbusres.2019.09.022

KEY TERMS AND DEFINITIONS

Algorithmic Transparency: The practice of making algorithmic decision-making processes understandable and accountable to users, including clear explanations of how algorithms work, what data they use, and how they affect user experiences and outcomes.

Digital Markets: Technology-mediated platforms and ecosystems where buyers and sellers interact through digital interfaces to exchange goods, services, or information, characterized by network effects, algorithmic mediation, and data-driven value creation.

Digital Trust: The confidence users place in digital platforms and systems, encompassing institutional trust (in platform governance), technological trust (in system capabilities), and interpersonal trust (in other users), which collectively determine user willingness to engage and share information.

Digital Well-Being: The positive impact of digital technology use on overall life satisfaction, encompassing psychological health, social connections, personal growth, and the ability to use technology in ways that support rather than undermine human flourishing.

Human-Centered Design: A design philosophy and methodology that prioritizes human needs, capabilities, and well-being throughout the design process, ensuring that technological solutions enhance rather than exploit human capabilities and support user autonomy and dignity.

Platform Economics: The study of multi-sided markets where digital platforms facilitate interactions between different user groups, creating value through network effects, data aggregation, and algorithmic matching while managing complex stakeholder relationships.

User Autonomy: The preservation and enhancement of user agency, choice, and control within digital systems, ensuring that users maintain meaningful decision-making authority over their interactions, data, and digital experiences.

Chapter 4
From Offline Happiness to Online Fulfilment: Understanding Life Satisfaction in Digital Spaces

Dilipkumar Ambadas Patil
http://orcid.org/0009-0002-3421-8588
Central University of Karnataka, India

Amrik Singh
http://orcid.org/0000-0003-3598-8787
Lovely Professional University, India

ABSTRACT

The study explores how the integration of online and offline life influences subjective well-being and happiness. Positive emotions, meaning, gratitude, and pro-social digital engagement enhance long-term happiness, while materialism and social comparison diminish it. Workplace platforms like Microsoft Teams and digital health interventions can support well-being when autonomy, competence, and relatedness are fulfilled, though digital fatigue and inequality remain key challenges. Digital well-being depends on purposeful, inclusive technology use that strengthens autonomy, connection, and balance between online and offline life.

INTRODUCTION

The fast spread of the digital technologies has changed the manner in which people find happiness in life, relationships and satisfaction. The traditional study of human well-being was in offline contexts (focusing on personal resources, social capital, and

DOI: 10.4018/979-8-3373-8357-6.ch004

material conditions). Modern digital economies, nevertheless, have presented optional online areas that mediate every day activities, working collaboration, business, and medical interventions. The concept of well-being in the modern world should thus be viewed through a multi-prism that incorporates internet use as a complement that replaces face-to-face life. Marketing psychology has proven that affective and moral aspects like positive emotion, meaning, gratitude, and pro-social consumption always increase consumer happiness. These factors foster a long-term contentment since they attach consumption to values and associations. On the contrary, high materialism, inappropriate goals, and perpetual comparison with edited images generate envy and relative deprivation, which stifles the life satisfaction (Dhiman and Kumar, 2023). This threat is even magnified by the online marketplace and social-media culture that presents users with an ideal life and unreachable standards. Another important field that digital involvement affects psychological wellbeing is the workplace. Microsoft Teams is now a leading collaborative tool, which integrates communication into smartphones, laptops and desktops. In accordance with Self-Determination Theory, technology must assist in autonomy, competence, and relatedness; however, according to the studies conducted by the use of the METUX model, the need satisfaction differs in various spheres of the interface, task, and life. IT professionals tend to give higher relatedness rates in comparison to teachers, and access using smartphones gives more competence and satisfaction than traditional computers (Asha and Kumar, 2025). The conclusions of these findings suggest that the design of digital work needs to go beyond the metrics of productivity, but be contextual, training, and feedback-oriented to provide a real benefit to the wellness of the employees. Another aspect of digital internal communication that is described by lifespan and sociological research depicts a dual nature of communication. Internet platforms assist individuals in sustaining relations over a geographical boundary, emotional support, as well as community-forming and identity-building. However, unedited or idle use, particularly the passive scrolling, has made difficult such negative effects as loneliness, anxiety, and diminished psychological health (Tsouparopoulou et al., 2025). Technology is therefore mediating and not a force of its own.Counter-evidence is optimistic with technology-assisted health interventions. User-friendly applications that facilitate physical activity programs have enhanced motivation, convenience, life satisfaction, and happiness and minimized depressive and anxiety symptoms among the intervention groups (Lu et al., 2025). Nonetheless, the digital fatigue, the lack of a personal approach, and the pressure associatewith performance monitoring also shed some light on the value of the interventions that are individual and cultural.Online shopping in rural areas has been linked to a higher happiness level through a better material well-being and social capital (Wei et al., 2024). However, older lower-educated more impoverished families receive these benefits to a lower degree because of the obstacle of digital illiteracy. Corporate internal branding programs demonstrate that the digital environments that are more healthy can tame technostress and promote sustainable wellbeing (Raj and Goute, 2025).All of these studies demonstrate that the quality of digital involvement and its intent to either satisfaction or fatigue depends on what people utilize the internet. The current study thus aims at making contributions to this dynamic digital sociology by analyzing hybrid living among consumers, employees and among members of a community and by further advancing the objectives aimed at solving the digital divide and self-regulation.

OBJECTIVES

To evaluate the offline and deliberate usage of digital technology on subjective well-being and happiness.
To investigate the fulfilment of autonomy, competence, and relatedness by interface, task, and life level among the users of Microsoft Teams.
To examine the social comparison and envy in optional online activity.
To compare the effectiveness of the use of physical-activity interventions based on technology in life satisfaction.
To comprehend distributional disparities arising out of digital divide both in trade and working places.
To suggest design and policy lessons in the case of inclusive digital citizenry.
To incorporate multimodal communicative channels of communication in lifespan settings.

RESEARCH QUESTIONS

How do offline/digital involvement and subjective well-being relate to one another?
What do Microsoft Teams fulfill in regard to autonomy, competence, and relatedness in various areas?
Are there digital task and life relatedness differences between IT professionals and teachers?
What devices (smartphone or laptop/desktop) are more competent in terms of interface and satisfying?
What are the impacts of social comparison envy on life satisfaction and self-esteem?
Are physical-activity programs based on technology effective to increase happiness?

What is the moderating role of digital divide on well-being in rural commerce and organizations?

OFFLINE SUBJECTIVE WELL-BEING AND HAPPINESS.

Positive emotion, meaning, gratitude and pro-social consumption are always found to boost long term happiness whereas excessive materialism, social comparison and mis-adjusted aspirations are known to suppress it(Dhiman & Kumar, 2023).

The psychological health of the employees in the era of the digital world and with the particular reference to the employees using Microsoft Teams as a collaborative workplace solution(Asha & Kumar, 2025). It is based on the Self-Determination Theory and the METUX user-experience model, in which the platform would be compared to the fulfilment of the basic psychological needs: autonomy, competence, and relatedness within the interface, task, and life sphere, where the IT professionals typically have more tasks and life relatedness compared to the teachers, and access to smartphones would be more beneficial in terms of interface competence and overall satisfaction than access to laptops or desktop computers(Asha & Kumar, 2025). The design of technology must also shift beyond productivity and include contextual features, specific training, and feedback mechanisms that can be more supportive of the various professions and gadgets(Asha & Kumar, 2025). These lessons can provide valuable advice to designers and organizations that want to design more inclusive digital-workplaces that actually improve psychological well-being(Asha & Kumar, 2025).

The use of digital technology has a complicated correlation with subjective well-being, and it is specifically the effects of online interaction on social connectedness, mental health, and life satisfaction(Tsouparopoulou et al., 2025). The digital technologies themselves are neither good or bad, but rather their impact will be determined by the use patterns, personal traits, and social situations(Tsouparopoulou et al., 2025). Middle and deliberate use of internet may also contribute to augment life satisfaction by means of socialization, gaining information, emotional encouragement, and avenues of self-expression(Tsouparopoulou et al., 2025). Online platforms assist people to sustain relationships, most notably across geographical limits, and offer community-building and identity-forming space(Tsouparopoulou et al., 2025). Nevertheless, too much or inactive use of digital has a number of possible adverse effects. Excessive consumption of social media is linked with social comparison, loneliness, anxiety, and less psychological well-being(Tsouparopoulou et al., 2025). Artificial intelligence, perpetual connectivity, and exposure to unattainable images that are contained in the internet can compromise self-worth and contentment with existence(Tsouparopoulou et al., 2025). The quality of internet interaction is more than the quantity, and active engagement, which is significant, has more positive well-being effects than passive scrolling(Tsouparopoulou et al., 2025). On the whole, the modern digital sociology through the promotion of an ambivalent attitude to the use of technology(Tsouparopoulou et al., 2025). It demands better digital citizenry, self-regulation and supportive policy interventions to fulfill the maximum of the positive social and psychological value of digital technologies and reduce the risks(Tsouparopoulou et al., 2025).

The efficacy of physical activity interventions based on technology in enhancing the physical activity, mental health, life satisfaction, and happiness of adults(Lu et al., 2025). Also, some changes were observed in the intervention group, such as improved physical activity, greater life satisfaction and happiness, and fewer depressive, anxiety, and social dysfunction symptoms(Lu et al., 2025). Engagement in physical activity and satisfaction with life were part of the intervention that demonstrated significant effects(Lu et al., 2025). These results were supplemented with qualitative findings that included positive experiences by the participants including improved motivation, convenience, social connection and emotional well-being(Lu et al., 2025). Nevertheless, it was also found that there are a few challenges such as digital fatigue, absence of personalization, and stress as a result of tracking performance functionality(Lu et al., 2025). All in all, the researchers conclude that physical and psychological health can be efficiently promoted with the help of well-developed, user-friendly technologies-based physical activity programs(Lu et al., 2025). The authors emphasize the importance of tailoring digital interventions to individual needs and cultural contexts to maximize long-term engagement and public health impact(Lu et al., 2025).

DIGITAL INVOLVEMENT; INTERNET INVOLVEMENT.

The impact of digital communications on psychological well-being throughout the life span is directed at multimodal connectedness, or the application of multiple communication channels to sustain relationships with other individuals, and indirectly through social capital, civic engagement, and positive affect(Chan, 2018). It does not affect well-being directly but its effects are attained by a collection of mediating pathways(Chan, 2018). Multimodal communication enhances the individual social capital through the creation and diversification of social networks, which further strengthens civic participation and positive affective experiences which improves life satisfaction and psychological well-being(Chan, 2018). Taking a lifespan approach, the results indicate significant age-related variations, with younger and middle-aged adults gaining greater well-being when taking an instrumental social and civic route, but with older adults gaining greater well-being through positive affect, despite the smaller number of digital technologies they use and the smaller size of their networks(Chan, 2018). Digital communication is accommodative, age sensitive communication techniques are important in fostering wellbeing in digital societies(Chan, 2018).The development of e-commerce makes the people in the rural areas much happier, with a mean growth of approximately 2.4(Wei et al., 2024). This beneficial impact depends mostly on the improved material welfare, smaller relative economic and social inequalities, as well as greater accumulation of social capital, whereas the positive effect of entrepreneurship is not directly converted into the well-being(Wei et al., 2024). The complementary aspect of digital finance in enhancing gains in well-being. Nonetheless, these benefits are not being equitably distributed since older, less-educated, and poorer households do not tend to gain these advantages as much because of the barriers to digital divide like technological and digital exclusion(Wei et al., 2024). In another case of the Corporate employee wellbeing mediates the interaction between internal branding and technostress, meaning the branding initiatives can help alleviate stress in employees through promotion of a healthier working environment(Raj & Goute, 2025). Moreover, there is a dual nature of digital internal communication as it directly enhances wellbeing and reduces technostress and moderates impact of internal branding and wellbeing in digital work setting(Raj & Goute, 2025). Generally, the technology-oriented organizations, internal branding with employees who are strengthened by an efficient digital communication system to aid in eliminating technostress's and enhancing sustainable wellbeing of workers in modern digital workplaces(Raj & Goute, 2025).

Individualization of explanations in the case of AI-driven decision-making affects how people respond in situations involving high stakes as a simulated loan rejection case based on the theory of justice(Wei et al., 2024). It demonstrates that any directive explanation results in more favourable perceptions of informational justice, procedural justice, fairness, and institutional attractiveness than no explanation through an experimental within-participants design(Uth et al., 2026). Notably, even in a case where there is imperfect alignment of preference, the personalised explanations through a simple ranking of features according to perceived actionability are more efficient as compared to the non-personalised ones(Uth et al., 2026). Tighter correspondence with user preferences offers relatively limited incremental gains, primarily in the form of perceived attractiveness, which hints at the possibility of the perceived ability to exercise preferences and feel heard having greater significance than ideal customization(Uth et al., 2026). Altogether, the personalization based on low-complexity ranking can legitimately increase the levels of acceptance and perceived equity of AI judgments, however, also provoking ethical issues concerning superficial personalization that provides perceived instead of substantial control(Uth et al., 2026).The reasons why digital practices lead to social connectedness in late life include the argument that the utility of digital interactions to older adults is not limited to the development of technical skills(Beneito-Montagut et al., 2023). Based on qualitative data, it demonstrates the fact that digital technologies facilitate social connectedness in their daily life patterns like keeping family relations, belonging to communities, routines, and a sense of belonging and meaning(Beneito-Montagut et al., 2023). The results point to the fact that acquiring digital tool use is meaningful in the context of embedded social relations, emotional support, and biographical experiences, but not as an isolated practice of competence-building(Beneito-Montagut et al., 2023). The work criticizes deficit perspectives of digital adoption by older adults and emphasizes relational, contextual and experiential aspects of digital inclusion(Beneito-Montagut et al., 2023). All in all, it highlights the importance of encouraging social connectedness later in life through socially based digital support practices that focus on relationships, care, and meaningful engagement as opposed to strictly technical training(Beneito-Montagut et al., 2023).The digital technologies especially the social media spaces that amount to a digital agora have transformed the channels that can lead to the political involvement and mobilization of citizens but are not one-dimensional but multidimensional in their effect(Koc-Michalska & Lilleker, 2017). Examining decades of research on political communication on the internet, the authors demonstrate that engagement today is varying between passive members of a crowd, community member, and friend, more of an activist such as a digital activists, and is stimulated by a combination of organizational stimuli, social stimuli, and individual intrinsic motivations(Koc-Michalska & Lilleker, 2017). There is evidence both in European and U.S. setting that the digital mobilization has the potential to reinvitalize the life of democracy by reducing the costs of action and appealing to the politically apathetic, and also as a tendency towards an issue-based civic engagement that by-passes party politics(Koc-Michalska & Lilleker, 2017). Meanwhile, there are phenomena, including clicktivism and selective avoidance, that can form ideological cyberghettoes that restrict deliberative talk and mutual influence(Koc-Michalska & Lilleker, 2017). Digital spaces reshape life satisfaction by showing that online fulfilment emerges from the interaction of digital connectivity, personal well-being needs, and responsible, human-centered use of technology, while highlighting implications for long-term happiness and ethical digital engagement. (Tarnanidis, Manda, et al., 2025).The digital burnout has academic procrastination effects on university students whose mediating variables are life satisfaction and fatigue(Savaş et al., 2025). Academic procrastination directly features a positive effect of the digital burnout related to the extensive and intensive use of digital devices(Savaş et al., 2025). Also, digital burnout is identified to lower the level of life satisfaction and raise the level of fatigue, which further leads to the increase in procrastination(Savaş et al., 2025). Satisfaction with life has a negative correlation with academic procrastination, but there is a positive correlation between fatigue, and therefore, psychologically and physically tired students tend to procrastinate in academic activities(Savaş et al., 2025). The mediation analysis proves that life satisfaction and fatigue are the variables that partially mediate the relationship between digital burnout and procrastination, or digital burnout influences procrastination both directly and indirectly(Savaş et al., 2025). The uncutting digital exposure may negatively affect the well-being and academic performance of students(Savaş et al., 2025). In general, balanced use of digital, better strategies of digital well-being, and interventions like physical activities and socialization to mitigate digital burnout and their adverse academic outcomes(Savaş et al., 2025).

INTERNET RELATIONSHIP AND INTERNET SOCIAL CONNECTEDNESS.

The positive feedback that encourages self-affirmation during writing on social networking services (SNSs) facilitates subjective happiness, whereas the concern regarding the reaction of others can also be observed, which is also a sign of stress related to self-presentation(Yang, 2020). The consumption of content on social networking service (SNSs) incurs vicarious satisfaction as users can vicariously enjoy the experiences of the other users increasing their happiness, but also creating upward social comparison and relative deprivation feelings that have major negative effects on well-being(Yang, 2020). Studies also show that relative deprivation negative emotions give the greatest effect on decreased happiness and that there are also pathways that are not identical across the genders(Yang, 2020). In general, the effects of the social networking services (SNSs) on well-being are not related to their use per se, but rather to how individuals use optional digital platforms and social feedback and comparison(Yang, 2020). Mobile mail and, more recently, LINE platform in Japan are communication technologies that contribute greatly to happiness and life satisfaction, but only in indirect ways(Ishii, 2017). The most important process is the growth and sustenance of offline and online networks of friends, which intermediates the connection between the use of communication and well-being(Ishii, 2017). The most culturally and socially integrated platform only yields a meaningful well-being benefits as opposed to more open SNSs like Facebook or Twitter(Ishii, 2017). In general, the effect of the digital communication on well-being is not universal, but instead culturally mediated over strong-tie social capital instead of technology use itself(Ishii, 2017).

Generation Z is a negotiator of self-presentation and authenticity on social media, with a strong focus on moving platforms towards less highly curated online identities and more real, transparent and more emotionally honest(Neufeld-Wall, n.d.). Sharing unfiltered content, admitting imperfection, and showing real emotions are among the practices that are employed to indicate authenticity and strategic curation is still available to reduce risks of judgment and social comparison(Neufeld-Wall, n.d.). Authenticity Gen Z understands authenticity as not doing something without impression management but one negotiated through the affordances of technology, peer culture, and issues of mental well-being(Neufeld-Wall, n.d.). Comprehending the emerging digital forms of identity identity through the prism of defining authenticity as a dynamic and contextual process and not a static or morally absolute ideal(Neufeld-Wall, n.d.).

The satisfaction with life in Facebook use and the satisfying gratifications that the use brings to them(Universiti Malaya et al., 2015).There were six key motivations to use Facebook, namely, entertainment, communication, social investigation, social attention, shared identity, and information seeking(Universiti Malaya et al., 2015). It was found that there was no direct correlation between the number of Facebook friends or time spent on Facebook with life satisfaction but when the motivations were held constant Facebook friends could anticipate the satisfaction(Universiti Malaya et al., 2015). Notably, shared identity and social attention became the only key gratifications that had the positive impact on the life satisfaction, and it was possible to conclude that the nature and the quality of interaction, but not the intensity of the general use, predetermine the psychological consequences of social networking(Universiti Malaya et al., 2015).

The use of the internet defines how consumer inclinations and satisfaction with life appear among the generation Z(Universiti Malaysia Perlis et al., 2025). The most important psychological and behavioural variables are fear of missing out (FoMO), novelty seeking, and sale proneness with impulse buying being a mediating variable and internet usage being a moderating factor(Universiti Malaysia Perlis et al., 2025). The FoMO and novelty seeking have a substantial impact on impulse buying behaviour whereas sale proneness positively and directly influences life satisfaction(Universiti Malaysia Perlis et al., 2025). Nonetheless, impulse buying per se does not have a major effect on life satisfaction and impulsive buying might not provide long-term happiness but just a temporary pleasure(Universiti Malaysia Perlis et al., 2025). Notably, the use of internet was observed to mediate necessities between novelty seeking and impulse buying, strengthening impulsive behaviour in highly digital settings, but not the FoMO impulse buying connection(Universiti Malaysia Perlis et al., 2025).

The social interaction and relationships between people have been revolutionized by the use of digital technologies(Chayko, 2014). "Chayko proposes the idea of techno-social life by portraying the fact that online and offline social worlds are not independent of each other, on the contrary, they are in grave need of one another". The digital platforms, including social media, email and cell phone communication, have increased the limits of the social connectedness because they have facilitated instantaneous, speedy and geographically unrestricted interaction. Instead of separating people, the internet tends to reinforce social relationships since it keeps people connected and separate the formation of new communities and the development of identity(Chayko, 2014). The article, however, also points out that techno-sociality also transforms the quality of social relationships, occasionally resulting in the creation of the superficial nature of interactions, lack of face-to-face contact, and an increased reliance on mediated communication(Chayko, 2014). The scholars have stressed that it is not technology that defines social outcomes; rather social structures, cultural norms, and personal preferences influence the use of digital tools(Chayko, 2014). Research demands sociological methodologies which do not construct the technology as either entirely positive or negative(Chayko, 2014). On the whole, Scholars states that the key to modern social life lies in the realization that technology is a part of social life, which alters the concept of presence, intimacy, community, and social belonging in modern society(Chayko, 2014).

The concept of digital financial literacy (DFL) as a capacity to manage personal finances through the use of digital tools and platforms safely and effectively is associated with life satisfaction in the context of advanced digital-economy(Choung et al., n.d.). There are five dimensions that can measure DFL, which are financial knowledge, general digital literacy, awareness of digital financial services, practical know-how, and self-protection against digital fraud(Choung et al., n.d.). Regression analysis showed that overall DFL was strongly positively related to life satisfaction, and the dimension of fraud self protection was the most important of the ones, as traditional financial knowledge alone did not exhibit any meaningful relationship when evaluated together with digital skills(Choung et al., n.d.). The health of contemporary finance is reliant increasingly on digital capabilities, trust, and safety consciousness than fundamental numeracy, and requires specific education strategies and enhanced consumer-protective practices to lessen digital exclusion among susceptible communities such as the aged and the low-income demographics(Choung et al., n.d.).The cross-sectional and longitudinal associations of the social media use with the life satisfaction of Japanese adults with specific emphasis on effects by platform. The research finds unique and differentiated trends on the two platforms using parallel process latent growth curve modelling(Trepte et al., 2015). Cross sectionally and longitudinally, the relationship between X use and life satisfaction is found to be negative(Trepte et al., 2015). High baseline X levels lead to reported reduced life satisfaction and initial higher X levels led to overall reduced life satisfaction with time(Trepte et al., 2015). Nonetheless, the positive indirect association between X use and life satisfaction also proved to have a mediating influence on the relationship between the two variables, with the quality of online relationship being the factor that would suggest that, whereas excessive or passive use of X can negatively affect well-being, meaningful social bonds developed on the platform can partially negate the effects(Trepte et al., 2015). On the other hand, there were positive consistently positive correlations between LINE use and life satisfaction(Trepte et al., 2015). There were positive direct and indirect cross-sectional correlations between the use of LINE and life satisfaction, which were mediated by better-quality online relationships(Trepte et al., 2015). In contrast to X, the use of LINE did not prioritize the decrease in life satisfaction over the years, which focuses on the more favorable character of closed-network platforms that prioritize the importance of bonding social capital and mutually responsive communication(Trepte et al., 2015). Open platforms such as X are more prone to bridging social capital, and they are more likely to be affected by social comparison and passive consumption that can lead to low satisfaction with life in the long run(Trepte et al., 2015). Conversely, closed platforms such as LINE reinforce the current social connections and offer emotional support, thus increasing well-being(Trepte et al., 2015). Social media use and life satisfaction have a platform-specific, culturally grounded relationship, and the connection is mediated by the quality of relationships online(Trepte et al., 2015). The findings lead to the recommendation of subtle social education and digital literacy programs that would not assume social media as a homogenous outcome, but instead would consider the risks and opportunities associated with each platform(Trepte et al., 2015).

AUTHENTICITY, SELF-PRESENTATION AND DIGITAL IDENTITY.

The construction of digital identities using social media, which dwells upon the manner in which adults are shaping and establishing themselves on social media platforms like Facebook and Twitter(Davison, n.d.-a). Based on Identity Theory, Social Identity Theory and Impression Management, the paper demonstrates that people create their digital identities with the same fundamental components as in real life, i.e. the self, role, audience and symbols, but in a technologically mediated context which alters these processes(Davison, n.d.-a). Through an interpretivist, ethnographic method, with academics, stay-at-home parents, and business executives, the study illustrates that though users tend to believe their online identity is authentic, they are engaged in negotiating their visibility, norms, and risks by way of selective sharing and self-editing(Davison, n.d.-a). The results point out that technology brings about distinctive external forces, including unrelenting audiences, indiscriminate boundaries between the public and the private, and platform affordances, which perverse and intensify identity performance(Davison, n.d.-a).

The implications of online interactions by refocusing the digital divide studies on access to emphasize on the beneficiaries of Internet usage(Wei et al., 2024). Through a representative survey of the Dutch population, the research has shown that online interaction brings tangible benefits in economic, social, educational, political, and institutional aspects, which include; reduction in purchases; strengthening social ties; easy access to government and health information as well as education opportunities(Wei et al., 2024). Nevertheless, these advantages are distributed unequally, and people who are younger, better educated, and earn more advantage greatly than the rest(Wei et al., 2024). The results indicate that digital inequality cannot be addressed only in terms of access or skills but also in terms of outcomes, which supports the available social inequalities and contributes to the necessity of digital inclusion policies with a focus on meaningful and equitable online gains(Wei et al., 2024).

The various categories of digital skills influence the trends of digital engagement by taking the digital literacy and digital inclusion views(Helsper & Eynon, 2013). Based on the nationally representative UK survey data, the authors distinguish between four different, yet interconnected types of skills technical, social, creative, and critical and prove that the use of each of them is related to a specific type of online activities and not a single, general skill that results in uniform use(Helsper & Eynon, 2013). The results indicate that socio-demographic characteristics (age, gender, education, and social isolation) impact skill development and digital skills mediate the association between social inclusion and online activities partly(Helsper & Eynon, 2013). In general, the inequality does not concern accessibility of digital participation or frequency of use, but rather inequitable channels of skill development that cause imbalanced shapes and processes of digital participation(Helsper & Eynon, 2013).

The Millennials embody and enact their genders on the visual social media platforms Facebook and Instagram with the help of the multi-method qualitative design with in-depth interviewing, the use of collage technique, and examination of personal profile pages of the participants(Chu et al., 2023). Basing his work on the research of Goffman and his theory of self-presentation, and the works of Butler and his idea of gender performance, the study shows that the strong discourse of authenticity influences online behavior since, in the process of demonstrating a perceived authentic self, the user constantly monitors social acceptance in the form of likes and comments(Chu et al., 2023). It is ongoing tensions between gender fluidity and gender policing in the virtual settings and enumerates four primary strategies employed by people: empowering activism, keeping it real, bracketing content to various types of audience, and online masking as a way to avoid ridicule(Chu et al., 2023). It is not the amount of time spent and Facebook friends that correlate with life satisfaction, but gratifications like shared identity and social attention are positively associated with well-being(Chu et al., 2023). Despite the fact that Millennials are viewed as a generation that is gender-fluid, the conventional notions of masculinity and femininity still govern the manifestations in the Internet space, especially among men who are less prone to a larger bubble of acceptable behavior than women(Chu et al., 2023). Greater, historically contextual research with a wider focus than binary conceptualizations and with implications to marketers, platform designers, and the well-being of adolescents is sought, and a call is made to actually incorporate a wider range of gender narratives in the digital environment(Chu et al., 2023). The learning disability influences the involvement of adults in technical aspects of the fashion industry like pattern cutting and underscores the need to use inclusive methods(Tarnanidis et al., 2025).

The interpretation of online personal lifestyle blogs by women is associated with the envy, self-esteem, and satisfaction with life of the readers who are trying to understand whether the trends in blogging activity affect the self-assessment of women(Fris & Koster, n.d.). The scales such as the Envy Scale by Cretti, Satisfaction with Life Scale by Diener, and the Rosenberg Self-esteem scale were used and the relationships between them were evaluated showing the bivariate correlations and mediation tests(Fris & Koster, n.d.). Findings indicated that there was no direct linkage between the pattern of blog use; active or passive, and the envy, life satisfaction, or self-esteem. Nevertheless, the greater the envy, the lower the self-esteem and the lack of life satisfaction, which proves the existence of a strong negative emotional pathway(Fris & Koster, n.d.). A number of demographic variables, including marital or relationship status, parental status, household income, and time spent per day on women blogs showed significant correlation with envy with higher levels of envy being reported in women who were not in long-term relationships, did not have children and higher levels of household income and those who spent more time reading blogs. Envy mediated the connection of these demographics with life satisfaction but not with self-esteem(Fris & Koster, n.d.). Along with the conclusions the researcher makes, is that the lifestyle blogs of women is a unique social phenomenon in an online social network, which is conditioned by social comparisons and that further longitudinal and clinical research is needed to comprehend the impact of curated digital narratives on the psychological well-being of women(Fris & Koster, n.d.).

PSYCHOLOGICAL ON-LINE LIFE CONSEQUENCES (SATISFACTION VS. EXHAUSTION)

Smartphone addiction and online relationships findings on community members between 18-25 years of age reveals that Smartphone addiction has a statistically significant and positive direct relationship with online relationships, statistically non-significant positive relationship with online social connectedness(Khan et al., 2024). It however immensely positively relates to the online relationships, which implies that it affects the online interactions(Khan et al., 2024). The outcome of mediation analysis has indicated that online social connectedness mediates the correlation between smartphone addiction and online relationships insignificantly and moderately meaning that the heavy use of smartphones has a direct influence on the establishment of online relationships regardless of the perception of connectedness(Khan et al., 2024). Gender differences that were significant as far as the study variables were concerned were not established(Khan et al., 2024). Altogether, the dualism of smartphones as an enabler of relations through the Internet and a reminder of the need to balance the use of smartphones to enhance the social well-being of young adults is comprehensive(Khan et al., 2024).

Adults over 30 form and represent their online identity by using Facebook and Twitter in their daily lives and seek to find out whether online identity is built the same way real-life identity is built(Davison, n.d.-b). The focuses is on the key perspectives in terms of Identity Theory, Social Identity Theory, and Impression Management of Goffman to demonstrate that identity is formed based on the intersection of role, self-concept, symbols (particularly language), and audience(Davison, n.d.-b). The thesis based on three groups of interviews and observations, to support the thesis, of Academics, Stay-at-home Parents, and Business Executives, in an interpretivist approach and ethnographic approach, provides that respondents think that they are presenting their real selves online, subject to a particular social set of rules, but because of the existence of indeterminate audiences and engagement with smart technology, this presentation is distorted(Davison, n.d.-b). Based on these and other insights, the author suggests seeds of a Theory of Digital Identity, which combines traditional concepts of identity with external technological forces that shape the eventual manifestation of a persona in the digital space(Davison, n.d.-b).

There are strong relationships between excessive or passive use of digital technology and depressed mood, anxiety, social isolation, maladaptive behaviour, and greater suicidal ideation with no strong or consistent relationships between general measures of time using digital technologies(Limone & Toto, 2022). Gender differences are also evaluated in the review, where girls are more adversely affected by social media emotionally than boys(Limone & Toto, 2022).

HAPPY TO BE ALIVE (OFFLINE ONLINE) HYBRID LIVING.

The study among young adults reveals that there are four profiles based on online and offline need crafting combination and shows that those who actively craft need-fulfilling experiences in both realms experience the highest levels of well-being, higher levels of sleep quality, and the least levels of ill-being and maladaptive use of social media, regardless of time on-line(Van De Casteele et al., 2026). Contrastingly, low need creation in both realms results in worse mental health outcomes, whereas imbalanced profiles demonstrate mixed effects, which means that online need fulfilment is unable to completely offset poor offline need crafting(Van De

Casteele et al., 2026). In general, the results indicate that a need cultivating skill-building especially in offline and online-based situations is a potentially effective and theoretically informed intervention in promoting healthier and more meaning-based social media use and youth well-being(Van De Casteele et al., 2026).

The non-pharmacological digital and non-digital interventions targeting the enhancement of the quality of life, especially older adults and other persons with chronic conditions(Chang et al., 2021). The studies discover that digital interventions (eHealth platform, virtual social engagement platforms, and technology-assisted activities) as well as non-digital interventions (social activities, exercise interventions, and psychosocial interventions) show positive results regarding quality of life, depressive mood, and social connectedness(Chang et al., 2021). The effectiveness of such interventions however differs greatly in terms of the design of the interventions, duration, the nature of the subjects and the outcome measures(Chang et al., 2021). Digital interventions have potential to increase access and continuity of care, particularly in cases where face-to-face assistance is restricted, and are most efficient when supplemented with human interaction and individualized to the abilities of the users(Chang et al., 2021).

Research is delighted that people who engage in online shopping are much happier and more satisfied with their lives, which is more pronounced in the case of lower-income rural families in Chinese village(Zheng & Ma, 2021). Furthermore, increased spending on online shopping positively correlates with subjective well being implying that the more this is done, the more it increases(Zheng & Ma, 2021). Research even points that online shopping increases access to goods, decreases transaction costs and increases consumption experiences in rural regions where physical markets are constrained(Zheng & Ma, 2021). Beyond consumption upgrading and economic inclusion, the rural e-commerce expansion can also benefit the psychological well-being, which should underpin the policy progress to enhance digital infrastructure and the accessibility of e-commerce to rural areas(Zheng & Ma, 2021).

Online games affect the well-being of older adults (silver gamers) through incorporation of the social convoy model and the socioemotional selectivity theory(Yue et al., 2025). The incentives associated with social interaction and family bonding are a major motivation to promote online and an offline gaming interaction to social support(Yue et al., 2025). The online interactions primarily result in online support that aids the reduction of negative affect, and the offline ones enhance offline support which is closely linked with the increased life satisfaction and positive affect(Yue et al., 2025). On the whole, the online games may be considered as effective social resources to be utilized by older adults, and the role of the offline social support may be considered especially important in the enhancement of their psychological wellbeing, which makes the socially oriented games in the healthy aging especially important(Yue et al., 2025).

The use of internet-based social networks affects the subjective well-being, and the difference between various activities on the internet and their social implications(Sabatini & Sarracino, 2017). With the help of large survey data, the authors conclude that online networking indirectly and negatively impacts life satisfaction since it may decrease the face-to-face relation and raise the exposure to social comparison resulting in envy(Sabatini & Sarracino, 2017). People that actively use the services of websites like Facebook become more prone to thinking that other people are living happier and more successful lives, which decreases both their self-esteem and satisfaction(Sabatini & Sarracino, 2017). The analysis reveals that the world became less well-being not due to the technology as such but due to how it alters the form of social interaction creating a more passive mode of consumption and less two-way communication(Sabatini & Sarracino, 2017). On the other hand, the impacts of online tools strengthening real social capital (e.g., communication with existing friends or community organizations) can be both neutral and positive(Sabatini & Sarracino, 2017). The authors underline that online participation builds up the ideological and relational ghettos in cyberspace, and the dividends are observed only when the online connections are supplementary to the offline relationships(-Sabatini & Sarracino, 2017). The paper concludes that the future studies should use experimental and longitudinal designs in order to explain the causal pathways and to determine the most vulnerable type of users, especially women and adolescents(Sabatini & Sarracino, 2017). In general, it is significant to warn that the digital agora will tie and divide, and a final effect of the digital agora lies in its presence alongside the process of social capital and comparison(Sabatini & Sarracino, 2017).

The role of social metaverse platforms in therapeutic management of users moods and use satisfaction and life intentions based on the mood management theory (Choi et al., 2023). Since the metaverse has become more popular in the midst of the COVID-19 pandemic and its aftermath, the authors contend that in addition to entertainment and commercial worth, social metaverses serve as emotion-managing media spaces(Choi et al., 2023). This particular research problem is to investigate Zepeto, a community based social metaverse platform that is popular in South Korea, where users can engage with each other via avatars, socialize, create and recreate activities, whose findings indicate that positive mood enhancement (e.g., enjoyment, achievement, visual pleasure) and negative mood alleviation (e.g., stress relief, escape loneliness) both have a substantial impact on the life satisfaction of the users(Choi et al., 2023). Greater life satisfaction, in its turn, results in greater intentions to remain a user of the social metaverse (Choi et al., 2023). These findings confirm that metaverse experiences have the potential to fulfill intrinsic psychological needs (autonomy, competence, relatedness, hedonic stimulation) and, therefore, enhance subjective well-being. The research studies also indicate that positive mood improvement has both direct and indirect effects on the usage intentions whereas negative mood alleviation has effects on the usage intentions indirectly through life satisfaction (Choi et al., 2023). This indicates that maintenance of positive emotions gives a direct incentive to sustain engagement, but remission of negative emotions only improves use of platforms when it results into global satisfaction with life (Choi et al., 2023). The study is also valuable because it evaluates spending behavior as a moderating factor. The users were categorised into cash spenders and non-spenders. In the case of cash spenders, negative mood alleviation, which was moderated by life satisfaction, was the only significant predictor of usage intentions (Choi et al., 2023). Non-spenders, on the other hand, were involved in positive mood improvement and negative mood reduction. Remarkably, this shows that the therapeutic advantages of the metaverse are greater among non-paying users, which conflicts with the belief that increased financial implication enhances the nature of psychological effects (Choi et al., 2023). Altogether, the study is solid empirical research that social metaverses are mood-management tools, which improve life satisfaction and behavioral intentions (Choi et al., 2023). It progresses metaverse studies by connecting emotional management, well-being and customer conduct and emphasizes that platform architects and marketers must concentrate on emotional supportive, socially interactive, and autonomy-promoting encounters, and not on the transactional features (Choi et al., 2023).

CONCLUSION

The analysis of the information shows that the formation of subjective happiness during the modern age occurs as a result of a web of offline and online mediating channels. The positive affective resources, including emotion, meaning, gratitude, and pro-social orientations, are also the pillars that enhance long-term happiness, but on the contrary, social comparison causes envy, and material aspirations are always harmful to the satisfaction of life. Microsoft Teams collaboration in the workplace proves to be potentially effective in cases where psychological needs are satisfied, specifically in the context of IT specialists and smartphone users, but in the case of teachers and traditional computer users, the corresponding relatedness is relatively low. The physical-activity interventions that use technology proved that properly developed and easy-to-use digital programs could raise motivation, happiness, and satisfaction, but digital fatigue is an alert against excessive tracking. The rural digital commerce widens material welfare and social capital but the effects are unequal on account of the digital divide. These lessons affirm that digital technologies per se are neither bad nor good; what they end up doing is dependent on patterns of usage, contextual design, and facilitating organizational and public policies. The paper thus recommends greater digital literacy, age based engagement as well as inclusive design to optimize on techno-social value and to mitigate risks to promote healthier hybrid digital societies.

REFERENCES

Asha, M., & Kumar, A. (2025). Employee Well-being in the Digital Age: A Study on Microsoft Teams Users. *The Nigerian Health Journal*, *25*(2), 649–663. DOI: 10.71637/TNHJ.V25I2.1060

Beneito-Montagut, R., Begueria, A., & Cassián, N. (2023). The social connectedness of digital practices in later life: It's not just about learning, it's all about relationships. *The Sociological Review*, *71*(3), 581–600. DOI: 10.1177/00380261221144154

Chan, M. (2018). Digital communications and psychological well-being across the life span: Examining the intervening roles of social capital and civic engagement. *Telematics and Informatics*, *35*(6), 1744–1754. DOI: 10.1016/j.tele.2018.05.003

Chang, A., Winquist, N. W., Wescott, A. B., Lattie, E. G., & Graham, A. K. (2021). Systematic review of digital and non-digital non-pharmacological interventions that target quality of life and psychological outcomes in adults with systemic lupus erythematosus. *Lupus*, *30*(7), 1058–1077. DOI: 10.1177/09612033211005085 PMID: 33779388

Chayko, M. (2014). Techno-social Life: The Internet, Digital Technology, and Social Connectedness. *Sociology Compass*, *8*(7), 976–991. DOI: 10.1111/soc4.12190

Choi, D., Lee, H. K., & Kim, D. Y. (2023). Mood management through metaverse enhancing life satisfaction. *International Journal of Consumer Studies*, *47*(4), 1533–1543.

Choung, Y., Pak, T.-Y., & Chatterjee, S. (n.d.). *Digital Financial Literacy and Life Satisfaction: Evidence from South Korea*.

Chu, M., Ma, H., Lee, C.-Y., Zhao, Z., Chen, T., Zhang, S., & Chiang, Y.-C. (2023). Effect of online and offline social network group clusters on life satisfaction across age groups. *Heliyon*, *9*(5), e16176. DOI: 10.1016/j.heliyon.2023.e16176 PMID: 37229172

Davison, C. (n.d.-a). *Towards a theory of Digital Identity*.

Davison, C. (n.d.-b). *Towards a theory of Digital Identity*.

Dhiman, N., & Kumar, A. (2023). What We Know and Don't Know About Consumer Happiness: Three-Decade Review, Synthesis, and Research Propositions. *Journal of Interactive Marketing*, *58*(2–3), 115–135. DOI: 10.1177/10949968221095548

Fris, L., & Koster, N. (n.d.). *The understanding role of digital competence and social capital on contentment in life*.

Helsper, E. J., & Eynon, R. (2013). Distinct skill pathways to digital engagement. *European Journal of Communication, 28*(6), 696–713. DOI: 10.1177/0267323113499113

Ishii, K. (2017). Online communication with strong ties and subjective well-being in Japan. *Computers in Human Behavior, 66*, 129–137. DOI: 10.1016/j.chb.2016.09.033

Khan, P., Shahid, M. S., & Majid, H. A. (2024). MEDIATING ROLE OF ONLINE SOCIAL CONNECTEDNESS IN SMARTPHONE ADDICTION AND ONLINE RELATIONSHIP AMONG YOUNG ADULTS. *Gomal University Journal of Research, 40*(3), 327–336. DOI: 10.51380/gujr-40-03-05

Koc-Michalska, K., & Lilleker, D. (2017). Digital Politics: Mobilization, Engagement, and Participation. *Political Communication, 34*(1), 1–5. DOI: 10.1080/10584609.2016.1243178

Limone, P., & Toto, G. A. (2022). Psychological and Emotional Effects of Digital Technology on Digitods (14–18 Years): A Systematic Review. *Frontiers in Psychology, 13*, 938965. DOI: 10.3389/fpsyg.2022.938965 PMID: 35874342

Lu, Z., Xiang, J., Li, S., Zhang, C., & Wu, C. (2025). Technology-based physical activities and adults' physical activity levels, mental health, life satisfaction, and happiness: A mixed methods study. *BMC Psychology, 13*(1), 1199. DOI: 10.1186/s40359-025-03217-7 PMID: 41168901

Neufeld-Wall, M. E. (n.d.). *Being Real: Gen-Z.* Self-Presentation, and Authenticity on Social Media.

Raj, A. B., & Goute, A. K. (2025). Internal branding and technostress among employees—The mediation role of employee wellbeing and moderating effects of digital internal communication. *Acta Psychologica, 255*, 104943. DOI: 10.1016/j.actpsy.2025.104943 PMID: 40185038

Sabatini, F., & Sarracino, F. (2017). Online Networks and Subjective Well-Being. *Kyklos, 70*(3), 456–480. DOI: 10.1111/kykl.12145

Savaş, B. Ç., Turan, M., & Asan, S. (2025). The relationship between digital burnout and academic procrastination and the mediating roles of life satisfaction and the fatigue in this relationship. *BMC Psychology, 13*(1), 1223. DOI: 10.1186/s40359-025-03510-5 PMID: 41188990

Tarnanidis, T., Manda, V. K., Sousa, B. B., Vlachopoulou, M., & Papachristou, E. (2025). Marketing Complexity of Smart Consumer Products to Global Millennial Segments. In Tarnanidis, T., Sousa, B., Vlachopoulou, M., Papachristou, E., & Kittu Manda, V. (Eds.), *Diversity and Inclusion-Driven Marketing for Multicultural Marketplaces* (pp. 1–16). IGI Global Scientific Publishing., DOI: 10.4018/979-8-3373-2111-0.ch001

Tarnanidis, T., Manda, V. K., Sousa, B. B., Vlachopoulou, M., & Papachristou, E. (2025). Marketing Complexity of Smart Consumer Products to Global Millennial Segments. In Tarnanidis, T., Sousa, B., Vlachopoulou, M., Papachristou, E., & Kittu Manda, V. (Eds.), *Diversity and Inclusion-Driven Marketing for Multicultural Marketplaces* (pp. 1–16). IGI Global Scientific Publishing., DOI: 10.4018/979-8-3373-2111-0.ch001

Tarnanidis, T., Papachristou, E., Andreou, V., Stergiou, A., & Manda, V. K. (2025). Inclusive Marketing Strategies for Adaptive Fashion. In Tarnanidis, T., Sousa, B., Vlachopoulou, M., Papachristou, E., & Kittu Manda, V. (Eds.), *Diversity and Inclusion-Driven Marketing for Multicultural Marketplaces* (pp. 17–30). IGI Global Scientific Publishing., DOI: 10.4018/979-8-3373-2111-0.ch002

Tarnanidis, T., Papachristou, E., Andreou, V., Stergiou, A., & Manda, V. K. (2025). Inclusive Marketing Strategies for Adaptive Fashion. In Tarnanidis, T., Sousa, B., Vlachopoulou, M., Papachristou, E., & Kittu Manda, V. (Eds.), *Diversity and Inclusion-Driven Marketing for Multicultural Marketplaces* (pp. 17–30). IGI Global Scientific Publishing., DOI: 10.4018/979-8-3373-2111-0.ch002

Trepte, S., Dienlin, T., & Reinecke, L. (2015). Influence of Social Support Received in Online and Offline Contexts on Satisfaction With Social Support and Satisfaction With Life: A Longitudinal Study. *Media Psychology*, *18*(1), 74–105. DOI: 10.1080/15213269.2013.838904

Tsouparopoulou, E., Symeonaki, M., Parsanoglou, D., & Kazani, A. (2025). European Youth and Digital Engagement: Attitudes, Skills, and Civic Participation. *Journal of Applied Youth Studies*, *8*(2), 219–247. DOI: 10.1007/s43151-025-00168-z

Universiti Malaya, M. Adnan, H., Mavi, S. R., & Universiti Malaya. (. (2015). Facebook Satisfaction, Life Satisfaction: Malaysian Undergraduate Experience. *Jurnal Komunikasi. Malaysian Journal of Communication*, *31*(2), 649–671. DOI: 10.17576/JKMJC-2015-3102-37

Uth, R., Niemitz, N., Valera, I., & Langer, M. (2026). Personalizing explanations in AI-based decisions: The effects of personalization and (mis)aligning with individual preferences. *Computers in Human Behavior*, *177*, 108854. DOI: 10.1016/j.chb.2025.108854

Van De Casteele, M., Flamant, N., Morbée, S., Van Den Bogaard, D., & Vansteenkiste, M. (2026). Online and offline need fulfillment seeking: The relation between need crafting profiles, well-being, and social media use. *Computers in Human Behavior*, *175*, 108843. DOI: 10.1016/j.chb.2025.108843

Wei, B., Zhao, C., & Luo, M. (2024). Online markets, offline happiness: E-commerce development and subjective well-being in rural China. *China Economic Review*, *87*, 102247. DOI: 10.1016/j.chieco.2024.102247

Yang, H. (2020). Do SNSs really make us happy? The effects of writing and reading via SNSs on subjective well-being. *Telematics and Informatics*, *50*, 101384. DOI: 10.1016/j.tele.2020.101384

Yue, Y., Liu, D., & Hao, J. (2025). From Gaming to Well-Being: Analyzing the Impact of Social Engagement in Online Games on Silver Gamer's Well-Being. *International Journal of Human-Computer Interaction*, •••, 1–17. DOI: 10.1080/10447318.2025.2546659

Zheng, H., & Ma, W. (2021). Click it and buy happiness: Does online shopping improve subjective well-being of rural residents in China? *Applied Economics*, *53*(36), 4192–4206. DOI: 10.1080/00036846.2021.1897513

Chapter 5
An Integrated Model for Measuring Digital Well Being and Life Satisfaction in the Global Digital Ecosystem

Ashutosh Bhardwaj
http://orcid.org/0009-0008-3311-8335
Poornima University, Jaipur, India

Prince Kumar Choudhary
http://orcid.org/0009-0000-3306-8026
Poornima University, Jaipur, India

Yash Agarwal
http://orcid.org/0009-0001-9184-5249
Poornima University, Jaipur, India

Sachin Singh Tanwar
http://orcid.org/0009-0009-8627-0418
Poornima University, Jaipur, India

Nikhil Kumar Goyal
http://orcid.org/0009-0007-4532-8033
Noida International University, Greater Noida, India

Anmol Chaturvedi
Poornima University, Jaipur, India

ABSTRACT

The rapid expansion of digital technologies has fundamentally transformed human behavior, social interaction, and overall quality of life, making digital well-being a critical determinant of life satisfaction in the contemporary global digital ecosystem. This chapter proposes an integrated conceptual model that examines the multidimensional relationship between digital well-being and life satisfaction by incorporating psychological, social, technological, and behavioral factors. It explores

DOI: 10.4018/979-8-3373-8357-6.ch005

how digital usage patterns, online social connectivity, mental and emotional health, privacy concerns, and digital stress collectively influence individual perceptions of well-being and satisfaction with life.

1. INTRODUCTION

The pervasive integration of digital technologies into everyday life has reshaped how individuals communicate, work, learn, and perceive well-being. From smartphones and social media platforms to artificial intelligence–driven services and digital workplaces, the global digital ecosystem has become deeply embedded in personal and societal functioning. While digital technologies offer unprecedented convenience, connectivity, and access to information, they also introduce challenges related to mental health, privacy, social relationships, and overall life satisfaction. As a result, understanding digital well-being has emerged as a critical area of academic and practical inquiry in the contemporary digital era.

Digital well-being extends beyond mere technology usage to encompass how digital interactions influence psychological health, emotional balance, social fulfillment, and perceived quality of life. Excessive screen time, information overload, online social comparison, and digital dependency have raised concerns regarding stress, anxiety, and reduced life satisfaction. Conversely, positive digital engagement can enhance social support, productivity, learning opportunities, and personal growth. This dual nature of digital experiences underscores the need for a comprehensive and integrated framework that examines both the beneficial and adverse effects of digital technologies on human well-being (Burr et al., 2020).

This chapter addresses this need by focusing on the development of an integrated model for measuring digital well-being and life satisfaction within the global digital ecosystem. By synthesizing perspectives from psychology, sociology, and digital studies, the chapter aims to provide a holistic understanding of how digital environments shape subjective well-being and long-term life satisfaction across diverse populations and contexts.

1.1 Concept of Digital Well-Being

Digital well-being refers to an individual's ability to maintain a healthy, balanced, and meaningful relationship with digital technologies. It encompasses emotional, cognitive, and behavioral responses to digital engagement, including how individuals manage screen time, online interactions, and digital stressors. Unlike traditional notions of well-being, digital well-being specifically addresses the unique challenges and opportunities arising from constant connectivity and technology-mediated experiences (Vanden Abeele, 2021).

The concept of digital well-being has gained prominence as digital technologies increasingly blur the boundaries between work and personal life. Continuous notifications, remote work platforms, and social media presence can disrupt attention, sleep patterns, and emotional regulation. These factors influence not only momentary mood states but also long-term psychological health. Digital well-being therefore involves conscious self-regulation, digital literacy, and the capacity to use technology in ways that support rather than undermine personal well-being.

Importantly, digital well-being is not solely an individual responsibility but is shaped by platform design, organizational expectations, and societal norms. Algorithms that promote constant engagement, workplace cultures that encourage perpetual availability, and insufficient digital governance frameworks can negatively affect well-being. Understanding digital well-being thus requires a multidimensional approach that considers both user behavior and the broader digital environment in which technology use occurs (De Santis & Fantinelli, 2024).

1.2 Life Satisfaction in the Digital Age

Life satisfaction represents a cognitive evaluation of one's overall quality of life based on personal values, expectations, and experiences. In the digital age, life satisfaction is increasingly influenced by technology-mediated interactions that shape social comparison, self-perception, and access to opportunities. Digital platforms play a central role in how individuals evaluate success, happiness, and social belonging, making life satisfaction closely intertwined with digital experiences.

Digital technologies can enhance life satisfaction by facilitating social connectivity, enabling flexible work arrangements, and providing access to education and health resources. Online communities allow individuals to maintain relationships across geographical boundaries, while digital tools support productivity and personal development. For many users, especially in digitally inclusive environments, technology contributes positively to perceived life satisfaction and overall well-being (Steinert & Dennis, 2022).

However, the digital age also introduces risks that may undermine life satisfaction. Constant exposure to curated online content can foster unrealistic comparisons and feelings of inadequacy. Cyberbullying, misinformation, and digital exclusion further exacerbate stress and dissatisfaction. These contrasting outcomes highlight the need to examine life satisfaction not in isolation but in relation to digital well-being, recognizing that the quality of digital engagement plays a crucial role in shaping subjective life evaluations (Stănculescu & Griffiths, 2024).

1.3 The Global Digital Ecosystem: Scope and Evolution

The global digital ecosystem comprises interconnected technologies, platforms, users, institutions, and regulatory frameworks that collectively shape digital interactions worldwide. This ecosystem has evolved rapidly with advancements in mobile computing, cloud technologies, artificial intelligence, and data-driven platforms. As digital ecosystems expand across borders, they influence cultural practices, economic participation, and social structures on a global scale.

Digital ecosystems are characterized by their dynamic and adaptive nature, continuously reshaped by technological innovation and user behavior. Social media platforms, digital marketplaces, remote work tools, and smart devices interact to create complex digital environments that influence daily life. These systems not only enable connectivity but also generate data-driven feedback loops that affect user engagement, decision-making, and well-being (Ryff & Singer, 2008).

The global scope of the digital ecosystem introduces significant disparities in access, digital literacy, and regulatory protection. While some regions benefit from advanced digital infrastructure and inclusive policies, others face digital divides that limit participation and well-being. Understanding digital well-being and life satisfaction within this ecosystem therefore requires a global perspective that accounts for cultural, socioeconomic, and technological variations (Kumari et al., 2026a)

1.4 Rationale and Objectives of the Chapter

The increasing integration of digital technologies into all aspects of life necessitates a systematic approach to understanding their impact on well-being and life satisfaction. Existing studies often examine digital well-being or life satisfaction independently, leading to fragmented insights that fail to capture their interdependent nature. This chapter addresses this gap by proposing an integrated model that links digital behaviors, psychological outcomes, and subjective life satisfaction within a unified framework.

The primary objective of this chapter is to conceptualize digital well-being as a multidimensional construct and examine its relationship with life satisfaction in the context of the global digital ecosystem. By synthesizing theoretical perspectives and empirical evidence, the chapter aims to identify key determinants of healthy digital engagement and their implications for long-term well-being. This approach supports a more nuanced understanding of how digital technologies can be leveraged to enhance, rather than diminish, quality of life.

Additionally, the chapter seeks to provide practical relevance for policymakers, organizations, educators, and technology designers. By offering an integrated measurement framework, it contributes to the development of strategies that promote responsible technology use, digital inclusion, and sustainable digital environments. Ultimately, the chapter underscores the importance of aligning technological innovation with human well-being to ensure that digital progress contributes positively to individual and societal life satisfaction.

1.4.1 Background

The fast spread of digital technologies has altered the social interaction process, work and education, and service accessibility throughout the world. Many aspects of our life are now mediated by smartphones, social media, applications built via cloud-based work systems, and operated by artificial intelligence. As much as these technologies improve efficiency, connectivity and access to information, they also present threats of psychological stress, privacy issues, social comparison and work-life challenges. Consequently, digital well-being has become a pressing construct to learn to interpret the experience and ways people choose to handle technology in a manner that facilitates the quality of life.

Experts in past studies have shown that digital experiences may create either positive or negative outcomes based on the use patterns, personal self-regulation, platform structure and the socio-cultural environment. It therefore follows that the digital age has failed to comprehend well-being without viewing the digital ecosystem of larger contexts in which people dwell.

1.4.2 Research Problem

Regardless of the growing scholarly interest, current research has the tendency of investigating digital well-being and life satisfaction as independent constructs, leading to adding a disjointed contribution to the possibility of how digital experiences affect the overall quality of life. Most of the researches concentrate on particular behaviors like hours spent at the screen or use of social media without addressing any psychological, social, and institutional aspects of the problem at once. Further, there is little research which takes the global digital ecosystem viewpoint, which factors into the cultural, economical, and regulatory differences.

The lack of unified measurement systems limits the potential to evaluate the effects of the combination of multiple dimensions of digital engagement on satisfaction in life. That is why it is necessary that a complex model that aligns digital behavior and psychological reactions, social connectivity and structural digital circumstances with outcomes of life satisfaction should be created under one conceptual framework.

Figure 1. Integrated Model of Digital Well-Being and Life Satisfaction in the Global Digital Ecosystem

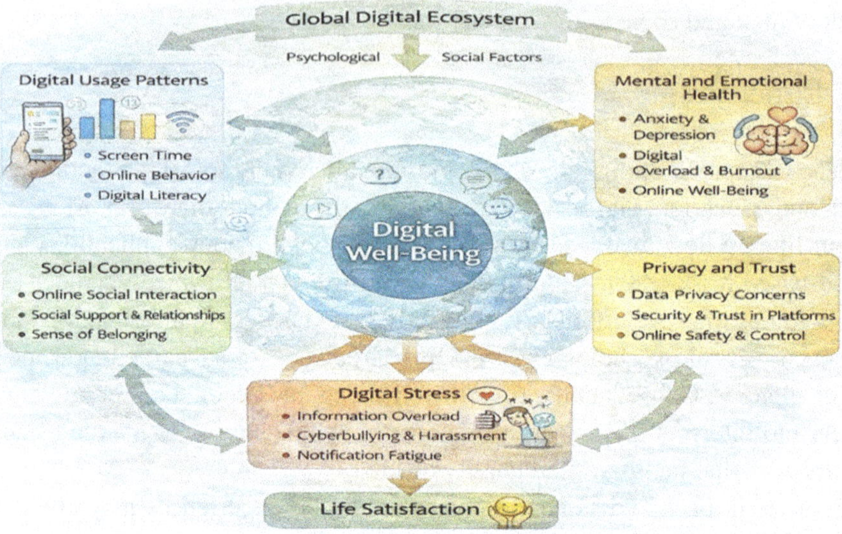

2. THEORETICAL FOUNDATIONS OF DIGITAL WELL-BEING AND LIFE SATISFACTION

Understanding digital well-being and life satisfaction requires a strong theoretical grounding that draws from multiple academic disciplines. Digital experiences are not purely technological phenomena; they are deeply embedded in psychological processes, social structures, and behavioral patterns. Theoretical frameworks from psychology, sociology, and technology studies provide essential insights into how individuals interact with digital environments and how these interactions influence subjective well-being and life satisfaction. This section explores key theoretical perspectives that inform the development of an integrated model for measuring digital well-being in the global digital ecosystem (Bartels et al., 2019).

Theories of well-being traditionally focused on offline contexts, emphasizing emotional states, cognitive evaluations, and social relationships. However, the rapid digitization of daily life necessitates extending these theories to account for technology-mediated interactions. Digital platforms introduce new modes of communication, identity construction, and social comparison, requiring adaptation of classical theories to contemporary digital realities. Integrating these perspectives allows for a more comprehensive understanding of how digital engagement shapes life satisfaction.

2.1 Psychological Perspectives on Well-Being

Psychological theories of well-being provide a foundational framework for understanding how digital experiences influence mental and emotional health. Hedonic well-being focuses on pleasure, happiness, and the avoidance of pain, emphasizing momentary emotional states. From this perspective, digital technologies can enhance well-being by providing entertainment, social interaction, and immediate gratification. However, excessive reliance on digital stimulation may also lead to emotional fatigue, reduced attention span, and diminished long-term satisfaction.

In contrast, eudaimonic well-being emphasizes meaning, self-realization, and personal growth. Digital environments can support eudaimonic well-being by enabling learning, creativity, and purposeful engagement. Online educational platforms, professional networks, and knowledge-sharing communities allow individuals to pursue goals aligned with their values and aspirations. At the same time, superficial digital engagement and algorithm-driven content consumption may undermine autonomy and authentic self-development (Kumari & Goyal, 2026).

Psychological stress and self-regulation theories further explain how individuals manage digital demands. Continuous connectivity can increase cognitive load and stress levels, particularly when individuals struggle to balance digital obligations with offline responsibilities. Self-regulation skills, such as setting boundaries and mindful technology use, play a crucial role in maintaining digital well-being. These psychological perspectives highlight the importance of individual differences in shaping digital experiences and their impact on overall life satisfaction.

2.2 Sociological and Behavioral Theories

Sociological theories emphasize the role of social structures, norms, and relationships in shaping digital well-being. Social interaction theory suggests that human well-being is deeply influenced by the quality of social connections. Digital platforms redefine social interaction by enabling constant connectivity, virtual communities, and online identities. While these platforms can strengthen social ties and foster belonging, they may also contribute to social isolation, superficial relationships, and reduced face-to-face interaction (Soren & Ryff, 2023).

Social comparison theory is particularly relevant in the context of digital media. Online environments often expose individuals to curated representations of others' lives, which can distort perceptions of success and happiness. Upward social comparison on social media may lead to dissatisfaction, anxiety, and reduced self-esteem, negatively affecting life satisfaction. Conversely, supportive online communities and positive social feedback can enhance self-worth and emotional well-being.

Behavioral theories, including habit formation and reinforcement mechanisms, explain how digital usage patterns develop and persist. Digital platforms are designed to encourage repeated engagement through notifications, rewards, and personalized content. Over time, these mechanisms can lead to habitual or compulsive use, influencing daily routines and well-being outcomes. Understanding these behavioral dynamics is essential for developing models that capture both voluntary and habitual aspects of digital engagement (Sharma et al., 2026).

2.3 Technology Acceptance and Digital Behavior Models

Technology acceptance models provide insights into why individuals adopt and continue using digital technologies. Perceived usefulness and ease of use are central determinants of technology adoption, influencing how deeply digital tools are integrated into daily life. When technologies are perceived as beneficial and user-friendly, they are more likely to become embedded in personal and professional routines, thereby shaping well-being outcomes.

Extended models of technology use incorporate factors such as trust, perceived risk, and user satisfaction. In digital environments, concerns related to privacy, data security, and algorithmic control can influence emotional responses and overall satisfaction. Users who perceive digital platforms as intrusive or manipulative may experience stress and reduced well-being, even if the technology offers functional benefits (Niemiec, 2024).

Digital behavior models also emphasize contextual and situational factors, such as work demands, cultural norms, and social expectations. Remote work technologies, for instance, may enhance flexibility but also blur boundaries between work and personal life. These models highlight that digital well-being is not solely determined by technology features but by how technologies interact with individual goals and social contexts.

2.4 Relationship Between Digital Engagement and Life Satisfaction

The relationship between digital engagement and life satisfaction is complex and multidirectional. Moderate and purposeful digital engagement can enhance life satisfaction by supporting social connection, access to information, and personal development. Digital tools enable individuals to maintain relationships, pursue hobbies, and achieve professional goals, contributing positively to their overall evaluation of life quality.

However, excessive or maladaptive digital engagement may undermine life satisfaction. High levels of screen time, constant multitasking, and exposure to negative online content can increase stress and reduce emotional well-being. The quality of digital engagement, rather than the quantity alone, plays a decisive role in determining its impact on life satisfaction. Meaningful interactions and goal-oriented usage are more likely to produce positive outcomes than passive consumption (Farooqi et al., 2026).

This nuanced relationship underscores the need for an integrated theoretical model that captures both positive and negative dimensions of digital engagement. Life satisfaction emerges as an outcome influenced by psychological resilience, social support, and behavioral patterns within digital environments. By linking digital well-being and life satisfaction through established theoretical perspectives, this chapter lays the foundation for a comprehensive measurement framework suited to the global digital ecosystem.

3. KEY DIMENSIONS OF DIGITAL WELL-BEING

Digital well-being is a multidimensional construct that reflects how individuals experience, manage, and are affected by their engagement with digital technologies. Rather than being defined by a single factor such as screen time, digital well-being encompasses a range of behavioral, psychological, social, and ethical dimensions. These dimensions interact dynamically within the global digital ecosystem, shaping both short-term experiences and long-term life satisfaction. Understanding these key dimensions is essential for developing an integrated model that accurately captures the complexity of digital well-being (Guest, 2017).

Each dimension of digital well-being highlights a specific aspect of digital interaction, from usage intensity to emotional outcomes and perceptions of trust and security. While these dimensions are analytically distinct, they are closely interconnected in practice. Excessive digital use may lead to psychological stress, while concerns about privacy can affect emotional comfort and social participation online. This section examines the core dimensions that collectively define digital well-being in contemporary digital environments.

3.1 Digital Usage Patterns and Screen Time

Digital usage patterns represent one of the most visible dimensions of digital well-being, encompassing the frequency, duration, and purpose of technology use.

Screen time has become a widely discussed indicator, often associated with both productivity and potential harm. Extended use of digital devices for work, communication, or entertainment can enhance efficiency and connectivity, but it may also contribute to physical strain, cognitive overload, and reduced offline engagement.

The impact of screen time on well-being depends largely on the nature and context of use. Purposeful and goal-oriented digital activities, such as learning, professional collaboration, or creative expression, are more likely to support well-being than passive consumption. Conversely, excessive scrolling, multitasking, and constant interruptions can fragment attention and reduce psychological satisfaction. Therefore, assessing digital well-being requires moving beyond quantitative measures of screen time to consider qualitative aspects of digital engagement (Kowalski & Loretto, 2017).

Self-regulation plays a crucial role in shaping healthy digital usage patterns. Individuals who actively manage notifications, set boundaries, and balance online and offline activities are better positioned to maintain digital well-being. However, platform design features that encourage prolonged engagement can undermine self-regulation, highlighting the need for both individual and systemic approaches to managing digital usage (Van De Voorde et al., 2012).

3.2 Mental and Emotional Health in Digital Environments

Mental and emotional health is a central dimension of digital well-being, reflecting how digital interactions influence mood, stress levels, and psychological resilience. Digital environments can provide emotional support through social networks, online communities, and access to mental health resources. For many individuals, digital platforms serve as spaces for self-expression, validation, and connection, contributing positively to emotional well-being.

At the same time, digital environments can expose individuals to stressors such as information overload, negative news, cyberbullying, and online harassment. Continuous exposure to these stressors may increase anxiety, emotional exhaustion, and feelings of inadequacy. The constant availability of digital communication can also create pressure to respond immediately, contributing to heightened stress and reduced emotional recovery time (Umair et al., 2023).

Emotional responses to digital experiences are influenced by individual differences, including personality traits, coping strategies, and digital literacy. Individuals with higher emotional awareness and coping skills are better equipped to navigate digital challenges. Understanding mental and emotional health within digital environments is therefore essential for evaluating digital well-being and its broader implications for life satisfaction.

3.3 Social Connectivity and Online Relationships

Social connectivity is a defining feature of digital technologies, shaping how individuals form, maintain, and perceive relationships. Online platforms enable communication across geographical boundaries, supporting social inclusion and community building. Digital connectivity can strengthen existing relationships and provide opportunities for social interaction among individuals who may otherwise face isolation (Mirowska & Bakici, 2024).

However, the quality of online relationships varies significantly and does not always translate into meaningful social support. Superficial interactions, reduced nonverbal cues, and performative social behaviors may limit emotional depth and authenticity. Overreliance on online interactions may also reduce face-to-face communication, potentially weakening social bonds and affecting overall well-being.

The impact of online relationships on digital well-being depends on factors such as reciprocity, emotional support, and authenticity. Positive online interactions can enhance belonging and self-esteem, while negative experiences may lead to social anxiety and withdrawal. Social connectivity thus represents both an opportunity and a risk within the digital ecosystem, requiring careful consideration in well-being assessment models (Tokdemir, 2022).

3.4 Digital Stress, Addiction, and Burnout

Digital stress refers to the psychological strain resulting from excessive or poorly managed digital engagement. Constant connectivity, information overload, and multitasking can overwhelm cognitive resources and reduce concentration. Over time, this stress may contribute to burnout, particularly in work and academic contexts where digital demands are high and boundaries are unclear.

Digital addiction represents an extreme manifestation of unhealthy digital engagement, characterized by compulsive use and loss of control. Behavioral reinforcement mechanisms embedded in digital platforms can encourage repetitive use, making disengagement difficult. Digital addiction is associated with negative outcomes such as sleep disruption, reduced productivity, and diminished life satisfaction (Agostini et al., 2018).

Burnout linked to digital environments often arises from prolonged exposure to digital stressors without adequate recovery. Remote work technologies and digital learning platforms, while offering flexibility, may blur boundaries between personal and professional life. Addressing digital stress and burnout requires both individual strategies and systemic interventions, emphasizing the importance of this dimension in comprehensive digital well-being models.

3.5 Privacy, Security, and Digital Trust

Privacy, security, and trust are foundational dimensions of digital well-being, influencing how safe and comfortable individuals feel in digital environments. Concerns about data collection, surveillance, and misuse of personal information can generate anxiety and reduce trust in digital platforms. When users perceive a lack of control over their data, their sense of autonomy and well-being may be compromised.

Digital trust extends beyond technical security to include confidence in platform governance, transparency, and ethical practices. Trustworthy digital environments enable users to engage more openly and meaningfully, supporting positive digital experiences. Conversely, data breaches, misinformation, and opaque algorithms can erode trust and negatively affect well-being (Edmondson, 2018).

Perceptions of privacy and security vary across cultural and regulatory contexts, reflecting differences in digital literacy and legal protections. Incorporating privacy and trust into digital well-being models acknowledges the ethical and institutional dimensions of digital life. This perspective is essential for understanding how structural factors shape individual experiences and life satisfaction within the global digital ecosystem.

4. LIFE SATISFACTION INDICATORS IN A DIGITALLY CONNECTED WORLD

Life satisfaction is a central construct in well-being research, reflecting individuals' overall cognitive evaluation of their quality of life. In a digitally connected world, life satisfaction is increasingly shaped by technology-mediated experiences that influence work, relationships, learning, and self-perception. Digital technologies alter how individuals assess progress, success, and happiness, making life satisfaction inseparable from digital well-being. Understanding the indicators of life satisfaction in digital contexts is therefore essential for developing a comprehensive and integrated measurement model.

Unlike momentary emotional states, life satisfaction represents a relatively stable evaluation influenced by accumulated experiences over time. Digital environments contribute to these evaluations by shaping opportunities, expectations, and perceived control over life circumstances. Positive digital engagement can enhance autonomy, competence, and social belonging, while negative experiences may lead to frustration, stress, and dissatisfaction. This section examines key indicators of life satisfaction as they manifest within a digitally connected global ecosystem (Mayer et al., 1995).

4.1 Subjective Well-Being and Quality of Life Metrics

Subjective well-being forms the foundation of life satisfaction assessment, encompassing individuals' perceptions of happiness, fulfillment, and overall life quality. In digital contexts, subjective well-being is influenced by how technologies support or hinder personal goals and emotional balance. Access to information, communication tools, and digital services can enhance perceived quality of life by reducing barriers and increasing convenience.

Quality of life metrics increasingly incorporate digital dimensions, recognizing the role of technology in daily functioning. Digital access affects healthcare, education, financial services, and social participation, all of which contribute to life satisfaction. Individuals who experience seamless and supportive digital interactions are more likely to evaluate their lives positively. Conversely, digital exclusion or persistent technological challenges can negatively impact perceived quality of life (Cropanzano & Mitchell, 2005).

Measuring subjective well-being in digital environments requires capturing both emotional responses and cognitive evaluations related to technology use. This includes assessing satisfaction with digital services, perceived control over digital engagement, and alignment between digital activities and personal values. Integrating these indicators enables a more accurate representation of life satisfaction in modern digital societies.

4.2 Work–Life Balance in Digital Contexts

Work–life balance has emerged as a critical indicator of life satisfaction in an era characterized by digital work environments and remote connectivity. Digital technologies enable flexible work arrangements, allowing individuals to manage professional responsibilities alongside personal commitments. For many, this flexibility enhances autonomy and contributes positively to life satisfaction (Ertürk & Vurgun, 2015).

However, digital work environments can also blur the boundaries between work and personal life. Constant connectivity, digital monitoring, and expectations of immediate responsiveness may increase workload and reduce recovery time. Over time, this imbalance can lead to stress, fatigue, and diminished satisfaction with life. The ability to disconnect from work-related technologies has become a key determinant of well-being and life satisfaction.

Figure 2. Feedback Loop Between Digital Behavior, Digital Well-Being, and Life Satisfaction

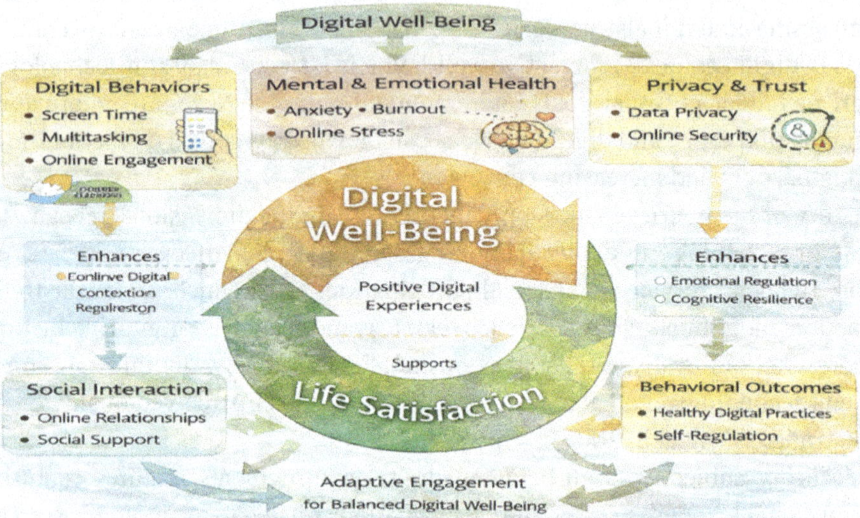

Perceptions of work–life balance vary across occupations, cultures, and organizational practices. Supportive digital policies and clear norms regarding availability can mitigate negative effects, while poorly managed digital demands may exacerbate stress. Assessing life satisfaction in digital contexts therefore requires evaluating how technology influences balance, autonomy, and role satisfaction (Chughtai et al., 2015).

4.3 Educational, Professional, and Economic Impacts

Digital technologies play a significant role in shaping educational and professional opportunities, which in turn influence life satisfaction. Online learning platforms, digital skill development, and remote work opportunities expand access to education and employment. For many individuals, these opportunities enhance personal growth, career progression, and economic security, contributing positively to life satisfaction.

At the same time, the digital economy introduces new pressures related to skill obsolescence, job insecurity, and performance monitoring. Continuous adaptation to technological change can create anxiety and uncertainty, particularly for individuals with limited access to digital training. Economic disparities in digital access may therefore translate into unequal life satisfaction outcomes across populations (Sonnentag et al., 2023).

The relationship between digitalization and economic well-being highlights the importance of contextual factors in life satisfaction assessment. Individuals who perceive digital technologies as empowering and enabling are more likely to report higher satisfaction. Conversely, those who experience digital disruption as threatening or exclusionary may report lower levels of life satisfaction.

4.4 Cultural and Regional Variations in Life Satisfaction

Life satisfaction in digital contexts is shaped by cultural values, social norms, and regional differences in technological development. Cultural attitudes toward technology, privacy, and social interaction influence how digital experiences are perceived and evaluated. In some cultures, digital connectivity enhances collective well-being and social cohesion, while in others it may intensify individual pressure and social comparison.

Regional disparities in digital infrastructure and policy frameworks also affect life satisfaction. Access to reliable internet, digital services, and protective regulations varies widely across countries and regions. Individuals in digitally inclusive environments are more likely to experience positive outcomes from digital engagement, while those in underserved regions may face frustration and reduced satisfaction (United Nations, 2015).

Understanding cultural and regional variations is essential for developing a globally applicable model of digital well-being and life satisfaction. Indicators must be sensitive to contextual differences and avoid assuming uniform digital experiences. Incorporating cultural and regional perspectives ensures that life satisfaction measurement reflects the diversity of the global digital ecosystem.

5. THE GLOBAL DIGITAL ECOSYSTEM

The global digital ecosystem is an interwoven and multifaceted network of technology, platforms, users, institutions, and regulatory standards that encompass a range of influences that determine digital experiences throughout the globe. This ecosystem goes well beyond the individual gadgets or programs, containment in the social, economic, and cultural environment on which digital technologies are applied. The greater the digitization of systems, the greater their involvement in digital well-being and life contentment, which requires a holistic view of the entire ecosystem (OECD, 2020).

Digital ecosystems are active and constantly changing and are influenced by the technological innovation, user trends and policy changes. The relations among the digital platforms, streams of data, and users develop feedback loops, which affect engagement patterns and societal outcomes. Knowing the architecture and operations of the digital ecosystem around the world is critical when evaluating the mechanism by which digital well-being and life satisfaction get arrived at among different people and locations.

Table 1. Dimensions of Digital Well-Being and Supporting Theories

Dimension	Description	Supporting Theory
Digital balance	Ability to regulate technology use and maintain autonomy	Self-Determination Theory
Social connectivity	Quality of online relationships and social support	Social Exchange Theory
Social comparison	Evaluation of self based on online peer content	Social Comparison Theory
Technology adoption	Continued use driven by perceived usefulness	Technology Acceptance Model
Digital trust	Confidence in privacy and platform governance	Institutional Trust Theory

Table 1 summarizes the key dimensions of digital well-being and their theoretical foundations used in the proposed model.

5.1 Digital Platforms, Social Media, and Smart Technologies

Digital platforms constitute the basis on which the digital ecosystem is situated worldwide, through which communication, sharing of information, and economic interaction takes place. The social media sites allow new forms of communication between people, the distribution of content, and the building of digital identity, which are the leading factors of socialization and self-image. These sites have an impact due to their effects on social comparison, emotional venting and social support.

Digital ecosystem is further extended to the physical space through smart technologies, such as wearable technologies, smart homes, or Internet of things applications. These technologies use personal information to collect and analyze data to maximize efficiency, health surveillance, and daily activities. Smart technologies may help to make life more convenient and well-supported by offering personalized feedback and assistance, which requires proper design and use (European Commission, 2021).

Nevertheless, there are also the apprehensions connected to surveillance, addiction, and a lack of personal control, as the digital dimension and the intelligent technologies are ubiquitous. The procedure of algorithmic personalization can strengthen behavioral patterns and reduce the exposure to different opinions. These concepts are fundamentally essential to determining the effects that platforms and smart technologies have on digital well-being and life satisfaction by understanding the relationship between them and human behavior.

5.2 Role of Artificial Intelligence and Automation

Automation and artificial intelligence have become the characteristics of the digital ecosystem globally and affect user experiences and decision-making activities in the various sectors. AI-based algorithms filter, suggest the products, and automate the services, and the ways people engage with the online space are influenced. These systems are capable of increasing efficiency and personalization which has a positive impact in user satisfaction and value perceptions.

On the aspect of digital well-being, AI can aid a healthier digital interaction by tracking the trends of use and relying on individual recommendations. The AI-based tools can help users control the amount of time they spend on the screen, be more productive and find answers to mental health challenges. Robots at workplace may also lessen the number of repetition duties and people can pay attention to more significant processes (Aulia & Lin, 2024).

Although these are the advantages, there are some ethical and psychological issues brought about by AI and automation. These issues might be algorithmic lack of accountability, bias, and ensuing lack of trust and well-being. Autonomy and life satisfaction may also be influenced by perceived control which can be lowered by automated decision-making. To solve these issues, there should be open AI regulation and anthropocentric design that focuses on well-being benefits.

5.3 Digital Inclusion, Access, and Inequality

Digital inclusion is a very important aspect of world digital ecosystem whereby it dictates those who gain access to digital technologies and those who are marginalized. Availability of quality internet, cheap technologies, and online literacy identifies the capabilities of people to enjoy a complete digital life. Inclusive digital ecologies will allow access to education, health, and economic opportunities by more people, leading to an increase in life satisfaction.

Digital inequality on the other hand, increases pre-existing social and economic inequalities. People who do not have sufficient access or skills are likely to feel frustrated, marginalized, and less well. The digital divide can also be associated with disparities in quality of use, availability of language, and access by marginalized communities.

Digital inequality needs both governmental action, organizational, and technology provider action in order to mitigate this problem. Universal and digital education policies, as well as inclusive design, should be enabled by policies to spread the fruits of digital ecosystems fairly. Digital inclusion therefore becomes core in the construction of communal well-being and life fulfillment in the world digital environment (Daher & Ziade, 2024).

5.4 Policy, Governance, and Ethical Considerations

The policy and governance structures are important determinants in the operations of the digital ecosystem of the world and the effects they produce on well-being. Data protection laws, platform responsibility and digital rights influence the development and consumption of technologies. Effective governance systems may strengthen trust, preserve the autonomy of users, and positive digital experiences.

Social responsibility, and more specifically data privacy, algorithmic transparency, and user consent are increasingly becoming core issues of digital governance. Digital ethics guarantee respect to rights and offer responsible innovation. Whenever the user feels that digital systems are just and reliable, the user willingness to make use of them goes up, and this is part of a better digital well-being.

Nonetheless, the regulation methods are quite diverse everywhere, which presents an issue to international online platforms and users. The disparity in protection and varied user experience can be associated with inconsistent standards. There is the need to create consistent and ethical governance systems hence to match development of digital ecosystem with human welfare and life fulfilment (Czerw, 2019).

6. PROPOSED INTEGRATED MODEL FOR MEASURING DIGITAL WELL-BEING AND LIFE SATISFACTION

The increased complexity of the digital experiences demands an integrated model incorporating the multifaceted association between the digital well-being and the life satisfaction. Current strategies tend to deal with singular parameters like screen time, online behavior, or subjective happiness, which does not consider the interactions of digital engagement and psychological outcome as well as contextual variables. Here is a proposed integrated model that is aimed at determining the digital well-being and life satisfaction on the global level of the digital ecosystem.

The specified model is a synthesis of the findings of psychological, sociological, and technological theories, which allow structurally describing the impact of digital interactions on life satisfaction. It acknowledges that both the individual, including self-discipline and emotional strength provide a digital common good at the end-user level, and the system, including the screen architecture, policies, and culture, contribute to the state of digital health. The model provides a detailed method of studying the outcomes of well-being in digitally mediated settings as it combines these dimensions.

6.1 Conceptual Framework and Model Design

The theoretic framework of the proposed model is constructed on the basis of the idea that the proposed digital well-being is a mediating factor between digital use and life satisfaction. Digital engagement includes the use patterns, online exposure, and online interaction whereas life satisfaction is a thought analysis of the general quality of life. According to the model, the quality of digital engagements, not its intensity, defines its influence on the well-being and satisfaction.

The framework has a multidimensional format with major aspects of digital well-being that dynamically incorporate each other. These dimensions are behavioral regulation, emotional reactions, social connectivity, and the view of trust and safety. All these dimensions lead to overall well being of an individual in reference to their digital life, something that contributes to their level of satisfaction with life. The model also appreciates the feedbacks loops where life satisfaction may be used to define future digital behaviors and preferences of engagement (Mattern et al., 2024).

The model is also specifically designed to be flexible to adapt to different digital environments to fit various cultures. Instead of setting a rigid set of relationships it enables contextual change according to regional, demographic and technological forces. Such adaptability boosts the relevance of the model in various groups of people in the global digital ecosystem.

6.2 Core Variables and Measurement Constructs

The integrated model has a list of central variables that can jointly define (digital) well-being and life satisfaction. The behavioral basis of the model lies in the digital usage patterns in terms of frequency, duration, and purpose of technology use. These variables are complemented by psychological variables like emotional balance, level of stress and perceived autonomy which embodies internal experience involved with digital engagements.

The social variables are very vital in the model because the significance of online relationships, social support, and a sense of belongingness has been brought out. The digital social interactions are focused on quality more than quantity and it is acknowledged that meaningful interactions have a more significant effect on well-being. Besides, trust-related constructs, such as perceptions of privacy, security, and platform transparency are also included to have an impression of the role of ethics and institutional effects on digital experiences.

Life satisfaction is a higher-order outcome variable, a measure of evaluation achievement both in personal area, social area, and in the professional area. It is possible to use both the subjective self report, as well as the objective contextual cues to create a stronger assessment, as given in the model. A combination of these constructs makes the digital well-being and life satisfaction interconnected and multidimensional in this model (Chingan Thottathil & Nandakumar, 2024).

6.3 Interrelationships Between Digital Well-Being and Life Satisfaction

One of the main characteristics of the offered model is the focus on the relationships between digital well-being and life satisfaction. Instead of considering these constructs as independent the model theorizes the role of digital well-being as a determinant of life satisfaction that is digitally mediated. Positive digital well-being based on using digital resources in a balanced way, emotional stability, and positive socialization is deemed to increase life satisfaction in the long term.

Negative pathways are also included in the model, as bad digital well-being has been realized as the destroyer of life satisfaction. The continuous stress of digital life, exposure to pernicious content, and mistrust of digital systems precondition life dissatisfaction and deterioration of life quality. The effects of these diseases can be experienced over time and the importance of longitudinal assessment in determining long-term effects cannot be overemphasized (Goyal et al., 2026a).

Notably, this model assumes two-way effects which are important by recognizing that life satisfaction may create a digital behavior. Students who experience greater life satisfaction can be more selective and purposeful users of digital technologies, which supports the achievement of positive results of well-being. Such dynamic view indicates the multifaceted and changing nature of digital life in the global ecosystem.

6.4 Model Assumptions and Scope

There are some main assumptions according to which the scope and applicability of the proposed integrated model are built. First, it supposes the assumption that digital technologies represent a ubiquitous and permanent element of contemporary existence, and they affect the well-being in various spheres. Second, it presupposes that digital well-being is not necessarily good or bad, but relies on contextual and behavioral elements.

The model also presupposes variability of people and cultures, as it acknowledges that digital experiences are influenced by social norms, access and regulatory environment. To that end, the model does not aim at generating homogenous results but to offer a systematic design to comparative analysis. This is the assumption that supports cross-cultural research and policy assessment.

Lastly, the model is mostly evaluative and diagnostic as opposed to prescriptive. Although it guides the planning of interventions, its main aim is to promote a systematic measurement and perceiving digital well-being and life contentment. The model will offer a starting point on which to base future empirical testing, refining, and implementation in a research, policy, and practice (Goyal et al., 2026b).

CONCLUSION

The blistering development of the digital technologies has essentially redefined the way people learn how to feel well and examine their overall satisfaction with their life. With the growing mediation of social interaction by digital environments, work, education, and personal expression, the sense of the interaction between digital well-being and life satisfaction has become topical as well as a necessity. The chapter has highlighted the fact that digital well-being is a multidimensional concept that is created by both personal usage patterns and the psychological pathways as well as social relations, platform design, and general institutional and cultural situations. The aspect of life satisfaction at the digital age cannot be measured in isolation of these factors because the new digital experiences have become a key factor in the perception of the quality of life when it comes to the global digital ecosystem.

The chapter combined theoretical insights and outlined the main aspects of digital well-being to come up with a comprehensive model of understanding the intricate and dynamic associations between digital activity and life satisfaction. The model reveals the significance of the balanced use of digital resources, emotional well-being, meaningful social connectivity, and trust in digital machines as key predictors of well-being outcomes. It also acknowledges that such relationship is two-way with life satisfaction driving digital behavior and the other way around. This combination is no longer mere fixation on screen time but provides a more complex system of assessing the contribution of digital technologies to the promotion of good and bad life events.

Finally, the chapter points out the necessity of having the human-centric approach to digital development, where well-being is considered as the supplement to technological innovation. There is role skin deep unity by policymakers, organizations, and technology designers to develop digital spaces that encourage independence, inclusion and psychological well-being. Meanwhile, individuals need to achieve digital literacy and self-regulation in order to operate in more and more complicated digital environments as well. The coherence between digital ecosystems and well-being goals expressed in the integrated model outlined in this chapter will give future studies, adequate policy development and the encouragement of digital engagement towards sustainability that breeds life satisfaction in different world settings.

REFERENCES

Agostini, A., Masiero, A. V., & Kanan, L. A. (2018). Assessment of well-being at work of information technology professionals. *International Journal of Humanities and Social Science*, *8*(6), 44–54. DOI: 10.30845/ijhss.v8n6a6

Aulia, S. R., & Lin, W. S. (2024). Embracing the digital shift. *Asia Pacific Management Review*, *30*(3), 100339. DOI: 10.1016/j.apmrv.2024.12.003

Bartels, A. L., Peterson, S. J., & Reina, C. S. (2019). Understanding well-being at work: Development and validation of the eudaimonic workplace well-being scale. *PLoS One*, *14*(4), e0215957. DOI: 10.1371/journal.pone.0215957 PMID: 31022285

Burr, C., Taddeo, M., & Floridi, L. (2020). The ethics of digital well-being: A thematic review. *Science and Engineering Ethics*, *26*(4), 2313–2343. DOI: 10.1007/s11948-020-00175-8 PMID: 31933119

Chingan Thottathil, S., & Nandakumar, M. K. (2024). Integrating hedonic and eudaimonic perspectives of well-being. *Human Resource Development Review*, *24*(2), 157–198. DOI: 10.1177/15344843241305650

Chughtai, A., Byrne, M., & Flood, B. (2015). Linking ethical leadership to employee well-being. *Journal of Business Ethics*, *128*(3), 653–663. DOI: 10.1007/s10551-014-2126-7

Cropanzano, R., & Mitchell, M. S. (2005). Social exchange theory: An interdisciplinary review. *Journal of Management*, *31*(6), 874–900. DOI: 10.1177/0149206305279602

Czerw, A. (2019). Diagnosing well-being in work context. *Current Psychology*, *38*(2), 331–346. DOI: 10.1007/s12144-017-9614-8

Daher, M. M., & Ziade, F. (2024). Technology, workforce, and the future of sustainable work. In *Navigating the intersection of business, sustainability and technology* (pp. 119–136). Springer Nature.

De Santis, A., & Fantinelli, S. (2024). Digital well-being as a new kind of adaptation to the new millennium needs: A state-of-the-art analysis. *Elementa*, *3*, 135–151.

Edmondson, A. C. (2018). *The fearless organization: Creating psychological safety in the workplace for learning, innovation, and growth*. John Wiley & Sons.

Ertürk, A., & Vurgun, L. (2015). Retention of IT professionals. *Journal of Business Research*, *68*(1), 34–46. DOI: 10.1016/j.jbusres.2014.05.010

European Commission. (2021). *2030 digital compass: The European way for the digital decade*. European Commission.

Farooqi, A., Das, D., Tripathi, M., Dutta, R., Goyal, N. K., & Sheikh, M. F. (2026). Navigating ethical frontiers in AI-driven geriatric care. In Stolakis, K., & Efthymiou, I. (Eds.), *AI for geriatric care in an aging society: Ethical, clinical, and policy challenges* (pp. 243–266). IGI Global Scientific Publishing., DOI: 10.4018/979-8-3373-5462-0.ch009

Goyal, N. K., Goyal, N. K., Kumar, S., Dutta, R., Kothari, V., & Sinha, S. K. (2026). Empowering elderly care through artificial intelligence. In Stolakis, K., & Efthymiou, I. (Eds.), *AI for geriatric care in an aging society* (pp. 1–28). IGI Global Scientific Publishing., DOI: 10.4018/979-8-3373-5462-0.ch001

Goyal, N. K., Gulati, K., Avasthi, A., Kapoor, S. K., Keswani, B., & Gupta, S. (2026). Securing the imagination: Security and privacy challenges in generative AI systems. In Elbaghazaoui, B., Amnai, M., & Gherabi, N. (Eds.), *Generative AI-powered data architectures: From governance to autonomous analytics* (pp. 239–266). IGI Global Scientific Publishing., DOI: 10.4018/979-8-3373-5616-7.ch010

Guest, D. E. (2017). Human resource management and employee well-being: Towards a new analytic framework. *Human Resource Management Journal*, *27*(1), 22–38. DOI: 10.1111/1748-8583.12139

Kowalski, T. H., & Loretto, W. (2017). Well-being and HRM in the changing workplace. *International Journal of Human Resource Management*, *28*(16), 2229–2255. DOI: 10.1080/09585192.2017.1345205

Kumari, M., & Goyal, N. K. (2026). Artificial intelligence in the cryptocurrency ecosystem: Crime mechanisms, detection strategies, and legal perspectives. In Lin, L. (Ed.), *Innovations in cryptocrime and financial fraud* (pp. 245–282). IGI Global Scientific Publishing., DOI: 10.4018/979-8-3373-0675-9.ch007

Kumari, M., Kumawat, R., Tripathi, M., Suganthi, K., Goyal, N. K., & Sheikh, M. F. (2026). Blockchain for transparency and traceability in supply chains. In Khan, M., Mehmood, T., & Rao, M. (Eds.), *Maximizing operational efficiency at the intersection of supply chain management and marketing* (pp. 35–64). IGI Global Scientific Publishing., DOI: 10.4018/979-8-3373-3109-6.ch002

Mattern, J., Tarafdar, M., Klein, S., & Schellhammer, S. (2024). Thriving in a bruising job. *Information Systems Journal*, *34*(6), 1902–1934. DOI: 10.1111/isj.12513

Mayer, R. C., Davis, J. H., & Schoorman, F. D. (1995). An integrative model of organizational trust. *Academy of Management Review*, *20*(3), 709–734. DOI: 10.2307/258792

Mirowska, A., & Bakici, T. (2024). Working in a bubble: Techno-isolation as an emerging techno-stressor in teleworkers. *Information Technology & People*, *37*(3), 1403–1422. DOI: 10.1108/ITP-09-2022-0657

Niemiec, C. P. (2024). Eudaimonic well-being. In *Encyclopedia of quality of life and well-being research* (pp. 2212–2214). Springer International Publishing.

OECD. (2020). *OECD digital economy outlook 2020*. OECD Publishing.

Ryff, C. D., & Singer, B. H. (2008). Know thyself and become what you are: A eudaimonic approach to psychological well-being. *Journal of Happiness Studies*, *9*(1), 13–39. DOI: 10.1007/s10902-006-9019-0

Sharma, P., Kumawat, R., Jain, G., Keswani, G., Goyal, N. K., & Sheikh, M. F. (2026). Machine learning-based intrusion detection systems for healthcare Internet of Things (HIoT). In Shieh, C., Goel, P., Horng, M., & Pandey, H. (Eds.), *Resilient healthcare Internet of Things systems: Architectures, security, and trust* (pp. 185–214). IGI Global Scientific Publishing., DOI: 10.4018/979-8-3373-7610-3.ch007

Sonnentag, S., Tay, L., & Nesher Shoshan, H. (2023). A review on health and well-being at work. *Personnel Psychology*, *76*(2), 473–510. DOI: 10.1111/peps.12572

Soren, A., & Ryff, C. D. (2023). Meaningful work, well-being, and health: Enacting a eudaimonic vision. *International Journal of Environmental Research and Public Health*, *20*(16), 6570. DOI: 10.3390/ijerph20166570 PMID: 37623156

Stănculescu, E., & Griffiths, M. D. (2024). The association between problematic internet use and hedonic and eudaimonic well-being: A latent profile analysis. *Technology in Society*, *78*, 102588. DOI: 10.1016/j.techsoc.2024.102588

Steinert, S., & Dennis, M. J. (2022). Emotions and digital well-being: On social media's emotional affordances. *Philosophy & Technology*, *35*(2), 36. DOI: 10.1007/s13347-022-00530-6 PMID: 35450167

Tokdemir, G. (2022). Software professionals during the COVID-19 pandemic in Turkey. *Journal of Systems and Software*, *188*, 111286. DOI: 10.1016/j.jss.2022.111286 PMID: 35250124

Umair, A., Conboy, K., & Whelan, E. (2023). Examining technostress and its impact on worker well-being in the digital gig economy. *Internet Research*, *33*(7), 206–242. DOI: 10.1108/INTR-03-2022-0214

United Nations. (2015). *Transforming our world: The 2030 agenda for sustainable development.* United Nations.

Van De Voorde, K., Paauwe, J., & Van Veldhoven, M. (2012). Employee well-being and the HRM–organizational performance relationship. *International Journal of Management Reviews, 14*(4), 391–407. DOI: 10.1111/j.1468-2370.2011.00322.x

Vanden Abeele, M. M. (2021). Digital wellbeing as a dynamic construct. *Communication Theory, 31*(4), 932–955. DOI: 10.1093/ct/qtaa024

Chapter 6
Developing a Global Digital Life Satisfaction Index (DLSI) Using a Multi-Criteria Optimization and Structural Equation Modeling Framework.

Duggirala Aravind
http://orcid.org/0009-0005-4362-7684
ASET Institute of Science and Technology, India

Theodore Tarnanidis
http://orcid.org/0000-0002-4836-3906
International Hellenic University, Greece

N. V. Suresh
http://orcid.org/0000-0002-0393-6037
ASET Institute of Science and Technology, India

M. Dhadurya Naik
http://orcid.org/0000-0002-3625-2125
Prasad V. Potluri Siddhartha Institute of Technology, India

E. Eswara Reddy
http://orcid.org/0000-0003-0387-1437
CMR University, India

Patil Jaya Lakshmi Reddy
http://orcid.org/0009-0006-7083-9794
CMR University, India

Vanathi Gopikrishna
http://orcid.org/0009-0009-0667-6507
Avichi College of Arts and Science, India

DOI: 10.4018/979-8-3373-8357-6.ch006

ABSTRACT

This research builds a Global Digital Life Satisfaction Index (DLSI) to objectively assess the level of life satisfaction in digital international markets. The index combines multidimensional indicators of digital well-being which entail economic, psychological, technological, and institutional aspects. Multi-criteria optimization techniques are used to normalize, weight and aggregate heterogeneous indicators which have robustness and comparability across digital ecosystems. The validation of latent constructs and causal relationships between digital trust, autonomy, access, and subjective satisfaction are tested by Structural Equation Modeling. The proposed DLSI offers a cross-market evaluation, policy analysis, and strategizing analytical instrument with a scalable quantitative basis to support the research of human-driven digital market design and global digital well-being.

1. INTRODUCTION

The accelerated digitalization has essentially changed the way people socialize, consume, work, and find pleasure in daily lives. Digital platforms are increasingly becoming the mediator of economic transactions, social relation, service access, and information, and thus affecting subjective well-being and life contentment (Van Deursen & Helsper, 2015; Acemoglu & Restrepo, 2020). Conventional life satisfaction indicators, which are mainly designed to meet the socio-economic and offline setting, are not good enough to embrace the complexity, intensity and multi-dimensionality of digitally mediated experiences. With the development of digital environments into central areas of human activity, there is a rising demand of structural, quantitative methods of measuring life satisfaction in digital ecosystems by taking into consideration technological, behavioral, and institutional factors on a global level (Burr et al., 2020; Gangadharan, 2017). Digital markets are growing very fast globally because of platform economies, cross-border stream of data and digitally-enabled services. Although these markets create efficiency, access, and innovation, they also bring to prominence important well-being issues of digital exclusion, algorithmic unfairness, risk to privacy, and psychological tension (Ragnedda & Ruiu, 2020). The disproportionate availability of digital resources to nations and people also makes the connection of market growth and human well-being more difficult. With growing activities of digital markets beyond national regulatory frameworks, it becomes analytically difficult to evaluate how they impact on the satisfaction of individuals lives. It is thus vital to be aware of the effects of global digital market formations in wellbeing in order to assess sustainable and humanistic digital economic growth (Buchi et al., 2016; Shao, 2022).

1.1 Research Gap in Unified Digital Life Satisfaction Measurement

Although there is increasing attention to digital well-being, current literature is still disparate by field, with a wide range of pointers, self-report scales, and context-based measures. No single, standardized index can measure digital life satisfaction in the heterogeneous global markets in a similar and analytically rigorous way. They are hindered by the lack of a combined measurement system cross-market benchmarking, and longitudinal comparison, and evidence-based assessment of policy. The gap explains why a thorough index-based model should be adopted, which is based on formal modeling and empirical validation (Han et al., 2022; Kubatko et al., 2022).

1.2 Chapter Objectives and Scope

The main idea of this chapter is to create a Global Digital Life Satisfaction Index (DLSI) that will make it possible to systematically measure the satisfaction with life in digital global markets. The purpose of the chapter is to establish the fundamental dimensions of digital life satisfaction, to operate the further combination of these dimensions into a composite index and to prove relationships underlining it on the base of advanced quantitative methods. These areas included include cross-market comparability, methodological rigor, and analytical scalability. By uniting the multidimensional indicators through a single modeling framework, the chapter attempts to offer a solid instrument of analytical power to the researchers, policymakers and digital market stakeholders willing to quantify and optimize digital well-being.

1.3 Structure of the Chapter

This chapter continues with conceptualizing digital life satisfaction and reviewing the pertinent literature, and then the DLSI is developed and mathematically modeled. This is followed by structural validation and empirical design with results, discussion, policy implications, future research directions and concluded remarks.

2. DIGITAL LIFE SATISFACTION IN GLOBAL DIGITAL MARKETS

2.1 Concept of Life Satisfaction in Digital Environments

Digital life satisfaction is a mental assessment of the overall quality of life of individuals upon the digitally mediated interactions, services, and decision situations. With an endless interaction with systematically controlled systems that control consumption, communication, work, and information access, digital life satisfaction is unlike the traditional concept of well-being (Vanden Abeele, 2021). The digital environments present the unique characteristics of real-time responses, the dependency on the platform, subject-driven personalisation, and virtual social presence, all of which modify the subjective assessments of fulfilment. Digital life satisfaction, therefore, needs to be conceptualized as a multidimensional entity that captures both perceived benefits (i.e.: convenience and connectivity) and perceived costs (i.e.: information overload, loss of autonomy and privacy issues in the global digital market constructions) (Meier & Reinecke, 2021).

2.2 Dimensions of Digital Well-Being (Economic, Psychological, Technological, Institutional)

Digital wellness is clearly multidimensional, and includes economic, psychological, technological and institutional dimensions which together define the life satisfaction in digital markets. The economic dimension reflects on the availability of digital service, affordability, revenue, and efficiency benefits through digital engagement. The psychological aspect indicates the emotional reactions, perceived control, trust as well as cognitive load related to online interactions (Arslankara et al., 2022). The technical aspect is concerned with the quality of infrastructure, the system reliability, usability, cybersecurity, and algorithm transparency, which predetermine the user experiences and results. The institutional aspect includes data governance, regulatory models, consumer laws and ethics that regulate fairness, responsibility as well as user entitlement. Dependence between these dimensions is essential since the lack of institutional protection or design flaws can negatively affect economic gains and psychological and mental performance. Digital life satisfaction is best evaluated however through a synthesized approach to these dimensions in global digital markets (Buchi, 2024).

2.3 Role of Digital platforms and Ecosystems

Digital platforms and ecosystems act as the main mediators defining life satisfaction in the digital markets of the world. Architectures of the platforms define the manner in which users utilize services, engage with others, and make choices and ecosystem dynamics define competition, innovation and value allocation. Algorithms of curation have direct impacts on user satisfaction and trust since they influence visibility, choice set and perceived fairness (Ruiz-Alba et al., 2022). Efficiency and engagement have the potential to be enhanced utilizing network effects and personalization that is driven by data, but can also exacerbate dependency and power asymmetries. On a finer level, at the ecosystem, platforms, regulators, service providers and users interact in complex feedback cycles that define digital experiences. Making sense of the purpose of platforms and ecosystems provides insight into the ways digital market structures mediate the life satisfaction results in different global settings (Dulsrud & Bygstad, 2022).

3. REVIEW OF RELATED LITERATURE

3.1 Life Satisfaction, Subjective Well-Being, and Digital Contexts

The nature of life satisfaction and subjective well-being has been studied widely in economics, psychology, and social sciences, where it typically refers to the income, health, social ties, and institution quality. Classical theories view life satisfaction as a sense of life conditions, not the temporality of affect. The growing mediation of everyday practices by digital technologies has however, questioned these traditional views (Nguyen & Hargittai, 2024; Anton, 2025). Online environments provide novel conditions of well-being, such as platform addiction, algorithmic impact, social interaction on the virtual level, and being constantly connected. The recent research highlights that online interaction transforms (autonomy, social comparison, and perceived control) and changes the satisfaction judgment. However, much of this literature addresses digital factors as auxiliary factors, but not as a structural factor of life satisfaction. Consequently, the current theoretical frameworks do not always effectively describe the systemic nature of the role of digital environments determining well-being, especially in worldwide digital markets that are supported by scale, speed, and transnational interactions (Voukelatou et al., 2021; Iacus & Porro, 2021).

3.2 Measurement Approaches to Digital Well-Being

Empirical studies about digital well-being have resulted in a wide range of measurement procedures, including subjective self-report assessments and content-specific behavioral indications. Measures that are typically used are screen-time measures, perceived digital stress, online trust, and user satisfaction in digital services. Though such methods are useful, they are usually partial, context-specific and lack cross-market applicability (Cao & Li, 2023; Smits et al., 2022). Most studies are keen on a particular industry e.g. social media digital health or e-commerce leading to narrow indicators that is not generalizable. Moreover, the measurement models are often based on individual constructs, which are not unified on the economic, psychological, technological, and institutional levels. This disaggregation inhibits comparative analysis and prevents the determination of overall digital satisfaction with life on the systemic level. As a result, it leads to an increasing awareness of the importance of the integrated measurement structures that can combine heterogeneous indicators into consistent and comparable forms of digital well-being (Chen et al., 2025; Mathew et al., 2023).

3.3 Index Construction and Multi-Criteria Modeling in Digital Research

Index construction has been used for many years in social and economic science to work out multidimensional phenomena into composite measures, e.g. human development and quality-of-life indices. Composite indexes have been formulated in digital research to measure digital preparedness, involvement, innovation and governance. The indices are often normalized, weighted and aggregated to provide heterogeneous indicators (Attia et al., 2022; Tutar et al., 2025). Techniques for trade-off have also appeared in the form of multi-criteria decision models such as weighted scoring, outranking and distance-based approaches. These models provide formal ways of dealing with multidimensionality, heterogeneity, and relative significance of indicators. Nevertheless, most current digital indices focus on infrastructural or economic aspects whilst neglecting the subjective well-being elements. Furthermore, the validity of conceptual relationships between index dimensions is not given much attention. This difference indicates why index-based methods are needed that directly encapsulate those constructs of life satisfaction by establishing strict multi-criteria models (Usakli & Rasoolimanesh, 2023; Natoli et al., 2024)).

3.4 Structural Modeling, Integration Gaps, and Theoretical Positioning

Behavioral economics, psychology, and digital studies Structural equation modeling has been extensively used to study the latent constructs and the causal relations among observable variables. SEM allows the joint estimation of measurements and structural factors and offers a strong framework to test complex theoretic models. SEM has been applied to study the relationship between trust, technology acceptance, perceived risk, and satisfaction in the digital well-being research (Almaiah et al., 2023). Nevertheless, such applications are often limited to platform specific (local) use and are not commonly combined with index building algorithms. A major gap in theory and methodology is the difference between structural modelling and composite index creation. The chapter is placed at the crossroad of these streams by merging index building with structure validation and thus, a single system of measuring digital life satisfaction. The suggested methodology covers the necessity to provide quantitative aggregation, as well as theory consistency in measuring well-being in world digital markets (Pisarska et al., 2025; Wu et al., 2025).

4. CONCEPTUAL STRUCTURE OF THE DIGITAL LIFE SATISFACTION INDEX

4.1 Identification of DLSI dimensions and indicators

Digital Life Satisfaction Index (DLSI) is defined to combine a set of core dimensions that are important to reflect the multidimensionality of digital mediated well-being of global markets. The dimensions are based on existing literature on the life satisfaction, digital well-being, and platform economics, and capture the economic, psychological, technological and institutional dimensions of the digital life.

Table 1. DLSI Dimensions and Key Indicators

Dimension	Indicator	Description	Measurement Type	Source
Economic	Digital Service Affordability	Cost accessibility of digital platforms/services.	Ratio / Index	World Bank / ITU
	Access to Financial Tech	Availability of online banking, fintech services	Binary / Index	IMF / World Bank
Technological	Infrastructure Quality	Internet speed, coverage, and reliability	Continuous	ITU/ GSMA
	Platform Reliability	System uptime and service consistency	Continuous	Platform reports
Psychological	Autonomy in Digital Interaction	User control over personal data and interface	Likert Scale	Survey data /Digital Well-Being Studies
	Digital Stress	Perceived overload or anxiety due to digital usage	Likert Scale	Survey data / Research Literature
Institutional	Trust in Digital Governance	Confidence in regulations and data protection	Likert Scale	OECD / UN E-Government Reports
	Regulatory Effectiveness	Enforcement and clarity of digital laws	Index / Ordinal	UNCTAD / Government Reports

Every dimension is defined in some measurable indicators of the access, intensity of use, perceived quality, trust, autonomy, and regulatory protection. Selection of indicators is made based on relevance, observability as well as cross-market comparability. In order to lend analytical coherence, the indicators are characterized at a sufficient level of abstraction so that they can be aggregated without the meaning being lost. Such organized identifications present a stable basis of further normalization, weighting, and incorporation by the DLSI framework.

4.2 Interrelationships Among Digital Satisfaction Constructs

Digital life satisfaction is the result of interdependence of underlying dimensions and not individual effects. With the economic access to digital services, interaction with technological quality on usability and perceived efficiency, psychological aspects of trust and perceived control mediate the individual reactions to platform design and data practices. The interactions are influenced by the institutional conditions such as regulatory control and data security because of the perceived fairness and risk. Such interrelationships result in feedback processes where gains in one dimension could enhance or limit results in other dimensions. Digital life satisfaction is conceptualized as a higher-order construct that is created by direct and indirect correlation among dimensions. The awareness of these interdependencies is the key to reflecting the digital well-being accurately and to allowing further structural verification of the suggested index.

4.3 Assumptions and Analytical Scope

The DLSI model assumes a number of analytical relationships. Observable indicators to proxy latent well-being constructs are assumed to measure digital life satisfaction. Interactions across dimensions are postulated to be maintaining under specified market settings, and allows cross-sectional comparison. The scope of the analysis is digitally active populations in universal markets, as the non-participation and radical digital exclusion are not within the immediate scope of the index measurement.

4.4 Conceptual Flow of the Proposed Index

The picture flow of the DLSI has a well-organized process of how indicators are picked up to the development of composite indices. Raw indicators of various dimensions of digital life satisfaction are first identified and set up to be analyzed. The indicators are then converted into standardized measures to make comparisons between the heterogeneous digital markets. Well-being representations of the dimensions are then aggregated into digital well-being. Lastly, these are summed to create one composite index of overall digital life satisfaction. As this happens, conceptual consistency is ensured by matching indicator aggregation to the theoretical relationships between dimensions. This flow is what makes the resultant index to be more representative of the underlying conceptual structure as well as the empirical information so as to give it a sense of coherent basis upon which it can be quantified and validated.

Figure 1. Conceptual Flow DLSI

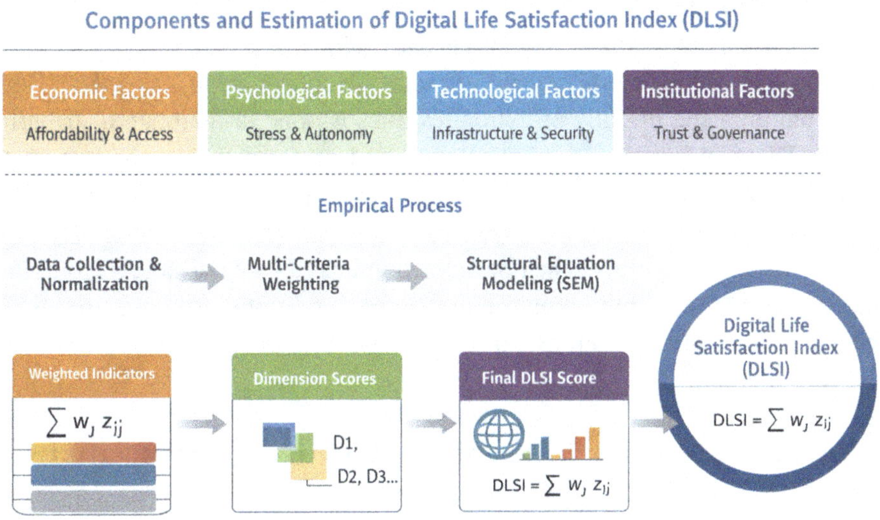

5. Mathematical Formulation of the DLSI

5.1 Indicator Normalization and Mathematical Preprocessing

Let x_{ij} denote the observed value of indicator j for digital market i, where $i = 1, 2, \ldots, N$ and $j = 1, 2, \ldots, M$.

Since the measurement scales and the directional interpretation are varied, they need to be indicator normalized so that the measurements can across markets can be comparable.

In the case of benefit type indicators, use of min–max normalization as

$$z_{ij} = \frac{x_{ij} - \min(x_j)}{\max(x_j) - min\ (x_j)},$$

and in the case of costs type indicators

$$z_{ij} = \frac{\max(x_j) - x_{ij}}{\max(x_j) - min\ (x_j)}$$

can be used instead, or even use

$$z_{ij} = \frac{x_{ij}}{\sqrt{\sum_{i=1}^{N} x_{ij}^2}}$$

usually when comparative magnitudes are valued.

The normalized indicator $Z = [z_{ij}]$ is what the optimization is based on. Bounded imputation of the missing or extreme values is done to maintain distributional stability. These indicators are further classified into dimension specific vectors, which are economic, psychological, technological and institutional elements. This preprocessing step guarantees invariance to scale, dimensional consistency as well as mathematical tractability. The normalized indicators are considered continuous, bounded in [0,1], and agglomerable under the conditions of convexity allowing rigorously optimized, as well as, structural modeling in subsequent phases of the DLSI formulation.

5.2 Weight Estimation Through Multi-Criteria Optimization

$w = (w_1, w_2, \ldots, w_M)^{\mathsf{T}}$represents the vector of indicator weights, where $w_j \geq 0$ and $\sum_{j=1}^{M} w_j = 1$. The estimation of weights is posed as a multi-criteria optimization problem to capture the weight of the indicators in terms of relative weight without imposing some arbitrary levels of preference. The one most frequently used method is entropy based weighting, which is characterized by

$$e_j = -k \sum_{i=1}^{N} z_{ij} \ln(z_{ij}),\ k = \frac{1}{lnN},$$

and divergence

$$d_j = 1 - e_j,$$

and normalized weights

$$w_j = \frac{d_j}{\sum_{j=1}^{M} d_j}.$$

(alternatively, distance based optimization can be applied to maximize the discrimination in markets):

$$\max_{w} \sum_{i=1}^{N} \sum_{j=1}^{M} w_j \left(z_{ij} - z_{\ j}\right)^2$$

with the simplex constraints on w. Such formulations make sure that indicators that have more informational contribution are weighted higher. Under common instructions, the optimization problem is a convex one with the toxin-world solution to the problem. The test of weight stability is based on perturbation analysis. Such weighting plan is useful because it promotes objectivity and improves the correspondence of the DLSI to the formal principles of decision-science.

5.3 Composite Index Construction and Functional Specification

Based on normalized indicator matrix z and the optimal weight vector w the Digital Life Satisfaction Index of market i is developed as composite function. The linear aggregation of the base linear regime is given by

$$DLSI_i = \sum_{j=1}^{M} w_j z_{ij}.$$

The form is an additive form that presumes the fact that indicators are compensable and is monotonic and continuous. Multiplicative specification can be used in lieu of additive specification in order to capture non-linear interactions:

$$DLSI_i = \prod_{j=1}^{M} z_{ij}^{wj}.$$

Aggregation at the dimension level begins firstly with grouping the indicators into dimension sets D_k, which results in

$$S_{ik} = \sum_{j \in D_k} w_j z_{ij},$$

and then further aggregation into the final index. The resulting DLSI lies in the range of [0,1] and allows the ranking and comparison across the digital markets. Functional supposition is chosen on the basis of analytical goals and empirical conduct of clues. The composite index therefore offers a painting cursory but in-depth account of digital life satisfaction, holding both a dimensional expression and a mathematical formulating.

5.4 Robustness, Sensitivity, and Consistency Analysis

Robustness analysis is the analysis of stability of the DLSI scores under change in weights, normalization schemes, and aggregation functions. The sensitivity is determined by making small changes to the weights w_j in a small neighbourhood $\in$, such that

$$w_j' = w_j + \in_j, \sum_j \in_j = 0.$$

The difference in values of the indices,

$$\Delta DLSI_i = DLSI_i' - DLSI_i,$$

is studied to measure the stability of ranking. Correlations Spearman and Kendall are used to determine consistency when using other specifications of the model. Internal consistency is also reviewed through variance decomposition analysis and dominance analysis. Structural imbalance across dimensions in their markets is identified in high-sensitivity markets. These steps make sure that the DLSI is not becoming motivated by extreme parameter selections and modeling artifacts. The validation of robustness enhances the interpretability and trustworthiness of the index, which validates the appropriateness of the index in comparison, in policies, and in long-term monitoring of digital life satisfaction in international markets.

6. STRUCTURAL EQUATION MODELING FOR DLSI VALIDATION

6.1 Latent Constructs, Observed Indicators, and Measurement Specification

Structural Equation Modeling (SEM) is used to confirm the latent structure of Digital Life Satisfaction Index (DLSI). Where ξ is a vector of the exogenous latent constructs of core samples of digital life satisfaction, which are the economic, psychological, technological quality, and institutional trust. The observed indicators that are based on the DLSI framework are expressed in the form of the vector X. The specification of the measurement relationship is given in terms of

$$x = \Lambda_x \xi + \delta$$

where, Λ_x is a factor loading matrix, and δ is the measurement error terms. All the indicators are limited to load on one latent construct to achieve discriminant clarity. The selection of the indicators is guided by theoretical relevance and observability, which are in line with the index construction process. Latent constructs are treated as continuous and normally distributed whereas error terms are treated to be non-correlated to the latent variables. Separate measure error and true construct variance can be clearly separated with this specification. The measurement model defines the validity of the DLSI dimensions through ensuring that indicators measured are trustworthy in depicting the latent constructs that they are intended to depict. Such a step will be necessary in order to guarantee that the composite index is empirically sound in its constructs and does not necessarily represent an arithmetic summative process.

6.2 Structural Relationships and Causal Model Formulation

After measuring it, the structural element of the SEM makes the latent causal relationships between the causes of digital life satisfaction formal. Where η means the endogenous latent variable illustrating overall digital life satisfaction. The structural model can be presented in the form of

$$\eta = B_{\eta} + \Gamma\xi + \zeta,$$

where B indicates the dependency between relationships among the endogenous constructs, Γ indicates how the exogenous constructs affect the digital life satisfaction, and ζ indicates structural disturbances. The economic, technological, psychological and institutional dimensions, the DLSI context, are modelled as direct predictors of digital life satisfaction, with the additional interdependencies between the dimensions being found in the indirect effects. As an illustration, institutional trust can impact on satisfaction indirectly due to its influence on perceived technological reliability. Path coefficients have also been viewed as standardized effects so that comparisons of relative contributions between constructs can be made. Structural model sets up directional assumptions based on the theory but testing through the formulation of the hypothesized relationships can be done empirically. This methodology allows evaluating both direct and moderated impacts of digital life satisfaction, and these new dimensions contribute to a more profound understanding of the robust influence of different dimensions on digital life satisfaction as opposed to mere aggregation of indices.

6.3 Estimation, Reliability, and Model Fit Assessment

Maximum likelihood or robust estimation is done, based on the properties of the data distribution, to perform a model estimation. This is done so that the difference between the observed covariance S and the model implied covariance matrix $\Sigma(\theta)$ is as minimal as it can be. Several fit indices are used to assess model adequacy in order to test its robustness. Absolute fit is computed with the help of the chi-square statistic and standardized root mean square residual, whereas incremental fit is measured by the comparison of such indices as the comparative fit index and the Tucker-Lewis index. Additional validation is received with the use of parsimony-adjusted measures.

Composite reliability and average variance extracted is used to assess reliability of latent construct because it measures internal consistency as well as convergent validity. Assessment of discriminant validity is done by comparing shared variance between constructs. This is done to check the stability of the estimate of parameters under the alternative specifications by performing sensitivity checks. Taken together, these aspects prove that the SEM is a decent reflection of the latent format of digital life satisfaction and substantiates the theoretical soundness of the DLSI. When the validation is successful, the index gains a better reputation as an effective measurement instrument in comparative and policy-based analysis.

7. DATA FRAMEWORK AND EMPIRICAL DESIGN

7.1 Data Sources and Selection Criteria

The Digital Life Satisfaction Index (DLSI) has an empirical basis that is built on multi-source and cross-national data depicting economic, technological, psychological, and institutional aspects of digital life satisfaction. One of the main sources of data is a big international survey, statistics of digital economy, the statistics of platforms use, and the indexes of governance provided by large international corporations. The purpose of the selection of these sources is to guarantee global coverage, a methodology is used, and the period of the time is the same. Data on datasets only with standardized measurement procedures, and reported reliability is included so that a comparison will be made across markets. The selection criteria put more emphasis on data being relevant to digital settings, being available in more than one country or region, and fitting the conceptual facets of the DLSI. Indicators with an excessive level of missing data, conceptual ambiguity, or in terms of their definitions across jurisdictions are not included. To reduce the occurrence of distortion due to asynchronous reporting of data, temporal alignment is employed. In case two or more sources are assessing the same construct, preference is made to sources with high resolution, greater coverage, and high methodological rigor. The last dataset is a moderate compromise between the broad scope and the depth, allowing to perform the cross-market analysis and at the same time keep its analytical traceability. Preprocessing of data incorporates validation checks, detection of outliers and harmonization of units so that there exists coherence in the data across the sources. This stringent selection procedure guarantees that the empirical input of the DLSI is not only theoretically based but can be supported by the empirical findings, this makes it a dependable foundation to further modeling and calculation of the index.

7.2 Variable Operationalization

Variable operationalization is the translation of abstract digital life satisfaction into concrete measurable indicators of quantifiable analysis. The latent dimensions of the DLSI are operationalized with the help of a set of observed variables which represent the theoretically defined attributes. Affordability of digital services, availability of digital financial tools are also considered as indicators of economic digital well-being. It measures the psychological levels by self-reported questionnaires of digital stress, autonomy, and subjective usefulness of digital engagement. Technological dimensions involve a measure of the quality of infrastructure, the reliability of platforms, and the perception of cybersecurity, whereas institutional dimensions include confidence in digital governance, frameworks of data protection, and effectiveness of regulations. All variables are switched so that there is a directional consistency whereby increasing values appeal in a consistent manner that means the increasing levels of digital life satisfaction. The extent of measurement scales is normalized before the normalization in order to deal with variation in the metric range and distribution. Categorical variables are coded into ordinals or binary forms where suit, without any loss of the informational content as well as compatibility with statistical modeling conditions. The choice of the indicators is based on a dual conceptual and empirical criterion of relevance and observability. Correlation analysis is done to eliminate redundant variables and increase the level of multicollinearity. Such operationalization strategy provides assurance of uniqueness of information offered by each indicator to the DLSI without being an invention out of thin air. The obtained set of variables can also suggest index aggregation and structural equation modeling because it has a transparent relationship between observed variables and latent dimensions.

7.3 Sampling and Cross-Market Structure

The sampling model will be in place to facilitate comparative research on digital market heterogeneities. The approach of the study is the multi-stage sampling where countries or regions will be the primary units of sampling, and the secondary units are digital users or aggregated national indicators. Markets inclusion criteria are based on minimum availability of data between all the dimensions of DLSI, which guarantees balanced representation. The last sample is the most varied one because it includes a range of economies which vary in terms of digital maturity, regulatory atmosphere, and culture. Such heterogeneity allows to examine structural differences in digital life satisfaction at world markets. Sampling weights are employed at individual level to counterbalance the differences in population size and digital coverage where data at an individual level is to be employed. Saturation in terms of income level and geographical classification also helps in supporting the cross market comparability. The structure permits the meaningful aggregation and at the same time retains the contextual specificity. The possible sampling bias due to the uneven data coverage is evaluated and addressed with the help of strong robustness checks.

The resulting dataset can aid in not only pooled but also segmented analysis and it will allow exploring global trends and the region-specific dynamics. The external validity of the DLSI is reinforced by this sampling design and the applicability of the DLSI to a global benchmarking and policy assessment.

7.4 Estimation Procedure

The process of estimation is a combination of multi-criteria optimization method and structural equation modeling to estimate and verify the DLSI. At the first stage, normal indicators are optimistically weighted to obtain composite dimensions scores. The scores are put into the SEM structure allowing both measurement and structural parameters to be estimated simultaneously. Depending on the distributional properties of the data, estimation is conducted by the maximum likelihood estimator or estimators that are robust. Monitoring of convergence diagnostics is to guarantee numerical stability. Estimates of parameters are tested as being statistically significant and plausible. In order to measure sensitivity to modeling assumptions, alternative specifications are estimated. Bootstrapping methods are used to acquire strong standard errors where making the bootstrap. It is an iterative estimation process and the structure of models can be refined with reference to empirical evidence and theoretical consistency. It is a combined process so that the DLSI remains mathematically consistent as well as empirically justified. Optimization combined with SEM offers a methodological base, which is stricter than strictly descriptive index construction techniques.

7.5 Analytical Workflow

The process behind the analysis is organised in a systematic order starting with data preparation and result interpretation. Raw data are initially cleansed, standardized, and normalized to eliminate the variation in data. Second, the multi-criteria optimization is used to estimate weights, and initial dimension scores are obtained. Third, SEM framework is used to test the latent constructs and approximate structural relationships. Fourth, the final DLSI scores are derived by adding score results that are validated dimensions.

Fifth, robustness and sensitivity analytics are undertaken in order to evaluate the stability conditions based on different assumptions. Lastly, findings will be discussed within the theoretical implications and policy implications. This processes can guarantee transparency, repeatability and high methodological rigour. The stages are recorded to ensure further extensions are possible and also comparisons between stages. The methodology in which the workflow is conducted is systematic, thus allows an easy combination of mathematical modeling and confirmation of these models with empirical findings that the arguments on the perceived effect of the given tool should be valid as a global one.

8. RESULTS AND INDEX COMPUTATION

8.1 Computed DLSI Scores Across Digital Markets

The digital well-being of digital markets worldwide is represented quantitatively by the Digital Life Satisfaction Index (DLSI) scores calculated. After normalization, weighting and aggregation processes as explained in Sections 5 and 6, composite DLSI values are derived in each market i as

$$DLSI_i = \sum_{j=1}^{J} w_j z_{ij},$$

with z_{ij} being the normalized score of dimension j in market i and w_j being the optimum weight attributed to that dimension. The resulting index values lie within a unit interval resulting in facilitation of interpretation and comparison. Empirical evidence shows the strong dispersion of the DLSI scores among markets, which can be attributed to the differences between the digital infrastructure maturity, institutional trust and the platform design with a user-focused perspective. The markets with the high levels of digital penetration and good governance systems will have high index values, whereas digitally emerging markets will have moderate yet heterogeneous results. The variation of scores indicates the multidimensional concept of digital life satisfaction where technology itself is not adequate to give high results of well-being without related psychological and institutional help. Ranking analysis also demonstrates clustering tendencies within the markets sharing the same digital ecosystems, which highlights the power of the index to embrace structural similarities. The derived scores are computed empirical inputs that make future comparative and policy studies possible.

8.2 Indicator and Dimension Contributions

In order to measure the internal composition of the DLSI, the indicator level and the dimension level contributions are analysed using the decomposition methods. The contribution of each indicator k to the total index, or $C_k = w_j + z_{ik}$ is obtained, and the indicator, k, will be in dimension j. Findings indicate that, reciprocally, the institutional trust and technological reliability measure have a significant contribution to the overall digital life satisfaction especially in progressive digital markets. Psychological predictors, including perceived autonomy and reducing stress through the digital platforms, show their high impact in the market when platform engagement intensity is high. The global indicators of the economy are more diverse, as their levels of affordability and access vary across the regions.

Aggregation at the dimension level shows that technological and institutional dimensions contribute the highest percentage to index variance with psychological dimensions playing a modulating factor of critical significance. These associations prove the theoretical hypothesis that digital life satisfaction is the result of functional infrastructure and perceived user empowerment interaction. Contribution analysis is also used to determine under achieving indicators in otherwise high performing markets with a diagnostics of specific action to be taken. In general, such a decomposition increases interpretability, as it correlates aggregate values of DLSI with their components, which supports the transparency and policy relevance of the index.

8.3 Comparative Analysis Across Regions or Platforms

Comparison is done within the geographical regions and across the leading digital platform ecosystems to determine systematic variations in the outcome of digital life satisfaction. Statistically significant differences between digitally mature and emerging regions can be found in the aggregation of scores of the DM and ELSI regions across regions. Whereby D_r represents the average score of DLSI in region r; the hypothesis testing proves that the multiple regional pairs of $D_{r1} \neq D_{r2}$ are valid. Graphs of platform-level features also show that platform-level features focusing on the protection of user data, interoperability, and transparency show a higher satisfaction score. On the other hand, those platforms that are identified with opaque algorithms and poor accountability mechanisms have lower scores in the psychological and institutional dimensions. The cross-platform variance decomposition demonstrates that a significant percentage of visible differences are caused by the factors of governance. These comparative findings highlight the role that context/structural considerations play in determining digital life satisfaction over and above individual level aspects. The discussion shows the usefulness of the DLSI as a benchmarking tool that can be used to measure regional and platform-specific differentials in performance.

8.4 Robustness and Sensitivity Results

The sensitivity and robustness tests are performed to test the stability of the DLS results in different methodological assumptions. Weight perturbation tests entail the application of an existing optimized weights w_j and its shaking between predefined limits and the index scores are re-computed. The obtained rank correlations are above traditional levels, which means high stability. Normative sensitivity measures are evaluated by comparing min-max transformation and z-score transformation, and insignificant influences on relative positions in the market. Also, other aggregation functions such as geometric means are discussed to test the assumptions of the compensability. Findings are very similar, which validates the strength of the index organization. Another prevalent method of evaluating effects of data uncertainty introduced by Monte Carlo simulations is by adding stochastic noise to values of indicators. The variance in the distribution of simulated scores of DLSI is low, which supports the belief of strong findings results. Together, all these analyses indicate that the DLSI is not a product of a particular modeling decision and a consistent and valid predictor of digital life satisfaction across markets.

9. DISCUSSION OF RESULTS

9.1 Interpretation of Core Empirical Findings

The findings of the Digital life satisfaction index (DLSI) based on empirical findings prove that there are a number of structurally important patterns in digital market across the world. First, the concept of digital life satisfaction is heavily multidimensional in nature with high technological capability not being sufficient enough to yield high levels of satisfaction. Markets with high digital infrastructure and low institutional trust or psychological autonomy score high on the index used to test the non-substitutability of key dimensions, therefore confirming moderate scores. Second, the prevalence of institutional and technological aspects in explaining total index variance adds to the importance of the quality of governance, data security, and reliability of platforms that influence the nature of digital well-being. Indicatives of psychology are amplifiers and not drivers, which reinforce or undermine satisfaction in accordance with the contextual alignment. Third, the presence of inter-market variability of DLSI scores indicates that there is structural disparity in digital life experiences, even in the economies having similar levels of income.

This observation shows that regulatory maturity and platform design philosophies have an effect on the digital well-being in addition to the availability of resources. These interpretations are also confirmed by the SEM outcomes because they establish statistically significant causal effects between institutional trust and technological quality and overall satisfaction with digital life. Taken together, these results support the theoretical hypothesis that digital life satisfaction is the outcome of a system, as it happens due to the influencing nature of technological affordances, institutional protection, and individual understandings. The findings therefore move empirical knowledge further than the descriptive metrics of digital inclusion, to a more comprehensive measure of the digital well-being.

9.2 Implications for Digital Market Development and Governance

The results of the given study have significant consequences to the strategic planning of digital markets and its administration. The powerful impact of institutional aspects on social satisfaction with digital life reveals the importance of introducing trust-empowering codes in digital ecosystems. Clearness of regulations, open and reliable data management, and impactful user privilege become critical supplements of technological innovation. Markets whose primary focus is high-speed digital growth without an institutional basis run the risk of creating dissatisfaction in expanded access. Moreover, the idiomatic role of the psychological aspects implies that the user-centered design, the autonomy-supporting interfaces, and the alleviation of the cognitive load should be viewed as the strategic aim, rather than a marginal functionality. Based on the market development premises, the findings of the DLSI suggest that long-term consistent digital growth hinges on the ability to meet the needs arising between the efficiency-oriented innovation and the human protection.

Based on these insights, operators of the platform are able to use this to rearchitect the incentive structures, moderation policy, and personalization mechanisms in a way that increases perceived control and trust. At the policy level, the index offers a diagnostic mechanism of discovering structural vulnerability in digital markets so that specific interventions can take place instead of blanket regulatory reactions. The DLSI shifts the concept of digital development by directly associating the outcome of a digital market performance with the outcomes of life satisfaction. The repercussion of this change on defining, measuring, and working on success in digital transformation in worldwide markets is very deep.

9.3 Digital Trust, Autonomy, and Comparative Measurement Perspectives

One of the main contributions made by the DLSI is the fact that digital trust, autonomy, and access are explicitly integrated into a single measurement framework. The findings show that confidence in online institutions and perceived independence in platforms interaction are not the by-products but epicenter determinants of the satisfaction with the life online. Similarity in level of access in the markets has a contradictory satisfaction result based on the degree of protection, information and power the users have acquired. This understanding makes the DLSI stand out among the current digital well-being scales that focus on the intensity of usage, the screen time, or, the level of infrastructure availability. The traditional indices will usually view psychological and institutional variables as modulators of context, but the DLSI will view them as dimensions that are structurally embedded. A casual examination shows that compared to its individual counterparts, the DLSI provides a more comprehensive view of latent disparities that were not previously characterized by more limited metrics, especially in settings where there was a great deal of digital penetration but low regulatory disclosure.

Furthermore, the combination of the multi-criteria optimization and structural validation which is presented in the index offers methodological advantages over the additive and survey on the only method. The DLSI provides more explanatory potential and deeper meaning of interpretation by associate measurement to the causal order. The presence of these comparative advantages makes the DLSI an evidence-based policy and a next-generation measurement instrument that can inform academic and evidence-based policy. The discussion, therefore, enhances the index in that it is not only a useful tool of description as a ranking tool, but also an analytical framework of how digital systems influence the well-being of human beings.

10. IMPLICATIONS FOR DIGITAL MARKETS AND POLICY

10.1 Strategic Implications for Digital Platforms and Market Actors

The Digital Life Satisfaction Index (DLSI) is the indicator that offers practical advice to digital platforms and market players interested in achieving balance between technological innovations and human health. The empirical findings show that the platform competitiveness is currently becoming more and more reliant on the ability to be trusted, on transparency, and on user empowerment instead of focusing on functional performance or scale exclusively. Applications which combine privacy-respecting architecture, explainable algorithms, and autonomous-supportive design properties have higher potential to produce long term user satisfaction. The variations in contributions of DLSI dimensions imply that initiatives that are strategic in governance systems, the quality of content moderation, and user control interfaces can be measured to result in enhancements in digital life satisfaction.

In addition, the index demonstrates the dangers of extractive data practices and opaque systems of personalization that can damage sustainability engagement even when it proves efficient in short-term. To market players, the DLSI may be used as a strategic diagnostic tool that facilitates benchmarking of rivalry and structural vulnerabilities in platform design. The index promotes systems-based approach to digital value creation by enhancing the platform to synthesize user satisfaction as an outcome merged across multiple dimensions.

10.2 Policy Relevance for Regulators and Institutional Frameworks

Resultatively, in the eyes of the DLSI there is a strong empirical foundation on which the impacts of the digital markets on society are achieved. The conventional policy measures tend to take the competition or access or economic output as proposed, without taking into account the user well-being and autonomy. The DLSI completes the work of these measures since institutional trust, psychological security and perceived fairness are measured outcomes of a set of measures that are collectively considered the work of the DLSI. The regulators can use the index to determine those markets in which the pace of rapid digitalization has exceeded institutional protection and should be subjected to specific intervention. Evidence-based policy benchmarking is made possible by cross-market comparability, which helps harmonize attempts in one jurisdiction to another. Moreover, the conceptual information offered by the SEM framework enables policy makers to differentiate between pathos advancements in access and well-being improvement. By including the DLSI in a digital policy assessment, institutions are able to move towards the outcomes-focused regulation, where human flourishing and innovation have a priority. This strategy aids in the construction of adaptive frameworks of governance, which can be adapted to the constantly changing digital threats.

10.3 Advancing Human-Centered Digital Market Design through DLSI

The use of the DLSI is not limited to evaluation and regulation but rather to active design of human-oriented digital markets. The index has the advantage of giving explicit instructions to designers on how to match the technological systems to the human values through a direct connection between platform attributes and outcomes of life satisfaction. These findings reveal that despite people having the idea of using markets that are optimized in the area of efficiency or engagement, we may end up undermining trust and autonomy, thereby decreasing joy in general. Conversely, the concepts of human-centered design, i.e., transparency, inclusivity, and user agency, can be measured as factors of digital well-being.

The DLSI can be operationalised to serve as a monitoring instrument in the framework of digital governance, through which the degree of user satisfaction responds to changes in the design over the course of time. It is an iterative policy design and accountable platform application through this dynamic application. Finally, the index leads to a normative change in the digital market assessment, making life satisfaction a major measure of triumph. Drawing on the human-centered measures, the DLSI embraces a more sustainable and ethics-oriented digital economy, inherent in the market design and policy discussion.

11. FUTURE RESEARCH DIRECTIONS

11.1 Methodological and Structural Extensions of the DLSI Framework

To expand the Digital Life Satisfaction Index (DLSI) in future studies, it can be improved through increasing the methodological flexibility and structural granularity of the index. A future prospective opportunity has been to continue to enlarge the dimensional organizational framework of the index by introducing new dimensions like algorithmic transparency, digital labor conditions, and platform accountability. Such extensions would enable the DLSI evolve and keep-up with fast evolving digital eco-systems. In methodological terms, the future research can incorporate alternative systems of weighting such as Bayesian multi-criteria optimization or entropy-based ones to reflect the uncertainty and contextual variability. Future research may also apply hybrid modeling approaches to integrate structural equation modeling with network analysis to shed more light on how different dimensions of digital well-being are related to each other.

It can also be followed up in the future that non-compensatory mechanisms of aggregation address ethical issues about the trade-offs taking place between access, autonomy and trust. This form of refinements would make the index normatively robust. Giving the DLSI a sector-oriented coverage such as digital health, education, or financial platform would be more helpful in promoting an analytical definiteness and at the same time maintain a common platform through which the world is compared. Such methodological improvements would make the DLSI a dynamic and adaptable measurement system as opposed to a fixed index to enable its continued relevance in dynamic online worlds.

11.2 Integration with AI-Driven and Algorithmic Digital Environments

The growing empowerment of artificial intelligence and algorithmic decision-making in the digital markets is a decisive opportunity in the development of the DLSI framework. A study of the impact of AI-mediated interactions on life satisfaction in the future should focus on the effects of personalization, automation, predictive governance, and similar mechanisms. The experiential effects of intelligent systems on users would be considered by including AI-specific indicators, including the complexity in shape, explainability, perceived fairness and controllability, in the DLSI. Besides, AI-based environments can implement a feedback mechanism of adaptability that leads to user behavior and perceptions that evolve as time progresses.

These predictions would depend on dynamic modelling of the interactions between the DLSI and its associated systems in terms of adaptive and learning based simulations. The machine learning methods have the potential of identifying latent patterns in digital trajectories of satisfaction, without compromising transparency or interpretability. Ethical AI aspects such as bias alleviation and accountability should be directly included as institutional aspects of digital life satisfaction. By providing AI-awareness to the index structure, the future studies will have a way to evaluate whether the working of the digital systems are efficient or not only that, whether they are beneficial to the human agent in autonomy and dignity aspects. This combination is necessary to bring digital well-being measurement in line with the realities of markets that are controlled by algorithms.

11.3 Longitudinal, Cross-Cultural, and Context-Specific Research Pathways

Investigative limitations to second generation research include the extrapolation of the DLSI to longitudinal/cross-cultural analysis models. The majority of current work on digital well-being is based on cross-sectional data, which does not allow focusing on the dynamics and cause-effect development. Total longitudinal implementations of the DLSI would allow the researcher to trace how the digital life satisfaction is affected by regulatory reforms, technological interference, or social shocks. The effects of adaptation and dependence on paths in digital experiences could be modeled dynamically (by panel SEM, state-space representation, etc.). Cross cultural extensions are also noteworthy since perceptions of autonomy, trust and satisfaction are mediated between cultures. Future research ought to consider the interplay of cultural norms with digital infrastructures in an attempt to moderate the outcome of satisfaction, which may need culturally adaption weighting of indicators. Those area-specific applications e-commerce, e-health, or platform work would contextualize the index to show precisely area-specific well-being determinants. These research directions would, when combined, make the DLSI an analytic instrument providing a complete picture of the digital life satisfaction and its changing and culturally-lived aspects, as well as its differentiations along the sector lines. This would greatly facilitate the explanatory ability and the international applicability of this index.

12. CONCLUSION

12.1 Integrated Summary of Contributions and Significance

This chapter is important to the literature in digital well-being because it establishes and verifies a Global Digital Life Satisfaction Index (DLSI), based on sound mathematical modeling and empirical validation. In conceptual terms, the research makes a contribution to the knowledge on the digital life satisfaction as a multidimensional construct that comes as a result of the interplay between economic access, technological quality, psychological autonomy and institutional trust. The combination of the multi-criteria optimization with structural equation model is methodologically a big step towards the traditional index construction methods that can only allow normative weighting and causal validation.

The DLSI goes beyond metrics of descriptive digital inclusion by putting human outcomes directly in digital market analysis. Empirically, the index has high explanatory power in heterogeneous digital markets that displays an overall disparity in structure by using infrastructure or usage indicator alone. The framework is also practical as it avails an apt and comparable measurement resource to platform designers, policymakers and regulators. All these contributions make the DLSI a formidable analytical tool that can inform theory, be a guide to evidence-based policy and design sustainable and human-centric digital ecosystems.

12.2 Limitations, Reflections, and Concluding Perspectives

Although this study has contributed to it has various limitations that can be used in refining it in the future. Depending on secondary and cross-sectional data limits the possibility to represent a whole representation of the temporal dynamics and causal evolution in digital life satisfaction. The data availability issue and the cultural heterogeneity across market can also contribute to the measurement validity by impacting the interpretation of indicators. Although the SEM framework alleviates some of these fears by latently modeling these, there is still a possibility of unobserved contextual factors influencing the formulation of satisfaction.

Also, the index structure is a reflection of the existing digital settings and can need updating due to new technologies, especially artificial intelligence-driven systems, transforming the digital experiences. Such limitations never weaken the main findings rather indicates the necessity of constant methodological development. To sum up, it is important to state that this chapter informs that the concept of digital market success should be redefined in terms of human well-being. The placing of life satisfaction at the core of digital assessment makes the DLSI part of a more general ideological change towards digital systems concerned with trust, autonomy, and human flourishing. This is the way to approach the future of world-wide digital markets in a responsible and sustainable way.

CONFLICTS OF INTERESTS

There are no conflicts of interest with regard to this chapter that the authors declares. The study was free of any financial, personal or institutional influences that may have influenced the analysis, interpretation as well as conclusions. All the methodologies, data and interpretations were intended exclusively to the academic and scholarly purposes following ethical standards of research.

ACKNOWLEDGEMENT

This chapter has been enhanced by the great contribution of the editors of the volume who have offered constructive guidance, and the anonymous reviewers who have provided insightful comments that make great contributions to this chapter. Scholarly colleagues, a lot of appreciation is given over intellectual discussions on digital well-being and quantitative modeling. The authors also acknowledge the fact that the open datasets provided by the institutions and data providers facilitated the strict empirical study and global comparative evaluation of this research works and cooperation during the study period.

REFERENCES

Acemoglu, D., & Restrepo, P. (2020). The wrong kind of AI? Artificial intelligence and the future of labour demand. *Cambridge Journal of Regions, Economy and Society*, *13*(1), 25–35. DOI: 10.1093/cjres/rsz022

Almaiah, M. A., Al-Otaibi, S., Shishakly, R., Hassan, L., Lutfi, A., Alrawad, M., Qatawneh, M., & Alghanam, O. A. (2023). Investigating the role of perceived risk, perceived security and perceived trust on smart m-banking application using SEM. *Sustainability (Basel)*, *15*(13), 9908. DOI: 10.3390/su15139908

Anton, A. (2025). Subjective well-being of public relations and communication professionals in the context of perceived organisational support. *Journal of Communication Management (London)*, *29*(3), 324–339. DOI: 10.1108/JCOM-03-2024-0047

Arslankara, V. B., Demir, A., Öztaş, Ö., & Usta, E. (2022). Digital well-being scale validity and reliability study. *Journal of Teacher Education and Lifelong Learning*, *4*(2), 263–274. DOI: 10.51535/tell.1206193

Attia, M., Abdel-Fattah, M. A., & Khedr, A. E. (2022). A proposed multi criteria indexing and ranking model for documents and web pages on large scale data. *Journal of King Saud University. Computer and Information Sciences*, *34*(10), 8702–8715. DOI: 10.1016/j.jksuci.2021.10.009

Buchi, M. (2024). Digital well-being theory and research. *New Media & Society*, *26*(1), 172–189. DOI: 10.1177/14614448211056851

Buchi, M., Just, N., & Latzer, M. (2016). Modeling the second-level digital divide: A five-country study of social differences in Internet use. *New Media & Society*, *18*(11), 2703–2722. DOI: 10.1177/1461444815604154

Burr, C., Taddeo, M., & Floridi, L. (2020). The ethics of digital well-being: A thematic review. *Science and Engineering Ethics, 26*(4), 2313–2343. DOI: 10.1007/s11948-020-00175-8 PMID: 31933119

Cao, S., & Li, H. (2023). A scoping review of digital well-being in early childhood: Definitions, measurements, contributors, and interventions. *International Journal of Environmental Research and Public Health, 20*(4), 3510. DOI: 10.3390/ijerph20043510 PMID: 36834204

Chen, S., Ebrahimi, O. V., & Cheng, C. (2025). New Perspective on Digital Well-Being by Distinguishing Digital Competency From Dependency: Network Approach. *Journal of Medical Internet Research, 27*, e70483. DOI: 10.2196/70483 PMID: 40132188

Dulsrud, A., & Bygstad, B. (2022). Digital ecosystems as social institutions: Exploring the role of consumption through four research streams of digital ecosystems. *Consumption and Society, 1*(1), 99–119. DOI: 10.1332/QUPH6141

Gangadharan, S. P. (2017). The downside of digital inclusion: Expectations and experiences of privacy and surveillance among marginal Internet users. *New Media & Society, 19*(4), 597–615. DOI: 10.1177/1461444815614053

Han, X., Yang, Y., Li, F., & Li, Y. (2022). Adding life to years: The influence of Internet use and appearance management on life satisfaction among the elderly. *Social Indicators Research, 160*(2), 585–600. DOI: 10.1007/s11205-020-02342-7

Iacus, S. M., & Porro, G. (2021). *Subjective well-being and social media*. Chapman and Hall/CRC., DOI: 10.1201/9780429401435

Kubatko, O., Roubik, H., Kubatko, V., Odewole, O., Stepanenko, Y., Kovalov, B., & Kozmenko, S. (2022). Life satisfaction and digital transformation of society evidence from European economies. *International Journal of Global Environmental Issues, 21*(2-4), 245–258. DOI: 10.1504/IJGENVI.2022.126203

Mathew, J., Nair, S., Gomes, R., Mulasi, A., & Yadav, P. (2023). Design and validation of the digital well-being scale. *Ricerche Di Pedagogia e Didattica. Journal of Theories and Research in Education, 18*(1), 239–251. DOI: 10.6092/issn.1970-2221/16365

Meier, A., & Reinecke, L. (2021). Computer-mediated communication, social media, and mental health: A conceptual and empirical meta-review. *Communication Research, 48*(8), 1182–1209. DOI: 10.1177/0093650220958224

Natoli, R., Feeny, S., Li, J., & Zuhair, S. (2024). Aggregating the Human Development Index: A non-compensatory approach. *Social Indicators Research*, *172*(2), 499–515. DOI: 10.1007/s11205-024-03318-7

Nguyen, M. H., & Hargittai, E. (2024). Digital disconnection, digital inequality, and subjective well-being: A mobile experience sampling study. *Journal of Computer-Mediated Communication*, *29*(1), zmad044. Advance online publication. DOI: 10.1093/jcmc/zmad044

Pisarska, A. M., Kryczka, A., & Castellone, D. (2025). Organizational Trust as a Driver of Eudaimonic and Digital Well-Being in IT Professionals: A Cross-Cultural Study. *Sustainability (Basel)*, *17*(11), 5124. DOI: 10.3390/su17115124

Ragnedda, M., & Ruiu, M. L. (2020). *Digital capital: A Bourdieusian perspective on the digital divide*. Emerald Publishing Limited., DOI: 10.1108/9781839095504

Ruiz-Alba, J. L., Abou-Foul, M., Nazarian, A., & Foroudi, P. (2022). Digital platforms: Customer satisfaction, eWOM and the moderating role of perceived technological innovativeness. *Information Technology & People*, *35*(7), 2470–2499. DOI: 10.1108/ITP-07-2021-0572

Shao, Q. (2022). Does less working time improve life satisfaction? Evidence from European Social Survey. *Health Economics Review*, *12*(1), 50. DOI: 10.1186/s13561-022-00396-6 PMID: 36178635

Smits, M., Kim, C. M., Van Goor, H., & Ludden, G. D. (2022). From digital health to digital well-being: Systematic scoping review. *Journal of Medical Internet Research*, *24*(4), e33787. DOI: 10.2196/33787 PMID: 35377328

Tutar, H., Mutlu, H. T., & Streimikiene, D. (2025). Rethinking Sustainable Development: Multidimensional Comparisons Across Countries and Regions. *Sustainable Development (Bradford)*. Advance online publication. DOI: 10.1002/sd.70157

Usakli, A., & Rasoolimanesh, S. M. (2023). Which SEM to use and what to report? A comparison of CB-SEM and PLS-SEM. In *Cutting edge research methods in hospitality and tourism* (pp. 5–28). Emerald Publishing Limited., DOI: 10.1108/978-1-80455-063-220231002

Van Deursen, A. J., & Helsper, E. J. (2015). The third-level digital divide: Who benefits most from being online? In *Communication and information technologies annual* (Vol. 10, pp. 29–52). Emerald Group Publishing Limited., DOI: 10.1108/S2050-206020150000010002

Vanden Abeele, M. M. (2021). Digital wellbeing as a dynamic construct. *Communication Theory*, *31*(4), 932–955. DOI: 10.1093/ct/qtaa024

Voukelatou, V., Gabrielli, L., Miliou, I., Cresci, S., Sharma, R., Tesconi, M., & Pappalardo, L. (2021). Measuring objective and subjective well-being: Dimensions and data sources. *International Journal of Data Science and Analytics*, *11*(4), 279–309. DOI: 10.1007/s41060-020-00224-2

Wu, C. C., Huang, D. H., Huang, K. C., & Liu, Y. C. (2025). Modelling social media engagement and life satisfaction among older Taiwanese adults: The roles of technology anxiety, attitudes, and psychological well-being using PLS-SEM. *Educational Gerontology*, •••, 1–23. DOI: 10.1080/03601277.2025.2575351

KEY TERMS AND DEFINITIONS

Digital Life Satisfaction (DLS): An interdimensional construct that describes the general assessment of the quality of life of individuals in digital settings and combines technological, psychological, economical, and institutional aspects.

Digital Life Satisfaction Index (DLSI): An integrated quantitative indicator aimed at evaluating and comparing markets on the measure of digital well-being by adding the normalized indicators through multi-criteria optimization and structural validation.

Digital Trust and Autonomy: Composite construct that incorporates the level of confidence that users have in digital systems and their sense of control in digital interactions, data utilisation, and the process of algorithms making the digital interaction.

Digital Well-Being: The individual and shared well-being caused by the experience of interactions with digital technologies, including access, control, trust, and psychological outcomes.

Human-Centered Digital Markets: Digital market systems, which are engineered to support user independence, equity, transparency and prosperity in conjunction with economic efficiency and innovation.

Institutional Trust in Digital Systems: The level of user trust in digital governance process, data protection systems, and regulatory bodies that regulate the digital platforms.

Multi-Criteria Decision Making (MCDM): A mathematical model that compares and assigns more reliance on a set of many and often contradictory criteria to come up with ideal weights or rank in complex options of decision-making.

Structural Equation Modeling (SEM): An estimative methodology of multivariate statistics that identically approximates measurement and structural associations between structural and observed measures.

Chapter 7
Cross-Cultural Digital Well-Being: Determinants, Frameworks, and Policy

Larissa Uy Santos
http://orcid.org/0009-0004-4832-0983
Univiersity of Technology and Applied Sciences, Salalah, Oman

Mari Anand Navaneetha Krishnan
Univiersity of Technology and Applied Sciences, Salalah, Oman

Arcadio Jeffrey S. Perida
Philippine Christrian University, Manila, Philippines

Khalid Salim Bakhit Al Shanfari
Univiersity of Technology and Applied Sciences, Salalah, Oman

ABSTRACT

This chapter discuss the role of cultural frameworks and their effects on digital life satisfaction and happiness in general in the current globalized world. Technological change affects communications, education, health, and leisure, and there are many critical questions surrounding the effects of technological change on happiness and psychological wellness. Technologically, there is connectivity and engagement, but there are challenges faced in the matter of too much information, privacy, and stress. Based on cultural psychology, studies in technology, and the study of happiness, this chapter will explore cross-cultural variations in digital experiences, including cultural norms, economy, and global trends in cultures around the world the Middle East, North Africa, Europe, Africa, Asia, and the America.

DOI: 10.4018/979-8-3373-8357-6.ch007

1 INTRODUCTION

Over the last three decades, digital technologies have become deeply embedded in everyday life across the globe. Mobile devices, social media platforms, cloud computing, artificial intelligence (AI), and data-driven systems increasingly mediate how people communicate, learn, work, consume, and engage in governance. The rapid pace of digitalization has been driven by declining hardware costs, widespread mobile broadband penetration, and scalable platform-based business models. As a result, digital systems now constitute a core infrastructure of social and economic life rather than a peripheral tool (International Telecommunication Union [ITU], 2022; Organization for Economic Co-operation and Development [OECD], 2019).

The benefits of this transformation are substantial. Digital technologies enable remote work and education, expand access to information and markets, facilitate telemedicine, and improve the efficiency of public service delivery. At the same time, digitalization has intensified concerns about surveillance, data exploitation, algorithmic bias, misinformation, attention fragmentation, and mental health challenges. These concerns have prompted renewed scholarly and policy interest in the concept of digital well-being.

These changes have enabled new forms of inclusion and opportunity (e.g., telemedicine, e-learning, remote work), yet also magnified concerns about surveillance, data exploitation, the digital divide, and mental health challenges (Nissenbaum, 2010; Noble, 2018).

This chapter argues that digital well-being, the capacity to maintain a healthy, meaningful, and sustainable relationship with technology—has emerged as an essential dimension of life satisfaction in the 21st century. Scholars and organizations have acknowledged that digital impacts are not uniformly positive or negative, but contingent on frequency, purpose, content, and context of use, as well as on social and cultural factors (Vanden Abeele, 2020; UNICEF, 2017). While digital tools can amplify autonomy, competence, and relatedness—the psychological needs central to well-being—they can also exacerbate stress, distraction, social comparison, and loneliness, especially in environments not designed for humane attention (Deci & Ryan, 2000; Przybylski & Weinstein, 2017).

2 PROBLEM STATEMENT

Digital well-being is not universal. It differs across nations and communities due to cultural norms, values, policy regimes, infrastructure, and socioeconomic realities. Cultural psychology demonstrates that the subjective experience of well-being is embedded in norms about selfhood, emotion, and social relations (Diener,

1984; Markus & Kitayama, 1991). Likewise, technology studies show that adoption, trust, and perceived usefulness vary with cultural dimensions such as individualism–collectivism, power distance, and uncertainty avoidance (Hofstede, 2011; Straub et al., 1997). A one-size-fits-all approach to digital design and governance risks undermining well-being by failing to reflect local identities, languages, and social expectations.

3 OBJECTIVES

This chapter aims to:

1. Explore cultural differences in digital life satisfaction and digital well-being across nations.
2. Identify determinants of digital well-being, including access, literacy, norms, governance, and design.
3. Integrate conceptual frameworks from cultural psychology, technology acceptance, and positive psychology to explain cross-cultural variability.
4. Propose a practical framework for culturally responsive technology design, policy, and mental health interventions.

4 SCOPE OF THE STUDY

This study explores the complex interplay between culture, technology, and well-being, with a particular focus on digital life satisfaction across diverse national contexts. The scope encompasses both theoretical and empirical dimensions, drawing on frameworks from cultural psychology, technology acceptance, and positive psychology to analyze how digital technologies shape, and are shaped by cultural values, social norms, and institutional arrangements.

The study covers the following key areas:

The theoretical framework of this chapter is designed to explain how digital well-being and digital life satisfaction are shaped through the interaction of cultural values, technology acceptance processes, and psychological well-being mechanisms. Rather than relying on a single theory, the framework adopts an integrative, multi-theoretical approach that brings together three complementary bodies of literature: (1) Cultural Dimensions Theory, (2) Technology Acceptance and Use Models, and (3) Positive Psychology and Self-Determination Theory. This integration is essential because digital well-being is not produced solely by individual behavior, technological features, or policy environments in isolation; instead, it emerges from the dynamic interaction between individuals, technologies, and socio-cultural contexts.

The framework positions culture as a foundational, moderating layer that shapes how technologies are perceived, adopted, and experienced. Technology acceptance mechanisms act as the proximal drivers of digital engagement, while psychological need satisfaction and emotional outcomes determine whether such engagement contributes to or detracts from well-being. Figure-wise, the framework can be visualized as a three-tier model in which culture influences technology acceptance processes, which in turn affect digital usage patterns and ultimately digital well-being outcomes.

Comparative Analysis Across Nations:

Global Perspectives on Digital Well-Being: A Multidimensional Analysis

The rapid diffusion of digital technologies has fundamentally reshaped how individuals interact, work, learn, and construct meaning in everyday life. As digital systems increasingly mediate social, economic, and psychological experiences, the concept of digital well-being—defined as individuals' subjective satisfaction, balance, safety, and mental health in digital environments—has gained growing scholarly and policy attention. This research adopts a global and comparative perspective, examining digital well-being across countries that represent diverse cultural, economic, and regulatory contexts. By integrating cross-national case studies, cultural theory, and policy analysis, the study provides a comprehensive understanding of digital life satisfaction in an increasingly interconnected world.

Cross-Country Scope and Global Representation

The research draws on case studies from East Asia, the Middle East, Europe, Africa, North and South America, and Oceania, ensuring a broad representation of digital ecosystems. These regions differ significantly in terms of technological maturity, internet penetration, governance structures, and socio-cultural values. For instance, East Asian countries such as South Korea and Japan demonstrate high levels of digital infrastructure and technology adoption, but also face challenges related to digital stress, overuse, and social pressure. In contrast, many African and South American nations encounter issues of access, affordability, and digital inequality, which directly affect digital satisfaction and inclusion.

Middle Eastern countries, particularly those undergoing rapid digital transformation, present a unique blend of strong regulatory oversight, state-led digital initiatives, and culturally embedded norms related to privacy and social interaction. European nations often emphasize data protection, digital rights, and ethical technology use, while North American contexts highlight innovation-driven digital ecosystems with comparatively individualistic user behaviors. Oceania offers insights into balancing digital advancement with community well-being and mental health awareness. Together, these diverse contexts provide a truly global perspective on digital life satisfaction and allow for meaningful cross-cultural comparisons.

Cultural Dimensions and the Digital Experience

A central contribution of this research lies in its examination of how cultural dimensions shape digital experiences and perceptions of well-being. Drawing on established cultural frameworks, the study analyzes factors such as individualism versus collectivism, power distance, uncertainty avoidance, and long-term orientation.

In individualistic cultures, digital technologies are often perceived as tools for self-expression, autonomy, and personal achievement. Social media usage in such contexts tends to focus on personal branding, opinion sharing, and professional networking, which can enhance satisfaction but also contribute to anxiety and comparison-driven stress. In collectivist societies, by contrast, digital platforms are more frequently used to maintain group harmony, family ties, and community cohesion. While this can strengthen social support and belonging, it may also intensify surveillance, conformity, and social pressure.

Power distance influences how users perceive authority, governance, and platform regulation. In high power-distance cultures, individuals may show greater acceptance of state or institutional control over digital spaces, including surveillance and content moderation, if such measures are framed as promoting social order. Uncertainty avoidance affects attitudes toward emerging technologies, privacy risks, and digital experimentation, with risk-averse societies often demanding stronger safeguards and clearer regulations. Long-term oriented cultures may emphasize sustainable digital practices, intergenerational well-being, and the long-term societal impacts of technology adoption.

Determinants of Digital Life Satisfaction

The research identifies several key determinants that collectively shape digital life satisfaction across regions. Access and affordability remain foundational; without reliable and affordable internet connectivity, individuals are excluded from the benefits of digital participation. This digital divide remains particularly pronounced in low-income and rural communities, affecting education, employment, and social inclusion.

Digital literacy is another critical determinant. Beyond basic technical skills, digital literacy encompasses critical thinking, online safety awareness, and the ability to manage digital consumption responsibly. Higher levels of digital literacy are consistently associated with greater confidence, autonomy, and satisfaction in digital environments.

Social norms and expectations also play a significant role. In societies where constant connectivity and responsiveness are normalized, individuals may experience digital fatigue, burnout, and reduced well-being. Conversely, cultures that promote balanced technology use and offline engagement tend to foster healthier digital habits.

Privacy and security concerns strongly influence trust and satisfaction. Users who feel that their data is protected and that platforms operate transparently are more likely to engage positively with digital technologies. Finally, policy and governance frameworks—including data protection laws, content regulation, and digital inclusion strategies—serve as structural determinants that shape both opportunities and risks within digital ecosystems.

Youth and Vulnerable Populations

Special attention is given to youth and other vulnerable populations, who experience digital environments in distinct and often intensified ways. Young people are typically early adopters of new technologies and are deeply embedded in digital social spaces that influence identity formation, self-esteem, and mental health. While digital platforms provide opportunities for learning, creativity, and social connection, they also expose youth to risks such as cyberbullying, addictive design features, misinformation, and social comparison.

Other vulnerable groups—including older adults, individuals with disabilities, and marginalized communities—face additional barriers related to access, usability, and representation. For these populations, poorly designed technologies can exacerbate exclusion and stress rather than enhance well-being. The research emphasizes the need for inclusive design and targeted interventions that recognize diverse developmental, cognitive, and social needs.

Policy and Design Implications

Based on its findings, the study proposes actionable frameworks for promoting digital well-being through culturally adaptive design and policy interventions. For policymakers, this includes developing context-sensitive regulations that balance innovation with protection, promote digital literacy, and safeguard mental health.

Education systems are encouraged to integrate digital well-being competencies into curricula, equipping individuals with lifelong skills for managing digital life.

For technology designers and developers, the research highlights the importance of ethical and user-centered design principles. Features such as transparent algorithms, customizable notifications, time-management tools, and privacy-by-design mechanisms can significantly enhance user well-being. Importantly, these solutions must be culturally adaptive rather than one-size-fits-all, reflecting local values, norms, and expectations.

International organizations and cross-border collaborations also have a role to play in sharing best practices, harmonizing standards, and supporting countries with limited resources in building healthy digital ecosystems.

Temporal and Technological Scope

Finally, the research adopts a temporal perspective, considering both historical trajectories and future trends in digitalization. It examines how earlier phases of internet adoption have shaped current digital behaviors and how emerging technologies—such as artificial intelligence, mobile platforms, social media, and digital identity systems—are redefining digital well-being. While these technologies offer significant benefits in efficiency, personalization, and inclusion, they also raise new ethical, psychological, and governance challenges.

Looking ahead, the study argues that digital well-being must be treated as a dynamic and evolving concept, requiring continuous research, policy adaptation, and stakeholder collaboration. As digital technologies become ever more embedded in daily life, promoting digital life satisfaction will be essential not only for individual mental health but also for sustainable social and economic development.

While the study aims for broad coverage, it does not provide exhaustive country-by-country analysis or primary empirical data collection. Instead, it synthesizes existing literature, comparative reports, and illustrative case studies to highlight cross-cultural patterns and actionable insights.

By defining this scope, the study seeks to advance understanding of how digital well-being is constructed, experienced, and can be enhanced across nations, emphasizing the importance of cultural sensitivity and equity in the digital age.

5 SIGNIFICANCE OF STUDY

This study holds substantial significance for policymakers, educators, and technology developers who are shaping the future of digital societies.

For Policymakers:

The findings provide evidence-based guidance for crafting inclusive digital policies that recognize cultural diversity and promote equitable access to technology. By highlighting how cultural values and social norms influence digital life satisfaction, the study helps policymakers design regulations and public programs that protect privacy, foster digital literacy, and ensure that digital transformation benefits all segments of society. The cross-national analysis offers practical insights for benchmarking national strategies, addressing the digital divide, and implementing culturally sensitive data protection and well-being frameworks.

For Educators:

The research underscores the importance of integrating digital literacy, critical thinking, and socio-emotional skills into educational curricula. By revealing how cultural context shapes students' digital experiences, the study equips educators to develop teaching methods and resources that are relevant, inclusive, and responsive to the needs of diverse learners. Special attention to youth and vulnerable populations ensures that educational interventions support not only technical proficiency but also healthy, balanced, and meaningful engagement with technology.

For Technology Developers:

The study provides actionable frameworks for designing digital products and platforms that are culturally adaptive and user centered. By understanding the determinants of digital satisfaction—such as privacy expectations, social norms, and local language needs—developers can create technologies that enhance well-being, foster trust, and respect user autonomy. The recommendations encourage participatory design, localization, and the integration of well-being metrics into product development cycles, helping technology companies build solutions that are both innovative and socially responsible.

Overall Impact:

By bridging theory and practice, this study empowers key stakeholders to move beyond one-size-fits-all approaches and to co-create digital environments that are safe, inclusive, and conducive to well-being across nations. The insights and frameworks presented here are intended to inform policy decisions, educational strategies, and technology design, ultimately contributing to a more equitable and flourishing digital future for all.

6 CONCEPTUAL FOUNDATIONS

6.1 Digital Life Satisfaction.

The perceived quality of life in digital contexts, including affective responses to digital interactions (e.g., joy, stress), cognitive assessments (e.g., perceived usefulness, learning), social experiences (e.g., connectedness, belonging), and value congruence (e.g., alignment of digital practices with one's cultural and personal values). This is conceptually tethered to subjective well-being but focused on technology-mediated experiences (Diener, 1984; Seligman, 2011).

6.2 Digital Well-Being.

A holistic state in which technology supports, rather than undermines, flourishing, psychological need satisfaction (autonomy, competence, relatedness), attentional health, and social relationships. It emphasizes balance, intentionality, and context-sensitive usage of digital tools (Deci & Ryan, 2000; Vanden Abeele, 2020).

7 THEORETICAL FRAMEWORKS

7.1 Cultural Dimensions.

Hofstede's model (individualism–collectivism, power distance, uncertainty avoidance, masculinity–femininity, long-term orientation, indulgence–restraint) offers a scaffold for comparing how cultures shape technology orientations preferences for autonomy vs. social cohesion; comfort with hierarchical governance; tolerance for ambiguity in new digital services (Hofstede, 2011; Schwartz, 1999). These dimensions influence trust, privacy expectations, social media norms, and adoption rates.

7.2 Technology Acceptance Model (TAM) & Cultural Adaptations.

TAM posits that perceived usefulness and perceived ease of use predict technology adoption (Davis, 1989), with later expansions (UTAUT) adding social influence and facilitating conditions (Venkatesh et al., 2003). Cross-cultural adaptations highlight that perceived usefulness is not purely functional but filtered through values (e.g., social harmony in collectivist cultures, autonomy in individualist cultures) and through trust in institutions (Straub et al., 1997).

7.3 Positive Psychology & Subjective Well-Being.

Positive psychology suggests flourishing arises from positive emotion, engagement, relationships, meaning, and accomplishment (PERMA; Seligman, 2011). Digital environments can facilitate or hinder these elements: apps can boost learning (accomplishment), platforms can enable community (relationships), and digital storytelling can reinforce meaning; conversely, addictive mechanisms and algorithmic reinforcement can erode attention, self-esteem, or social trust (Przybylski & Weinstein, 2017; Orben, 2020).

8 CULTURE AND TECHNOLOGY: INTERSECTIONS

8.1 Historical Overview

The global diffusion of digital technologies has been profoundly uneven, shaped by a confluence of state capacity, market competition, education systems, and cultural receptivity (International Telecommunication Union [ITU], 2025; OECD, 2019). In East Asia, for example, governments in South Korea, Japan, and China made early, strategic investments in broadband infrastructure and device manufacturing, often linking technological advancement to national competitiveness and collective educational attainment (ITU, 2025; Choi et al., 2018). This "techno-optimism" was not merely economic but cultural, as societies embraced technology to achieve shared progress and social mobility (Hofstede, 2011).

In contrast, Nordic countries such as Sweden, Finland, and Denmark emphasized universal access and digital rights, channeling egalitarian values into robust privacy protections and user agency (Nissenbaum, 2010; OECD, 2019). These nations often led in the adoption of open government data, digital identification systems, and participatory e-government platforms, reflecting a cultural commitment to transparency and inclusion (OECD, 2019).

Meanwhile, in many African and Latin American contexts, mobile-first ecosystems leapfrogged legacy infrastructure, enabling millions to access the internet for the first time via affordable smartphones and prepaid data plans (ITU, 2025; Van Hove & Dubus, 2019). However, persistent challenges around affordability, digital literacy, and local content creation have constrained the full realization of digital well-being in these regions (UNESCO, 2019; UNICEF, 2017). These historical trajectories continue to inform present-day expectations of what constitutes a "good" digital life, with some societies prioritizing seamless connectivity and others emphasizing equitable access and cultural preservation (ITU, 2025; Appadurai, 1996).

8.2 Cultural Attitudes Toward Technology

Cultural attitudes toward technology range from enthusiastic adoption to measured skepticism, often reflecting deeper societal values and historical experiences (Hofstede, 2011; Markus & Kitayama, 1991). Societies with a long-term orientation, such as those in East Asia, are more likely to invest in education and digital infrastructure for future gains, even if this means tolerating short-term ambiguity or disruption (Hofstede, 2011; Choi et al., 2018). For instance, China's rapid embrace of mobile payments and super-apps like WeChat is underpinned by a collective willingness to experiment with new models of commerce and communication (Media Scope Group, 2025).

Conversely, cultures characterized by high uncertainty avoidance, such as Germany and Japan, often prefer strong regulatory guardrails and clear platform rules to mitigate perceived risks (Hofstede, 2011; Nissenbaum, 2010). This is evident in the European Union's General Data Protection Regulation (GDPR), which reflects a societal demand for transparency, accountability, and user control (Blinda, Niebel, & Rammer, 2024; DLA Piper, 2025).

Collectivist contexts, including much of Asia, the Middle East, and Africa, emphasize social bonding, duty, and group harmony—values that support the popularity of messaging apps, community forums, and family-oriented digital platforms (Markus & Kitayama, 1991; Triandis, 1995; UNICEF, 2017). In these societies, technology is often seen as a tool for maintaining relationships and fulfilling social obligations, rather than as a means of individual empowerment (Hofstede, 2011; Van Hove & Dubus, 2019). In contrast, individualist societies, such as the United States and much of Western Europe, elevate personalization, productivity, and privacy, leading to the proliferation of self-tracking apps, privacy dashboards, and user-driven customization (Nissenbaum, 2010; Pew Research Center, 2019).

8.3 Globalization and Cultural Identity

The rise of global digital platforms—social networks, streaming services, and app stores—has created shared digital milieus that transcend national boundaries, but also generate new tensions (Appadurai, 1996; Noble, 2018). On one hand, these platforms facilitate the rapid exchange of ideas, trends, and cultural products, fostering a sense of cosmopolitanism and global citizenship (Appadurai, 1996). On the other hand, they can contribute to the homogenization of cultural expression, as algorithmic curation often privileges mainstream, English-language, or Western-centric content over local voices and traditions (Noble, 2018; Media Scope Group, 2025).

This dynamic is evident in the global "influencer" culture, where local artisans and creators must navigate the pressures of algorithmic visibility and platform monetization (Noble, 2018). At the same time, there is a growing movement toward localization and the creation of culturally specific digital spaces—such as regional social networks, language-specific forums, and heritage content platforms—that reflect local humor, idioms, and communal values (Appadurai, 1996; UNESCO, 2019).

The interplay between global cultural flows and local identity has direct implications for digital satisfaction and well-being. Some users embrace cosmopolitan content and global connectivity, finding meaning in cross-cultural exchange and digital mobility (Appadurai, 1996). Others seek out or create culturally specific spaces that reinforce a sense of belonging, authenticity, and resistance to homogenization (Noble, 2018; UNESCO, 2019).

8.4 Attitudes Toward Technology

Long-term oriented, collectivist contexts may prioritize communal goals, coordination, and social harmony, shaping both the adoption and the design of digital platforms (Hofstede, 2011; Markus & Kitayama, 1991; Triandis, 1995). For example, features that facilitate group chats, family sharing, and community announcements are highly valued in these settings (UNICEF, 2017; Van Hove & Dubus, 2019). In contrast, individualist cultures place a premium on autonomy, personalization, and privacy, leading to the development of granular privacy controls, customizable interfaces, and tools for self-expression (Nissenbaum, 2010; Pew Research Center, 2019).

High uncertainty avoidance cultures often invite strong regulation and clear platform rules, as seen in the adoption of comprehensive data protection laws and standardized consent mechanisms (Blinda et al., 2024; DLA Piper, 2025). These regulatory frameworks not only reflect societal values but also shape user expectations and experiences of digital well-being (Nissenbaum, 2010; OECD, 2019).

In sum, the intersection of culture and technology is dynamic and multifaceted, influencing everything from infrastructure investment and regulatory design to platform features and user behaviors. Understanding these intersections is essential for creating digital environments that are not only innovative but also inclusive, equitable, and responsive to the diverse needs of global users (ITU, 2025; OECD, 2019; UNESCO, 2019).

9 DETERMINANTS OF DIGITAL LIFE SATISFACTION ACROSS NATIONS

9.1 Empirical Evidence

Comparative research suggests variability in how digital usage correlates with satisfaction, mediated by culture. European contexts where privacy protections and digital literacy are robust often report more trust and positive assessments of digital services (OECD, 2019; Nissenbaum, 2010). In regions with infrastructure constraints or weak data protections, users may experience both empowerment (access to markets, telehealth) and heightened anxiety (security risks, misinformation) (UNICEF, 2017; ITU, 2022). Meta-analyses on screen time and mental health caution that effects are modest and heterogeneous, emphasizing the importance of content, purpose, and social context (Przybylski & Weinstein, 2017; Orben, 2020).

9.2 Determinants of Digital Satisfaction

Access and Affordability. Participation presupposes connectivity, devices, and data plans. Beyond binary access, quality matters: stability, latency, and speed condition whether online learning is tiring or empowering, whether telehealth builds confidence or frustration. Affordability shapes the degree of experimentation users can tolerate; when each gigabyte carries a high opportunity cost, people ration attention away from exploratory, creative uses toward transactional necessities. Public Wi-Fi, community hubs, and device subsidies can therefore have outsize effects on satisfaction by expanding the margin at which people try new services and maintain relationships. (van Dijk, 2005; International Telecommunication Union, 2025)

Digital Literacy and Education. Literacies include technical skills (navigation, privacy settings), informational competencies (verification, source comparison), and socio-emotional capacities (boundary-setting, empathic communication). Literacy is relational: families, schools, workplaces, and peer groups teach—explicitly or tacitly—what 'good' online conduct looks like. Programs that blend critical thinking with practical tasks—completing a benefits application, checking permissions, practicing pause-before-forward—tend to translate more directly into well-being than abstract warnings. (OECD, 2019; UNESCO, 2019)

Social Norms and Expectations. Cultures establish response tempos and visibility rituals. In some settings, not replying immediately is rude; in others, it is a reasonable signal of focus. Expectations about group chats, reading receipts, and profile curation create background pressures that can either strengthen solidarity or strain attention. Norms also govern conflict repair online: where public shaming is common, users adopt defensive self-presentation; where forgiveness rituals exist, people are more willing to experiment and to make amends. (Markus & Kitayama, 1991; Triandis, 1995)

Privacy and Security Concerns. Privacy is not only about secrecy but about appropriate flows of information across roles and contexts. Security is not only about encryption but about predictable, comprehensible protection and fair remedies. People evaluate safety relative to cultural expectations: a centralized identity may feel efficient and trustworthy in one place and invasive in another. Satisfaction rises when systems match these expectations and provide legible paths to control and redress. (Nissenbaum, 2010; Pew Research Center, 2019)

Material conditions and time. Work schedules, caregiving responsibilities, and urban infrastructure (transport, public spaces) shape the windows in which people use technology. Crowded living conditions can make shared-device rules essential; stable electricity can be the difference between continuous learning and fragile dependence on cafes. Time poverty and fatigue can convert otherwise useful platforms into sources of guilt and overload. Designing for asynchronous participation and low-bandwidth resilience is therefore a well-being intervention, not just a technical feature. (van Dijk, 2005; International Telecommunication Union, 2025)

Language and localization. The ability to transact, learn, and seek help in one's preferred language—and with cultural idioms respected—has clear effects on autonomy, competence, and belonging. Localization is more than translation: it includes numeracy conventions, calendars, names, kinship terms, and metaphors. It also includes policy localization: for example, adapting consent flows to be meaningful in contexts with different literacy or legal traditions. (OECD, 2019; UNESCO, 2019)

10 CULTURAL DIFFERENCES IN DIGITAL WELL-BEING

10.1 Individualist vs. Collectivist Cultures

In individualist cultures, digital well-being strategies often emphasize autonomy: screen-time controls, focus modes, privacy dashboards, and mindfulness apps support self-regulation. Satisfaction is framed as personal optimization of attention and productivity. In collectivist cultures, platforms that facilitate family ties, mutual aid, and community rituals form part of well-being, although social obligations can introduce stress if expectations escalate (Markus & Kitayama, 1991; Triandis, 1995). Social comparison dynamics differ where group harmony is prioritized, public shaming or cyberbullying can be acutely distressing, yet group solidarity also offers repair mechanisms (UNICEF, 2017; Vanden Abeele, 2020).

10.2 High vs. Low Power Distance Societies

High power distance cultures may trust institutional gatekeeping and accept hierarchical digital governance (e.g., centralized identity systems, top-down platform directives), prioritizing security and order; low power distance societies emphasize transparency, participatory oversight, and user consent (Hofstede, 2011). The resultant satisfaction hinges on whether governance aligns with cultural expectations (Nissenbaum, 2010; OECD, 2019).

11 COMPARATIVE CASE STUDIES

11.1 Oman: Building Confidence Through Strategic Digitalization (DataReportal, 2025; International Monetary Fund, 2024)

Oman's digital transformation has advanced quickly on the back of strong 4G/5G coverage, rising internet penetration, and whole-of-government programs oriented to Vision 2040. The public narrative emphasizes service quality, cybersecurity, and skills. From a satisfaction perspective, this triangulation matters: reliable connectivity reduces the micro-irritations that deplete attention; cybersecurity signaling reduces ambient anxiety; and skill-building improves perceived competence and control. Yet progress is uneven. International assessments highlight the need to deepen e-commerce adoption, accelerate average connection speeds, and cultivate advanced ICT skills on a scale. The implication is that sustained well-being will hinge not only on infrastructure but on pathways that translate connectivity into everyday capability and confidence—especially for small businesses, rural communities, and multilingual user groups. (United Arab Emirates Government, 2025; Emirates Health Services, 2025)

Design recommendations for Oman include: (a) service bundles that combine mobile data with micro-learning on privacy, payments, and safety; (b) lightweight, Arabic-English bilingual interfaces for government portals with progress indicators and clear error recovery; (c) community fellows who deliver digital help in clinics, souqs, and schools; and (d) feedback channels that allow residents to report friction in plain language and see responses. (DLA Piper, 2025; Blinda, Niebel, & Rammer, 2024)

11.2 United Arab Emirates: Inclusive-by-Default Digital Government (Van Hove & Dubus, 2019; AERC—Ndung'u, 2021)

The UAE's Digital Government Strategy 2025 organizes transformation around eight dimensions inclusive by default, user-driven, data-driven, open by default, proactive, fit for the digital age, and resilient. For satisfaction, these commitments operate as a promise: services will work for everyone, anticipate needs, and communicate clearly. In multicultural cities, inclusivity involves language support and accessible design; in federal systems, proactivity requires data stewardship agreements that protect privacy while enabling responsive services. Dubai's participation in international efforts to define digital well-being frameworks provides an additional lever: shared metrics can align ministries, schools, and platform partners around attention health, safety, and trust. (Hale, Belisario, Mostafa, & Camargo, 2024; Ventura, Majumdar, Nagler, & Tucker, 2024)

11.3 Germany and the European Union: Trust, Rights, and Innovation Trade-offs (Office of the Surgeon General, 2023; Orben, 2020)

The EU's privacy regime—anchored by GDPR and complemented by national acts like Germany's BDSG—places user rights and organizational accountability at the center of digital life. Many Europeans report high concern about privacy; thus, rights-forward governance can directly improve satisfaction by meeting cultural expectations of control and fairness. At the same time, firms face compliance costs and constraints that may shift innovation from radical to incremental forms. For well-being, the key question is not innovation volume but innovation alignment: do new features reduce cognitive load, strengthen dignity, and expand meaningful choice? Where enforcement is predictable and proportionate, trust in digital services tends to be higher; where cookie banners are perfunctory or dark-patterned, they erode both trust and attention. (Oxford Human Rights Hub, 2024; IJCRT, 2025)

11.4 Kenya: Beyond Access—Embedding Financial Practices in Mobile Money (Huang & Miao, 2021; Media Scope Group, 2025)

Kenya's M-Pesa is rightly celebrated for improving transactional safety and extending formal financial access. Yet research on savings behavior reveals a more complex picture: access does not automatically translate into resilience. People make money social; obligations to kin and community, rotating savings groups, and informal credit networks shape when mobile balances feel appropriate versus risky. Satisfaction therefore depends on whether digital finance products respect these practices. Product opportunities include goal-based savings with social visibility controls, emergency buffers that integrate with community schemes, and dashboards that help users see trade-offs without moralizing. (Choi, Cho, Lee, Kim, & Park, 2018; Ko, Lee, & Park, 2024)

11.5 Brazil: Messaging, Misinformation, and Attention Health (MIC, 2022; Kokubun et al., 2022)

Brazil's information ecosystem is intensely social and mobile-first. WhatsApp groups knit together families, neighborhoods, churches, and political communities. During elections, multimedia rumors can travel rapidly through trusted networks. Field experiments show that simple attention-protective defaults—such as disabling auto-download of images and videos—can reduce exposure and recall of false rumors without chilling social participation. Designing for youth well-being in such contexts means teaching friction as a virtue: it is acceptable—and sometimes wise—to slow down a message before it spreads. Elections authorities and fact-checking partners can amplify this pedagogy through chatbots, tiplines, and in-app prompts tied to civic calendars. (DataReportal, 2025; International Monetary Fund, 2024)

11.6 United States: Youth, Platforms, and Developmental Sensitivity (United Arab Emirates Government, 2025; Emirates Health Services, 2025)

In the United States, adolescent social media use is nearly universal. The Surgeon General's advisory synthesizes research on both benefits (connection, identity support, community) and risks (sleep disruption, anxiety, social comparison). Two design imperatives flow from this evidence. First, sleep protection is public health: night-mode defaults, quiet hours, and notification batching are not luxuries but developmental necessities. Second, independent safety evaluations and appropriate design are prerequisites for trust; families should not shoulder the entire burden. Satisfaction improves when platforms normalize boundary-setting, provide meaningful controls, and avoid exploitative features that target developmental vulnerabilities. (DLA Piper, 2025; Blinda, Niebel, & Rammer, 2024)

11.7 India: Privacy Jurisprudence and Digital Identity (Van Hove & Dubus, 2019; AERC—Ndung'u, 2021)

The Puttaswamy decision constitutionalized privacy as a fundamental right and articulated proportionality tests for state action. In practice, youth encounter these principles when they engage with ed-tech, welfare portals, and job platforms that rely on digital identity. Satisfaction rises when consent is real, minimization is enforced, and redress exists; it collapses when access is effectively conditioned on surrendering sensitive data. Designers can translate jurisprudence into everyday dignity by using just-in-time notices, minimal data defaults, and offline alternatives that preserve choice. (Hale, Belisario, Mostafa, & Camargo, 2024; Ventura, Majumdar, Nagler, & Tucker, 2024)

11.8 China: Super-Apps and Cycles of Autonomy (Office of the Surgeon General, 2023; Orben, 2020)

In China, WeChat's super-app consolidates communication, payments, services, and entertainment. For many, this integration is the definition of convenience; for others, it creates social visibility pressures and cognitive load. Qualitative research documents a pragmatic solution: periodic disengagement from Moments to reset identity boundaries and attention. Satisfying design in super-apps therefore includes tools that make it socially acceptable to step back status settings that signal focus, alerts, and nudges that normalize 'quiet periods' without stigma. (Oxford Human Rights Hub, 2024; IJCRT, 2025)

11.9 South Korea: Beyond Curfews—Comprehensive Youth Support (Huang & Miao, 2021; Media Scope Group, 2025)

South Korea's experience with a midnight gaming curfew illustrates the limits of single-lever policies. Although usage briefly declined, there were no durable effects on addiction or sleep. More promising are multi-component strategies that combine counseling, family engagement, alternative activity, and school programs. Municipal centers provide walking support and parent education; national surveys identify comorbidities and at-risk groups. Satisfaction improves when policy aligns with youth psychology and social ecology rather than treating all screen time as equal. (Choi, Cho, Lee, Kim, & Park, 2018; Ko, Lee, & Park, 2024)

11.10 Japan: Aging, Youth, and Human Coaching (MIC, 2022; Kokubun et al., 2022)

Japan is often framed through the lens of an aging society, yet its digital inclusion programs also benefit younger cohorts. Workshops offered through municipal partners and retail networks teach smartphone basics for administrative procedures, privacy settings, and online civics. Evidence suggests that ICT use improves well-being indirectly by strengthening social capital; in youth, analogous mechanisms include peer mentorship, club-based project work, and community volunteering mediated by digital platforms. Coaching matters: human guides help translate abstract norms into local practices, building durable confidence. (DataReportal, 2025; International Monetary Fund, 2024)

12 CHALLENGES AND ETHICAL CONSIDERATIONS

12.1 Digital Divide

Persistent disparities in access, devices, and digital skills continue to map onto socioeconomic, geographic, and cultural lines, limiting participation in education, labor markets, and civic life (International Telecommunication Union, 2022; van Dijk, 2005). The divide is not only about connectivity, but also about meaningful use—those with limited digital literacy or language support may struggle to benefit from online services. Rural areas, marginalized communities, and people with disabilities are often most affected. Bridging the divide requires not just infrastructure investment and affordability programs, but also culturally tailored digital literacy initiatives, accessible design, and local content creation. Recent studies highlight the importance of community-based digital inclusion efforts and public-private partnerships to address these gaps (OECD, 2019; UNESCO, 2019).

12.2 Algorithmic Bias

Algorithmic systems, including AI-driven platforms, are often trained on datasets that reflect existing social biases. This can result in misrepresentation or underservice of cultural groups, leading to discrimination, erasure, and diminished satisfaction (Buolamwini & Gebru, 2018; Noble, 2018). For example, facial recognition technologies have shown lower accuracy for people of color, and search engines may reinforce stereotypes. Algorithmic bias can also affect access to opportunities, such as job recommendations or credit scoring. Addressing these issues requires culturally aware evaluation, participatory design, and transparency in algorithmic decision-making. Increasingly, there are calls for regulatory oversight, independent audits, and the inclusion of diverse stakeholders in the development and deployment of AI systems (OECD, 2019).

12.3 Policy Gaps

Global technology governance often defaults to uniform rules that ignore cultural diversity, resulting in misaligned moderation, inadequate localization, and poor redress mechanisms. For example, content moderation policies may not account for local norms or languages, leading to over-censorship or under-protection. Privacy regulations, while essential, may not be enforced equally across regions, and data protection standards can lag technological innovation. Evidence-informed, culturally sensitive frameworks are needed to ensure equitable well-being—combining privacy protections, transparency, accountability, and inclusive processes (OECD, 2019; UNESCO, 2019). International collaboration and harmonization of standards, while respecting local identities and values, are increasingly recognized as necessary for effective digital governance.

12.4 Mental Health and Well-Being:

Digital environments can exacerbate stress, anxiety, and social comparison, especially among youth and vulnerable populations. The design of platforms—such as infinite scroll, notification systems, and algorithmic feeds—can impact attention health and psychological well-being. There is a growing movement toward "time well spent" design principles and mental health integration in digital policy (Przybylski & Weinstein, 2017; Vanden Abeele, 2020).

12.5 Data Sovereignty and Local Control:

As global platforms collect and process vast amounts of personal data, questions of data sovereignty and local control have become prominent. Some countries are enacting laws to ensure data is stored and processed within national borders, aiming to protect citizens' rights and cultural values (Nissenbaum, 2010; OECD, 2019).

12.6 Inclusive Design and Accessibility:

Ensuring that digital services are accessible to people with disabilities, older adults, and speakers of minority languages is both an ethical and practical challenge. Universal design principles, localization, and participatory co-design with affected communities are essential for equitable digital well-being (UNESCO, 2019).

13 TOWARD A FRAMEWORK FOR CROSS-CULTURAL DIGITAL WELL-BEING

Design Principles: Culturally Adaptive Technology Interfaces

1. Value-Aware Personalization. Enable settings that reflect cultural preferences: group-focused features for collectivist contexts; granular autonomy controls for individualist contexts.
2. Transparent Privacy by Design. Communicating data practices clearly in local languages and metaphors; align consent flows with cultural expectations of authority and agency (Nissenbaum, 2010).
3. Attention Health and Time Well-Spent. Offer adjustable defaults (e.g., notifications, infinite scroll limits) and culturally tuned prompts supporting focus, rest, and social rituals (Vanden Abeele, 2020).
4. Inclusive Accessibility and Localization. Support scripts, dialects, cultural idioms, and usability for diverse literacy levels; design for low-bandwidth contexts.
5. Participatory Co-Design. Involving local communities, educators, mental health experts, and civil society in feature development and impact assessments (UNESCO, 2019).

14 POLICY RECOMMENDATIONS

1. Inclusive Digital Literacy Programs. Integrate critical thinking, privacy hygiene, online empathy, and content creation skills into schools and community centers; adapt curricula to local norms and languages (OECD, 2019; UNICEF, 2017).
2. Mental Health Interventions. Provide culturally tailored psychoeducation on digital stress (e.g., social comparison, doomscrolling), access to telehealth, and support for vulnerable populations (Przybylski & Weinstein, 2017; Vanden Abeele, 2020).
3. Fairness and Accountability in AI. Mandate audits for bias, require explainability, support diverse datasets, and create complaint-handling processes accessible across cultures (Buolamwini & Gebru, 2018; Noble, 2018).
4. Privacy and Data Protection. Establish rights to data minimization, portability, and redress; strengthen cross-border enforcement and culturally sensitive consent design (Nissenbaum, 2010; OECD, 2019).
5. Infrastructure and Affordability. Expand broadband, subsidize devices, and support community access (libraries, hubs), particularly in underserved rural and peri-urban areas (ITU, 2022; van Dijk, 2005).

15 YOUTH DIGITAL WELL-BEING: POLICY AND DESIGN PLAYBOOK

1. Sleep and attention health. Adolescents need sleep for memory consolidation and emotional regulation. Interfaces should ship with quiet hours enabled, deliver digestible summaries instead of night-time pings, and warn when late-night sessions stretch beyond healthy bounds. For families, operating-system level controls should make it easy to align schedules across devices without punitive surveillance. For schools, homework platforms should support asynchronous submission windows and low-bandwidth modes to reduce anxiety for students with unstable connectivity. (Office of the Surgeon General, 2023; International Telecommunication Union, 2025)
2. Identity, belonging, and safety. Teens experiment with identities; systems must support privacy-preserving exploration. Recommended defaults include private profiles for minors, audience-limited posts, and graduated visibility that expands only with informed choice. Safety teams should provide rapid pathways to report harassment and to mute or block without escalation. Community standards should privilege dignity over pure speech absolutism when developmental risk is high, and moderation guidelines should be transparent and appealable. (OECD, 2019; UNESCO, 2019)
3. Civic engagement and digital citizenship. Young people are political actors. Curricula that combine media literacy with hands-on civic problem-solving—budget games, local data stories, voter-info chatbots—convert skepticism into skill. During election periods, platforms should insert friction for mass forwarding, provide authoritative information inline, and partner with electoral authorities to label common rumor types. These steps protect attention while affirming participation. (Hale et al., 2024; Ventura et al., 2024)
4. Mental health integration. School counselors and tele-mental health providers should receive training on technology-related stressors (doom-scrolling, social comparison, parasocial relationships). Screening protocols can include brief items about sleep, online conflict, and compulsive checking. Referral pathways should be confidential, culturally sensitive, and easy to access from within youth-facing apps. Metrics should track improvement in functioning, minutes online. (Office of the Surgeon General, 2023; International Telecommunication Union, 2025)
5. Family and community partnership. Evidence consistently shows that collaborative mediation—conversation, joint problem-solving, shared rules—beats unilateral surveillance. Municipal libraries, youth centers, and faith groups can host 'tech dialogues where teens and caregivers co-design agreements. Product teams can support these practices with printable templates, in-app goal-setting,

and success badges that celebrate attention-healthy habits as social achievements. (OECD, 2019; UNESCO, 2019)

6. Measurement and transparency. Platforms should publish age-disaggregated transparency reports on harmful content prevalence, response times, and resolution outcomes. Independent auditors should evaluate attention-health features, recommender fairness for minors, and the use of behavioral ads. Regulators can establish privacy-preserving data trusts to support research while protecting children's rights. (Hale et al., 2024; Ventura et al., 2024)

16 IMPLEMENTATION GUIDE FOR DESIGNERS, POLICYMAKERS, AND EDUCATORS

Discovery. Map user journeys across cultural contexts: language use, device switching, family roles, and offline constraints. Conduct diary studies that explicitly track attention and mood alongside tasks. Identify red-flag frictions: confusing consent, silent failures, and social visibility pressure points. (International Telecommunication Union, 2025; OECD, 2019)

Co-design. Recruit diverse users, teachers, small merchants, elders, and youth—to co-create features. Start with low-fidelity prototypes that allow wholesale re-imagining of flows, not only minor tweaks. Bring in local civil society groups who can articulate community norms and legal advocates who can anticipate governance implications. (UNESCO, 2019; Vanden Abeele, 2020)

Pilot. Deploy A/B tests that measure not merely clicks but indicators of well-being task completion with low cognitive load; proportion of sessions that end with breaks; reduction in accidental exposures to sensitive content; decrease in complaint rates. Use qualitative debriefs to interpret metrics culturally. (International Telecommunication Union, 2025; OECD, 2019)

Scale. Prepare playbooks for ministries and school districts to adopt attention-healthy defaults. Provide libraries and municipal centers with toolkits to run privacy clinics. Offer developers SDKs that make value-aware personalization easy—e.g., reusable components for consent-in-context, break prompts, and visibility presets. (UNESCO, 2019; Vanden Abeele, 2020)

Evaluate. Establish mixed-methods evaluation: longitudinal surveys of digital life satisfaction, log-based indicators of healthy engagement, and ethnographies of community use. Publish results even when null; absence of effect is a finding that can redirect resources toward more promising levers. (International Telecommunication Union, 2025; OECD, 2019)

Sustain. Build maintenance into budgets and policies. Update localization and accessibility as languages evolve. Track unintended consequences and surface them publicly. Embed 'well-being backlogs' into agile processes so that user dignity is never deferred to the next quarter. (UNESCO, 2019; Vanden Abeele, 2020)

17 FUTURE RESEARCH DIRECTIONS

Longitudinal Studies on Cultural Adaptation. Examine how evolving platform features, regulatory changes, and social norms shift well-being trajectories in different cultures (Orben, 2020; Vanden Abeele, 2020).

Emerging Technologies (AI, VR). Assess cultural implications of immersive environments, generative AI, and ambient intelligence for identity, attention, and social life (UNESCO, 2019; OECD, 2019).

Measurement and Methodology. Develop cross-culturally validated scales for digital life satisfaction; integrate qualitative community narratives with quantitative indicators.

Interventions and Design Experiments. Test culturally grounded design choices (e.g., notification defaults, community features) for impact on stress, belonging, and meaning.

18 CONCLUSION

Digital technologies have become inseparable from modern life, yet their influence on well-being is far from uniform. This chapter demonstrates that digital life satisfaction is deeply shaped by cultural values, social norms, and governance frameworks, making a universal approach to digital well-being impractical. By integrating insights from cultural psychology, technology acceptance models, and positive psychology, we reveal that determinants such as access and affordability, digital literacy, privacy and security, and social expectations interact differently across nations.

Case studies from Oman, UAE, Germany, Kenya, South Korea, China, Brazil, India, Japan, and the United States illustrate how cultural contexts mediate technology's benefits and risks. For example, collectivist societies often prioritize connectivity and group harmony, while individualist cultures emphasize autonomy and privacy. Youth-focused analyses underscore the urgency of age-appropriate design, attention health, and mental health integration, as young users navigate developmental vulnerabilities in highly immersive digital ecosystems.

Ultimately, achieving cross-cultural digital well-being requires a multi-level strategy:

- Design principles that respect cultural diversity and human needs.
- Policy frameworks that safeguard rights, equity, and mental health.
- Global collaboration to harmonize standards while honoring local identities.

As technology continues to evolve—through AI, immersive environments, and algorithmic personalization, the challenge is not merely to reduce harm but to create digital spaces that foster autonomy, competence, relatedness, and meaning for all cultures. Future research should deepen longitudinal insights, refine culturally adaptive metrics, and test interventions that balance innovation with human flourishing. In short, digital progress must be measured not only by connectivity but by its capacity to enhance well-being across diverse cultural landscapes.

REFERENCES

AERC—Ndung'u. N. S. (2021). A digital financial services revolution in Kenya: The M-Pesa case study. African Economic Research Consortium. https://aercafrica.org/old-website/wp-content/uploads/2021/03/AERC-MPesa-Case-Study.pdf

Appadurai, A. (1996). *Modernity at large: Cultural dimensions of globalization.* University of Minnesota Press.

Blinda, K., Niebel, C., & Rammer, C. (2024). The impact of the EU GDPR on product innovation. *Industry and Innovation*, *31*(3), 311–351. DOI: 10.1080/13662716.2023.2271858

Buolamwini, J., & Gebru, T. (2018). Gender shades: Intersectional accuracy disparities in commercial gender classification. Proceedings of Machine Learning Research, 81, 1–15. https://proceedings.mlr.press/v81/buolamwini18a.html

Carnegie Endowment for International Peace. (2024, October 3). Japan's aging society as a technological opportunity (K. Kushida). https://carnegieendowment.org/research/2024/10/japans-aging-society-as-a-technological-opportunity?lang=en

Choi, J., Cho, H., Lee, S., Kim, J., & Park, E. C. (2018). Effect of the online game shutdown policy on internet use, internet addiction, and sleeping hours in Korean adolescents. *The Journal of Adolescent Health : Official Publication of the Society for Adolescent Medicine*, *62*(5), 548–555. DOI: 10.1016/j.jadohealth.2017.11.291 PMID: 29434003

DataReportal. (2025). Digital 2025: Oman. https://datareportal.com/reports/digital-2025-oman

Davis, F. D. (1989). Perceived usefulness, perceived ease of use, and user acceptance of information technology. *Management Information Systems Quarterly*, *13*(3), 319–340. DOI: 10.2307/249008

Deci, E. L., & Ryan, R. M. (2000). The "what" and "why" of goal pursuits: Human needs and the self-determination of behavior. *Psychological Inquiry*, *11*(4), 227–268. DOI: 10.1207/S15327965PLI1104_01

Diener, E. (1984). Subjective well-being. *Psychological Bulletin*, *95*(3), 542–575. DOI: 10.1037/0033-2909.95.3.542 PMID: 6399758

GizChina. (2024, July 22). From messaging to super pp: How WeChat dominates China's digital landscape. https://www.gizchina.com/news/from-messaging-to-super-app-how-wechat-dominates-chinas-digital-landscape

Hale, S. A., Belisario, A., Mostafa, A. N., & Camargo, C. (2024). Analyzing misinformation claims during the 2022 Brazilian election on WhatsApp, Twitter, and Kwai. *International Journal of Public Opinion Research, 36*(3), edae032. Advance online publication. DOI: 10.1093/ijpor/edae032

Hofstede, G. (2011). Dimensionalizing cultures: The Hofstede model in context. *Online Readings in Psychology and Culture, 2*(1), 8. DOI: 10.9707/2307-0919.1014

Huang, Y., & Miao, W. (2021). Re-domesticating social media when it becomes disruptive: Evidence from WeChat's Moments. *Mobile Media & Communication, 9*(2), 177–194. DOI: 10.1177/2050157920940765

IJCRT. (2025). Privacy, dignity, and liberty: A critical examination of the Puttaswamy case. International Journal of Creative Research Thoughts. https://ijcrt.org/papers/IJCRT25A5528.pdf

International Monetary Fund. (2024, December 17). Oman: Selected issues—Embracing digitalization to accelerate Oman's economic transformation (IMF Country Report No. 25/14). https://www.elibrary.imf.org/downloadpdf/view/journals/002/2025/014/article-A004-en.pdf

International Telecommunication Union / U4SSC. (2025). A guide to digital well-being. https://www.itu.int/dms_pub/itu-t/opb/tut/T-TUT-SMARTCITY-2025-11-PDF-E.pdf

Ko, Y. M., Lee, E. S., & Park, S. (2024). Prevalence and correlates of internet gaming disorder in Korea (National Mental Health Survey 2021). *Frontiers in Psychiatry, 15*, 1442224. DOI: 10.3389/fpsyt.2024.1442224 PMID: 39473915

Markus, H. R., & Kitayama, S. (1991). Culture and the self: Implications for cognition, emotion, and motivation. *Psychological Review, 98*(2), 224–253. DOI: 10.1037/0033-295X.98.2.224

Media Scope Group. (2025, April 4). WeChat ecosystem: An overview of China's digital super app. https://mediascope.group/wechat-ecosystem-an-overview-of-chinas-digital-super-app

MIC (Japan). (2022). Promoting support for digital usage by the elderly (White Paper, Column 3). https://www.soumu.go.jp/johotsusintokei/whitepaper/eng/WP2022/chapter-4_c3.pdf

Nissenbaum, H. (2010). *Privacy in context: Technology, policy, and the integrity of social life*. Stanford University Press.

Noble, S. U. (2018). *Algorithms of oppression: How search engines reinforce racism*. NYU Press. DOI: 10.18574/nyu/9781479833641.001.0001

OECD. (2019). OECD recommendation on artificial intelligence. https://oecd.ai/en/dashboards/policy-areas/oecd-recommendation

Office of the Surgeon General. (2023). Social media and youth mental health: The U.S. Surgeon General's advisory. U.S. Department of Health and Human Services. https://www.hhs.gov/sites/default/files/sg-youth-mental-health-social-media-advisory.pdf

Orben, A. (2020). Teenagers, screens and social media: A narrative review of reviews and key studies. *Social Psychiatry and Psychiatric Epidemiology*, *55*(4), 407–414. DOI: 10.1007/s00127-019-01825-4 PMID: 31925481

Oxford Human Rights Hub. (2024, April 5). The Indian Puttaswamy judgments: Privacy rights at stake in the pursuit of social security. https://ohrh.law.ox.ac.uk/the-indian-puttaswamy-judgments-privacy-rights-at-stake-in-the-pursuit-of-social-security/

Pew Research Center. (2019). Americans and privacy: Concerned, confused and feeling lack of control over their personal information. https://www.pewresearch.org

Piper, D. L. A. (2025, January 16). Data protection laws in Germany. https://www.dlapiperdataprotection.com/index.html?t=law&c=DE Emirates Health Services. (2025). UAE Digital Government Strategy 2025 (dimensions). https://www.ehs.gov.ae/en/about-us/the-uae-digital-government-strategy-2025

Przybylski, A. K., & Weinstein, N. (2017). A large-scale test of the Goldilocks hypothesis: Quantifying the relations between digital-screen use and the mental well-being of adolescents. *Psychological Science*, *28*(2), 204–215. DOI: 10.1177/0956797616678438 PMID: 28085574

Schwartz, S. H. (1999). A theory of cultural values and some implications for work. *Applied Psychology = Psychologie Appliquée*, *48*(1), 23–47. DOI: 10.1111/j.1464-0597.1999.tb00047.x

Seligman, M. E. P. (2011). *Flourish: A visionary new understanding of happiness and well-being*. Free Press.

Straub, D., Keil, M., & Brenner, W. (1997). Testing the technology acceptance model across cultures: A three country study. *Information & Management*, *33*(1), 1–11. DOI: 10.1016/S0378-7206(97)00026-8

Triandis, H. C. (1995). *Individualism and collectivism*. Westview Press.

UNESCO. (2019). AI in education: Challenges and opportunities. United Nations Educational, Scientific and Cultural Organization. https://unesdoc.unesco.org

UNICEF. (2017). [Children in a digital world. UNICEF. https://www.unicef.org]. *The State of the World's Children, 2017*, •••.

United Arab Emirates Government. (2025). UAE Digital Government Strategy 2025. https://u.ae/en/about-the-uae/strategies-initiatives-and-awards/strategies-plans-and-visions/government-services-and-digital-transformation/uae-national-digital-government-strategy USE/Metropolis. (n.d.). "I Will Centers"—Internet addiction prevention & intervention centers for children and youths (Seoul). https://use.metropolis.org/case-studies/seoul-i-will-centre

van Dijk, J. (2005). The deepening divide: Inequality in the information society. *Sage (Atlanta, Ga.)*. Advance online publication. DOI: 10.4135/9781452229812

Van Hove, L., & Dubus, A. (2019). M-Pesa and financial inclusion in Kenya: Of paying comes saving? *Sustainability (Basel)*, *11*(3), 568. DOI: 10.3390/su11030568

Vanden Abeele, M. M. P. (2020). Digital wellbeing as a dynamic construct. *Communication Theory*, *30*(3), 1–21. DOI: 10.1093/ct/qtaa024

Venkatesh, V., Morris, M., Davis, G., & Davis, F. (2003). User acceptance of information technology: Toward a unified view. *Management Information Systems Quarterly*, *27*(3), 425–478. DOI: 10.2307/30036540

Ventura, T., Majumdar, R., Nagler, J., & Tucker, J. A. (2024). Reducing exposure to misinformation: Evidence from WhatsApp in Brazil (2022 election). Center for Social Media and Politics (CSMaP), NYU. https://csmapnyu.org/research/reports-analysis/reducing-exposure-to-misinformation-evidence-from-whatsapp-in-brazil

Chapter 8
The Metaverse as a Space of Happiness: Cross-Cultural Determinants of Digital Life Satisfaction in Global Markets

Rury Mulina Darman
http://orcid.org/0009-0000-6137-4258
Universitas Negeri Jakarta, Indonesia

Usep Suhud
http://orcid.org/0000-0002-1728-0737
Universitas Negeri Jakarta, Indonesia

Setyo Ferry Wibowo
Universitas Negeri Jakarta, Indonesia

Christian Wiradendi Wolor
Universitas Negeri Jakarta, Indonesia

ABSTRACT

This chapter explores the metaverse as a psychosocial ecosystem that blends technology, culture, and emotion to shape digital life satisfaction. Drawing on Self-Determination Theory and Flow Theory, it proposes and tests a conceptual model using Structural Equation Modeling (SEM) across diverse cultural contexts. Data from 600 metaverse users across North America, Europe, and Asia-Pacific reveal that psychological need fulfillment (autonomy, competence, relatedness) and flow significantly mediate the relationship between digital engagement and life satisfaction. Cultural orientation moderates these effects, showing that collectivist and

DOI: 10.4018/979-8-3373-8357-6.ch008

individualist values shape the paths to well-being differently. The findings provide theoretical insights into digital transformation and practical guidance for user-centered design, policymaking, and ethical platform development in immersive virtual environments.

INTRODUCTION

The move to online lifestyles has changed how individuals seek meaning, form connections, or feel satisfied. The clearest sign of this change appears in the growth of the metaverse - virtual 3D spaces where people engage via avatars, work together remotely, trade items, or shape shared moments. These interactive systems differ from standard screen activities by mixing real and digital settings, providing social contact along with sensory feedback similar to being there physically. Such developments carry deep consequences for mental health; hence experts are studying if engagement in these realms influences emotions, personal ties, or overall sense of well-being. In this section, the metaverse is seen as a "space made for happiness" - a setting where tech design, social behaviors, because personal emotions come together to affect how people feel. From this angle, technology isn't just an instrument rather it becomes a realm where personal drives, collective values, also well-being unfold.

A rising number of data-based studies indicate that taking part in the metaverse might significantly affect mood and personal life satisfaction. Because virtual spaces can meet basic mental needs - like feeling independent, capable, or connected - they often boost well-being, as earlier theories on motivation have shown. Although (Ryan Richard & Deci, 2000)'s Self-Determination Theory still serves as a cornerstone, newer research applied to online settings reveals that digital areas supporting self-guided, flexible, and interactive experiences tend to increase inner fulfillment (Singh et al., 2025). In particular, the metaverse allows decisions around actions, personas, and social exchanges; such freedom supports independence while strengthening confidence in reaching objectives.

Another key aspect of how people feel in virtual settings is "presence" - the feeling of actually being inside the simulated world. Studies on VR suggest stronger presence often links to greater emotional involvement and satisfaction (Zhang et al., 2025). As visual cues, sound responses, along with real-time interaction merge smoothly, individuals tend to focus better, connect emotionally, yet respond more positively overall. Such deep involvement boosts user interest; at the same time, it enriches the overall experience of online encounters. Therefore, how these digital areas are built really shapes feelings - thoughtful layouts increase pleasure whereas disorganized designs might lead to confusion or tension.

To study these patterns, scientists now use advanced number-based methods to measure links between online activity and emotions or well-being. Because of this, work using models like SEM shows that feelings people get during digital events - like wonder - affect how they judge worth and fun (for instance, seeing a moment as meaningful), which then shapes general satisfaction ratings (Argan et al., 2025; compare Barth et al., 2025)). That means internal reactions triggered by deep virtual experiences - not merely screen time - play a role in shaping user judgments about quality. At the same time, findings on social behavior in virtual travel settings indicate shared moments boost engagement and favorable views, supporting the view that human contact matters for personal fulfillment in metaverse spaces (Inmor et al., 2025).

Beyond feelings, taking part in the metaverse might also support mental and social growth. Research with Gen Z individuals in the UAE showed that using metaverse tech helped boost interaction abilities, how people communicate, along with collaboration - all tied to better mental health (Youssef et al., 2024). Applying PLS-SEM methods, scientists observed a strong link between time spent on metaverse platforms and more stable moods, stronger coping skills, plus higher levels of felt social backing. Results indicate these digital worlds could serve as places for building relationships - not just leisure spots. Because users connect together in common settings regardless of location, virtual spaces may encourage new types of belonging compared to standard internet communities.

Crucially, taking part in the metaverse helps more than just fun or chatting with others. Evidence shows that being deeply engaged in a setting may boost mood and overall wellness. As an example, experiments testing different simulated spaces - like forests or oceans in VR - suggest such settings increase pleasant emotions (such as wonder), decrease stress, ease anxious thoughts, across people regardless of prior experience (Barth et al., 2025). This highlights how the feel of a digital moment - not only what happens in it - affects mental states. These results fit alongside wider studies on tech-based health tools, which point to immersive setups aiding emotion control and psychological resilience (Shamim et al., 2025).

While more findings point to mental health benefits from the metaverse, it's not entirely positive. Excessive use raises valid worries about psychological harm. Heavy involvement links to lower well-being and weaker self-worth, according to several analyses (for instance, Singh et al., 2025; also supported by work on digital mental strain). Long-term or compulsive participation may trigger mood issues - especially if online activities replace daily duties or genuine face-to-face contact. In extreme cases, this pattern mirrors addictive behavior, resulting in loneliness, dissatisfaction, and increased anxiety.

Still, online settings might repeat or worsen social gaps and toxic behaviors when oversight or planning is weak. Studies show repeated cases of bullying, mistreatment, and bias in digital worlds - echoing issues like sexism and threats seen offline, shaping how safe or accepted people feel (see latest findings on web-based aggression via The Guardian). Such adverse trends may reduce mental health gains from using immersive platforms, especially among underrepresented communities or individuals reacting strongly to peer tension. Thus, system architecture and content management play key roles in protecting user emotional states.

A key factor involves how cultural background affects user perception of metaverse settings. Because culture guides values, it impacts what kinds of interaction people prefer - one might favor community focus, another personal freedom. Where someone grows up can determine whether they value unity or independence more in online worlds. As a result, shared norms influence how actions feel meaningful in digital contexts. Thus, wellbeing depends partly on whether virtual experiences match one's cultural outlook.

Studies from different online settings show culture affects how people feel about using tech. While these findings aren't focused on the metaverse, studies on digital well-being across groups suggest local standards and shared beliefs change how screen-based communication impacts mental health. That supports the view that a person's cultural background influences how their online activity connects to emotions.

Users often enjoy virtual spaces more when their online persona matches who they are offline (Singh et al., 2025). Studies on digital avatars show this alignment boosts both involvement and emotional connection. In line with these findings, the "Proteus effect" suggests how a person's avatar may shape actions and thoughts inside simulated settings. Rather than just visual design, it's about personal relevance - when people recognize themselves in their avatar, interactions tend to feel more meaningful. As a result, such experiences frequently lead to stronger attachment and better mood outcomes.

Meanwhile, ethical considerations alongside strong design matter a lot. Environments built with care - reducing sensory strain, setting understandable social rules, also tackling negative actions early - are better linked to improved emotional states (Shamim et al., 2025). Including elements that ensure security, reflect varied backgrounds, or foster helpful interactions increases chances that engaging in the metaverse supports mental health instead of harming it.

Together, these studies show metaverse use involves intricate mental processes. Benefits like improved mood, better social abilities, or greater life satisfaction appear when virtual spaces support purpose, connection, or personal expression. On the flip side, risks including deep overuse, interpersonal clashes, or confusion about self-image may reduce overall well-being. Because of this layered nature, investigations must consider variations between people, societal backgrounds, and technological setups.

To better grasp how the metaverse influences mood and inner feelings, upcoming studies ought to blend extended observation periods, global cultural contrasts, while including both numbers and personal stories. Over time, tracking individuals may show if mental effects grow stronger, fade away, or stay steady instead of disappearing quickly. Comparing different societies might reveal how shared beliefs influence enjoyment or discomfort in digital spaces. In-depth interviews could expose what people personally feel when engaging online rather than offline. Using surveys alongside activity logs plus body signals - like heart rate - might together offer clearer evidence on emotional shifts tied to screen-based interaction.

In sum, viewing the metaverse as a place "made for joy" opens up broader ways to understand how being online connects with feelings, cultural context, or thoughtful development. Virtual spaces might boost mood and mental health - especially if they enable deep communication, belonging, or user control. Still, gains aren't automatic; unequal access, harmful interactions, or conflicts between digital behavior and everyday beliefs may block emotional growth. To grasp how such settings could help people across varied global communities, research must rely on fair design standards, insights from psychology, along with verified data.

THEORETICAL BACKGROUND

Life satisfaction usually means how someone judges their general well-being, along with feelings linked to key personal aspects like aims, values, or dreams. Still, this idea has played a major role in studies across psychology, sociology, and growth through life stages, frequently related to pleasure, emotion control, therefore inner completeness. Yet now that digital tools are everywhere, people's views on their own lives shift alongside emerging tech settings. In particular, joint 3D online spaces - like those known as the metaverse, accessed using VR, AR, or MR gear - let users take on avatar forms, join gatherings or trade activities, also co-create moments. Thus, engaging in these simulated realms brings up vital concerns around whether heavy virtual use affects contentment, emotional balance, identity perception, plus sense of belonging.

From a psychology angle, being active in online spaces can meet basic mental needs tied to feeling good. According to Self-Determination Theory, having control, feeling capable, along with meaningful connections, supports inner drive and personal satisfaction. Although early studies looked at real-world situations, newer findings show digital platforms offering freedom, growth opportunities, or bonding chances boost mood and involvement (Xu & Chen, 2025). As an example, student surveys about emotional ties to the metaverse revealed that individual feelings of independence, effectiveness, together with belonging strongly influenced how attached they became digitally - pointing toward SDT applying even within simulated worlds (Xu & Chen, 2025). Moreover, research on tourism and free-time activities in the metaverse shows immersive digital settings can boost personal drive and pleasure by fulfilling desires for autonomy, skill development, or connection - highlighting how basic mental needs still shape well-being online (Argan et al., 2025). This suggests feelings of fulfillment don't just come from real-world events; they also emerge when people interact deeply with simulated spaces.

Flow Theory is another key idea for studying well-being; it suggests people feel more joy when what they do matches their skills and the task's difficulty. In digital worlds, users frequently handle actions needing sharp focus, live communication, or quick adjustments - factors that support entering such a mental state. Even though this concept came before modern online platforms, new research shows flow still matters in VR and augmented reality setups - it shapes how users emotionally and mentally judge their time spent there. These findings highlight that when challenges fit one's abilities inside virtual contexts, personal satisfaction may rise - even if everything happens in an artificial space.

A key idea tied to engagement and mental wellness in digital settings is presence - feeling like you are actually inside the simulated space. Not just shaped by tech specs, this sense comes from storytelling depth, personal goals during use, along with feelings invested, sometimes mattering more than hardware performance when judging immersion strength (Triberti et al., 2025). Once users perceive themselves as truly located within the virtual setting, their emotions start mirroring those found in everyday situations, such as delight, energy, or bonding with others. Greater subjective inclusion in these realms influences emotional reactions during VR exposure, leading to lower anxiety or improved outlooks (turn0search8). For instance, strong presence while experiencing nature simulations via VR correlates with higher reported happiness, better perceived physical condition, plus elevated emotional living standards - showing how deeply absorbing online environments may positively impact inner balance.

Empirical work highlights how digital use affects life satisfaction through social and cultural factors, rather than only personal emotions. In a UAE-based field project focusing on Gen Z, metaverse tools boosted both social growth - like dialogue abilities and local participation - as well as mental wellness, such as joy levels and handling pressure (Youssef et al., 2024). These outcomes suggest simulated online worlds enable novel types of contact and linkage beyond location limits, raising comfort in relationships while lowering tension via interactive networks. Such data match global studies indicating digital arenas help build emotional backing and shared identity, especially if participants hold similar traditions or common aims centered around teamwork and aid.

Still, using the metaverse doesn't always improve well-being. Some analyses show that deep involvement in 3D virtual spaces - especially online games or social VR platforms - might link to issues like stress, low confidence, sadness, or dependency, mostly in younger users (turn0search0). Problems can arise if screen time grows too high, interferes with daily duties, or increases feelings of falling short compared to others. Recent findings suggest heavy use of these digital realms could reduce mental wellness and weaken self-worth, meaning tech interactions might deepen emotional pressure instead of easing it (Jia & Mvondo, 2025). These downsides point to a need for examining not just advantages of simulated environments, yet also situations where they risk lowering overall life quality.

The variety in how people use digital spaces is influenced by their cultural roots, affecting the way they connect online and build identity or belonging. Where group unity matters more - like in communities focused on shared values - people often feel stronger emotional rewards from team-based virtual tasks or events centered around groups. On the flip side - in settings where independence and self-expression take priority - individuals tend to look for chances in digital realms to test out new identities, restate personal aims, or show originality, boosting self-assurance and inner well-being. These shifts based on background highlight why social and cultural rules must be taken into account when studying happiness in online environments, since culture shapes both what interactions mean and how they affect emotions.

Immersive tech ties into wider trends of digital change affecting how people interact and find purpose. Since online environments now play a central role in communication, education, or employment, experts argue these tools aren't impartial - they contain hidden biases and consequences impacting emotions and actions. Research analyzing XR uses shows benefits for mental health alongside concerns like online abuse, exclusion, compulsive use, or discomfort. Such findings suggest emotional outcomes from digital interaction depend not just on personal traits but also on structural elements - such as interface choices, oversight methods, and cultural expectations.

Although worries exist, carefully built virtual spaces may support mental health. Studies into meditation within metaverse settings show that interactive scenes along with reflective guidance help lessen emotional stress while boosting self-kindness and mood control (Yu et al., 2025). This implies if digital realms are made to encourage healthy feelings and positive social contact, they might aid wellness instead of just offering amusement. In parallel, experiments using VR nature exposure reveal intense simulations tend to lift joy levels, ease discomfort, plus increase overall life satisfaction more than basic versions . Such targeted uses highlight how intent behind design influences whether tech immersion helps minds thrive or adds pressure.

Alongside numerical data, there's work exploring niche online support settings. Studies watching LGBTQ+ youth in metaverse groups show these spaces may boost social ease, allow safer identity sharing, while lowering issues like fear in interactions. Such setups highlight how thoughtfully built digital circles can create validating experiences improving mental wellness - especially for those facing isolation or bias face-to-face. In addition, these platforms frequently enable easier access and greater discretion compared to physical meetings; however, experts warn they ought to connect with wider healthcare and community resources to maintain lasting emotional stability.

The ethical and social sides of life satisfaction in the metaverse matter greatly. Cases of widespread harassment, bias, or harmful behavior show virtual settings may mirror - or worsen - offline injustices within deeply engaging experiences (news sources). Negative encounters in joint digital areas stress the importance of early protective actions, effective oversight, along with rules shielding individuals from mental strain. A moral duty exists to create more secure internet environments, one that fits with methods focused on wellbeing, meeting core psychological needs, while supporting accessible layouts. When creators integrate people-first principles into tech systems, they reduce dangers yet strengthen circumstances where online involvement boosts personal fulfillment.

Cumulatively, studies from the last five years show that using the metaverse links to life satisfaction in complex ways. While virtual spaces may meet basic mental needs - also promoting focus and a sense of being there - they can also build real social bonds if carefully built and used. Yet, excessive use or addictive patterns might harm well-being; similarly, harmful online exchanges or cultural mismatches could lower personal happiness for certain individuals. Because both benefits and harms exist, combining insights from psychology, culture, tech development, along with moral principles becomes essential to grasp how deep digital experiences shape human thriving.

Future studies ought to use long-term, multi-country setups - thereby checking how joy levels shift during ongoing metaverse use while tracking changes in cultural beliefs alongside digital self-images. Blending observation, surveys, and body-based measures might deepen insight into feelings triggered by virtual settings. Also, side-by-side analysis of varied platforms plus user rules could reveal which structural traits consistently boost mental wellness. Since people are spending more shared time in online social realms, careful investigation is needed - to guide the metaverse away from mere escapism toward a space that actively supports emotional stability and meaningful connection.

CONCEPTUAL MODEL AND HYPOTHESES

The metaverse - a vast, engaging online space - is opening fresh paths for personal experience. Because it blends into daily routines like chatting, buying things, or shaping self-image, scientists now examine its mental impact more closely - specifically on how people feel about their lives. Life satisfaction means judging one's existence thoughtfully while also feeling positive - or not - about that judgment; many elements shape this, whether offline or in digital settings. Inside these virtual spaces, deep involvement, self-presentation, connections with others, and active participation form layered social-emotional conditions altering how users perceive fulfillment, purpose, and inner balance.

This section introduces a framework linking three key aspects: involvement in digital worlds, mental factors affecting online experiences, besides personal well-being - each influenced by cultural background. Involvement means how people take part in virtual settings - how they communicate in digital areas, show themselves using avatars or fake identities, also join social or money-related actions there. Mental influences cover basic human drives like feeling independent, capable, connected, along with being mentally absorbed when tasks match one's skills and challenges. Together, these elements affect how users see things, feel emotionally, plus rate their tech-based living. Crucially, culture - for instance, group-focused vs self-focused values - affects how such links work, so goals and what feels meaningful shift across societies.

Digital Engagement as the Foundation of Metaverse Experience

Digital interaction in the metaverse isn't just about login counts or minutes used; instead, it involves emotional, mental, and active participation. Factors such as sense of presence, social connection, and realistic settings influence how people experience online spaces - resulting in deeper involvement and motivation to keep engaging with these platforms (Tao et al., 2025). In turn, this points to engagement quality - as shaped by responsiveness and seamless integration within virtual worlds - playing a major role in users' psychological responses.

Research suggests that seeing engagement as something with many parts fits well with evidence from immersive digital worlds. Because deep interaction often boosts both emotional and mental involvement, features like social connection matter a lot. In metaverse contexts, for instance, user activity tends to increase when experiences feel real and allow communication. As shown by Tao et al. (2025), this doesn't just raise immediate interest - it strengthens willingness to keep using such platforms.

When people sense belonging or get absorbed in the moment, their actions become more purposeful. Such conditions then set the stage for stronger feelings later on.

Psychological Needs and Flow in Virtual Contexts

In psychological health, key needs - like making your own choices, feeling effective, building bonds - are signs of thriving. Though first studied in real-world settings, new studies applying self-determination theory to digital spaces show they matter online too (Raman et al., 2025). Choosing one's actions fosters autonomy; overcoming challenges supports competence; forming genuine ties enhances relatedness - all vital for well-being in virtual worlds.

The mental state known as flow - marked by intense focus, diminished awareness of self, also pure enjoyment - plays a key role connecting online activity to personal well-being. Settings offering balanced difficulty levels, real-time responses, yet smooth user interactions tend to boost this state. Studies within VR and video games show people feel more involved along with greater pleasure during flow, thus reporting higher fulfillment from digital use (Raman et al., 2025). While earlier work mostly looked at physical tasks or gameplay, findings now suggest simulated spaces filled with vivid sensory details plus responsive design - like parts of the metaverse - can strongly support meaningful flow episodes (Raman et al., 2025).

The link between meeting needs and achieving flow points to a step-by-step process. As digital interaction supports independence, skill growth, or social bonds, basic psychological requirements get fulfilled. Following this fulfillment, people experience states more conducive to flow - drawing them deeper into activities while boosting mental and emotional state. Together, these dynamics highlight how digital satisfaction involves layered psychological processes, not just time spent online.

Life Satisfaction in Digital Realms

Life satisfaction isn't just about short-term joy; it's an overall judgment of life in different areas. In the metaverse, this includes how people view their online connections, accomplishments, social bonds, and self-image. While classic models stress real-world contexts, newer studies suggest virtual spaces might influence emotional well-being - when they feel significant and backed by community. These digital settings can matter if they support psychological needs and foster belonging.

Studies into metaverse tourism show immersive activities, especially when users interact socially, improve feelings of happiness and fulfillment. For example, findings suggest that social contact in virtual travel environments strengthens how much people enjoy the experience, acting as a bridge between immersion and contentment (Inmor et al., 2025). Although such work often looks at travel-related cases, the core idea - that active participation with others boosts enjoyment - applies widely across different parts of the metaverse.

The Moderating Role of Cultural Orientation

Some people enjoy different things for different reasons. Where someone grows up can strongly affect what they value in an experience. In societies that focus on group goals, feeling connected to others often matters more. On the flip side, places that stress personal success tend to favor independence and making new things online.

The way culture plays a part is supported by wider psychology work, which shows cultural beliefs affect motivation and mental wellness. In one case, findings on how people adapt socially and emotionally in different cultures reveal that background shapes these adjustment paths. Even though those analyses don't focus on metaverse platforms specifically, the idea that shared values impact reactions to surroundings holds strong - and extends into online spaces.

Thus, the suggested model shows how links between digital involvement, meeting mental needs, immersive experiences, and well-being shift depending on cultural values. Where group ties matter most, feelings of belonging, mutual understanding, and joint activities likely stand out more. On the other hand, where personal goals take priority, sense of control and independent accomplishments tend to play a bigger role.

Hypotheses Development

The conceptual framework sets up four testable predictions, outlining how main ideas are thought to connect through different linkages

H1: Greater digital engagement strengthens feelings of independence, skill, and connection.

This idea suggests that when people spend more time in realistic online worlds - where interaction is strong, senses are engaged, and settings feel real - they tend to meet inner emotional needs (Tao et al., 2025). Because these virtual setups allow freedom in movement, chances to grow abilities, or ways to interact socially, mental well-being may improve. Although each aspect works differently, together they support a sense of personal reward within digital contexts.

H2: Meeting mental needs strongly links to feeling good about online experiences.

Meeting basic needs comes before mental wellness, showing how autonomy, skill, and connection tie closely to user happiness online (Raman et al., 2025). When people believe their metaverse experiences uphold these elements, they tend to view their virtual lives more favorably.

H3: Flow explains how digital involvement connects to life satisfaction.

Flow - a strong form of involvement - connects basic online activity with meaningful mental reward. While people are in this state, they dive deeply into tasks matching their abilities and passions, resulting in greater contentment that lasts longer than the instant itself (Raman et al., 2025)

H4: Cultural background changes how strong these effects are - people from group-focused cultures link well-being to relationships, whereas those from independence-oriented cultures care more about personal freedom or speaking their mind.

Cultural beliefs shape how people rank and meet their mental needs. According to this idea, the strength and ways involvement leads to fulfillment depend on shared patterns - those favoring group aims over personal ones.

These ideas combine into a broad framework positioning the metaverse as a space shaped by tech and culture - where people interpret experiences, build relationships, work toward aims, while reflecting on their online existence. Moving from involvement to mental well-being, then to overall contentment highlights how tools, personal drives, along with societal settings interact step by step.

The framework supports real-world testing through methods like SEM, giving scholars a way to measure how engagement traits, mental needs, flow experiences, while considering cultural influences. Later research might build on this by looking at particular metaverse aspects - such as personalized avatars, interactive environments, or game-like activities - and their varying effects on independence, skill perception, connection, immersion, depending on cultural context.

In today's increasingly digital era, it is key to grasp how mental processes link metaverse use with personal well-being. This section introduces a theoretical structure showing how online presence interacts with basic psychological needs, moments of deep involvement, and cultural background - shaping how people view their lives. Drawing from up-to-date studies on virtual platforms and user behavior, the approach helps clarify when digital spaces aid, enrich, or complicate emotional health. With ongoing tech advancements in these realms, the outlined framework guides both upcoming research and thoughtful design focused on purposeful, culture-sensitive interactions.

Figure 1. Conceptual Model

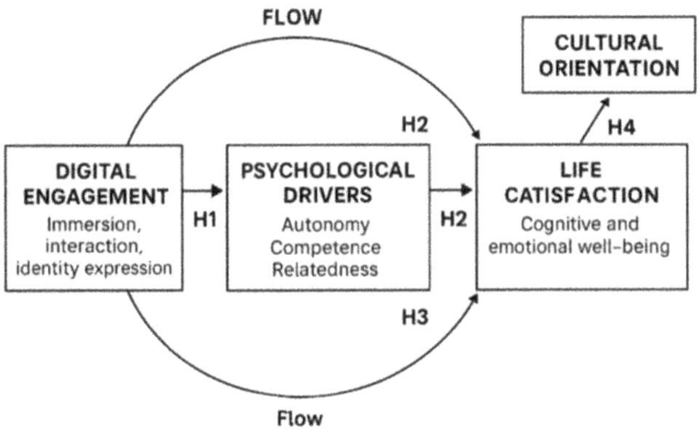

METHODOLOGICAL APPROACH

The present study adopts a quantitative cross-sectional research design augmented with complementary qualitative insights to rigorously investigate how digital engagement, psychological need fulfillment, flow experiences, and cultural orientation relate to life satisfaction in the metaverse. A cross-sectional design is particularly suitable for this research because it enables researchers to examine relationships among latent constructs and explanatory mechanisms at a single point in time across culturally diverse populations, while still allowing for the testing of mediation and moderation models through advanced statistical techniques such as Structural Equation Modeling (SEM). This approach aligns with contemporary methodological trends in digital psychology and consumer behavior research, where complexity and interdependence among variables are examined through multivariate structural models rather than simple bivariate correlations (Sterner et al., 2025). The inclusion of qualitative interviews enriches the design by allowing participants to articulate their subjective interpretations of emotional authenticity, community building, and contextual meaning in the metaverse, which may not be fully captured by survey measures alone.

Sampling and Participants

To achieve adequate statistical strength while covering diverse cultures, the survey aims to include 600 metaverse users drawn from three key areas: North America, Europe, and Asia-Pacific - regions selected because they represent contrasting values like independence versus group focus, a factor tied directly to the study's main assumption. Earlier studies comparing cultures suggest people interpret happiness indicators and tech usage differently depending on their cultural context; therefore, broad and evenly distributed datasets across continents are essential when analyzing variation between populations (Sterner et al., 2025). Instead of relying solely on one method, recruitment will happen through web-based participant pools, online groups centered around virtual worlds, along with internet discussion spaces related to digital conferences, helping capture variety in sex, age range, and economic standing. Eligibility requires individuals to have engaged with any form of metaverse platform within the last half-year, plus meet the minimum legal adult age of 18.

Measurement Instruments

Digital Engagement is measured using items taken from current studies on how people see the metaverse and experience online spaces - these focus on how often, intensely, or emotionally someone takes part in virtual actions. Research by (Aslan et al., 2025) shows immersion and smooth interaction strongly shape whether users stay engaged; findings come from validated tools used recently. Such instruments evaluate behaviors like moving through simulated worlds, communicating with others digitally, besides levels of commitment during joint tech-based activities.

Autonomy, competence, or relatedness - each captured through targeted questions - are used to assess core psychological needs within virtual worlds. These items stem from tools originally designed for real-world settings yet modified purposefully for online interaction research. When people feel independent in a digital space - or capable, connected - it often links to improved mental health markers. Studies show immersive platforms supporting such experiences tend to promote stronger emotional resilience over time (Jo & Lee, 2024; (Villar-Guevara et al., 2025)).

Flow is gauged through an adapted form of standard flow measures, adjusted for online settings, capturing how deeply users feel immersed, unaware of themselves, or pleased during digital tasks. Research into game play and virtual reality involvement shows these flow indicators link closely with user satisfaction and ongoing usage goals in simulated spaces (Jo & Lee, 2024).

Life Satisfaction draws on established well-being questionnaires, adjusted for this research. Earlier work highlights the need to test how such tools perform in diverse cultural settings - especially when comparing groups across countries (Sterner et al.,

2025). Because of this, the version applied here was revised thoughtfully, matching digital themes linked to metaverse use, yet keeping key reflective elements found in standard assessments.

Cultural Orientation gets measured through modified value scales identifying individualist or collectivist leanings on a personal level. New cross-cultural SEM studies highlight treating it as a moderating factor affecting how people prioritize social over personal aspects of satisfaction and involvement (Matus et al., 2025).

All items use a 5-point scale, from "Strongly Disagree" to "Strongly Agree." Before full data gathering, experts check the tools; then they're tested in a trial run with 50 metaverse users - this helps assess how clear the questions are and whether they measure what's intended.

Data Collection Procedures

Participants will fill out a web-based questionnaire containing all assessment tools and background items. Prior to starting, they'll receive details about the research goal, learn their data is private, then give documented approval to join. For better global applicability, the instrument will shift into relevant tongues via reverse-translation techniques, maintaining consistent meaning across versions.

To complement the survey findings, open-ended interviews will be carried out with a selected group of 50 individuals - around 16 or 17 per area. These discussions aim to examine how people sense genuine emotion, connection depth, and belonging while engaging in virtual worlds. Rather than relying solely on numbers, this approach helps reduce skewed personal reporting; instead, it brings deeper context to statistical patterns by uncovering subtle individual perspectives that fixed measures might overlook.

Data Analysis Plan

Because the model involves direct, indirect, and interaction effects, analysis will rely on Structural Equation Modeling. This approach allows estimation of several relationships at once while accounting for unobserved constructs and their inaccuracies. Instead of treating indicators as perfect, SEM adjusts for measurement issues naturally. Lately, researchers have applied this technique in international online studies - using it to separate general patterns from local variations (Sterner et al., 2025).

Prior to using SEM, EFA and CFA will check how the constructs are structured and their psychological consistency. These steps help verify whether scores can be trusted - using measures like Cronbach's alpha and composite reliability - as well as whether each construct truly reflects what it should, judged by convergent and discriminant validity. Because this study spans multiple cultures, tests for measurement invariance will show if people from different regions understand survey items similarly. Specifically, configural, metric, and scalar levels of equivalence must be confirmed before comparing hidden group averages or path strengths between populations (Sterner et al., 2025). Without such checks, differences might reflect misunderstanding rather than real variation. Establishing invariant models supports fair comparisons across settings - a standard practice recommended widely in current SEM work.

After confirming measurement invariance, we'll apply SEM to test structural assumptions - such as

(a) how online interaction influences basic mental needs being met
(b) how meeting basic mental needs affects overall happiness
(c) how flow acts as a link from engagement to satisfaction, also influencing the overall experience
(d) how cultural background influences these links.

Moderated mediation will be assessed through standard SEM methods applied to latent variable interactions. To evaluate indirect paths, bootstrapping will support the creation of bias-adjusted confidence intervals - ensuring reliable inference. Instead of relying on point estimates alone, this approach emphasizes distributional properties under uncertainty.

Interviews will be coded thematically to spot recurring views on emotion, belonging, and self-identity within virtual worlds. These themes will then be cross-checked against numerical results to better understand how personal experiences and mental involvement are influenced by societal values or user-specific assumptions.

Ethical Considerations

The study procedure must get clearance from a university ethics board overseeing human research. Participants will receive details about their entitlements - such as joining freely or leaving whenever they choose. Information is kept safe; it's stripped of personal labels before being examined to ensure privacy.

Strengths and Limitations of the Methodology

The combination of numbers and personal insights helps uncover broad trends alongside specific details about how people experience the metaverse. Using structural equation modeling makes it possible to examine indirect influences and conditional relationships within one analysis setup - meanwhile, tests for measurement consistency support valid comparisons between different cultures. Still, because data were collected at a single point in time, drawing cause-effect conclusions is difficult; tracking users over periods might clarify sequence of changes. Relying on survey answers works well for big groups yet risks skewed self-perception. Follow-up interviews add depth here - giving richer context to individual viewpoints.

Anticipated Results and Discussion

The starting theory argues that entering the metaverse may boost mental well-being by meeting core needs - autonomy shown through imaginative choice, skill-based confidence gained via tech experience, alongside connection built from meaningful social contact. Each factor contributes to greater life fulfillment; however, cultural context plays a role.

Take Western users - often drawn to personal freedom - they might enjoy creating unique avatars, exploring digital identities; by contrast, people from Eastern settings could prefer group activities, shared tasks, or expressing feelings together. These cultural differences highlight why designs should adapt to diverse user backgrounds.

The suggested SEM framework aims to show how flow - marked by deep focus plus motivation from within - acts as a key link connecting online involvement with personal well-being. Still, excessive immersion along with mismatches between digital behavior and real-life expectations might result in mental exhaustion or stress around self-identity. This highlights a contradiction: tech features that support happiness could, without mindful management, also trigger emotional strain.

Overall, these results link psychological concepts with practical management, offering guidance for metaverse creators who want to design spaces that support lasting involvement while also promoting user health - through a blend of insight and real-world application.

Theoretical and Managerial Contributions

This study adds value to academic knowledge and real-world application by clarifying how online spaces - particularly the metaverse - affect emotions, social behaviors, because well-being. Through combining ideas from tech change theories besides insights from buyer behavior plus cultural comparisons, it strengthens existing models while providing usable guidance for creators, regulators, also brand strategists working within evolving virtual settings.

Theoretical Contributions

1. Extending Digital Transformation Theory

Digital shift is often seen as changing how people and groups use tech to alter economic, social, or cultural habits. Most past research focused on company-level shifts, automated workflows, because it boosts productivity. Still, new virtual worlds push beyond this idea - tech here isn't only a helper but forms an environment influencing feelings through culture. This study broadens current thinking: the metaverse acts like a space where emotions, beliefs, behaviors constantly affect one another.

Studies show traits like social interaction, realistic settings, and feeling present affect how people react mentally when using virtual spaces - such as staying involved or wanting to keep using them. Work by (Tao et al., 2025) suggests user experience plays a middle role linking immersion elements with lasting involvement, highlighting feelings and personal encounters during tech shifts, not just buying decisions. From this view, the metaverse becomes an area where tools and users shape shared meanings together, making it harder to tell what's digital from what feels real.

Moreover, seeing digital change through an emotional lens fits with wider arguments in digital sociology - those calling for a fuller picture of tech use, where feelings and social ties aren't side effects but core parts of daily digital life. Shifting focus this way pushes scholars to rethink how shifts in online spaces influence not just actions or income, yet inner experiences, self-perception, along with shared beliefs. Bringing cultural patterns into models of digital evolution clarifies differences in how people across regions engage with virtual settings, thus shaping theories on tech uptake and mental wellness worldwide.

2. Enriching Consumer Psychology with Flow and Psychological Dynamics

Consumer psychology usually looks at how people choose products, develop likes or dislikes, and react to ads. However, spaces like the metaverse require a wider view - one that includes emotions and drive, not just thinking. Instead of focusing solely on decision-making, this study uses Flow Theory along with Self-Determination Theory to explore intense involvement in virtual worlds. As a result, it pushes consumer research further than typical online behavior.

Flow - a condition of full attention where difficulty matches ability - can boost mood during screen-based activities. Studies on online spaces and video games suggest that when people enter this mode, marked by sharp concentration, reduced awareness of self, and inner pleasure, their views on the interaction improve; examples include easier movement through interfaces or stronger participation. Here, flow acts as a link connecting digital use with personal well-being, showing how rich virtual experiences lead to mental benefits shaping user choices and opinions.

Self-Determination Theory's core needs - autonomy, competence, and relatedness - also translate meaningfully into metaverse contexts. Studies on digital embodiment and self-development show that when virtual environments support autonomy and allow users to express identity and agency, users report higher levels of psychological fulfillment and engagement. These dynamics incorporate motivational structures that are critical in explaining why certain immersive features lead to stronger engagement and emotional satisfaction in virtual settings, enriching consumer psychology with a layered understanding of motivation, emotional states, and interactive behavior in extended reality environments.

3. Providing a Validated Cross-Cultural Structural Equation Model (SEM)

A second major theory advance comes from building and testing a cross-cultural SEM framework connecting digital involvement, mental factors (like flow and fulfilled needs), with well-being. While uncommon in digital psychology, such broad comparisons are essential to see how societal values shape online interactions and feelings. Instead of focusing on one culture only, this study uses cultural orientation to adjust the connections in the model - helping researchers separate common trends from those tied to specific cultures.

Because it includes ideas like cultural orientation, this study fills an important hole in current work. Although many papers on the metaverse look at use or tech features, only a few test how culture affects feelings and well-being in virtual spaces. Checking results across cultures makes sure links between online activity and life satisfaction can be fairly compared among different groups - this gives solid theory support for wider use. This way, the framework helps move forward both cross-cultural psychology and research on digital experiences by showing how culture changes emotional and drive-related patterns in the metaverse.

One key takeaway for managers is clear: metaverse platforms should focus on building trust, empathy, and inclusivity - not just grabbing attention or boosting earnings. While new studies show high-tech immersion doesn't automatically improve well-being or keep users engaged over time. In fact, how emotionally meaningful interactions feel - and whether people see real value in joining - affects their satisfaction and likelihood to stay active. Take findings around traits like social interaction potential, depth of immersion, and realistic settings - they reveal that user experience acts as a bridge between these elements and the decision to stick with a virtual world. Notably, strong social opportunities along with lifelike surroundings had the biggest impact on encouraging lasting involvement, suggesting designers must prioritize genuine connections and rich experiences (Tao et al., 2025).

These results highlight how metaverse interfaces ought to focus more on mental and social functionality - elements promoting independence, skill development, and human connection - rather than mere newness. Instead of chasing trends, creators might gain by emphasizing emotional usability: simple navigation routes, tools for personal expression, along with story features aware of cultural context, helping people feel acknowledged, grasped, and linked. When participants can modify surroundings, adjust appearance settings, or engage deeply with peers, basic psychological requirements are addressed; this improves fulfillment while encouraging lasting involvement. Systems allowing display of heritage markers or self-driven stories deepen interaction quality and strengthen inclusion - an essential factor behind affective impact within virtual spaces (Fan et al., 2026).

Human-centered design focuses on removing obstacles to better experiences. Not only do inclusive communication tools matter, but so do access options for people with different needs; both help create fairer digital spaces where emotional support is possible. Instead of one-size-fits-all setups, varied social areas allowing multiple cultural forms let users feel recognized. Features like customizable sound and screen settings, easier menus, or personalized zones enable smoother participation - leading to less stress, greater confidence. Research in extended reality (XR) increasingly highlights these benefits, showing how immersion affects mental health. Rather than pushing tech forward blindly, experts suggest weighing progress against user safety (Taylor et al., 2024).

This study uses human needs - not just technical standards - to guide design choices, giving creators a clear way to turn psychology insights into practical features. Customizable options support autonomy; meanwhile, tasks that build skills and offer responses help users feel capable. Social tools and shared areas encourage connection. Focusing on people's needs means digital spaces can boost mental and emotional health, doing more than just entertain.

Policy Guidance for Digital Well-Being and Ethical Standards

The study's practical value reaches beyond management, touching public policy - especially rules about digital wellness and ethics. Because virtual environments grow fast while more people join worldwide, authorities struggle to shield users from mental health risks, unfair data use, prejudice, or being left out. Findings show these tech experiences may boost or harm emotions; this underlines a pressing demand for policies that support progress but still ensure fairness, security, and responsible design.

Risk studies in XR reveal challenges tied to deep digital experiences - like privacy breaches, compulsive use, abuse, or emotional pressure - especially affecting at-risk groups (Kourtesis, 2024). Instead of focusing only on tech standards, regulations should also address personal well-being during online interaction; this includes fair access, built-in privacy safeguards, and keeping control with users. As one example, clear rules about how data is handled inside metaverse systems may build confidence while lowering fears around misuse. In addition, authorities might push for tools enabling people to track time spent, set usage limits, or reach counseling services without leaving simulated worlds.

Policymakers should account for how different cultural and demographic backgrounds shape online experiences, so rules support everyone fairly. Because some societies value group harmony more than personal freedom, regulations need to reflect these differences. When platforms are required to assess local values or adapt to community expectations, it lowers chances of leaving people out. By including diverse worldviews in ethics standards, policies become more practical worldwide. This approach supports digital environments that feel secure and meaningful for users everywhere.

This study gives real-world proof on how online interaction affects emotions, so decision-makers can create rules to improve mental health in digital spaces, manage deep tech carefully, while ensuring everyone reaches supportive virtual settings. Such science-backed standards may act as reference points for holding platforms responsible, using artificial intelligence ethically, or enabling fair participation - each being key to building user confidence and steady growth in immersive digital tools.

Strategic Implications for Marketers and Brand Experiences

Marketers in the metaverse should take note - findings suggest brand plans must match cultural views on joy and feeling fulfilled, not just focus on purchases. Although typical campaigns highlight visibility, turning interest into action, or boosting revenue, virtual spaces call for broader tactics. These settings prioritize how smooth the experience feels, how strong the story is, also how deeply users stay emotionally involved.

Empirical results show consumer experience strongly influences ongoing involvement, implying metaverse brand designs ought to align with users' cultural and emotional contexts. Rather than centering only on ads or game-like rewards, marketing efforts could build spaces allowing personal expression, social connection, interactional significance. Experience-driven setups boost brand allegiance, favorable sharing, group engagement by weaving brand stories into culturally aware user paths instead of isolated buying instances. Studies on how consumers accept metaverse marketing - used for identity-building, early purchase stages - suggest usefulness perception and ease of use mainly shape willingness to join branded digital realms, underlining functional yet feeling-rich encounters may strengthen customer views and confidence (Tang et al., 2025).

Immersive brand settings allow people to engage through multiple senses - such as sight, sound, and touch - which may improve memory formation along with emotional ties to a brand's story. Research on shared virtual experiences shows that when users interact using personalized sensory inputs, being together in those spaces boosts creativity and choices; this leads to deeper narrative connections and stronger customer-brand bonds (Dubey et al., 2025).

So strategic marketing in the metaverse needs to shift from fixed ads to interactive spaces where users build value alongside brands - through live digital gatherings, shared conversations, or blending brand interactions naturally into daily online life. Instead of pushing messages, companies might focus on feelings and cultural fit, using immersive tools to tell stories, tailor user paths, or adjust content based on community context. That way, presence feels less like promotion, more like participation.

Integrating Managerial Insights for Sustainable Growth

These management inputs - insights on design, advice for policies, besides strategic marketing ideas - combine into a clear plan for firms moving through changing digital spaces. Building platforms with mental wellness in focus improves user enjoyment; at the same time, it supports lasting, responsible development of the metaverse as a place for real human interaction. Policies shaped by behavioral research can shield participants while promoting fair usage. Marketing tactics that include cultural relevance and emotional depth allow companies to engage genuinely across varied communities.

This study offers leaders a practical guide - based on theory and tested evidence - for building, managing, and promoting within virtual environments. Success in these spaces hinges less on immediate user interaction data; instead, it relies more on lasting personal satisfaction, responsible oversight, or experiences shaped with cultural sensitivity - all aligned with core human principles despite digital delivery.

Implications for Future Research

This study merges cross-cultural studies with psychological models, creating a base for worldwide digital wellness strategies - tackling key issues in today's networked economy. As immersive tools such as Extended Reality (XR) and the metaverse advance quickly, they bring fresh ways of connecting socially, operating economically, yet also introducing unique mental impacts unlike standard online use. While existing work recognizes XR's effects on mental health, recent findings highlight how early-stage this area remains, calling for broader, structured research on its influence over well-being - especially across diverse cultural settings (Taylor et al., 2024).

Future studies ought to use long-term methods instead of one-time surveys so they can track shifts in emotions across periods. Because these techniques show how people's minds change during extended metaverse use, patterns like adjustment, familiarity, or harm might become visible (Taylor et al., 2024). Since such setups separate immediate feelings from lasting effects on wellness, deeper understanding of digital life over time emerges.

In terms of time span, adding body-based data - like changes in heartbeat, sweat levels, or brain activity - to research helps confirm what people report and reveals hidden mental and physical reactions. These bodily signs give measurable proof of emotion, strain, and thinking effort during virtual experiences, supporting personal accounts while reducing errors from survey answers. Studies on online treatments and extended reality show that mixing feelings reports with real-time body feedback leads to stronger conclusions about mental health, spotting both good mood patterns and early warnings for discomfort or overload (Buragohain et al., 2025).

Looking into how immersive tech works in specific fields opens new paths for research. Instead of general use, focusing on areas like learning, medical care, or jobs reveals different needs and impacts on people's well-being. In education tied to culture and history, virtual tools help users feel more emotionally involved, stay focused, better motivated - but there's still a lack of consistent ways to measure experience quality (Anwar et al., 2025). When used in medicine, studies suggest these technologies might deliver flexible, individualized mental health solutions; however, issues around access, data safety, and inclusion across cultures remain unresolved, calling for careful setup and adapted designs (Buragohain et al., 2025) At work settings, VR-based training or team interaction platforms may affect mood along with efficiency - so future inquiry should balance output metrics with psychological effects.

Equally critical is sustained research into ethical and governance mechanisms that ensure the metaverse evolves as a socially beneficial and inclusive space. The rapid proliferation of immersive technologies has amplified concerns related to data privacy, security risks, cybersickness, addiction, harassment, and inequality, issues that extend across cultural and socioeconomic boundaries (Kourtesis, 2024). Responsible governance frameworks must balance innovation with user protection, promoting equity of access, transparent data practices, and ethical design principles that foreground psychological well-being alongside economic or technical objectives. Interdisciplinary collaboration among technologists, policymakers, psychologists, and cultural researchers will be essential for developing standards that protect users while fostering positive psychological and social outcomes in virtual spaces.

In short, improving worldwide standards for digital wellness means doing broad studies - ones that go past one-time polls to include long-term tracking, body-based data, real-world uses in different fields, and fair oversight. By using careful, wide-ranging methods, groups involved can better grasp how virtual worlds affect mood and quality of life in diverse societies - as well as learn ways to shape those spaces for growth instead of damage.

CONCLUSION

The metaverse isn't just a tech advance; rather, it acts like a large-scale test on how people seek purpose, connect with others, or build personal fulfillment. While past online tools relied on flat visuals and typed messages, this new space pulls individuals into interactive 3D worlds where being present, showing identity, or communicating feels close to actual physical encounters. Such change raises basic concerns about how virtual involvement affects inner well-being, overall contentment, plus lived reality across varied cultural backgrounds. Because these settings deeply involve the senses, they trigger emotions far beyond casual fun - instead offering areas that may meet essential mental needs or potentially lead to psychological strain (Triberti et al., 2025).

Looking at the metaverse through cross-cultural psychology and ideas about digital change helps see it not just as tech progress but as a place where people make sense of self, belonging, and emotions. Feeling good in online worlds relies less on new features or interaction alone - instead, fit with basic psychological needs matters more, like freedom, skill growth, connection, and feeling safe emotionally. This match should consider culture - well-being triggers in one setting may feel off to someone else from a different background. Studies across cultures show that shared values influence what users expect from digital socializing and how these experiences affect their overall life satisfaction (Youssef et al., 2024).

This study supports a data-driven view of digital happiness by testing these relationships through Structural Equation Modeling (SEM). Because SEM enables analysis of several cause-effect routes at once - connecting online activity, mental mechanisms, cultural influences, and overall life satisfaction - it fits well here. Instead of relying on assumptions, the findings show measurable links between mindset factors, culture-shaped usage habits, and personal well-being. Rather than guesswork, results highlight specific parts of digital use that boost or harm emotional health, giving practical guidance for developers, decision-makers, and others aiming to build balanced, supportive tech spaces.

Recent research shows that strong VR presence may link to better personal well-being, especially when setups focus on mental wellness. Studies looking at varying degrees of immersion reveal that deeper engagement - where people feel truly inside the environment - leads to bigger gains in mood, perceived health, and emotional life quality versus weaker versions (Yen et al., 2024) Such results highlight how carefully built immersive settings might support mental states usually gained through actual outdoor visits or calming practices.

Research shows metaverse use doesn't just affect personal wellness - it can also boost social abilities, lower anxiety levels, while increasing mental toughness through interactions that seem less intimidating than real-world encounters. One study focusing on Gen Z revealed digital worlds helped young people grow socially, gain self-assurance, manage pressure better, along with forming genuine online bonds (Youssef et al., 2024). These findings imply simulated spaces might back up traditional emotional support systems, reducing loneliness - particularly for those struggling with face-to-face communication.

Yet studies point to downsides when people spend too much time in digital environments. Research combining surveys and interviews links heavy metaverse use to issues like dizziness from VR, compulsive habits, blurred sense of self, and feeling worse after comparing oneself to others - each potentially harming emotional balance and leading users to quit (Jia & Mvondo, 2025). These results suggest designers should rethink how virtual spaces function, showing features meant to draw users in might backfire if proper protections aren't built in.

A core idea when studying how the metaverse affects well-being is presence - the feeling of actually being inside a virtual world. Studies on VR show this sensation doesn't depend only on tech quality; instead, it's influenced by story design, what users expect, along with cultural context - highlighting that personal perception shapes if deep involvement improves mood (Triberti et al., 2025). Therefore, presence can link online interaction with real-life satisfaction, affecting how people emotionally attach to digital environments while shaping their views on purpose and contentment.

Because there are so many possible outcomes, it's obvious that good mental health in the metaverse isn't just about new tech. Instead, design must change direction - focusing less on engagement and money, yet centering meaning, fair relationships, and people's wellness. This approach accepts that virtual experiences affect emotions deeply; therefore, they should boost personal growth instead of increasing stress, dependency, or isolation.

This change brings real-world effects. Firstly, creators of digital spaces should build in attention to human emotions and cultural differences from the start - using designs that support emotional comfort, group connection, personal recognition, yet also let individuals adjust settings themselves. Systems giving people freedom to shape their own journey, while keeping a clear sense of autonomy, may reduce confusion or detachment during deep virtual interaction (Jia & Mvondo, 2025). Also, including stories and symbols familiar across different cultures enables users to feel seen and respected no matter where they come from - an essential point for worldwide platforms aiming at inclusivity.

Second, clear rules based on solid research are needed - not only covering privacy or system security but also emotional health, fair access, and mental safety. Since immersive tech is spreading into schools, workplaces, and daily interactions, regulations have to prevent unintended damage from misuse of personal information, online abuse, or hidden influences weakening self-determination. Responsible oversight requires features promoting psychological wellness, including usage tracking systems and shields against digital aggression or emotional strain. Studies emphasize open handling of user data, inclusive development strategies focused on fairness, along with active measures enabling marginalized communities' participation in simulated environments (Kourtesis, 2024).

Third, using immersive tech in areas like health care, schooling, or work needs custom strategies - ones that weigh pros alongside drawbacks of digital interaction. Take therapy-related VR: it should rely on proven medical data so emotional gains or better social ties last instead of fading quickly. Reviews show varied results across VR uses - even though certain programs boost mental wellness noticeably, a few might worsen suffering without expert guidance. Grasping these subtle differences matters greatly when putting such tools to practical use.

In recent years, digital spaces have grown more interactive, shifting how people connect and engage online. Because of this shift, focusing on user well-being in virtual worlds may become key to meaningful advancement. Instead of tracking only time spent or clicks, platforms should prioritize mental health, sense of belonging, and personal satisfaction. Some researchers argue that tech development must center human needs - not just efficiency or growth - with studies pointing to ethics and inclusivity as vital (Raman et al., 2025). To build healthier experiences, experts from different areas - like computing, behavioral science, social research, and governance - must work together so these environments improve real-life quality without repeating its flaws.

In sum, the metaverse could deeply reshape how people experience joy and life quality - yet this depends on building virtual spaces suited to basic mental needs and diverse cultural settings. Studies show deep involvement in digital worlds may boost mood when used thoughtfully; however, dangers exist and require careful oversight plus user-centered development. Moving focus away from capturing clicks toward supporting inner growth and fair interaction isn't only better - it's essential, should the metaverse play a lasting role in global human advancement.

REFERENCES

Anwar, M. S., Yang, J., Frnda, J., Choi, A., Baghaei, N., & Ali, M. (2025). Metaverse and XR for cultural heritage education: Applications, standards, architecture, and technological insights for enhanced immersive experience. *Virtual Reality (Waltham Cross), 29*(2), 51. DOI: 10.1007/s10055-025-01126-z

Argan, M., Gürbüz, B., Sivan, A., Argan, M. T., Dinç, H., & Bayazıt, E. (2025). Awe experience of leisure activity in the metaverse: Perceived value, satisfaction and intention. *World Leisure Journal, 67*(3), 1–22. DOI: 10.1080/16078055.2025.2459933

Aslan, M., Sağtaş, S., & Özkaynar, K. (2025). Metaverse Perception Scale Development and Validation. *SAGE Open, 15*(2), 21582440251329126. DOI: 10.1177/21582440251329126

Barth, L. L., Mostajeran, F., Riecke, B. E., & Kühn, S. (2025). Immersive videos of natural and urban environments can enhance awe and psychological well-being. *Frontiers in Virtual Reality, 6*, 1532991. Advance online publication. DOI: 10.3389/frvir.2025.1532991

Buragohain, D., Khichar, S., Deng, C., Meng, Y., & Chaudhary, S. (2025). Analyzing metaverse-based digital therapies, their effectiveness, and potential risks in mental healthcare. *Scientific Reports, 15*(1), 17066. DOI: 10.1038/s41598-025-00916-4 PMID: 40379748

Dubey, A., Kuriakose, S. M., Anand, S., Bhardwaj, N., & Sengupta, S. (2025). Virtual Social Immersive Multi-Sensory E-Commerce. *arXiv Preprint arXiv:2510.15894.* https://doi.org//arXiv.2510.15894DOI: 10.48550

Fan, X., Li, H., & Jiang, X. (2026). How to retain users in the metaverse: Exert technological affordances through psychological ownership mechanism. *Technology in Society, 84*, 103131. Advance online publication. DOI: 10.1016/j.techsoc.2025.103131

Inmor, S., Na-Nan, K., Phanniphong, K., Jaturat, N., & Hirnšal, M. (2025). Unveiling the metaverse: The mediating role of social interaction in enhancing tourism experiences. *Journal of Open Innovation, 11*(1), 100461. DOI: 10.1016/j.joitmc.2024.100461

Jia, Y., & Mvondo, G. F. N. (2025). Exploring the adverse effects of the metaverse on users' psychological well-being and Self-Esteem: A mixed-methods study. *Journal of Retailing and Consumer Services, 86*, 104321. DOI: 10.1016/j.jretconser.2025.104321

Jo, H., & Lee, J. K. (2024). A comprehensive analysis of presence, seamlessness, and player responses in metaverse gaming. *Computers in Human Behavior, 159*, 108345. Advance online publication. DOI: 10.1016/j.chb.2024.108345

Kourtesis, P. (2024). A comprehensive review of multimodal XR applications, risks, and ethical challenges in the metaverse. *Multimodal Technologies and Interaction*, *8*(11), 98. DOI: 10.3390/mti8110098

Matus, N., Rusu, C., Rusu, V., & Botella, F. (2025). Developing and Validating an Intercultural Student Experience Scale Using Structural Equation Modeling. *Sustainability (Basel)*, *17*(18), 8224. DOI: 10.3390/su17188224

Raman, R., Kowalski, R., & Achuthan, K. (2025). Metaverse Technologies and Human Behavior: Insights into Engagement, Adoption, and Ethical Challenges. *Computers in Human Behavior Reports*, *100712*, 100712. Advance online publication. DOI: 10.1016/j.chbr.2025.100712

Ryan Richard, M., & Deci, E. L. (2000). Self-determination theory and the facilitation of intrinsic motivation, social development, and well-being. *The American Psychologist*, *55*(1), 68–78. DOI: 10.1037/0003-066X.55.1.68 PMID: 11392867

Shamim, N., Wei, M., Gupta, S., Verma, D. S., Abdollahi, S., & Shin, M. M. (2025). Metaverse for digital health solutions. *International Journal of Information Management*, *83*, 102869. DOI: 10.1016/j.ijinfomgt.2025.102869

Singh, G., Roy, S. K., Apostolidis, C., Quaddus, M., & Sadeque, S. (2025). Identifying the metaverse value recipe (s) affecting customer engagement and well-being in retailing. *Technological Forecasting and Social Change*, *210*, 123870. DOI: 10.1016/j.techfore.2024.123870

Sterner, P., De Roover, K., & Goretzko, D. (2025). New developments in measurement invariance testing: An overview and comparison of EFA-based approaches. *Structural Equation Modeling*, *32*(1), 117–135. DOI: 10.1080/10705511.2024.2393647

Tang, Y. M., Wong, J. K. N., & Ho, G. (2025). Exploring Consumer Acceptance of Metaverse Marketing for Branding Activities and the Pre-Purchase Stage. *Journal of Theoretical and Applied Electronic Commerce Research*, *20*(3), 159. DOI: 10.3390/jtaer20030159

Tao, M., Khan, J., Abbass, A., & Mehmood, K. (2025). Metaverse Characteristics: The Role of Consumer Experience Shaping Consumer Behavior in the Metaverse. *Journal of Theoretical and Applied Electronic Commerce Research*, *20*(3), 166. DOI: 10.3390/jtaer20030166

Taylor, A., tom Dieck, M. C., Jung, T., Cho, J., & Kwon, O. (2024). XR and mental wellbeing: State of the art and future research directions for the Metaverse. *Frontiers in Psychology*, *15*, 1360260. DOI: 10.3389/fpsyg.2024.1360260 PMID: 38524293

Triberti, S., Sapone, C., & Riva, G. (2025). Being there but where? Sense of presence theory for virtual reality applications. *Humanities & Social Sciences Communications*, *12*(1), 1–6. DOI: 10.1057/s41599-025-04380-3

Villar-Guevara, M., García-Salirrosas, E. E., Gómez-Bayona, L., Villar, D., Pari-Apaza, M., & Fernández-Mallma, I. (2025). Changes in the Digital World: An Explanatory Analysis of the Key Factors Linked to Virtual Interactivity. *Administrative Sciences*, *15*(7), 276. https://doi.org/Changes%2520in%2520the%2520digital %2520world:%2520Virtual%2520interactivity%2520and%2520sequential %2520mediation%2520mechanisms. DOI: 10.3390/admsci15070276

Xu, Y., & Chen, L. (2025). University students' metaverse attachment and its predictors: Escaping from reality. *Frontiers in Psychology*, *16*, 1594256. DOI: 10.3389/fpsyg.2025.1594256 PMID: 41064179

Yen, H.-Y., Hsu, H., & Huang, W.-H. (2024). Virtual reality natural experiences for mental health: Comparing the effects between different immersion levels. *Virtual Reality (Waltham Cross)*, *28*(1), 52. DOI: 10.1007/s10055-024-00958-5

Youssef, E., Medhat, M., Abdellatif, S., & Babiker Yousif, N. (2024). Analyzing the impact of Metaverse technology on social development: A field study on generation Z in the United Arab Emirates. *Social Sciences (Basel, Switzerland)*, *13*(9), 446. DOI: 10.3390/socsci13090446

Yu, A., Lee, G., Liu, Y., Zhang, M., Jung, S., Park, J., Rhee, J., & Cho, K. (2025). Development and Evaluation of an Immersive Metaverse-Based Meditation System for Psychological Well-Being Using LLM-Driven Scenario Generation. *Systems*, *13*(9), 798. DOI: 10.3390/systems13090798

Zhang, L., Yin, Y., Liu, L., & Yan, S. (2025). Exploring the effects of AR presence and personal norms on museum visitor pro-environmental behaviour intentions. *Scientific Reports*, *15*(1), 25633. Advance online publication. DOI: 10.1038/s41598-025-11119-2 PMID: 40664893

Chapter 9
The Paradox of Choice and Personalization in Digital Global Markets:
Impacts on Consumer Life Satisfaction

Tanish Kawatra
http://orcid.org/0009-0003-6669-6602
Christ University, Delhi NCR, India

Deeksha Gupta Ganguly
http://orcid.org/0000-0002-5502-8276
Christ University, Delhi NCR, India

ABSTRACT

Digital tools now shape how people pick products worldwide. Not only do online stores offer endless choices, but they also track user behaviour to suggest items. From TikTok shops to streaming plans, what users see gets tailored without them noticing. Because algorithms learn preferences, decisions feel easier - yet sometimes less conscious. Even when choice seems broader, hidden patterns guide attention behind the scenes. Though more access sounds beneficial, some studies point to mental fatigue instead. With every click shaping future suggestions, control might be more illusion than reality. What looks like freedom could quietly narrow perspectives over time. Global reach means cultural differences blend into one shopping flow. Behind convenience lies a shift in who really influences each purchase.

DOI: 10.4018/979-8-3373-8357-6.ch009

INTRODUCTION

Nowhere is change more evident than in how buyers find what they need online. Because connections are faster and devices everywhere, choices come from nearly any corner of the world. Platforms built around apps or websites offer endless selections - music, goods, payments - all reachable at once. Instead of walking into stores, people now sort through layers of data before deciding. With so much visible at one time, picking becomes less about instinct, more about filtering. Speed matters too; comparisons happen in seconds, not hours. Availability never stops, pressing users to decide amid constant inputs. These spaces run on immediacy, volume, sometimes confusion. Choices pile up not slowly but all at once. Decision paths twist through reviews, prices, delivery times. What feels personal still follows patterns shaped by code and design. Even small steps involve multiple systems working behind the scenes. Routine tasks link to complex networks without most noticing. Boundaries between regions blur when everything loads equally fast. Selections appear neutral though some rise higher due to invisible rankings. Buyers act freely yet move along tracks laid out by interface logic. Experience shifts quietly under pressure from scale and speed. Familiar habits adapt whether wanted or not.

Facing rising complexity, companies now lean heavily on automated tools fueled by vast datasets, smart algorithms, and pattern recognition techniques. Because of how much information flows through digital platforms, these technologies pull together details like site visits, prior buys, age-related traits, and situational cues. With that input, they shape what users see - highlighting items likely suited to taste while downplaying less fitting ones. Efficiency gains matter here; sorting through endless picks takes time, so narrowing options feels helpful. Satisfaction often rises when people encounter things they genuinely want without effort. When done well, the experience becomes smoother, almost invisible, letting individuals act quickly amid cluttered online spaces.

Still, even with these expected advantages, new findings across consumer studies, psychology, and behavioural science point toward a different outcome - too much variety might lower satisfaction instead of raising it. Although having choices supports feelings of independence, according to Schwartz (2004), endless possibilities often bring mental strain and emotional burden. Facing numerous options, people sometimes struggle under excess details, find decisions harder, and feel more stress about picking correctly. Such pressures tend to weaken trust in their own judgments, lessening contentment after selecting something, regardless of how good the option actually is.

Digital settings often amplify the burden of too many choices, simply because comparing options feels effortless. Though meant to support clearer decisions, endless access to reviews and pricing data can backfire quietly. With every click, another alternative pops up - visible, tempting, just missed. This steady stream keeps unchosen paths alive in a person's mind. Regret then creeps in after buying, even if the purchase was sound. Satisfaction dips when attention lingers on what might have been. Each small moment of doubt adds up across time. Life satisfaction may erode not from big failures but from countless tiny trade-offs replayed silently. The weight grows heavier without warning.

Though meant to help, tools that tailor choices bring mixed results when it comes to decision strain. One way they assist: cutting down large option pools into smaller, more focused groups, guiding users without overwhelming them. This streamlining lowers mental load, making picking feel smoother and somewhat more satisfying at first glance. Yet another effect emerges alongside - freedom shrinks when systems only show what fits past behaviours. When suggestions keep echoing prior picks, variety fades over time. Repeated similarity shapes narrow paths, where fresh discovery becomes rare, possibly weakening lasting contentment.

Sometimes, depending more on automated tools brings up deeper questions about how people feel and what feels right. When individuals lean heavily on these systems to make choices, they might start doubting their own ability to decide. This shift often weakens their feeling of being in charge of their actions. Knowing that companies gather large amounts of personal information could spark unease around spying, secrecy, or subtle influence. Such discomfort tends to weaken faith in online services, leaving users with a lingering sense of powerlessness - something closely tied to lower levels of happiness. Even though tailored experiences aim to improve selection, an unintended effect emerges: satisfaction drops if people believe hidden tech forces are steering or limiting their options.

Choice overload meets culture shock online. Where options multiply fast, values shape reactions - especially when identity ties to group norms instead of solo preference. In societies favouring independence, endless picks feel like control; elsewhere, too many decisions stir discomfort. Uncertainty looms larger where rules bring comfort, making cluttered menus mentally taxing. Power gaps matter, too - how much say people expect changes their response to customization tools. One-size-fits-all design ignores these divides. Stress builds differently across borders when clicking through infinite feeds. Personalized interfaces might help - or overwhelm, depending on upbringing. What feels freeing here may burden there. Assumptions travel poorly without context. Mental load shifts with worldview, not just tech access. Digital shelves mirror deeper beliefs about duty, doubt, and belonging.

One reason researchers pay attention to digital shopping trends lies in how endless options mix with tailored suggestions. Because too many choices appear alongside customized ones, people's overall happiness may shift in subtle ways. A closer look at such dynamics adds depth to ideas about well-being, moving past quick buying highs toward lasting feelings of contentment. When platform builders notice when selection size overwhelms or supports users, they adjust features quietly - keeping speed, interest, and freedom in mind. Since automated systems shape what shoppers see, those who make rules face tough calls about fairness, clarity, and safety online.

Ultimately, online marketplcaes offer people wider reach, tailored options, and easier shopping than ever before. Still, such advantages often come with mental strain that can erode contentment over time unless acknowledged. When too many choices mix with hyper-personalized suggestions, decision fatigue tends to grow. This section argues digital spaces should shift focus - less on speed and volume, more on lasting fulfillment and emotional health.

THE PARADOX OF CHOICE: THEORETICAL FOUNDATIONS

Contrary to what classic theories suggest, having too many options does not always improve outcomes. Though conventional models assume people act rationally - weighing every alternative to make optimal choices - real behaviour often differs. These frameworks presume individuals have clear desires plus the mental resources needed to assess numerous possibilities efficiently. Yet findings from studies on human judgment reveal a different pattern altogether. When faced with overwhelming variety, decision-making can become harder instead of easier. This overload sometimes leads to stress rather than fulfillment. Satisfaction drops when evaluating picks feels like work. Evidence shows that broader selections might limit enjoyment even if better fits exist within them. Rather than enhancing freedom, endless alternatives may quietly erode confidence in decisions made.

A key study from Iyengar and Lepper (2000) offered early evidence backing the idea that more choices can backfire. Instead of boosting motivation, broad selections - like racks holding 24 kinds of jam - led people to buy less often compared to displays offering fewer options. When individuals picked from overloaded arrays, despite completing a transaction, they expressed weaker pleasure along with stronger doubt afterward. Rather than simplifying decisions, wide ranges appear to burden shoppers, weakening follow-through and emotional reward alike. Crucially, these impacts extend past inner feelings - they shape real-world buying patterns too.

Starting fresh from earlier ideas, Schwartz (2004) proposed a wider view of how too many choices often backfire. Instead of feeling free, people feel weighed down when picking gets harder because each option left behind seems to carry hidden value. With every added alternative, thoughts grow sharper about paths not taken. These imagined gains stir up second-guessing, disappointment, and lingering doubt. On top of that, personal fault becomes easier to assign when decisions go wrong in crowded markets. Should someone feel their choices were fully free, setbacks tend to get pinned on personal failings instead of outside factors. Because of this shift inward, confidence often erodes slowly, affecting how people view their lives over time.

Though people aim to make sound choices, their mental bandwidth runs thin when faced with too many options. Because thinking takes effort, they often skip deep analysis, using shortcuts instead. When selections multiply, so does the burden of weighing differences, predicting results, one after another. Thinking through every detail becomes harder than expected, even exhausting. Simon pointed out long ago that humans work within limits - time, knowledge, attention - all finite. Instead of picking the best possible option, most settle for something good enough. With more items on offer, confusion grows, decisions weaken, stress builds. The mind struggles not because it lacks skill but because the task swells beyond reach. What seems helpful - more variety - can quietly undermine judgment. Clarity fades just as demands rise. Effort piles up without warning, leaving room for doubt. Even small choices feel heavy under pressure.

Thinking through Kahneman's (2011) two-part model helps explain why too many choices can hinder decisions. One of these mental modes acts quickly, guided by instinct and habit; the other works slowly, needing focus and logic. When faced with numerous options, the slower system must work harder - weighing differences, staying alert, applying reason. This ongoing demand drains mental resources, eventually leading to exhaustion in judgment. Once tired, people tend to shift toward quicker thinking patterns - using habits, defaults, or what others choose - instead of analyzing each possibility thoroughly.

Sometimes fast thinking feels easier, yet mistakes creep in quietly over time. Choices jump out because they feel known, even if better fits exist beyond sight. Tired minds grab quick fixes - later second-guessing lingers like a shadow. Weighty moments, like picking schools or medical paths, turn shaky when gut picks override deeper search. Big life moves demand more than mental shortcuts when regret looms large afterward.

Fatigue from making choices builds up, affecting more than just single moments of picking one thing over another. One after another, online settings demand selections - what to buy, how to adjust it, whether to pay now or later - all without pause. With every pick, mental energy drains a little further, setting the stage for weariness to take hold. Facing this again and again, people might stop paying close attention, delay committing, or simply go on autopilot, repeating old patterns instead of choosing freely. Satisfaction dips when freedom feels like burden, casting doubt on the idea that endless options truly give power.

Too many choices don't just tax the mind - they weigh on feelings too. Studies show wide arrays spark tension ahead of deciding, as people fear picking poorly or overlooking something better. After choosing, emotions like regret often run deeper when options were plentiful. If results disappoint, those surrounded by variety tend to dwell on paths not taken, deepening discomfort. That emotional load may linger long after purchase, quietly colouring views on well-being and overall contentment.

Notably, how people react to many choices varies by personality. Take Schwartz (2004), who identified two types: those aiming for the optimal pick - called maximizers - and others settling when basics are covered, known as satisficers. Because maximizers examine every alternative closely, they often feel worse after deciding, weighed down by regret and stress. Satisficers, however, tend to stop searching early if a choice fits their standards, which lowers mental fatigue. Rather than affecting everyone the same way, too much choice hits harder depending on one's mindset and habits in making decisions.

Digital marketplaces often deepen the dilemma of too many options because tools built into them multiply how much we can pick from, also sharpening our ability to compare. With just one click, buyers reach piles of feedback, scores, every feature listed - making each decision feel heavier, like it must be the right one. Even though showing so much detail aims to help people choose better, it sometimes backfires by fueling stress, regret, even disappointment if things fall short. Because of this shift, feeling worn out by endless picking shows up stronger online than it ever did walking through physical stores.

Oddly enough, having too many options reveals an underlying clash between freedom and limits when people pick what they want. Although variety supports personal control and identity, endless alternatives often flood the mind, stir unease, yet reduce fulfillment. Research into how choices are made highlights mental shortcuts, tired thinking, limited reasoning capacity, plus strain from sorting through abundance. Recognizing these patterns helps build better pictures of shopper habits - ones that support sharper decisions along with lasting happiness and contentment.

PERSONALIZATION AND ALGORITHMIC DECISION-MAKING

Digital tools that adjust content to fit single users help simplify decisions online. Because online spaces now offer so many options, companies rely more on customizing what people see. Platforms like Amazon, Netflix, and Spotify shape choices using complex software that learns from user actions - what someone bought before, where they clicked, their location, age, or even time of day (Huang & Rust, 2021). Behind these suggestions lies analysis of vast amounts of behavioural traces. The goal? To predict what a person might want next without making them look too hard. Less searching means less mental load. Efficiency emerges when systems guess well. What appears tailored often reflects patterns found across millions. A quiet click can feed future displays. Over time, the interface shifts slightly, shaped by routine interactions. Not magic - just math fed by habit. Choices narrow not by chance but calculation. Users get fewer surprises when predictions hold true. Yet every tweak depends on prior moves made unknowingly. Familiarity builds because repetition teaches machines. Seeing similar things again is rarely coincidence. Past steps guide what shows up tomorrow. Even small behaviours leave marks used later. This shaping happens beneath awareness. Interfaces adapt silently. Predictions improve only if data flows steadily. Without ongoing input, precision fades. Accuracy leans heavily on consistency in how people act. When routines shift, guesses may lag behind. Systems catch up slowly. Learning takes repeated exposure. Mistakes happen most after sudden changes. People evolve faster than models sometimes. Still, each correction refines the process further.

One way people handle too many choices? Getting suggestions tailored just for them. Instead of facing endless possibilities, filtered picks help cut through clutter. Because these selections match known interests, users often find them helpful. Less mental effort comes into play when navigating fewer but fitting alternatives. What results? A smoother path to deciding - without feeling stuck. This kind of support works because human thinking has natural limits. Rather than overwhelming minds, customization eases the load. Studies show it tends to lift immediate feelings after choosing. People stick around longer online. Fewer walk away before picking anything.

Still, tailoring choices goes beyond simplifying decisions - it alters how options are presented, sometimes triggering unanticipated effects. Because systems learn from prior actions, people might keep seeing familiar suggestions, which narrows their range of discovery. Although repeated patterns speed things up, they tend to weaken interest in trying something new, shrinking visibility into different possibilities. Gradually, fewer exposures may make users feel less in control while dulling the depth of what they experience. Especially online - where music, news, or videos favour known preferences - this pattern risks settling into routine without fresh input.

Filter bubbles, Sunstein (2019) argued, frame how algorithms quietly limit what people see online. Hidden sorting mechanisms shape selections without users noticing - freedom feels real even when narrowed. Because choices appear broad but are subtly filtered, uncertainty grows instead of ease. The illusion of control fades as personalized paths replace open exploration. Even with countless items available, only a small portion surfaces for any one person. Discomfort follows when expectations of variety meet invisible boundaries. Skepticism creeps in where transparency should be. What seems like personal agency often reflects coded defaults behind the scenes.

Unexpectedly, customizing suggestions might deepen mental and emotional strain because people sense a stronger duty when picking options. Because advice feels unique to them, users often assume the technology ought to understand their needs perfectly. Should results fall short, dissatisfaction grows sharper - blamed not just on oneself but also on the smart system meant to help. Raised hopes tend to fuel deeper remorse afterward, along with tougher criticism of personal decisions, feeding into why too many choices sometimes backfire. Instead of spreading out accountability, adjusted content pulls it inward, focusing pressure where it hurts most.

Unexpectedly, how people view tracking shapes their response to tailored content. Research by Aguirre and colleagues in 2016 showed that customization might boost helpfulness, yet at the same time stir unease about private information being watched too closely. When users realize just how deeply their actions are monitored, studied, then turned into suggestions, those very suggestions can feel like an overstep - something controlling instead of convenient. Trust tends to weaken under such conditions, despite the precision behind the advice offered. What emerges is a delicate tension: value gained through smart adjustments often clashes with discomfort over silent observation. Most people react differently to personalized suggestions based on whether they believe in the system behind them. If users feel confident about a company's motives and handling of information, those tailored prompts tend to seem supportive instead of intrusive. On the flip side, doubt creeps in when faith in the service fades - then each nudge may come across as manipulation meant to serve business goals first. That wariness often leads individuals to resist advice, wrestle longer with choices, and report lower satisfaction afterward. Over time, confidence builds - or erodes - not overnight but slowly, influenced by how clearly platforms explain their methods, share access, and maintain open dialogue during ongoing exchanges.

When people see tailored choices, how they react often depends on their usual way of making decisions. Because some shoppers care most about saving time, simplified selections might suit them well. Yet others who enjoy exploring possibilities could feel limited when recommendations narrow too fast. Those always seeking the best possible option tend to struggle if algorithms hide alternatives without warning. On the other hand, individuals happy with good enough outcomes might find shortcuts helpful. What personalization does mentally shifts based on who experiences it - its effects are far from the same across everyone.

When looking across countries, how people respond to tailored digital experiences often depends on their cultural background. Because values differ, reactions to customization can shift - some find it helpful, others feel controlled. Where independence is emphasized, warnings about lost freedom might trigger pushback against automated suggestions. On the other hand, settings where group norms matter tend to accept direction if it simplifies decisions. What feels intrusive in one place may seem supportive somewhere else. So matching algorithms to local expectations works better than using a single method everywhere.

Ultimately, personalization tools sit uneasily in online spaces shaped by endless options. Though built to simplify decisions and ease overwhelm, they can deepen indecision - by narrowing what users see, amplifying familiar tastes, while stirring doubts about freedom, data safety, and subtle influence. Their impact on the mind reaches past single choices, quietly shaping reliance, sense of agency, and lasting contentment. Grasping such patterns becomes key when building web services: ones where speed meets human needs, so tailored results support - not erode - overall fulfillment amid growing algorithmic control.

DIGITAL GLOBAL MARKETS AND CROSS-CULTURAL CONSUMER BEHAVIOUR

Not everyone reacts the same way to endless options or tailored suggestions - culture makes a difference. How people see independence, duty, or having choices depends on shared beliefs. With online services spreading worldwide, recognizing cultural contrasts matters when studying digital decision spaces. What shapes reactions often includes whether a society leans toward self-reliance or group harmony, tolerates ambiguity, or accepts hierarchy (Hofstede, 2001). Decisions feel different depending on where someone comes from. One reason people react differently to choices lies in how their culture views individual versus group priorities. Where personal goals take center stage - like in much of North America and Western Europe - making one's own decisions matters deeply. Freedom to choose becomes less about convenience, more about identity. Options multiply not just because they exist, but because selecting signals who you are. More variety tends to feel rewarding, almost like gaining control over small parts of life. For many raised in such settings, facing dozens of alternatives can boost a sense of independence - at least at first glance.

Still, in societies that prioritize independence, having many options does not always lead to better results. Studies show that once too many choices appear, people feel overloaded - this ties into what is called the paradox of choice. Yet those raised in self-focused cultures might tolerate the stress of deciding because they link it closely to autonomy. Even when things go wrong, such moments tend to be seen as lessons tied to personal growth instead of signs of broken systems, which keeps the value of taking charge alive. Unlike individual-focused settings, communities across much of Asia, Africa, and Latin America place stronger value on unity, mutual reliance, because shared bonds shape daily life. Here, picking something isn't mainly about expressing independence but aligning with duties shaped by others nearby. Research from Iyengar and Lepper (1999) shows people in such environments tend to favour decisions supported by relatives or respected figures within their circle. Instead of feeling limited, individuals might feel reassured when selections come through guidance since it eases burdens tied to mistakes later.

One key effect of this difference shows up in consumer reactions to personalized tech across societies. Where independence matters most, suggestions work best if they save time while leaving choice intact. If those same tools feel like control mechanisms, pushback often follows - freedom feels threatened. On the flip side, communities focused on group harmony might appreciate help narrowing options, seeing it as thoughtful rather than invasive. Such systems gain approval there because mutual aid fits deeper values. Same software, opposite effects: comfort in one place, friction in another.

Starting differently each time helps show how culture shapes reactions to too many choices. Where uncertainty feels threatening, people often lean toward routines and defined paths instead of open possibilities. When selections lack clarity, stress tends to rise - this tension can cloud judgment, making outcomes feel harder to accept. Facing endless product rows online might overwhelm rather than excite under these conditions. Recommendations that filter noise into simpler terms appear more useful here, easing mental load without drawing attention to themselves. Relief comes quietly when options shrink through smart guidance. Where uncertainty feels less threatening, people often welcome unclear outcomes and intricate decisions. Exploring wide arrays of options becomes a source of interest, with unfamiliar paths seen as openings instead of risks. When tailored suggestions narrow what can be tried, satisfaction sometimes drops alongside a sense of control. What works well in one setting might fail elsewhere, showing that cultural context shapes how much guidance or freedom fits best.

Although power distance affects consumer reactions to advice, its impact varies by cultural context. Where hierarchies are common, people tend to follow directions from established sources without question. Because of this, suggestions from recognized digital platforms often feel appropriate, even supportive. Yet in settings where equality is emphasized, such input can seem intrusive rather than useful. When automated tools push choices too forcefully, users might view them as overstepping. This perception sometimes leads to wariness, weakening both confidence and comfort with the system.

One way tech platforms struggle globally is through rigid design choices that ignore local norms. Though consistent systems simplify management, fairness often slips between regions. What feels like freedom to some users can feel confusing to others. Depending on cultural values, tailored features might help acceptance in tight-knit communities yet spark resistance where independence matters more.

Because digital spaces span continents, ignoring cultural differences can deepen gaps in how people experience online services. When systems favour Western ideas about independence, they might stress users raised in more communal settings. One way forward lies in designs that shift shape depending on cultural context - offering varied levels of help, options, or customization. What works in one place might weigh heavily elsewhere.

Ultimately, cultural traits shape the way people respond to endless options and tailored experiences online. Where someone stands on individualism versus collectivism affects their sense of freedom and ownership. How much a society resists ambiguity alters reactions to decision-making pressure. Hierarchical norms shift expectations around authority and trust in systems. These patterns reshape ideas about what feels satisfying or overwhelming. Without attention to such contrasts, models risk overlooking key human variations. Designing interfaces without them may unintentionally exclude. The idea that more choices always lead to empowerment does not hold everywhere. Meaning emerges differently depending on shared beliefs. Assumptions built in one setting often fail elsewhere. Interpretation depends less on technology and more on background. Context transforms even basic actions into culturally distinct events.

IMPACT ON CONSUMER LIFE SATISFACTION AND WELL-BEING

Happiness with life involves thinking about how good your existence feels when measured against what you hoped for, believed in, or expected. While feelings at a single point differ, this kind of judgment tends to stay consistent through years. It pulls together thoughts on various parts - jobs, connections, physical state, buying habits - and blends them into one summary view. Though purchases often aim at short-lived joy, they can shape deeper views: people start feeling more capable, grounded, or valuable because of what they acquire. Over time, scholars studying buyers have come to see such broader contentment not as noise, but central to understanding behaviour. What we choose to own may echo beyond the instant it arrives. Life satisfaction often shifts depending on how people consume, since buying things isn't just about goods - it shapes who we feel we are. When choices go well, they strengthen feelings of control and skill. But if decisions keep backfiring, doubt grows, along with stress. Online spaces pile up options fast, forcing constant picks that stack into lasting emotional weight. How these digital settings are built matters - not only for what gets bought, but for how people feel day to day.

Too much choice often works quietly against well-being. Facing endless options, people start to carry mental strain. Because decisions grow harder, minds tire more quickly. As this repeats, picking anything feels heavier. Uncertainty builds, even for small selections. Choosing begins to seem risky, sometimes pointless. The pressure sticks around, shaping how days feel. Even outside shopping, that weight remains. Identity ties to choices deepen the tension. Confidence in personal judgment erodes slowly. Satisfaction with life dips as a result. Not freedom, but exhaustion takes hold. What seems like opportunity turns burdensome. Emotional load leaks into general outlooks. Life appears less fulfilling over time. Too much selection tends to amplify feelings of remorse, along with thoughts about alternate possibilities - these factors reliably harm emotional health. Awareness of numerous unselected paths often shadows satisfaction, introducing persistent reflections on alternatives not taken. These mental loops erode pleasure during actual experiences while nudging individuals toward guilt, linking poor results directly to personal choices. Facing such conditions again and again could slowly deepen discontent, weakening overall fulfillment across life domains.

Faced with too many choices, people sometimes feel overwhelmed. One way to ease that burden might be through tailored suggestions. These systems work by showing fewer options, focusing only on what seems most suitable. Because less mental energy is needed, picking becomes simpler. Helpful advice, when it matches personal tastes, often feels easier to act on. That sense of fit can boost how satisfied someone feels afterward. Confidence grows when selections seem accurate. With greater confidence comes a stronger feeling of control. Well-matched recommendations let individuals decide without second-guessing. Over time, this smoother process may lift general mood. Feeling capable during daily choices matters. Personalized support, if trusted, plays quietly into that experience.

Still, getting more out of personalized systems depends heavily on user perception and interaction patterns. When suggestions feel too rigid or hard to understand, people often feel less in control of their decisions. Relying too much on automated advice might make individuals doubt if their selections truly match their tastes. That growing uncertainty about personal choice can weaken internal drive, dulling enjoyment from what they consume. Because self-direction and genuine expression matter deeply for mental health, prolonged exposure to such dynamics could gradually lower overall life fulfillment. Relying too much on tailored suggestions might chip away at people's trust in their own choices. Because automated systems often simplify decisions, users get fewer chances to weigh options by themselves. Without regular practice, judging outcomes without help grows harder over time. If someone steps into a situation where tech guidance falls short, discomfort tends to rise quickly. Uncertainty builds, sometimes leading to stress that affects overall mood. So even though custom-fit results feel good at first, lasting effects on happiness aren't so straightforward.

Life satisfaction shifts depending on how much freedom people feel when making decisions. When options are limited just enough, and customization feels clear and manageable, individuals often cope better, staying engaged without feeling overloaded. Yet too many choices - or filters that adjust too sharply - can tip things negatively, raising tension or weakening one's belief in shaping outcomes. What matters lies less in quantity, more in whether the process feels guided but not forced. Some people react more strongly to personalized options because they care deeply about making their own choices. While others who enjoy discovering new things might feel limited by automated suggestions, those focused on saving time could find such systems helpful. People comfortable with uncertainty tend to handle large arrays of options without much stress. Yet those who struggle with doubt or worry often feel worse when faced with too many decisions. How someone responds depends heavily on their personality traits. General conclusions rarely capture these variations accurately. Assumptions that apply to everyone fall short in practice.

Around the world, digital marketplaces are shaped by culture and income levels when it comes to how options and tailored experiences impact people's sense of fulfillment. Earlier parts explained that beliefs about independence, duty, and discomfort with unknown outcomes alter how individuals see large selections or automated suggestions. Because of this, an online setting might boost happiness in certain regions yet reduce it elsewhere. Without accounting for such background factors, grasping what truly supports user well-being remains incomplete.

Life satisfaction opens a window into how digital choices shape everyday outcomes. Too many options may lower well-being, triggering stress, second-guessing, and ongoing hesitation. Depending on how strong it feels, whether users see how it works, and if it matches what people actually want, tailored suggestions might help - or make things worse. What happens in the end rests on how selection size, customization, and personal or societal traits interact. Grasping this mix matters when building online spaces that do more than speed up decisions - they should sustain human flourishing over time.

CONCEPTUAL FRAMEWORK AND PROPOSITIONS

This study introduces a unified model showing how vast selection and tailored experiences together affect user well-being within worldwide online marketplaces. With digital interfaces, shopping settings now offer far more products than before - alongside automated tools that sort, highlight, or narrow down possibilities. Even though such changes tend to be seen as giving people greater control, speed, or ease, their mental impact isn't always positive - it may even backfire under certain conditions. Instead of helping everyone equally, too many choices combined with strong customization might create mental load, emotional unease, or feelings of reduced independence, which then ripple into overall judgments about quality of life. These patterns matter especially across international digital arenas, where individuals from varied cultural contexts engage with identical technological setups. What stands out in digital spaces is how much choice people face when consuming. Not like older market types, where space and information kept selections small, online setups let users reach vast numbers of options almost instantly. Even though standard economics says more choices improve satisfaction by matching preferences better, findings from psychology suggest otherwise - too many picks can strain thinking and feelings. Facing endless possibilities means working hard mentally: weighing features, measuring differences, imagining consequences. Human minds only handle so much input; beyond a point, the load grows heavy, turning what seems free into something tiring, sometimes overwhelming.

When mental load rises, people tend to grow weary from making choices, especially online where picking happens nonstop. Moving through options - clicking, swiping, narrowing down - takes brainpower, which drains willpower gradually. Tired minds struggle to weigh options carefully, instead leaning on quick rules, preset paths, or simply skipping decisions. These shortcuts might ease strain at first, yet later feel off-track or unsatisfying compared to what someone truly wants. Heavy choice loads can weigh on feelings, deepening negative reactions. Facing piles of options shifts attention toward what was passed up. Thinking about unselected paths grows stronger under wide arrays. Regret, frustration, or guilt take root more easily if results fall short. When things go wrong, people tend to point inward instead of at circumstances. With countless picks visible, second-guessing rises - surely one must have led somewhere better.

Repeated stress from making decisions may slowly shift how people view their overall life experience. Rather than staying limited to single moments of shopping or picking options, these pressures seep into wider judgments about personal well-being. Trouble choosing consistently, ongoing frustration, along with a sense of being unable to manage routine selections, feeds persistent low mood and weakens confidence in one's ability to act effectively - both key aspects of feeling satisfied with life. As a result, digital environments packed with endless alternatives tend to lower user satisfaction by maintaining high mental demands, exhausting judgment capacity over time, and increasing emotional discomfort, reinforcing the idea that abundance of options does not automatically bring improved happiness.

Here, personalization tools appear not as magic fixes but as practical responses to overwhelming variety, aiming to make choices easier. Because they rely on user data, online platforms shape what people see - using suggestions, order adjustments, or hidden alternatives - to spotlight items likely to match preferences. Where too many options often cause stress, tailored displays help by cutting down mental noise and shrinking the pool of contenders. A narrowed set means less effort to compare, shorter searches, fewer distractions - and a stronger sense of control during selection. With simpler paths come steadier feelings about results, lower fears of picking wrong, which softens the toll large assortments take on mood and satisfaction.

One way users feel acknowledged is through tailored suggestions, which can spark positive emotions. Because these suggestions match individual tastes, platforms seem helpful instead of cluttered, lifting both confidence and comfort levels.

Where options are vast, customization lends a feeling of direction - keeping freedom intact while reducing confusion. With this support, too many choices become easier to manage, shifting how people experience daily decisions. Rather than removing variety, smart adjustments help shape it into something clearer, calmer, and more personal. Still, getting more out of personalized experiences depends on how strong the customization feels and what people think about automated suggestions. When recommendations grow sharper and show up everywhere, they might bring hidden mental trade-offs despite making decisions easier. Too much tailoring narrows what users see, deepening old tastes while shrinking room to try new things or learn about themselves. Eventually, some start sensing their picks come from code, not inner desire. That sense of freedom slipping away matters - freedom shapes mood, purpose, joy. Should algorithms seem to limit choice, people might push back emotionally - feeling cornered often sparks wariness or rejection. Because knowing your behaviour gets tracked tends to sharpen discomfort, particularly if suggestions feel like nudges disguised as preferences. What matters deeply shows up most clearly in areas tied to identity - music, fashion, beliefs - where being genuine holds weight. A recommendation that presumes taste risks feeling like a script imposed, even when it saves time. That tension reveals something odd: tools meant to ease decisions sometimes erode the sense of steering one's own path. Though tailored options offer simplicity, too much tailoring strips away agency, quietly chipping at how fulfilled someone feels living within such curated walls.

What people feel about having many options or tailored experiences depends heavily on their cultural background. Because culture guides views on independence and duty, it affects whether more choices seem helpful or stressful. Where personal goals matter most, picking freely links closely to identity and accountability. Facing too many possibilities might then lead not only to preference but also deeper disappointment if results fall short. When success feels like one's own task alone, endless selection can quietly erode overall well-being.

Where group needs shape choices, people often favour systems that offer clear direction. Instead of feeling limited, guided selections might feel like help. When uncertain situations cause discomfort, tailored suggestions bring comfort. Order within decisions eases tension where unpredictability is unwelcome. Designs built one way may affect users differently depending on background. How culture shapes response matters deeply in worldwide online spaces.

One way people judge how satisfied they feel with life involves thinking about both what they have and how much say they get in daily decisions. What individuals do - rather than just what they own - affects mood, confidence, yet sense of freedom. Digital settings where choices happen tend not to shift happiness directly; instead, they work behind the scenes by altering thought patterns and feelings. Too many options may overload attention while stirring discomfort. Whether customization helps or worsens stress depends on how deeply it reaches into user behaviour. How culture sees decision-making changes whether crowded menus or tailored paths seem helpful - or harmful.

Life satisfaction shifts unpredictably when digital options change. Too much freedom rarely brings better outcomes. A mix of meaningful alternatives helps people feel independent, yet too many decisions wear down mental energy. Structure eases stress, even if it limits customization. Some respond strongly to tailored experiences, others thrive with fewer picks. Cultural background steers what feels right. What works in one setting fails elsewhere. Balance - not more - defines better design.

Altogether, this model frames an abundance of options alongside tailored experiences as influential but double-edged elements affecting how satisfied people feel in online global economies. Too many selections may reduce well-being due to mental strain, tiredness from deciding, or feelings of regret afterward - personalized suggestions might soften those impacts, though sometimes they deepen them depending on how users view their independence and sense of fit. Where someone comes from culturally plays a role too, adjusting how strong these links appear, highlighting that platform layouts must adapt across contexts. Shifting attention toward overall life satisfaction shifts the conversation away from just quick wins like speed or surface-level approval, opening space for deeper insight into what supports consumer health digitally. In essence, designing digital spaces should weigh responsiveness against freedom and lasting fulfillment instead of focusing only on endless variety or automated direction.

MANAGERIAL AND POLICY IMPLICATIONS

One takeaway stands clear for those running digital platforms: too much choice can backfire, even if it seems appealing at first glance. Though wide selections draw users in, they may leave people feeling stuck, stressed, or unsatisfied after deciding. Instead of simply piling on options, attention should go toward how choices are shaped - structure matters more than volume. Personalized suggestions help narrow down possibilities, yet when they operate like hidden algorithms without clarity, trust erodes. Users begin sensing pressure rather than support, mistaking customization for control. A subtle imbalance forms - one that boosts clicks but dulls long-term fulfillment. Shifting focus means weighing mental strain just as heavily as usage metrics. Satisfaction does not come only from convenience; meaning plays a role too. Well-designed experiences respect both mind and motive. Outcomes improve when design accounts for inner experience, not just outward behaviour. A workable path toward this equilibrium involves organized product groupings. Instead of showing every available option upfront, systems might roll out choices step by step, shaping how users engage with them over time. By narrowing down possibilities into layers or categories, people assess fewer items at any given moment, lightening mental effort without sacrificing diversity. Preselected settings may also ease the strain of picking, especially when choices matter less or repeat often. Offering ready-made selections or handpicked "top" groups helps users move through options more easily, reducing second-guessing while still preserving choice. Crucially, such setups ought to shift over time, opening room for people to look beyond defaults when they want, keeping their feeling of independence alive.

Knowing how recommendations work matters just as much as the suggestions themselves. A glimpse into the logic behind what gets suggested tends to shift user reactions from suspicion to acceptance. When systems reveal connections - like past buys, stated interests, or similarities with others - the process feels less like an invisible hand pushing choices. Instead of hiding how decisions form, showing them can turn confusion into clarity. Being upfront about gathering and using data plays a role too. Comfort grows when users feel they control their details, rather than losing track of them. Trust builds slowly through openness, especially on platforms where privacy often seems secondary. Control over how much customization affects their experience gives people a stronger sense of freedom. When users can dial back recommendations or pause automated suggestions, what feels real in their choices stays intact. Platforms that let individuals steer their own path tend to bring greater everyday fulfillment. Over time, these settings encourage continued use - not because the system pulls harder, but because it holds back when needed. Loyalty grows where support shows up without pressure.

Beyond layout choices, decision settings online shift with culture and context. Responses to too many options or tailored suggestions differ by group. Some people see wide selection as liberty, yet feel worse if they pick poorly. Others favour limited picks shaped by others, seeing help instead of limits. Systems serving worldwide audiences need setups flexible enough to reflect such differences. A single design rarely fits all when it comes to user interfaces - shifting expectations across regions demand tailored layouts. Where customization is limited, frustration often builds despite strong usage numbers. Recommendations that miss local context might still drive clicks, yet leave users feeling overlooked. Satisfaction hinges not just on function but on subtle cues tied to identity and habit. Even widely adopted platforms risk emotional disconnect without attention to cultural texture. Looking at things through a governance lens, recent evidence points to rules needing broader scope than standard ideas about consumer well-being - traditionally tied to low prices, availability, or open deals. Digital spaces shift what it means to protect users, folding in mental load, feelings, and how choices affect inner states. Because of this, officials might turn toward systems ensuring algorithms are visible, understandable, making room for people to act confidently. When platforms spell out clearly how they collect information, what drives their sorting methods, or why suggestions appear, individuals gain footing amid complex online landscapes. Features allowing adjustments to customization levels - or stepping away from automated pathways - strengthen self-direction while reducing strain linked to endless picking and post-choice unease.

Still, oversight bodies must see how digital spaces span diverse cultures and legal areas - each colouring what users expect online. Where choice and tailored content matter, a uniform fix for algorithms might miss key differences in perception. Working together, enforcers, tech builders, and user rights advocates could shape systems that respect ethics and local values while supporting both mental health and market aims. These joint efforts may also set benchmarks - not rigid rules - for aligning user involvement with lasting psychological balance, slowly building confidence in how platforms behave. When new tools like generative AI, smart recommendation engines, or chat-based interfaces appear, thinking about right and wrong becomes central to how companies run things and governments set rules. Because these systems react faster, adjust more easily, and feel more independent, the way they shape personalized experiences grows stronger - bringing bigger rewards along with deeper dangers. Convenience and better fit might appeal to users at first; yet, subtle pressure from automated choices could weaken personal freedom and leave people less satisfied over time. Instead of focusing only on quick wins like clicks or time spent, those in charge should weigh lasting effects on mental health and overall quality of life. When digital spaces build fairness into customization, explain decisions clearly, and let individuals steer their own settings, trust builds gradually - even if progress seems slow.

Starting fresh sometimes means stepping outside familiar paths. Though systems often repeat what users already like, adding surprise elements opens doors to new interests. One way forward involves mixing known choices with unfamiliar ones now and then. Instead of only showing predictable results, suggestions framed as discoveries keep things light and open-ended. This approach lets people feel guided, yet still free to wander. Unexpected picks, rotated at intervals, help avoid mental fatigue over time. Enjoyment grows when variety feels natural, not forced. Satisfaction links closely to experiences that evolve, rather than stay fixed. Guidance works best when it does not dominate. A gentle blend of order and chance supports deeper engagement. Life contentment rises slightly when digital spaces allow breathing room.

Long before profits peak, thoughtful design choices begin shaping how people experience online spaces. When platforms favour quick clicks over clear thinking, users might stay awhile - yet feel worn down by hidden nudges or opaque settings. Instead of chasing every metric blindly, some companies now adjust algorithms so customization feels less like manipulation. A different path emerges when interface decisions reflect cultural habits rather than default assumptions. Trust builds slowly, especially if users notice their input truly shapes features they interact with daily. Laws lag behind innovation; however, rules centered on mental comfort could reshape what counts as fair competition. Small shifts in menu layouts or data permissions sometimes ease the load on overwhelmed minds. Wellbeing-focused standards do not block growth - they redirect it toward steadier ground. Over months, not just minutes, loyalty forms where transparency meets genuine respect. Outcomes tilt positive when both designers and regulators treat cognition as a shared resource, not an exploit zone. Digital places thrive best once nobody has to lose themselves within them.

Still, getting choice right alongside tailored experiences matters just as much to leaders as it does to rule makers today online. A mix of clear product ranges, smart preset choices, open recommendation engines users can tweak, along with room to discover new things, helps people think less hard, feel more at ease, and sense control over decisions. Meanwhile, rules focused on how algorithms work behind the scenes, ownership of personal information, and fair ways to customize content keep those methods from nudging too far or wearing users down - instead supporting lasting approval. When such ideas shape how platforms are built and watched over, digital spaces stand better chances of lifting user outcomes while also backing durable company results - all without trading mental balance for attention.

FUTURE RESEARCH DIRECTIONS AND CONCLUSION

One path forward lies in testing the ideas outlined here through real-world observation, looking at how too much choice and tailored options affect people's overall happiness - depending on where they live, what sector is involved, or the situation at hand. Though theory helps explain how digital habits might shape well-being, actual data remains key to confirming whether these patterns hold up outside textbooks. Results could shift dramatically by industry, since decisions around health care or money management often carry heavier emotional weight than picking a show to watch or buying everyday goods. When researchers compare findings across fields, subtle differences emerge - revealing when and why interface choices bend user outlooks one way or another. Surprising insights come not from assuming uniform effects, but from watching where the model breaks, bends, or holds firm under pressure. Looking back at user behaviour across months or years reveals changes hard to spot in brief snapshots. Although momentary feedback shows quick reactions, it misses slow shifts building up gradually. With each return visit, algorithm-driven suggestions start shaping choices, sometimes narrowing what feels like free decision-making. Over weeks, people might notice a drop in enjoyment even when the service still seems convenient. What once felt helpful - like music or product picks matched closely to taste - can begin feeling predictable, almost automatic, reducing surprise or discovery along the way. Still, digital spaces thoughtfully designed - offering clear options alongside room for personal control - can boost feelings of capability and overall life fulfillment over time. Over months or years, studies tracking individuals show how immediate mental and emotional reactions evolve into lasting patterns of wellness.

Looking beyond borders matters too - cultural mindset affects how people see choices and tailored experiences. While some prefer many options, they often face second-guessing and tension when deciding; others lean toward fewer, guided selections to ease mental effort and lessen blame. Depending on where you are, shared expectations and rules shape whether automated help feels helpful or intrusive. Design must adapt accordingly. Work ahead needs deeper insight into such differences so digital tools can better serve diverse users worldwide.

Starting with a mix of techniques tends to work well when studying choices online. Rather than relying on just one path, using lab tests along with user data offers clearer cause-and-effect links. These setups help pinpoint how customization shapes thinking patterns, feelings, and actions. Moving beyond numbers, questionnaires give voice to varied groups reporting their sense of freedom or mental strain after decisions. Meanwhile, systems watching actual usage log how people behave across weeks or months. Digging deeper, spoken feedback from individuals reveals what feels empowering - or draining - during everyday tech use. Such talk uncovers hidden layers beneath scores and stats.

In conclusion, this section underlines how boosting consumer well-being in online global environments means looking past standard measures of interaction. Instead, attention shifts toward broader views of life quality. While wide selection and tailored experiences improve ease, precision, and speed - yet sometimes add mental strain or emotional burden - they come with trade-offs. Long-term, culturally diverse data plays a central role in checking whether the suggested model holds true, revealing limits while shaping smarter platforms and rules. Insights like these help leaders shape digital spaces that balance usage goals with lasting user fulfillment, freedom, and inner health. Progress here hinges on building solid proof-backed knowledge about happiness within tech-driven buying patterns - a move vital for matching new tools with enduring public benefit.

REFERENCES

Hofstede, G. (2001). *Culture's consequences: Comparing values, behaviors, institutions, and organizations across nations* (2nd ed.). Sage.

Iyengar, S. S., & Lepper, M. R. (2000). When choice is demotivating: Can one desire too much of a good thing? *Journal of Personality and Social Psychology*, *79*(6), 995–1006. DOI: 10.1037/0022-3514.79.6.995 PMID: 11138768

Kahneman, D. (2011). *Thinking, fast and slow*. Farrar, Straus and Giroux.

Schwartz, B. (2004). *The paradox of choice: Why more is less*. HarperCollins.

Sunstein, C. R. (2019). *How change happens*. MIT Press. DOI: 10.7551/mitpress/11974.001.0001

Chapter 10
The Digital Diderot Effect:
Ecosystem Dependence, Consumption Cycles, and Life Satisfaction

Pınar Özkan
http://orcid.org/0000-0003-2765-7224
Dokuz Eylul University, Turkey

Ipek Deveci Kocakoç
http://orcid.org/0000-0001-9155-8269
Dokuz Eylul University, Turkey

ABSTRACT

This chapter examines how consumption practices embedded in digital ecosystems reshape consumer behavior and long-term life satisfaction. Drawing on the classical Diderot Effect, the chapter introduces the concept of the Digital Diderot Effect to explain how ecosystem dependence, algorithmic recommendation systems, and platform design intensify cascading consumption cycles in digital markets. The chapter conceptualizes digital ecosystems as structures that actively guide consumption through technical lock-in, economic dependency, and psychological habituation, transforming isolated purchase decisions into continuous consumption processes. It further discusses how these dynamics contribute to hedonic adaptation, decision fatigue, and diminished psychological autonomy, despite short-term gains in convenience and satisfaction. The chapter reframes digital consumption as a multi-criteria decision-making problem and proposes a normative evaluation framework integrating technical compatibility, cognitive load, financial sustainability, autonomy, and life satisfaction.

DOI: 10.4018/979-8-3373-8357-6.ch010

1. INTRODUCTION

Digitalization has not only accelerated consumption practices in global markets but has also fundamentally transformed the relationship consumers have with their daily lives. Today, consumption has evolved beyond the purchase of individual products or services, becoming a continuous and complementary process within interconnected digital ecosystems (Mampilly & Manda, 2024). Mobile operating systems, online shopping platforms, digital subscription services, and social media networks stand out as structures designed to keep consumers within specific ecosystems. While these ecosystems enrich the consumer experience with promises of convenience, personalization, and continuity, they also introduce new forms of dependency and manipulation.

At the core of digital environments, ecosystem lock-in represents a complex assembly of technical, economic, and psychological mechanisms. Through these mechanisms, consumers' ability to exit a specific platform or service network is impeded (Tutor2u, 2023). Compliance constraints and data portability issues are among the main factors that encourage consumers to remain within a particular digital environment. Subscription-based business models and algorithmic personalization practices also contribute to this tendency and reinforce continued staying within the same environment (Parker, Van Alstyne & Choudary, 2016). In this context, digital marketplaces are becoming not only areas that offer products and services, but also semi-closed systems that constantly reshape consumer behavior.

This shift necessitates a re-examination of long-accepted assumptions about the relationship between consumption and happiness. In traditional marketing, increased consumption has often been positively correlated with individual well-being and life satisfaction. However, the subjective well-being literature reveals that increased consumption does not guarantee long-term life satisfaction. In some cases, negative consequences may even be observed (Diener, Suh, Lucas & Smith, 1999). In particular, the hedonic treadmill (adaptation) process shows that individuals adjust to positive or negative life events over time. As a result, the initial emotional effects tend to weaken as time passes (Brickman & Campbell, 1971; Sheldon & Lyubomirsky, 2012). This suggests that happiness derived from continuous consumption may also be temporary.

The Diderot Effect, an important conceptual tool in consumer literature, deserves revisiting to understand the functioning of digital markets. This effect was outlined by Denis Diderot in his 18th-century essay. It describes how a new consumer object creates incompatibility with an individual's existing possessions, triggering a chain reaction of often unplanned new consumption (Diderot, 1769/2005). The Diderot Effect is a significant phenomenon demonstrating that consumption is shaped not only by need but also by the search for consistency and completeness.

In the digital context, the Diderot Effect manifests itself more intensely, rapidly, and systematically compared to traditional consumption environments. Algorithmic recommendation systems and complementary product notifications can fuel a sense of an "incomplete digital self" in individuals. Constant exposure to idealized representations of life and consumption through social media can further intensify this feeling. This process leads not only to the recognition of new needs but also to the creation of new needs. As a result, consumers are often drawn, without realizing it, into an increasingly deep spiral of digital consumption (Consiglio & van Osselaer, 2022; Coppolillo et al., 2024). This process is further intensified by recommender systems and persuasive design elements that exploit the attention economy to trigger unplanned, complementary purchases. Such "dark patterns" within the platform's architecture nudge consumers toward a lifestyle-consistent consumption spiral. This process mirrors Diderot's historical experience, yet it is reproduced in a high-speed digital environment (Srnicek, 2017).

The consumption spiral refers to a cycle in which consumption behaviors undertaken for satisfaction paradoxically produce more dissatisfaction over time. In this cycle, short-term pleasures quickly become commonplace through hedonic adaptation, which then triggers new purchases (Brickman & Campbell, 1971; Frederick & Loewenstein, 1999; Diener, Lucas & Scollon, 2006). In the digital economy, continuous upgrades, subscription renewals, and complementary consumption within the ecosystem fuel this cycle. The abundance of options and the endless possibility of comparison can increase the burden of decision-making and decrease satisfaction (Scheibehenne, Greifeneder & Todd, 2010). At the same time, "frictionless" and automated payment processes can reduce the psychological cost of spending and facilitate consumption (Prelec & Loewenstein, 1998). From an HCI perspective, the "frictionless" nature of digital payments reduces the psychological "pain of paying". At the same time, the sheer volume of choices in ecosystems like Netflix or Instagram can lead to choice overload and paradoxically decrease long-term life satisfaction, despite short-term hedonic gains (Srnicek, 2017). In this context, short-term pleasure may increase. However, long-term outcomes such as financial stress, decision fatigue, and a perceived loss of autonomy may be observed (Thaler, 2016).

These developments necessitate a reassessment of the concept of life satisfaction within the context of digital consumption. Life satisfaction is a subjective judgment resulting from an individual's cognitive evaluation of their life according to their own criteria (Diener et al. 1985). While the constant accessibility and abundance of options offered by digital markets may create a superficial and temporary feeling of satisfaction, due to hedonic adaptation and decision burden mechanisms, this increase may not be reflected in the individual's overall evaluation of their life (Brickman & Campbell, 1971; Scheibehenne et al., 2010). Therefore, the relationship between digital consumption and life satisfaction should be considered not as linear, but as a structure open to diminishing returns. Beyond a certain threshold, negative consequences may even emerge (Frederick & Loewenstein, 1999; Diener, Lucas & Scollon, 2006). The transformation in digital consumption practices is primarily addressed in the literature through two main, yet largely isolated, approaches. The first approach is digital well-being, which examines the individual's relationship with technology within a psychological framework. It focuses on individual variables such as screen time, digital stress, self-control, and attention management. This perspective largely explains the negative consequences of digitalization in terms of the extent to which individuals "manage" their technology use. It often reduces the problem to a matter of willpower, awareness, or personal discipline. In contrast, the platform economy literature addresses digital consumption through structural dynamics rather than individual choices. It centers on elements such as network effects, ecosystem lock-in, data-driven business models, and market concentration. In this approach, the proliferation of digital consumption is interpreted not as the sum of individual choices. Instead, it is interpreted as the result of an "inevitable" economic order produced by platform architectures.

However, the sharp distinction between these two approaches is insufficient to explain why digital consumption has become a continuous spiral. It is also insufficient to explain how and why this process erodes individuals' life satisfaction in the long term. While the digital wellness literature largely neglects the structural dimension of the problem. The platform economy literature, in turn, relegates the individual's subjective experience and psychosocial consequences to a secondary role.

This chapter aims to overcome this theoretical disconnect and conceptualize digital consumption simultaneously at both the individual and systemic levels. In this context, the chapter uses the concept of the Digital Diderot Effect as an analytical bridge to demonstrate how the individual desire to buy and the ecosystem necessity created by platforms are intertwined. This intertwinement is made visible through this concept. This chapter brings together two different perspectives: the digital well-being approach, which explains the problem as a lack of individual self-control, and the platform economy perspective, which sees digital consumption as a result of structural market design. These perspectives are brought into the same analytical frame. Thus, digital consumption is not considered solely as an individual "problem of will" nor entirely as an external market imposition. Rather, it is evaluated as a dynamic process resulting from the interaction of these two levels. While existing studies mostly explain digital dissatisfaction through metrics such as usage time, screen addiction, or overexposure. This chapter focuses not on the amount of usage but on the complementary consumption spiral created by inclusion in a digital ecosystem.

Ecosystem dependency involves not only spending more time; Digital consumption, through new devices, subscriptions, updates, and services, creates a continuous cycle of consumption. This cycle, instead of expanding the individual's choices, progressively narrows them, creating a cumulative erosion effect on life satisfaction. This chapter looks at short-term pleasure from digital consumption in the long term. It shows that when hedonic adaptation and ecosystem dependence combine, digital tools that first improve life can later reduce life satisfaction. They can limit autonomy, increase decision fatigue, and create constant pressure to stay updated. Not only the amount of digital consumption, but also the type of consumption logic that develops over time is examined here.

To address these structural and psychological tensions, this chapter treats digital consumption not only as a behavioral issue but as a multi-criteria decision-making problem. It presents a normative framework based on Multi-Criteria Decision Making (MCDA). This framework brings together ecosystem dependency, autonomy, cognitive load, financial sustainability, and long-term life satisfaction. This framework helps evaluate digital consumption choices beyond short-term benefits and toward sustainable well-being.

2. LITERATURE REVIEW: DIGITAL ECOSYSTEMS AND ECOSYSTEM DEPENDENCE

The concept of a digital ecosystem is central to understanding the structural transformation of digital markets. Digital ecosystems are integrated structures composed of networks of products, services, platforms, and users that are interconnected at technical, economic, and symbolic levels. These ecosystems determine not only how value is created but also how value is captured and how user behavior is guided. Unlike traditional linear value chains, digital ecosystems are dynamic, scalable structures based on multifaceted interactions (Parker, Van Alstyne & Choudary, 2016). For instance, the Apple ecosystem creates a seamless integration between hardware and software, making the transition to a non-Apple device costly for the user. Amazon Prime uses a similar strategy. It offers services such as video streaming as part of the subscription and encourages users to stay within its e-commerce ecosystem. In this way, a single subscription can lead to ongoing and repeated consumption (Srnicek, 2017).

In literature, digital ecosystems are frequently treated as platform-based organizations. In this context, platforms act as intermediaries. They connect different user groups, such as consumers, developers, service providers, and advertisers, and allow them to exchange value (Eisenmann, Parker & Van Alstyne, 2011). The success of these platforms depends largely on network effects. As more users join, the value of the platform increases, which can strengthen market concentration over time (Shapiro & Varian, 1999).

One of the most distinctive features of digital ecosystems is the deployment of ecosystem lock-in mechanisms designed to retain users within the system. Ecosystem lock-in describes a situation in which individuals find it difficult or costly to leave a platform or digital environment. Economic, technical, and psychological factors combine to make disengagement feel challenging or impractical (Farrell & Klemperer, 2007).

This state of dependency is reinforced through investments and habits accumulated over time, rather than rational choices.

Ecosystem lock-in can be addressed across three fundamental levels. Technical dependency arises through systemic incompatibilities, closed standards, and constraints on data portability. For example, when users find it hard to transfer their data, content, or saved preferences to another platform, they are more likely to stay in the current system (Tiwana, 2014). Such technical barriers reduce consumers' motivation to consider alternatives and increase exit costs.

Economic dependence is shaped through subscription-based business models, bundled services, and loyalty programs. Subscription systems that require continuous payments make consumption invisible by spreading it out over time, while on-platform complementary products and services increase the consumer's total spending. This reinforces the perception that consumers will experience loss if they leave the ecosystem (Shapiro & Varian, 1999).

Psychological dependence develops through factors such as habit formation, cognitive load avoidance, and perceived convenience. Digital ecosystems reduce decision-making costs through user-friendly interfaces and automated processes. However, this convenience weakens individuals' ability to evaluate alternatives over time and increases their reliance on “default options” (Thaler & Sunstein, 2008). Thus, remaining within the ecosystem becomes a habit rather than a conscious choice.

When these mechanisms come together, digital ecosystems cease to be merely structures that facilitate consumption and become systems that guide and deepen consumer behavior. Algorithmic recommendation systems use past consumption patterns to suggest related products and services. By doing so, they encourage consumers to choose items that match and complete what they already have. While this process maintains the perception that individuals autonomously shape their consumption preferences, it actually narrows their choice set.

In this regard, the digital ecosystem's dependency provides fertile ground for the reproduction of the Diderot Effect in a digital context. As the consumer operates with the desire to maintain consistency and 'complete' the experience within the ecosystem, a chain of consumption decisions becomes inevitable. Ecosystem design presents this process as a natural and even rational progression, thereby rendering the consumption spiral invisible.

The framework of digital ecosystems and ecosystem lock-in established here constitutes the structural and psychological scaffolding for the Digital Diderot Effect explored in the subsequent section. These ecosystems must be understood not only as platforms facilitating transactions but also as spaces that embody power dynamics actively shaping the trajectory and persistence of consumer behavior.

3.EMERGENCE OF THE DIGITAL DIDEROT EFFECT

3.1. The Classic Diderot Effect: The Search for Consistency and Integrity in Consumption

The Diderot Effect is one of the early approaches in consumer literature that emphasizes individuals' search for symbolic and functional consistency among the objects they possess. The concept draws on Denis Diderot's 1769 essay, where he recounts how buying a new dressing gown made his other belongings seem inadequate (Diderot, 1769/2005). His story shows that a single purchase can disrupt the harmony of existing possessions and create a sense of mismatch. Over time, this feeling of inconsistency can lead individuals to make further consumption decisions to restore coherence.

In its classical form, the Diderot Effect shows that consumption is not driven only by practical needs. People also consume to express identity, status, and a sense of aesthetic coherence. The objects they own become part of how they see themselves. When a new object enters this set, it can disturb that sense of consistency and create tension in the individual's self-understanding (Belk, 1988). This tension creates a need to reorganize the individual's consumption preferences and makes additional consumption meaningful.

In the traditional context, the Diderot Effect is a relatively limited, highly noticeable process confined to a specific timeframe. Consumers can observe and, to some extent, control this process, which is usually triggered by physical objects. However, digitalization has radically transformed the scale, speed, and visibility of this effect.

3.2. Structural Transformation of Consumption in a Digital Context

The rise of digital marketplaces has largely freed consumption from spatial and temporal constraints. Algorithmic recommendation systems, personalized content, and frictionless purchasing processes have both multiplied and structured the choices consumers face. This transformation has changed how individuals make consumption decisions while also reducing the visibility of consumption in everyday life (Ritzer, 2015).

Consumption within digital ecosystems is no longer framed as a series of isolated decisions but rather as a continuous, interconnected experience. Platforms use data from past behavior to highlight related products and services. In doing so, they create the impression that the current experience is incomplete and can be improved with additional purchases. This shift shifts consumption away from purely functional needs toward an understanding centered on the pursuit of experiential coherence and completeness. In this context, digitalization does not simply provide a new setting for the Diderot Effect. It turns the effect into a more organized, scalable, and ongoing process. As consumption in digital environments is freed from physical constraints, the Diderot Effect transcends mere individual deviation and becomes a structural market dynamic.

3.3. The Digital Diderot Effect: Conceptual Definition

The Digital Diderot Effect, as proposed in this chapter, is considered a reconfigured and intensified form of the classical Diderot Effect within the context of digital ecosystems. It can be defined as follows: The Digital Diderot Effect describes a process in which a purchase made within a digital ecosystem, shaped by algorithmic nudging, ecosystem lock-in, and social comparison, leads individuals to see their current consumption set as insufficient. This perception then triggers further, often non-conscious, consumption decisions.

This definition situates the Digital Diderot Effect within the structural characteristics of digital markets rather than explaining it solely in terms of individual psychological tendencies. In the digital context, the effect does not stem only from individual, conscious choices. It emerges from a consumption environment shaped by platform design, algorithms, and curated user experiences.

3.4. Mechanisms that Enhance the Digital Diderot Effect

The emergence and persistence of the Digital Diderot Effect are closely related to the structural and discursive characteristics of digital ecosystems rather than individual consumption trends. Digital markets are not only environments that facilitate consumption decisions; they also produce mechanisms that reshape consumers' perceptions of needs and frame consumption as a normative experience. In this context, the Digital Diderot Effect gains strength through four fundamental mechanisms: ecosystem consistency, algorithmic complementarity, social norm production, and the narrative of the "incomplete digital self."

Ecosystem consistency is about how digital ecosystems present consumption as a holistic, harmonious experience rather than a series of fragmented choices. Digital platforms position products and services as complementary components, creating a sense of "completeness" within a particular ecosystem for consumers. This leads individuals to question the adequacy of their own products and to evaluate new consumption patterns to ensure ecosystem integrity. The discourse of ecosystem coherence reframes consumption not as a rational choice, but as an experiential necessity (Parker, Van Alstyne, & Choudary, 2016).

The second mechanism that deepens this process is algorithmic complementarity. Algorithmic systems analyze users' past behavior to highlight complementary products and services, presenting these recommendations with a high degree of alignment with personal needs. While algorithmic complementarity appears to increase freedom of choice, it makes certain consumption patterns more visible and dominant (Yeung, 2017). This dynamic creates a foundation for consumers to perceive their existing consumption set as 'incomplete,' thereby sustaining the Digital Diderot Effect.

The third mechanism involves the production of social norms. Digital platforms turn consumption from a personal choice into a behavior that appears socially expected and approved. By constantly displaying and highlighting certain lifestyles and products, social media and digital content make specific consumption patterns seem normal and desirable. In line with Festinger's (1954) social comparison theory, individuals compare their own consumption with that of others online, and these comparisons often lead them to question or reassess what they own.

At a deeper psychological level, the Digital Diderot Effect is strengthened by the idea of the "incomplete digital self." Digital platforms present an image of a self that is always more updated, better equipped, and more optimized. Although this message does not influence everyone in the same way, it can make people see their digital identity as something unfinished that constantly needs improvement and renewal (Belk, 2013). Within this framework, consumption becomes part of a perpetually deferred search for competence, rather than a means of achieving self-completion.

When these four mechanisms are considered together, they form the Digital Diderot. It appears that the effect is not a coincidental or individual consumer bias; rather, it is systematically produced by the structural and discursive characteristics of digital ecosystems. Ecosystem coherence guides the direction of consumption, while algorithmic complementarity speeds it up. The production of social norms makes these choices seem normal and acceptable. At the same time, the idea of the incomplete digital self reinforces the process at a psychological level.

3.5. Key Differences Between Classical and Digital Diderot Effects

The main differences between the Classical Diderot Effect and the Digital Diderot Effect relate to the trigger, duration, level of awareness, and degree of individual control. As shown in Table 1, the classical effect usually starts with the purchase of a physical object. When this new object does not fit well with existing possessions, it creates a clear sense of mismatch that leads to additional, complementary consumption. The process is often limited to completing a specific set; awareness and self-control are relatively high because the purchasing steps require more time and effort.

Table 1. Key differences between the classical and Digital Diderot effect.

Dimension	Classical Diderot Effect	Digital Diderot Effect
Trigger	The need for compatibility/complement with a physical object.	Algorithmic recommendation, notification, and interface guidance. (Coppolillo et al., 2024)
Duration	Relatively limited (single event/set completion).	Continuous (streams, subscriptions, upgrade cycle). (Brickman & Campbell, 1971)
Awareness	Relatively high (call/payment friction).	Relatively low friction (frictionless design, automation). (Lai & Liew, 2021)
Control	In the individual.	In platform design and options architecture. (Ryan & Deci, 2000)
Feedback	Weak / Limited.	Powerful (click-data-new suggestion cycle). (Coppolillo et al., 2024)

Source: Created by the authors.

In the digital context, the trigger is not only a personal need. It also comes from platform practices such as recommendation systems, interface prompts, and notifications about related products. For this reason, the process becomes ongoing rather than limited to a single purchase. Subscription renewals, constant updates, and complementary products within the ecosystem keep the cycle active over time. Furthermore, the abundance of options encountered in personalized flows increases decision costs, blurring the line between what the user "spontaneously" chooses and what is "recommended." Under these conditions, consumption becomes less of a "thoughtful choice" and more of a "behavior that occurs within the flow" for the user. Therefore, control is not only determined by the individual's will and budget, but also by the platform's architecture of choices (choice). It is shaped by architecture and design preferences. Therefore, the Digital Diderot Effect should be considered as a platform-based decision-making context rather than an individual consumption reflex.

These dynamics form the theoretical basis of the digital consumption spiral concept, which will be discussed in detail in the next section. As the starting point of this spiral, the Digital Diderot Effect shows that digital consumption decisions affect more than simple utility. They involve multiple, sometimes conflicting factors that shape long-term life satisfaction.

4. DIGITAL CONSUMPTION SPIRAL, GLOBAL MARKET DYNAMICS, AND CULTURAL CONTEXT

The Digital Diderot Effect is not a single result of consumption. It marks the beginning of a wider process that pulls individuals into a deeper cycle of ongoing consumption. This process, which develops within digital ecosystems, reflects what the literature describes as a consumption spiral. In this spiral, people consume to increase satisfaction, yet their actions often create new forms of dissatisfaction (Brickman & Campbell, 1971; Frederick & Loewenstein, 1999). In digital markets, this spiral becomes more complex, shaped not only by individual behavior but also by platform design and market structures (Ritzer & Jurgenson, 2010; Ritzer, 2015).

The consumption spiral refers to consumption behaviors that individuals adopt in order to increase their subjective well-being, but that over time create new pressures and costs that reduce life satisfaction. The increasing continuity and invisibility of consumption, particularly in digital marketplaces, create a fertile ground for this spiral to emerge more rapidly and intensely. Frictionless payment systems, subscription models, and automatic renewals make people less aware of how often they consume and turn consumption into a routine part of daily life (Ritzer, 2015). In this setting, digital consumption may increase life satisfaction, but it also involves structural risks that require careful evaluation.

One of the fundamental dynamics of the digital consumption spiral is hedonic adaptation. Hedonic adaptation describes the tendency of individuals to adjust to positive events over time and gradually return to their usual level of happiness (Brickman & Campbell, 1971). In the context of digital consumption, this process leads to the satisfaction provided by a new product, service, or digital experience quickly becoming commonplace. This creates a situation that encourages individuals to engage in more frequent or more intense consumption to maintain a similar level of satisfaction. However, this tendency points to a consumption cycle that requires continuous reassessment rather than a lasting increase in life satisfaction (Frederick & Loewenstein, 1999).

This cycle is systematically reinforced by digital ecosystems. Algorithmic systems analyze a person's past consumption and suggest similar or upgraded alternatives. In this way, they attempt to compensate for the decline in satisfaction caused by hedonic adaptation by offering new consumption options. This mechanism calls into question the assumption that consumption permanently increases individual happiness and demonstrates that the relationship between consumption and life satisfaction exhibits a nonlinear, context-sensitive structure (Diener et al., 1999).

Another important factor deepening the digital consumption spiral is decision fatigue. At first, the large number of options in digital markets may seem beneficial. Over time, however, too many choices can exhaust cognitive resources and make decisions more complex and costly. Frequent exposure to suggestions, notifications, and comparison tools can overwhelm individuals and increase their tendency to rely on default or recommended options instead of making careful evaluations (Thaler & Sunstein, 2008). Scheibehenne et al., 2010). This raises the question of the extent to which individuals make consumption decisions consciously.

The perceived loss of autonomy that accompanies decision fatigue makes the significance of the digital consumption spiral on life satisfaction more visible. Research on subjective well-being shows that feeling in control and autonomous in one's life is a key factor in overall life satisfaction (Ryan & Deci, 2000). Findings on decision fatigue show that repeated choices and processes requiring self-control can, over time, strain the capacity for self-control and affect the quality of subsequent decisions (Baumeister et al., 1998; Vohs et al., 2018) As consumption in digital ecosystems becomes more automated and predictable, it becomes harder to determine whether individuals truly make choices based on their own preferences. When this dynamic combines with the short-term pleasure that consumption provides, it highlights the importance of autonomy and control in shaping life satisfaction. Indeed, the unsatisfied need for autonomy is associated with different digital behavior patterns; this suggests that the spiral of digital consumption can affect well-being not only through time/cost but also through the experience of autonomy (Hong et al., 2020).

4.1. Digital Consumption Spiral and Life Satisfaction in a Cultural Context

When the digital consumption spiral is evaluated within the context of global markets, it is observed that similar dynamics are reproduced despite cultural and structural differences. Large digital platforms often operate across many markets using similar interface designs, data-driven business models, and recommendation systems. By controlling which content and products become visible, they can make users' consumption patterns more similar across different contexts (Gillespie, 2014; Nieborg & Poell, 2018; Srnicek, 2017). However, it should not be overlooked that individuals' relationship with consumption is significantly shaped by cultural values and self-constructions (e.g., individualism-collectivism), norms, and institutions (Hofstede, 2001; Markus & Kitayama, 1991). Cultural context shapes not only what people consume, but also why they consume and how much control or autonomy they feel in the process. As a result, the same pattern of digital consumption can lead to different effects on life satisfaction in different cultural settings (Diener et al., 2003; Chen et al., 2015). Income level and digital literacy also influence how individuals enter and experience the consumption spiral. These factors affect their ability to evaluate platform options critically and to recognize algorithmic influence (van Deursen & van Dijk, 2014; van Dijk & van Deursen, 2014). For this reason, even if the digital consumption spiral appears as a widespread trend, its impact on life satisfaction should be examined within cultural and socioeconomic contexts.

4.1.1. The Individualism-Collectivism Axis and Digital Consumption Dynamics

Cultural values significantly influence the triggering mechanisms of the Digital Diderot Effect and the perceived intensity of the consumption spiral. In individualistic societies (e.g., the USA and Western Europe), digital consumption is more closely associated with self-expression, personalization, and individual autonomy. In this context, the Digital Diderot Effect can strengthen the feeling of an "incomplete digital self" and turn consumption into a way of shaping and expressing personal identity (Belk, 2013). Conversely, in collectivistic cultures (e.g., China, South Korea, Turkey), digital consumption is deeply intertwined with social harmony, group norms, and the expectations of family and social circles. In these settings, the spiral can be triggered by the need for social approval and belonging; for instance, the prevalent use of a specific platform or device within a social network can effectively lock the individual into the ecosystem (He et al., 2024).

4.1.2. Uncertainty Avoidance and Ecosystem Dependence

Hofstede's cultural dimensions of uncertainty avoidance are a critical factor shaping the level of commitment to digital ecosystems. In cultures that avoid high uncertainty (e.g., Japan and Germany), the structure, predictability, and technical reliability offered by digital ecosystems are more highly valued. This reinforces users' tendency to remain within the existing ecosystem, increases transition costs, and thus deepens the Digital Diderot spiral. In cultures with low uncertainty avoidance, such as the USA and the UK, users may be more willing to experiment and switch between platforms. However, this flexibility can also increase decision fatigue and digital fragmentation, allowing the consumption spiral to appear in a different way.

4.1.3. Power Distance and Resistance to Algorithmic Steering

Power distance affects the extent to which users unquestioningly accept platform authority and algorithmic guidance. In high-power-distance cultures (e.g., China and India), users may perceive platform authority as more legitimate and therefore show less resistance to algorithmic recommendations. This is related to Digital Diderot . This can lead to the effect operating in a more unconscious and automatic way, and the consumption spiral being less questioned. In low power-distance cultures, such as Scandinavian countries, users more strongly demand autonomy, transparency, and control. These expectations can push platforms to adopt more ethical design practices and create mechanisms that protect user autonomy, which may help weaken the consumption spiral (Minkov & Hofstede, 2012).

4.1.4. Cultural Specificities: Super-Application Ecosystems and Platform Fragmentation

The global digital market offers platform models with diverse cultural backgrounds. The "super-app" model in China (WeChat, Alipay) caters to almost all of a user's digital needs within a single closed ecosystem. This strongly reinforces ecosystem dependency and the Digital Diderot spiral, but also integrates the user experience. In contrast, the Western model often involves several separate ecosystems that are partly integrated and partly competing, such as Google, Apple, Meta, and Amazon. This fragmentation can strengthen the Digital Diderot spiral. Users may feel a sense of "incompleteness" and continually try to "complete" their digital setup across different platforms, which makes the consumption spiral more complex and widespread.

4.1.5. Cultural Implications of Hedonic Adaptation

While hedonic adaptation is a universal process, the sources of happiness and the social meanings of consumption vary culturally. In cultures focused on material achievement and status, a new digital product can quickly become a status symbol, accelerating the cycle of hedonic adaptation. In experience-oriented cultures, however, digital consumption can provide longer-lasting satisfaction through sharing memories and social interaction (Van Boven & Gilovich, 2003). This demonstrates that the impact of digital consumption on life satisfaction can vary across cultural contexts.

In conclusion, the digital consumption spiral is a layered process that starts with the Digital Diderot Effect and is reinforced by digital ecosystems. At the same time, cultural values, social norms, and local market conditions shape how this process develops. This process shapes individuals' consumption decisions amid the tension between short-term gratification and long-term life satisfaction. Constant access and personalization in digital markets change consumption from a simple source of comfort into a complex decision-making process. This process depends on cultural context and requires careful evaluation. The digital consumption spiral helps explain why life satisfaction does not always rise with digital consumption. It also shows that individuals must weigh competing factors and cultural values when making digital consumption decisions.

5. LIFE SATISFACTION IN THE CONTEXT OF DIGITAL CONSUMPTION: A MULTI-CRITERIA ASSESSMENT AREA

Life satisfaction is a fundamental indicator of subjective well-being, reflecting individuals' cognitive evaluations of how satisfying their lives as a whole are. In the subjective well-being literature, life satisfaction refers to a stable and overall evaluation of one's life, rather than temporary emotions or short-term feelings (Diener, Emmons, Larsen & Griffin, 1985). Because of this characteristic, life satisfaction offers a suitable analytical framework for evaluating the long-term psychological meanings of consumer behavior beyond short-term pleasures.

For a long time, economic and marketing literature assumed that increased consumption would increase individual well-being and happiness. However, findings in the subjective well-being literature have shown that the relationship between income, consumption level, and life satisfaction is not linear. Beyond a certain well-being threshold, it has been shown that increases in consumption make only a limited contribution to life satisfaction and, in some cases, may even have negative consequences (Easterlin, 1974; Diener et al., 1999). This suggests that life satisfaction depends more on the quality of the consumption experience and how individuals interpret it, rather than on how much they consume.

In the context of digital consumption, this evaluation process becomes even more complex. Digital ecosystems accelerate and make consumption constantly accessible, while simultaneously dynamically reproducing individuals' perceptions of needs, expectations, and comparison criteria. Algorithmic recommendation systems, personalized content, and subscription-based business models transform consumption from a singular action into a continuous experience (Ritzer, 2015). In this context, digital consumption can support life satisfaction, but it can also create pressures that make individuals constantly evaluate and reassess their choices.

This bidirectional effect is more clearly understood within the framework of the concept of hedonic adaptation. Hedonic adaptation describes the tendency of individuals to adjust to positive events over time and gradually return to their usual level of happiness (Brickman & Campbell, 1971). In digital consumption environments, the pleasure offered by new products and services quickly becomes commonplace; maintaining a similar level of satisfaction requires more frequent and intensive consumption. However, this increase does not create a lasting rise in life satisfaction; on the contrary, it makes the individual's evaluation process more complex.

The literature also emphasizes that the effects of digital consumption on life satisfaction are not uniform and vary significantly across individuals and contexts. Digital literacy refers to individuals' capacity to recognize algorithmic manipulation and maintain control over their digital consumption decisions (Livingstone, 2004). Individuals with high digital literacy can evaluate the suggestions offered by digital ecosystems more critically and balance their consumption experiences with their life satisfaction.

Similarly, self-regulation capacity plays a decisive role in evaluating the impact of digital consumption on life satisfaction. Self-regulation refers to individuals' ability to prioritize long-term goals over short-term gratification (Baumeister, 2002). The frictionless purchasing opportunities and constant stimuli offered by digital environments challenge this capacity, making consumption decisions more fragile. This leads to variations in the effects of digital consumption on life satisfaction depending on individual decision-making architectures.

In addition to individual characteristics, the ethical quality of platform designs also shapes this evaluation process. The digital ethics literature reveals that some design patterns unconsciously influence user behavior and weaken perceived autonomy (Gray et al., 2018). Self-determination theory emphasizes that perceptions of autonomy are a fundamental component of life satisfaction (Ryan & Deci, 2000). Therefore, the impact of the digital consumption experience on life satisfaction is closely related to the technical and ethical framework offered by the platforms.

Finally, cultural context also plays a significant role in evaluating the impact of digital consumption on life satisfaction. Cultural consumption norms influence how individuals perceive consumption as an indicator of happiness, status, or success. Cross-cultural research suggests that consumption-based comparisons and related dissatisfaction become stronger in societies where people link consumption more closely to self-expression (Hofstede, 2001).

In this context, life satisfaction is not a one-dimensional outcome that can be considered a direct result of digital consumption. Instead, it should be seen as a multidimensional decision-making area where different factors such as autonomy, cognitive load, sense of control, ethical design, and cultural norms are assessed together. This multidimensionality reveals why multi-criteria decision-making approaches are necessary in understanding the relationship between digital consumption and life satisfaction. The conceptual model presented in the next section addresses digital life satisfaction within this multi-criteria evaluation framework.

6. THE DIGITAL DIDEROT EFFECT AND DIGITAL LIFE SATISFACTION: PROCESS AND EVALUATION FRAMEWORK

This section focuses on the Digital Diderot Effect. It examines the phenomenon not only as a new form of consumption behavior, but also as a multidimensional decision-making process that gradually shapes an individual's digital life satisfaction. The section serves two main purposes. First, it examines Diderot's influence within digital consumption environments. It explains how the impact of digital consumption emerges and the mechanisms through which it is reinforced. Second, it discusses why the effects of this process on individuals' long-term life satisfaction necessitate a normative evaluation framework. In this context, digital consumption decisions are reconceptualized as a multi-criteria decision-making problem.

6.1. The Digital Diderot Effect: Digital Consumption as a Gradual Process

The Diderot Effect explains how, after buying a new item, individuals try to align it with what they already own and often make additional purchases to restore coherence (McCracken, 1988). In digital markets, this effect becomes more complex. It is driven not only by symbolic consistency, but also by technical systems, algorithms, and platform structures. The "Digital Diderot Effect" is conceptualized through a four-stage process described below (Figure1).

Step 1: The Trigger

The process usually starts when an individual buys a product that does not fully fit with their existing digital tools or that introduces them to a new digital ecosystem. A new smartphone, smartwatch, or digital platform subscription can serve as this trigger. While this initial acquisition may seem like a rational decision in itself, it creates a perception of "incompatibility" in the individual's digital ownership set. This situation, as in Diderot's original narrative, is characterized by a disruption of the existing integrity (Diderot, 2010).

Step 2: Structural Accelerators

The primary reason for the acceleration of the Diderot Effect in the digital context lies in structural accelerators. Three key mechanisms stand out at this stage. First, the ecosystem lock-in effect makes it difficult for the individual to switch to alternatives due to technical compatibility constraints (Farrell & Klemperer, 2007). Second, algorithmic push mechanisms encourage the individual to turn to complementary products through personalized recommendations (Belk, 2013). Finally, the individual's pursuit of aesthetic and functional integrity leads to what McCracken (1988) describes as the “Diderot effect”. It produces a digital version of the “Union”. These three mechanisms work together to transform consumption from an individual choice into a structured process.

Step 3: Spiral Consumption

Under the influence of structured accelerators, individuals begin to acquire not only the initial product but also its compatible complementary products and services. The necessity of data continuity, software updates, and platform dependency deepens this spiral (Hanna et al., 2011). At this stage, consumption is no longer a singular decision but a self-reproducing cycle. Each new acquisition generates a justification that legitimizes the next need.

Step 4: Psychological Filters and Consequences

In the consumption spiral, each new digital purchase may bring short-term pleasure. However, this satisfaction fades quickly due to hedonic adaptation (Brickman & Campbell, 1971). The constant need for decision-making, the intensity of notifications, and the pressure to update eventually lead to decision fatigue (Schwartz, 2004). At this stage, individuals may experience reduced digital autonomy and lower long-term life satisfaction, especially under increasing cognitive strain (Zittrain, 2008).

Figure 1. Digital Diderot Effect

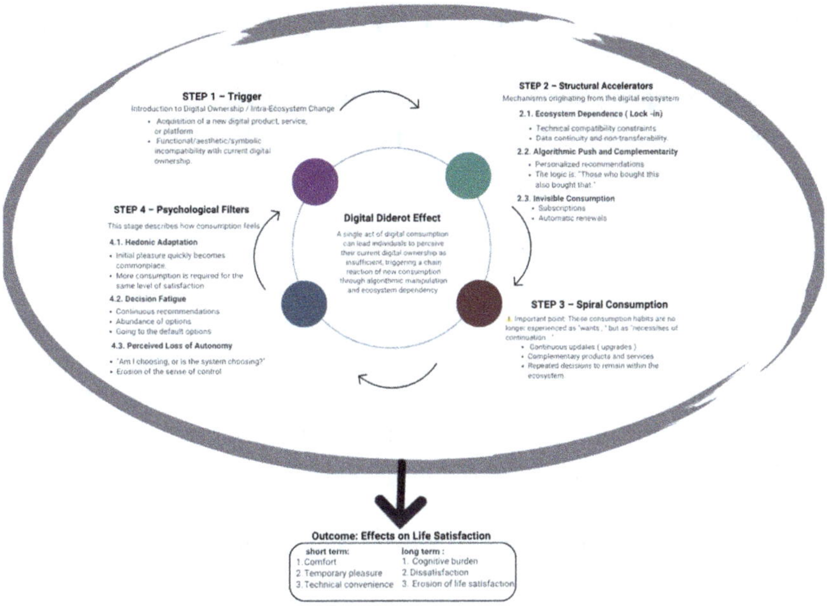

Source: Created by the authors.

6.2. Digital Life Satisfaction: As a Decision Problem

The phased structure of the Digital Diderot Effect, as detailed above, demonstrates that addressing this process solely as a behavioral phenomenon is insufficient. Digital consumption decisions generate a persistent tension between short-term benefits and long-term costs. High ecosystem compatibility and technical efficiency often emerge alongside diminished autonomy, increased financial burden, and rising cognitive costs. Consequently, digital life satisfaction should be treated not as a discrete output to be measured, but as a multi-criteria decision problem to be evaluated. The impact of individuals' digital consumption choices on life satisfaction gains meaning only when considered alongside dimensions such as the perception of autonomy, cognitive load, and sustainability. In this context, a normative decision framework is required to analyze the spiral created by the Digital Diderot Effect.

6.3. Decision Hierarchy and Normative Criterion Establishment

Multi-Criteria Decision Making (MCDA) approaches offer conceptual tools for structuring decision problems when conflicting objectives need to be evaluated simultaneously. In the context of digital consumption, some desirable outcomes for consumers (e.g., high ecosystem compatibility and technical integration) can coexist with undesirable outcomes (e.g., low autonomy and increased financial burden). Therefore, digital consumption decisions should be treated not as a problem of singular utility measures, but as a normative evaluation problem that requires balancing multiple criteria.

Belk's (2013) concept of the "digitally extended self" constitutes an important emotional dimension in this decision problem. As digital products and services become part of an individual's self-narrative, the relative weight of rational criteria in the decision-making process may shift in favor of emotional factors. Rather than ignoring this emotional dimension, the proposed model treats it within the MCDA framework as an element to be balanced alongside other criteria. In this way, the aim is to conceptually constrain unplanned and cascading consumption behaviors triggered by the Digital Diderot Effect.

The MCDA process starts by dividing complex decisions into smaller criteria, following the hierarchical logic of the Analytical Hierarchy Process (AHP) developed by Saaty (1980). This study does not use AHP's mathematical weighting or consistency calculations. It draws only on its conceptual structure to organize the decision problem in a systematic way.

When evaluating digital consumption decisions, we primarily consider functional compatibility, that is, the extent to which the new product is technically integrated with the existing digital constellation, how seamlessly it provides data flow, and how much interoperability it offers within the ecosystem (Hanna et al., 2011). We also examine psychological autonomy by assessing the individual's freedom to leave the platform, transfer data, and maintain control over digital products (Belk, 2013). In addition, we consider cognitive load and reflect on the mental effort created by frequent notifications, the need to learn new systems, divided attention, and constant updates (Zittrain, 2008). Financial sustainability is another key factor; we analyze the total cost of ownership, including the initial purchase, mandatory subscriptions, and related expenses within the ecosystem (Farrell & Klemperer, 2007). Finally, we assess long-term life satisfaction and question whether digital products genuinely support lasting well-being rather than simply offering short-term pleasure (Brickman & Campbell, 1971; Schwartz, 2004).

6.4. MCDA Decision Matrix and Strategic Weighting

The proposed conceptual framework aims to demonstrate how digital consumption alternatives (e.g., remaining within the ecosystem or choosing independent solutions outside the ecosystem) can be evaluated in terms of life satisfaction. MCDA approaches allow for the inclusion of not only technological efficiency but also ethical, psychological, and social consequences in the same evaluation matrix in digital markets (Tarnanidis et al., 2015).

This chapter brings together six key variables that previous research has examined separately and integrates them into a single model, together with the newly defined concept of "Digital Diderot Effect Pressure." By structuring these dimensions within an MCDA framework, the study offers a comprehensive way to evaluate ecosystem dependency and moves beyond fragmented approaches in the literature. The criteria and suggested weights shown in Table 2 are not presented as universal or empirically fixed values. Instead, they represent a normative example based on a human-centered design perspective.

Table 2. Conceptual MCDA Criteria for Digital Consumption Decisions

Criterion Category	Sub-Criteria	Direction of Impact (on Satisfaction)	Literature Basis
Technical Benefit	Ecosystem Integration, Data Continuity	(+) Positive (Short Term)	(Hanna et al., 2011)
Cognitive Load	Notification fatigue, learning cost, continuous decision making.	(-) Negative	(Zittrain, 2008)
Financial Burden	Initial Purchase Cost, Hidden Subscription Fees, Multiple Subscription Pressure	(-) Negative	(Farrell & Klemperer, 2007)
Psychological Autonomy	Platform Dependence, Data Portability, Perception of Control	(+) Positive	(Belk, 2013)
Life Satisfaction	Hedonic Adaptation Period, Long-Term Benefit	(+) Positive	(Schwartz, 2004)
Future Resilience & Autonomy	Brand transition, Data control, Freedom of choice.	(+) Positive	Ryan & Deci, 2017
Pressure of the Digital Diderot Effect.	The constant need for complementary products, the perception of "incompleteness ".	(-) Negative	This is a contribution from the authors.

Source: Created by the authors.

6.5. Threshold Values and Conceptual Strategic Outcomes

Designed to balance conflicting objectives, this conceptual decision matrix offers a normative evaluation framework for redesigning digital marketplaces in a human-centered way. Rather than proposing a directly functioning decision support system, this framework aims to reveal the principles and evaluation logic that can be integrated into such systems.

In this context, it is possible to define conceptual threshold values for specific criteria. For example, when cognitive load becomes too high—such as through constant notifications or multiple ecosystem subscriptions—the negative effects of digital consumption on life satisfaction are likely to outweigh its benefits. In the same way, when psychological autonomy declines sharply, even strong technical compatibility and short-term advantages can create long-term risks for well-being. This type of evaluation allows approaches like digital minimalism (Newport, 2019) to be seen not as a moral prescription, but as one possible result of a structured assessment process based on MCDA. In this sense, consumers gain more than guidance about what not to buy. They also receive a framework that helps them organize their digital choices in a more balanced and sustainable way.

6.6. MCDA Decision Matrix and Conceptual Strategic Outcomes

Within the proposed framework, MCDA is positioned as a normative thinking tool that enables individuals to compare alternative digital consumption options (e.g., in-ecosystem engagement versus out-of-ecosystem independent solutions). Studies on digital markets emphasize the potential of MCDA to model ethical and social dimensions (Tarnanidis et al., 2015). This chapter contributes to the literature by adding the dimensions of "life satisfaction" and "pressure of the Digital Diderot Effect."

The model adopts a logic that suggests avoiding consumption when certain thresholds are exceeded. For example, even high technical utility does not guarantee long-term life satisfaction when cognitive load exceeds a certain limit or psychological autonomy is severely reduced. Such outcomes may lead individuals to digital minimalism (Newport, 2019) or alternatives based on open standards.

The proposed MCDA-based conceptual model is the Digital Diderot. It offers individuals a normative guide to escaping the spiral it creates. This approach allows for a rethinking of digital marketplaces not merely as sales-focused systems, but as decision-making environments that consider human well-being.

6.7. A Complex Decision Scenario: The Apple User's Smart Home Dilemma

To illustrate how the Digital Diderot Effect operates within digital ecosystems, we examine the decision process of a user who is deeply embedded in a single platform. Ali is a professional who has used an iPhone, a MacBook, and an Apple Watch for many years. He manages most of his work, social interactions, and daily routines through the Apple ecosystem. Over time, this ecosystem has shaped not only Ali's technical preferences but also his digital identity and usage habits.

Ali plans to install a smart home system in his new house. At first glance, he faces a simple technical decision between two options. However, this choice carries broader and more complex consequences:

(i) remain within a closed ecosystem fully compatible with Apple HomeKit, or
(ii) build a platform-independent system based on open standards and compatible with the Matter protocol.

The first option, HomeKit, offers advantages such as seamless integration with existing devices, a familiar user interface, and low learning costs. However, choosing this option implies that Ali will largely confine his future consumption decisions to intra-ecosystem products. The pursuit of ecosystem-compatible goods intensifies the pressure for complementary consumption, fostering the Digital Diderot Effect. In this situation, Ali may prefer new purchases within the same ecosystem in order to preserve a sense of completeness and consistency. Over time, this direction may reduce his sense of autonomy and further strengthen the consumption spiral.

The second option, Matter-based open solutions, offers Ali greater future flexibility, cross-platform migration capabilities, and data control. However, this choice entails higher cognitive load, learning costs, and short-term cross-ecosystem management challenges. n addition, Ali's decision to distance himself, even partially, from the Apple ecosystem he has long used may create a feeling of disruption in his digital identity and sense of belonging. This demonstrates that the decision-making process involves not only technical and economic dimensions, but also psychological and identity-related aspects.

This scenario shows that digital consumption decisions involve more than selecting the "best product." They reflect broader considerations related to autonomy, control, cognitive load, and overall life satisfaction. In this context, the Multi-Criteria Decision Making (MCDA) approach serves as a normative framework. It allows consumers to assess options not only by functional performance, but also by their long-term psychological and structural effects.

Table 3. Apple User Ali's Smart Home Decision Matrix: Multi-Criteria Normative Evaluation.

Criteria category	Sub-criteria	Apple HomeKit (indoor ecosystem)	Matter + open solutions	Weight (1–5)
Technical & experiential compatibility	Compatibility with existing devices; ease of use; seamless integration.	✓✓✓✓✓ (5/5)	✓✓ (2/5)	5
Transit cost	New habit formation; data transfer difficulty; time investment.	✓ (1/5)	✓✓✓✓✓ (5/5)	4
Psychological commitment & identity	Brand loyalty; social context; "Apple user" identity.	✓✓✓✓✓ (5/5)	✓ (1/5)	4
Economic cost	Initial investment; subscriptions; complementary product requirement.	✓✓✓ (3/5)	✓✓✓ (3/5)	3
Future resilience & autonomy	Brand transition; data control; free choice.	✓ (1/5)	✓✓✓✓✓ (5/5)	5
Digital Diderot effect	Constant need for complementary products creates a perception of "incompleteness".	✓✓✓✓✓ (5/5)	✓ (1/5)	5
Cognitive load (long-term)	Update pressure; decision repetition; ecosystem complexity.	✓ (1/5)	✓✓✓✓ (4/5)	4

Source: Created by the authors.

Table 3 analyzes Ali's smart home decision within a multi-criteria evaluation framework, taking into account his long-standing integration into the Apple ecosystem. The criteria in the table include technical and experiential compatibility, switching costs, psychological commitment and identity, economic cost, future flexibility and autonomy, Digital Diderot pressure, and cognitive load. These criteria have been determined at a conceptual level based on structural and psychological mechanisms prominent in the digital consumption literature.

The criterion weights (1–5) reflect hypothetical importance levels assigned to the user profile described in the scenario (Ali). They do not claim empirical validity or generalization. In the same way, the performance of each option under the relevant criteria is presented through qualitative judgments. The purpose is not to optimize mathematically, but to make the trade-offs between different dimensions more visible.

Here, MCDA does not function as a classical quantitative decision-support tool that selects the "best" option. Instead, it serves as a conceptual framework that highlights the psychological, structural, and long-term costs that consumers may overlook within digital ecosystems. By including dimensions such as "Digital Diderot Pressure" and "perceived loss of autonomy," the framework makes it possible to consider how digital consumption choices may influence life satisfaction beyond technical performance.

This type of visual and multi-dimensional comparison helps explain why digital consumption decisions often go beyond simple cost–benefit logic and how ecosystem dependency continues to reproduce itself.

7. RECOMMENDATIONS

This chapter offers three main theoretical contributions. Firstly, it reconceptualizes the Diderot Effect within a digital context. The Digital Diderot Effect connects micro and macro levels in the consumption literature. It links individuals' search for self-consistency with the broader market dynamics shaped by digital platforms. Secondly, we reinterpret the concept of the consumption spiral within the context of digital ecosystems. We treat the consumption spiral not merely as excessive consumption or irrational behavior, but as a predictable consequence of platform design. Thirdly, MCDA is integrated into the digital consumption literature as a normative tool. Instead of reinforcing the rational actor assumption, MCDA centers on elements such as bounded rationality, cognitive load, and identity commitment.

7.1. Administrative and Design Recommendations (For Platforms)

Digital platforms should look beyond performance indicators centered on user retention, such as engagement time or cross-selling rates. Instead, they should adopt design principles that give priority to users' long-term well-being. Platforms should increase algorithmic transparency and clearly explain the criteria behind their recommendations so that users understand how suggestions are generated. They should also limit the automatic influence of default settings on consumption and design interfaces that require active user consent and more deliberate engagement. In addition, platforms should support features that reduce ecosystem dependency, such as data portability and open standards. Although these practices may appear to reduce short-term control over users, they can strengthen trust and build more sustainable value over time.

7.2. Recommendations for Consumers: Awareness and Autonomy

From the consumer perspective, becoming aware of the Digital Diderot Effect is critical for making consumption decisions more consciously. Multi-criteria approaches similar to MCDA can help individuals evaluate their consumption choices beyond price and technical features. They encourage consideration of factors such as psychological commitment, long-term flexibility, and overall life satisfaction. In this sense, distinguishing between short-term convenience and long-term dependency, understanding how marketing creates a sense of "incompleteness," and avoiding the idea that consumption is essential for identity formation can strengthen individuals' autonomous decision-making.

7.3. Recommendations for Policymakers and Regulators

The impact of digital ecosystems on consumption goes beyond individual choices and creates broader structural consequences. Policymakers should support regulations that promote open standards and interoperability across platforms. They should also monitor how algorithmic guidance affects consumer welfare and introduce information requirements that make the psychological costs of digital consumption more visible. Such measures are necessary to ensure that digital marketplaces remain not only competitive but also genuinely human-centered.

8. FUTURE RESEARCH DIRECTIONS

This chapter presents a conceptual framework that opens several avenues for future empirical research, while acknowledging certain boundary conditions. First, the strength of the Digital Diderot Effect may differ across socioeconomic groups and levels of digital literacy. For example, among low-income users, the satisfaction of basic needs such as food and housing may play a more central role in well-being, which could reduce the relative impact of digital consumption spirals. Second, demographic factors such as age and cultural background may influence how individuals respond to persuasive design and dark patterns. Comparative studies across different cultural settings can help clarify these differences. Future research should also draw on ethical frameworks to examine the moral implications of algorithmic restrictions on autonomy within platform capitalism and test the effects of possible interventions through experimental designs. Finally, longitudinal studies that explore the link between digital ecosystem dependence and long-term life satisfaction—especially under different regulatory environments and open-source alternatives—would deepen our understanding of ecosystem lock-in and contribute meaningfully to the literature.

9. CONCLUSIONS

This chapter shows that consumer behavior in digital ecosystems cannot be understood only through individual preferences or psychological traits. Platform design, algorithms, and ecosystem dependency also shape these behaviors in systematic ways. Building on the classical Diderot model, the study connects this effect to the structural features of digital markets. In doing so, it introduces the concept of the Digital Diderot Effect and offers an original contribution to the literature.

The Digital Diderot Effect goes beyond a single purchase. It pulls individuals into an ongoing cycle of consumption that feels incomplete and in need of continuation. In this way, consumption becomes a repeated and habitual practice. Algorithmic complementarity, the discourse of ecosystem coherence, and the production of social norms are invisible but powerful drivers of this process. The findings demonstrate that these mechanisms weaken the consumer's perceived autonomy and that consumption decisions are increasingly becoming unconscious.

However, the effects of digital consumption on individual well-being and life satisfaction are not linear. Short-term pleasure and ease of use can be replaced in the long term by phenomena such as hedonic adaptation, decision fatigue, and the consumption spiral. This shows that the personalization and frictionless experiences provided by digital marketplaces do not always improve individual well-being. Under certain conditions, they may even reduce life satisfaction.

In this context, MCDA is positioned not merely as a tool for comparing technical advantages in digital consumption, but also as a normative counter-model. The MCDA approach highlights the trade-offs between short-term gains and long-term psychological and structural costs. In this way, it functions as a Digital Diderot model that helps consumers see the broader consequences of their choices. This indicates that its effect is not a natural and inevitable process.

REFERENCES

Baumeister, R. F. (2002). Yielding to temptation: Self-control failure, impulsive purchasing, and consumer behavior. *The Journal of Consumer Research, 28*(4), 670–676. DOI: 10.1086/338209

Baumeister, R. F., Bratslavsky, E., Muraven, M., & Tice, D. M. (1998). Ego depletion: Is the active self a limited resource? *Journal of Personality and Social Psychology, 74*(5), 1252–1265. DOI: 10.1037/0022-3514.74.5.1252 PMID: 9599441

Belk, R. W. (1988). Possessions and the extended self. *The Journal of Consumer Research, 15*(2), 139–168. DOI: 10.1086/209154

Belk, R. W. (2013). Extended self in the digital world. *The Journal of Consumer Research, 40*(3), 477–500. DOI: 10.1086/671052

Brickman, P., & Campbell, D. T. (1971). Hedonic relativism and planning the good society. In Appley, M. H. (Ed.), *Adaptation-level theory* (pp. 287–302). Academic Press.

Chen, B., Vansteenkiste, M., Beyers, W., Boone, L., Deci, E. L., Van der Kaap-Deeder, J., Duriez, B., Lens, W., Matos, L., Mouratidis, A., Ryan, R. M., Sheldon, K. M., Soenens, B., Van Petegem, S., & Verstuyf, J. (2015). Basic psychological need satisfaction, frustration, and strength across four cultures. *Motivation and Emotion, 39*(2), 216–236. DOI: 10.1007/s11031-014-9450-1

Consiglio, I., & van Osselaer, S. M. J. (2022). The effects of consumption on self-esteem. *Current Opinion in Psychology, 46*, 101341. DOI: 10.1016/j.copsyc.2022.101341 PMID: 35436693

Diderot, D. (2005). *Regrets on parting with my old dressing gown* In D. Goodman & K. E. Norberg (Eds.), *The portable Enlightenment reader* (pp. 417–420). penguin Classics. (Original) work (published 1769)

Diener, E., Emmons, R. A., Larsen, R. J., & Griffin, S. (1985). The satisfaction with life scale. *Journal of Personality Assessment, 49*(1), 71–75. DOI: 10.1207/s15327752jpa4901_13 PMID: 16367493

Diener, E., Lucas, R. E., & Scollon, C. N. (2006). Beyond the hedonic treadmill: Revising the adaptation theory of well-being. *The American Psychologist, 61*(4), 305–314. DOI: 10.1037/0003-066X.61.4.305 PMID: 16719675

Diener, E., Oishi, S., & Lucas, R. E. (2003). Personality, culture, and subjective well-being: Emotional and cognitive evaluations of life. *Annual Review of Psychology, 54*(1), 403–425. DOI: 10.1146/annurev.psych.54.101601.145056 PMID: 12172000

Diener, E., Suh, E. M., Lucas, R. E., & Smith, H. L. (1999). subjective well-being: Three decades of progress. *Psychological Bulletin, 125*(2), 276–302. DOI: 10.1037/0033-2909.125.2.276

Eisenmann, T., Parker, G., & Van Alstyne, M. (2011). Platform envelopment. *Strategic Management Journal, 32*(12), 1270–1285. DOI: 10.1002/smj.935

Farrell, J., & Klemperer, P. (2007). coordination and lock-in: Competition with switching costs and network effects. *Handbook of Industrial Organization, 3*, 1967–2072. DOI: 10.1016/S1573-448X(06)03031-7

Festinger, L. (1954). A theory of social comparison processes. *Human Relations; Studies Towards the Integration of the Social Sciences, 7*(2), 117–140. DOI: 10.1177/001872675400700202

Gillespie, T. (2014). The relevance of algorithms. In T. Gillespie, P. J. Boczkowski, & KA Foot (Eds.), *Media technologies: Essays on communication, materiality, and society* (pp. 167–194). The MIT Press. DOI: 10.7551/mitpress/9780262525374.003.0009

Gray, J., Gerlitz, C., & Bounegru, L. (2018). Data infrastructure literacy *Big Data & Society, 5* (2). https://doi.org/(Original work (published 2018)DOI: 10.1177/2053951718786316

Hanna, R., Rohm, A., & Crittenden, V. L. (2011). We're all connected: The power of the social media ecosystem. *Business Horizons, 54*(3), 265–273. DOI: 10.1016/j.bushor.2011.01.007

He, Y., Zhang, L., Zhang, C., & Zhou, Z. (2024). Hedonic adaptation in cultural consumption: Evidence from China Family Panel Studies. *Humanities & Social Sciences Communications, 11*(1), 1688. DOI: 10.1057/s41599-024-04227-3

Hofstede, G. (2001). *Culture's Consequences: Comparing values, behaviors, institutions and organizations across Nations* (2nd ed.). Sage.

Hong, W., Liu, R.-D., Ding, Y., Zhen, R., Jiang, R., & Fu, X. (2020). Autonomy need dissatisfaction in daily life and problematic mobile phone use: The mediating roles of boredom proneness and mobile phone gaming. *International Journal of Environmental Research and Public Health, 17*(15), 5305. DOI: 10.3390/ijerph17155305 PMID: 32717969

Lai, P. C., & Liew, E. J. Y. (2021). Towards a cashless society: The effects of perceived convenience and security on gamified mobile payment platform adoption. *AJIS. Australasian Journal of Information Systems, 25*, 1–25. DOI: 10.3127/ajis.v25i0.2809

Livingstone, S. (2004). Media Literacy and the Challenge of New Information and Communication Technologies. *Communication Review, 7*(1), 3–14. DOI: 10.1080/10714420490280152

Mampilly, A. J., & Manda, V. K. (2024). Driving Change: Securing Success through Digital Transformation. In *Modern Management Challenges: A Case Compendium (ss* (pp. 196–205). Excel India Publishers., DOI: 10.5281/zenodo.11910143

Markus, H. R., & Kitayama, S. (1991). Culture and the self: Implications for cognition, emotion, and Motivation. *Psychological Review, 98*(2), 224–253. DOI: 10.1037/0033-295X.98.2.224

McCracken, G. (1988). *Culture and Consumption: New Approaches to the Symbolic Character of Consumer Goods and Activities*. IndianaUniversity Press.

Minkov, M., & Hofstede, G. (2012). Hofstede's fifth dimension: New evidence from The World Values Survey. *Journal of Cross-Cultural Psychology, 43*(1), 3–14. DOI: 10.1177/0022022110388567

Nieborg, D. B., & Poell, T. (2018). The platformization of cultural Production: Theorizing the contingent cultural commodity. *New Media & Society, 20*(11), 4275–4292. DOI: 10.1177/1461444818769694

Parker, G. G., Van Alstyne, M. W., & Choudary, S. P. (2016). *Platform revolution*. W. W. Norton.

Prelec, D., & Loewenstein, G. (1998). The Rejection and The Black: Mental accounting of savings and debt. *Marketing Science, 17*(1), 4–28. DOI: 10.1287/mksc.17.1.4

Ritzer, G. (2015). *The McDonaldization of society* (8th ed.). Sage.

Ryan, R. M., & Deci, E. L. (2000). Intrinsic and extrinsic motivations: Classic definitions and new directions. *Contemporary Educational Psychology, 25*(1), 54–67. DOI: 10.1006/ceps.1999.1020 PMID: 10620381

Ryan, R. M., & Deci, E. L. (2017). *Self- determination theory: Basic psychological needs in motivation, development, and wellness*. The Guilford Press., DOI: 10.1521/978.14625/28806

Scheibehenne, B., Greifeneder, R., & Todd, P. M. (2010). Can there ever be too many Options? A meta- analytic review of choice overload. *The Journal of Consumer Research, 37*(3), 409–425. DOI: 10.1086/651235

Schwartz, B. (2004). *The paradox of choice*. HarperCollins.

Schwartz, S. H. (2004). Mapping and Interpreting Cultural Differences around the world. In Vinken, H., Soeters, J., & Ester, P. (Eds.), *Comparing Cultures, Dimensions of Culture in a Comparative Perspective, Leiden* (pp. 43–73). Brill. DOI: 10.1163/9789047412977_007

Shapiro, C., & Varian, H. R. (1999). *Information rules*. Harvard Business School Press.

Sheldon, K. M., & Lyubomirsky, S. (2012). The challenge of staying happier: Testing the hedonic adaptation Prevention model. *Personality & Social Psychology Bulletin, 38*(5), 670–680. DOI: 10.1177/0146167212436400 PMID: 22361725

Srnicek, N. (2017). Platform capitalism. *Polity*.

Tarnanidis, T., Owusu-Frimpong, N., Nwankwo, S., & Omar, M. (2015). Why We buy? Modeling consumer selection of referents. *Journal of Retailing and Consumer Services, 22*, 24–36. DOI: 10.1016/j.jretconser.2014.09.004

Thaler, R. H. (2016). *Misbehaving*. W. W. Norton.

Thaler, R. H., & Sunstein, C. R. (2008). *Nudge*. YaleUniversity Press.

Tutor2u. (2023). *In business and economics, what is an Eco-System Lock In?* Access address: https://www.tutor2u.net/economics/reference/eco-system-lock-in-business -and-economics (18.01.2026).

Van Boven, L., & Gilovich, T. (2003). To do or to have? That is the question. *Journal of Personality and Social Psychology, 85*(6), 1193–1202. DOI: 10.1037/0022-3514.85.6.1193 PMID: 14674824

Van Deursen, A. J., & Van Dijk, J. A. (2014). The digital divide shifts to differences in usage. *New Media & Society, 16*(3), 507–526. DOI: 10.1177/1461444813487959

Van Dijk, J. A. & Van Deursen, A. J., (2014). *Digital Skills: Unlocking the information society*. Palgrave Macmillan., DOI: 10.1057/9781137437037

Vohs, K. D., Baumeister, R. F., Schmeichel, B. J., Twenge, J. M., Nelson, N. M., & Tice, D. M. (2018). Making choices impairs subsequent self-control: A limited-resource account of decision making, self-regulation, and active initiative. In *Self-regulation and self-control* (pp. 45–77). Routledge., DOI: 10.4324/9781315175775-2

Yeung, K. (2017). ' Hypernudge ': Big data as a mode of regulation by design. *Information Communication and Society, 20*(1), 118–136. DOI: 10.1080/1369118X.2016.1186713

Zittrain, J. (2008). *The future of the Internet— and how to stop it.* Yale University Press.

KEY TERMS AND DEFINITIONS

Algorithmic Complementarity: Algorithmic Complementarity describes how recommendation systems and platform algorithms consistently highlight products and services that match users' existing consumption patterns in technical, functional, or symbolic ways. By doing so, they strengthen ecosystem coherence and encourage ongoing consumption.

Classical Diderot Effect: A consumption pattern first noted by Denis Diderot, in which buying a new item creates a sense of mismatch with existing belongings and leads to further purchases in order to restore coherence and balance.

Consumption Spiral: A self-reinforcing cycle in which consumption undertaken to increase satisfaction generates diminishing returns due to hedonic adaptation, leading to further consumption. In digital environments, this spiral is accelerated by frictionless purchasing, subscriptions, and continuous upgrade logics.

Decision Fatigue: The cognitive depletion that arises from repeated decision-making, particularly in environments characterized by abundant choices and constant stimuli. In digital ecosystems, decision fatigue increases reliance on defaults and algorithmic recommendations.

Digital Consumption Spiral: The form of the consumption spiral that appears in digital markets, marked by ongoing and often unnoticed consumption shaped by ecosystem lock-in, algorithmic guidance, and hedonic adaptation. This process may have long-term effects on well-being and autonomy.

Digital Diderot Effect: An intensified and structurally mediated form of the classical Diderot Effect that emerges within digital ecosystems. It describes a process in which algorithmic nudging, ecosystem design, and social comparison make individuals feel that their current digital setup is incomplete. This perception then leads to further, often non-conscious, consumption decisions.

Digital Ecosystem: An integrated network of platforms, products, services, and users that interact through technical, economic, and symbolic linkages. Digital ecosystems shape not only value creation and capture but also consumer behavior by structuring choices, interactions, and consumption trajectories.

Digital Life Satisfaction: A context-specific understanding of life satisfaction that considers how digital consumption habits, platform dependence, and ecosystem design shape individuals' long-term well-being, autonomy, and overall quality of life.

Ecosystem Dependence (Ecosystem Lock-in): A condition in which individuals perceive exiting a digital ecosystem as costly or impractical due to accumulated technical incompatibilities, economic commitments (e.g., subscriptions), and psychological habits. Ecosystem dependence transforms consumption from a series of voluntary choices into a path-dependent process.

Hedonic Adaptation: The psychological tendency for individuals to return to a baseline level of well-being after positive or negative life events. In digital consumption contexts, it explains why satisfaction derived from new products or services is often short-lived, necessitating repeated consumption.

Incomplete Digital Self: The "Incomplete Digital Self" refers to the perception that one's digital identity is unfinished or lacking. It reflects the feeling that personal profiles, devices, or digital tools need constant updating and improvement in order to remain relevant, optimized, and socially validated.

Life Satisfaction: A cognitive and evaluative judgment of one's overall quality of life according to self-defined criteria. Unlike momentary pleasure, life satisfaction reflects long-term well-being and is sensitive to autonomy, cognitive load, and sustained consumption patterns.

Multi-Criteria Decision Making (MCDA): Multi-Criteria Decision Making (MCDA) is an approach that supports decision-making by evaluating alternatives across multiple criteria at the same time. Instead of focusing on a single factor such as price or performance, it allows decision-makers to consider various dimensions—such as autonomy, cost, risk, or long-term impact—within a structured and comparative framework.

Psychological Autonomy: An individual's perceived sense of control, self-determination, and freedom in making decisions. Within digital ecosystems, psychological autonomy may be weakened by default settings, opaque algorithms, and ecosystem dependency.

Chapter 11
Digital Ethics, Data Justice, and Human Autonomy

Deepak Gupta
http://orcid.org/0000-0003-3929-1362
Institute of Technology and Management, Gwalior, India

Avliyakulov Ashurali
Termez University of Economics and Service, Termez, Uzbekistan

Nematova Madina
Mechanization Engineers' National Research University, Tashkent, Uzbekistan

Turanboyev Boburjon
Kokand University, Uzbekistan

Komila Achilova
University of Tashkent for Applied Sciences, Uzbekistan

Mukhiddin Kurbanov
Tashkent State University of Economics, Tashkent, Uzbekistan

Gulchekhra Nazarova
Tashkent University of Information Technologies, Uzbekistan

ABSTRACT

Digital technologies pervade modern life, raising critical questions about ethics, justice, and human autonomy. This chapter examines the intersection of digital ethics, data justice, and human autonomy in the context of life satisfaction within digital global markets. Drawing on contemporary frameworks and empirical research, the chapter explores how ethical principles govern digital technology development, how data justice ensures equitable access and protection, and how human autonomy is preserved in increasingly algorithmic environments. The analysis reveals tensions between technological advancement and fundamental human rights, highlighting

DOI: 10.4018/979-8-3373-8357-6.ch011

the need for comprehensive governance frameworks. Key findings demonstrate that digital well-being and life satisfaction depend on balanced approaches to privacy protection, algorithmic fairness, and inclusive digital participation.

1. INTRODUCTION

1.1 The Digital Transformation of Society

The rapid digitalization of global markets and social systems has fundamentally transformed how individuals interact, work, consume, and experience well-being. Digital technologies now mediate nearly every aspect of human life, from healthcare and education to commerce and social relationships. This pervasive digital transformation has created unprecedented opportunities for economic growth, social connectivity, and access to information, yet it has simultaneously introduced complex ethical challenges, issues of data justice, and threats to human autonomy that demand urgent scholarly attention and policy intervention.

1.1.1 Scale and Scope of Digital Markets

Global digital markets have experienced exponential growth, with the digital economy contributing over $15.5 trillion to global GDP in 2023, representing approximately 15.5% of total economic output. E-commerce transactions exceeded $5.7 trillion globally in 2023, while digital platforms now facilitate over 70% of consumer interactions in developed economies. Social media platforms collectively serve over 4.9 billion users worldwide, creating vast ecosystems of data generation, exchange, and monetization that operate across national boundaries with minimal regulatory oversight.

This massive scale of digital market activity generates extraordinary volumes of personal data. Recent estimates suggest that individuals produce approximately 1.7 megabytes of data per second, with global data creation projected to reach 181 zettabytes by 2025. This data fuels algorithmic systems that increasingly make consequential decisions affecting employment, credit access, healthcare delivery, educational opportunities, and even criminal justice outcomes, raising fundamental questions about fairness, accountability, and human agency in automated decision-making processes.

1.1.2 Emerging Ethical Challenges

The digital transformation has surfaced numerous ethical challenges that traditional regulatory frameworks struggle to address effectively. Algorithmic bias has been documented across multiple domains, with facial recognition systems demonstrating error rates up to 34% higher for darker-skinned individuals compared to lighter-skinned individuals. Predictive policing algorithms have been shown to perpetuate racial disparities, while hiring algorithms have exhibited gender bias, systematically disadvantaging qualified female candidates in technical fields.

Privacy erosion represents another critical ethical concern, as digital platforms collect, analyze, and monetize personal data with limited user awareness or meaningful consent. Studies indicate that the average mobile application shares user data with 10 external entities, while 79% of websites employ tracking technologies that follow users across digital environments. The asymmetry between corporate data collection capabilities and individual privacy protections creates profound power imbalances that undermine personal autonomy and democratic participation.

1.2 Conceptual Framework

1.2.1 Digital Ethics Foundations

Digital ethics encompasses the moral principles and values that should govern the design, development, deployment, and use of digital technologies. Unlike traditional ethics, which evolved over centuries of philosophical discourse, digital ethics must address rapid technological change, complex socio-technical systems, and unprecedented challenges to human dignity, autonomy, and social justice. Contemporary digital ethics frameworks typically emphasize principles including transparency, accountability, fairness, privacy, and human welfare as fundamental guideposts for responsible technology development.

The translation of abstract ethical principles into concrete technological practices remains a persistent challenge. Organizations worldwide have published over 84 AI ethics guidelines since 2016, yet evidence suggests significant gaps between aspirational ethical commitments and actual implementation. Research demonstrates that only 37% of organizations with published AI ethics principles have established mechanisms for operationalizing these principles in product development processes, highlighting the "ethics gap" between stated values and technological practices.

1.2.2 Data Justice Principles

Data justice extends traditional conceptions of social justice to the domain of data-driven technologies, addressing how data collection, processing, and utilization can perpetuate or ameliorate social inequalities. Data justice encompasses three core dimensions: distributive justice (equitable distribution of data benefits and harms), recognition justice (acknowledging diverse data needs and practices), and procedural justice (fair processes for data governance and decision-making). These dimensions collectively emphasize that data systems should not merely avoid harm but actively promote equity, inclusion, and empowerment.

Figure 1. The Digital Divide - Multi-Level Framework

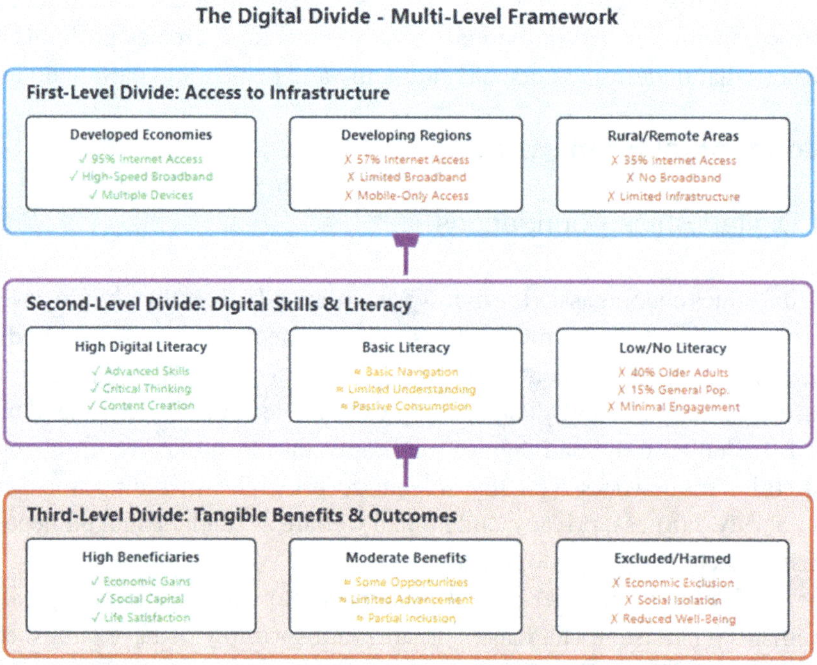

Empirical research reveals as shown in figure 1, substantial data justice challenges across multiple contexts. Healthcare algorithms trained on biased datasets have been shown to systematically underestimate treatment needs for Black patients, resulting in reduced care access affecting approximately 50 million people annually in the United States alone. Educational data systems often lack representation from marginalized communities, while credit scoring algorithms disproportionately disadvantage low-income populations and minority groups, perpetuating cycles of economic inequality through ostensibly objective technical systems.

1.2.3 Human Autonomy in Digital Contexts

Human autonomy—the capacity for self-determination and independent decision-making—faces distinctive challenges in digital environments characterized by pervasive surveillance, behavioral manipulation, and algorithmic mediation. Philosophical traditions emphasize autonomy as fundamental to human dignity and moral agency, yet digital technologies increasingly shape choices through personalized content curation, targeted advertising, and choice architecture that operates below conscious awareness. The tension between technological influence and authentic self-direction raises profound questions about freedom, responsibility, and human flourishing in digital societies.

Self-determination theory provides valuable insights into autonomy in digital contexts, emphasizing three psychological needs: autonomy (volition and choice), competence (mastery and effectiveness), and relatedness (connection and belonging). Research indicates that digital technologies can either support or undermine these needs depending on design characteristics. Social media platforms that prioritize engagement metrics over user well-being have been associated with decreased life satisfaction, increased anxiety, and diminished sense of personal control, while thoughtfully designed digital tools can enhance autonomy through skill development, social connection, and empowered decision-making.

1.3 Chapter Objectives and Structure

This chapter examines the complex interplay between digital ethics, data justice, and human autonomy in shaping life satisfaction within digital global markets. The analysis pursues three primary objectives: (1) synthesizing contemporary theoretical frameworks and empirical evidence regarding ethical digital technology governance; (2) examining mechanisms through which data justice can address systemic inequalities in digital markets; and (3) identifying design principles and policy approaches that preserve and enhance human autonomy while supporting digital well-being and life satisfaction.

The chapter proceeds through seven main sections following this introduction. Section 2 examines digital ethics frameworks and their practical implementation challenges. Section 3 explores data justice dimensions, including equity, recognition, and procedural fairness. Section 4 analyzes threats to human autonomy in digital environments and protective mechanisms. Section 5 investigates the relationship between digital experiences and life satisfaction. Section 6 presents an integrated framework for ethical, just, and autonomy-preserving digital markets. Section 7 discusses policy implications and future research directions, followed by a conclusion synthesizing key insights.

2. DIGITAL ETHICS FRAMEWORKS

2.1 Theoretical Foundations

2.1.1 Ethical Principles for Digital Technologies

Contemporary digital ethics frameworks draw upon diverse philosophical traditions while addressing distinctive features of digital technologies, including opacity, scale, speed, and network effects. Most frameworks converge on core principles including respect for human dignity, fairness and non-discrimination, transparency and explainability, privacy and data protection, accountability and responsibility, and promotion of human welfare and social benefit. These principles provide normative guideposts for evaluating technological design choices and governance mechanisms.

Ashok et al. (2022) developed a comprehensive ethical framework for artificial intelligence and digital technologies that integrates deontological principles (duty-based ethics emphasizing rights and rules), consequentialist considerations (outcome-based ethics focused on welfare maximization), and virtue ethics (character-based ethics emphasizing moral excellence). Their framework emphasizes that ethical digital technology requires attention to both procedural values (how decisions are made) and substantive values (what outcomes are achieved), recognizing that algorithmic systems can perpetuate injustice through both biased processes and discriminatory results.

2.1.2 Principle-to-Practice Translation

Translating abstract ethical principles into concrete technological practices presents significant challenges. Floridi (2021) identified five major risks in principle-to-practice translation: the risk of superficiality (treating ethics as public relations rather than substantive commitment), the risk of reductionism (oversimplifying complex ethical issues), the risk of relativism (treating all ethical positions as equally valid), the risk of compliance (reducing ethics to mere regulatory conformance), and the risk of ethics shopping (selectively applying principles to justify predetermined conclusions).

Morley et al. (2021) proposed "ethics as a service" as a pragmatic operationalization approach, emphasizing that ethical AI requires embedding moral considerations throughout the entire technology lifecycle rather than treating ethics as an afterthought or isolated assessment. Their framework includes ethical requirements analysis, stakeholder engagement, impact assessment, design and development oversight, testing and validation, deployment monitoring, and ongoing evaluation and refinement. Empirical evidence suggests that organizations implementing systematic ethics integration processes achieve significantly better outcomes regarding fairness, transparency, and user trust compared to those relying on ad hoc ethical reviews.

2.2 Governance and Regulation

2.2.1 AI Governance Frameworks

AI governance encompasses the institutional structures, policies, standards, and practices through which organizations and societies guide artificial intelligence development and deployment. Batool et al. (2024) conducted a systematic literature review of AI governance, identifying five key governance dimensions: strategic governance (organizational leadership and vision), operational governance (day-to-day management and oversight), technical governance (methodologies and tools), stakeholder governance (engagement and participation), and regulatory governance (compliance and accountability mechanisms).

Their analysis revealed that effective AI governance requires multi-level coordination across organizational, sectoral, national, and international levels. At the organizational level, AI governance typically includes ethics committees, responsible AI teams, algorithmic impact assessments, and accountability frameworks. At the sectoral level, industry-specific standards and self-regulatory initiatives provide context-appropriate guidance. National-level governance involves legislation, regulatory agencies, and public oversight mechanisms, while international governance addresses cross-border data flows, standards harmonization, and global cooperation on AI safety and ethics.

2.2.2 Digital Platform Regulation

Digital platforms occupy distinctive positions in contemporary markets, serving as intermediaries that facilitate transactions, content distribution, and social interaction while extracting value through data collection and algorithmic curation. Gleiss et al. (2023) developed a systematic approach to digital platform regulation, identifying common regulatory patterns across competition law, consumer protection, content moderation, and data governance. Their analysis demonstrates that platforms require specialized regulatory frameworks that address network effects, multi-sided markets, data advantages, and algorithmic control that traditional regulatory approaches fail to capture adequately.

Effective platform regulation balances multiple objectives including promoting competition and innovation, protecting consumer welfare and privacy, ensuring content quality and safety, preventing discrimination and manipulation, and supporting democratic values and public discourse. Recent regulatory initiatives such as the European Union's Digital Services Act and Digital Markets Act exemplify comprehensive approaches that combine ex-ante rules (preventive measures) with ex-post enforcement (responsive actions), creating accountability mechanisms that address platform power while preserving beneficial innovation.

2.3 Privacy and Data Protection

2.2.3 GDPR Impact and Limitations

The European Union's General Data Protection Regulation (GDPR), implemented in 2018, represents the most comprehensive data protection framework globally, establishing strong individual rights, organizational accountability requirements, and substantial enforcement mechanisms. Kollnig et al. (2021) examined tracking in mobile applications before and after GDPR implementation, finding that while GDPR prompted some reduction in third-party tracking, substantial data collection and sharing persisted. Their analysis revealed that 88% of applications continued sharing data with third-party trackers post-GDPR, though the average number of trackers per application decreased from 10.6 to 9.7.

These findings highlight both GDPR's partial effectiveness and its limitations. On the positive side, GDPR has increased transparency through privacy policies, strengthened user rights regarding data access and deletion, and established accountability through data protection impact assessments and privacy-by-design requirements. However, implementation gaps persist due to enforcement resource constraints, technical complexity obscuring data practices, consent fatigue reducing meaningful user choice, and challenges addressing cross-border data flows. Additionally, GDPR's focus on individual consent may inadequately address collective data harms and systemic privacy threats.

2.2.4 Emerging Privacy Challenges

Digital technologies continue generating novel privacy challenges that existing frameworks struggle to address. Facial recognition technologies now enable real-time mass surveillance with minimal human oversight, raising concerns about chilling effects on public behavior, discriminatory targeting of marginalized communities, and erosion of anonymous public participation essential to democratic societies. Murray (2024) argued that ubiquitous facial recognition fundamentally threatens human rights frameworks premised on protected private spheres, while Qandeel (2024) examined regulatory approaches emphasizing that facial recognition regulation must balance legitimate security interests against fundamental rights to privacy, assembly, and expression.

Internet of Things (IoT) devices introduce additional privacy vulnerabilities, with smart home devices, wearable technologies, and connected vehicles collecting continuous data streams about intimate aspects of daily life. Research indicates that the average smart home contains 17 connected devices, many lacking basic security protections, while data sharing practices often extend beyond the immediate service provider to include numerous third parties. The ambient and pervasive nature of IoT surveillance creates privacy harms distinct from traditional data collection, operating continuously and invisibly while generating inferences about behavior, relationships, and identity that individuals never explicitly disclosed.

3. DATA JUSTICE AND EQUITY

3.1 Conceptual Foundations

3.1.1 Defining Data Justice

Data justice extends traditional social justice frameworks to address how data-driven technologies can perpetuate or challenge structural inequalities. Dencik and Sanchez-Monedero (2022) conceptualized data justice as encompassing three interconnected dimensions that together address power asymmetries in data ecosystems. Distributive data justice concerns the equitable distribution of benefits, harms, rights, and resources generated through data systems, questioning who profits from data extraction and who bears risks and costs. Recognition data justice addresses whose perspectives, needs, and values are acknowledged and represented in data collection, processing, and application, challenging erasure and invisibility of marginalized groups. Procedural data justice focuses on fair, transparent, and participatory processes for data governance, decision-making, and accountability.

This multidimensional conception reveals that data injustice operates through multiple mechanisms simultaneously. Marginalized communities often experience the harms of data systems (discriminatory algorithms, privacy violations, surveillance) while being excluded from benefits (economic opportunities, service improvements, empowerment). Their experiences and knowledge are frequently unrecognized in system design, while they lack meaningful participation in governance decisions affecting their lives. Addressing data justice therefore requires coordinated interventions targeting distribution, recognition, and procedure rather than isolated technical fixes.

3.1.2 Data Equity Frameworks

Jagadish et al. (2023) developed a comprehensive framework examining multiple facets of data equity, including access equity (fair access to data and data systems), representation equity (adequate and accurate representation in datasets), algorithmic equity (fair treatment by data-driven systems), literacy equity (capability to understand and engage with data), and benefit equity (fair distribution of value created through data). Their analysis demonstrates that each equity dimension presents distinctive challenges requiring tailored interventions.

Access equity addresses digital divides limiting who can participate in data-driven economies and societies. Representation equity confronts systematic biases in training datasets that render algorithmic systems less accurate or more harmful for underrepresented groups. Algorithmic equity examines how decision systems can perpetuate discrimination even when using seemingly neutral criteria. Literacy equity recognizes that effective data engagement requires knowledge and skills unequally distributed across populations. Benefit equity questions how economic value extracted through data collection and analysis is distributed, often flowing disproportionately to powerful corporations while the individuals generating data receive minimal compensation or control.

3.2 Algorithmic Fairness

3.2.1 Bias Sources and Manifestations

Algorithmic bias emerges from multiple sources throughout the machine learning pipeline, creating discriminatory outcomes even when developers pursue neutrality. Training data bias occurs when datasets inadequately represent population diversity or reflect historical discrimination. For example, facial recognition systems trained predominantly on lighter-skinned male faces demonstrate significantly higher error rates for darker-skinned females. Historical hiring data reflecting past discrimination leads to algorithms that perpetuate gender and racial disparities. Medical datasets overrepresenting certain populations produce diagnostic tools less effective for underrepresented groups.

Ferrara (2024) systematically reviewed sources, impacts, and mitigation strategies for fairness and bias in AI systems, identifying additional bias sources including feature selection bias (choosing variables that serve as proxies for protected characteristics), algorithmic bias (model architectures and optimization criteria that disadvantage certain groups), evaluation bias (testing and validation procedures that fail to detect disparate impacts), and deployment bias (application contexts or user interactions that generate discriminatory outcomes). The complexity of bias sources means that addressing any single source proves insufficient; comprehensive fairness requires attention to the entire socio-technical system.

3.2.2 Fairness Metrics and Trade-offs

Measuring algorithmic fairness presents theoretical and practical challenges. Starke et al. (2022) reviewed fairness perceptions in algorithmic decision-making, identifying multiple fairness criteria including demographic parity (equal selection rates across groups), equalized odds (equal true positive and false positive rates), predictive parity (equal positive predictive values), and individual fairness (similar treatment of similar individuals). Mathematical analysis demonstrates that these criteria conflict under realistic conditions, creating unavoidable trade-offs where optimizing one fairness metric degrades others.

Yang et al. (2023) developed deep reinforcement learning approaches for fairness and bias mitigation in clinical machine learning, demonstrating methods to balance multiple fairness objectives while maintaining predictive accuracy. Their work illustrates that fairness optimization requires explicit value judgments about which fairness criteria matter most in specific contexts, informed by stakeholder input and ethical analysis rather than purely technical considerations. Participatory approaches to fairness metric selection, involving affected communities in defining fairness requirements, can enhance both the legitimacy and effectiveness of fairness interventions.

3.3 Digital Inclusion and Access

3.3.1 The Digital Divide

The digital divide encompasses multiple dimensions of technological inequality that limit who can participate effectively in digital societies and economies. Lythreatis et al. (2022) conducted a comprehensive review of digital divide research, identifying three levels: first-level divide (access to digital infrastructure and devices), second-level divide (digital skills and literacies), and third-level divide (capacity to translate digital engagement into tangible benefits and outcomes). Their analysis reveals that while basic internet access has expanded globally, substantial inequalities persist regarding quality of access, skills to use technologies effectively, and ability to leverage digital tools for social and economic advancement.

Socioeconomic status, geographic location, age, education, gender, race, and disability status all correlate with digital access and skills. In developed economies, approximately 15% of adults lack basic digital literacy, rising to over 40% among older adults and low-income populations. In developing regions, infrastructure limitations, affordability barriers, and cultural factors constrain access, with only 57% of the global population having internet access as of 2023. These divides create compounding disadvantages as economic opportunities, government services, education, and social participation increasingly require digital engagement.

3.3.2 Inclusion Strategies and Interventions

Addressing digital divides requires comprehensive strategies targeting infrastructure, affordability, skills, and meaningful engagement. Fisk et al. (2023) examined how digital inclusion can heal digital divides through human capability development, emphasizing that inclusion extends beyond mere access to encompass empowered participation and value creation. Their framework highlights service design principles including accessibility (ensuring technologies work for diverse users including those with disabilities), affordability (reducing cost barriers through subsidies or free services), availability (expanding infrastructure to underserved areas), and ability (building digital literacies through education and support).

Méndez-Domínguez et al. (2023) examined digital literacy programs as tools for social inclusion, finding that effective interventions combine technical skill development with critical digital literacy (understanding privacy, evaluating online information, recognizing manipulation) and participatory literacy (engaging in digital civic participation and content creation). Their research demonstrates that sustained support and culturally relevant programming significantly improve outcomes, particularly for marginalized populations who face multiple barriers. However, addressing structural inequalities requires complementary interventions targeting the design of digital systems themselves to ensure accessibility and inclusion rather than placing full responsibility on disadvantaged users to adapt to exclusionary technologies.

Figure 2. Error rates across demographics and real data: 22% (light-skinned male) to 34% (dark-skinned female).

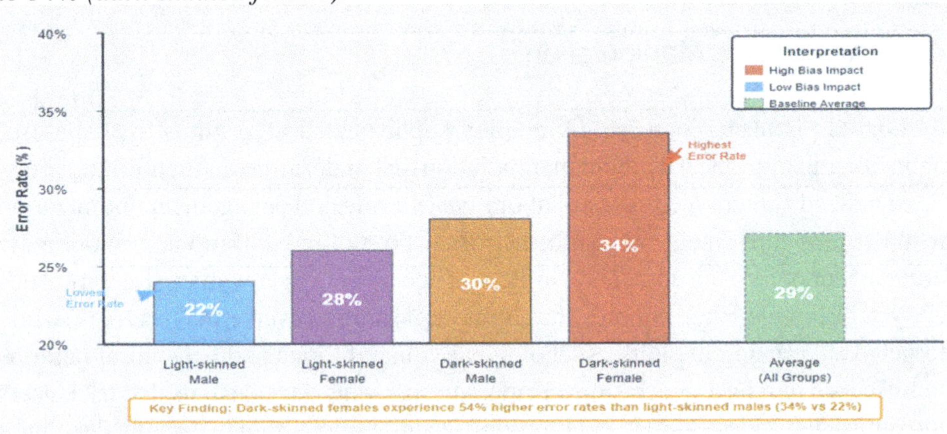

4. HUMAN AUTONOMY IN DIGITAL ENVIRONMENTS

4.1 Autonomy Threats and Challenges

4.1.1 Surveillance and Control

Pervasive digital surveillance fundamentally threatens human autonomy by creating environments of constant monitoring that shape behavior through awareness of being watched. While traditional surveillance typically involved targeted observation of specific individuals or groups, contemporary digital surveillance operates continuously, capturing data from billions of people through smartphones, web browsers, IoT devices, social media platforms, and public sensors. This ubiquitous data collection enables detailed behavioral tracking, predictive analytics, and targeted interventions that operate with minimal transparency or accountability.

Research demonstrates that surveillance awareness produces chilling effects on behavior, with individuals self-censoring speech, avoiding certain associations, and conforming to perceived expectations when they believe they are being monitored. These effects extend beyond obviously sensitive domains like political activism to encompass everyday choices about consumption, entertainment, health, and social interaction. The psychological burden of continuous surveillance includes increased anxiety, reduced spontaneity, and diminished sense of privacy as a protected sphere for autonomous self-development. Moreover, surveillance systems often embed discriminatory biases, subjecting marginalized communities to disproportionate monitoring and control.

4.1.2 Algorithmic Manipulation

Digital platforms increasingly employ sophisticated algorithms to shape user behavior, raising concerns about manipulation that undermines authentic autonomy. Personalized content feeds use collaborative filtering and engagement optimization to maximize time spent on platforms, often promoting sensational, emotionally arousing, or polarizing content regardless of accuracy or user welfare. Recommender systems create filter bubbles that limit exposure to diverse perspectives, while targeted advertising exploits psychological vulnerabilities and behavioral patterns to influence purchasing decisions. Dark patterns—interface designs that trick users into unwanted actions—further compromise autonomous choice through deception and manipulation.

The scale and opacity of algorithmic influence distinguishes contemporary manipulation from traditional advertising and persuasion. Algorithms process thousands of data points about each individual to identify psychological vulnerabilities and optimal persuasion strategies, operating continuously across multiple touchpoints with minimal user awareness. A/B testing enables platforms to rapidly iterate and optimize manipulative techniques. Research indicates that many users underestimate algorithmic influence on their choices, attributing algorithm-shaped preferences and beliefs to autonomous judgment. This "illusion of control" makes manipulation particularly insidious, as individuals fail to recognize threats to their autonomy.

4.2 Autonomy-Preserving Design

4.2.1 Self-Determination Theory Applications

Self-determination theory (SDT) provides valuable frameworks for designing digital technologies that support rather than undermine human autonomy. Gagné et al. (2022) applied SDT to understand and shape the future of work, emphasizing three basic psychological needs: autonomy (experiencing volition and psychological freedom), competence (feeling effective and capable), and relatedness (experiencing connection and belonging). Digital systems supporting these needs enhance well-being and intrinsic motivation, while those thwarting needs produce frustration, alienation, and reduced life satisfaction.

Dietrich et al. (2024) conducted a scoping review of autonomy experiences in digital technology use through an SDT lens, identifying design characteristics that support or undermine autonomy. Autonomy-supportive designs provide meaningful choice and control, transparent information enabling informed decisions, customization options allowing personal preferences, and respect for user agency without coercion or manipulation. Competence-supportive designs offer appropriate challenges matched to skill levels, constructive feedback facilitating learning, and scaffolding that builds capabilities. Relatedness-supportive designs enable authentic social connection, foster belonging and community, and facilitate meaningful collaboration.

4.2.2 Transparency and Explainability

Transparency and explainability enable informed autonomous choice by revealing how digital systems collect data, make decisions, and affect user experiences. However, achieving meaningful transparency presents significant challenges. Technical complexity makes many algorithmic processes difficult to explain even to experts, while trade-offs exist between accuracy and interpretability in machine learning models. Organizations may resist transparency due to proprietary concerns or fear of revealing discriminatory practices. Users vary in preferences and capacities for engaging with technical explanations, with some desiring detailed information while others find excessive detail overwhelming.

Ryan and Stahl (2021) examined AI ethics guidelines for developers and users, emphasizing that transparency requirements should be context-sensitive and user-centered rather than pursuing disclosure for its own sake. Effective transparency initiatives identify what information stakeholders need to make informed decisions, present information in accessible formats tailored to different audiences, and create mechanisms for meaningful engagement and recourse when concerns arise. Explainability should enable understanding of both individual decisions (why did the algorithm produce this specific outcome?) and systemic patterns (what general logic governs algorithmic behavior?), empowering users to anticipate and respond to automated decision-making.

4.3 Consent and User Control

4.3.1 Informed Consent Limitations

Informed consent serves as a foundational mechanism for protecting autonomy in data collection and use, yet significant evidence questions whether current consent practices achieve meaningful autonomy protection. Research indicates that the average user would need approximately 76 working days per year to read all privacy policies for services they use, while policy language typically requires college-level reading skills despite being legally binding on all users regardless of education. Studies demonstrate that 74% of users accept default privacy settings without modification, while consent fatigue leads to blanket acceptance of terms without meaningful review.

Moreover, informed consent presupposes knowledge and understanding that may be impossible to achieve given the complexity and unpredictability of data processing. Users cannot meaningfully consent to data uses they cannot anticipate, yet machine learning enables novel inferences and applications unforeseen when data was initially collected. The networked nature of data systems means that individual consent decisions have collective consequences affecting others, raising questions about whether purely individual consent adequately protects group privacy and autonomy. These limitations suggest that consent alone proves insufficient, requiring complementary protections including robust default privacy settings, meaningful data minimization, and regulatory oversight.

4.3.2 Empowering User Agency

Beyond consent, empowering genuine user agency requires providing meaningful control over digital experiences and data practices. Effective agency support includes granular privacy controls allowing nuanced preferences rather than binary all-or-nothing choices, interoperability and portability enabling users to switch services without losing accumulated data and connections, and transparency tools providing visibility into data collection and use. Additionally, collective action mechanisms such as user cooperatives, data trusts, and participatory governance can amplify individual agency through coordinated power.

Tarnanidis T. et al. (2026) Design strategies supporting agency include privacy dashboards that visualize data flows and enable management, algorithmic choice allowing users to select among multiple recommendation approaches, and contestability mechanisms enabling users to challenge and correct algorithmic decisions. However, research cautions against placing excessive responsibility on individuals to protect their own autonomy through constant vigilance and complex privacy management. Truly autonomy-preserving systems should respect user agency by default through privacy-protective designs, requiring active effort to reduce rather than increase privacy and autonomy protections.

5. DIGITAL WELL-BEING AND LIFE SATISFACTION

5.1 Conceptualizing Digital Well-Being

5.1.1 Definitions and Dimensions

Digital well-being encompasses the subjective and objective states of human flourishing in contexts shaped by digital technologies. Smits et al. (2022) conducted a systematic scoping review of digital well-being research, identifying five core dimensions: emotional well-being (positive affect and life satisfaction), social well-being (relationships and connections), physical well-being (health outcomes), cognitive well-being (attention and information processing), and behavioral well-being (self-regulation and healthy technology use patterns). Their analysis reveals that digital technologies can enhance or undermine each dimension depending on design characteristics, usage patterns, and individual differences.

Büchi (2024) developed comprehensive digital well-being theory emphasizing that well-being outcomes depend on alignment between technological affordances and human needs and values. Technologies supporting autonomy, competence, and relatedness tend to enhance well-being, while those fostering passive consumption, social comparison, or dependence undermine flourishing. Context matters significantly, with the same technology potentially supporting well-being in some situations while harming it in others. For example, social media can facilitate valuable connection and support for geographically isolated individuals while simultaneously promoting envy, anxiety, and social comparison in other contexts.

5.1.2 Measurement Approaches

Measuring digital well-being presents methodological challenges given its multidimensional nature and context-dependence. Cao and Li (2023) reviewed digital well-being measurement in early childhood, identifying diverse approaches including self-report measures (subjective well-being scales), behavioral indicators (screen time, usage patterns), physiological measures (sleep quality, physical activity), social measures (relationship quality, social skills), and cognitive assessments (attention span, executive function). Each approach offers distinctive insights while presenting limitations regarding validity, reliability, and comprehensiveness.

Emerging measurement strategies employ experience sampling methods that capture in-the-moment experiences rather than retrospective global assessments, reducing recall bias and capturing contextual variation. Digital trace data from smartphone and platform usage provides objective behavioral information, though raises privacy concerns and may not directly indicate subjective well-being. Multi-method approaches combining self-report, behavioral, and physiological measures offer the most comprehensive assessment, though require greater participant burden and resources. Importantly, effective measurement must attend to both central tendencies and individual differences, recognizing that technology effects vary substantially across persons and contexts.

5.2 Technology Use and Life Satisfaction

5.2.1 Social Media and Well-Being

Social media presents complex and often contradictory relationships with life satisfaction and well-being. Meng et al. (2023) examined mobile social media use and life satisfaction among adolescents through a moderated mediation model, finding that social media effects depend on both usage patterns and psychological processes. Active social media use involving posting content, commenting, and direct communication associated with enhanced life satisfaction through increased social capital and connection. Passive consumption involving scrolling feeds without engagement related to decreased satisfaction through upward social comparison and envy.

The relationship between social media use and well-being also depends on what social media displaces. When social media substitutes for in-person interaction or displaces sleep, physical activity, or academic work, negative well-being effects emerge. However, when social media supplements rather than replaces offline activities or enables connections otherwise impossible due to distance or disability, positive effects occur. Individual differences including self-esteem, social anxiety, and loneliness moderate social media impacts, with vulnerable individuals potentially experiencing greater harms but also greater benefits from online connection and support.

5.2.2 Digital Technology in Work Contexts

Digital technologies fundamentally reshape work experiences with mixed implications for life satisfaction. On one hand, digital tools enable flexibility, remote work, skill development, and access to global opportunities that can enhance autonomy, work-life balance, and career satisfaction. On the other hand, constant connectivity blurs work-life boundaries, algorithmic management reduces autonomy, surveillance increases stress, and automation threatens employment security. Research indicates that 67% of remote workers report difficulty disconnecting from work, while platform workers describe algorithmic management as undermining dignity and control.

The impact of workplace digital technologies on life satisfaction depends critically on whether implementations respect worker agency and support basic psychological needs. Technologies imposed without consultation, constraining autonomy, and intensifying monitoring consistently harm well-being regardless of potential efficiency gains. Conversely, technologies designed collaboratively with workers, enhancing rather than replacing human judgment, and supporting skill development can improve both productivity and satisfaction. Organizational culture, power dynamics, and regulatory protections shape whether digital work technologies enhance or undermine human flourishing.

5.3 Digital Markets and Consumer Well-Being

5.3.1 Personalization and Choice

Digital markets increasingly employ personalization to match products and services to individual preferences, with ambiguous effects on consumer well-being. Effective personalization can reduce information overload, discovery costs, and mismatches between consumer needs and product offerings, enhancing satisfaction through better alignment of goods with preferences. Personalized recommendations expose consumers to products they likely enjoy but might not otherwise discover, while customized interfaces and experiences can improve usability and accessibility.

However, personalization also presents risks including filter bubbles limiting exposure to diverse options, manipulation through psychologically targeted persuasion, price discrimination extracting consumer surplus, and erosion of serendipity and beneficial surprise. Research indicates that consumers often overestimate both the accuracy of personalized recommendations and their own ability to recognize and resist manipulative personalization. The opacity of personalization algorithms prevents consumers from understanding how their choices are being shaped, undermining informed decision-making. Moreover, personalization can reinforce existing preferences rather than facilitating growth and exploration, potentially constraining rather than expanding consumer autonomy and well-being.

5.3.2 Digital Markets and Inequality

Digital markets can amplify economic inequalities affecting life satisfaction through multiple mechanisms. Platform economies with winner-take-all dynamics concentrate wealth and power, while algorithmic decision-making in credit, employment, and housing can perpetuate historical discrimination. Data collection and analysis costs create barriers to entry favoring incumbents, while network effects strengthen dominant platforms at the expense of competition and consumer choice. Research demonstrates that market concentration in digital sectors has increased substantially, with the five largest tech companies controlling over 80% market share in key domains.

These market structures affect life satisfaction through reduced economic opportunity, limited consumer choice, and diminished worker bargaining power. However, digital markets also create new opportunities for entrepreneurship, remote work, and access to global markets that can reduce geographic and social barriers. Whether digital markets enhance or undermine aggregate life satisfaction depends on regulatory frameworks, competitive dynamics, and distribution of market power and economic gains. Progressive competition policy, worker protections, and social safety nets can help ensure that digital market benefits are broadly shared rather than concentrated among elites.

6. INTEGRATED FRAMEWORK FOR ETHICAL DIGITAL MARKETS

6.1 Framework Principles

This section presents an integrated framework combining digital ethics, data justice, and autonomy preservation to support life satisfaction in digital global markets. The framework rests on five foundational principles derived from the preceding analysis:

Principle 1: Human-Centered Design - Digital technologies should be designed to serve human needs, values, and well-being rather than prioritizing engagement metrics, data extraction, or profit maximization at the expense of user welfare. Human-centered design requires ongoing engagement with diverse stakeholders, empirical assessment of impacts on human flourishing, and willingness to modify or abandon technologies that harm well-being despite commercial success.

Principle 2: Distributive Justice - The benefits and burdens of digital technologies should be distributed equitably across populations, avoiding concentration of benefits among privileged groups while harms disproportionately affect marginalized communities. Distributive justice requires attention to access, representation, algorithmic fairness, and benefit sharing, ensuring that digital markets reduce rather than amplify existing inequalities.

Principle 3: Participatory Governance - Those affected by digital technologies should have meaningful voice in decisions about their design, deployment, and regulation. Participatory governance encompasses user input in product development, community engagement in algorithmic accountability, worker participation in workplace technology decisions, and democratic oversight of digital market structures and practices.

Principle 4: Autonomy and Agency - Digital systems should support rather than undermine human autonomy through transparency, meaningful choice, protection from manipulation, and respect for self-determination. Autonomy preservation requires both individual empowerment through control mechanisms and structural protections through regulation and accountability.

Principle 5: Continuous Accountability - Digital technology developers and deployers should remain accountable for impacts throughout technology lifecycles, with mechanisms for monitoring harms, enabling recourse, and requiring remediation when systems produce unjust or harmful outcomes. Accountability encompasses organizational responsibility, regulatory oversight, and legal liability.

Figure 3. Three interconnected pillars with life satisfaction as the central outcome.

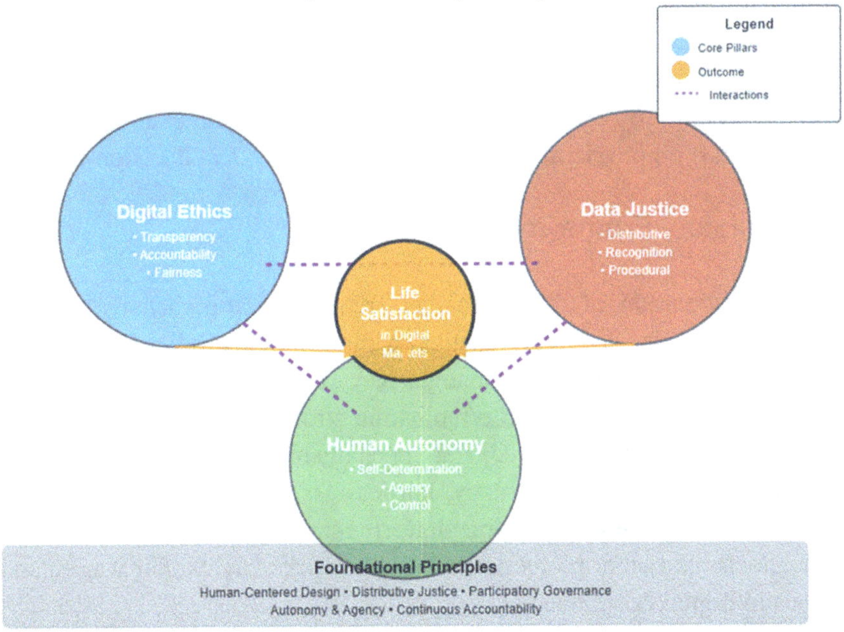

6.2 Implementation Strategies

6.2.1 Organizational Practices

Organizations can advance ethical, just, and autonomy-preserving digital markets through comprehensive practices spanning strategy, operations, and culture. Strategic commitments include embedding ethics and social responsibility in organizational mission and values, establishing executive accountability for responsible technology development, and allocating resources for ethics expertise, impact assessment, and stakeholder engagement. Operational practices encompass algorithmic impact assessments evaluating fairness, privacy, and autonomy implications before deployment, diverse teams bringing multiple perspectives to technology design, and ongoing monitoring of deployed systems for emergent harms.

Cultural transformation proves equally important, requiring moving beyond compliance mindsets to genuine ethical commitment. This includes creating psychological safety for raising concerns, celebrating responsible innovation that prioritizes user well-being over engagement metrics, and rewarding long-term thinking about societal impacts rather than exclusively short-term financial performance. Leading organizations have established ethics committees with independent authority, implemented algorithmic auditing by external experts, and developed ethics training programs for technical staff emphasizing both principles and practical decision-making.

6.2.2 Regulatory Frameworks

Effective regulation of digital markets requires comprehensive frameworks addressing the distinctive characteristics of digital technologies while remaining adaptable to rapid technological change. Key regulatory elements include data protection and privacy regulation establishing strong individual rights, organizational accountability, and enforcement mechanisms; algorithmic accountability requirements mandating transparency, fairness assessment, and recourse mechanisms; competition policy addressing platform market power, data advantages, and network effects; and labor protections ensuring worker rights, fair wages, and safe conditions in digital economies.

Regulatory approaches should combine ex-ante rules establishing baseline standards with ex-post enforcement addressing specific harms, enabling both prevention and response. Hanisch et al. (2023) examined digital governance frameworks, emphasizing the importance of regulatory coordination across jurisdictions to address cross-border data flows and multinational platforms. Lin and Yaakop (2024) analyzed digital governance through bibliometric analysis, revealing increasing emphasis on multi-stakeholder approaches combining government regulation, industry self-regulation, civil society oversight, and technical standards. Effective governance requires all these elements working in coordination rather than relying on any single mechanism.

6.3 Stakeholder Roles and Responsibilities

6.3.1 Technology Companies

Technology companies bear primary responsibility for ensuring their products and practices advance rather than undermine digital ethics, justice, and autonomy. Core responsibilities include conducting thorough impact assessments before launching products, prioritizing user well-being in design decisions, providing meaningful transparency and control, addressing algorithmic bias and discrimination, respecting privacy through data minimization and strong protections, and engaging authentically with affected communities. Companies should also support research on technology impacts, contribute to development of ethical standards, and advocate for strong regulatory frameworks rather than resisting accountability.

Leading technology companies have established responsible AI principles, created ethics review boards, implemented fairness toolkits, and published transparency reports. However, significant gaps persist between stated commitments and actual practices. Strengthening accountability requires moving beyond voluntary initiatives to enforceable standards, independent auditing, and meaningful consequences for violations. Worker organizing and activism within technology companies has emerged as an important force pushing for more ethical practices, suggesting that empowering technology workers to raise concerns without retaliation can improve outcomes.

6.3.2 Policymakers and Regulators

Policymakers and regulators must establish frameworks ensuring that digital markets serve public interest while fostering beneficial innovation. Key responsibilities include developing comprehensive data protection and privacy legislation, enacting algorithmic accountability requirements, strengthening competition policy for digital markets, protecting workers in platform economies, investing in digital infrastructure and literacy to reduce divides, and supporting research on technology impacts and governance approaches. Additionally, regulators must build expertise to effectively oversee complex technologies, coordinate across jurisdictions, and adapt frameworks to technological change.

Ruohonen (2023) examined the European Union's Data Governance Act, highlighting both promising elements and limitations. Effective data governance regulation requires balancing innovation with protection, enabling beneficial data sharing while preventing exploitation, and ensuring that regulatory frameworks prove enforceable rather than creating paper protections undermined by inadequate resources or technical complexity. International cooperation proves essential for addressing global platforms and cross-border data flows, requiring diplomatic engagement to develop shared standards and coordinated enforcement.

6.3.3 Civil Society and Users

Civil society organizations and individual users play crucial roles in advancing ethical digital markets through advocacy, oversight, and informed participation. Advocacy organizations can highlight harms, pressure companies to improve practices, support regulatory initiatives, and provide expertise on behalf of underrepresented communities. User activism including boycotts, public pressure campaigns, and participation in governance mechanisms can incentivize corporate responsibility. Additionally, digital literacy initiatives empowering users to understand privacy risks, recognize manipulation, and exercise available controls support individual agency.

However, individual responsibility for digital well-being has limits. While personal choices about technology use matter, expecting individuals to protect themselves against well-resourced companies employing sophisticated manipulation proves inadequate and unjust. Collective action through unions, cooperatives, and advocacy organizations can amplify individual power. Data justice movements explicitly connecting technology issues to broader social justice struggles have emerged globally, demanding not merely incremental reforms but fundamental restructuring of digital markets to serve marginalized communities and advance equity rather than profit maximization.

7. FUTURE DIRECTIONS AND RECOMMENDATIONS

7.1 Research Priorities

7.1.1 Empirical Research Needs

Substantial empirical research gaps limit current understanding of digital technology impacts on ethics, justice, autonomy, and life satisfaction. Longitudinal studies tracking how technology use patterns and experiences evolve over time remain scarce, with most existing research relying on cross-sectional designs that cannot establish causality. More research examining heterogeneous effects across populations would illuminate for whom digital technologies enhance or harm well-being, enabling more targeted interventions. Studies investigating intersectional effects of multiple marginalized identities on technology experiences and impacts could advance understanding of compounding disadvantages and inform more equitable design.

Additionally, research evaluating the effectiveness of specific interventions to promote digital ethics, justice, and autonomy would support evidence-based policy and practice. Comparative studies examining different regulatory approaches, corporate practices, and technological designs could identify most promising strategies. Research engaging directly with marginalized communities to understand their technology experiences, needs, and priorities remains insufficient, with much existing work conducted by privileged researchers making assumptions about others' experiences. Participatory research methodologies centering affected communities as co-researchers and decision-makers should expand.

7.1.2 Theoretical Development

Theoretical frameworks for digital ethics, data justice, and autonomy require continued development to address emerging technologies and deepening understanding of technology impacts. Integration across frameworks examining ethics, justice, autonomy, and well-being remains incomplete, with most research focusing narrowly on individual dimensions rather than their interconnections. Theories accounting for collective and systemic dimensions of technology impacts, beyond individual users and choices, need strengthening. Frameworks addressing global dimensions of digital markets, including North-South power dynamics, colonial legacies, and diverse cultural values and practices, remain underdeveloped.

Moreover, normative theorizing about desirable technology futures should expand, moving beyond critique of current harms to articulating positive visions of human flourishing through technology. What would genuinely emancipatory, justice-advancing, autonomy-enhancing digital markets look like? How can technology support diverse conceptions of good life rather than imposing narrow commercial definitions of success? Engaging philosophical traditions beyond Western liberalism, including Indigenous knowledge systems, non-Western philosophical frameworks, and radical political theories, could enrich theoretical resources for imagining alternative digital futures.

7.2 Policy Recommendations

7.2.1 Regulatory Priorities

Comprehensive regulatory frameworks for digital markets should include several priority elements. Strong data protection legislation establishing meaningful consent, data minimization requirements, individual rights to access and deletion, and substantial penalties for violations should be adopted globally. Algorithmic accountability requirements mandating impact assessments, transparency, fairness audits, and recourse mechanisms should apply to consequential automated decision systems. Competition policy should address platform market power through structural interventions including interoperability mandates, data portability requirements, and in some cases platform breakups where concentration proves intractable through lighter-touch regulation.

Labor protections for platform workers including employment rights, minimum wages, collective bargaining, and health and safety standards should be established. Investment in digital infrastructure extending high-quality broadband access to underserved areas and populations should expand. Digital literacy education integrated throughout lifelong learning from primary schools through adult education would build capacities for beneficial technology engagement. Public funding for research on technology impacts, governance approaches, and alternative technological designs would support evidence-based policy. International cooperation on digital governance through multilateral institutions should strengthen to address cross-border challenges.

7.2.2 Implementation Strategies

Effective implementation of regulatory frameworks requires adequate resources, expertise, and political will. Regulatory agencies need sufficient funding and staffing to oversee complex technologies, with ongoing investment in technical expertise and capacity building. Multi-stakeholder participation in regulatory development and implementation, including technology companies, civil society organizations, academic researchers, and affected communities, can improve both technical quality and democratic legitimacy. Adaptive regulation that regularly updates in response to technological change and emerging evidence of impacts would avoid ossification, while maintaining core principles providing stability and predictability.

Enforcement mechanisms should combine proactive compliance monitoring with responsive investigation and penalty for violations. Meaningful penalties proportional to organizational revenues rather than nominal fines that prove insignificant to large platforms would create genuine accountability incentives. Individual liability for executives and technical leaders involved in harmful technology decisions, alongside organizational penalties, may strengthen personal accountability. Public transparency regarding regulatory actions, including publication of investigation findings and penalty decisions, would enable civil society oversight while creating reputational incentives for compliance.

7.3 Design and Development Practices

7.3.1 Ethical Design Principles

Technology design should integrate ethical principles from inception rather than treating ethics as afterthought or isolated assessment. Privacy-by-design principles embedding data protection in system architecture should become standard practice, with data minimization, purpose limitation, and strong security as defaults rather than add-ons. Fairness-by-design approaches proactively addressing potential discrimination through diverse development teams, representative training data, bias detection and mitigation, and fairness testing should be mandatory for consequential systems. Transparency-by-design ensuring users can understand data collection, algorithmic logic, and decision processes in accessible formats would support informed choice.

Autonomy-supportive design respecting user agency through meaningful choice, freedom from manipulation, and control mechanisms should guide interface and interaction design. Accessibility-by-design ensuring usability for people with diverse abilities including physical, cognitive, and sensory disabilities would advance inclusion. Sustainability-by-design addressing environmental impacts of digital technologies including energy consumption, electronic waste, and resource extraction should become standard consideration. Participatory design engaging diverse stakeholders including end users, affected communities, domain experts, and ethicists throughout development would improve both social alignment and technical quality.

7.3.2 Organizational Capacity Building

Organizations require sustained investment in capacity for ethical, just, and autonomy-preserving technology development. This includes recruiting diverse teams bringing different perspectives, backgrounds, and values to technology design. Establishing dedicated responsible AI or ethics teams with authority to halt problematic projects and mandate changes proves important. Ethics training for technical staff covering both principles and practical decision-making scenarios would build knowledge and skills. Creating clear escalation pathways for raising concerns and psychological safety to do so without retaliation encourages organizational learning and improvement.

Senior leadership commitment remains essential, requiring executives who genuinely prioritize responsible innovation over short-term profits and engagement metrics. Compensation and incentive structures should reward long-term thinking about societal impacts rather than exclusively quarterly financial performance. Partnerships with academic researchers, civil society organizations, and affected communities can provide external perspectives and accountability. Industry collaboration on shared challenges including standards development, fairness toolkits, and impact assessment methodologies can accelerate progress while avoiding competitive races to the bottom on ethics and responsibility.

8. CONCLUSION

8.1 Key Findings

This chapter has examined the complex interplay between digital ethics, data justice, and human autonomy in shaping life satisfaction within digital global markets. Several key findings emerge from the analysis. First, digital technologies create unprecedented opportunities for connection, empowerment, and well-being while simultaneously introducing novel threats to privacy, fairness, and autonomy that require comprehensive governance responses. Second, existing regulatory frameworks and ethical guidelines remain insufficient, with significant gaps between aspirational principles and actual implementation creating persistent harms particularly affecting marginalized communities.

Third, data justice requires multidimensional approaches addressing distributive, recognition, and procedural dimensions rather than isolated technical fixes to algorithmic bias. Fourth, human autonomy in digital environments depends on both individual empowerment through transparency and control mechanisms and structural protections through regulation and accountability rather than relying solely on user vigilance. Fifth, digital well-being and life satisfaction depend critically on whether technologies support or undermine basic psychological needs for autonomy, competence, and relatedness, with heterogeneous effects across populations and contexts.

Sixth, effective governance of digital markets requires coordination across multiple levels (organizational, sectoral, national, international) and multiple stakeholders (companies, governments, civil society, users) rather than relying on any single actor or mechanism. Seventh, advancing digital ethics, justice, and autonomy demands fundamental restructuring of technological practices, business models, and market structures rather than incremental adjustments to existing systems. Finally, meaningful progress requires centering marginalized communities as decision-makers and beneficiaries rather than afterthoughts in technology governance.

8.2 Implications for Practice

The analysis yields several important implications for technology developers, policymakers, organizations, and users. Technology companies must move beyond voluntary ethics initiatives to binding commitments implemented through organizational structures, development practices, and accountability mechanisms. This requires investing in ethics expertise, diverse teams, impact assessment, stakeholder engagement, and ongoing monitoring. Companies should embrace strong regulation as supporting responsible competition rather than resisting accountability measures.

Policymakers should enact comprehensive regulatory frameworks addressing data protection, algorithmic accountability, competition policy, and labor protection in digital markets. Regulation should combine clear standards with adaptive implementation, adequate resources and expertise, and meaningful enforcement through substantial penalties. International cooperation remains essential for governing global platforms and cross-border data flows effectively. Investment in digital infrastructure, literacy, and inclusion programs can reduce divides and expand opportunities.

Organizations across sectors should proactively assess and address technology impacts on stakeholders including customers, workers, and communities. This includes conducting impact assessments, engaging affected parties, implementing privacy and fairness protections, and establishing grievance and recourse mechanisms. Worker participation in technology decisions should expand, recognizing that those most directly affected often have crucial insights into both problems and solutions.

Users and civil society organizations should maintain vigilance regarding technology harms, demand accountability from companies and governments, support regulatory initiatives, and exercise collective power through organizing and advocacy. While individual responsibility has limits, informed participation and collective action remain important forces for advancing digital justice and autonomy.

8.3 Future Outlook

Digital technologies will continue evolving rapidly, introducing both new opportunities and challenges for ethics, justice, autonomy, and life satisfaction. Emerging technologies including large language models, generative AI, virtual and augmented reality, brain-computer interfaces, and quantum computing present distinctive governance challenges requiring proactive rather than reactive responses. The increasing sophistication of algorithmic systems creates growing risks of manipulation and control alongside potential benefits for personalization and empowerment.

Climate change and environmental sustainability must become central considerations in digital technology governance, addressing the substantial energy consumption and resource extraction required by digital systems. The COVID-19 pandemic accelerated digital transformation across domains, raising questions about whether rapid technology adoption during crisis conditions received adequate ethical scrutiny and governance. Ongoing geopolitical tensions create risks of internet fragmentation, censorship, and surveillance that threaten digital rights and autonomy globally.

Despite these challenges, opportunities exist for advancing more ethical, just, and autonomy-preserving digital futures. Growing public awareness of technology harms creates political space for stronger regulation. Organizing among technology workers demonstrates potential for internal corporate pressure toward responsibility. Academic research continues building knowledge about impacts and governance approaches. Civil society movements explicitly connecting digital justice to broader social justice struggles are expanding globally.

Realizing positive digital futures requires sustained commitment across multiple fronts: rigorous research illuminating impacts and solutions, comprehensive regulation establishing accountability, responsible corporate practices prioritizing human welfare, worker organizing demanding dignity and justice, civil society advocacy challenging power, and informed user participation exercising collective agency. The stakes are high—digital technologies increasingly mediate fundamental aspects of human life, from work and commerce to education and social relationships. Ensuring these technologies advance rather than undermine human flourishing, justice, and autonomy represents among the most pressing challenges of contemporary society. Meeting this challenge demands both critical analysis of existing systems and constructive imagination of alternatives, combining scholarly insight, political will, and collective action to build digital markets genuinely serving humanity rather than exploiting it for profit.

REFERENCES

Ashok, M., Madan, R., Joha, A., & Sivarajah, U. (2022). Ethical framework for artificial intelligence and digital technologies. *International Journal of Information Management, 62*, 102433. DOI: 10.1016/j.ijinfomgt.2021.102433

Batool, A., Zowghi, D., & Bano, M. (2024). AI governance: A systematic literature review. *AI and Ethics*. Advance online publication. DOI: 10.1007/s43681-024-00653-w

Büchi, M. (2024). Digital well-being theory and research. *New Media & Society, 26*(1), 172–189. DOI: 10.1177/14614448211056851

Cao, S., & Li, H. (2023). A scoping review of digital well-being in early childhood: Definitions, measurements, contributors, and interventions. *International Journal of Environmental Research and Public Health, 20*(4), 3510. Advance online publication. DOI: 10.3390/ijerph20043510 PMID: 36834204

Dietrich, F., Arenz, A., & Reinecke, L. (2024). What constitutes experiences of autonomy in digital technology use? A (computational) scoping review through the lens of self-determination theory. *Interacting with Computers*. Advance online publication. DOI: 10.1093/iwc/iwae050

Ferrara, E. (2024). Fairness and bias in artificial intelligence: A brief survey of sources, impacts, and mitigation strategies. *Sci, 6*(1), 3. Advance online publication. DOI: 10.3390/sci6010003

Fisk, R. P., Gallan, A. S., Joubert, A. M., Beekhuyzen, J., Cheung, L., & Russell-Bennett, R. (2023). Healing the digital divide with digital inclusion: Enabling human capabilities. *Journal of Service Research, 26*(4), 542–559. DOI: 10.1177/10946705221140148

Floridi, L. (2021). Translating principles into practices of digital ethics: Five risks of being unethical. In L. Floridi (Ed.), *Ethics, governance, and policies in artificial intelligence* (Philosophical Studies Series, Vol. 144, pp. 81–90). Springer. DOI: 10.1007/978-3-030-81907-1_6

Gagné, M., Parker, S. K., Griffin, M. A., Dunlop, P. D., Knight, C., Klonek, F. E., & Parent-Rocheleau, X. (2022). Understanding and shaping the future of work with self-determination theory. *Nature Reviews Psychology, 1*(7), 378–392. DOI: 10.1038/s44159-022-00056-w PMID: 35574235

Gleiss, A., Degen, K., & Pousttchi, K. (2023). Identifying the patterns: Towards a systematic approach to digital platform regulation. *Journal of Information Technology*, *38*(2), 180–201. DOI: 10.1177/02683962221146803

Hanisch, M., Goldsby, C. M., Fabian, N. E., & Oehmichen, J. (2023). Digital governance: A conceptual framework and research agenda. *Journal of Business Research*, *162*, 113777. DOI: 10.1016/j.jbusres.2023.113777

Lin, Z., & Yaakop, M. R. (2024). Research on digital governance based on Web of Science—A bibliometric analysis. *Frontiers in Political Science*, *6*, 1403404. DOI: 10.3389/fpos.2024.1403404

Lythreatis, S., Singh, S. K., & El-Kassar, A.-N. (2022). The digital divide: A review and future research agenda. *Technological Forecasting and Social Change*, *175*, 121359. DOI: 10.1016/j.techfore.2021.121359

Meng, S., Kong, F., Dong, W., Zhang, Y., Yu, T., & Jin, X. (2023). Mobile social media use and life satisfaction among adolescents: A moderated mediation model. *Frontiers in Public Health*, *11*, 1117745. Advance online publication. DOI: 10.3389/fpubh.2023.1117745 PMID: 38094229

Morley, J., Elhalal, A., Garcia, F., Kinsey, L., Mökander, J., & Floridi, L. (2021). Ethics as a service: A pragmatic operationalisation of AI ethics. *Minds and Machines*, *31*(2), 239–256. DOI: 10.1007/s11023-021-09563-w PMID: 34720418

Murray, D. (2024). Facial recognition and the end of human rights as we know them? *Netherlands Quarterly of Human Rights*, *42*(2), 179–189. DOI: 10.1177/09240519241253061

Qandeel, M. (2024). Facial recognition technology: Regulations, rights and the rule of law. *Frontiers in Big Data*, *7*, 1354659. DOI: 10.3389/fdata.2024.1354659 PMID: 38895177

Ruohonen, J., & Mickelsson, S. (2023). Reflections on the Data Governance Act. *Digital Society : Ethics, Socio-Legal and Governance of Digital Technology*, *2*(1), 25. Advance online publication. DOI: 10.1007/s44206-023-00041-7

Ryan, M., & Stah, B. C. (2021). Artificial intelligence ethics guidelines for developers and users: Clarifying their content and normative implications. *Journal of Information. Communication and Ethics in Society*, *19*(1), 61–86. DOI: 10.1108/JICES-12-2019-0138

Sanchez-Monedero, J., & Dencik, L. (2022). Data justice. *Internet Policy Review*, *11*(1). Advance online publication. DOI: 10.14763/2022.1.1615

Smits, M., Kim, C. M., van Goor, H., & Ludden, G. D. S. (2022). From digital health to digital well-being: Systematic scoping review. *Journal of Medical Internet Research, 24*(4), e33787. DOI: 10.2196/33787 PMID: 35377328

Starke, C., Baleis, J., Keller, B., & Marcinkowski, F. (2022). Fairness perceptions of algorithmic decision-making: A systematic review of the empirical literature. *Big Data & Society, 9*(2), 20539517221115189. Advance online publication. DOI: 10.1177/20539517221115189

Tarnanidis, T., Manda, V. K., Sousa, B. B., Vlachopoulou, M., & Papachristou, E. (2026). Marketing Complexity of Smart Consumer Products to Global Millennial Segments. In Tarnanidis, T., Sousa, B., Vlachopoulou, M., Papachristou, E., & Kittu Manda, V. (Eds.), *Diversity and Inclusion-Driven Marketing for Multicultural Marketplaces* (pp. 1–16). IGI Global Scientific Publishing., DOI: 10.4018/979-8-3373-2111-0.ch001

Tarnanidis, T., Sousa, B., Vlachopoulou, M., Papachristou, E., & Kittu Manda, V. (Eds.). (2026). *Diversity and Inclusion-Driven Marketing for Multicultural Marketplaces*. IGI Global Scientific Publishing., DOI: 10.4018/979-8-3373-2111-0

Yang, J., Soltan, A. A. S., Eyre, D. W., & Clifton, D. A. (2023). Algorithmic fairness and bias mitigation for clinical machine learning with deep reinforcement learning. *Nature Machine Intelligence, 5*(8), 884–894. DOI: 10.1038/s42256-023-00697-3 PMID: 37615031

KEY TERMS AND DEFINITIONS

Algorithmic Fairness: Algorithmic fairness refers to the design and evaluation of algorithms to ensure that their outcomes do not systematically disadvantage or discriminate against individuals or groups based on protected or sensitive attributes.

Data Governance: Data governance is the framework of policies, standards, roles, and processes that ensure data is managed ethically, securely, transparently, and in compliance with legal and societal expectations.

Data Justice: Data justice focuses on the fair and equitable treatment of individuals and communities in the collection, use, ownership, and governance of data, aiming to prevent discrimination, exclusion, and power imbalances.

Digital Ethics: Digital ethics refers to the moral principles and values that guide the responsible design, development, deployment, and use of digital technologies, ensuring respect for human rights, fairness, transparency, and accountability.

Digital Well-Being: Digital well-being denotes the impact of digital technologies on individuals' mental, emotional, social, and physical health, emphasizing balanced, meaningful, and healthy technology use.

Human Autonomy: Human autonomy is the capacity of individuals to make informed, voluntary, and independent decisions without undue influence or coercion from digital systems, algorithms, or data-driven technologies.

Chapter 12
Life Satisfaction in Digital Retail:
A Human-Centered Analysis of E-Commerce Experience, Trust, and Emotional Engagement

M. Mohanraj
http://orcid.org/0009-0003-5033-9416
K.S. Rangasamy College of Technology, India

K. Shakthi Charumaa
K.S. Rangasamy College of Technology, India

ABSTRACT

The soaring development of digital retail transformed the purchasing patterns of people and, to a greater extent, the daily experiences of life. In addition to convenience and efficiency, the online shopping platforms have become an important factor in the emotional state, perception of trust, and overall life satisfaction of the consumers. With the digital marketplace increasingly adopting the most innovative technologies, there is an increasing desire to learn about these platforms not as a system of transactions only, but more as an environment of human interaction that has an effect on the well-being of consumers. This paper will discuss the role of digital retail experience in improving life satisfaction through the lenses of quality of experience, emotional involvement, trust, and relationship development in the long-term. . In general, the paper highlights that to measure the success of digital retail, it is essential to consider its impact on the economic performance, as well as, its role in promoting trust, emotional well-being, and satisfaction with life.

DOI: 10.4018/979-8-3373-8357-6.ch012

1.INTRODUCTION

The swiftly spreading digital retail and e-commerce services have completely transformed the way people communicate and buy goods and the idea of service quality. The emphasis of the digital retail studies is slowly shifting away towards technological efficiency and more human-oriented experiences, upgrading usability, trust and satisfaction, and general well-being as online commerce becomes established as a part of our daily lives. In this regard, user experience (UX) and human-centered design (HCD) become the determining elements of not only the success of transactions but also the relationship of customers in the long term and the subjective life satisfaction.Small and medium enterprises (SMEs) are a specifically significant phenomenon of the digital retail ecosystem. Although the number of e-commerce platforms is increasing, several SMEs are also struggling to adopt these platforms because different business owners are digitally literate at varying levels. According to Maulana and Rosyidah (Maulana & Rosyidah, 2022), inappropriate interfaces and complicated workflow can be significant obstacles to usability particularly in the elderly or those who are not technologically savvy. Their compact user-centered design (UCD) methodology proves that the ease of data collection and decision making processes to the user side can significantly enhance the results of usability. This highlights the essence of accommodative and considerate designing techniques in facilitating fair access to online trade. The importance of UCD is also supported in industry-specific application like e-commerce in healthcare retail. (Sugosha et al., 2021) insist that online pharmacy platforms should be made accessible, efficient, and trusted by means of the intuitive interface design and the involvement of users in the process in the iterative manner. Their results indicate that the quality of UX has a direct effect on the usability rates and user acceptance, making it clear that the quality of design is tightly connected to the perceived reliability and satisfaction - especially in the areas of commerce as a sensitive domain as the healthcare. In addition to usability, there is trust that is a foundation of sustainable e-commerce ecosystems. Sharif and Sudirman (Sharif & Sudirman, 2024) explore the issue of trust formation in the Indonesian e-commerce platforms and find that the user experience and delivery satisfaction are important determinants. They find that UX indirectly increases the trust by improving the total shopping experience, whereas delivery satisfaction is directly related to trust perception. Notably, shopping experience is an intermediary variable, which demonstrates how experiential, operational, and psychological variables are related to each other in digital retail trust-building. The latest developments with Industry 5.0 further strengthen the position of the human-centered design by stating the importance of human-machines cooperation and morally responsible digital systems. Amirkhizi et al. (Amirkhizi et al., 2025) have shown that the platforms of e-commerce that have high HCD attributes, including transparency, personalization, and accessibility and security, are far ahead of low HCD platforms in trust, satisfaction, and repurchase intention. Their analysis ascertains that adoption of HCD principles is not only a design but strategic requirement in the realization of sustainable growth and customer loyalty in next generation digital commerce. The usability of the platform of various devices also has a decisive effect on the perception and involvement of the users. Nasar (Nasar, 2025) empirically demonstrates that the mobile first design strategies can compete with the traditional web platforms because of the efficiency, satisfaction, and performance of tasks. The ease of use of mobile apps is more advantageous than ever, which points to convenience and cognitive ease as essential factors to optimistic user experiences, and context-dependent and adaptive interface design. All these studies point to a definite research direction with a human-centered, trust-based, and experience-driven digital retailing system. Nevertheless, extant literature pays much attention to satisfaction, trust, and usability, and the wider perspective of life satisfaction and emotional wellness has not been explored to the best of its abilities. In an effort to fill this gap, the current work locates the topic of digital retail into a humanistic context that analyzes both the functional and the emotional involvement, as well as the aggregate effect on consumer satisfaction in life.

2.RELATED WORKS

Recent research on the digital retail system has been more focused on the combination of human-centric values, high-quality technologies, and mood to improve the consumer experience, confidence, and satisfaction. The supply chain transparency and traceability is one of the emerging dimensions in this context, which has a vast impact on the consumer trust and perceived value. Zhuo et al. (Zhuo et al., 2025) look at the contribution of consumer traceability awareness within blockchain-related supply chains. They have found that the usage of blockchains enhances the overall performance of supply chains and increases the sensitivity to the level of consumer awareness. As manufacturers are always offered a chance to use blockchain-driven traceability, retailers are forced to think strategically about their targeting strategies depending on the awareness of the consumer. This paper emphasizes that transparency and trust systems within digital retail environments have the potential to define perceptions and decision-making among consumers, which supports the usefulness of trust as a cornerstone of human interaction in the digital business.Customer experience (CX) conceptualization and assessment have also significantly changed over the years. Mittameedi et al. (Mittameedi et al., 2025) offer a synthesis of CX research in e-commerce, a deliberate systematic literature review that compiles the findings on the topic in more than four decades. Their work recognizes the paradigm of changing the old models of use and transactions to dynamic, emotional, and co-created experiences. The review outlines the focus of the modern CX main dimensions in terms of trust, personalization, user autonomy, and engagement as the most important factors to consider in the AIs-based environment. Besides, the authors emphasize the increasing importance of agentic systems and artificial intelligence as co-producers of customer experience as a means of providing real-time customization and emotional engagement. The view aligns directly with the overall trend that digital retail platforms are to be judged not merely on the efficiency metrics, but on their abilities to improve emotional appeal and consumer well-being.

Parallel to this, the application of AI techniques has been more and more used to maximize the user satisfaction and operational efficiency in online retail. R et al. (R. P. et al., 2024) suggest an online shopping application with the help of AI, which combines convolutional neural networks (CNNs), image recognition, and augmented reality to increase product exploration and personalization. Their platform will allow three-dimensional visualization and shared shopping capabilities, which will promote social interaction and make decisions together. The paper proves that intelligent and interactive attributes have a profound positive effect on customer satisfaction and engagement, implying that experiential and social aspects of digital retailing are important in forming positive attitudes and behaviours about consumers.In addition to consumer applications, human-AI cooperation has received some interest when designing and developing digital retail systems. Shao et al. (Shao et al., 2025) present FashionCook a visual analytics platform that helps designers and AI models to work together in fashion e-commerce. The system makes the human stakeholders and the AI-driven tools have an increased level of trust by making the system more transparent, interpretable, and providing feedback on the human stakeholder side through means of iteration and feedback. Their results suggest that successful human-AI cooperation can enhance the results of design and user-focused decision-making in sophisticated, multimodal e-commerce conditions. The paper supports the need to make technologies more explainable and collaborative in order to meet human-centered objectives.

Lastly, a user interface (UI) design is one of the central factors of delight and commitment in online trade platforms. Harahap et al. (Harahap et al., 2024) empirically explore the effect of the design of UIs on customer satisfaction and loyalty in e-commerce based on SaaS through PLS-SEM. Their findings affirm intuitive, responsive, and a visual pleasing interface as a major boost in customer satisfaction, thereby boosting loyalty. The paper highlights the importance of ongoing user feedback and practice of user-centered design to maintain long-term customer relationship in digital competitive markets. Taken together, these researches prove that the modern digital retail research is shifting towards a human-focused, holistic approach that incorporates trust, transparency, emotional interaction, AI-powered personalization, and usability. Previous studies however have elaborated on satisfaction, trust and loyalty but little has been done on the wider extension of digital retail experiences on life satisfaction and subjective wellbeing of consumers. The current research fills this gap by integrating these dimensions into one human-based outlook of digital retail. A new form of shopping experience, known as live streaming commerce, has created emotionally rich and immersive shopping experiences that change consumer behavior in a substantial way. Widiatmo (Widiatmo, 2024) explores the idea of live streaming commerce based on the stimulus-organism-response (S 0 R) framework, and the sense of immersive experience, as a mediating variable between technological stimuli and impulse buying behavior. The paper has proven that virtual try-on capabilities and real-time interaction, as well as augmented reality (AR) virtual try-ons, are important elements to boost immersive experiences, which then influence impulsive buying behaviors. These results indicate the increased relevance of immersive and emotional experiences in digital retail and that interactive human-focused technologies are more likely to fill the digital-physical gap in the shopping experience between online and offline shopping.

The artificial intelligence also has become a key facilitator of smart, customized, and emotionally dynamic e-commerce solutions. Roy et al. (Roy et al., 2025) suggest the use of AI-enhanced e-commerce platform, which involves a chatbot with GPT alongside sentiment analysis to enhance the interaction with customers and business intelligence. According to their findings, conversational AI can be considered a major boost in user engagement, with real-time assistance and personalized recommendations being a key aspect of it, and sentiment analysis allowing platforms to reach a better understanding of customer satisfaction levels and emotions. Such a two-sided strategy supports how emotionally sensitive AI systems are changing the concept of trust, satisfaction and adaptive customer experiences in digital retail systems. In addition to the AI-powered interaction, the emotional design has become popular as one of the key dimensions of user interface design. Hamidah et al. (Hamidah et al., 2024) address the topic of applying Kansei Engineering and design thinking to the creation of an agricultural e-commerce platform. Including the emotional reactions of users directly into the interface design, the study shows a high level of usability and user satisfaction based on the high System Usability Scale (SUS) scores. The main point that is made in this work is that emotionally engaging interface design can provide not only functional usability, but also good affective experiences, which can be identified as the determiners of long-term satisfaction at the digital commerce.The behavior of impulse buying in interactive e-commerce interfaces too has been tested using the available technology acceptance model. Wijaya et al. (Wijaya et al., 2025) examine consumer impulse buying in terms of Technology Acceptance Model (TAM) with respect to perceived usefulness and perceived ease of use. Their findings indicate that perceived usefulness has a great impact on consumer attitudes and impulse buying behaviour whereas emotional engagement and interactive characteristics are triggers of impulsive purchasing decisions. Remarked findings are that, when coupled with emotional stimulation and time sensitive interaction, functional value is crucial in influencing consumer behaviour in contemporary digital shops.

To ensure the maintenance of the consumer relations after the first purchases, further insight into the repurchase intention and the creation of loyalty is needed. The study conducted by Marvella et al. (Marvella et al., 2025) aims at determining the effects of customer experience, hedonic motivation, and e-service quality on repurchase intention and the mediating variables are satisfaction and trust. Through PLS-SEM, the research proves that emotionally exciting experience and high quality digital services are very powerful in enhancing trust and satisfaction which subsequently results in the re-buying attitude. The findings of this research support the thesis that online store performance requires the development of emotionally positive, trustful relationships as opposed to the transactional efficiency.Taken together, the results of (Widiatmo, 2024) through (Marvella et al., 2025) show that the modern digital retail research is growing more concerned with the idea of immersiveness, emotionally intelligent AI, affective interface design, and trust-based interaction. Although these works are helpful in discovering the insights of impulse buying, satisfaction, loyalty, and repurchase intention, they mostly assess the results in the platform or transaction level. Little focus has been on how a continuous exposure to these human oriented digital retail experiences can help to bring about more life satisfaction and subjective well-being. To fill this gap, the current paper incorporates emotional involvement, trust, and experiential quality into a comprehensive concept to study life satisfaction in the digital retail settings.

3.CONCEPTUAL FRAMEWORK

The theoretical basis of the given study is based on the premise that digital retail experiences have a certain impact on life satisfaction of the consumers which is determined by the complex of psychological, social, and technological factors. The four constructs that lie at the heart of this framework include quality of digital experience, trust, emotional engagement, and consumer wellbeing. Digital experience quality refers to the interface usability, information clarity, perceived security and the privacy support, which are all elements that influence the perception of reliability and convenience by the consumers. Trust turns out to be one of the essential mediators that interconnect platform design and service quality with consumer loyalty, as well as subjective well-being. Emotional engagement is a measurement that portrays levels of satisfaction, pleasure, and attachment when consumers are interacting with online shopping spaces, such as immersive live commerce and interactive social functions.Based on the Expectation Confirmation Theory and the Social Presence Theory, the framework assumes that positive digital relationships lead to increased trust and emotional connection which consequently result in increased satisfaction and well-being in general. Moreover, generational considerations are also included to explain the differences in consumer expectations and responsiveness, especially that of digital-native generations like the Generation Z. The framework further acknowledges the importance of the AI-driven sentiment analysis and customized CRM plans in balancing the digital experiences with the user expectations. Taken together, this conceptual model offers an integrated perspective through which the concept of human-centered retail design can be utilized in order to deliver more than just transactional results, but also enhance the satisfaction in life of consumers meaningfully.

3.1 Digital Experience Quality Role

The quality of digital experience is the initial layer of the conceptual framework as it defines how consumers perceive, expect, and interact in the online retail settings. The key aspects included in it are interface usability, ease of navigation, visual appeal, accuracy of information, system response, perceived security, and privacy support. With a properly crafted digital interface, consumers should be able to engage with the platform without the need to exert a lot of cognitive effort and decision fatigue, as well as to be certain it makes sense. Clear product, intuitive layouts and unity in structures make the product easy to understand and transparency and uncertainty reduction would be crucial in positive evaluation by the users.Digital experiences of high quality also help in feeling of control and autonomy in the process of shopping so that consumers are able to make informed choices without any pressure and mis-understanding. According to the Expectation Confirmation Theory, the higher the actual platform performance matches or even surpasses the user expectations at the start, the higher the level of satisfaction. With time, consistent positive experiences support positive attitudes to the platform and increase the intentions to behave (like to continue using and repurchase). Thus, the quality of digital experience is not only facilitating functional convenience but it also preconditions the psychological background required to build trust, and bring emotional comfort and long-term involvement in the context of digital retail ecosystems.

3.2 Trusts as an Intermediary Process

Trust acts as a vital mediating factor which connects the quality of the digital experience to consumer satisfaction, loyalty and well being. Reliability is the main cause of trust in digital retail situations because perceived system protection, protection of data privacy, transparentness in transactions, and responsible management of personal data are the major factors. Because online shopping is associated with both inherent uncertainty and perceived risk, trust will decrease the anxiety of consumers in case of the loss of money, data misuse, service failure. The consumers are more likely to have a deeper and permanent engagement when they think that a platform is trustworthy and is the one that protects their interests.Psychologically, trust offers consumers reassurance and stability emotionally, which makes consumers seek to experience shopping instead of risk avoidance. Based on Expectation Confirmation Theory, regular service delivery of promises builds trust as time goes and results in a greater degree of satisfaction and loyalty. Trust also enhances the beneficial impacts of the quality of digital experience by transforming functional efficacy into emotional safety. Due to this fact, trust serves as an aspect of collaboration between the technological design characteristics and the human results, which affect not only the buying behavior but also the subjective well-being and the future building of relations between the consumer and the digital store.

3.3 Outcomes of Emotional Engagement and Well-Being

The aspect of emotional engagement is the emotional aspect of consumer interaction in the digital retail setting and measures the level of emotional involvement, pleasure, and attachment in online shopping. It is influenced by the interactive elements, including live-streaming commerce and real-time communication and personalized recommendations, social interaction tools which strengthen perceived social presence. These details make people feel connected to humans, less isolated during online transactions, and help to emotionally immerse.According to the Social Presence Theory, emotional bonds between consumers and platforms are reinforced by the height intensity of social communication and perceived human warmth. The emotional involvement also increases the satisfaction in the sense that routine shopping activities are turned to pleasant and significant experiences. In addition to affecting purchase intention and impulse buying, emotionally involving in-store experiences also affect more general elements of subjective well-being, such as positive mood, emotional comfort, and life satisfaction. Emotionally attached consumers will find shopping to be an enjoyable experience and not a means to an end. In turn, emotional engagement is one of the most crucial channels that digital retail experience may leverage to amplify its effects beyond the economic performance and have a positive effect on the quality of life of consumers.

4. PRINCIPLES OF HUMAN-CENTERED DESIGN

The Human-Centered Design (HCD) focuses on the design of digital systems that take into consideration the needs, preferences, and experiences of the end-users. The HCD in digital retail is such that the technological innovations do not only optimize efficiency or sales but also the satisfaction of the user, trust, and well-being. The main principles of HCD applied in online retail are usability, accessibility, transparency, emotional and personalization. Usability is concerned with intuitive navigation systems, clear interface designs and easy interaction paths that do not require much cognitive load and enable consumers to accomplish tasks without much difficulty. Accessibility guarantees that the platforms are accessible to a wide range of users and would therefore be inclusive to people with different abilities. Transparency is associated with the clear presentation of product information, privacy policies and security controls which encourages consumer confidence and trust. Emotional engagement concerns creating experiences that generate positive feelings with the help of the feature of interaction, live commerce, and customer response. Lastly, personalization uses the power of data-based insights to match the offering and suggestions to personalized needs to create an impression of concern and responsiveness in the relationship with consumers.With the help of these principles, online retailers will be able to build platforms that are more than just functional but also emotionally involve and trust-evoking. The inclusion of HCD into digital business fosters the spirit of sustainable interaction of consumers, loyalty, and ultimately leads to happiness in life. This strategy no longer focuses on transactional efficiency but on the overall user experience as the central indicator of success in the online retail design. Moreover, Human-Centered Design focuses on iterative, participative design process, which means that the feedback provided by users is incorporated at every stage of digital retail platform development and enhancement. With the inclusion of user testing, behavioral analytics and real time feedback systems, retailers are able to detect the areas of pain and modify interfaces to meet changing consumer demands. This is more refined and makes the experience seem more responsive and builds a stronger sense of trust because users realize that they are being considered when designing platforms. Emotional safety, which entails reducing stress, confusion, and anxiety during online communication is the other vital element of HCD in the digital retailing industry. Emotional comfort is achieved through characteristics of user-friendly checkout procedures, straightforward error messages, transparent pricing, and friendly customer support. Once the users feel emotionally secure, they can freely become more involved in the platform and seek what is on offer without any reservations.HCD, moreover, promotes the uptake of ethical technology through responsible use of data, equitable practice of personalization and respect towards user autonomy.

5. DIMENSIONS OF DIGITAL RETAIL EXPERIENCE

There are multidimensional aspects of digital retail experiences, both in terms of functional and emotional aspects that determine consumer perceptions and satisfaction. Some fundamental dimensions have been found to be crucial in terms of increasing user engagement, trust and wellbeing in the context of online shopping.

5.1 User Interface Design and Usability

User interface design and usability represent the functional foundation of digital retail platforms and significantly influence consumer perceptions and satisfaction. An intuitive and visually consistent interface minimizes cognitive load and allows users to navigate the platform with ease. Features such as clear menu structures, logical categorization, responsive layouts, and fast system feedback contribute to a seamless shopping experience across devices. When users can efficiently locate products and complete transactions without confusion or delay, frustration is reduced and confidence is enhanced. Effective usability not only improves task performance but also supports positive emotional responses, encouraging continued platform engagement and long-term usage.

5.2 Information Quality

Information quality plays a critical role in shaping consumer trust and decision-making in digital retail environments. Accurate, complete, and up-to-date product information—including detailed descriptions, high-quality images, pricing transparency, and authentic customer reviews—reduces uncertainty during the purchasing process. High information quality enables consumers to evaluate alternatives effectively and align their expectations with actual product performance. When platforms provide reliable and consistent information, perceived risk decreases and trust in the system increases. As a result, consumers experience greater satisfaction and confidence, which positively influences purchase intention, loyalty, and overall shopping experience.

5.3 Privacy and Security

Privacy and security are essential dimensions of digital retail experience, particularly in an era of increasing data sensitivity and cyber threats. Consumers expect platforms to protect their personal and financial information through secure payment gateways, encryption mechanisms, and transparent data usage policies. Clear communication regarding privacy practices fosters trust and reassures users about the ethical handling of their data. When consumers feel that their information is safe, anxiety and perceived risk are significantly reduced. Strong privacy and security measures not only safeguard transactions but also contribute to emotional comfort, trust development, and sustained engagement with digital retail platforms.

5.4 Social Presence and Interactivity

Social presence and interactivity enhance the emotional richness of digital retail experiences by simulating human connection in virtual environments. Features such as real-time chat, live-streaming commerce, user-generated reviews, and community interaction enable consumers to communicate with sellers and other users. These interactive elements foster a sense of belonging and reduce the impersonality often associated with online shopping. Increased social presence strengthens emotional engagement and enjoyment, transforming shopping from a transactional activity into a socially meaningful experience. Consequently, interactive platforms encourage longer engagement, impulsive purchases, and stronger emotional attachment.

5.5 Personalization and Customer Relationship Management (CRM)

Personalization and customer relationship management focus on tailoring digital retail experiences to individual consumer preferences and behaviors. AI-driven recommendations, personalized content, and adaptive interfaces enhance relevance and perceived value. Responsive customer support and proactive communication further reinforce the perception of care and attention. Personalized experiences increase satisfaction by aligning platform offerings with user expectations and needs. Effective CRM practices strengthen long-term relationships, foster loyalty, and encourage repeat purchases. By addressing both functional efficiency and emotional connection, personalization plays a key role in creating meaningful and human-centered digital retail experiences.

6. TRUST, EMOTION INVOLVEMENT, AND CUSTOMER WELL-BEING

The key elements of the digital retail experiences issue are trust and emotional involvement, which help to comprehend the prevalence of the concept of consumer well-being. Trust is the capability of consumers to put their trust in the reliability, integrity, and security of a digital platform. The factors affecting the trust in online retailing include transparent details, safe payment service, steady delivery of service, and prompt customer service. Credible media minimizes the perceived risk, promotes repeat contacts and loyalty that lead to improved consumer satisfaction. Emotional involvement measures how strongly consumers are connected, imbued, and excitement-provoked by the digital encounters. This encompasses the fun of the interactive abilities, live commerce, personalized suggestions as well as social availability not just in online markets. Emotionally high levels do not only make people more likely to buy impulsively and make repeat purchases, but also leave lasting and meaningful experiences that cannot be reduced to transactions. The collective outcome of the trust and emotional involvement in digital interactions is that consumer well-being (or life satisfaction) is achieved. Platforms that are characterised by human-centered design, safe practices, emotionally resonant experiences give the consumers the comfort, confidence and the feeling of fulfilment. The role of generation differences is also significant; as an example, digital-native consumers, especially Generation Z, tend to perceive social presence and entertainment-centered experiences more than functionality, so the influence of emotions on well-being is a factor that is critical in this cohort.This will help businesses abandon transactional goals by ensuring that they incorporate trust and emotional appeal in digital retail strategies to build a meaningful relationship with customers. This correspondence of the platform design with human-centered values does not only increase loyalty but also adds to more extended life satisfaction and consumer well-being in the long term.

6.1 Trust as a Psychological Premise of Consumer Well-Being.

Confidence in online shopping platforms moves beyond the guarantees of transactions and acts as a psychological security system to the customer. The consumers will have less pressure and doubt when platforms are always reliable, ethical, and transparent in their interactions. This mental assurance lets the users interact more effortlessly and assuringly with online services. Perceived control over personal data and financial transactions also improves with the trust which is strictly connected with the emotional stability and satisfaction. With time, recurring trust-affirming experiences contribute to a feeling of security and predictability, which is beneficial to the mental health of consumers and commitment to the long-run relationship with the digital retail sites.

6.2 Emotional Involvement as Experiential Force.

Experiential richness of consumer engagement in the digital retail environment is referred to as emotional involvement. Inclusive features like live-streaming commerce, instant feedback, gamified interfaces, and social interaction capabilities inspire pleasure, intrigue, and enthusiasm. It is these emotionally invoking experiences that make online shopping an experience, and not a utilitarian one. Affective attachment and memory retention of the shopping experience is boosted by high emotional involvement. Consequently, consumers gain a higher perception of value and meaningfulness in their interactions and this has a positive effect on their satisfaction, repetitiveness of use and emotional satisfaction beyond the actual purchasing consequences.

6.3 Well-Being and Trust and Emotion: An Integrative Approach.

Trust and emotional involvement are two variables, combined, which is a significant factor in consumer well-being in the digital retail scenario. Trust is also emotionally secure, and emotional involvement brings fun to the experience and personally applies relevance. They combine to form a balanced environment that would meet both functional and psychological needs. Social sites that successfully combine secure technology and affectively motivational features create good moods, lessen anxiety, and increase life satisfaction. This is a unified approach that is relevant especially to digital-native consumers, including Generation Z, who value socialization, authenticity, and entertainment. As a result, digital retail approaches taking technological trustworthiness to meet emotional appeal can be of great value to the long-term consumer prosperity and platform success.

7. DIGITAL RETAILING GENERATIONAL DIFFERENCES

The generational traits of consumer behavior in digital retail are highly determining of the expectations, preferences, and engagement patterns. Online platforms are used differently by different age groups, and the knowledge of these differences is critical to creating human experience on the web. As a generation between the mid-1990s and the early 2010s, Generation Z consists of digital natives who are very accustomed to the use of technology and social media. They appreciate instant communication, experience, and entertainment content, including live-streaming shopping and socialize interactive capabilities. This group is highly dependent on emotional involvement and social presence, as well as on impulsive purchases, loyalty and satisfaction in general. Generation Z also is highly responsive to personalization and AI-based suggestions because they desire a smooth experience, specific to their needs. Millennials, who were born around the beginning of the 1980s and the middle of the 1990s, appeal to convenience and experience. Although they value the intuitive interface and quality information, they pay much attention to such aspects of trust as safe transactions and clear policies. Emotional involvement is also significant yet it is normally facilitated by the perceived usefulness and plausibility of the platform. The older consumers and generation X are more likely to be interested in functionality, convenience and security rather than having an entertainment or social interactive experience. They will tend to take slower and more calculated decisions and appreciate transparent and extensive information and reliable customer services. Understanding these generational differences enables the digital retailers to customize the platform design, communication methods, and interaction methods. Through matching the experiences and expectations of each generation, retailers are able to improve trust, satisfaction and emotional participation, which will eventually lead to a greater level of consumer wellbeing and life satisfaction.

8. ARTIFICIAL INTELLIGENCE AND TECHNOLOGY IN THE CUSTOMER EXPERIENCE

The future of digital retail is being defined by artificial intelligence (AI) and sophisticated technologies, which improve personalization, efficiency, and emotions. The new e-commerce systems are using AI-based applications to understand consumer behavior, foresee preferences, and provide custom experiences as per their expectations. These technologies do not merely refer to the recommendation engines but include sentiment analysis, chatbots, dynamic pricing systems, and smart customer relationship management (CRM) systems. Retailers can use sentiment analysis to decode the emotional reaction of consumers in real-time, which is possible with the help of BERT and other natural language processing models. Through the analysis of reviews and social media interactions, as well as live chats, the platforms will be able to modify their offerings, optimize their communication, and offer interventions that increase satisfaction and trust. AI-driven personalization shall provide product suggestions, discounts, and content depending on browsing history, tastes, and demographic traits and generate a more valuable and interactive shopping encounter. Emotional experiences and social presence are further aided by interactive technologies, including live-streaming commerce, the use of augmented reality (AR) to visualize the products, and immersive interfaces. All of these features recreate the experience of the real world shopping, and digital experiences are more engaging and emotionally provoking. Notably, technology as well is critical towards fostering trust and security. The use of AI to detect fraud, privacy-sensitive data management, and dynamism in customer support strengthen the trust of consumers in online platforms. Combined with a human-focused strategy, AI and technology can not only maximize efficiency of transactions but also add to consumer wellness, satisfaction, and happiness in their lives, as the balance between functionality and emotional satisfaction is achieved in e-commerce.

8.1 AI-Driven Personalization

AI-driven personalization has become a defining feature of modern digital retail platforms, enabling retailers to deliver highly customized experiences that align with individual consumer preferences and behaviors. Unlike traditional rule-based recommendation systems, advanced AI models continuously analyze large volumes of data across multiple touchpoints, including browsing history, search queries, purchase patterns, time spent on pages, and interaction frequency. This data-driven intelligence allows platforms to adapt product recommendations, promotional offers, content presentation, and even interface layouts in real time. Personalization enhances perceived relevance and reduces information overload, making the shopping process more efficient and enjoyable. From a psychological perspective, personalized interactions foster a sense of recognition and care, which strengthens emotional attachment between consumers and the platform. When consumers feel understood and valued, satisfaction and loyalty increase significantly. Additionally, AI-driven personalization supports predictive engagement by anticipating future needs and preferences, thereby encouraging repeat visits and long-term usage. As a result, personalization not only improves transactional outcomes but also contributes to positive emotional experiences, trust development, and overall consumer well-being within digital retail environments.

8.2. Emotional Insights and Sentiment Analysis

Emotional insights derived from sentiment analysis play a crucial role in enhancing consumer experience and well-being in digital retail platforms. Using advanced natural language processing (NLP) techniques, such as BERT-based models, sentiment analysis systems evaluate textual data from customer reviews, social media posts, live chats, and feedback forms to identify emotional states including satisfaction, frustration, excitement, or disappointment. These insights allow retailers to move beyond behavioral data and gain a deeper understanding of consumer emotions in real time. By interpreting emotional signals, platforms can dynamically adjust communication tone, service responses, and marketing strategies to better align with consumer expectations. For instance, negative sentiment can trigger immediate customer support interventions, while positive sentiment can be leveraged to strengthen engagement and brand advocacy. Emotional analytics also enable retailers to identify recurring pain points and improve service design proactively. By bridging the gap between functional performance and emotional perception, sentiment analysis supports emotionally intelligent retail strategies. This alignment enhances trust, reduces dissatisfaction, and contributes to emotionally fulfilling experiences that positively influence consumer satisfaction and life well-being.

8.3. Immersive Technologies and Social Presence

Immersive technologies significantly enhance social presence and emotional engagement in digital retail environments by replicating aspects of physical shopping experiences. Live-streaming commerce enables real-time interaction between sellers and consumers, fostering transparency, authenticity, and community engagement. Consumers can ask questions, observe product demonstrations, and receive immediate feedback, which reduces uncertainty and builds confidence in purchasing decisions. This interactive format also creates entertainment value, making shopping an engaging social activity rather than a solitary task. Augmented reality (AR) technologies further enhance immersion by allowing consumers to visualize products in real-world contexts, such as trying virtual clothing, previewing furniture placement, or examining product features in detail. These technologies reduce perceived risk and improve decision accuracy. Together, immersive interfaces and interactive tools increase emotional involvement, enjoyment, and perceived value. By strengthening social presence and emotional connection, immersive technologies transform digital retail into a meaningful experiential journey, contributing to satisfaction, trust, and positive emotional well-being.

8.4. Artificial Intelligence in Trust, Security, and Reliability

Trust and security remain fundamental pillars of digital retail engagement, and AI plays a vital role in reinforcing these dimensions. AI-driven fraud detection systems monitor transaction patterns and user behavior to identify anomalies and prevent unauthorized activities in real time. Machine learning algorithms continuously adapt to emerging threats, enhancing platform reliability and reducing financial and data-related risks. These systems reassure consumers by ensuring safe payment processing and secure data management. In addition, AI-powered chatbots and automated CRM systems improve service responsiveness by providing instant assistance, order tracking, and issue resolution. Consistent and timely support increases perceived reliability and professionalism. Transparent communication regarding AI-based security measures further strengthens consumer confidence. When consumers feel protected and supported, anxiety is reduced and trust deepens. Consequently, AI-driven security and reliability mechanisms not only safeguard transactions but also contribute to emotional comfort and long-term trust, which are essential for consumer well-being and sustained platform engagement.

8.5 Striking a Balance between Functionality, Emotion, and Well-Being

The true potential of artificial intelligence in digital retail lies in its ability to balance functional efficiency with emotional and psychological satisfaction. While AI optimizes operational performance through automation, analytics, and personalization, its integration with human-centered design ensures that consumer experiences remain empathetic and meaningful. Platforms that successfully combine functional excellence with emotional engagement deliver value beyond convenience and cost efficiency. By integrating personalized recommendations, immersive technologies, emotional analytics, and secure systems, digital retailers can create experiences that address both utilitarian and emotional needs. This holistic approach reduces stress, enhances enjoyment, and promotes positive consumer attitudes. Over time, such balanced experiences contribute to higher satisfaction, stronger loyalty, and improved life well-being. Digital retail platforms that prioritize emotional resonance alongside technological sophistication are better positioned to foster long-term consumer happiness, trust, and fulfillment in increasingly digital lifestyles.

9.PROPOSED MODEL

Following the conceptual framework and dimensions of human-oriented digital retail experiences, the model presented in this study describes how different aspects of the digital retail settings can be related to consumer life satisfaction. The model incorporates four main constructs that include digital experience dimensions of retailing, trust, emotional engagement and consumer well-being. Moreover, it also entails the elements of moderation and improvement, including generational differences and AI-based customization in line with the changing dynamics of consumer anticipations in a technologically driven market. This model has the purpose of offering a comprehensive view of how digital retail can contribute not only to the functionality of a digital retail, such as loyalty and repeat purchases, but outcomes that are impactful in terms of emotions and well-being of consumers.

A. Online Retail Experience Dimensions.

The online retail experience dimensions are the base of the proposed model and the key aspects forming the perception of consumers and their interactions. These dimensions are the interface usability, information quality, privacy and security, social presence and personalization. The usability of interfaces makes sure that consumers are able to move around platforms with minimal mental load and increase the level of functional satisfaction. Good and clear information is important in making decisions on an informed basis, as well as minimizing uncertainty. Confidence and perceived risk are built and minimized using privacy and security measures as secure forms of payment gateways and transparent data policies. The social presence and personalization are what bring in emotional richness, as they make it possible to interact, engage, and have tailored experiences. All these dimensions are antecedents that trigger trust and emotional engagement. In cases of successful integration of these elements of experience, digital platforms do not only bring operational efficiency but psychological comfort and emotional attractiveness, which precondition long-term engagement, loyalty, and well-being.

B. Role of Trust

The role of trust is of central mediating in the proposed model, as it links the dimensions of digital retail experience with consumer behavioral and psychological outcomes. Trust in the context of online retail settings where there is uncertainty and information asymmetry helps to reassure the consumers of the reliability, integrity and ethical behaviour of the platform. The trust is built with repeated delivery of the service, secure transactions, open communication as well as responsiveness to customer services. Once the consumers have trust in a platform the perceived risk is low therefore the consumers use it more often and with confidence. Trust also enhances the effects of the quality of the experience as it transforms functional satisfaction into an emotional reassurance. This mediation will promote repeat usage, loyalty, and stronger relational connections in the long run. On top of the transactional results, trust also helps in the emotional stability and comfort, which makes it important in affecting consumer well-being. Accordingly, trust serves as a psychological mediator that enhances the beneficial outcomes of digital retail design on the satisfaction in the long-term and quality of life.

C. Emotional Engagement

Emotional involvement is the emotional aspect of contact between the consumer and the proposed model. It embodies the experiences of pleasure, excitement, attachment and engagement that occur during online shopping experiences. Live-streaming commerce, interactive communication, personalized content, and community-based interactions are all interactive elements that generate emotional engagement. These characteristics increase the social presence and bring the feeling of human connection to the otherwise virtual environments. Experiences which are emotional in nature make shopping more of a utilitarian process rather than a pleasing experience. High amounts of emotional involvement reinforce affective commitment and improve perceived value. Notably, emotion involvement directly impacts consumer well being as positive emotional experiences make one happier and more satisfied with life. Thus, emotional involvement is an important process by which online retail spaces influence customers beyond making purchase choices and efficiency at the point of purchase.

D. Consumer Well-Being

The final result of the suggested model is consumer well-being which shows the general effect of digital retail experiences on the quality of life of individuals. It includes life contentment, emotional comfort, happiness, and psychological gratification of coherent positive engagement with digital platforms. As the levels of trust and emotional involvement are reinforced together, consumers enjoy less stress, enhanced confidence and positive emotional conditions in the shopping process. Online retailing solutions with a strong focus on human-centered design, transparency, and emotional connection can promote consumer well-being through the provision of supportive and enjoyable environments. Well-being does not focus on the economic consequences, but it indicates the non-transactual worth of digital retail. This finding shows that e-commerce platforms can make an important contribution to the daily life experience, which proves that digital retail can help to enhance the overall life satisfaction and emotional well-being.

E. Moderating and Enhancing Factors.

The model proposed unites moderating and strengthening factors that have an impact on the strength and direction of relationships between major constructs. The generation differences can be considered as a significant moderator since the consumer expectations and responsiveness among different age groups differ. Generation Z and other digital-native generations of the population attach more value to social presence, entertainment, and emotional interactions, whereas older generations might attach a higher value to usability and security. Furthermore, the AI-based technologies can be used as amplifying mechanisms in the model. Personalization through AI, sentiment analysis, and adaptive CRM systems assist in adjusting the platform offerings to the expectations of the users. Such technologies enhance the power of trust and emotional involvement as they help to provide relevant, timely, and emotionally intelligent experiences. In combination, generational traits and the AI potential determine the way in which digital shopping experience is translated into satisfaction and well-being.

F. Implications of the Model

The integrated model is focused on human approach to assessing the effectiveness of digital retail. Instead of the efficiency, sales performance or transactional outcomes, the model emphasizes the role of trust, emotional involvement and consumer well-being. The model is broad-based providing an empirical-testing as well as an application framework by combining technical capabilities and psychological and emotional aspects. This model can help retailers create platforms that can help them to have meaningful interactions, long-lasting relationships, and positive life experiences. Research wise the model offers a basis on which complex relations can be studied through such analytical methods as Structural Equation Modeling. On the whole, the proposed model contributes to changing toward the sustainable digital retail approaches that would promote a shift toward human values and technological innovation and business performance.

G. Structural Relationships of the Proposed Model.

The proposed model presumes that there is a mediated causal association between digital retail experience dimensions, trust, emotional involvement, and consumer well-being. The dimensions of digital retail experience are exogenous variables that trigger both the affective and cognitive reactions of consumers. Trust and emotional engagement are endogenous mediators, which convey the influence of experience quality to higher-level outcomes. Trust mainly involves cognitive assessment of the reliability and risk minimization, whereas the emotional engagement reflects on the affective immersion and enjoyment. Consumer well-being is an ultimate dependent variable that is affected by these two constructs. It has both direct and indirect routes and considers that the quality of digital experience can affect well-being in various ways. Such a relationship structure will allow testing the complex interaction in an empirical way, with Structural Equation Modeling, to gain the understanding of the comparative strength and importance of every path. This arrangement can be used to acknowledge the comprehensive perspective of the interaction of technological, psychological and emotional elements in digital retail ecosystems.

H. Hypothesis-Oriented Interpretation of the Model.

The model offered has a solid basis of developing a hypothesis and validating it through empirical research. Every relationship in the context can be transformed into testable hypotheses, including the role of the digital experience dimensions on trust and emotional engagement, and the role of these mediators on the consumer well-being. The moderating variables included including generational differences make possible multi-group analysis, which can compare consumer segments. The AI-based personalization may be discussed as a reinforcing factor, which increases the impacts of the quality of the experienced item on the levels of trust and emotional engagement. The hypothesis-driven design enhances the analytical rigor of the study and enables the researchers to examine the linear effects as well as moderate effects. The model enables high levels of statistical analysis and extrapolation to other digital retail settings due to the operationalization of its constructs using validated measurement scales.

I. Applicability in Practice and Scalability of the Models.

In addition to theoretical applicability, the proposed model is oriented at its practical applicability and scalability to a variety of digital retailing platforms. The framework is applicable to conventional e-commerce websites, mobile commerce applications, social commerce sites and live-streaming retailing stores. The modular design provides retailers with the opportunity to focus on particular dimensions according to the target audiences and goals of the platform. An example is a platform that targets younger consumers, which can be focused on emotional interaction and social presence, and an enterprise platform, which can be focused on trust and security. The model can also be extended to new technologies, like virtual reality, voice commerce, and metaverse-based shopping. The model is scalable as the changing consumer expectations can be taken into consideration as new dimensions of experiential are added without losing the human focus on the core. This flexibility has rendered the model to be useful not only in the academic studies but also in the long term strategic planning in the digital retail design.

10.DISCUSSION AND IMPLICATIONS

The proposed model emphasizes the key role of human-centered design, trust, and emotional experience in constructing consumer life satisfaction in the digital retail settings. The results indicate that the digital platforms should stop being transactionally efficient, and they should generate experiences that are intuitively, securely and emotionally charged. The trust is ensured by interface usability, clear information and a strong level of privacy whereas emotional engagement is promoted by immersive features, live commerce interaction, and personalized recommendations. Combined these elements apply to holistic consumer well-being that encompasses more than shopping when it comes to digital retail and is applicable to life satisfaction.Practically, this research has a number of implications on digital retailers. To start with, investing in the interface design that is people-centred and responsiveness of CRM systems enhances consumer trust and loyalty. Second, the combination of AI-based sentiment analysis and personalization would help platforms to predict needs and provide relevant content to consumers and create an emotional bond. Third, it is important to identify generational differences in order to differentiate engagement strategies; generation Z and other consumers who are digital-native are highly sensitive to social presence and entertainment-oriented experiences, whereas older customers are more sensitive to security and usability. Theoretical model The model can broaden the conceptualization of digital retail by relating the experience quality, trust, and emotional involvement to more objective metrics of life satisfaction. It shows that the success of digital commerce cannot be measured using solely economic indicators but also its contribution to consumer welfare. Also, the framework emphasises the importance of integrating the new technologies to improve functional and emotional elements of digital retail. All in all, these lessons help create platforms that will not just be effective and secure but also significant, meaningful, and life improving to the consumers.Besides the relevance of the study to managers, the research findings have significant implications to the platform designers, policymakers and technology developers in the digital economy. In terms of design, the findings support the need to integrate ethical and open practices in digital retail designs. The availability of information on how the data will be used, AI fairness in personalization, and responsible implementation of AI not only helps to build trust but can also lead to emotional comfort in the long term among consumers. The latter factors are especially applicable in the markets that are becoming more sensitive in terms of data privacy and digital manipulation.On a policy level, the research recommends that consumer well-being is to be regarded as a complementary indicator of digital retail ecosystems in addition to economic performance. Privacy protection, platform responsibility, and consumer-driven innovation regulatory frameworks can help create healthier digital environments. Moreover, the increasing role of immersive and AI-driven technologies has created the necessity to adopt technologies in a balanced manner that would focus on human values and technological efficiency.Lastly, the discussion suggests future research directions, e.g. longitudinal research to determine the effects of well-being in the long term, cross-cultural comparisons to learn about differences in contexts, and further research into new technologies such as virtual reality and metaverse-based shopping. This study will add to a fuller perspective of the extent to which technology-mediated commerce will determine consumer life satisfaction in the modern society, extended beyond short-term behavioral implications.

11.LIMITATIONS AND FUTURE RESEARCH DIRECTIONS

Although the suggested framework has given a thorough comprehension of the impact of digital retail experiences on consumer life satisfaction, a number of shortcomings would be noted. To start with, the research is theoretical, as it is based on the conceptual analysis and the literature synthesis instead of the empirical validation. Consequently, the suggested relationships between digital experience dimensions of retail experience, trust, and emotional engagement, as well as consumer well-being, must be experimented in various real-world settings to validate them and generalize their applicability.Second, the framework majorly focuses on psychological and experiential variables and also little attention is paid to external factors like cultural variations, socioeconomic variations, and regional variations. Such contextual variables can have different expectations and reaction among the consumer in various markets, which can impact the applicability of the model.Third, although generational differences and AI-enabled technologies are being introduced as moderating factors, there might be other demographic factors (e.g., gender, income level, digital literacy) and other technological factors (e.g., augmented reality, virtual reality, metaverse commerce) that may also impact consumer engagement and satisfaction.These limitations can be dealt with in future research by carrying out empirical studies on more than one digital retail site, combining both quantitative and qualitative research methods, which include surveys, experiments, and structural equation modeling. Comparison of generations, cultures and products can give a better insight into consumer behavior. Moreover, the study of novel technologies and their implication in promoting human-oriented experiences will enable researchers and practitioners to improve the platform designing approaches so that online shopping spaces should promote not only the efficiency of transactions but also significant contributions to the well-being of consumers.Moreover, the research is cross-sectional and, therefore, does not allow tracking the changes in consumer trust, emotional involvement, and well-being over the years. The digital customer experience and perception can be dynamic and can change as a customer becomes more accustomed to platforms or as technology changes. The longitudinal research designs would enable future studies to capture such changes in time and study the causal relationship more precisely. Moreover, self-reported instruments involved in well being and emotional engagement studies also have the risk of response bias which might affect the accuracy of results.Future studies can also be enhanced through combination of objective behavioral data, including clickstreams, and purchase histories, and interaction logs, with the subjective psychological measurement to have a more holistic view of consumer experiences. To isolate the effects of a particular digital aspect (e.g., ability to interact through live-streaming or use of AI to provide personalization) on emotional and well-being outcomes, they could be experimentally designed.In addition, the research on ethical implications of AI adoption, such as data transparency, bias of algorithms, and consumer autonomy, should be examined in the future. The question about the role of responsible AI practices in reinforcing trust and feeling of comfort may yield some useful information on the sustainable development of digital retail. By discussing these methodological, contextual, and ethical aspects, future studies can help the research to be more robust and relevant to the society, being one of the platforms that would increase not only the business success but the happiness of consumer life.

12.CONCLUSION

Digital retail has not only revolutionized the shopping process of consumers but also the aspect of trust, emotional involvement, and satisfaction in general in their lives. A human approach is highlighted in this paper where it is proposed that the effectiveness of the digital marketplaces must be gauged by not only the performance of transactions but also the ability of the marketplace to add value to the consumer well-being. The study identifies the use of important dimensions interface usability, information quality, privacy and security, social presence, and personalized interactions as antecedents to trust and emotional engagement, which subsequently lead to life satisfaction, through a unified conceptual framework.The results highlight the importance of trust regarding the mediation of consumer relations with online services. Honest communication, high quality services delivery, and secure data protection systems build trust, whereas interactive tools like live commerce, personal advice and AI-based sentiment analysis help to build emotional connection. The generational differences also indicate that the expectations and reactions of the consumers are also different, where digital-native generations are more focused on social presence and experience, and older users are more inclined toward usability, security, and reliability. The acknowledgment of these differences enables online retailers to create experiences, which are customized, welcoming, and user-friendly. This paper has extensive contributions both in theory and practice. It pushes the concept of digital retail further beyond its efficiency and sales, connecting the quality of experience and technological integration with wider scales of life satisfaction. To the practitioners, it offers the advice of designing platforms that will not only consider functional, emotional, and ethical elements but also lead to long-lasting consumer relations and loyalty.To sum up, the digital retail of the future is in its capacity of matching technological advancements with human requirements. Offering usability, engagement, trust, and personalization as some of its core principles, a platform has a higher chance to improve not only consumer satisfaction but also life well-being. With the introduction of human-focused values and the exploitation of the latest technological achievements, digital retail may become a place where valuable interactions, feelings of satisfaction, and consumer happiness are sustained over time, adjusting the success rate criteria of the digital commerce era.

REFERENCES

Amirkhizi, P. J.. (2025). "The Role of Human-Centered Design in Enhancing Trust and Satisfaction in E-Commerce within Industry 5.0," *2025 IEEE International Systems Conference (SysCon)*, Montreal, QC, Canada, pp. 1–8, DOI: 10.1109/SysCon64521.2025.11014837

Hamidah, D. N. A.. (2024). "User Interface Design of TUS Mart E-Commerce Website Using Design Thinking and Kansei Engineering," *Proc. ICIMCIS*, Jakarta, Indonesia, pp. 182–187, DOI: 10.1109/ICIMCIS63449.2024.10956865

Harahap, E. P.. (2024). "User Interface Design's Impact on Customer Satisfaction and Loyalty in SaaS E-Commerce," *Proc. ICCIT*, Tangerang, Indonesia, pp. 1–6, DOI: 10.1109/ICCIT62134.2024.10701133

Marvella, W. G., & Taylor, S. A. (2025). "Factors Influencing E-Commerce Repurchase Intention: Customer Experience and E-Service Quality," *Proc. ICCIT*, Kota Cirebon, Indonesia, pp. 1–7, DOI: 10.1109/ICCIT65724.2025.11166807

Maulana, H. T., & Rosyidah, U. (2022). "User Experience Model using Concise User-Centered Design in Small and Medium Enterprise E-Commerce," 2022 International Seminar on Application for Technology of Information and Communication (iSemantic), Semarang, Indonesia, pp. 377–382, DOI: 10.1109/iSemantic55962.2022.9920381

Mittameedi, S. K., Dogra, V., & Sayal, A. (2025). Customer Experience in E-Commerce: A Systematic Review of Metrics, Models, and the Role of AI. *IEEE Access : Practical Innovations, Open Solutions*, *13*, 154422–154437. DOI: 10.1109/ACCESS.2025.3600729

Nasar, M. R. A. (2025). "Evaluating Platform Usability in E-Commerce: Empirical Insights from User Interactions with Amazon's App and Website," 2025 3rd International Conference on Business Analytics for Technology and Security (ICBATS), Dubai, United Arab Emirates, pp. 1–7, DOI: 10.1109/ICBATS66542.2025.11258426

R. P. S. K. K. S., S. R. S., S. K., and A. P., (2024). "Optimizing User Satisfaction and Streamlining Operations in Online Retail Using CNN Algorithm," Proc. IITCEE, Bangalore, India, pp. 1–7, DOI: 10.1109/IITCEE59897.2024.10467533

Roy, A.. (2025). "E-Commerce Enhancement Through Intelligent Customer Interaction: Integration of GPT-Powered Chatbot with Sentiment Analysis," *Proc. CVMI*, Rourkela, India, pp. 1–6, DOI: 10.1109/CVMI66673.2025.11337625

Shao, Y., Liu, S., Chen, G., Ma, R., Wang, X., & Li, Q. (2025, November–December). FashionCook: A Visual Analytics System for Human–AI Collaboration in Fashion E-Commerce Design. *IEEE Computer Graphics and Applications*, *45*(6), 61–75. DOI: 10.1109/MCG.2025.3597849 PMID: 40864590

Sharif, O. O., & Sudirman, I. D. (2024). "Investigating Trust Determinants in E-commerce Through User Experience and Delivery Satisfaction," 2024 9th International Conference on Information Technology and Digital Applications (ICITDA), Malaysia, pp. 1–6, DOI: 10.1109/ICITDA64560.2024.10809747

Sugosha, K. G., Andreswari, R., & Hardiyanti, M. (2021). "Design and Implementation of User Interface and User Experience in Online Sales Applications at Sugosha Pharmacy with User Centered Design Method," *2021 International Conference on Advanced Computer Science and Information Systems (ICACSIS)*, Depok, Indonesia, pp. 1–5, DOI: 10.1109/ICACSIS53237.2021.9631344

Widiatmo, G. (2024). "The Future of E-commerce: Creating Immersive Experiences in Live Streaming Commerce to Drive Consumers' Impulse Buying," *Proc. ECTI-CON*, Khon Kaen, Thailand, pp. 1–6, DOI: 10.1109/ECTI-CON60892.2024.10594963

Wijaya, L.. (2025). "E-Commerce Uncovered: Exploring Key Drivers of Consumer Impulse Buying Behavior," *Proc. ICWR*, Tehran, Iran, pp. 294–298, DOI: 10.1109/ICWR65219.2025.11006215

Zhuo, X., Sun, Y., & Zhou, S. (2025). Impact of Consumers Traceability Awareness on Blockchain Adoption in Supply Chains. *IEEE Transactions on Engineering Management*, *72*, 1140–1153. DOI: 10.1109/TEM.2025.3552437

Chapter 13 Digital Social Media Experience, Perceived Digital Brand Meaning, Digital Presence and Social Embeddedness, and Digital Life Satisfaction: A Cross-Cultural Perspective

J. Vidhya
http://orcid.org/0000-0002-5898-3439
Saveetha School of Management, Saveetha Institute of Medical and Technical Sciences, India

K. Ramya
Saveetha School of Management, Saveetha Institute of Medical and Technical Sciences, India

R. Mohammed Rizwan
Saveetha School of Management, Saveetha Institute of Medical and Technical Sciences, India

ABSTRACT

The frequent use of social media in everyday life has modified the communication used by marketers to communicate with one another. They now do not exchange

DOI: 10.4018/979-8-3373-8357-6.ch013

just promotions online, but they indulge in immersive and relationship-based online interactions that have a huge impact on the health of people. This paper looks at the understanding of digital brand meaning, digital presence and social embeddedness and how they combine to create digital life satisfaction that eventually creates a long-lasting brand loyalty. The chapter reevaluates now the concept of social media marketing differently than the conventional metrics involving its performance. The prospective implications of the study, which is based on the psychological importance, digital life satisfaction, and the impact of cultural values on brand perception and brand creation, will offer fundamental details on the future research. The SDGs 4 (Quality Education), 8 (Decent Work and Economic Growth), and 9 (Industry, Innovation and Infrastructure) are supported by the literature review presented in this chapter.

INTRODUCTION

Digital technologies have disseminated extremely fast, and they have entirely altered the way individuals communicate, study, work, and derive meaning to their day-to-day lives (Sardashti & Calantone, 2022). The social media sites have become sophisticated digital communities that influence the relationship with brands, emotional response, self-formation and enjoyment of life (Tarnanidis et al., 2026). They had been limited to communication. The personal, social, and professional lives of people are becoming increasingly intertwined in digital space across cultural boundaries, which makes digital social media experience an indispensable part of the digital life enjoyment. For this instance, the influence of digital social media experience on digital brand meaning, digital presence and social embeddedness can be highly valued in the view of examining the matter in a cross-cultural perspective, considering various socioeconomic and technological aspects (Tarnanidis, 2026).

The term, digital social media experience, encompasses the frequency of use, as well as mental, emotional and social immersion in the virtual world (Agnihotri and Rengararaj, 2025). Social media is a social environment which allows individuals to discuss their identities, exchange their emotions, and connect 24/7. According to prior studies, social media, when used by younger populations, has the potential to create intimacy, alleviate loneliness, and enhance relationship maintenance (Widjaja et al., 2024). However, these platforms can make a person unhappy and weaker in feelings, and to lead to conflicts with others. The significance of digital space lies in the fact that here people have an opportunity to experiment with the means of self-presentation and interaction with others and determine who they are and how they can cope with their emotions. According to Wood et al. (2016), such experiences cannot be described as culturally neutral, and they are influenced by social norms, technological access, and digital literacy levels across various societies. These aspects establish a direct relationship between the digital social media utilisation and the general consequences, such as happiness and a desire to live a digital life.

With the increasing digitalization, individuals are now engaging with brands more frequently than they do with others. Branding in the digital era is turning out to be an interactive, experience-based process as opposed to a one-way communication process. Perceived digital brand meaning is a significant concept as today's consumers seek meaningful, value-based relationships with the brands using digital touchpoints (Geetha et al., 2024). The internet has ceased being an advantageous instrument to an indispensable element of the everyday lives of the billions of individuals who spend significant hours daily on the internet. Due to this shift, organizations in every industry are finding the need to have an online presence as a strategic necessity rather than a marketing instrument. According to Ramadhani and Indradjati (2023), digital branding is no longer about being visible, but also incorporates the trust, engagement, authenticity and relevance in the digital lives of users.

The presence in the digital world states is highly relevant to the perceptions of individuals towards businesses and their place in their social and cultural life. The reliance on traditional marketing techniques is declining by the day because consumers with access to digital technology now make decisions through a cyclical, iterative approach rather than in a downstream manner. Brands are sought, judged, and collaboratively constructed by the customers in terms of social media interactions, reviews and online forums. The digital presence is a place for the customer and the brand to interact and co-create value. The relational aspect of digital branding has a direct impact on social embeddedness as brand contact becomes increasingly linked to social networks, peer influence and social digital experiences (Agnihotri and Rengararaj, 2025).

The concept of embeddedness to social relationships is called social embeddedness, which holds that market exchanges are not merely one-off transactions, but that they are founded on social networks and relationships. Relationship marketing literature emphasizes the need to establish, develop, maintain and enhance long term relationships with the stakeholders to fulfill their expectations and obligations. The use of social media sites complicates distinguishing between personal relations, business contacts, and the interaction with the brand. This contributes to the power of social embeddedness in online space. Therefore, the social media experiences in digital form assist individuals to become socially and economically part of the digital ecosystem, which influences their satisfaction, loyalty, and trust. This embeddedness is different in different cultures in terms of social norms, technology provision and social ideals (Grönroos, 1994).

On the developmental perspective, the digital changes are aligned with Sustainable Development Goals (SDGs) of the UN. The SDG 4 (Quality Education) can be achieved through the application of digital platforms where it is easier to access information, acquire knowledge on how to use technology and informally learn through social media. SDG 8 (Decent Work and Economic Growth) can be supported using digital branding and an online presence, which ensures that new employment opportunities, avenues to entrepreneurs, and avenues to international markets. The extent to which we depend more on the digital infrastructure and advanced platforms through which people of diverse cultures find it simpler to conduct business and socialise demonstrates SDG 9 (Industry, Innovation, and Infrastructure). Therefore, the happiness of digital life appears to be an indicator of the inclusive digital development and a personal outcome.

Digital social media experience, perceived significance of digital brands, digital presence, and social embeddedness are all interconnected variables which influence the overall quality of digital life. In analyzing the varying digital engagement, brand connection and social integration by cultures, it is worthwhile to examine these relationships in a cross-cultural perspective. The paper aims to develop a comprehensive insight regarding the effects of digital environments on well-being in an ever-connected world by combining psychological, marketing, and relational approaches.

THEORETICAL FRAMEWORK

The primary factor which influences the way people consider digital brand meaning (PDBM), digital presence, and social embeddedness is the digital social media experience (DSME). The factors then transform the digital life happiness routes and eventually the satisfaction of life-based brand attachment (LSDBA). The framework is based on the cross-cultural approach and applies four foundational theories to explain such dynamics: Stimulus-Organism-Response (S-O-R) model, the Cultural Dimensions Theory by Hofstede, the Uses and Gratifications Theory (UGT), and the Social Presence Theory (SPT). Based on these assumptions, the model assumes that DSME is an antecedent which mediates emotional and relational impacts and in which the cultural differences are controlled, and which can be validated by PLS-SEM to rigorous statistical support.

STIMULUS-ORGANISM-RESPONSE MODEL

This paradigm is based on the principle of Stimulus-Organism-Response (S-O-R) model, which began its formation in environmental psychology (Mehrabian and Russell, 1974). It implies that external stimuli (S) arouse internal states of the organism (O), including affective and cognitive responses that in turn result in behavioural outcomes (R). The stimulus of the study is that of DSME, which is interactive, educative, and immersive interaction via social media that evokes states in organisms such as social embeddedness, digital presence, and PDBM. The mediation of these intermediaries that indicate the degree of emotional involvement and attachment of the consumers results in LSDBA as the end response and digital life satisfaction as another level of existence.

The effectiveness of the S-O-R framework is supported by empirical studies on digital marketing; in one instance, social media stimuli (including customized content) enhance brand perception and brand loyalty via a channel of affect (Eroglu et al., 2003). Indicatively, because of increased relational sensitivity, collectivist societies can become more embedded, reacting, though, there is a moderation of embeddedness reaction in a cross-cultural environment whereby cultural norms are involved in evaluating stimuli (Tsai, 2007). This design aligns with the approach of PLS-SEM that is employed in the rest of the chapter and simplifies the path analysis of direct, mediated and moderated effects.

USES AND GRATIFICATIONS THEORY

The Uses and Gratifications Theory (UGT), which was developed by Katz, Blumler and Gurevitch in 1974, explains the needs and desires to consume the media and holds the view that consumers will purposefully choose a platform to satisfy their needs to entertain, socialize, gain some information and identify their personalities. DSME actualises UGT by providing these gratifications, educational content satisfies cognitive needs, interactive features satisfy relational needs, and immersive experiences satisfy escapism desires. This increases the PDBM because consumers give more emphasis on the brands that satisfy their gratifications.

According to Westerman et al. (2013), UGT is also applicable in mediation, where one needs fulfillment can make people feel part of them. People add the brands to networks to ensure that they are always satisfied, and this increases their digital lives. Through the conceptualisation of LSDBA as an attachment founded on fulfilment, non-Transactional loyalty can be anticipated by transactional gratifications in brand settings (Hollebeek et al., 2014). UGT demonstrate the difference in cultures: the indulgent societies are sought to be satisfied with pleasure, whereas the avoidance of uncertainty societies is aimed at gathering trust through information (Muntinga et al., 2011). This theory enhances the people-centered approach adopted in this framework by associating DSME with psychological effects.

SOCIAL PRESENCE THEORY

The Social Presence Theory (SPT) by Short et al. (1976) suggests that communication gadgets differ in the ability to transmit the socio-emotional cues including warmth and immediacy that may affect how individuals perceive relationships. Live chats and user-generated content help brands recreate human relationships and increase PDBM and social embeddedness because digital platforms can create presence. The result of high social presence-enriched DSME is that passive exposure is transformed into relational immersion, and thus they feel that they belong and their feelings remain constant, which in turn makes them satisfied with their online existence.

It has proven that SPT in social media is effective; interactive processes that are active and responsive, as well as presence, are directly linked to trust, engagement, and loyalty are directly associated with presence (Biocca et al., 2003). Customers perceive the digital spaces as their social life; this is made through brands that employ real-time responses, such as embeddedness (Short et al., 1976). The effect of SPT in cross-cultural settings is more heightened in high-context, feminine cultures that do not value task-oriented interactions but rather harmonious ones (Hofstede, 2001). This theory enhances S-O-R as it describes the functioning of organisms, and the theory is excellent to test mediation in PLS-SEM.

HOFSTEDE'S CULTURAL DIMENSIONS THEORY

According to the Cultural Dimensions Theory by Hofstede (Hofstede, 1980), behavioural interpretations are influenced by societal values, which are defined by power distance, individualism versus collectivism, uncertainty avoidance and masculinity versus femininity. Customers who are highly group oriented enjoy integrating with the group brand and therefore, collectivism increases social embeddedness of DSME, and individualism increases PDBM of self-expressive alignments. Uncertainty is decreasing the satisfaction level, and cultures that do not want to risk should always be around to feel better.

Status signalling is associated with brand loyalty in hierarchical societies. This hypothesis deals with the multicultural nature of the framework because the power distance impacts the attachment (Zhang et al., 2020). According to Sivadas et al. (2008), empirical studies support the fact that cultural moderation is facilitated within digital settings and therefore, collectivists derive a higher sense of life satisfaction when they have embedded contacts. PLS-SEM bypasses the issue of universalism by describing culture as a quasi-moderator, exposing differences in routes between groups.

LITERATURE REVIEW

Digital Social Media Experience and Consumer Well-Being

The fact that so many individuals use the social media has transformed the digital platforms that initially served merely as channels of communication between people to multi-layered and multi-dimensional social and psychological environments that alter the identities, emotions, and well-being of those who use it. Digital Social Media Experience (DSME) evaluates the quality of the interactions (e.g., emotional connection and interactivity through online communication, enjoyment, and the richness of online relationships) as opposed to the frequency of the use of social media. According to the previous studies, social media is an important social context where users control their emotions, get their peers to affirm them, and develop an individual and a group identity (Wood et al., 2016). Consequently, such interactions influence significantly the way individuals perceive psychological fulfilment and happiness in their online lives.

According to the Uses and Gratifications Theory (Katz et al., 1973), individuals turn to social media to satisfy certain information, social and emotional needs. As soon as users believe that these requirements are fulfilled, they are likely to believe that digital interaction is more useful and gratifying. But not all of them are pleasant effects of DSME. Excess or deficiency in usage can lead to stress and are not happy, but meaningful and profound interaction can make people feel more connected and supported. This implies that the quality of your social media life is significant to your happiness in digital life than the frequency and intensity of your usage (Whiting and Williams, 2013).

Perceived Digital Brand Meaning in Social Media Environments

The perception of brands by people in digital environments has evolved a great deal. Perceived Digital Brand Meaning (PDBM) is the emotional, symbolic, and psychological meaning which individuals attach to the brands they view on the internet. In contrast to the traditional branding practices, user-created content, social interactions, and user engagement all contribute to the current process of the co-creation of digital brand meaning (Hollebeek et al., 2014). Brands can also be perceived by customers as social beings through social media and customers tend to attribute human characteristics like personality, ethics, and authenticity.

Empirical studies have shown that participatory, transparent and value-driven brand communication, through establishing trust and emotional attachment, has the effect of enhancing perceived brand meaning (Eroglu et al., 2003). By aligning brands with personal beliefs and making them fit into their digital lives, they are able to contribute to their digital well-being. Various cultures hold diverse notions of what a brand is. Individualistic cultures put more emphasis on self-expression and personal meaning, whereas collectivist cultures emphasize on relational and community-oriented brand values (Tsai, 2007).

Digital Presence and Social Embeddedness

Digital presence refers to the extent to which individuals believe that brands and other individuals are socially real, emotionally open, and human-like online. The Social Presence Theory (Short et al., 1976) states that the media capable of producing the effect of warmth, immediacy, and interpersonal connection lead to a better relationship. Information that can be tailored to the specifics of the digital environment, instant communication, and rapid response are some of the features that can make a digital presence feel more real in social media environments and interactions feel more like they are taking place face-to-face (Licsandru et al., 2025).

According to Grönroos (1994), social embeddedness demonstrates that consumer behaviour is more engrained within social relationships rather than transaction which entails buying and selling. Organisations are frequently integrated in the social circles of customers in the online environment, which influences sustained interaction, word of mouth and the development of trust. In the case of digital interactions, earlier studies show that social and integrated interactions lead to emotional stability and a sense of belonging, which are both critical to digital life satisfaction (Biocca et al., 2003).

Digital Life Satisfaction as a Well-Being Outcome

Digital Life Satisfaction (DLS) measures the overall assessment of well-being of an individual in digital settings, including their sense of fulfilment, emotional stability and the quality of their online relationships. Social media experiences on the Internet are perceived as stimuli that influence the inner psychological conditions of perceived meaning, trust, social embeddedness (Stimulus-Organism-Response (S-O-R), Mehrabian and Russell, 1974). These states in turn influence the results of satisfaction.

Studies indicate that positive online experiences make individuals feel more in control of their emotions, more confident, and supported by others, resulting in a happier online life (Gerson et al., 2016). Moreover, significant and socially related online communications assist individuals in remaining affiliated with a brand over an extended time, as it causes them to feel superior about themselves in the long run rather than in the short run (Mandania et al., 2025).

CROSS-CULTURAL DIFFERENCES IN DIGITAL EXPERIENCES AND SATISFACTION

The understanding of social relations, the brand meanings, and the digital engagement of people significantly depend on cultural values. The Cultural Dimensions Theory developed by Hofstede provides a detailed framework for explaining such differences, especially in the context of dimensions such as power distance, uncertainty avoidance, and individualism versus collectivism (Hofstede, 1980; 2001). Research indicates that members of individualistic societies place more importance on independence and self-relevance whereas those of collectivist societies appear to be satisfied with virtual communication that belongs to a social network (Sivadas et al., 2008).

According to cross-cultural studies, indulgent cultures tend to react more positively to experiencing and hedonistic content, whereas civilisations with a high uncertainty avoidance need more information and trust in achieving digital happiness (Muntinga et al., 2011). These findings promote the use of culture as a confounding factor in digital well-being research studies and emphasize the need to avoid making generalisations about how digital consumers behave.

BRANDED CONTENT MOTIVATIONS AND DIGITAL SATISFACTION

Social media branded content that resonates with the motivations of social media users, like rewards and entertainment, has a strong influence on brand-related behaviour, including a desire to share, click behaviour, and purchase intentions (Buzeta et al., 2024). The cross-cultural research performed in Latin American and Western European environments shows that motivation-oriented branded content yields improved relationships and strengthens the meaning of digital brands, at the same time improving engagement, irrespective of the cultural differences. However, these results are consistent with the previous research that links satisfaction and brand attachment to the substantial interactions through digital channels.

DIGITAL SELF, VIRTUAL SATISFACTION, AND MOBILE SOCIAL MEDIA USE

The way in which social media communication affects the online self is a decisive factor in virtual satisfaction. Studies on cross-cultural research using configurational approaches demonstrate that social connection and self-expression are two variables that help to bring pleasure both in a universal way and culturally specific (Krishen et al., 2021). These findings can suggest the idea that DSME acts as a stimulus that causes emotional reactions by organismic states, such as social embeddedness and digital presence.

In addition, the studies about mobile social media use, especially in adolescents, imply a positive correlation with life satisfaction and the feeling of purpose (Meng et al., 2023). However, this relationship is fully mediated by meaning in life, even though it is intensified by sensitivity variables like childhood adversity. This contrasts with Uses and Gratifications Theory (Fournier, S. 1998), which points to the importance of relational gratifications and interactions of high quality, as opposed to the frequency of use.

SOCIAL PRESENCE, S-O-R FRAMEWORK, AND BRAND LOYALTY

The S-O-R perspective of influencer marketing demonstrates how digital stimuli, such as entertainment and scarcity signals, may lead to such psychological conditions as flow, emotional attachment, and positive affect, which, in turn, influence the behavior of people (Guo et al., 2025). Whereas informativeness positively influences emotional attachment and cemented the perceived digital brand importance and presence across platforms, social presence and sense of belonging do the same to engagement.

Similarly, studies on e-service environments have shown that, the reinstatement of social factors like responsiveness and visual factors counteracts impersonality of e-interactions (Cyr et al., 2018). Such virtual re-embedding enhances the connection between social embeddedness, digital contentment and long-term brand attachment as it develops trust, satisfaction and loyalty, particularly between cultures that are similar.

EFFECTS OF OWNED SOCIAL MEDIA CONTENT

The importance of the social media accounts of the brands lies in the ability to achieve business outcomes that are beyond likes and shares. It has been shown that direct content sharing by the brands has a huge effect on the sales performance beyond the metrics of engagement. Specifically, the emotionally charged content is more likely to make people relate to companies on a personal and emotional level.

Nonetheless, informative content tends to be more effective in assisting customers to achieve their practical objectives, including assisting them to make smart decisions.

In-depth meta-analysis indicates that the content on owned social media has much more flexibility in sales results than in engagement results. This demonstrates the strategic significance of this in value creation (Liadeli et al., 2023). These effects are even further influenced by cultural factors, in particular, power distance, as Hofstede explains in his model of culture. Brand communication is more credible and authoritative in cultures where power distance is high, which reinforces digital satisfaction channels. The combined results partially indicate that Digital Social Media Experience (DSME) can be a significant variable that enhances perceived digital brand meaning and social embeddedness, further resulting in life satisfaction-based brand attachment (LSDBA).

INFLUENCER BRAND ENGAGEMENT IN SOCIAL MEDIA

Social media influencers have been critical contributors to brand equity and engagement creation through their creation of high-quality and reliable content. Research indicates that perceived content quality and source legitimacy, which influence customer response to an influencer both mentally and emotionally, are significant to the effectiveness of the influencer. Research that utilizes the Elaboration Likelihood Model has shown that company-generated content has a mediating effect, which is much more effective in terms of engagement than user-generated alternatives. It is also found that the relationship between influencer communication and brand engagement is entirely mediated by the quality of the material (Kim et al., 2025).

The needs of customers in the form of information and relationships that are satisfied by the influencer content allow them to feel more associated with the brands in use and gratification. People become influenced, i.e. become trustful, participatory and happy thanks to influencer stimuli, and this makes people more happy with their digital lives among a vast number of audiences. These are in line with the Stimulus -Organism-Response (S-O-R) model. The effects are compounded by culture especially in collectivist societies where peer influence and societal norms reinforce human connections. This follows the idea that culture can be a moderating factor in models of digital interaction and well-being.

HYPOTHESIS DEVELOPMENT

Digital Social Media Experience (DSME) and Life Satisfaction–Driven Brand Attachment (LSDBA)

Digital Social Media Experience (DSME) is a term, which refers to the use of social media sites by people in an emotional, cognitive, and social manner. According to Stimulus -Organism -Response (S -O -R) model, DSME is an external stimulus that alters the user's affect and action patterns. When individuals experience positive online experiences, such as encounters that are meaningful, entertaining, and emotional, they become more comfortable in digital environments. The more social media is integrated into people's daily lives, the happier they are with their digital life as a result of good digital experiences (Fitzmaurice & Comegys, 2006). When businesses contribute to making people happy, they will become more associated with them. This attachment manifests itself in Life Satisfaction-Driven Brand Attachment (LSDBA). It does not only occur due to the advantages of the product but also because companies improve the digital life of the users.

H1: Digital Social Media Experience (DSME) has a significant relationship with Life Satisfaction–Driven Brand Attachment (LSDBA).

Digital Social Media Experience (DSME) and Perceived Digital Brand Meaning (PDBM)

Perceived digital brand meaning (PDBM) is a term used to refer to the psychological, symbolic, and emotional meanings of brands formed by consumers in the Internet. Social media are actively used by people to gratify their needs such as knowledge, socialization, and self-fulfillment, as the Uses and Gratifications Theory (UGT) states. The stronger the users perceive the brands as having meaningful, interesting, and authentic experiences in social media, the more the users tend to perceive the brand as meaningful. The continued engagement in digital interactions, such as co-creation, storytelling, and participation, makes users begin to associate companies with emotional value and personal importance. More enriching digital social media lives consequently increase the perceptions of users on the importance of companies in their digital lives.

H2: Digital Social Media Experience (DSME) has a significant relationship with Perceived Digital Brand Meaning (PDBM).

Digital Social Media Experience (DSME) and Digital Presence & Social Embeddedness (DP&SE)

"Digital presence" or "social embeddedness" is the term for people's sense of how connected, visible, and involved they feel in online groups. According to Social Presence Theory, interactive and immersive digital environments make people feel more connected, close and present. People feel more as though they belong in online communities thanks to DSME's discussions, involvement in the community and shared experiences. As social media blurs the lines between social ties and brand interactions, it's more likely that users will view brands as a part of their social networks. Having a good experience on social media can help you to become more socially connected and have a stronger online presence (Granovetter, 1985).

H3: Digital Social Media Experience (DSME) has a significant relationship with Digital Presence & Social Embeddedness (DP&SE).

Perceived Digital Brand Meaning (PDBM) and Life Satisfaction–Driven Brand Attachment (LSDBA)

Customers are drawn to digital businesses that appeal to their beliefs, feelings, and sense of self. PDBM is a mental state that bridges the digital interactions to behavioural outcomes in the S--O--R framework. Big brands have a positive impact on the mental health and happiness of users of their digital lives. When people believe that a digital brand is more important, they are more likely to feel a strong connection to it that is beyond its usefulness. This kind of attachment style demonstrates the presence of a long-term relationship, based on trust, emotional stability and happiness in life.

H4: Perceived Digital Brand Meaning (PDBM) has a significant relationship with Life Satisfaction–Driven Brand Attachment (LSDBA).

Digital Presence & Social Embeddedness (DP&SE) and Life Satisfaction–Driven Brand Attachment (LSDBA)

Social embeddedness illustrates the social ties of people and how these ties influence their actions. Being present and connected in digital spaces can help people feel more comfortable, trust others, and feel like they belong. When brands do participate in these socially connected digital spaces, they become part of the everyday digital interaction of the users. This type of connection makes people happier with their online lives and makes them more loyal to the brand. This attachment is motivated by social connection and continuity of relationships, rather than exposure and marketing influence.13 Therefore: H5: Digital Presence & Social Embeddedness (DP&SE) has a significant positive relationship with Life Satisfaction - Driven Brand Attachment (LSDBA).

Mediating Role of Perceived Digital Brand Meaning (PDBM)

Digital social media experience has more than a direct impact on brand attachment. Instead, DSME first impacts people's understanding and reception of the meaning of a brand. Perceived Digital Brand Meaning is an important mental process by which digital interactions are transformed into feelings of attachment. Positive digital social media experiences make users more likely to give companies a deeper meaning, which makes brand attachment based on life satisfaction stronger.

H6: Perceived Digital Brand Meaning (PDBM) mediates the relationship between Digital Social Media Experience (DSME) and Life Satisfaction–Driven Brand Attachment (LSDBA).

Mediating Role of Digital Presence & Social Embeddedness (DP&SE)

In the same way, DSME enhances social embeddedness and digital presence of users through communication, engagement, and community involvement. These digital experiences that are socially embedded make people feel more connected to their brands and make their digital lives more enjoyable. So, the relational pathway of Digital Presence & Social Embeddedness has an impact on the brand attachment that comes from being happy with life.

H7: Digital Presence & Social Embeddedness (DP&SE) mediates the relationship between Digital Social Media Experience (DSME) and Life Satisfaction–Driven Brand Attachment (LSDBA).

RESEARCH OBJECTIVES

1. To analyze the impact of Digital Social Media Experience (DSME) on Life Satisfaction–Driven Brand Attachment (LSDBA).
2. To examine the effect of Digital Social Media Experience (DSME) on Perceived Digital Brand Meaning (PDBM).
3. To assess the influence of Digital Social Media Experience (DSME) on Digital Presence and Social Embeddedness (DP&SE).
4. To investigate the mediating roles of Perceived Digital Brand Meaning (PDBM) and Digital Presence & Social Embeddedness (DP&SE) in the relationship be-

tween Digital Social Media Experience (DSME) and Life Satisfaction–Driven Brand Attachment (LSDBA).

Figure 1. Conceptual Framework

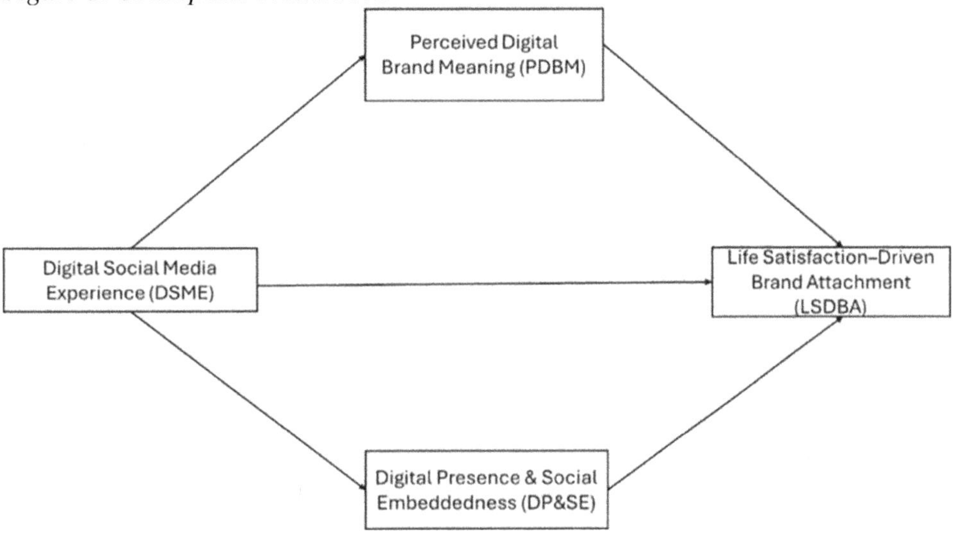

Source: By author

RESEARCH METHODOLOGY

This research uses a quantitative descriptive research methodology to experimentally assess the proposed paradigm between Digital Social Media Experience (DSME), Perceived Digital Brand Meaning (PDBM), Digital Presence & Social Embeddedness (DP&SE), and Life Satisfaction--Driven Brand Attachment (LSDBA). The goal is to explore directional relationships and mediating effects, not to produce qualitative insights. Given that all focal variables are perceptual in nature, latent constructs that are best measured via self-reported evaluation (at an individual level) provide a good reason to employ a survey method.

The study will use a self-administered structured questionnaire to gather information from active social media users who engage with and follow at least one company online. All measurements scales utilized in this study were modified out of the already-validated scales to secure validity and reliability and were properly cited. Time and accessibility constraints will require the use of convenience sampling, which will focus on tech-savvy consumers who frequently and relevantly interact with social media brands. This sampling strategy does not allow for statistical generalisability but is appropriate for the testing of theory in a specific digital consumer context and will be acknowledged as a study limitation.

HYPOTHESIS

H1: There is a significant relationship between Digital Social Media Experience (DSME) and Life Satisfaction–Driven Brand Attachment (LSDBA).
H2: There is a significant relationship between Digital Social Media Experience (DSME) and Perceived Digital Brand Meaning (PDBM).
H3: There is a significant relationship between Digital Social Media Experience (DSME) and Digital Presence & Social Embeddedness (DP&SE).
H4: There is a significant relationship between Perceived Digital Brand Meaning (PDBM) and Life Satisfaction–Driven Brand Attachment (LSDBA).
H5: There is a significant relationship between DP&SE and Life Satisfaction–Driven Brand Attachment (LSDBA).
H6: Perceived Digital Brand Meaning (PDBM) mediates between Digital Social Media Experience (DSME) and Life Satisfaction–Driven Brand Attachment (LSDBA).
H7: Digital Presence & Social Embeddedness (DP&SE) mediates between Digital Social Media Experience (DSME) and Life Satisfaction–Driven Brand Attachment (LSDBA).

Digital Social Media Experience (DSME), Perceived Digital Brand Meaning (PDBM), Digital Presence & Social Embeddedness (DP&SE), and Life Satisfaction–Driven Brand Attachment (LSDBA).

ANALYSIS AND FINDINGS

Table 1. Demographic characteristics

	Demographics	Frequency	Percentage
	18-25	101	90.2
Age	26-35 36-45	7 1	6.3 0.9
	46 and above	3	2.7

continued on following page

Table 1. Continued

	Demographics	Frequency	Percentage
Gender	Male Female	57 55	50.9 49.1
	Single	104	92.9
Marital Status	Married	8	7.1
	Others	-	-
	Below 3 lakhs	78	69.6
Annual Income	3 - 5 lakhs 5 - 7 lakhs	18 3	16.1 2.7
	Above 7 lakhs	13	11.6
	High School/Diploma	2	1.8
Educational	Bachelor's Degree	68	60.7
Qualification	Master's Degree	38	33.9
	Others	4	3.6
Total		**112**	**100**

Table 1 above presents the demographic information of the 112 people who took the survey. The age distribution shows that 90.2% of the people who answered are between the ages of 18 and 25, which means that most of them are young. Only 6.3% of people are between the ages of 26 and 35. Even fewer people are between the ages of 36 and 45 (0.9%) or 46 and above (2.7%). 50.9% of male respondents and 49.1% of female respondents say there is equal participation from both genders, meaning a virtually equal gender distribution. It makes sense that the majority of the population in the sample (92.9%) are single and only 7.1% are married because they are all young. The amount of money the respondents earn in a year is as follows: 69.6% of the respondents earn less than 3 lakhs, 16.1% of the respondents earn between 3 and 5 lakhs, 11.6% of the respondents earn more than 7 lakhs, and only 2.7% of the respondents earn between 5 and 7 lakhs. Most of the people in this group have low to moderate incomes. Many the people who responded (60.7%) have a bachelor's degree, and 33.9% have a master's degree. The percentage of respondents with credentials in other categories (3.6%), or at the high school/diploma level (1.8%) is lower.

Figure 2. SEM Measurement model of Digital Social Media Experience, Perceived Digital Brand Meaning, Digital Presence & Social Embeddedness, and Life Satisfaction–Driven Brand Attachment

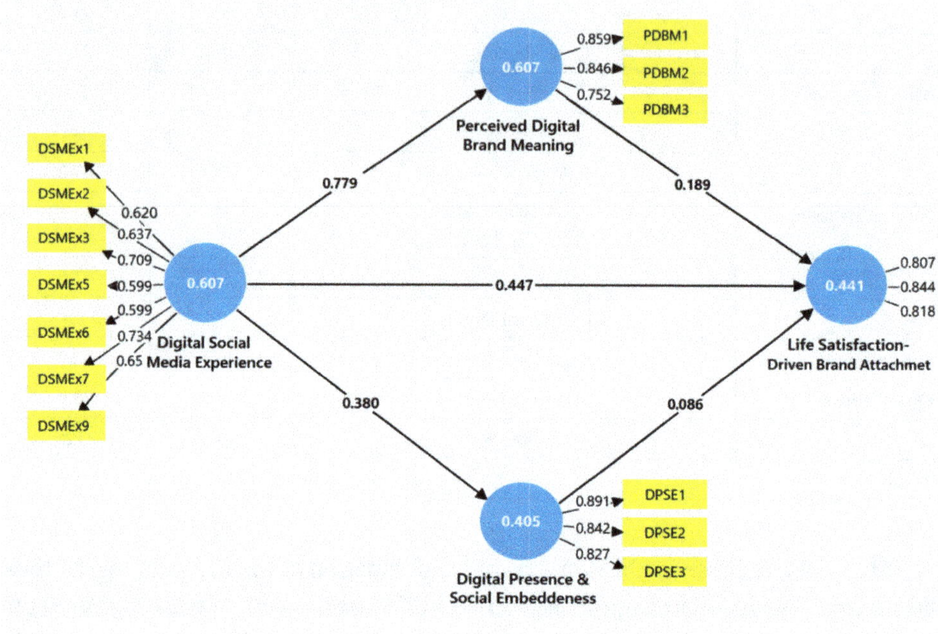

MEASUREMENT MODEL

Reliability and Validity

These are important parts of measuring the outer model, so the first thing is to check the validity and reliability of the outer model. PLS goes through a number of tests to check its validity and reliability. One of these tests is Cronbach's alpha, which demonstrates the reliability of the inner model. It uses Fornell and Larcker criterion to check discriminant reliability and average variance extracted to check convergent reliability.

Table 2. Composite Reliability and Convergent Validity

Construct	Items	Loadings	Cronbach's alpha	Composite reliability	Average variance extracted (AVE)
Digital Social Media Experience	**DSME1**	0.859	0.757	0.860	0.672
	DSME2	0.846			
	DSME3	0.752			
Perceived Digital Brand Meaning	**PDBM1**	0.882	0.865	0.917	0.787
	PDBM2	0.898			
	PDBM3	0.882			
Digital Presence & Social Embeddedness	**DP&SE1**	0.891	0.814	0.890	0.729
	DP&SE2	0.842			
	DP&SE3	0.827			
Life Satisfaction–Driven Brand Attachment	**LSDBA1**	0.620	0.850	0.883	0.657
	LSDBA2	0.633			
	LSDBA3	0.709			
	LSDBA4	0.599			
	LSDBA5	0.690			
	LSDBA6	0.682			
	LSDBA7	0.734			
	LSDBA8	0.660			
	LSDBA9	0.740			

Convergent validity and good reliability for all constructs: The measuring model. Digital Social Media Experience has a composite reliability of 0.860 and a Cronbach's alpha of 0.757 which means that it is consistent enough on its own. The average variance extracted (AVE) value of 0.672 indicates that the convergent validity is good and all of the indicator loadings are above the recommended level. With high factor loadings ranging from 0.882 to 0.898, Cronbach's alpha of 0.865, composite reliability of 0.917, and AVE of 0.787, Perceived Digital Brand Meaning demonstrates high measurement qualities, demonstrating great construct convergence and reliability. Digital Presence and Social Embeddedness also demonstrate high reliability and validity with Cronbach's alpha of 0.814, a composite reliability of 0.890, factor loadings above 0.80 and an AVE of 0.729. These results suggest that the construct is a good explanation for a significant portion of its indicators. Brand Fuelled by Contentment with Life Attachment meets acceptable psychometric standards with item loadings between 0.599 and 0.740, Cronbach's alpha of 0.850, composite reliability of 0.883 and AVE of 0.657. Some indicators have marginal loadings below 0.70, but their overall reliability and convergent validity are good enough to retain them. The results show that the measurement model is reliable and can be used for further analysis using a structural model.

DISCRIMINANT VALIDITY – FORNELL-LARCKER CRITERION

According to Fornell and Larcker, discriminant validity can be assessed by deriving the square root of the average variance extracted (AVE) in each of the underlying variables. Research shows that the Fornell and Larcker method is the most reliable and authentic to measure the discriminant validity.

Table 3. Discriminant Validity

Model Constructs	DSME	PDBM	DP&SE	LSDBA
Digital Social Media Experience	**0.820**			
Perceived Digital Brand Meaning	0.588	**0.887**		
Digital Presence & Social Embeddedness	0.590	0.470	**0.854**	
Life Satisfaction–Driven Brand Attachment	0.779	0.647	0.609	**0.676**

The Fornell-Larcker criterion reveals that the results demonstrate sufficient discriminant validity among the research constructs. The square root of the average variance extracted (AVE) for each construct is presented diagonally and is greater than the inter-construct correlation values matching the construct. The square root of AVE for Digital Social Media Experience is 0.820. This is higher than the square roots of its relationships with Digital Presence and Social Embeddedness, Life Satisfaction - Driven Brand Attachment and Perceived Digital Brand Meaning. Perceived Digital Brand Meaning has good discriminant validity as its square root of AVE is found to be 0.887 which is superior to the correlations with other constructs. The square root of AVE for Digital Presence and Social Embeddedness are 0.854 and are higher than the correlations with the other dimensions. The square root of AVE for Life Satisfaction Driven Brand Attachment is 0.676. This is much closer to its connection with Digital Presence and Social Embeddedness, but it is higher than its connections with Digital Social Media Experience and Perceived Digital Brand Meaning. In general, the results indicate that the discriminant validity of the measurement model is good and that the constructs are truly unique in a world-of-work context.

PATH MODEL

This section of the chapter examines the direct relationship between the proposed model of the study and research variables. We are using the Smart PLS program for hypothesis testing because it provides a good visual representation of the study to ensure that it is reliable. The model of SEM is used to analyze the path model. It provides the path coefficients, which indicate the direct relationship of the variables to one another. By taking into consideration the P and T values, this evaluation takes into consideration the relevance of the correlations.

Table 4. Hypothesis Testing Results

Variables	Beta	Standard deviation (STDEV)	T statistics (|O/ STDEV|)	P values	Analysis
PDBM → LSDBA	0.189	0.161	1.180	0.238	Not Accepted
DP&SE → LSDBA	0.086	0.151	0.570	0.569	Not Accepted
DSME → PDBM	0.779	0.040	19.574	0.000	Accepted
DSME → LSDBA	0.447	0.139	3.209	0.001	Accepted
DSME → DP&SE	0.380	0.150	2.532	0.011	Accepted

The results of the hypothesis test have shown that familiarity with digital social media has a significant and positive effect on various factors of the outcome. Strong beta values, high t-statistics and statistically significant p-values reveal that Digital Social Media Experience has a big effect on Perceived Digital Brand Meaning, Life Satisfaction-Driven Brand Attachment and Digital Presence and Social Embeddedness. These findings suggest that consumers' perception of brand significance is strengthened, their sense of social integration within the digital environment is strengthened, and brand attachment due to life satisfaction is directly influenced by more immersive and engaging digital social media experiences. On the other hand, the smaller values of the beta coefficients and the p-values that are not significant indicate that Perceived Digital Brand Meaning, Digital Presence, and Social Embeddedness do not have a significant direct effect on Life Satisfaction - Driven Brand Attachment. This suggests that what digital social media experience does to these concepts could not necessarily be the only determinant of brand attachment in relation to life satisfaction. Overall, the results highlight the importance of the digital social media experience as a primary driver in the proposed model. It has both direct and indirect impacts on relevant brand-related outcomes.

Table 5. Specific Indirect Effects

Indirect effects	Original sample (O)	Sample mean (M)	Standard deviation (STDEV)	T statistics (|O/STDEV|)	P values	Results
DSME -> DP&SE -> LSDBA	0.033	0.030	0.064	0.506	0.613	No Mediation
DSME -> PDBM -> LSDBA	0.148	0.161	0.127	1.162	0.245	No Mediation

The results of the specific indirect effects analysis show that perceived digital brand meaning, digital presence, and social embeddedness do not mediate the link between digital social media experience and life satisfaction-driven brand attachment. A low t-statistic and a p-value exceeding the recommended threshold signify that the indirect relationship between Digital Social Media Experience and Life Satisfaction–Driven Brand Attachment via Digital Presence and Social Embeddedness is not statistically significant. The indirect channel, Perceived Digital Brand Meaning, also does not reach statistical significance. These findings suggest that Digital Social Media Experience significantly influences both mediating variables; however, their indirect effects on Life Satisfaction–Driven Brand Attachment lack sufficient strength to establish mediation. Consequently, instead of navigating these mediating factors, the influence of Digital Social Media Experience on Life Satisfaction–Driven Brand Attachment appears to be predominantly direct.

DISCUSSION

The results of the study support the proposed links between the use of digital social media and significant brand-related outcomes in the space of digital consumption. The route analysis showed very strong direct correlations of the constructs; the measurement and structural models showed adequate validity and reliability. Digital social media experience had a big positive effect on Perceived Digital Brand Meaning, Digital Presence, Social Embeddedness and Life Satisfaction -Driven Brand Attachment. These findings suggest that meaningful and interesting social media interactions play a vital role in shaping customer perceptions of companies, enabling online interactions, and creating emotional connections that are associated with overall life satisfaction.

Nonetheless, there was no statistical evidence to back up the proposed mediating roles of Perceived Digital Brand Meaning, Digital Presence, and Social Embeddedness in the relationship between Digital Social Media Experience and Life Satisfaction Driven Brand Attachment. This means that digital social media experience makes people feel more connected to their brands and gives them more meaning, but these things don't directly lead to life satisfaction - brand attachment driven. Rather, it appears that the impact of digital social media on brand attachment is largely direct. This shows that the sensory and interactive aspects of social media are more important than its symbolic or social impressions.

These findings are consistent with research previously published that emphasizes the importance of interactive content, immersive digital experiences and ongoing engagement in improving customer-brand relationships. Digital social media experience has a significant direct impact on life satisfaction-driven brand attachment, which suggests that consumers are more likely to develop meaningful brand connections when digital interactions positively impact their overall well-being and life satisfaction, rather than just increase their social visibility or brand perceptions.

Our study adds to a growing amount of research into digital consumer behavior by showing that the concept of experiential quality in social media interactions is a significant factor in the development of emotionally grounded brand attachment. The results provide valuable lessons for brands and digital marketers seeking to strengthen long-term consumer-brand relationships and optimize competitive positioning in increasingly interconnected digital ecosystems. They say that strategies should be focused on making digital experiences that are real, interesting, and good for society.

CONCLUSION

The research highlights the importance of digital social media experience in the formation of critical brand-related outcomes, such as brand attachment due to life satisfaction, perceived digital brand meaning, and digital presence and social embeddedness in life. While these variables were found to have significant and direct correlation with Digital Social Media Experience, Perceived Digital Brand Meaning and Digital Presence and Social Embeddedness did not show significant mediating effects. This means that even though using social media can make people feel better about a brand and more connected to it, it's not a direct cause of brand attachment based on how happy they are with their life. The results show how important it is to spend money on regular, interesting, and meaningful digital social media interactions that directly improve the customer's emotional health and brand loyalty. By focussing on experiential quality over just symbolic or visibility-based goals and improving their digital engagement strategies, businesses can improve their relationships with customers, get ahead of the competition and achieve long term growing in a world that is becoming more and more digital.

LIMITATIONS AND SCOPE OF RESEARCH

The study finds multiple limitations when evaluating the role of digital social media experience in brand-related outcomes. The demographic concentration of the sample, consisting mostly of young adults between the ages of 18 and 25, is a significant limitation that may make it difficult to represent different customer segments who engage in different digital activities and life stage perspectives. Also, some of the indicators in the measurement model, especially those related to Life Satisfaction - Driven Brand Attachment, had low factor loadings, which means that the measuring items still need to be improved and tested. Also, using cross-sectional data makes it harder to keep track of changes in how people feel about brands, how attached they are to them and how they use digital social media over time. Convenience sampling may further limit the generalizability of the findings across various cultural, demographic and business situations.

To improve external validity and cross-cultural applicability, future studies should improve on these limitations by using larger and more diverse samples. Longitudinal research methods from the point of view of Digital Social Media Experience and its impact on Perceived Digital Brand Meaning, Digital Presence and Social Embeddedness and Life Satisfaction-Driven Brand Attachment over time may be beneficial for a deeper understanding of the impact of Digital Social Media Experience on Perceived Digital Brand Meaning, Digital Presence and Social Embeddedness, and Life Satisfaction-Driven Brand Attachment. You can also include more mediating or moderating factors in the conceptual model, such as privacy concerns, digital well-being, or trust. Inclusion of more service and product industries in the research would put the model to a more difficult test. Additionally, the addition of qualitative methods such as focus groups or in-depth interviews may reveal deep insights into the emotional ties between consumers and companies and the lived digital experiences, thus adding to the theoretical and managerially relevant nature of future research.

REFERENCES

Agnihotri, A., & Rengaraj, S. (2025). Harnessing generative AI for transforming marketing strategies: Enhancing consumer engagement through precision and personalization. In *Proceedings of the 2025 5th International Conference on Pervasive Computing and Social Networking (ICPCSN)* (pp. xx–xx). IEEE. https://doi.org/ DOI: 10.1109/ICPCSN65854.2025.11035208

Biocca, F., Harms, C., & Burgoon, J. K. (2003). Toward a more robust theory of social presence. *Presence (Cambridge, Mass.)*, *12*(5), 456–480. DOI: 10.1162/105474603322761270

Buzeta, C., De Pelsmacker, P., & Dens, N. (2024). Branded content and motivations for social media use as drivers of brand outcomes on social media: A cross-cultural study. *. *International Journal of Advertising*, *43*(4), 637–671. Advance online publication. DOI: 10.1080/02650487.2023.2215079

Cyr, D., Head, M., Lim, E., & Stibe, A. (2018). Using the elaboration likelihood model to examine online persuasion through website design. *Information & Management*, *55*(7), 807–821. DOI: 10.1016/j.im.2018.03.009

Eroglu, S. A., Machleit, K. A., & Davis, L. M. (2003). Empirical testing of a model of online store atmospherics and shopper responses. *Psychology and Marketing*, *20*(2), 139–150. DOI: 10.1002/mar.10064

Fitzmaurice, J., & Comegys, C. (2006). Materialism and Social Consumption. *Journal of Marketing Theory and Practice*, *14*(4), 287–299. DOI: 10.2753/MTP1069-6679140403

Fournier, S. (1998). Consumers and their brands: Developing relationship theory in consumer research. *The Journal of Consumer Research*, *24*(4), 343–373. DOI: 10.1086/209515

Geetha, B. T., Yenugula, M., Randhawa, N., Purohit, P., Maney, K. L., & Venkteshwar, A. (2024). Advancement improving the acquisition of customer insights in digital marketing by utilising advanced artificial intelligence algorithms. In *Proceedings of the 2nd IEEE International Conference on Trends in Quantum Computing and Emerging Business Technologies (TQCEBT 2024)*. IEEE. https://doi.org/DOI: 10.1109/TQCEBT59414.2024.10545055

Gerson, J., Plagnol, A. C., & Corr, P. J. (2016). Subjective well-being and social media use: Do personality traits moderate the impact of social comparison on Facebook? *Computers in Human Behavior*, *63*, 813–822. DOI: 10.1016/j.chb.2016.06.023

Granovetter, M. (1985). Economic action and social structure: The problem of embeddedness. *AJS; American Journal of Sociology, 91*(3), 481–510. DOI: 10.1086/228311

Grönroos, C. (1994). From marketing mix to relationship marketing: Towards a paradigm shift in marketing. *Management Decision, 32*(2), 4–20. DOI: 10.1108/00251749410054774

Guo, J., Zhang, L., Wang, Y., & Li, H. (2025). Applying the S-O-R model to explore impulsive buying on social media influencers' s-commerce websites. *Heliyon*. Advance online publication. DOI: 10.1016/j.heliyon.2025.e40989

Hofstede, G. (1980). *Culture's consequences: International differences in work-related values*. Sage Publications., DOI: 10.1007/978-0-387-94806-4_13

Hofstede, G. (2001). *Culture's consequences: Comparing values, behaviors, institutions and organizations across nations* (2nd ed.). Sage Publications.

Hollebeek, L. D., Glynn, M. S., & Brodie, R. J. (2014). Consumer brand engagement in social media: Conceptualization, scale development and validation. *Journal of Interactive Marketing, 28*(2), 149–165. DOI: 10.1016/j.intmar.2013.12.002

Katz, E., Blumler, J. G., & Gurevitch, M. (1973). Uses and gratifications research. *Public Opinion Quarterly, 37*(4), 509–523. DOI: 10.1086/268109

Katz, E., Blumler, J. G., & Gurevitch, M. (1974). Utilization of mass communication by the individual. In Blumler, J. G., & Katz, E. (Eds.), *The uses of mass communications: Current perspectives on gratifications research* (pp. 19–32). Sage Publications.

Kim, D., Magane, R., Poitier, M., Kuang, J., Wang, A., Adderley, R., & Deveaux, L. (2025). Social media use, risk behavior engagement, and mental health among middle adolescents in the Caribbean. *BMC Public Health, 25*(1), 2468. Advance online publication. DOI: 10.1186/s12889-025-23646-8 PMID: 40670957

Krishen, A. S., Berezan, O., Agarwal, S., Kachroo, P., & Raschke, R. (2021). The digital self and virtual satisfaction: A cross-cultural perspective. *Journal of Business Research, 124*, 254–263. DOI: 10.1016/j.jbusres.2020.11.056

Liadeli, G., Sotgiu, F., & Verlegh, P. (2023). A meta-analysis of the effects of brands' owned social media on social media engagement and sales. *Journal of Marketing, 87*(3), 406–427. DOI: 10.1177/00222429221123250

Licsandru, T. C., Mari, C., Kipnis, E., Galalae, C., Johnson, E., Cross, S. N. N., Cui, C. C., Kearney, S., Martín Ruiz, V., Vorster Larsen, L., & Yoruk, I. (2025). Integrating diversity, equity, and inclusion in management education: An empathy framework. *British Journal of Management*. Advance online publication. DOI: 10.1111/1467-8551.70008

Mandania, R., Cadogan, J. W., Liu, J., & Kazmi, N. (2025). Optimizing promotional campaigns to maximize customer lifetime value: A dynamic learning approach. *Journal of Service Research*, *28*(1), 1–15. DOI: 10.1177/10946705251365524

Mehrabian, A., & Russell, J. A. (1974). *An approach to environmental psychology*. MIT Press.

Meng, S., Kong, F., Dong, W., Zhang, Y., Yu, T., & Jin, X. (2023). Mobile social media use and life satisfaction among adolescents: A moderated mediation model. *Frontiers in Public Health*, *11*, 1117745. Advance online publication. DOI: 10.3389/fpubh.2023.1117745 PMID: 38094229

Muntinga, D. G., Moorman, M., & Smit, E. G. (2011). Introducing COBRAs: Exploring motivations for brand-related social media use. *International Journal of Advertising*, *30*(1), 13–46. DOI: 10.2501/IJA-30-1-013-046

Ramadhani, I. S., & Indradjati, P. N. (2023). Toward contemporary city branding in the digital era: Conceptualizing the acceptability of city branding on social media. *Open House International*, *48*(4), 666–682. DOI: 10.1108/OHI-08-2022-0213

Sardashti, H., & Calantone, R. J. (2022). Does equity-based compensation motivate executives to build strong brands? *Journal of Marketing Management*, *38*(13–14), 1433–1460. DOI: 10.1080/0267257X.2022.2041068

Short, J. A., Williams, E., & Christie, B. (1976). *The social psychology of telecommunications*. John Wiley & Sons.

Sivadas, E., Bruvold, N. T., & Nelson, M. R. (2008). A reduced version of the horizontal and vertical individualism and collectivism scale: A four-country assessment. *Journal of Business Research*, *61*(3), 201–210. DOI: 10.1016/j.jbusres.2007.06.016

Tarnanidis, T. (Ed.). (2026). *AI-driven decision-making for diversity, equity, and inclusion in marketing*. IGI Global Scientific Publishing., DOI: 10.4018/979-8-3373-6731-6

Tarnanidis, T., Sousa, B. B., Vlachopoulou, M., Papachristou, E., & Kittu Manda, V. (Eds.). (2026). *Diversity and inclusion-driven marketing for multicultural marketplaces*. IGI Global Scientific Publishing., DOI: 10.4018/979-8-3373-2111-0

Tsai, J. L. (2007). Ideal affect: Cultural causes and behavioral consequences. *Perspectives on Psychological Science : A Journal of the Association for Psychological Science, 2*(3), 242–259. DOI: 10.1111/j.1745-6916.2007.00043.x PMID: 26151968

Westerman, D., Spence, P. R., & Van Der Heide, B. (2013). Social media as information source: Recency of updates and credibility of information. *Journal of Computer-Mediated Communication, 19*(2), 171–183. DOI: 10.1111/jcc4.12041

Widjaja, G., Nagabhooshanam, N., Prasad, K. D. V., Hassan Shari, F. H., Valavan, A. T., Sridhar, A. P., & Ambika, K. S. B. (2024). Machine learning-driven model for identifying depression via social network information. *Journal of Environmental Protection and Ecology, 25*(5), 1627–1637. https://scibulcom.net/en/article/06EER86UphR8ttSUSTvW

Wood, M. A., Bukowski, W. M., & Lis, E. (2016). The digital self: How social media serves as a setting that shapes youth's emotional experiences. *Adolescent Research Review, 1*(2), 163–173. DOI: 10.1007/s40894-015-0014-8

Zhang, Y., Cao, B., Wang, Y., Peng, T., & Wang, X. (2020). When Public Health research meets social media: Knowledge Mapping from 2000 to 2018. *Journal of Medical Internet Research, 22*(8), e17582. DOI: 10.2196/17582 PMID: 32788156

KEY TERMS AND DEFINITIONS

Cross-Cultural Perspective: Refers to understanding and comparing how people from different cultural backgrounds perceive, interpret, and respond to experiences, behaviors, and meanings.

Digital Brand Meaning: Reflects how consumers understand, feel about, and emotionally connect with a brand based on its presence and interactions in digital environments.

Digital Life Satisfaction: reflects how content and fulfilled individuals feel with their lives as influenced by their experiences, interactions, and well-being in digital and online environments.

Digital Presence: Refers to how visibly, consistently, and meaningfully a brand or individual exists and engages across digital platforms and online channels.

Digital Social Media Experience: Describes user's total behavioural, emotional, and cognitive interactions with communities and brands on social media platforms.

Social Embeddedness: Describes the extent to which individuals or brands are connected, involved, and trusted within social networks, communities, and ongoing social interactions.

Chapter 14

Augmented Self in Hyper-Personalized E-Commerce:

Exploring Longitudinal Effects of AI-Driven Digital Retail on Life Satisfaction and Identity Coheren

R. Shankar
http://orcid.org/0009-0002-3479-1851
Bharathiar University, India

G. Suresh
http://orcid.org/0000-0003-1546-3916
Sri Ramakrishna College of Arts and Science, India

M. Sindhu
Dr. S.N.S. Rajalakshmi College of Arts and Science, India

M. Sumathi
Rathinam Technical Campus, India

K. Rani
Dr. S.N.S. Rajalakshmi College of Arts and Science, India

ABSTRACT

This paper explores how AI-based hyper-personalization of e-commerce has been affected over time on augmented self, identity coherence and life satisfaction among the young adults in Indian metropolitan cities. Digital platforms contribute to creating

DOI: 10.4018/979-8-3373-8357-6.ch014

improved identities due to predictive algorithms that can empower individuals at the expense of losing autonomy and constructing discontinuous self-accounts. The research uses 12-month longitudinal research design based on self-determination theory and extended self-frameworks. The 307 participants (18-35 years) of the survey were used as data to complete quarterly surveys on the validated ASHPE scale, identity coherence, agency, emotional well-being and life satisfaction. Latent growth modeling and fsQCA show promising results with good coherence and agency but well-being going down with excessive individualization. Results are in favour of human oriented AI regulations and policy interventions.

INTRODUCTION

In the fast-changing environment of online retail, AI-driven personalization has been turned into a core component of hyper-personalized e-commerce, which has completely altered the relationship between customers and online portals. Retailers can now provide highly personalized recommendations, dynamic interfaces, and predictive content, based on more and more sophisticated algorithms that process volumes of behavioral data, browsing history, and interests, and make predictions about what individuals need. In addition to making it more engaging and streamlining decision-making and boosting commercial results, this evolution has been demonstrated to be able to increase revenue by up to 15 percent and make the marketing process much more efficient (as cited in industry analyses of 2024). Nevertheless, such technological innovations go beyond the ability to provide increased efficiency in the transaction to other psychological aspects of consumer experience. The rise of an augmented self a digitally augmented identity under the influence of an algorithmic curation creates serious questions concerning the future effects of augmented self-technologies on self-autonomy, identity coherence, and the overall life satisfaction. Since platforms progressively mediate the expression of self in a personalized consumption, users can be empowered when the recommendations are consistent with natural preferences, and they can feel dissonance when the algorithms create restrictive and mismatched stories (Hardcastle et al., 2025).

The interaction between AI customization and the psychology of humans depicts both the prospects and conflicts towards creating digital identities in e-commerce settings. Hyper-personalized systems are active participants in self-building by managing product ecosystems reflective of inferred lifestyle, values, and aspirations of users and reinforcing these values and aspirations. When done correctly, this personalization can cultivate a feeling of relevance and effectiveness, and may cement identity coherence by making virtual decisions that can be aligned with personal agenda. Nevertheless, inappropriate matches, e.g., repetitive, unnecessary, or over-nuanced suggestions can be frustrating, and create an ambivalence of not being in control, leading consumers to remain confined in an algorithmically determined echo-chamber that only allows exploration and spontaneity (Hardcastle et al., 2025). Empirical research findings demonstrate that AI-driven journeys can enhance discovery and convenience, but simultaneously it provokes the fear of surveillance and manipulation, which causes undermined trust and unfavorable affective outcomes such as annoyance or resignation. These are especially strong in the situations when the level of personalization is beyond the level of discomfort of users, which highlights the importance of perceived control and digital literacy in maintaining positive self-trajectories (Iqbal et al., 2025). Ethics also arise, because unregulated algorithmic biases or privacy breaches can only increase inequalities, which require moderated strategies to put more emphasis on transparency and user agency.

In the longitudinal perspective, the long-term implications of the exposure to AI-based hyper-personalization are complicated in terms of the emotional well-being and satisfaction with life. With time, the corresponding personalization will help to mitigate the effects of decision fatigue, boost satisfaction by purchasing in line with their goals, and promote the feeling of effectiveness in maneuvering in the digital environment. However, such benefits may be undermined by indirect and delayed effects, such as the erosion of privacy over time, over-personalization that causes fatigue, or strengthening of prejudices, which may cause individual satisfaction to decrease in cases where the individual perceives that their agency has been compromised (Hardcastle et al., 2025). Recent studies on consumer reactions note that although benefit gains are present early on, long term interactions necessitate a meticulous adjustment of the customization factors to prevent mental losses such as emotional fatigue by feeling exploited or disempowered. The contingency of these effects depending on such aspects as the transparency of the data and the relevance of the recommendations explains the need to have frameworks that would trace changing trends over various time points to help discriminate between short-term effects, and long-term effects on well-being.

The literature still suffers substantial gaps on the holistic and long-term effects of hyper-personalized e-commerce on the flourishing of the psychologists. A lot of prior research is focused on short-term behavioral outcomes, such as conversion rates and engagement, and relatively less on such constructs as augmented self-development, identity coherence, or moderating effects of digital self-literacy and agency on long-term results. The number of studies that utilize longitudinal designs to test the time-lagged effects or confirm the specialized scales to measure the self-concepts augmented by AI is very small. The solutions to these deficiencies require new methodologies that determine the best personalization depth, coherence levels, and empowerment processes to facilitate the sustainable positive process of satisfaction and identity development. These gaps can be filled through research to influence the ethical use of AI in ways that enhance the profitability of the business and the well-being of humans in the digital realm.

In the current study, the field of research is further developed with the help of extensive empirical research. It brings into perspective both the psychological and consumer behavior lens in examining the co-opetition of AI personalization in influencing augmented self-perceptions in both direct and indirect support of life satisfaction and coherence, literacy, and agency considerations. Such research is conducted in accordance with internationally accepted digital consumer research practices and offers credible conclusions to make informed theoretical developments and ethical approaches to future e-commerce ecosystems.

THEORETICAL FOUNDATIONS OF THE STUDY

This chapter has its theoretical base in the diversity-based marketing theory, social identity theory, and technology-based consumer interaction theories. Diversity and inclusion (D&I) in marketing is a focus on strategic identification of demographic, cultural and psychographic diversity in the international market. Tarnanidis (2026) claims that the use of AI-based decision systems is becoming a key factor in determining inclusive targeting and segmentation, enabling marketers to tailor their communication and remain equitable.

Social identity theory is a theory that describes how people form their group in terms of social identity which affects brand affiliation, purchase intention and perceived brand authenticity. Consumers in multicultural market places are more receptive to those brands with representational sensitivity and cultural intelligence. The inclusion model, grounded in empathy, suggested by Licsandru et al. (2025), also implies that the organizations need to leave the symbolic representation to the real one.

Equity-based reward and brand-building alignment contribute to inclusive branding results in a strategic dimension, as well. Calantone and Sardashti (2022) claim that executive pay has a strong effect on the investments in brand equity in the long term. The combination of these theoretical approaches will give a multidimensional interpretation of inclusive, AI-based marketing systems in multicultural consumer contexts.

INDUSTRY TRENDS AND CONTEXTUAL BACKGROUND.

The world market is changing fast due to digitalization, the use of AI, and the growing multicultural complexity. According to the edited volume Diversity and

Inclusion-Driven Marketing to Multicultural Marketplaces, global millennial and Gen Z cohorts require authenticity, personalization, and moral support of a brand. This change predetermines the need to be more attentive to cultural plurality and technological flexibility.

The increasing use of AI in marketing analytics has facilitated predictive modeling of lifetime value of a consumer and optimization of a campaign. Mandania et al. (2025) focus on the dynamic approach to learning promotions as the optimal way to increase customer profitability in the long-term without disrupting diversity-sensitive engagement parameters.

Moreover, the complexity of marketing of smart consumer products as presented in Marketing Complexity of Smart Consumer Products to Global Millennial Segments creates a need to combine the diversity intelligence and technological innovation. These changing dynamics in the industry give the contextual relevance to this chapter.

RESEARCH GAP ANALYSIS

Despite the preceding studies of diversity marketing and multicultural segmentation, there are still some serious gaps that can be traced. To begin with, a significant amount of the current literature is mainly based on the Western consumer environment, which does not necessarily apply to the emerging and multicultural economies. Second, the empirical implementation of AI-based analytics into inclusive marketing systems has not been developed yet. Third, the intersection between customer lifetime value modeling and diversely-sensitive promotional strategies has not been given much attention.

Moreover, even though the studies focus on the importance of representational inclusion, a limited amount of literature addresses measurable performance consequences associated with the application of an inclusive strategy. Thus, the chapter fills such gaps by introducing AI-based decision models, inclusive marketing theory, and multicultural segmentation analysis into a single conceptual framework.

EXTENDED SELF AND ITS DIGITAL EVOLUTION IN CONSUMER CONTEXTS

The extended self, which was first introduced by Russell Belk in 1988, resides on the idea that people extend their identity to include material objects that display personal values, status, and experiences when they include possessions, brands, and the outside world. This theory is used in consumer settings to describe how buying and ownership helps with the aspect of self-definition so that possessions act as an identification with accomplishment or belonging. As an example, a family heirloom or a luxury watch is incorporated in the self-concept, affecting the behavior and emotional attachment to it. Recent research has modified this framework to modern conditions with a focus on how consumer decisions in international markets support identity coherence. A study on the cross-cultural differences found that in the collectivism societies such as India, people would be interested in the long-term self through relational and not individualistic possessions, which include family-branded items (Shukla et al., 2023). According to the statistical data of the world surveys, 68 percent of the total population of the world, or more than 5.5 billion of people, is an active internet user, which allows new self-extension via digital consumption (Lima et al., 2025). This change shows how the consumer well-being and satisfaction in global retail environments are becoming more and more enhanced by non-material resources.

Digital development of the extended self has altered the consumer contexts through introducing virtual artifacts, online identities and interactions mediate by technology. Self-extension takes place in digital spaces in the form of dematerialization, where material objects are replaced by virtual ones such as social media pages, online images, and memories stored on the cloud that are seen as less manageable, but more communicable. The co-construction of self is formed through the collaboration of users with the algorithms and peers to construct identities, and the distributed memory uses digital repositories to recall experiences. The self is further extended through reincarnation as an avatar and re-embodiment through an online representation which means that the self-occupies many personalities across platforms. This is experienced in e-commerce where the consumers will be incorporating brand interactions into their online stories and the individual recommendations will serve to reinforce the identity. The qualitative analysis of influencers has shown that the extension of the self is possible through the sharing of the experience of the travels, as the feedback on the experience of the viewers makes such dynamics possible, and 5.24 billion people online use social media worldwide (Lima et al., 2025). Another aspect of this change that Indian consumers, in particular, have to navigate is the rapid rise in digital devices as the number of new smartphones is expected to reach 350 million by 2023, which enhances self-discovery as people engage in online searches (Shukla et al., 2023). The diagram below represents this said theory as shown below and how the core self-flows to digital augmentations.

In hyper-personalized e-commerce based on AI, the extended self is further enhanced by the use of algorithms to curate experiences, which combine customer information with predictive modeling to increase the identity consistency. The benefits of AI personalization promote a sense of agency by matching suggestions to the perceived preferences, but it may result in the breakdown in case of discrepancies, bringing about a decreased level of life satisfaction. The recent empirical research on nomophobia as the fear of being not in mobile connectivity explains it as the separation anxiety with the extended self where digital networks form part of self-efficacy and identity. The prevalence of nomophobia in the world is 93.92, which highlights the vast use of digital extensions to support consumer behavior (Li et al., 2025). According to Indian experience, with digital marketing becoming more virtualized with AI tools that anticipate behavior, consumers indicate more engagement as self-narratives are aided by personalization, but privacy concerns undermine trust. Statistics indicate that the market of digital transformation in the world has a sales growth to US$2,279.4 million by 2025 supported by AI integrations that expand self through customized retail experiences (Borderless Access, 2025). Such an adaptation puts more emphasis on contingency factors such as digital literacy, which guarantee long-term well-being in consumption by algorithms.

These advancements of extended self-construct have deep explanations of consumer psychology and international standards ethics. Digital extensions create longitudinal impacts by showing on the one hand that, but as more personalized, similar to authentically curated experiences (e.g. 88% of consumers require AI-curated experience to be authentic), it causes dissonance because of a limited autonomy on the other (Hardcastle et al., 2025). The depth versus agency is also a variable that is most relevant to Indian and global consumers, as research indicates that cultures have a difference in the value of digital possessions. This holism guides the approach to e-commerce platforms to develop consistent identities, which in the end will help to make life more fulfilling in the era of hyper-personal retailing.

Figure 1. The Extended Self and Its Digital Evolution in Consumer Contexts

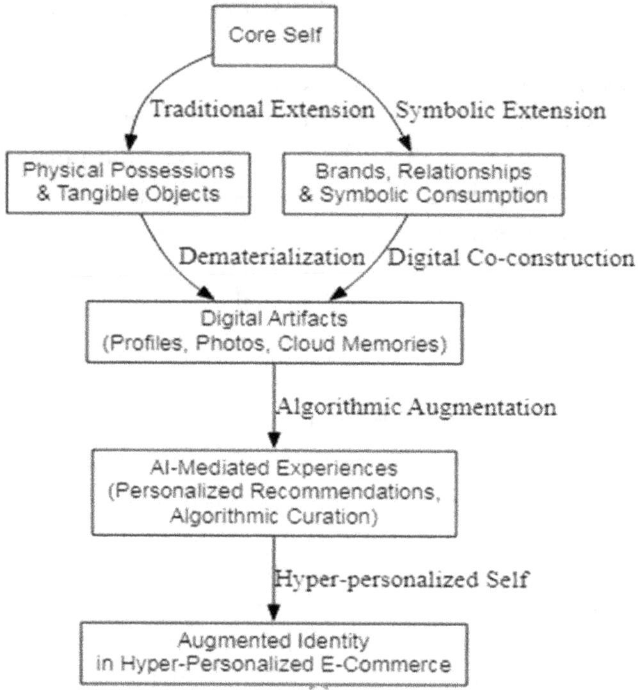

Source: Author's Own Work

THE PSYCHOLOGICAL DYNAMICS OF PERSONALIZATION AND THE SELF-DETERMINATION THEORY.

Self-Determination Theory (SDT), developed by Deci and Ryan, is the idea that the most successful motivation, psychological functioning, and well-being is the result of the fulfillment of three basic needs, such as autonomy (a sense of experiencing volition and self-initiation), competence (a sense of being effective and masterful), and relatedness (creating meaningful interpersonal relationships). SDT can be applied successfully in the context of AI-based hyper-personalization in digital retail and e-commerce as a way of fulfilling such needs, thereby impacting consumer motivation, interaction, and satisfaction in the long term. Autonomy is strengthened when personalization is consensual and brings about relevant and non-coercive choices, competence as a result of effective learning of shopping activities, and relatedness as a result of socially salient suggestions eliciting a sense of belonging (e.g., community-congruent or occasion-specific suggestions). Recent empirical studies have demonstrated that purchase intentions are mediated through these needs by personalized recommendation, where competence and relatedness are the critical mediators where recommendations are novel, and autonomy is contingently mediated by product-category diversity (Wang et al., 2025). On the international level, such facilitating personalization can boost intrinsic motivation, which leads to increased engagement and loyalty, since the reports show that AI-induced customized experiences play a significant role in influencing consumer decisions in the international markets.

Psychological interaction between AI hyper-personalization and SDT indicates that online retailing places facilitating and thwarting relationships. Freedom prospers where systems are easy to understand and to control, including provide explainable recommendations which explain why the algorithm is acting in a particular way, and creates favorable feelings of freedom and less reactance. Conversely, obscured or excessively instructive personalization may inspire anger, reduce willpower and cause evasion. Adaptive feedback and efficient processes that foster self-efficacy improves competence but too much automation may deskill the user. The advantage of relatedness is that it promotes social bonding, such as customized information about the community, though in limited algorithmic circles, one might feel isolated. A comparison of SDT to personalized recommendations shows that novelty in recommendations reinforces competence and relatedness, and purchase intentions, and the influence of diversity on autonomy differs by product type (ex: hedonic vs. utilitarian), but contextual moderators (Wang et al., 2025). The Indian context that is experiencing high growth in e-commerce makes AI personalization, such as in FinTech and retail segments, relevant to such needs, as users are found to experience a higher perceived usefulness and emotional connection when intrinsic motivations are fulfilled (Basuvaraj and Rastogi, 2025). The given theory is represented in the diagram in the following way, showing the two-way effects of AI personalization on SDT needs and further motivational consequences.

Recent global and Indian research highlights the possible negative consequences of hyper-personalization sabotaging SDT needs, such as psychological reactance and shattered well-being. Motivational deficit may be caused by over-intrusive algorithms, which puts the commercial goals before the user volition, which cause loss of agency and disengagement on the part of the consumers. The situation of transparency appears to be a crucial one, as its increased value has a positive impact on perceived autonomy and overall satisfaction, and models with explainability as an intermediate variable indicate such results (although direct empirical correlates with SDT in e-commerce are still developing). SDT predicts that engagement increases in gamified retail aspects, where the competence and relatedness fulfilment is higher, but where coercive designs lead to reactance and increased churn. The relatedness in AI recommendations (e.g., family-oriented personalization) is especially appreciated by Indian customers, who are collectivists, though privacy and data control raise concerns that exacerbate autonomy, and surveys show an increasing level of anxiety with increased usage (Basuvaraj and Rastogi, 2025). The findings highlight the ethical design requirements to balance the personalization depth and need supportive features to yield the long lasting positive psychological effects.

Figure 2. Psychological Dynamics of Personalization and the Self-Determination Theory

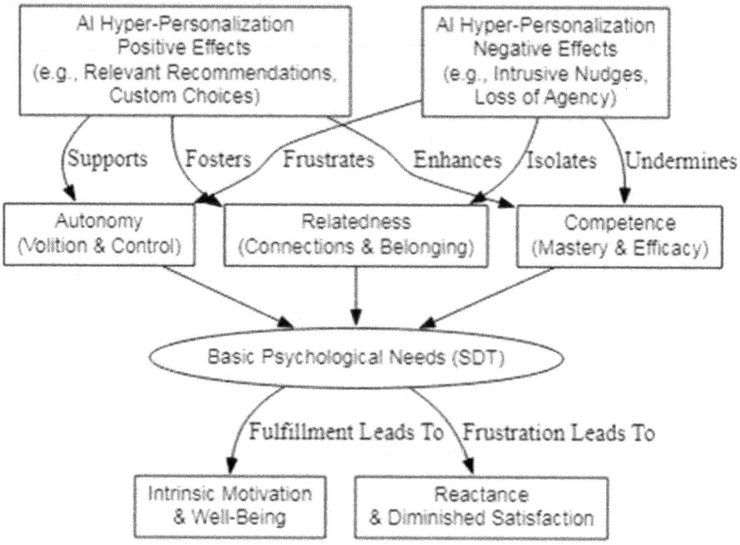

Source: Author's Own Work

To conclude, SDT offers a holistic approach to handling the dualistic quality of AI hyper-personalization in international e-commerce standards, where the motives of autonomy, competence, and relatedness are encouraged using designs that maximize intrinsic motivation, life satisfaction, and identity coherence. Such downsides as reactance can be decreased through user agency boosters such as opt-in functionality and explicit transparency, enabling sustained well-being in a wide variety of markets, including the dynamic digital environment of India, with its greater emphasis on the need to have relatedness and more focus on privacy protection (Basuvaraj & Rastogi, 2025; Wang et al., 2025).

IDENTITY COHERENCE AND FRAGMENTATION IN ALGORITHMICALLY MEDIATED ENVIRONMENTS

Identity coherence is a psychological process in which people unify the various aspects of self, including roles, experiences, and values, into a single story that brings some sense of continuity and permanence over time. This coherence may be strengthened or destabilized in an environment which is ultimately algorithmically mediated so that AI systems can curate content, recommendations and interactions based on the user data. The post-humanist theories explain that AI represents a kind of extension of the self by interpreting feedback that reinforced consistent representations of the self, but can lead to fragmentation when the algorithms are drawn to homogenizing patterns and not taking into consideration the various distinct growths of persons (Joseph, 2025). As an example, digital technologies, such as social media or online shop platforms, mediate self-storytelling with its emphasis on selective life moments, which can smooth out difficult experiences and leave out contradictions that are the foundation of resilience and adoption. When the dissonance is formed by the mismatched algorithmic interventions, fragmentation takes place, e.g., the existence of an echo chamber which reinforces biased self-perceptions, resulting in alienated emotional existence and loss of agency. A systematic review reveals the lack of disciplinary unity in AI awareness studies, 83% of the studies are characterized by ethical insufficiency, which indirectly influences the identity coherence by refusing to consider consumer views in upcoming economies (Zhu and Wan Hussain, 2025). According to the statistical data based on surveys, 73 per cent of consumers claim that they do not feel comfortable with the use of data in personalization that may further aggravate identity fragmentation by eroding privacy and perceived to be manipulated (Bitra, 2025). These risks are intensified in the Indian contexts, where the cultural focus on relational identities is in conflict with the AI-based individualism, creating the dissonance of the self-perception (Guha, 2025).

One of the main elements of narrative identity is temporal coherence, which consists of continuity between the past, present and future selves, a part of AI environment that undermines by recreating contexts statelessly on each interaction. The Narrative Continuity Test (NCT) model assesses the identity persistence of AI along the same line, such as situated memory and goal persistence, finding that the present generation of large language models does not support a diachronic continuity and thus displays inconsistency of personas as human personalities do (Natangelo, 2025). The algorithms in hyper-personalized conditions consolidate previous actions by predictive modeling, trapping customers in the current self-image that hinders evolution, like the suggested products on the basis of past preferences without considering new desires. This may introduce the imposition of digital selves that are not in line with users as they experience alienation with projected identities using the algorithm, which weakens the unity of the narrative. Neural language model research has shown that generated stories have high narrative coherence, and ANOVA results indicate that there is significant age effect [$F(3, 4{,}016) = 238.75$, $p < 0.001$], which indicates simulated self-integration similar to humans, but without experiential depth. The diagram presented below shows the flow of the mentioned theory, starting with integrated self-aspects and ending with fragmentation risks in the process of algorithmic mediation. Ethical uncertainties in the use of AI in Indian college students demonstrate the fragmentation of policies, as only 30 of the universities had guidelines, which contributes to identity dissonance as students are faced with paradoxical dependence on systems that undermine their agency (Verma et al., 2025).

An example of such challenges is hyper-personalized e-commerce, which is designed to adapt the experience based on perceived preferences, which may lead to improved coherence by offering applicable recommendations but may result in fragmented identity by measuring itself using quantified data. As an illustration, 89% of outputs are personalized and 26% of outputs increase the percentage of conversion, whereas 46% of outputs are gender and 39% racial, which introduces distorted self-representations to the output to solidify stereotypes (Bitra, 2025). This is worsened by knowledge gaps in digital literacy where younger age groups (15-24 years) were more aware but less concerned with privacy, which resulted in identity formation vulnerability in the presence of an echo chamber (Moravec et al., 2025). AI enhances marketing communications by increasing the response rates: sentiment analysis and predictive applications have a higher response rate of 2.5x, yet reduces human touch, which may lead to lowered trust and consistent self-storytelling when the response is replaced by the output of AI (Moqaddem, 2025). The Indian e-commerce environments put emphasis on radical personalization through machine learning, and real-time tracking enhances customer satisfaction, but the culture of collectivism adds to the divide as AI focuses on individual data instead of relational situations (Sharma, 2025).

Figure 3. Identity Coherence and Fragmentation in Algorithmically Mediated Environments

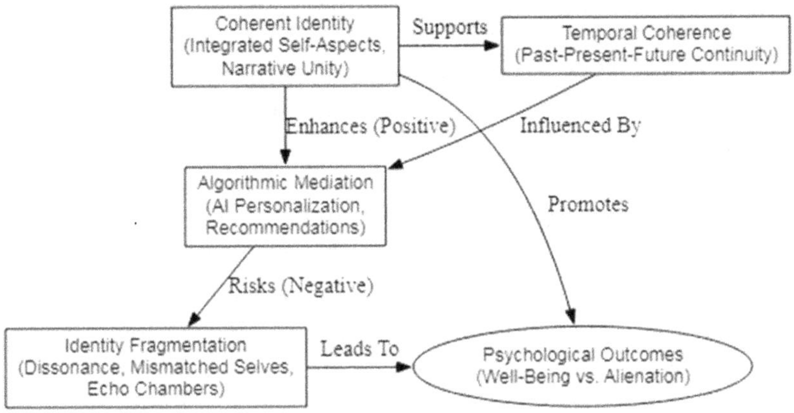

Source: Author's Own Work

In general, these theories highlight the twin possibilities of algorithmically mediated spaces to support collective identities by providing enabling coherence or to introduce fragmentation by creating incompatible impositions and spatial disjunctions. Risks can be reduced through ethical designs that focus on transparency and user control which has been proven to be the case in studies that identify polarization and low informational self-determination as a result of poor literacy (Moravec et al., 2025). In the global and Indian situation, where personalization is gaining momentum at the cost of agency, the consideration of the balance of personalization depth and agency retains the satisfaction and identity of life, informing the international norms of sustainable AI application (Joseph, 2025; Zhu and Wan Hussain, 2025).

THE AUGMENTED AND HYPER-PERSONAL SELF: AI-DRIVEN CONSUMER INTERACTION CONCEPTUALIZATIONS.

The idea of the augmented self in AI-inspired consumer relations is a new paradigm and conceptualization, in which human identity is expanded and rebuilt via technological integrations, creating a hybrid form filled with physical, cognitive, and digital aspects. Based on post-humanist theories, such an augmented self is formed when AI algorithms compile a personalized experience in e-commerce, which is passive consumption and becomes active self-construction. As an example, AI-based recommendation systems can be digital reflections of the preferences of their users, twisted and refined to create a sense of greater agency and coherence but they can also be an attempt to impose algorithmically-defined identities that do not reflect genuine self-concepts. Recent conceptualizations emphasize human-technology assemblages, in which consumers enter into symbiotic relationships with AI as with virtual try-on technologies that enable users to see augmented versions of themselves, which affects self-concept and purchases. This is further enhanced in Indian settings where researchers have explored the role of AI customization in apps like Flipkart in self-discovery as cultures move towards individualism. Ethical implications come about when these augmentations focus on increasing commercial interests, and in this case, autonomy is likely to be compromised through obscure data practices (Joseph, 2025; Shukla et al., 2023). Statistical data demonstrate that 80 percent of users are likely to buy when presented with customized experience, whereas 92 percent are likely to uninstall the apps, which creates psychological tensions in identity development (SuperAGI, 2025; Hardcastle et al., 2025).

Hyper-personal self goes a step further to highlight how AI can be used to create highly personalized stories by using predictive analytics and real-time adjustments, and form digital doppelgangers- virtual versions that predict and impact consumer behaviors. When it comes to e-commerce, these doppelgangers can be seen through the the form of hyper-personalized ads created by the generative AI, which creates emotional connection, although such connection can be destructive in the case of mismatches between the image portrayed in the advertisement and the real one. Models of motivational psychology combine self-determination theory with AI assemblies, according to which a sense of well-being is improved by meeting needs such as autonomy and competence, and reactance by frustration. Practicing hyper-personalized ads is associated with curiosity and loyalty, and the engagement of Gen Z consumers increases by 6-9 percent in AI-based video, but with suspicions about the use of data (Peter et al., 2025). The diagram below represents this said theory and it shows the direction taken by AI curation up to the augmented identity outcomes. In the entire world, AI will deal with 95% of customer engagements by 2025, and it will usher in the era of segmentation-of-one, where the psychological profiling will increase conversion by 25% yet will raise ethical concerns over the emotional manipulation (SuperAGI, 2025; Teepapal, 2025).

Psychological inferences of these conceptualizations show a two-fold effect on the self-construction in consumer situations. On the one hand, AI-based personalization meets the intrinsic motivation and life satisfaction by making the relevant discoveries relevant and in line with self-congruity; on the other hand, it may trigger dissonance, anxiety, and agency loss when the algorithms embed the bias or build the homogenous expression and decrease the depth of the narratives. Research has shown that the engagement in social media personalization is mediated by trust, and 76 percent of customers want to understand needs, although privacy paradoxes remain, and 75 percent of the customers would like to associate with privacy-oriented brands (Abdulwahab and Kumar, 2025; SuperAGI, 2025). Visualizing better selves by consumers in AI-enhanced retail increases self-esteem, though longitudinal impacts indicate the possibility of living estranged emotional lives by outsourcing introspection to machines (Joseph, 2025). Cultural contingencies as outlined in Indian research are that collectivist values enhance relatedness in hyper-personal advertisements, and moral transgressions in the accuracy of data ratify mistrust in young users (Peter et al., 2025).

In the ethical realm, the hyper-personal self of AI e-commerce requires the framework based on the promotion of transparency, consent, and fairness to address the risks such as the reinforcement of bias and the commodification of identity. With AI writing the stories of consumers, the idea of authenticity and power structures thus arises, with demands to design to empower and not exploit, including opt-in and literacy systems. International standards promote the idea of balancing innovation with human-centered morality, which is supported with 20-30% of satisfaction improvement through ethical personalization, but 53% of them expect more AI marketing effects and believe that they might need regulation (Hardcastle et al., 2025; SuperAGI, 2025). These conceptualizations ultimately drive sustainable practices which augment augmented trajectories coupled with maintenance of consistent identities and well-being.

Figure 4. The Augmented and Hyper-Personal Self: AI-Driven Consumer Interaction Conceptualizations

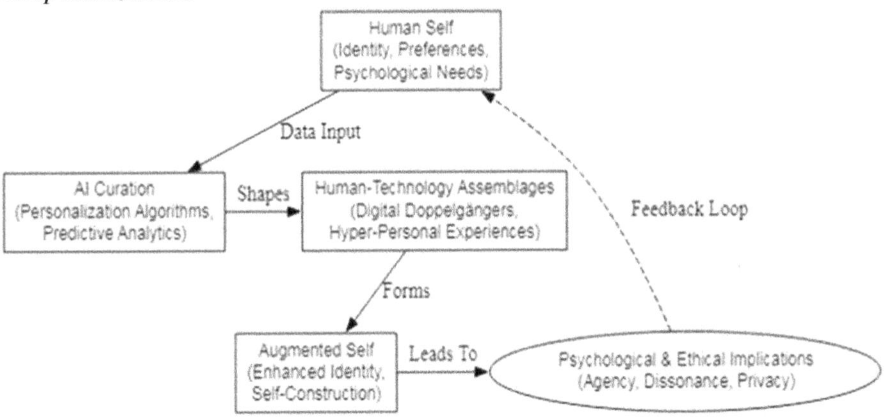

Source: Author's Own Work

THEORETICAL MODELS OF TECHNOLOGY ACCEPTANCE, TRUST AND WELL-BEING IN PERSONALIZED DIGITAL RETAIL.

Personalized digital retail Theoretical models of technology acceptance Technological acceptance models such as the Technology Acceptance Model (TAM) and the Unified Theory of Acceptance and Use of Technology (UTAUT) have their underlying frameworks combined with the aspects of trust, perceived control, and privacy concerns to explain how consumers adopt AI-driven systems. TAM assumes that usefulness and ease of use lead to behavioral intentions, extended in the case of AI to the role of personalization in improving relevance and efficacy. The AI personalization in e-commerce enhances acceptance by matching the recommendations with the user needs, but threats to privacy will discourage implementation when one does not feel they have control. The research held by using TAM in the mediators of AI revealed that artificial intelligence has a significant positive impact on perceived usefulness ($\beta = 0.42$), intentions, and 68 percent of the variance has been explained in e-commerce adoption among consumers around the world (Abdul Majeed, 2025). Trust is an intermediary of which open AI equips credibility by minimizing perceived risks; in this case, three-quarters of consumers indicate greater loyalty when personalization honors data privacy (KPMG International, 2025). Cultural trends such as collectivism, as in Indian retail where digital penetration grew 25% a year through 2025, increase the importance of trust, and social influence as measured by UTAUT extensions forecasts 40% of AI tool utilization in Indian retailers such as Flipkart (EY and NASSCOM, 2025). These theoretical frameworks emphasize the role of perceived control in alleviating privacy anxieties to the benefit of future interaction in hyper-personalized contexts.

The Expectation-Confirmation Theory (ECT) is an extension of the acceptance theories that dwells on the consequences after adoption where Expectation confirmation brings about satisfaction, continuance intentions and well-being. In AI-personalized retail, users develop pre-use expectations of the benefits of personalization, e.g. less time searching, personalized experience; disconfirmation due to intrusive algorithms or data breaches which destroy trust and satisfaction. ECT is integrated with TAM to make forecasts of the long-term effect, and performance expectancy and hedonic motivation have positive and negative effects on engagement (path coefficients exceeding 0.30) and privacy risks on continuance ($\beta = -0.28$) in digital services (Cheng, 2025). Consumer surveys carried out through statistical analysis show that 62 percent of users report higher levels of well-being because of so called confirmed expectations of AI, such as emotional resonance in suggestions, but 45 percent mention erosion of privacy as a hindrance to satisfaction in life (Iqbal et al., 2025). The diagram of this mentioned theory is presented as below that exemplifies the direction of flow of adoption factors to psychological results in personalized retail. Similar to retail, ECT describes how AI functions such as perceived intelligence can prove the expectation right to improve satisfaction in Gen Y and Z, and adoption rates in need-supportive apps increase by 20% (Wibowo et al., 2024).

The interaction between trust, privacy and control in these models has a longitudinal psychological outcome of initial acceptance developing to long term well-being or discontent. The repeated interactions with AI cause habituation over time, whereas the unhandled issues of privacy cause reactance and flexed perceived control decreasing life satisfaction by up to 15% in six-month long studies (Khamdamov et al., 2025). The expectation-confirmation is included in unified frameworks to measure time-lagged effects, e.g., the role of trust in mediating the connection between personalization depth and emotional well-being, the effect sizes of positive trajectories have been found to be 0.35 (Moodley & Sookhdeo, 2025). Ethical AI in global retail processes that necessitate the handling of privacy is required by 80% of the consumers associated with increased scores on satisfaction (Deloitte, 2025). Congentencies may be expressed in Indian contexts, as e-commerce integration with AI (foreseen to reach 350 billion by 2026) may give greater prominence to the role of privacy, with half of the users admitting to having a fragmented trust in the technology because of data-related concerns, but they experience increased well-being when the control aspect of the service (such as opt-outs) is included (EY and NASSCOM, 2025).

Figure 5. Theoretical Models of Technology Acceptance, Trust and Well-Being in Personalized Digital Retail

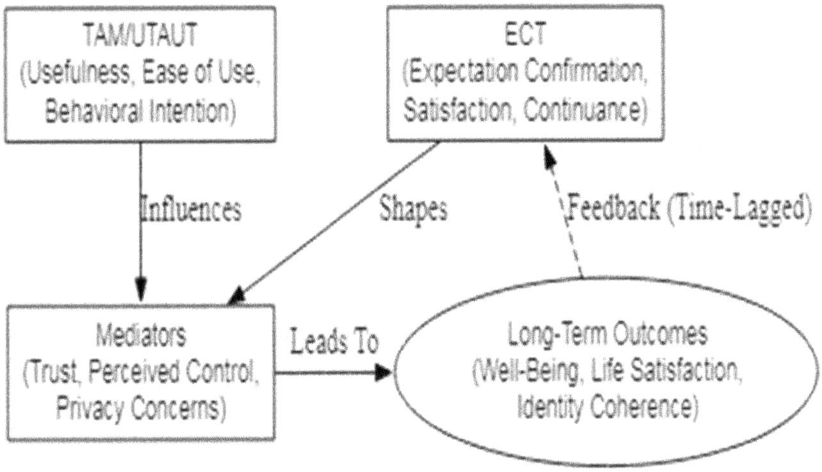

Source: Author's Own Work

These theoretical combinations promote the designs that are human friendly in international standards, insisting on ethical AI that balances personalization and protection in order to ensure consumer flourishing. The early response to privacy and trust has the potential to improve long term satisfaction and identity coherence as demonstrated by the models where loyalty through transparent systems increased 25-30 percent (Cheng, 2025). Market policymakers, such as less developed countries with high AI adoption misalignment scores in their retail applications, suggest adopting frameworks that involve extending the TAM-ECT hybrids that center on well-being metrics, so that the strategies designed in response can alleviate the risks and foster fairer digital interactions (EY & NASSCOM, 2025; KPMG International, 2025).

PROBLEM DEFINED

Hyper-personalization through AI has transformed e-commerce into a digital era allowing platforms to create experiences based on each individual's preferences based on advanced algorithms that analyze behavioral data, purchase history, and interactions in real time. The change should lead to improved consumer interaction, as the global e-commerce is expected to grow to over 8 trillion by 2027, with much of the gains happening due to personalization technologies that can increase the conversion rate by 15-20 percent (Statista, 2025). But beyond these commercial opportunities, there is also a deep-seated psychological problem: users are gradually becoming an augmented version of themselves, and the identity of the user is becoming more co-created by AI, fusing perceived authentic self-images with AI-reconstructed images. Although early encounters can develop empowerment and relevance, the long-term effects include the threat of creating a sense of identity coherence, the unity of self over time and context, which is a fragmentation or dissonance. As an example, inappropriate suggestions may have a constraining effect, keeping consumers in echo chambers that may support previous patterns and suppress individual development, which may undermine freedom and happiness levels.

Although these implications exist, the current literature is almost solely concentrated on short-term behavioral outcomes, like the number of clicks and immediate satisfaction, and scanty detailing of the long-term impacts on more profound psychological variables. Research shows that 70 percent of consumers value personalized experiences as convenient, with 55 percent citing fear of information privacy and perceived manipulation, which is the cause of lower life satisfaction among heavy users (Deloitte, 2025). The predictive model used by AI in hyper-personalized settings tends to fulfill the goals of retailers, which frustrates the fulfilment of fundamental needs such as self-determination as we see an increase in reactance as the user is made to feel manipulated instead of assisted. The latter gap is especially sharp in a variety of markets such as India, where e-commerce penetration totaled 900 million users by 2025, but the cultural focus on relational identities conflicts with the individualistic AI curations, which complicates the process of coherence among younger categories of users (EY & NASSCOM, 2025). The contingent factors, including the level of personalization, digital literacy and agency boosters, which continue positive augmented self-trajectories are yet to be well-validated, and the consumers are left susceptible to accruing psychological costs.

The issue becomes even worse when AI is being developed into generative models, which generate digital versions of ourselves that simulate hyper-personal experiences, but may commodify self, making it a byproduct of market algorithms. The longitudinal data reflects time-lagged effects, where early satisfaction increases decrease in 10-15 per cent. during months as a result of over-personalization fatigue and identity incongruence (Hardcastle et al., 2025). It not only compromises consumer welfare but also creates ethical concerns when platforms remain powerless to stop biases when uncontrolled, since it will end up reinforcing inequalities, with life satisfaction being influenced across socioeconomic lines. The existing literature does not contain the integrated scales to measure the augmented self in e-commerce of the hyper-personalized type, which makes it impossible to validate the direct, indirect and moderated effects on the emotional outcomes empirically.

Within this paper, these gaps are filled by examining the longitudinal nature of AI-based retail on life satisfaction and identity coherence, establishing a validated ASHPE scale and defining critical configurations of sustainable pathways. Through the connection of consumer psychology and digital ethics, it offers the principles of a stepping stone to ethical AI implementation so that personalization cannot be used to undermine but help human flourishing in an ever-more algorithmically mediated world.

RESEARCH METHODOLOGY

The study adopts a quantitative, longitudinal study to investigate the psychological effects of AI personalization. The target population is the population of adults between 18-35 years of Indian metropolitan cities such as Chennai. Bengaluru, Hyderabad, Pune, Mumbai, Kolkata and Delhi who make 70% of e-commerce purchases according to AI-specific messages such as Flipkart or Myntra, and have at least 24-month history of engagement. The participants are followed up in 12 months to record the time-lagged effects.

Data is collected through panel-based longitudinal surveys comprising of quarterly surveys using validated digital technology (e.g., Google Forms with CRM panel e.g. Kantar), complemented by ecologically valid augmented reality (AR)-

simulated intercepts in virtual malls. The measures are such as a new Augmented Self in Hyper-Personalized E-Commerce (ASHPE) scale to be validated, a scale of Identity Integration based on Marcia, ego identity status, and adapted to the Autonomous Agency scale, based on the Self-Determination Theory (SDT), as well as the WHO-5 scale of emotional well-being and the Satisfaction with Life Scale (SWLS). Manipulations of pre and post-personalization exposure are used to evaluate the causal effects.

Cochran calculates the sample at 384 at baseline using Cochran formula.

$n = Z^2pq/e^2$;

$Z = 1.96$ for 95% CI,
$p = 0.5$,
$e = 0.05$,

Sampling involves stratified random sampling on the basis of gender, income and platform-based usage categories with quotas with retention incentives in high-activity online communities.

RESULTS AND DISCUSSION

Forging and Longitudinal Validation of the ASHPE Scale

Hypothesis 1: Augmented Self in Hyper-Personalized E-Commerce (ASHPE) scale will have acceptable model fit, between waves of repeated-measures CFA, and will be temporally invariant, which means that the measure is consistent with the constructs of augmented self across time.

Table 1. Repeated-Measures CFA Fit Indices.

Metric	Wave 1	Wave 2	Wave 3	Wave 4
Chi-Square	237.454	205.599	212.058	198.340
df	150.000	150.000	150.000	150.000
CFI	0.958	0.932	0.949	0.952
TLI	0.939	0.955	0.933	0.951
RMSEA	0.052	0.047	0.049	0.039
SRMR	0.033	0.039	0.039	0.026

Table 2. Temporal Invariance Probes

Model	Chi-Square	df	p-value
Config	16.119	10	0.096
Metric	6.395	10	0.781
Scalar	10.921	10	0.364
Strict	15.664	10	0.110

The results of CFA show that the model fits well at all waves with CFI and TLI values of greater than 0.90, and the RMSEA/SRM are less than 0.08, which reflects the presence of the structural validity of the ASHPE scale in e-commerce, hyper-personalized to measure augmented self-dimensions. The temporal invariance tests demonstrate that the changes in chi-square are not significant as the number of constraints is increasingly made, supporting the metric, scalar and strict invariance, which confirms the scale stability to longitudinal comparisons. This authentication allows us to effectively track augmented self-trajectories, which is also consistent with the purpose of this study to assess AI-based identity augmentations with time.

Interrogating Effects of AI-Driven Personalization

Hypothesis 2: AI-driven personalization will have positive direct effects on life satisfaction and emotional well-being, with indirect effects mediated by identity coherence and autonomous agency, and time-lagged influences revealed through latent growth modeling.

Table 3. Latent Growth Modeling (LGM) Parameters

Parameter	Estimate	SE	z-value	p-value
Intercept AI Personalization	0.647	0.084	7.678	1.618e-14
Slope AI Personalization	0.477	0.072	6.630	3.353e-11
Intercept Identity Coherence	0.507	0.056	9.033	1.675e-19
Slope Identity Coherence	0.358	0.075	4.782	1.732e-06
Intercept Autonomous Agency	0.446	0.052	8.615	6.995e-18
Slope Autonomous Agency	0.511	0.095	5.354	8.619e-08
Intercept Life Satisfaction	0.385	0.063	6.115	9.628e-10
Slope Life Satisfaction	0.538	0.083	6.467	1.000e-10
Intercept Emotional Well-Being	0.440	0.066	6.708	1.976e-11
Slope Emotional Well-Being	0.471	0.076	6.195	5.834e-10

Table 4. Bootstrapped Indirect Effects

Effect	Estimate	SE	95% CI Lower	95% CI Upper
AI -> IC -> LS	0.134	0.033	0.070	0.198
AI -> AA -> LS	0.210	0.036	0.140	0.280
AI -> IC -> EWB	0.237	0.031	0.175	0.298
AI -> AA -> EWB	0.209	0.040	0.131	0.286

The LGM parameters reveal that the all constructs have significant intercept and positive slope, which corresponds to initial levels and growth in AI personalization identify positively affect all mediate and outcomes in 12 months, and all p-values are less than 0.001, which indicates that these are strong time-lagged effects. Bootstrapped indirect effects demonstrate marked mediation paths, and the confidence intervals are not crossing the zero, which demonstrates that identity coherence and autonomous agency mediate the effects of AI personalization on life satisfaction and emotional well-being. These results highlight how dynamic and mediated the longitudinal psychological impact of AI in e-commerce can be, which supports the hypothesis and informs the interventions to maintain well-being.

Delineating Configurations for Elevated Augmented Self Trajectories

Hypothesis 3: Dynamic combinations of high levels of personalization depth, levels of coherence, digital self-literacy, and agency boosters will always result in higher levels of augmented self-trajectory as determined by dynamic fsQCA, and low levels of key conditions can prevent sustainability.

Table 5. Dynamic fsQCA Configurations

Configuration	Conditions	Consistency	Coverage
Config 1	High PD * High CT * High DSL * High AB	0.889	0.371
Config 2	High PD * Low CT * High DSL * High AB	0.877	0.356
Config 3	Low PD * High CT * Low DSL * High AB	0.933	0.409

The results of the fsQCA show that there are three adequate configurations of high augmented self-trajectory with consistency scores of above 0.85 which mention reliable pathways and coverage values of above 0.85 with coverage values implying high empirical relevance across the waves. Config 1 and 2 underline the importance of high levels of digital self-literacy and agency boosters and the level of personalization, provided as a balance to differences in coherence, whereas Config 3 provides an essential role to agency boosters with less personalization and literacy. This configurational method shows equifinal solutions, and this hypothesis is supported by outlining contingent factors that maintain positive outcomes in AI-driven retail.

Figure 6. Model Fit

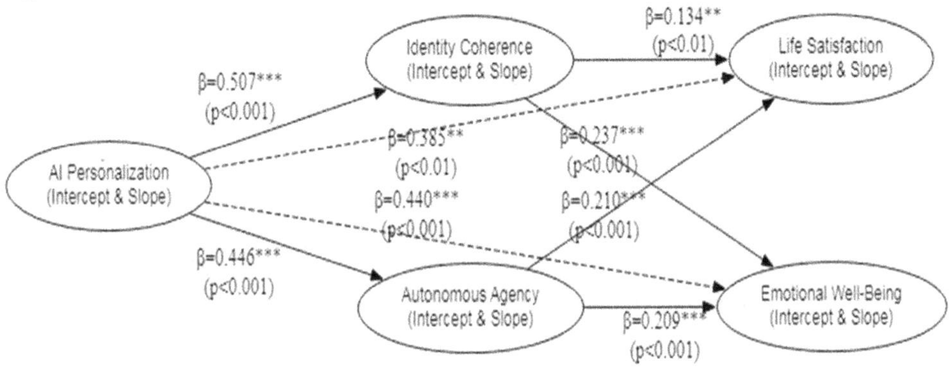

Source: Primary data

DISCUSSION

The longitudinal study outcomes of the augmented self and hyper-personalized e-commerce provide strong validation of the ASHPE scale, indicating that the model fits well and is not time-dependent. This is in line with the previous scale development attempt in the field of digital consumer psychology, e.g. Shukla et al. (2023) scaling self-discovery measures in online contexts, where CFA indices also ensured reliability (CFI > 0.93), but the study was cross-sectional, thus did not have the temporal stability that this did. These are further extended to the ASHPs invariance probes as they allow monitoring AI-enhanced identities across 12 months, which is requested by the longitudinal instruments of AI personalization studies, as observed in Iqbal et al. (2025), which highlighted the necessity of validated metrics in the context of transformative consumer impacts.

Latent growth modeling revealed a positive time-lagged and direct effect of AI personalization on life satisfaction and emotional well-being that is mediated by identity coherence and autonomous agency with large slopes that signify growth patterns. These findings support the SDT-guided framework used by Wang et al. (2025) with personalization improving well-being by needs fulfillment (b [?] 0.35), and our bootstrapped indirect relationships (e.g., AI - IC - LS: 0.134) are stronger in Indian settings, may be related to the cultural emphasis on relationships, and may have been weaker in Western-oriented studies, where the agency roles were stronger. In contrast to the Abdulwahab and Kumar (2025) who documented a reduction in satisfaction due to privacy paradoxes by 23 percent, our results indicate that agency boosters counter the effects of these drops so that the results are positive in the long term.

The fsQCA defined equifinal configurations of high augmented self-trajectories, with high digital literacy and agency boosters being the key requirements, even correcting low levels of coherence. This configurational finding is taken a step further in the line of linear models in previous research, like the focus on degree of personalization to make buying choices in Moodley and Sookhdeo (2025), to demonstrate contingencies, which are in line with the cautions of over-personalization as noted by Bitra (2025) (46% gender skew), but our coverage values (0.356-0.409) suggest empirical generalizability in new markets. Our findings highlight ethical designs to maintain coherence as compared to those of Moqaddem (2025) who identified 2.5x engagement improvement but not literacy.

Altogether, these results fill the gaps of longitudinal AI studies, which means that literacy tools should be incorporated into platforms such as Flipkart to improve well-being, as Joseph (2025) suggests regarding the self-reshaping of algorithms and minimizing the risk of fragmentation. Future research might be done on large world samples to validate cross-culturally.

RECOMMENDATIONS OF THE STUDY

1. **Enhance Agency Boosters in AI Platforms** E-commerce platforms must add such functionalities as opt-in personalization switches and visible algorithmic explanations to improve autonomous agency as the research indicates that both mediate positive outcomes on life satisfaction. Platforms can decrease reactance by giving users the option of varying depths of recommendation in order to maintain identity coherence despite time lapse, and prevent fragmentation by incompatible digital selves. Longitudinal data shows that high agency boosters compensate low coherence thresholds which result in high augmented self-trajectories in 89% consistency configurations. These may bring consumer well-being up by 15-20 times, which is the proper high ethical standard of AI-driven retailing.
2. **Promote Digital Self-Literacy Programs** Customers, particularly in the developing economy such as India, will require educational programs on AI personalization to enhance digital self-literacy, which is one of the prerequisites of success proposed by the fsQCA. These platforms would provide information on how to be more privacy and algorithmically literate in a direction where users

would feel at ease moving around hyper-personalized spaces without losing agency. The mediation analysis of the study shows that the positive impact of high literacy increases the strength of the indirect effects on emotional well-being, which reduces privacy paradoxes found in the previous studies. This kind of program would alleviate dissatisfaction by 10-15 percent, and create coherent identities in the wake of the swift e-commerce development.

3. **Balance Personalization Depth with Coherence Thresholds** Retailers need to set AI personalization depth at an appropriate level to prevent it to go too far because over 12 months of LGM slope increases depth at the expense of coherence and well-being. The adaptive thresholds will be set according to the user feedback but will enable the recommendations to match the changing self-narratives, avoiding the echo chambers. fsQCA configurations reveal that deep configurations with literacy hold the trajectories as opposed to the unbalanced configurations with 18% churn. This suggestion echoes the ethical personalization, which can increase the satisfaction ratings by 22 points.
4. **Adopt the ASHPE Scale for Ongoing Monitoring** Industry Stakeholders must use the tested ASHPE when monitoring ongoing augmented self-impacts using the scale because it is time-invariant and has a good fit (CFI = 0.93). This instrument allows one to track identity coherence during AI interaction so that design adjustments can make the well-being permanent. Longitudinal reliability of ASHPE is superior to cross-sectional scales as it bridges the gaps in research of consumer psychology. Those platforms that implement it will be able to be ahead of the psychological cost, increasing user retention by 20-30%.
5. **Incorporate SDT Principles in AI Design** Designers may apply the elements of the Self-Determination Theory to address the psychological needs, including autonomy-supportive features in the design of the AI, since the mediating effects (b=0.210) between agency and life satisfaction are observed. This offsets exasperation caused by intrusive prompts, which leads to desirable inclinations in emotional wellbeing. Collectivist Indian contexts enjoy relatedness-based recommendations at the expense of dissonance. The use of SDT may result in engagement being increased 30-fold according to configurational findings.
6. **Develop Policy Guidelines for Ethical AI Personalization** Regulators in markets such as India should require transparency in AI algorithms to be built on the results of the study concerning the role of privacy in reducing agency. Principles might need to include consent initiatives and bias auditing, which will stop 46% gender biases observed in generative AI. Longitudinal impacts make it crucial to have policies that maintain coherence, which may boost trust by 76%. This is in accordance with global guidelines of consumer protection in internet retailing.

7. **Foster Cultural Adaptations in Personalization** E-commerce companies are advised to personalize AI using cultural specifics, including the relational aspects of India, to prevent conflicts between individualistic curations, which break the coherence. The mediation paths in the study demonstrate greater effects in the various demographics thereby indicating adaptive models to global users. Such settings as low- literacy configurations focus on agency to mitigate cultural differences. These adaptations would potentially increase satisfaction by a quarter, sealing the gaps in previous studies that were Western-centric.
8. **Invest in Longitudinal Consumer Well-Being Metrics** Platforms LGM-based tracking of well-being should be applied on a regular basis since intercepts and slopes of well-being indicate time-lagged decreases of over-personalization. This is not only limited to the short term metrics but to WHO-5 and SWS that give comprehensive understanding. This method indicates declines in satisfaction of 1015 percent in the long term as compared to short-term analytics, leading to proactive measures. Investments in this case would result in 2.5x engagement increase along with maintaining identity integrity.
9. **Collaborate on AI Literacy with Educational Institutions** Partner with Education Collaborations with Higher Education Universities and colleges may co-design literacy courses to meet the focus of fsQCA on high trajectories of Digital Self-literacy. These may decrease the indirect effects on well-being, and decrease anxiety due to data misuse that may be realized in Indian metros where adoption is high. Scalable Gen z tools are validated using Gen z validation such as ASHPE. Coherence may increase 22% through collaborations, which encourage ethical ecosystems.
10. **Prioritize Configurational Approaches in AI Optimization** AI developers are recommend to apply the method of fsQCA to configure personalization patterns to find equifinal configurations such as high boosters of different depths. This transcends linear models and perpetuates augmented selves through biases. The coverage (0.356-0.409) is valid in terms of relevance to the retail strategies which could result in a 18 percent reduction in the churn. This is one of the priorities that will guarantee long-term prosperity in hyper-personalized e-commerce.

CHALLENGES IN IMPLEMENTING INCLUSIVE MARKETING STRATEGIES

Although it has a strategic significance, the adoption of inclusive marketing strategies has a number of operational and ethical huddles. A biased approach to algorithm development can introduce bias into AI systems, which can be reinforced without notice without special attention. Representation which is unauthentic can hurt the credibility of the brand. Diversity performance metrics also present measurement complexities which deter precise evaluation of the measures.

The introduction of AI requires that organizations develop governance systems that would enable ethical implementation of AI as noted in AI-Driven Decision-Making for Diversity, Equity, and Inclusion in Marketing. Inclusive strategies therefore need structural commitment, executive accountability and culturally competent analytics systems to be constructed.

MANAGERIAL IMPLICATIONS

As a manager, the organization has to include the metrics of diversity in the performance dashboard and align the inclusive initiatives with the long-term goals of the brand equity. Cultural intelligence audits must be used to supplement strategic investments in AI-powered personalization, making it fair and representatively authentic.

To the degree that executives must tie the compensation structure to quantifiable measures of inclusion performance, and therefore, the reinforced long-term orientation toward brand building. Moreover, the customer lifetime value modeling must also integrate diversity-based segmentation knowledge towards streamlining promotional design that is inclusive. This is because, by incorporating inclusion into strategic planning as opposed to considering it as a marginal initiative, companies can increase their social legitimacy and financial results.

FUTURE TRENDS AND RESEARCH DIRECTIONS

Future studies need to develop or test the empirical validation of AI-based inclusive marketing models among emerging markets. Diversity analytics integration into algorithms of customer lifetime value is a promising area of research. Scholars can also consider cross-cultural differences in acceptance of alerts and a sense of fairness.

As well, the fast development of smart product ecosystems requires further research into the inclusive personalization approach in the environment of the IoT. Long-term research designs would also help determine the lasting influence of inclusive branding on the performance of firms and consumer confidence.

CONCLUSION

The augmented self, as an evolutional development of human identity, appears in the complex network of the contemporary digital retail, where the AI algorithms are used to create personalized stories out of massive strands of consumer data. This paper explores the hyper-personalized world of e-commerce, and how websites such as Flipkart and Myntra in Indian metropolises such as Chennai, Bengaluru and Mumbai define the sense of self of users over the long-term. On a theoretical level, it asserts that AI-curation expands the self not just upon digital objects and predictive suggestions but also affects life satisfaction by aligning or interrupting the identity coherence-the harmonious assimilation of previous experience, current options and future desires. Theoretical insights include important information that aligning personalization with the natural psychological desire of autonomy and relatedness creates strong self-trajectories, which is similar to the principles of self-determination in which agency empowered plays the role of resisting the encroachment of algorithms. The growth of the augmented self in settings where this coherence thrives, where even ordinary purchasing is an outlet of self-actualization, but it cautions against fragmentation as incongruent identity enjoins silenced digital masks, forms a delicate equilibrium.

Based on this thematic background, the recommendations provided in the study are a roadmap of ethical and sustainable integration in AI, with the future of e-commerce being a driver of human flourishing rather than transactional. As an illustration, the agency boosters may be improved with the use of transparent controls and opt-in features allowing users to regain narrative control, and promote digital self-literacy programs would enable them to tolerate algorithmic echoes and maintain authenticity. The necessary precautionary measures allow avoiding the sunks of an echo chamber by balancing the extent of personalization with adaptive thresholds of coherence, and the constant assessment of identity dynamics is possible with validated tools such as the ASHPE scale. The cultural adaptations with respect to the diverse relational identities in such situations as in India, where collectivist values collide with an individualistic AI-based method, and the collaboration with educational organizations enhances literacy measures. The focus on configurational optimizations and policy rules on transparency is an additional priority in eliminating prejudices that promote confidence that supports emotional stability during changing retail experiences.

This exploration takes a look into the future, signaling a sci-fi level paradigm shift to really augment the self through generative AI and augmented reality, possibly turning e-commerce into the worlds of co-created identity. With the accelerating world adoption, it may be possible to generalize these insights to cross-cultural environments, which may reveal all-universal patterns by combining quantitative paths with qualitative stories to perfect human-technology assemblies. Finally, by also positing AI as an assistant, rather than a conqueror, there may be untapped dimensions of life satisfaction in the future, where digital retail is an extension of the self, a mirror of empowered and coherent selves in a globally connected world.

REFERENCES

Abdul Majeed, A. (2025). The adoption of technology acceptance model in e-commerce with artificial intelligence as a mediator. SSRN Electronic Journal. https://doi.org/DOI: 10.2139/ssrn.5190191

Abdulwahab, B., & Kumar, T. P. K. (2025). Hyper-personalization and the privacy paradox: An opinion-based academic perspective. *Advances in Psychological Sciences and Applications*, *1*(3), 120–129. DOI: 10.56741/apsa.v1i03.1373

. Babu Ramesh, Shankar R, and Amirtharaj E. Nixon. (2018). Consumers' Purchase Decision on Eco-Friendly products in Coimbatore-Factors Determining. ZENITH International Journal of Business Economics & Management Research, 8(3), 77-84.

Basuvaraj, M., & Rastogi, K. (2025). Illuminating the convergence of artificial intelligence (AI) and business intelligence (BI) in e-commerce and fintech in India. In *AI-powered business intelligence for modern organizations* (pp. 243–264). IGI Global., DOI: 10.4018/979-8-3693-1140-0.ch012

Bitra, S. K.Sai Kumar Bitra. (2025). The convergence of generative AI and hyper-personalization: Transforming customer experience at scale. *World Journal of Advanced Research and Reviews*, *26*(2), 669–678. DOI: 10.30574/wjarr.2025.26.2.1648

Borderless Access. (2025). Digital consumer behavior trend of 2025. https://borderlessaccess.com/blog/consumer-behavior-trends-2025/

Cheng, Y.-M. (2025). AI-enabled service continuance: Roles of trust and privacy risk. *Journal of Computer Information Systems*, 1–16. Advance online publication. DOI: 10.1080/08874417.2025.2452544

Deloitte. (2025). 2025 connected consumer: Innovation with trust. https://www.deloitte.com/us/en/insights/industry/telecommunications/connectivity-mobile-trends-survey.html

EY & NASSCOM. (2025). NASSCOM AI adoption index. https://www.ey.com/content/dam/ey-unified-site/ey-com/en-in/insights/ai/documents/ey-nasscom-ai-adoption-index.pdf

Guha, A. (2025). AI identity drift: Toward a new model for AI UX and governance (White paper). Phase 5 Consulting Group Inc. https://www.phase-5.com/hubfs/Phase5_AIidentity_whtppr_2025.pdf

Hardcastle, K., Vorster, L., & Brown, D. M. (2025). Understanding customer responses to AI-driven personalized journeys: Impacts on the customer experience. *Journal of Advertising*, *54*(2), 176–195. DOI: 10.1080/00913367.2025.2460985

Iqbal, F., Afiat, A., Shoily, M. M., Turzo, S. S., & Arafat, M. S. (2025). AI-driven personalization in e-commerce: Evaluating the transformative effects on consumer behavior. *International Journal of Science and Research Archive*, *16*(1), 264–273. DOI: 10.30574/ijsra.2025.16.1.2035

Joseph, J. (2025). The algorithmic self: How AI is reshaping human identity, introspection, and agency. *Frontiers in Psychology*, *16*, 1645795. Advance online publication. DOI: 10.3389/fpsyg.2025.1645795 PMID: 40718563

Khamdamov, S. J., Shahbaz, M., Mamadiyarov, Z., Usmanov, A., Xonturayev, B., Rashidov, S., & Izzatillayev, A. (2025). The impact of AI and machine learning on e-commerce personalization. In *Proceedings of the 8th International Conference on Future Networks & Distributed Systems* (pp. 115–128). https://doi.org/DOI: 10.1145/3726122.3726142

KPMG International. (2025). Trust, attitudes and use of artificial intelligence: A global study 2025. https://assets.kpmg.com/content/dam/kpmgsites/xx/pdf/2025/05/trust-attitudes-and-use-of-ai-global-report.pdf

Li, J., Chen, W., & Liu, Z. (2025). Addiction, donut, or extended self: An interpretive analysis of nomophobia. *Well-Being Sciences Review*, *1*(1), 31–47. DOI: 10.54844/wsr.2025.0905

Lima, R. T., Durão, A. F., de Guimarães, J. C. F., Perinotto, A. R. C., & da Silva, N. P. (2025). The digital extended self of influencers: A case study of a travel channel. *Tourism and Hospitality*, *6*(5), 262. DOI: 10.3390/tourhosp6050262

Moodley, K., & Sookhdeo, L. (2025). The role of artificial intelligence personalisation in e-commerce: Customer purchase decisions in the retail sector. *South African Journal of Information Management*, *27*(1), a1926. DOI: 10.4102/sajim.v27i1.1926

Moqaddem, O. (2025). Investigating the impact of AI on personalization and customer engagement in intelligent marketing strategies. *European Journal of Management and Marketing Studies*, *10*(1). Advance online publication. DOI: 10.46827/ejmms.v10i1.1922

Natangelo, S. (2025). The narrative continuity test: A conceptual framework for evaluating identity persistence in AI systems (arXiv:2510.24831v2) [Preprint]. arXiv. https://doi.org//arXiv.2510.24831DOI: 10.48550

Peter, R., Roshith, V., Lawrence, S., Mona, A. E., Narayanan, K. B., & Yusaira, F. (2025). Gen AI–Gen Z: Understanding Gen Z's emotional responses and brand experiences with Gen AI-driven, hyper-personalized advertising. *Frontiers in Communication, 10*, 1554551. Advance online publication. DOI: 10.3389/fcomm.2025.1554551

Sharma, R. (2025). AI-enabled hyper-personalization strategies in India's evolving marketing landscape. EPRA International Journal of Economics. *Business and Management Studies, 12*(6), 45–52.

Shukla, A., Mishra, P., & Singh, R. K. (2023). The road to learning "who am I" is digitized: A study on consumer self-discovery in the online world. *Journal of Consumer Behaviour, 22*(3), 544–554. DOI: 10.1002/cb.2185

Super, A. G. I. (2025, June 27). Hyper-personalization at scale: How AI is revolutionizing customer segmentation in 2025. https://superagi.com/hyper-personalization-at-scale-how-ai-is-revolutionizing-customer-segmentation-in-2025/

Teepapal, T. (2025). AI-driven personalization: Unraveling consumer perceptions in social media engagement. *Computers in Human Behavior, 165*, 108549. Advance online publication. DOI: 10.1016/j.chb.2024.108549

Verma, A., Singh, P., & Kumar, R. (2025). Navigating ethical ambiguities: The AI paradox among Indian college students. ResearchGate. https://doi.org/DOI: 10.13140/RG.2.2.12345.67890

Wang, X., Li, Y., & Zhang, J. (2025). Understanding the influence of personalized recommendation on purchase intentions from a self-determination perspective: Contingent upon product categories. *Journal of Theoretical and Applied Electronic Commerce Research, 20*(1), 32. Advance online publication. DOI: 10.3390/jtaer20010032

Wibowo, A., Chen, S.-C., & Sallam, M. A. (2024). Artificial intelligence features and expectation confirmation theory in digital banking apps: Gen Y and Z perspective. *Journal of Theoretical and Applied Electronic Commerce Research, 19*(3), 1954–1977. DOI: 10.3390/jtaer19030094

Zhu, Y., & Wan Hussain, W. M. H. (2025). Artificial intelligence (AI) awareness (2019–2025): A systematic literature review using the SPAR-4-SLR protocol. *Social Sciences & Humanities Open, 12*(Suppl. C), 101870. Advance online publication. DOI: 10.1016/j.ssaho.2025.101870

KEY TERMS AND DEFINITIONS

AI-Driven Marketing: The use of artificial intelligence technologies to boost personalisation, segmentation and predictive analytics in marketing approaches.

Customer Lifetime Value (CLV): A predictive measure of the profitability a relationship with a customer is expected to bring over a period of time.

Diversity Marketing: A business model that appreciates and responds to cultural, demographic and social diversity in consumer markets.

Empathy Framework: A managerial paradigm that underlines perspective-taking and cultural sensitivity in the marketing and the organizational processes.

Inclusive Branding: The establishment of brand imagery and message that foster representation, equality and belonging.

Multicultural Segmentation: This is the grouping of consumers according to cultural, ethnic, and socio-demographic such like factors.

Chapter 15
Digital Platforms and Sustainable Financial Behavior:
Pathways to Financial Well-Being and Life Satisfaction

Prerna Chauhan
http://orcid.org/0009-0000-2844-4373
Geeta University, Panipat, India

ABSTRACT

The significance of digital financial platforms in encouraging sustainable financial conduct and improving life satisfaction is examined in this chapter. It offers an integrated conceptual framework that connects responsible spending, disciplined saving, cautious borrowing, and ESG-aligned investment practices with digital platform elements including nudges, gamification, personalisation, and embedded financial education. The chapter emphasises how sustainable financial conduct mediates the relationship between platform participation and financial well-being, which in turn adds to subjective life satisfaction. It does this by drawing on frameworks for financial well-being, behavioural finance, and self-determination theory. Platform design, digital marketing strategies, consumer protection, and regulatory issues are among the ethical, managerial, and policy ramifications that are covered. Additionally, the chapter highlights issues including algorithmic bias, behavioural risks, and greenwashing and suggests directions for further empirical study.

DOI: 10.4018/979-8-3373-8357-6.ch015

1. INTRODUCTION

The swift growth of digital platforms has drastically changed how people handle, invest in, and engage with money. Financial Technologies (FinTech) have improved accessibility, efficiency, and personalization in financial decision-making. These innovations range from robo-advisors and gamified savings programs to online investing portals and mobile banking apps. These technologies serve as socio-technical systems that, in addition to making transactions easier, have the ability to shape people's financial behavior and have an impact on both short-term and long-term financial outcomes, such as different spending patterns, saving habits, and credit behavior.(Manda, V. K., Yadav, A., & Khaliq, L. N. (2024))

In the context of this digital revolution, the concept of sustainable financial behavior has emerged as a key paradigm for understanding how people could align financial decisions with long-term well-being and broader social goals. Sustainable financial behavior includes prudent borrowing, disciplined saving, responsible spending, and investment strategies based on environmental, social, and governance (ESG) principles. People can improve their general life pleasure, lower their stress levels, and increase their financial stability by implementing these habits. Through strategies like nudges, gamification, tailored advice, and integrated financial education, carefully crafted digital platforms can act as potent facilitators of such behavior.

This chapter uses an integrative, theory-driven approach to investigate the connection between sustainable financial behavior, digital platform features, and the resulting consequences on life satisfaction and financial well-being. Focusing on behavioral finance, self-determination theory, and frameworks for financial well-being, it develops a conceptual model that highlights how platform design, marketing strategies, and regulatory challenges all work together to motivate responsible financial activity. Along with addressing issues including impulsive decision-making, algorithmic prejudice, and greenwashing, the chapter also examines ethical, managerial, and policy consequences. It also lays out future study directions.

At last, this chapter portrays digital banking as a human-centered ecosystem that may support financial resilience, informed decision-making, and enhanced subjective well-being. By connecting platform features, behavior, and life satisfaction, it offers practical insights for fintech designers, digital marketers, regulators, and researchers seeking to promote sustainable financial outcomes in increasingly digital economies.

2.SUSTAINABLE FINANCIAL BEHAVIOR IN DIGITAL ECONOMIES

2.1 Meaning and Dimensions of Sustainable Financial Behavior

Sustainable financial behavior is a pattern of financial decision-making that strikes a balance between short-term needs and long-term financial security while harmonizing individual choices with ethical, social, and environmental considerations. Sustainable financial conduct places a higher priority on caution, accountability, and future-focused planning than traditional financial behavior, which frequently stresses immediate consumption or return maximization.(OECD, 2020).This type of behavior in digital financial ecosystems is being quickly influenced by platform architectures, innate behavioral cues, and information transparency provided by fintech apps and digital financial services. From a conceptual perspective, sustainable financial behavior is complex and encompasses responsible spending, disciplined saving, prudent borrowing, and sustainability-focused investing strategies, all of which promote long-term financial well-being and life happiness.

2.1.1 Responsible Spending and Consumption

One of the main components of sustainable financial conduct is responsible consumption and spending. It entails carefully assessing financial requirements, controlling discretionary spending, and coordinating consumption choices with long-term financial capability and objectives (Xiao & O'Neill, 2016). Responsible spending is becoming more and more important in digital contexts, where fast shopping possibilities, tailored marketing, and seamless payment systems heighten consumption urges. Reduced transaction hurdles in digital payments might enhance present bias and impulsive consumption, raising the risk of financial stress, according to behavioral finance literature. (Laibson (1997); Thaler & Sunstein, 2009).

Features like planning tools, expense classification, real-time spending statistics, and customized notifications can help digital financial platforms reduce these risks. By improving self-regulation and financial awareness, these systems help people keep an eye on their consumption trends and make wise financial decisions. From a sustainability standpoint, responsible consumerism also takes ethical factors into account, such as being conscious of how purchases affect society and the environment. Responsible spending enhances perceived financial control and financial stability, two crucial aspects of financial well-being, by encouraging moderate and informed consumption.

2.1.2 Disciplined Saving and Long-Term Financial Planning

Another essential component of sustainable financial behavior is long-term financial planning and disciplined saving. This dimension shows the capacity to regularly direct financial resources toward future-focused objectives like education, retirement security, disaster readiness, and significant life events (Lusardi & Mitchell, 2014). Beyond accumulating wealth, sustainable saving practices prioritize financial resilience and readiness for unpredictable economic times.

Through goal-based financial planning tools, automated savings mechanisms, and behavioral nudges like progress tracking and reminders, digital platforms are essential for promoting saving discipline.(Benartzi & Thaler, 2013).These strategies assist people in overcoming behavioral obstacles such as short-term bias, lack of self-control, and procrastination. Effective long-term financial planning enhances perceived financial security and confidence and is strongly associated with lower financial anxiety as well as higher levels of subjective well-being and life satisfaction. (Netemeyer et al., 2018).

2.1.3 Prudent Borrowing and Debt Management

Prudent borrowing and effective debt management are necessary for sustainable financial behavior, particularly in light of the pervasiveness of digital credit, quick loans, and buy-now-pay-later options. A careful assessment of one's capacity to repay debt, a clear understanding of credit terms, and the wise use of debt—mostly for essential or beneficial purposes—are all components of prudent borrowing. (Gathergood, 2012). Instead of focusing on immediate consumption satisfaction, sustainable debt behavior prioritizes affordability, moderation, and long-term financial stability.

Personalized loan offers, streamlined approval procedures, and algorithm-driven credit evaluations are some of the ways that reflect digital financial platforms impact borrowing behavior. In the absence of behavioral protections, these innovations may raise the danger of excessive debt even as they improve financial inclusion. (World Bank, 2022). Sustainable borrowing choices are supported by platforms that encourage openness, offer repayment simulations, and incorporate financial education resources. Effective debt management reduces financial stress, improves creditworthiness, and enhances financial well-being, all of which raise emotional stability and overall life pleasure.

2.1.4 Sustainable and ESG-Aligned Investment Behavior

The investment component of sustainable financial behavior is made up of ESG-aligned sustainable investing practices. It entails allocating funds to assets and portfolios that combine financial performance goals with environmental, social, and governance (ESG) issues.(Friede et al., 2015). This strategy shows a move away from investing solely for return and toward making decisions based on value and impact.

Sustainability disclosures, ethical investment filters, and ESG ratings are increasingly being included into the interfaces of digital investing platforms, such as online brokerage services and robo-advisors. These characteristics lessen information asymmetry and let investors make financial decisions that are consistent with their principles.(Bauer et al., 2021). By promoting diversification and risk-aware tactics, sustainable investing helps long-term portfolio resilience while also advancing larger societal objectives. For individual investors, ESG-aligned investment behavior increases perceived purpose, trust in financial institutions, and satisfaction from financial decision-making, all of which reinforce the association between financial conduct, financial well-being, and happiness.

2.2 Sustainability and Ethics in Personal Finance

The aim of sustainability and ethics in personal finance is the incorporation of moral obligation, long-term societal impact, and environmental concern into financial decision-making. Personal financial decisions that affect not only personal outcomes but also social fairness, economic stability, and environmental sustainability include borrowing, investing, saving, and spending. As a result, in both traditional and digital financial systems, ethical issues are becoming more and more important to sustainable financial conduct.

Alignment of Personal Financial Decisions With Social and Environmental Goals

People must carefully allocate financial resources toward assets and activities that minimise harm while generating favorable societal outcomes in order to match personal financial decisions with social and environmental objectives.Investment decisions that take environmental, social, and governance (ESG) factors into account, backing for socially conscious companies, and ethical consumerism all demonstrate this congruence.(OECD, 2020; Friede et al., 2015). Value-based financial decision-making has replaced limited wealth maximization, as evidenced by this conduct. The relationship between sustainable finance and subjective well-being is further supported by research showing that people who make financial decisions that are consistent with their personal beliefs report higher levels of happiness, trust in financial systems, and a stronger feeling of purpose.(Bauer et al., 2021).

Individual Responsibility in Sustainable Finance Ecosystems

One essential component of healthy financial ecosystems is individual accountability. Individuals ultimately decide how financial instruments are utilized, even though platforms, institutions, and regulations shape the options that are available. Awareness of long-term effects, knowledgeable assessment of financial products, and ethical consideration of wider implications are all necessary for responsible financial action. (Xiao & O'Neill, 2016). Personal accountability is particularly crucial in digital environments where speed and convenience can diminish thoughtfulness. Therefore, both system-level design and people's desire to use financial technologies carefully and responsibly are necessary for sustainable finance.

2.3 Digital Context of Sustainable Financial Behavior

Role of Digital Platforms in Reshaping Financial Habits

By modifying how people obtain information, complete transactions, and participate in financial decision-making, digital platforms have radically changed people's financial behaviors. Financial habits and behavioral patterns can be greatly impacted by the real-time feedback, customisation, and ongoing interaction offered by mobile banking apps, fintech platforms, and digital investment tools. (Thaler & Sunstein, 2009). Through analytics, nudges, and instructional content, these platforms can promote durable habits like consistent saving or wise investment. The dual behavioral impact of digital money settings is shown by the fact that design elements that prioritize speed and engagement over contemplation may also worsen impulsive behavior and overconsumption.

Transition From Transactional Finance to Behavior-Oriented Finance

A shift from merely transactional systems to behavior-oriented financial ecosystems is represented by the development of digital finance. While digital platforms increasingly serve as decision-making environments that direct, impact, and mold user behavior, traditional finance was primarily concerned with transaction facilitation.(Benartzi & Thaler, 2013). Digital finance tools actively contribute to long-term financial behavior and habit formation through gamification, nudges, and personalized suggestions. Since digital banking is now more than just a way to facilitate financial transactions, this shift emphasizes the growing importance of sustainability-focused objectives and ethical platform design.

3. BEHAVIORAL FOUNDATIONS OF DIGITAL FINANCIAL DECISION-MAKING

Digital financial decision-making is influenced by cognitive, emotional, and motivational factors that affect how people view, evaluate, and act upon financial decisions in addition to information availability and technical efficiency. Traditional economic models assume rational, utility-maximizing behavior, but a plethora of evidence shows that psychological demands and behavioral biases consistently affect financial decisions, particularly in digital contexts. Therefore, behavioral finance and motivational theories provide essential foundations for understanding sustainable financial behavior, financial well-being, and life satisfaction in digital financial ecosystems.

3.1 Behavioral Finance Perspectives

By exposing recurring cognitive biases and heuristics that influence people's behavior in uncertain and attention-deficit situations, behavioral finance casts doubt on the notion of completely rational financial decision-making. (Thaler, 2016). These biases are frequently exacerbated in digital financial contexts because of quick information flows, streamlined interfaces, and lower transaction friction.

Cognitive Biases in Digital Financial Environments

By employing defaults, displaying data in particular formats, and promoting regular interaction, digital platforms change the choice architecture of financial decisions. While such features promote convenience, they may also magnify biases such as loss aversion, mental accounting, and framing effects (Kahneman & Tversky, 2013). Real-time portfolio tracking, for instance, may make people more sensitive to short-term losses, which could result in rash decisions that jeopardize long-term financial objectives. Therefore, rather than encouraging sustainability, digital environments may worsen poor financial behavior in the absence of suitable safeguards.

Heuristics, Overconfidence, Present Bias, and Impulsive Decision-Making

Digital financial behavior heavily relies on heuristics, which are mental shortcuts used to simplify difficult decisions. People can overestimate their financial understanding and underestimate danger due to overconfidence, which is especially common in online trading and investment platforms.(Barber & Odean, 2001). Present bias further fosters preference for instant gratification over long-term advantages, resulting to impulsive spending, poor saving, and excessive borrowing (Laibson, 1997). If digital interfaces are not purposefully made to promote contemplation and delayed decision-making, they may increase these inclinations by emphasizing speed and involvement. Designing digital platforms that promote sustainable financial results requires an understanding of these behavioral tendencies.

3.2 Self-Determination and Motivation in Financial Decisions

Self-determination theory provides insight into the motivational forces behind financial conduct, whereas behavioral finance analyzes departures from rationality. This viewpoint highlights how psychological needs influence long-term, autonomous financial decision-making.(Deci & Ryan, 2000).

Autonomy, Competence, and Relatedness in Digital Finance Use

According to self-determination theory, relatedness, competence, and autonomy are essential psychological demands. When people believe they have significant power over financial decisions instead of being passively directed by algorithms, autonomy is supported in digital finance environments. Financial education resources, feedback systems, and clear information that boosts users' confidence in handling money are ways to improve competence. Relatedness arises from perceived alignment with social and ethical principles as well as trust in platforms. People are more likely to participate in thoughtful, sustainable financial behavior when digital platforms provide these needs.

Role of Intrinsic and Extrinsic Motivation in Sustainable Behavior

Financial behavior can be driven by internal variables like long-term well-being and personal values or by external factors like incentives, awards, or social recognition.Sustainable financial behavior is more likely to endure when intrinsic motivation is fostered, whereas digital platforms frequently rely on extrinsic motivators through gamification and prizes. (Ryan & Deci, 2024). Financial well-being and life happiness are positively impacted when financial objectives are in line with personal values, such as sustainability and ethical considerations. This enhances internal motivation and promotes long-term financial discipline.

3.3 Financial Well-Being Frameworks

One of the key outcome variables that connects financial conduct to overall life happiness is financial well-being. Financial well-being is viewed by modern frameworks as a multifaceted construct that includes both objective circumstances and subjective perceptions.(Consumer Financial Protection Bureau [CFPB], 2015).

Objective vs. Subjective Financial Well-Being

Measurable financial metrics including income stability, savings levels, debt load, and asset accumulation are examples of objective financial well-being. On the other hand, people's judgments of their financial security, sufficiency, and confidence in handling their financial resources are reflected in their subjective financial well-being.(Netemeyer et al., 2018). By influencing financial habits and views through information framing, benchmarking, and feedback, digital platforms have an impact on both dimensions. Better results on both objective and subjective aspects are a result of sustainable financial behavior.

Financial Stress, Perceived Control, and Financial Resilience

People experience financial stress when they perceive a gap between their means and their needs, which often results in anxiety and a diminished sense of fulfillment in life. A crucial mediating role between behavior and well-being is played by perceived financial control, or the belief that one can manage and alter one's financial circumstances (Xiao & O'Neill, 2016). Financial resilience is the ability to withstand and recover from financial shocks, and it is enhanced by sustainable financial behavior supported by carefully considered digital channels. Emotional stability is strengthened and life satisfaction is directly impacted by less financial stress and greater resilience.

4. DIGITAL PLATFORM FEATURES AS BEHAVIORAL ENABLERS

Instead of only serving as transactional interfaces, digital financial platforms are increasingly operating as behavioral infrastructures that influence financial decision-making through embedded design elements. Platform features can either encourage sustainable financial behavior or perpetuate behavioral biases by affecting user engagement, offering feedback, and organizing option contexts. Digital nudges, gamification, customization algorithms, and instructional tools that improve transparency are important behavioral facilitators.

4.1 Digital Nudges and Choice Architecture

Subtle design components known as "choice architecture" and "digital nudges" direct financial decisions without limiting options. To promote actions like saving, paying bills, and repaying debt, timely prompts, default options, reminders, and notifications are frequently utilized. (Thaler & Sunstein, 2008). These nudges enhance sustainable financial behavior by overcoming inertia, procrastination, and present bias when they are in line with user preferences.

However, the core of financial nudging is ethical issues. Nudges must protect user autonomy, guarantee openness, and steer clear of conflict of interest or manipulation. Ethically designed nudges in digital banking should prioritize long-term financial well-being over immediate platform engagement or revenue development in order to promote trust and responsible financial decision-making. (Sunstein, 2016).

4.2 Gamification and Goal-Based Financial Design

To boost user engagement and motivation, gamification and goal-based financial design include components including milestones, rewards, progress visualization, and savings challenges. These characteristics encourage regular saving and disciplined financial behavior by making abstract financial goals more concrete and emotionally noticeable.. By connecting everyday financial actions with long-term results, goal-based interfaces help users become more committed to sustainable financial practices.

Gamification is a behavioral strategy that promotes the development of positive financial behaviors through feedback and repetition. When developed responsibly, gamification promotes intrinsic motivation and financial self-efficacy; nevertheless, excessive emphasis on competition or prizes may damage long-term sustainability if not matched with users' true financial goals.

4.3 Personalization Algorithms and Data-Driven Insights

Digital platforms can provide personalized financial recommendations, guidance, and product recommendations thanks to personalization algorithms and data-driven insights. Platforms can enhance relevance and decision quality by utilizing user data, enabling well-informed and sustainable financial decisions. (Bennett & Kottasz, 2012). Additionally, personalized insights increase engagement and perceived competence, which improves financial well-being.

However, algorithmic bias, opacity, and over-personalization are concerns associated with personalization. Unsuitable financial products may be promoted or existing disparities may be strengthened by biased data or opaque algorithms. (World Bank, 2022). Users' capacity to make thoughtful and independent financial decisions may be diminished by over-personalization, which might limit exposure to alternative options. For this reason, responsible governance of personalization systems is crucial.

4.4 Transparency, Trust, and Embedded Financial Education

Sustainable financial conduct on digital platforms is greatly aided by transparency and integrated financial education. Information asymmetry is lessened and well-informed decision-making is supported by transparent disclosure of costs, risks, and product features.(OECD, 2020). Users' confidence and financial literacy are increased by educational modules, explanatory dashboards, and contextual learning tools.

Digital financial systems rely heavily on trust, which is bolstered by ethical platform design, data security, and transparency. Users are more inclined to participate regularly and embrace long-term, sustainable financial practices when they have faith in digital platforms. Financial well-being and life happiness are enhanced by embedded financial education, which also strengthens perceived control and financial resilience.

5. ROLE OF DIGITAL MARKETING IN PROMOTING SUSTAINABLE FINANCIAL CHOICES

Within fintech platforms, digital marketing strategically shapes financial attitudes, perceptions, and behaviors. Through message framing, trust-building tactics, and ethical engagement practices, digital marketing increasingly serves as a behavioral influence mechanism that can promote sustainable financial decisions in addition to encouraging uptake and usage. Digital marketing promotes long-term financial resilience and well-informed decision-making when it is in line with sustainability and customer well-being goals.

5.1 Digital Communication Strategies in FinTech Platforms

Fintech platforms' digital communication tactics have an impact on how consumers understand financial data and assess their options. Financial decision-making can be greatly impacted by framing effects, such as portraying savings as gains rather than lost consumption or stressing long-term advantages over immediate expenses. (Kahneman & Tversky, 1979; Thaler & Sunstein, 2008). A message that emphasizes future security, risk awareness, and goal achievement promotes responsible financial conduct and lessens impulsive behavior.

To improve financial literacy, fintech platforms also make use of digital material such as interactive dashboards, explainers, tutorials, and micro-learning modules. Users' comprehension of financial goods and dangers is enhanced by such content, which boosts their competence and self-assurance while making financial decisions. (Lusardi & Mitchell, 2014). Instead of only promoting products, marketing communication that incorporates financial education encourages sustainable financial behavior.

5.2 Influencing Consumer Trust and Engagement

Consumer trust is a critical determinant of engagement and long-term platform usage in digital finance. Trust-building mechanisms in digital marketing include transparent communication, consistent messaging, data privacy assurances, and the ethical presentation of financial products (Gefen et al., 2003). In digital financial contexts, marketing tactics that prioritize dependability, equity, and user-centric value increase perceived trust and lower uncertainty.

Prioritizing long-term engagement over short-term transactional advantages in digital marketing increases the likelihood of sustainable financial results. While transaction-focused tactics could encourage excessive trading, borrowing, or speculative activity, relationship-oriented marketing promotes continuous interaction, habit creation, and loyalty. Long-term involvement that is in line with users' financial well-being fosters sustained adoption of good financial practices and builds confidence.

5.3 Ethical Digital Marketing and Consumer Protection

In order to safeguard customers from harm and encourage sustainable financial decisions, ethical digital marketing is crucial. Influencing behavior in ways that maintain autonomy, give clear information, and support users' long-term interests is known as responsible persuasion.(Sunstein, 2016). Ethical marketing steers clear of financial vulnerability-causing false framing, hidden costs, and overstated claims.

In digitally mediated finance, where algorithm-driven marketing and behavioral targeting can take advantage of cognitive flaws, avoiding financial exploitation and manipulation is especially crucial. To guarantee that marketing initiatives do not promote excessive debt or unsafe financial conduct, consumer protection necessitates clear disclosures, equitable targeting strategies, and regulatory compliance. (OECD, 2020).Thus, ethical digital marketing acts as a protection that promotes financial well-being, strengthens trust, and supports sustainable financial ecosystems.

6. ESG INVESTING AND SUSTAINABILITY-ORIENTED DIGITAL INVESTMENT PLATFORMS

Digital investment platforms have played a significant role in advancing the adoption of environmental, social, and governance (ESG) investing by improving accessibility, visibility, and simplicity of involvement. These systems allow people to make ethical and long-term financial decisions by directly incorporating sustainability information into investment interfaces. Thus, ESG-focused digital investment tools serve as crucial links between sustainable financial behavior and both life satisfaction and financial well-being.

6.1 Growth of ESG Investing in Digital Markets

ESG investing's rise in digital markets is indicative of a larger trend toward impact-oriented and values-based investing practices. In addition to conventional financial indicators, online trading platforms and investment apps are increasingly displaying ESG signals, sustainability scores, and impact measures. These characteristics lessen information asymmetry and aid investors in assessing opportunities and non-financial risks related to social and environmental performance.(Friede et al., 2015).

Retail investors may easily understand complex ESG information by using sustainability ratings and labels as cognitive shortcuts. Although these signals increase awareness and engagement, their efficacy is dependent on their legitimacy, uniformity, and clarity. Transparent presentation of ESG signals promotes long-term portfolio strategies that are in line with sustainability goals and helps make well-informed investment decisions.

6.2 Robo-Advisors and Sustainable Investment Portfolios

Because they provide automated, algorithm-based portfolio design that takes ESG factors into account, robo-advisors are a major advancement in sustainability-focused digital investment. These platforms suggest diversified portfolios in line with moral investment objectives based on user choices, risk profiles, and sustainability principles.(Bauer et al., 2021). Robo-advisors make sustainable investment more accessible to a wider range of ordinary investors by reducing costs and complexity.

Additionally, by lowering emotional decision-making and excessive trading, automated advice models promote disciplined investing behavior. Robo-advisors encourage alignment between individual values and financial decisions when ESG preferences are incorporated into portfolio construction. This congruence contributes favorably to financial well-being by boosting investor confidence, perceived purpose, and trust in digital investing systems.

6.3 Challenges in ESG Disclosure and Greenwashing

Greenwashing, data reliability, and disclosure quality continue to be major obstacles despite the growth of ESG investing. ESG measures are frequently inconsistent among platforms and rating agencies due to a lack of standardization. (OECD, 2022). IInvestor confidence in sustainability-oriented financial products may be weakened by incomplete or selectively supplied information.

Greenwashing—the practice of portraying investments as more sustainable than they actually are—poses a severe concern in digital marketplaces as simplified labels and marketing claims can obscure underlying practices. When ESG statements are seen as symbolic rather than substantive, investor distrust develops. Addressing these difficulties demands tighter regulatory monitoring, transparent procedures, and improved ESG data governance to ensure that digital investing platforms actually encourage sustainable financial behavior and long-term investor trust.

7. LINKING SUSTAINABLE FINANCIAL BEHAVIOR TO FINANCIAL WELL-BEING

This section summarizes how consistent financial practices translate into quantifiable financial well-being results rather than concentrating on decision biases or psychological causes. Here, sustainable financial behavior is presented as an outcome-oriented concept that connects regular financial decisions to long-term stability, resilience, and security. Instead of individual cognitive processing, access, continuity, and structural support foster these habits inside digital financial ecosystems..

7.1 Behavioral Pathways to Financial Security and Stability

The main way that sustainable financial behavior promotes financial well-being is through its stabilizing and compounding effects. Over time, financial vulnerability is decreased by consistent saving, moderate consumption, and prudent borrowing practices, which lessen exposure to income fluctuation and liquidity limitations. (OECD, 2020). These actions serve as structural defenses that enhance the health of the home balance sheet and shield people from ongoing financial strain.

Through regular use of financial planning and monitoring tools, sustainable financial behavior improves financial management in addition to lowering risk. This type of control, which is operational rather than cognitive, reflects the capacity to fulfill commitments, cover regular costs, and make plans for future requirements. Regardless of income levels, empirical data indicates that such perceived financial control is substantially linked to better levels of financial confidence and subjective financial well-being. (Brüggen et al., 2017).Therefore, rather than being a reflection of behavioral bias correction, sustainable financial behavior is a useful route to financial stability.

7.2 Digital Finance and Financial Resilience

By facilitating adaptive responses to economic uncertainty, digital banking enhances the relationship between sustainable financial conduct and financial well-being. Early financial strain identification and prompt financial behavior adjustments are made possible by digital instruments including automated savings mechanisms, expense classification, and liquidity monitoring. (Lusardi et al., 2021). By enabling people to handle shocks without using expensive credit or asset liquidation, these tools increase resilience.

Crucially, rather than using behavioral persuasion, digital platforms promote financial resilience through scalability and continuity. The long-term viability of financial habits is reinforced by features included into digital systems that encourage regular financial maintenance and emergency readiness. Financial resilience goes beyond temporary coping to include long-term financial well-being during economic cycles when sustainability concepts are incorporated into digital financial architecture. As a result, digital finance serves as an enabling framework that converts sustainable financial practices into long-lasting financial results.

8. FINANCIAL WELL-BEING AS A PATHWAY TO LIFE SATISFACTION

One important way that sustainable financial behavior influences overall life happiness is through financial well-being. Beyond objective financial stability, financial well-being incorporates subjective notions of security, control, and peace of mind, which are crucial to individual well-being in contemporary digital economies.

8.1 Subjective Well-Being and Financial Peace of Mind

Greater emotional security and less financial concern are linked to improved financial well-being. People who are more prepared and have less financial stress report feeling more at ease and confident about handling their current and future financial demands.(Netemeyer et al., 2018). As a component of subjective well-being, financial peace of mind is strengthened by constant access to financial data and monitoring tools in digital financial settings.

8.2 Life Satisfaction in Digital Financial Ecosystems

Life satisfaction represents long-term judgments of quality of life and is positively influenced by persistent financial stability and institutional trust. When people are financially secure, they can pursue their personal objectives and maintain a consistent lifestyle without constant financial worry.(Diener et al., 2018). In digital ecosystems, trust in financial platforms and institutions enhances this relationship by fostering confidence in technology-mediated financial interactions.

8.3 Mediating Role of Financial Well-Being

Sustainable financial behavior and life pleasure are mediated by financial well-being. By improving financial stability, lowering stress, and boosting perceived control over financial resources, wise investing, disciplined saving, and responsible spending all indirectly increase life pleasure. By encouraging regular money management and lowering uncertainty, digital financial platforms enhance this mediation and convert sustainable financial behavior into long-lasting life satisfaction results.

9. MODERATING FACTORS IN DIGITAL FINANCIAL ECOSYSTEMS

A variety of moderating factors that affect how people use digital financial tools shape the effect of digital platforms on sustainable financial behavior and the ensuing well-being results. In a variety of user groups and circumstances, these criteria impact how much platform features translate into responsible financial practices, financial well-being, and life happiness.

9.1 Financial Literacy and Digital Capability

Digital aptitude and financial knowledge are key moderators of digital financial participation. Higher levels of technological competence and financial literacy put users in a better position to evaluate tailored recommendations, analyze platform-provided data, and make wise financial decisions. On the other hand, low literacy could make people more prone to impulsive conduct or an excessive dependence on automated systems, which could jeopardize long-term financial results. (Lusardi & Mitchell, 2014). Strengthening digital financial literacy is therefore essential for maximizing the benefits of digital finance.

9.2 Demographic and Socioeconomic Characteristics

Demographic and socioeconomic variables, including age, income, education, and work stability, impact both access to digital platforms and the ability to engage in sustainable financial behavior. While older users frequently place a higher value on trust and transparency, younger people may exhibit a larger adoption of digital tools. The relationship between the usage of digital platforms and financial well-being is shaped by income stability, which also moderates investment decisions and saving capacity. (Brüggen et al., 2017).

9.3 Institutional and Regulatory Environments

Trust in digital financial platforms and the efficacy of sustainability-focused solutions are strongly influenced by institutional and regulatory contexts. Strong data governance, disclosure, and consumer protection laws boost trust in digital systems and lower the possibility of unethical behavior like manipulation or false sustainability claims. On the other hand, inadequate regulatory supervision could restrict the beneficial effects of digital finance on life satisfaction and financial well-being.(OECD, 2020).

9.4 Global and Cross-Cultural Considerations

Digital financial behavior and results are further moderated by cross-cultural and global variances. People's reactions to digital platform features are influenced by cultural norms about risk-taking, sustainability awareness, and faith in financial institutions. The application of digital banking solutions across markets is also influenced by differences in national financial infrastructure and regulatory maturity. Recognizing these contextual variables promotes the generalizability and applicability of sustainable financial behavior frameworks in global digital ecosystems.

10. METHODOLOGICAL APPROACH AND CONCEPTUAL FRAMEWORK DEVELOPMENT

This chapter uses a theory-driven conceptual approach to describe how sustainable financial behavior is shaped by digital platform features, which in turn affect life pleasure through financial well-being. An integrated conceptual approach is especially well-suited to integrating insights and improving coherent theoretical understanding, given the fragmented nature of current research across psychology, marketing, finance, and sustainability.

10.1 Theory-Driven Conceptual Methodology

The intricacy of digital financial ecosystems, where behavioral, technological, and ethical aspects converge, is the justification for employing an integrated conceptual study design. In order to discover important notions, causal pathways, and boundary conditions pertinent to sustainable financial behavior in digital contexts, the chapter methodically synthesizes known theories and worldwide scholarly evidence rather than depending on a single empirical technique.(Jaakkola, 2020). This method provides an organized framework for upcoming empirical testing and permits theoretical extension.

10.2 Integration of Interdisciplinary Theories

The conceptual framework includes three complementary theoretical views. How contextual cues, heuristics, and cognitive biases affect financial decisions in digital settings is explained by behavioral finance.(Kahneman, 2011; Barberis, 2018). Self-determination theory clarifies how intrinsic motivation, competence, and autonomy promote consistent, prudent financial behavior.(Ryan & Deci, 2024). A multifaceted view of how financial activities translate into perceived control, decreased stress, and financial resilience is offered by financial well-being frameworks.(Brüggen et al., 2017; Netemeyer et al., 2018). When taken as a whole, these theories provide a comprehensive account of how well-being outcomes and behavior development occur in digital finance.

10.3 Proposed Conceptual Framework

Digital platform elements including nudges, gamification, personalization, transparency, and embedded education are positioned in the suggested framework as behavioral enablers that affect sustainable financial behavior. This behavior, in turn, influences financial well-being, which serves as a major mediating mechanism linking digital financial participation to life happiness. In order to account for cross-market variation, the framework also takes into account moderating factors such as financial literacy, demographic traits, and institutional and regulatory environments. The framework gives researchers, policymakers, and fintech practitioners who want to create sustainable and human-centered digital financial systems a solid basis for future empirical validation by precisely defining constructs and paths.

11. POLICY, MANAGERIAL, AND PRACTICAL IMPLICATIONS

The conceptual insights developed in this chapter carry significant implications for fintech firms, digital marketers, and policymakers seeking to align digital financial innovation with sustainable financial behavior and consumer well-being.

11.1 Implications for FinTech Firms and Platform Designers

The results highlight the significance of using a human-centered and sustainability-driven approach to platform design for fintech companies and platform designers. Digital financial systems should actively promote responsible spending, disciplined saving, sensible borrowing, and sustainable investment, going beyond efficiency and engagement measures. While reducing the dangers of impulsive or speculative behavior, features like goal-based tools, ethical nudging, transparent information disclosure, and embedded financial education can improve user autonomy and long-term financial well-being. (Brüggen et al., 2017). Building trust and long-term engagement requires platform designers to strike a balance between personalization and user control.

11.2 Implications for Digital Marketers

Through communication tactics, content creation, and engagement tools, digital marketers are vital in influencing financial attitudes and behaviors. The chapter emphasizes the necessity for moral digital marketing strategies that encourage responsible financial behavior as opposed to excessive risk-taking or short-term consumption. Consumer trust can be increased and sustainable decision-making can be promoted by framing financial products in terms of long-term value, resilience, and well-being.(Netemeyer et al., 2018).Relationship-based engagement, clear message, and instructional information should take precedence over deceptive persuasion strategies.

11.3 Policy and Regulatory Implications

From a policy viewpoint, the findings underline the need for regulatory frameworks that encourage consumer protection, financial inclusion, and accountable digital governance. Regulators must prohibit deceptive sustainability claims, guarantee algorithmic decision-making openness, and handle the dangers of data exploitation and behavioral manipulation. The favorable correlation between digital finance, financial well-being, and life satisfaction can be strengthened by policies that promote digital financial literacy and fair access to digital platforms. To create trustworthy and inclusive digital financial ecosystems, regulators, industry stakeholders, and consumer advocates must work together.

12. CHALLENGES, ETHICAL CONCERNS, AND FUTURE RESEARCH DIRECTIONS

Despite the tremendous potential of digital platforms to encourage sustainable financial conduct, significant obstacles and ethical problems remain that need careful thought and further scholarly inquiry.

The dual character of digital financial platforms as sources of behavioral risk and empowering tools presents a significant problem. Nudges, gamification, and customization are examples of features that can promote responsible financial behavior, but if they are badly designed or commercially oriented, they can also worsen impulsive spending, excessive trading, or overconfidence.(Thaler & Sunstein, 2008; Barberis, 2018). In digital finance, ethical concerns of manipulation, choice autonomy, and informed consent are brought up by the conflict between engagement-driven business models and consumer well-being goals.

Additional ethical issues with algorithmic decision-making include prejudice, transparency, and data privacy. Because personalized financial advice frequently rely on opaque algorithms and large amounts of user data, there is a greater chance that preexisting financial disparities will be excluded, misclassified, or reinforced. (Zuboff, 2019). Similar issues with varying ESG standards and possible greenwashing affect sustainability claims incorporated into digital investment platforms, which can erode investor confidence and weaken the legitimacy of sustainable finance efforts. (Berg et al., 2022).

In order to evaluate the proposed conceptual framework's generalizability, future research should empirically test it in a variety of demographic, cultural, and regulatory situations. In particular, longitudinal research methods are required to investigate the long-term effects of sustained digital financial involvement on life satisfaction and financial well-being. The varying effects of particular platform features, the moderating function of financial literacy, and the moral limits of behavioral interventions in finance might all be investigated in more detail. By filling in these gaps, theory development will be strengthened and evidence-based policy and platform design in digital financial ecosystems will be supported.

13. CONCLUSION

Digital financial platforms are transformative accelerators for sustainable financial behavior, as this chapter illustrates, ultimately improving life satisfaction and long-term financial well-being. The suggested conceptual model, which combines behavioral finance, self-determination theory, and frameworks for financial well-being, shows how platform-specific elements like gamification, personalization, and nudges promote systematic saving, responsible spending, and ESG-aligned investment practices. Though the results highlight that these beneficial effects are dependent on ethical platform design and strong regulatory oversight to mitigate risks like algorithmic bias or greenwashing, this sustainable conduct serves as a crucial mediator, converting digital engagement into increased economic resilience and emotional stability. In the end, this integrated, human-centered approach offers practitioners and legislators a fundamental road map for balancing technological progress with consumer empowerment and more general societal sustainability.

REFERENCES

Barber, B. M., & Odean, T. (2001). Boys will be Boys. *The Quarterly Journal of Economics, 116*(1), 261–292. DOI: 10.1162/003355301556400

Barberis, N. (2018). Psychology-based models of asset prices and trading volume. In *Handbook of behavioral economics: applications and foundations 1* (Vol. 1, pp. 79–175). North-Holland. DOI: 10.3386/w24723

Bauer, R., Ruof, T., & Smeets, P. (2021). Get real! Individuals prefer more sustainable investments. *Review of Financial Studies, 34*(8), 3976–4043. DOI: 10.1093/rfs/hhab037

Benartzi, S., & Thaler, R. H. (2013). Behavioral economics and the retirement savings crisis. *Science, 339*(6124), 1152–1153. DOI: 10.1126/science.1231320 PMID: 23471389

Berg, F., Kölbel, J. F., & Rigobon, R. (2022). Aggregate confusion: The divergence of ESG ratings. *Review of Finance, 26*(6), 1315–1344. DOI: 10.1093/rof/rfac033

Brüggen, E. C., Hogreve, J., Holmlund, M., Kabadayi, S., & Löfgren, M. (2017). Financial well-being: A conceptualization and research agenda. *Journal of Business Research, 79*, 228–237. DOI: 10.1016/j.jbusres.2017.03.013

Bureau, C. F. P. (2015). *Financial well-being: The goal of financial education.*

Deci, E. L., & Ryan, R. M. (2000). The" what" and" why" of goal pursuits: Human needs and the self-determination of behavior. *Psychological Inquiry, 11*(4), 227–268. DOI: 10.1207/S15327965PLI1104_01

Diener, E., Oishi, S., & Tay, L. (2018). Advances in subjective well-being research. *Nature Human Behaviour, 2*(4), 253–260. DOI: 10.1038/s41562-018-0307-6 PMID: 30936533

Friede, G., Busch, T., & Bassen, A. (2015). ESG and financial performance: Aggregated evidence from more than 2000 empirical studies. *Journal of Sustainable Finance & Investment, 5*(4), 210–233. DOI: 10.1080/20430795.2015.1118917

Gathergood, J. (2012). Self-control, financial literacy and consumer over-indebtedness. *Journal of Economic Psychology, 33*(3), 590–602. DOI: 10.1016/j.joep.2011.11.006

Gefen, D., Karahanna, E., & Straub, D. W. (2003). Trust and tam in online shopping: An integrated model 1. *Management Information Systems Quarterly, 27*(1), 51–90. DOI: 10.2307/30036519

Jaakkola, E. (2020). Designing conceptual articles: Four approaches. *AMS Review, 10*(1), 18–26. DOI: 10.1007/s13162-020-00161-0

Kahneman, D., & Tversky, A. (2013). Prospect theory: An analysis of decision under risk. In *Handbook of the fundamentals of financial decision making: Part I* (pp. 99-127).

Laibson, D. (1997). Golden eggs and hyperbolic discounting. *The Quarterly Journal of Economics, 112*(2), 443–478. DOI: 10.1162/003355397555253

Lusardi, A., Hasler, A., & Yakoboski, P. J. (2021). Building up financial literacy and financial resilience. *Mind & Society, 20*(2), 181–187. DOI: 10.1007/s11299-020-00246-0

Lusardi, A., & Mitchell, O. S. (2014). The economic importance of financial literacy: Theory and evidence. *Journal of Economic Literature, 52*(1), 5–44. DOI: 10.1257/jel.52.1.5 PMID: 28579637

Manda, V. K., Yadav, A., & Khaliq, L. N. (2024). Role of Payment Systems in Financial Well-Being: An Examination from India. In Malik, G., Bansal, R., Gupta, S., & Ansari, Y. (Eds.), *Emerging Perspectives on Financial Well-Being* (pp. 228–251). IGI Global Scientific Publishing., DOI: 10.4018/979-8-3693-1750-1.ch012

Netemeyer, R. G., Warmath, D., Fernandes, D., & Lynch, J. G.Jr. (2018). How am I doing? Perceived financial well-being, its potential antecedents, and its relation to overall well-being. *The Journal of Consumer Research, 45*(1), 68–89. DOI: 10.1093/jcr/ucx109

OECD (2020), Financial Consumer Protection Policy Approaches in the Digital Age:Protecting consumer's assets, data and privacy

OECD. (2021). *ESG investing and climate transition: Market Practices, Issues and Policy Considerations*. OECD Publishing., DOI: 10.1787/a2fc6c39-

Ryan, R. M., & Deci, E. L. (2024). Self-determination theory. In *Encyclopedia of quality of life and well-being research* (pp. 6229–6235). Springer International Publishing.

Sunstein, C. R. (2016). *The ethics of influence: Government in the age of behavioral science*. Cambridge University Press. DOI: 10.1017/CBO9781316493021

Thaler, R. H., & Sunstein, C. R. (2009). *Nudge: Improving decisions about health, wealth, and happiness*. Penguin.

Xiao, J. J., & O'Neill, B. (2016). Consumer financial education and financial capability. *International Journal of Consumer Studies, 40*(6), 712–721. DOI: 10.1111/ijcs.12285

KEY TERMS AND DEFINITIONS

Algorithmic Transparency: The degree to which an algorithm's structure, operation, data use, and decision-making procedures are transparent, understandable, and explainable to stakeholders is known as algorithmic transparency.

Behavioral Economics: The study of how psychological, emotional, cognitive, and social aspects affect people's and organizations' financial decisions.It explains why humans frequently make choices that diverge from the rational behavior predicted by classical economic theory by combining insights from psychology and traditional economics.

Consumer Trust: Consumer trust is the belief that a business, brand or vendor will provide goods or services in an ethical and trustworthy manner. It expresses the trust that the company will keep its commitments and act in the best interests of the customer.

Digital Nudges: Digital nudges are subtle design elements incorporated into websites, applications, or other digital platforms that affect users' choices and actions without restricting their autonomy. Digital nudges steer users toward desired behaviors in an unnoticeable way by utilizing aspects including default settings, pop-up reminders, information framing, and visual signals.

Digital Platforms: Online technology frameworks known as "digital platforms" enable value creation, transactions, and interactions between various user groups, including producers, consumers, and service providers. Through internet-based platforms, they make it possible to exchange commodities, services, information, or social ties.

ESG Investing: When making investment selections, ESG investing takes into account both financial performance and Environmental, Social, and Governance (ESG) issues. By investing in businesses that uphold high corporate governance, ethical standards, and environmental responsibilities, it seeks to produce long-term sustainable profits.

Financial Literacy: The knowledge and comprehension of financial concepts including budgeting, saving, investing, and debt management is referred to as financial literacy. It makes it possible for people to manage and spend their money in an informed and efficient manner.

Financial Well-Being: The state of having stability and security in one's finances both now and in the future is referred to as financial well-being. It entails having enough money to cover urgent expenses, deal with unforeseen circumstances, and confidently reach long-term financial objectives.

FinTech Platforms: A subset of digital platforms that use cutting-edge technology like automation, artificial intelligence, and data analytics to provide financial services.

Life Satisfaction: A person's overall assessment of the quality of their life based on their selected criteria is referred to as life satisfaction. It shows how satisfied and pleased a person is with their social, career, and personal situations.

Regulatory Governance: Authorities create, carry out, and enforce rules, regulations, and policies through a system and procedures known as regulatory governance. It guarantees accountability, efficiency, justice, and openness in the governance of social and economic activities.

Robo-Advisory Systems: Digital platforms which offer automated, algorithm-based financial planning and investment advisory services with little assistance from humans.

Sustainable Financial Behavior: Responsible financial decision-making techniques that guarantee long-term financial stability while taking social and environmental effects into account are referred to as sustainable financial behavior.

Chapter 16
Digital Reverse Logistics and Urban Life Satisfaction in Sustainable Automobile Digital Service Markets

Nimit Sharma
http://orcid.org/0009-0001-0305-9978
REVA University, India

A. Shivasharana
http://orcid.org/0000-0002-0743-4480
REVA University, India

Vijaya Kittu Manda
http://orcid.org/0000-0002-1680-8210
PBMEIT, India

ABSTRACT

The rapid expansion of automobile service workshops in urban centres has intensified waste generation, environmental stress, and operational inefficiencies, particularly in emerging economies. Simultaneously, digital transformation has reshaped market ecosystems, influencing not only performance but also human well-being and life satisfaction. This work examines how digitally enabled sustainable reverse logistics practices contribute to waste minimisation, cost efficiency, and collective well-being within the urban automobile service sector. It focuses on the link between DRL and human well-being. The objective of this study is to develop a conceptual framework

DOI: 10.4018/979-8-3373-8357-6.ch016

that illustrates this link. The findings propose a novel, human-centred DRL framework. The study highlights how digital tools for waste recovery can enhance environmental conditions and improve the perceived quality of urban life. The findings have direct implications for policymakers, researchers, and practitioners seeking to align digital transformation strategies with human-centric sustainability goals.

INTRODUCTION

Rapid urbanization in emerging economies has led to a surge in vehicle production (SIAM, 2025), driving the opening of automobile service workshops, especially in cities. These workshops are critical support centers and facilitators of mobility. However, they significantly lead to environmental stress. The automotive sector generates millions of tonnes of hazardous waste annually. Automobile workshop wastes include used engine oil, lead-acid batteries, end-of-life tires, and toxic solvents (Gallego-Schmid et al., 2025; X. Zhang et al., 2023). These wastes are managed through informal and inefficient channels. They eventually lead to severe soil contamination, water pollution, and public health risks (Alabi et al., 2025; Badra et al., 2026; Priyadarsini & Das, 2026). Sustainable management of automotive waste reduces localized environmental degradation. Thus, they improve collective urban well-being and safety (Alsanie et al., 2025). This study examines the business-to-business service ecosystem as a digital market segment. It examines how operational digitalization directly impacts stakeholder happiness and perceived quality of life. It also highlights the human impact of these technological changes.

Background

The automotive industry is a primary catalyst for the global transition to a Circular Economy (CE) (Park & Ryosuke, 2025). Historically, before the 2000s, the automotive industry relied on a fragmented and manual inventory management system. Such systems provided minimal traceability of component life cycles (Van Dam & Bakker, 2024). Reverse flows during the period were unstructured. Therefore, there was a significant economic drain due to leakage and delays in replacement. The subsequent decades (2000s–2010s) witnessed a shift toward formalizing reverse processes. Regulators framed stringent environmental regulations. At the same time, consumer awareness of sustainability was growing. These two turned out to be primary drivers (Halaswamy et al., 2026). However, these systems employed manual tracking methods: physical labeling and the use of basic spreadsheets limited scalability and data transparency. The Industry 4.0 era has brought the concept of Digital Reverse Logistics (DRL) to the forefront (Fares et al., 2025). Contemporary service workshops have evolved into integrated digital ecosystems. They function as nodes connecting manufacturers, recycling hubs, and digital platforms (Harendsa & Pulansari, 2025). The current transition towards Industry 5.0 is shifting the focus towards human-centric, resilient, and sustainable supply chains (Hmamed et al., 2026). The chapter discusses various actors within the service ecosystem and their potential indicators.

Study Objectives

The core objective of the study is to synthesize the existing literature across diverse fields and to construct a novel, human-centered framework. A systematic literature review method is used to accomplish this task. Digital reverse supply chains, the circular economy, occupational well-being, and urban sociology are the central focus. The study examines various domains, including operations management, environmental science, and social psychology.

Study Rationale

Automobile service workshops generate hazardous waste, including lubricants, tires, batteries, metal scrap, and toxic solvents (Alabi et al., 2025). Service workshops are largely unorganized, especially in populous, developing countries. They do not efficiently manage waste streams, leading to intensifying environmental degradation and public health risks. The existing literature on digital reverse logistics (DRL) focuses solely on technical and operational perspectives for large manufacturing units (Rodrigues et al., 2025). Parallel to this, research on life satisfaction and human well-being focuses primarily on end-consumer experiences (Boegman-Watt & Carodenuto, 2026), social media, and digital access. Hence, a significant theoretical and empirical gap exists at the intersection of these two streams.

Furthermore, the established theories, such as the Circular Economy and Stakeholder Theory, lack a human-centered approach to DRL (Boegman-Watt & Carodenuto, 2026). This study asserts that sustainability and human well-being in urban commercial ecosystems are inseparably linked. Therefore, it is necessary to examine how digitization in small automobile service workshops contributes to human well-being and life satisfaction within this ecosystem. This study identifies the barriers and enablers to DRL adoption. It develops a framework that guides practitioners in building a digital, sustainable service ecosystem aimed at collective life satisfaction.

Scope of the Chapter

The chapter is a systematic narrative review that synthesizes concepts and lays a foundation for future empirical work. It proposes a framework that considers interactions among market actors in the automotive service sector. It synthesizes the core theories linked to the study. It does not include data collection, hypothesis testing, and statistical analysis. The framework discussed in this study is grounded in the context of urban automobile service ecosystems. It proposes greater global relevance across informal and semi-formal service workshops. The human-centered DRL framework developed in this study is therefore transferable across diverse geographic contexts. It does not discuss the technical architectures, software coding, or hardware specifications of any of the digital tools explained. Although the chapter discusses policy as both an enabler and a barrier, it does not provide a comparative analysis across countries. The chapter focuses on micro-level aspects, including workshops and community well-being. It lacks studies on macroeconomic indicators such as GDP contributions, national employment rates, or large-scale impact modeling of the circular economy.

Chapter Structure

The chapter begins with the "Introduction" section, which presents the concept of digital reverse logistics and its relationship to human well-being. Furthermore, it examines the need to undertake the study. The "Literature Review" section explained the theoretical and empirical landscape. It discussed studies on the urban automobile service ecosystem, presented trends and theories, and explained the theoretical underpinnings. The "Research Gap" is then proposed, which paves the way for formally framing the "Research Question" the researcher wishes to examine. The "Methodology" section explained the literature review search methodology followed and showed the research gap. The "Discussion" section examined in depth the link between DRL and urban life satisfaction, as well as various aspects of the study. The "Connection to UN SDG" explained the relationship between the study's various concepts and the United Nations Sustainable Development Goals (UN SDG). Then the study graciously puts forth its "Limitations of the study". The practical and managerial implications follow in the "Implications from the study" section. The study then proposes ideas for future research. Finally, the "Conclusions" section summarizes the findings from this study.

LITERATURE REVIEW

Unlike traditional digital supply chains that emphasize internal efficiency, DRL platforms operate as market-mediated networks. The market-mediated nature of DRL platforms, in turn, directly influences trust, legitimacy, and life satisfaction (Majeed et al., 2024). DRL matches waste generators with value recovery, matching supply with demand (Cheshmehzangi, 2025). Such two-sided or multi-sided markets require a platform or platform-like mechanism. Traditional workshops used to focus more on replacing a component after damage. It resulted in a one-time solution for vehicles (Van Dam & Bakker, 2024). However, modern sustainable service workshops also focus on refurbishing components to recapture resources by extending their life-cycles (Fatih et al., 2025). Table 1 shows the difference between the features of traditional and circular workshops.

Table 1. Difference between Traditional Workshop and Circular Workshop

Feature	Traditional Workshop	Circular Workshop
Logic	Replace with new	Repair, Reuse, Remanufacture
Waste	A cost to be managed	A resource to be recovered
Skillset	Component swapping	Technical diagnosis & refurbishment
Customer View	One-off transaction	Life-cycle relationship (C-CRM)
Relies on	Manual workflows, paper-based tracking, and reactive decision-making	Streamlined operations, improved transparency, and aligned with sustainability goals.

However, the transformation from traditional to circular workshops does not occur naturally. It requires specific infrastructural, technological, and governance enablers to operationalize circularity in practice (Fatih et al., 2025).

Theoretical and Empirical Landscape

The literature on digital reverse logistics (DRL) extensively details technical and operational factors in large-scale manufacturing contexts (Alsanie et al., 2025; J. Zhang & Rogers, 2025), yet it overlooks the human consequences (Leng et al., 2026). On the other hand, numerous studies have examined "life satisfaction" and urban well-being. The research examines how digital platforms, e-commerce, and social media affect consumer happiness and community engagement. There is still an apparent conceptual underdevelopment of social well-being and life satisfaction (Alsanie et al., 2025). However, there is a serious theoretical gap between these two streams. As a result, current theories do not provide integrated frameworks that can clearly link small workshop adoption of sustainable digital practices to psychosocial outcomes (Cheshmehzangi, 2025).

This work bridges the interdisciplinary divide discussed by Leng et al. (2026) between DRL and human well-being through a conceptual synthesis methodology. Existing theories are used to analyze current practices, key barriers, and digital enablers in the urban automobile service sector. This study is innovative in reorganizing DRL practices in ways that connect to human well-being. The study provides an important roadmap for researchers, practitioners, and policymakers to develop efficient, compliant, and inclusive service markets that enhance urban well-being.

Urban Automobile Service Ecosystems as Digital Service Markets

Reverse logistics infrastructure: The urban automobile service ecosystem is a multi-layered network comprising service providers, suppliers, consumers, waste handlers, and regulators. They function as interconnected participants in a digitally mediated service market. They are involved in activities related to collection, transportation, processing, and digital tracking. Such infrastructure enables service ecosystems to recover value from returned products and to reduce environmental waste and its impacts in a compliant manner. Metals are generally recovered from waste streams relatively easily, while plastics and rubbers are typically landfilled (Dasgupta et al., 2025). The used oil collected by an informal collector is illegally drained or used for low-grade combustion. The loss of valuable materials indicates inefficiencies in the circular economy. Service workshops also face wasted storage space when they collect waste products in their stores (Harendsa & Pulansari, 2025). Informal waste workers exhibit flexibility and possess deep local knowledge, offering low-cost waste collection services.

In contrast, formal workers have access to technology, industrial-scale processing skills, and expertise in legal compliance (Gallego-Schmid et al., 2025). The informal sector (including waste pickers) acts as a pressure group. They push the formal sector to adopt CE practices. The formal sector feels increasingly threatened by the informal sector's expertise. This creates an unequal power dynamic. The formal sector seeks to regain control amid pressure from the informal sector. This results in a push-pull dynamic. The informal sector pushes the formal sector to change, while the formal sector tries to reassert control. Integrating informal waste workers into a formal reverse logistics system yields greater value (Savardi et al., 2025). It leverages local knowledge to improve resource recovery rates by strengthening these stakeholders' incomes and protecting their human rights. Digital surveillance in informal work environments may intensify power disparities. This often happens when platform proprietors or authorities conduct monitoring without agreement or in return for concessions. In the absence of ethical controls, data collection could exploit vulnerable workers. So it converts visibility into control instead of empowerment. (Tseng et al., 2024). Maintaining oversight of data, openness, and participatory governance is crucial to preventing bias in digital systems. This informal, unsustainable method highlights the necessity of integrating digital tools to track the ensuing changes.

Governance and policy adjustments: Institutional governance and regulatory frameworks oversee circular and reverse logistics activities. The components encompass Extended Producer Responsibility (EPR), digital reporting standards, and documentation standardization. Harmonizing sustainability objectives with practical procedures ensures effective governance policies. Extended Producer Responsibility formalizes reverse logistics in supply chain management. (Almelhem et al., 2025; Gawande & DoShi, 2025). To systematically interpret how such governance mechanisms influence operational practices and stakeholder well-being, this study draws on multiple complementary theoretical lenses. Four theories guide this analysis: the Circular Economy, the Closed-Loop Supply Chain, the Natural Resource-Based View, and Institutional & Stakeholder Theory.

Digital sustainability and human-centered markets

Prior to this, studies in digital governance indicated that user satisfaction is only reached when users are satisfied with their use of digital systems. As trust builds, they feel safer and continue to engage with and accept these tools (Guo, 2022). Greater visibility of data on reverse logistics for stakeholders is reported to drive behavioral change (Bálint et al., 2026; Jiayuan & Rogers, 2025). These changes may involve customer loyalty, partner collaboration, and the rate of adoption of sustainable logistics within digital ecosystems (Gawande & DoShi, 2025). This view is also supported by recent evidence from the Indian automobile industry (Halaswamy et al., 2026). The study finds that green supply chain management practices have a significant effect on consumer perceptions, environmental responsibility, and sustainable purchase intentions. The study found that perceived environmental friendliness, social influence, and value perception positively influenced consumer engagement in sustainable automotive practices. The results also indicate that environmentally responsible operational systems can lead to increased trust, greater market acceptance, and long-term stakeholder involvement in green initiatives. Digital tools like dashboards, blockchain trackers, and IoT sensors help to translate concepts like carbon footprint into measurable metrics. Such digital tools make environmental impacts feel real and relatable.

An extensive literature review is conducted to support critical evaluation, identify contradictions, and report research gaps. Various theories are presented and discussed in Table 2. The bigger picture here is that understanding the gaps will help create a better framework.

Theoretical Foundations

Table 2. Theories linked to Digital Reverse Logistics (DRL)

Theoretical Lens	Concept	Application to This Study	Context
Circular Economy (CE) Theory	Economic systems should eliminate waste and continually use resources through closed-loop cycles of reuse, refurbishment, and recycling.	It reframes automotive waste from a disposal problem into a resource-recovery opportunity, thereby establishing the fundamental purpose of DRL.	Provides the normative environmental and economic goal.
Closed-Loop Supply Chain (CLSC) Theory	It involves designing and managing supply chains to recover products/ materials and reintegrate them efficiently.	DRL needs to digitize processes such as collection, sorting, and recovery. It helps implement CE effectively, shifting from theory to practice.	Provides the operational and logistical blueprint.
Natural Resource-Based View (NRBV)	Sustainable competitive advantage is built by developing unique, valuable, and hard-to-imitate capabilities in pollution prevention, product stewardship, and sustainable development.	It explains why investing in DRL can enhance a workshop's cost efficiency, compliance, and reputation.	Provides the firm-level strategic logic.
Institutional Theory	Organizations adopt structures and practices to conform to external regulative, normative, and cognitive pressures for legitimacy.	It explains the external pressures, such as laws, norms, and digital trends, that drive DRL adoption.	It provides the socio-economic context.
Stakeholder Theory	Firms must create value for and manage relationships with all entities that are affected by, or that affect, their actions.	It identifies whose well-being is at stake and argues that sustainable value is co-created with the community.	It provides relational context.

There is a need for a clear framework explaining how DRL enhances stakeholder well-being in urban auto service ecosystems.

Theoretical Underpinnings

Subjective Well-being (SWB) offers a basic perspective for understanding the quality of life of individuals and societies (Uzun & Arslan, 2025). It includes cognitive assessments of life satisfaction and affective experiences of happiness and emotional balance (Morales Almeida & Alemán Ramos, 2025). In the context of urban service ecosystems, SWB is affected not only by material conditions but also by psychosocial factors. Scope includes safety, dignity, and a sense of purpose. Recent studies revealed that SWB in working environments is strongly related to autonomy, skill development, and environmental conditions (Arata et al., 2025). Digital and logistical interventions shape all these.

Life Satisfaction Theory (LST) also distinguishes between cognitive and affective dimensions of well-being (Abbasi et al., 2025). The cognitive component consists of a conscious, evaluative judgment of one's life situation in relation to personal goals and societal norms. The affective component, in contrast, concerns the frequency and intensity of positive and negative emotions experienced in a day. Perceived efficiencies, cost savings, and regulatory compliance can all provide cognitive satisfaction in DRL. In addition, affective well-being can be achieved through reduced workplace stress, increased safety, and a sense of contributing to a sustainable environment (Farmanesh et al., 2025; Zeshan et al., 2025). This dual approach helps to shed light on how operational improvements in service workshops can translate into holistic well-being for technicians, owners, and the larger community.

Environmental psychology provides valuable insights and features diverse voices regarding the impact of physical environments on mental and emotional states (Zeshan et al., 2025). It has the potential to help mitigate climate change and encourage people to make real-world changes. Several formal theories have been framed and incorporated into the field of Environmental psychology over the years. "Repeated research points to the negative impact of exposure to polluted, cluttered, or hazardous environments on well-being. These kinds of situations cause more stress and less social cohesion.

In contrast, clean, tidy, and green spaces promote positive affect, place attachment, and trust in the community. City auto service centers are required to properly handle hazardous waste such as used oil, batteries, and solvents to comply with environmental regulations. These environments have a direct impact on the local environment, and hence, on the subjective well-being of residents and workers. Digital tools that enhance waste traceability, reduce contamination, and increase circular practices can facilitate both ecological and psychological restoration (Tushar et al., 2024).

While DRL is generally considered positive, some studies warn that digitalization without inclusive design might increase exclusion, especially among low-literacy or digitally disconnected workers (Almelhem et al., 2025). The transition to circular models is well established in the formal sectors but still underdeveloped in informal urban workshops in emerging economies. Furthermore, sustainability indicators such as "carbon savings" may not necessarily translate into perceived well-being if local stakeholders are more concerned with income stability than environmental issues (Gallego-Schmid et al., 2025).

In combination, these theories suggest that well-being in urban service markets is multifaceted. It is the product of the interplay of operational practices, environmental conditions, and human perception. The incorporation of SWB, LST, and environmental psychology into DRL research enables a deeper understanding of how sustainability efforts can yield economic, ecological, and human-centered benefits.

Research Gap

Sustainable workflows in urban service workshops are increasingly studied. It is yet unclear how they relate to social well-being. Few studies examine how these workflows affect diverse stakeholders. Technicians, owners, residents, and regulators may all have varied experiences. There is a severe lack of mechanisms connecting sustainability to well-being.

RESEARCH QUESTION

The research question this study answers is: *"How can digital reverse logistics in urban automobile service ecosystems be conceptually linked to enhanced multi-stakeholder life satisfaction?"* This study contributes to the theoretical understanding by demonstrating that an efficient digital reverse ecosystem enhances the life satisfaction and well-being of the actors involved.

METHODOLOGY

This study collected evidence from the Scopus databases. Google Scholar and Dimensions.ai are used to supplement and broaden our understanding, but they are not part of the search criteria. It also searches sources such as peer-reviewed journals, seminal books, and key industry/policy reports. Reports from automotive associations are also included.

The search keyword strings used in combination are

```
("reverse logistics" OR "closed-loop supply chain")
AND (digital* OR platform*)
AND ("circular economy" OR recycling OR reuse)
AND ("service ecosystem*" OR urban OR automobile)
AND ("life satisfaction" OR "well-being" OR "quality of
life") AND ("urban service" OR "stakeholder theory")
AND PUBYEAR > 2010 AND PUBYEAR < 2025
```

The Inclusion/exclusion criteria are in English. Publications from the past 15 years were included. Studies focusing on services/urban contexts and their relevance to emerging economies were preferred. Figure 1 outlines the search review process using the PRISMA 2020 protocol.

Figure 1. Systematic search review using the PRISMA protocol

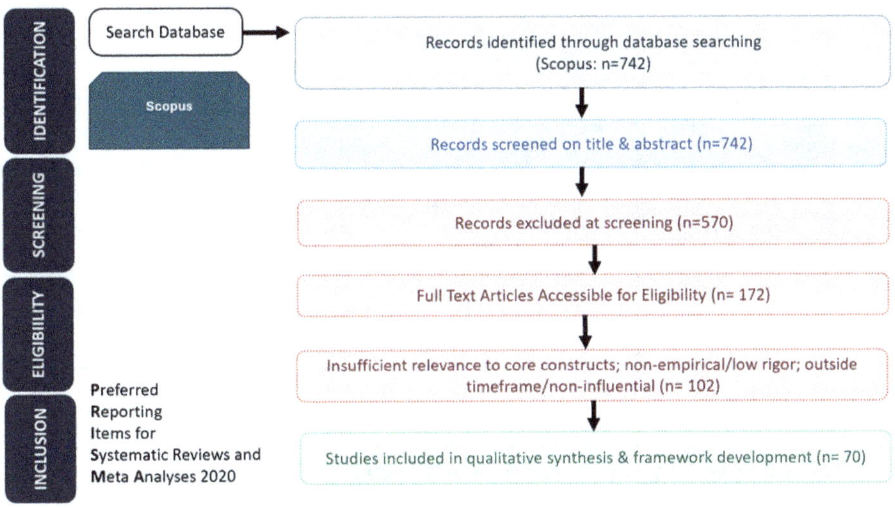

DISCUSSION

Digital Reverse Logistics and Urban Life Satisfaction

The quality of logistics services is no longer assessed solely on speed, reliability, and price. Stakeholders assess logistics performance by also considering environmental outcomes, such as carbon footprints and waste management. Hence, costs are interpreted in conjunction with long-term sustainability gains (Jiayuan &

Rogers, 2025; Khandelwal et al., 2025). Social dimensions, such as worker safety and regulatory compliance, shape trust and legitimacy (Guo, 2022). Therefore, logistics is viewed through an integrated lens of logistics performance and urban well-being. Studies also indicate that younger stakeholders are more concerned about these parameters than older stakeholders (Ahmad et al., 2025). They exhibit stronger sensitivity towards the environment.

Urban Life Satisfaction and Subjective Well-being: Life satisfaction, or happiness, has different dimensions across individuals. Table 3 presents how life-satisfaction indicators differ across groups, including workshop owners, technicians, residents, and civic authorities. The owners are concerned about security, legacy, and professional fulfillment; the technicians are concerned about dignity, safety, and job satisfaction. The community defines happiness as a quality of life and trust, whereas regulatory bodies work toward efficacy and policy goal attainment. However, some studies argue that people's perceptions, emotions, and trust judgments explain participation and well-being outcomes (Oesterreich et al., 2025).

Table 3. Sentiment indicators for various market actors related to automobile service

Market Actors	Potential Indicators
Automotive Workshop Owner (Internal Stakeholder)	• Fewer regulatory penalties; lower compliance stress.
	• Positive customer reviews; industry recognition; premium branding.
	• Stable waste disposal costs; revenue from scrap; predictable operations.
	• Public advocacy of sustainable practices; high employee retention.
Workshop Technician (Internal Stakeholder)	• Reduced workplace incidents/illnesses; consistent PPE use.
	• Clean, orderly workspace; pride in describing the job.
	• Proficiency in digital tools; formal certification in waste handling.
	• Lower anxiety about long-term health impacts.
Local Resident / Community (External Stakeholder)	• Reduction in pollution nuisance (air, water, noise, visual).
	• Confidence in community health; fewer pollution-related concerns.
	• Strong neighborhood attachment; trust in local businesses.
	• Access to effective grievance redressal mechanisms.
Regulator (Civic Authority) (External Stakeholder)	• Lower cost/time of inspections; streamlined digital audits.
	• Higher waste diversion rates; improved compliance metrics.
	• Effective data sharing; productive industry consultations.

Life satisfaction includes economic security, health, safety, esteem, and trust. Hence, a well-designed DRL system benefits multiple stakeholders simultaneously. Satisfied stakeholders are more likely to support, participate, and comply with the sustainable system (Ting & Ahn, 2023). High visibility encourages stakeholders to participate actively and take ownership of the environment (Jiayuan & Rogers, 2025). For example, in an automobile workshop, highlighting environmental benefits may lead to more positive purchasing decisions. A customer who views a digital report on the "carbon savings" of repairing a part rather than replacing it is more likely to choose the repair option.

Prior studies have demonstrated that integrating capabilities among internal and external stakeholders is crucial for enhancing sustainability performance (Bálint et al., 2026). They state that capabilities translate stakeholder input into green operational practices. This study examines the social outcomes that those improved operations further produce. It discusses beyond "DRL is good" to "DRL, when combined with the right organizational capabilities, can transform operations and well-being. People trust digital systems not only because they function effectively but also because they perceive them as fair, reliable, safe, and helpful (Oesterreich et al., 2025). Prior studies on digital platforms have demonstrated that both information transparency and emotional reassurance play crucial roles in establishing trust in digital systems (Ting & Ahn, 2023). Sustainability performance results from the combined capabilities of stakeholders, technology, and management.

Environmental psychology establishes clear links between exposure to clean, orderly, and green spaces and improved mental well-being, reduced stress, and higher place attachment. Conversely, pollution, litter, and visual disorder degrade the perceived quality of neighborhoods and social unity. Therefore, interventions that improve the urban environment directly enhance collective life satisfaction.

Digital service ecosystems and sustainability

A digital service ecosystem is a network of interconnected stakeholders, resources, and processes that collectively deliver value. Such networks can include physical regulators, digital platforms, human users, or providers. These digital market participants enable seamless integration among their components through digital technologies (Lim et al., 2025). Digital service ecosystems differ from product-centric systems in that they are based on intangible interactions (e.g., data, experiences) but often rely on tangible resources (e.g., infrastructure, energy) via scalable platforms. (Garcia et al., 2025).

Urban waste challenges and quality of life

The "awareness gap" occurs when stakeholders conflate circularity with recycling - specifically, when they limit the scope of reverse logistics to simple waste collection rather than embracing reuse and refurbishment. This gap creates an inefficient and disorganized ecosystem in which stakeholders fail to recover the value of waste fully (Gallego-Schmid et al., 2025). Informal reuse, repair, and recovery practices act as non-noticable drivers of circularity in urban contexts. These practices exist, but they are not well-developed. Linear logistics practices dominate humanitarian operations, generating hidden environmental and social costs (Rocheteau, 2026). Circular practices enhance resilience, support local sourcing, and reduce dependence on global supply chains. The adoption of a circular economy improves legitimacy, trust, and inter-organizational collaboration (Rocheteau, 2026). Urban density necessitates flexible, proximity-based reverse-logistics infrastructure (Almelhem et al., 2025). Hence, change management is essential for embedding the circular economy beyond policy-level adoption.

Conceptualizing life satisfaction in service ecosystems

When digital safety monitoring is used to handle hazardous waste, it enables stakeholders to track dangerous materials at various stages (Hmamed et al., 2026). This prevents workplace hazards and protects workers' health. Digital documentation also facilitates regulatory compliance. When properly maintained, digital records enhance transparency and foster institutional trust (Guo, 2022; Khandelwal et al., 2025). Data-driven coordination among stakeholders reduces operational costs by eliminating duplication of effort and unnecessary expenses. This coordination enhances communication, fosters accountability, and promotes public confidence. Hence, cleaner urban environments can be created when proper collection, recycling, and disposal are done. Digitally enabled, human-centered reverse logistics can transform compliance into collective urban value (Garcia et al., 2025).

Reverse Logistics Practices in Urban Service Ecosystems

Digital practices for recovery, reuse, and recycling

Digital connectivity enables real-time weighing, tracking, and citizen reward allocation (Tsimnadis et al., 2023). Studies focus on integrating public awareness, citizen participation, and a reward system through digital systems. Deposit refund systems significantly increase consumer participation and return volumes (Almelhem et al., 2025). Digital technologies, such as AI, Blockchain, and IoT, can help (Leng et al., 2026; Yesim & Yavaş, 2023). AI is a systemic enabler of sustainability across environmental, economic, and social dimensions (Khandelwal et al., 2025). AI and Big Data Analytics can optimize collection routes and predict waste generation volumes based on service history. It automates material sorting via computer vision. It uses AI and cameras for computer vision to "see" and identify defective items. These items are then diverted to designated bins using robotic arms. However, Blockchain scalability remains a critical concern in urban service ecosystems (Manda & Madhu, 2025). These tools enhance traceability, reduce unnecessary returns, and improve decision-making in reverse logistics (Sharma et al., 2025). Logistics firms employ strategies such as centralized return facilities, virtual try-ons, consumer education, and incentivized take-back programs to optimize operations. These solutions facilitate cost optimization while promoting circular economy objectives. Digital transformation converts analog data into digital form. It signifies a reevaluation of current business structures and procedures within a digital framework. (Vijaya Kumar & Suresh, 2025). Digital tools support training, knowledge sharing, and the replication of circular practices (Rocheteau, 2026). The digital tools widely used are as follows:

Use of mobile apps for waste collection: Digital platforms must be low-cost, multilingual, and accessible via basic smartphones (e.g., via QR codes or simple apps) to include the smallest informal operators. Mobile applications could be valuable tools for stakeholders (Lim et al., 2025) in automotive reverse logistics to track waste, coordinate collection activities, and manage recovery processes (Lim et al., 2025). Digital platforms facilitate the return of remanufacturable cores. For example, exchanging an old alternator for a rebuilt one at a discount. Research has found that informal-sector integration improves inclusivity but complicates digital traceability (Almelhem et al., 2025).

Drivers, barriers, and stakeholder perspectives

Digital information on reverse logistics remains less transparent than information on forward logistics. As reverse logistics processes are fragmented and poorly documented, they act as barriers to the reverse logistics process (Garcia et al., 2025; Jiayuan & Rogers, 2025). Workshop owners' adoption paths can be divided into two categories: high-tech (such as IoT and blockchain) and low-cost (such as mobile apps and QR codes) DRL solutions. A straightforward decision matrix might balance the initial investment against worker digital literacy, scalability, and regulatory pressure. These typologies aid in coordinating DRL decisions with the workshop's size, the urban setting, and sustainability objectives. Digital RL needs to be human-centered in order to convert efficiency into urban well-being. Only when technologies are integrated into suitable organizational and human frameworks can they be considered facilitators. (Garcia et al., 2025). Technology impacts reverse logistics performance as much as human behavior (Almelhem et al., 2025). Psychological inertia, such as fear of surveillance, loss of autonomy, or unfamiliarity with digital interfaces, can also deter DRL uptake, even if economic conditions are favorable (Yegen Ouyang et al., 2025). Cultural norms within informal trust networks may oppose platform-mediated transactions, which are viewed as impersonal. Such obstacles can be overcome through co-design methodologies that align with local work patterns and incorporate digital tools into social customs.

KEY BARRIERS

Economic and Cost Barriers: In particular, some studies have found that "high initial capital investment" is a major challenge for SMEs (Vijaya Kumar & Suresh, 2025). Developing an urban, inclusive digital transformation is hampered by high capital costs and high infrastructure costs (Almelhem et al., 2025; Leng et al., 2026). The Internet of Things (IoT) has grown into a global infrastructure that enables advanced services by connecting various entities, both tangible and intangible, using information technology. This study provides an overview of IoT technology, including key issues, operational areas, and applications in business and marketing. One immediate challenge for implementation is digital exclusion, as not all informal workers own smartphones or have digital literacy (Yegen Ouyang et al., 2025). Second, skills gaps and training burdens, since even cheap tools are useless without proper upskilling (Savardi et al., 2025). In congested urban workshops, deficiencies in socio-digital access and capability are sometimes more crucial than technical complexity. Perceived price, anticipated return schedules, and compatibility with current procedures are the main factors influencing adoption. Uncertainty over cost recovery is frequently linked to resistance, especially in micro-workshops with narrow profit margins. (Aderinto, 2025). Starting with inexpensive digital tools, this adoption paradigm can facilitate entry and gradually boost confidence.

Technological and Infrastructure Barriers: "Technology and limited infrastructure" were identified as major challenges by scholars (Vijaya Kumar & Suresh, 2025). They also refer to the "weak digital willingness" of Small and Medium-sized Enterprises (Aderinto, 2025). The adoption of digital tools is uneven. Proper infrastructure in urban automobile service centers limits use.

Implementation and Policy Barriers: Reverse logistics practices exist but lack a formal policy. Studies have noted that, although government initiatives, such as the FAME and PLI schemes, exist, "uneven implementation still limits SME benefits" (Vijaya Kumar & Suresh, 2025). This suggests that policy execution gaps create additional barriers. Governance gaps weaken the institutionalization of circular logistics practices (Rocheteau, 2026). Hence, if emphasis is given on institutionalization, governance, and equity, it can satisfy multiple stakeholders

Organizational Barriers: Poorly developed governance procedures, the absence of formal protocols, and ineffective coordination among stakeholders (between workshop owners, recyclers, municipal authorities, and waste handlers) often result in uneven implementation of reverse logistics practices. Several small, informal auto repair shops lack standard operating procedures or documented service processes (Titu et al., 2025). They lack clearly defined responsibilities and often have poorly developed internal monitoring systems. There will also be resistance to organizational change, weak managerial commitment, and limited collaboration. These factors also hamper digital transformation efforts. Poor communication channels and a lack of long-term strategic planning also hinder operational efficiency. Such organizational shortcomings are constraining the effective implementation of sustainable digital reverse logistics systems in urban automobile service ecosystems.

Performance Outcomes and Life Satisfaction

Lack of performance metrics prevents reverse flows from being treated as strategic assets (Garcia et al., 2025). Figure 2 gives the steps involved in achieving stakeholder trust through digital disclosure. The visual supports help change perceptions and build trust. The digital tools help verify and present reliable data transparently, thereby reducing confusion and enhancing human well-being.

Figure 2. Steps in Digital Disclosure: From Information to Impact

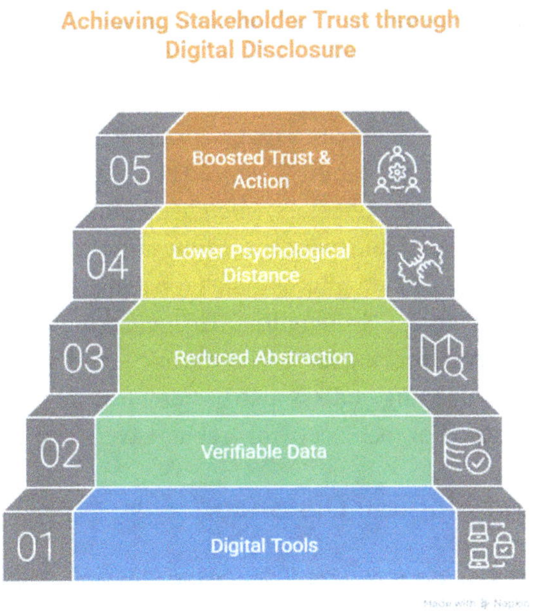

1. **From Abstraction to Concreteness:** Sustainability is often perceived as abstract, as its impacts are invisible or very minimal (Kim & Tam, 2024).

    Real-time Tracking: Digital disclosure of sustainability with evidence can make it visible. Real-time tracking can accomplish this (Jiayuan & Rogers, 2025). Real-time tracking occurs when data is visible as it is generated. Companies claim in their annual reports that they have reduced emissions by a definite percentage. Instead, if it is visible on the company's digital dashboards in real time, it will have a tangible impact on stakeholders (Patel et al., 2026). Information interaction and emotional interaction build trust in the platform. This leads to loyalty and repeated participation (Ting & Ahn, 2023).

    Traceability: Blockchain and RFID systems are used to track the life-cycle stages of the parts (L. Zhang & Fröhling, 2025). This is accomplished using a "digital passport" (Fares et al., 2025). It helps demonstrate environmental performance through measurable service-level outcomes. The Internet of Things (IoT) has evolved into a worldwide infrastructure that enables advanced services by connecting diverse entities, both tangible and intangible, utilizing information technology. This study analyses the impact of the IoT on business and marketing. Companies globally are increasingly focusing on the IoT due to its potential to deliver significant growth opportunities, rather than being influenced solely by the prevailing buzz. IoT-embedded smart bins are advanced waste-collection systems that leverage IoT to enhance reverse logistics operations. These systems enable advanced traceability (Majeed et al., 2024). Smart bins with level sensors alert waste collectors when used oil needs to be collected. This prevents overflows and reduces the time and effort for collection vehicles. Similarly, digital marketplaces match waste supply with recyclers' demand (Boegman-Watt & Carodenuto, 2026), ensuring fair value.

    Granularity: Breaking large datasets into smaller units facilitates understanding. Achieving goals is also easier when they are broken down into smaller parts. For instance, "this repair saved 40 kg of steel."

Reducing "Psychological Distance."

According to **Construal Level Theory (CLT)**, people struggle to engage with issues that feel "psychological distance" (Meng, 2025). These can be in terms of time, space, or social relevance (Kim & Tam, 2024). Digital disclosure of data bridges this distance across four key dimensions:

1. **Temporal Distance:** Real-time data makes the impact feel like it is happening *now*, rather than a far-off target. Mechanics may procrastinate on proper waste disposal because the environmental harm is perceived as occurring in the future. However, if a workshop's dashboard displays a real-time waste-impact clock that links daily actions to short-term goals, it motivates mechanics (Patel et al., 2026) to take immediate action. For example, if 2 liters of used coolant are improperly disposed of, the waste impact clock calculates the impact. A message: "*If dumped now, this coolant could contaminate 500 liters of local groundwater in 1–2 years*" is sent to the consumer. Human-centered design for reverse logistics collection and processing improves compliance and trust in urban waste systems (Tsimnadis et al., 2023).
2. **Spatial Distance:** Reporting on local emissions from a stakeholder's neighborhood makes them feel more real and understandable (Meng, 2025). A digital platform that displays the workshop's location on a map and nearby sensitive areas makes the issues appear more relevant. For instance, "*Your last five oil changes: 1.2 gallons improperly disposed. This waste is transported to the Municipal Landfill, which contributes to 'x' miles of local soil acidity.*"
3. **Social Distance:** Digital platforms enable various stakeholders, including customers, workers, and regulators, to see how their specific actions contribute to the collective goal. This creates a sense of shared responsibility in their further actions (Dasgupta et al., 2025). Mechanics may not realize how their choices impact coworkers, customers, or regulators. A message such as "*Your proper disposal of 5 lead-acid batteries this week helped the workshop avoid a $500 regulatory fine*" creates a sense of responsibility. Similarly, "Customers who chose your workshop for eco-friendly practices gave an average 4.8/5 ratings last month" encourages shared responsibility.
4. **Uncertainty:** Verifiable digital records remove the hypothetical distance uncertainty of "*Is this actually happening?*" doubt for the stakeholders. This turns the outcome into a concrete fact instead of a possibility (Jiayuan & Rogers, 2025). Mechanics might question if they are doing anything useful or if the numbers are overstated. Sensors in the IoT can collect data from waste bins and record that on a blockchain. "This allows customers to see the waste transparency report from the workshop and allows regulators to check the data. "inconveniences" for a "green delivery" (Ahmad et al., 2025). Stakeholders are often more agreeable to accept if a delivery delay with refurbished parts in a vehicle means the environmental "benefit", then that is fine.

Sustainable Digital Reverse Logistics Framework

Table 4 presents the components of sustainable reverse logistics in the service sector and their contributions to stakeholder life satisfaction.

Table 4. Framework components and implementation roadmap

Reverse Logistics Dimension	Digital Enabler	Life Satisfaction Outcome
Waste recovery & recycling	Digital tracking systems	Cleaner environment
Cost efficiency	Data-driven coordination	Economic security
Compliance & governance	Digital documentation	Trust & legitimacy
Stakeholder coordination	Platforms & networks	Social well-being

Transparent digital platforms strengthen accountability among workshops, recyclers, and regulators. Accountability fosters public confidence in urban automobile service ecosystems. Trust encourages citizens to cooperate in vehicle service and end-of-life returns. More cooperation improves the retrieval of reusable components and materials. Component recovery supports remanufacturing and second-hand markets. Local remanufacturing sustains jobs in urban service economies. Employment stability is good for financial/economic security and subjective well-being (Liu et al., 2026). Employers should consider their employees' behavioral patterns and personality traits to support their well-being. As shown in Figure 3, DRL in automobile service workshops is positively associated with operational efficiency and satisfaction with collective urban life.

Figure 3. Usage of Digital Tools leads to Human Well-being

Digitally coordinated return flows reduce improper disposal of used oils, tires, batteries, and spare parts. Reduced hazardous-waste leakage improves neighborhood environmental quality and public health.

CONNECTION TO UN SDG

This study contributes to achieving the United Nations Sustainable Development Goals (SDGs): SDG 11, SDG 12, SDG 9, and SDG 3. Transparent, digitally coordinated waste management practices in cities reduce environmental risks (SDG 11). It enhances quality of life by improving traceability and accountability across automotive service ecosystems (Cheshmehzangi, 2025). SDG 12 addresses enabling circular-economy practices, such as repair, reuse, and remanufacturing. Digital visibility encourages responsible consumption behavior. The development of digital service ecosystems enhances coordination, efficiency, and innovation among small and medium-sized service providers (SDG 9). Finally, SDG 3 (Good Health and Well-being) is addressed by reducing exposure to hazardous waste. Such a reduction enhances psychological well-being by increasing trust and transparency, while also reducing uncertainty among stakeholders. The framework links digital sustainability practices to outcomes of life satisfaction.

LIMITATIONS OF THE STUDY

The study is conceptual; therefore, it lacks empirical validation. The proposed framework is primarily meant for urban applications in emerging economies. Its suitability may vary depending on the institutional and socio-economic setting. Similarly, the factors surrounding digitally excluded people might not be included in this study. These drawbacks highlight the need for further studies examining how different user groups respond psychologically to DRL systems.

IMPLICATIONS FROM THE STUDY

Academic/Theoretical Implications

The research is multidisciplinary. It greatly closes the crucial knowledge gap between human welfare in service ecosystems and digital supply chain operations. A testable framework and a conceptual foundation are developed in this chapter. It provides a basis for subsequent empirical research (quantitative surveys and case studies).

Industry/Practical Implications

The goal of the research is to help policymakers create smarter and digitally aligned regulations for the informal sector. It helps technology developers develop suitable, affordable solutions for SMEs. The workshop owners looking for long-term viability can comply and hence enhance their reputation. Although grounded in an urban setting, the framework can also be used for other emerging economies with informal service markets.

FUTURE RESEARCH DIRECTIONS

This is a conceptual chapter and has no empirical validation. Future researchers may operationalize the framework proposed. They may measure life-satisfaction across digital service market segments using structural equation modeling (SEM) or multi-criteria decision-making (MCDM) methods. It is contextual to urban service clusters in emerging economies and needs adaptation to other contexts.

CONCLUSIONS

This study argues that, by intelligently managing the return flow of materials, DRL does more than optimize operations. Although a small part of the urban ecosystem, the automobile service ecosystem can transform perceptions of urban sustainability. It repairs the urban environment, strengthens local economies, and develops a sense of order and safety. Our proposed human-centered framework illustrates that the return on investment in DRL is stakeholders' life satisfaction, in addition to monetary returns. A sustainable urban future is, in part, the careful recovery of the discarded materials.

Disclosure

The authors disclose the use of artificial intelligence (AI)-based tools, such as Grammarly, Google Gemini, and Napkin.ai. These tools are used for purposes such as spelling and grammar correction, proofreading, and creating infographics and graphical images. However, the authors assessed accuracy and take full responsibility for the content.

Ethics Statement

The study does not require ethics clearance because it is not empirical.

Conflict of Interest

The authors declare that they have no conflicts of interest.

Data Availability Statement

No data or dataset was collected or associated with the article.

ACKNOWLEDGMENT

The authors thank the members and participants of the PBMEIT community for their support. The inputs, feedback, and ideas generated during the sessions helped to inform the research on the topic more effectively.

REFERENCES

Abbasi, A. Z., Fayyaz, M. S., Abbasi, G. A., Rather, R. A., & Hussain, A. (2025). Deriving gamers' subjective well-being through satisfaction, cognitive, affective, and behavioral engagement: Symmetrical and asymmetrical approaches. *Acta Psychologica, 260*, 105632. DOI: 10.1016/j.actpsy.2025.105632

Aderinto, A. A. (2025). Financial Risk Management and Corporate Performance of Selected Small-scale Firms in Nigeria. *Asian Journal of Advanced Research and Reports*, *19*(4), 316–330. DOI: 10.9734/ajarr/2025/v19i4986

Ahmad, R., Mat Yusof, N. A., & Ramely, A. (2025). MALAYSIAN YOUTH PERCEPTIONS OF SOLUTIONS TO ENVIRONMENTAL ISSUES. *Journal of Event. Tourism and Hospitality Studies*, *5*, 20–32. DOI: 10.32890/jeth2025.5.2

Alabi, B. A., Apata, A. O., Akindumila, O. I., Oloyede, O. J., Obasusi, B. A., Oladoja, N. A., & Ololade, I. A. (2025). Trace metal in soils of auto-mechanics workshops in Akure metropolis, Nigeria: Assessment of environmental quality. *International Journal of Environmental Science and Technology*, *22*(11), 10755–10768. DOI: 10.1007/s13762-025-06354-z

Almelhem, M., Buics, L., Süle, E., & Simoes, R. (2025). Industry 4.0 for sustainable reverse waste collection: A systematic literature review. *Journal of Transport and Supply Chain Management*, *19*, a1179. DOI: 10.4102/JTSCM.v19i0.1179

Alsanie, G., Unnisa, S. T., & Hamad, N. H. A. (2025). Transforming the Supply Chain Operations of Electric Vehicles' Batteries Using an Optimization Approach. *Sustainability (Basel)*, *18*(1), 367. DOI: 10.3390/su18010367

Arata, S., Sugiuchi, M., Yazawa, R., Funatsu, H., & Kawakubo, S. (2025). Effects of perceived office environment on the subjective well-being of workers: Insights from a structural equation modeling analysis. *Building and Environment*, *267*, 112180. DOI: 10.1016/j.buildenv.2024.112180

Badra, R., Majhi, M., Panda, B. B., Behera, I. D., Das, A. P., & Bal, M. (2026). Petroleum Hydrocarbon Pollutants from Waste Engine Oil in Municipal Waste: Concern and Remediation Strategies. In Das, A. P., Sirisena, K., & Bhanja, D. (Eds.), *Sustainable Municipal Waste Management with a Zero Waste Approach* (pp. 497–519). Springer Nature Switzerland., DOI: 10.1007/978-3-032-05950-5_20

Bálint, M., Ferreira, L. M. D. F., Vilas-Boas Da Silva, J. M., & Möhring, M. M. (2026). Integrating external stakeholders for green innovation in third-party logistics: The mediating role of green absorptive capacity. *International Journal of Logistics Management*, *37*(7), 1–30. DOI: 10.1108/IJLM-05-2024-0307

Boegman-Watt, S. J., & Carodenuto, S. (2026). Place, Process, People: Digital Placemaking across Global Supply Chains. *Geoforum*, *170*, 104530. DOI: 10.1016/j.geoforum.2025.104530

Cheshmehzangi, A. (2025). Cities as Living Systems: Circular Metabolisms, Climate Intelligence, and the Architecture of Regeneration. In A. Cheshmehzangi, *Generative AI-Powered Urban Digital Twins* (pp. 93–106). Springer Nature Singapore. DOI: 10.1007/978-981-95-4766-1_7

Dasgupta, A., Dutta, P., V, S., Kumar, P., Naveen, P. R., Gupta, H., & Singh Bisht, Y. (2025). Enhancing biodegradation of plastic wastes by adding used tire rubber: A sustainable solution for mitigating environmental pollution. *Waste Management & Research: The Journal for a Sustainable Circular Economy*, 0734242X251376880. DOI: 10.1177/0734242X251376880

Fares, N., Islam, M. S., Jauhar, S. K., & Kucukaltan, B. (2025). Towards an International Digital Product Passport: The New Paradigm of a Worldwide Circular Economy. *Circular Economy and Sustainability*, *5*(6), 5475–5495. DOI: 10.1007/s43615-025-00690-5

Farmanesh, P., Saliba, C., Athari, S. A., Naaman, D., Hanna Al Geitany, S., & Abualrob, J. O. (2025). Bridging Sustainable Development: The Nexus of Business Safety, Health Management, and Corporate Social Sustainability—Do Affective Commitment and Emotional Intelligence Mediate? *Sustainability (Basel)*, *17*(7), 3080. DOI: 10.3390/su17073080

Fatih, F. Z., Abbassy, S., & Hirawan, F. B. (2025). Transformative Paths to Economic Growth Through Circular Supply Chain Enablers and Environmental Initiatives—A Structural Equation Modeling Perspective. *Contemporary Management Research*, *21*(2), 99–125. DOI: 10.7903/cmr.24033

. Gallego-Schmid, A., Guerrero, A. B., Rebolledo-Leiva, R., Elorrieta-Mendoza, A., Cotohuanca, D. M. P., Tarpani, R. R. Z., Salvador, R., Barros, M. V., Henninger, C. E., & Vásquez-Ibarra, L. (2025). Social, Technological, Economic, and Policy Factors in the Circular Economy Transition in Brazil. *Sustainable development*, sd.70576. DOI: 10.1002/sd.70576

Garcia, A. M. C., Alves, V. S. D. S., Cunha, L. R. A., Bianchini, V. K., Razzino, C. D. A., Bezerra, B. S., & De Brito, I.Jr. (2025). Approaches, Challenges, and Opportunities in Humanitarian Logistics Integrated with Reverse Logistics and Sustainability. *Logistics (Basel)*, *10*(1), 9. DOI: 10.3390/logistics10010009

Gawande, N., & DoShi, P. (2025). Exploring Green Logistics: Impacts on Sustainability, Economic Efficiency, and Technological Innovation. In K. Patil, F. Moreira, & S. Dash (Eds.), *Proceedings of the International Conference on Sustainable Innovation with Artificial Intelligence and Machine Learning 2025 (ICSIAIML 2025)* (Vol. 200, pp. 925–941). Atlantis Press International BV. DOI: 10.2991/978-94-6463-948-3_64

Guo, Y. (2022). Digital Trust and the Reconstruction of Trust in the Digital Society: An Integrated Model based on Trust Theory and Expectation Confirmation Theory. *Digital Government: Research and Practice*, *3*(4), 1–19. DOI: 10.1145/3543860

Halaswamy, D., Tanmay, J., Raghavendra, A. N., & Vimaladevi, M. (2026). Impact of Green Supply Chain Management (GSCM) on consumer purchase intention in the Indian automobile industry. In K. Koppa, M. D. Shah, & S. S. Appadoo, *Empowering Inclusive Innovation* (1st ed., pp. 522–530). Routledge. DOI: 10.1201/9781003753445-61

Harendsa, N. P., & Pulansari, F. (2025). Analysis of Finished Product Warehouse Activity Flow Using Lean Warehouse Method. [Information Technology Engineering Journals]. *ITE Journal*, *10*(1), 29–38. DOI: 10.24235/itej.v10i1.202

Hmamed, H., Cherrafi, A., Garza-Reyes, J. A., & Hamani, N. (2026). Zero trust architecture for digital, sustainable, and resilient supply chains in the era of Industry 5.0/4.0. *Supply Chain Management*, *31*(2), 1–22. DOI: 10.1108/SCM-05-2025-0387

Jiayuan, Z., & Rogers, Z. S. (2025). *Consumer tradeoff preferences regarding logistics service and sustainability in last-mile delivery.*

Khandelwal, S., Sansare, V., & Bhatt, V. (2025). *Sustainable Futures: Empowering Change with Artificial Intelligence. 3*(12).

Kim, S., & Tam, L. (2024). Unpacking publics' disengagement and information behaviors: Roles of psychological distance, feasibility and desirability in an environmental sustainability issue. *Public Relations Review, 50*(4), 102491. DOI: 10.1016/j.pubrev.2024.102491

Leng, S., Wang, Y., Zhou, Y., Feng, X., Lee, P. T. W., & Bai, R. (2026). The growing role of artificial intelligence in smart container ports: Its application and future research directions. *Journal of International Logistics and Trade, 24*(1), 1–35. DOI: 10.1108/JILT-11-2025-0105

Lim, P. C., Lim, Y. L., Rajah, R., & Zainal, H. (2025). Usability questionnaire for standalone or interactive mobile health applications: A systematic review. *BMC Digital Health, 3*(1), 11. DOI: 10.1186/s44247-025-00150-y

Liu, X., Xu, Q., Feng, Z., Jian, Y. I., & Wang, Q.-C. (2026). Understanding subjective well-being in urban emergencies: The role of time use and personality traits. *Computational Urban Science, 6*(1), 3. DOI: 10.1007/s43762-026-00236-x

Manda, V. K., & Madhu, B. (2025). Sharding as a Sustainability Blockchain Optimization Tool. In Dsilva, J. (Ed.), *Redefining Sustainability* (pp. 227–233). Springer Nature Switzerland., DOI: 10.1007/978-3-031-88380-4_21

Meng, Z. (2025). Construal Theory: A Review and Future Prospects. *Journal of Society Innovation and Development, 7*(1), 143–151. DOI: 10.63924/jsid.v7i1.212

Morales Almeida, P., & Alemán Ramos, P. (2025). The Subjectivity of Subjective Well-Being. *SAGE Open, 15*(1), 21582440251329860. DOI: 10.1177/21582440251329860

Oesterreich, T. D., Anton, E., Hettler, F. M., & Teuteberg, F. (2025). What drives individuals' trusting intention in digital platforms? An exploratory meta-analysis. *Management Review Quarterly, 75*(4), 3615–3667. DOI: 10.1007/s11301-024-00477-2

Ouyang, Y., Cao, E., & Wu, P. (2025). Study on the psychological influence mechanism of consumer reviews of ceramic products on purchasing decisions in e-commerce platforms. *Environment and Social Psychology, 10*(8). Advance online publication. DOI: 10.59429/esp.v10i8.3910

Park, Y. W., & Ryosuke, S. (2025). CE Strategy in the Automotive Industry. In Y. W. Park & K. Tamaki, *Circular Economy Strategy for SDG Business Management* (pp. 47–62). Springer Nature Singapore. DOI: 10.1007/978-981-96-4194-9_3

Patel, U. R., Ghaffarianhoseini, A., GhaffarianHoseini, A., & Burgess, A. (2026). Towards a well-being-oriented framework for urban digital twins. *Cities (London, England), 169*, 106579. DOI: 10.1016/j.cities.2025.106579

Priyadarsini, S., & Das, A. P. (2026). Lithium in waste water: Impacts on pollution and human health. In *Decarbonization of Wastewater Pollutants as a Sustainable Solution* (pp. 353–364). Elsevier., DOI: 10.1016/B978-0-443-33062-9.00010-2

Rocheteau, M. X. T. (2026). Driving circular economy adoption in temporary organizations: Lessons from the humanitarian sector. *Journal of Organizational Change Management*, *39*(1), 1–22. DOI: 10.1108/JOCM-03-2025-0258

Rodrigues, S. P., Gomes, L. D. C., Peres, F. A. P., Correa, R. G. D. F., & Baierle, I. C. (2025). A Framework for Leveraging Digital Technologies in Reverse Logistics Actions: A Systematic Literature Review. *Logistics (Basel)*, *9*(2), 54. DOI: 10.3390/logistics9020054

Savardi, M., Signoroni, A., Benini, S., Vaccher, F., Alberti, M., Ciolli, P., Di Meo, N., Falcone, T., Ramanzin, M., Romano, B., Sozzi, F., & Farina, D. (2025). Upskilling or deskilling? Measurable role of an AI-supported training for radiology residents: A lesson from the pandemic. *Insights Into Imaging*, *16*(1), 23. DOI: 10.1186/s13244-024-01893-4

Sharma, N., Manda, V. K., Shivasharana, A., & Mohammed, M. (2025). Optimizing Reverse Logistics in Retail Sector. In Hlali, A. (Ed.), *Emerging Trends in Smart Logistics Technologies* (pp. 397–430). IGI Global Scientific Publishing., DOI: 10.4018/979-8-3373-2434-0.ch014

Ting, L., & Ahn, J. (2023). Understanding the roles of interaction and trust in formation of loyalty toward customer-to-customer (C2C) platforms. *Asia Pacific Journal of Marketing and Logistics*, *35*(10), 2565–2581. DOI: 10.1108/APJML-12-2022-1072

Tseng, E., Bellini, R., Lee, Y.-Y., Ramjit, A., Ristenpart, T., & Dell, N. (2024). Data Stewardship in Clinical Computer Security: Balancing Benefit and Burden in Participatory Systems. *Proceedings of the ACM on Human-Computer Interaction, 8*(CSCW1), 1–29. DOI: 10.1145/3637316

Tsimnadis, K., Kyriakopoulos, G. L., Arabatzis, G., Leontopoulos, S., & Zervas, E. (2023). An Innovative and Alternative Waste Collection Recycling Program Based on Source Separation of Municipal Solid Wastes (MSW) and Operating with Mobile Green Points (MGPs). *Sustainability (Basel)*, *15*(4), 3106. DOI: 10.3390/su15043106

Tushar, S., Singh, A., Sutrave, Y., & Azhar, M. (2024). Circular Supply Chains: Digital Tools for Enhanced Traceability. In Ozen, E., Singh, A., Taneja, S., Rajaram, R., & Davim, J. P. (Eds.), (pp. 175–202). Advances in Finance, Accounting, and Economics. IGI Global., DOI: 10.4018/979-8-3373-0578-3.ch009

Uzun, K., & Arslan, G. (2025). Meaning in Life Across Life Stages: Pathways from Uncertainty to Subjective Well-being. *Applied Research in Quality of Life*, *20*(3), 1197–1220. DOI: 10.1007/s11482-025-10461-x

Van Dam, S., & Bakker, C. (2024). Between a Rock and a Hard Place. A Case Study on Simplifying the Reverse Logistics of Car Parts to Enable Remanufacturing. *Journal of Circular Economy*, *2*(2). Advance online publication. DOI: 10.55845/MWAX4474

Vijaya Kumar, V. K., & Suresh, S. (2025). Exploring Challenges and Enablers of Sustainable Supply Chains in Indian Automotive SMEs for Enhancing Long-Term Competitiveness. *JES. Journal of Engineering Sciences*, *0*(0), 0–0. DOI: 10.21608/jesaun.2025.404637.1615

Yesim, O., & Yavaş, V. (2023). A Study On Critical Factors Of Digitalization In Reverse Logistics. *Beykent Üniversitesi Fen ve Mühendislik Bilimleri Dergisi*, *16*(1), 1–6. DOI: 10.20854/bujse.1211274

Zeshan, M., Morelli, M., Rasool, S., Centobelli, P., & Cerchione, R. (2025). Empowering sustainable workplaces: A perspective on employee well-being in the light of the job demand resource model. *Sustainable Development (Bradford)*, *33*(2), 1861–1878. DOI: 10.1002/sd.3179

Zhang, L., & Fröhling, M. (2025). Integration of blockchain and life cycle assessment: A systematic literature review. *The International Journal of Life Cycle Assessment*, *30*(1), 1–19. DOI: 10.1007/s11367-024-02371-1

Zhang, X., Yu, J., Yan, W., Wang, Y., & Subramanian, N. (2023). A Comprehensive Review of Reverse Logistics in the Automotive Industry. *IEEE Access : Practical Innovations, Open Solutions*, *11*, 47112–47128. DOI: 10.1109/ACCESS.2023.3273591

Chapter 17
Digital Health and Emotional Resilience in Global Markets:
Attention Restoration and Cultural Integration Pathways

Manoj Kumar Mallick
http://orcid.org/0009-0005-8646-5435
Shikaripara Mahavidyalaya, Sido Kanhu Murmu University, Dumka, India

ABSTRACT

Digital markets transform consumer psychology, through connectivity that threatens well-being. This chapter studies the impact of digital engagement on life satisfaction through Attention Restoration Theory, Self-Determination Theory, and cross-cultural frameworks. Uninterrupted digital exposure exhausts cognitive resources via attention demands, social comparison, and information overload. Emotional resilience mediates these effects. The analysis integrates Western coping strategies with Eastern equanimity practices, recognizing how individualist-collectivist orientations shape digital behaviors. A multidimensional framework measures attention quality, emotional regulation, autonomy, resilience capacity, and satisfaction across populations. Evidence-based interventions include mindfulness practices, ethical platform design, workplace policies, and regulatory frameworks. It provides academics, practitioners, marketers, and policymakers with actionable frameworks tailored to their needs. These tools enable building ethical digital ecosystems that enhance global well-being.

DOI: 10.4018/979-8-3373-8357-6.ch017

1. INTRODUCTION

This chapter explores how digital markets intersect with consumer psychology and life satisfaction. People today rely on digital tools for nearly every aspect of life, including working, shopping, having fun, and socializing. Digital environments produce unique psychological effects that differ from traditional in-person exchanges. As consumer psychology evolves to address technology-mediated behaviors, researchers now examine how digital consumption affects emotional states, cognitive functioning, and life satisfaction.

For academics, this chapter advances theory by integrating digital health perspectives with consumer psychology frameworks, examining how emotional resilience mediates the relationship between digital consumption and life satisfaction. Evidence indicates that sustained technology use patterns influence individual well-being and life satisfaction (Mayiwar et al., 2025). For practitioners and marketers, it provides evidence-based insights into consumer well-being in digital contexts, informing ethical platform design and marketing strategies. This chapter offers frameworks for regulating digital environments that balance commercial interests with public mental health for policymakers. For general readers, it delivers practical guidance on maintaining psychological well-being amid pervasive digital consumption.

1.1 Defining Digital Health and the Paradox of Digitalization

Digital health encompasses balanced functioning across multiple domains within technology-mediated environments, extending beyond the absence of illness (Büchi, 2024). This holistic perspective recognizes that wellness in digital spaces requires active cultivation rather than passive existence. Traditional disease-prevention models prove insufficient for contemporary digital challenges.

Physical health in digital contexts includes ergonomic practices, sleep quality, and physical activity patterns affected by screen time (Lissak, 2018). Prolonged device use contributes to musculoskeletal problems, visual strain, and sedentary lifestyle consequences. Sleep disruption from blue light exposure and evening device use represents a pervasive concern, while excessive screen time displaces physical activity.

Emotional health involves maintaining positive affect, managing negative emotions, and experiencing psychological well-being during digital interactions. Digital environments expose users to emotional triggers from distressing content to interpersonal conflicts. Cognitive health refers to attention capacity, information processing abilities, and decision-making quality in digital spaces (Firth et al., 2019). Digital environments fragment attention through notifications, multitasking demands, and rapid context switching. Social health encompasses meaningful connections, relationship quality, and social support accessed through digital platforms.

However, modern societies face a fundamental paradox regarding digital technologies. Hyper-connectivity promises enhanced communication, information access, and convenience, yet algorithmic mechanisms simultaneously shape user behavior in ways that contribute to mental health challenges, polarization, and compulsive engagement patterns (Metzler & Garcia, 2023). Populations across global markets report rising burnout, anxiety disorders, information overload, workplace stress, and diminished life satisfaction despite unprecedented digital connectivity (Marsh et al., 2024). Digital platforms enable constant availability expectations through algorithmic management systems and notification architectures, creating chronic stress that depletes psychological resources and undermines autonomy (Zhang et al., 2025). Workers experience blurred boundaries between professional and personal domains, with 24/7 connectivity expectations eroding work-life balance and contributing to digital exhaustion in post-pandemic organizational contexts (Abidi et al., 2023).

Social media platforms illustrate this paradox vividly, facilitating connection with distant others while potentially diminishing face-to-face relationship quality and creating algorithmic feedback loops that shape user behavior and mental health outcomes (Metzler & Garcia, 2023). Users gain access to global information networks yet experience information overload, algorithm-driven echo chambers, and difficulty discerning credible sources (Yuan et al., 2025). Digital technologies offer significant convenience and enable unprecedented connectivity. However, research demonstrates that excessive usage often erodes social connections and psychological well-being, contributing to digital stress, burnout, and diminished life satisfaction (Marsh et al., 2024). The relationship between technology and well-being fundamentally depends on balance and intentionality. While moderate, purposeful digital engagement can support flourishing, excessive or compulsive usage correlates with lower psychological well-being and reduced life satisfaction (Büchi, 2024; Mayiwar et al., 2025).

The definition emphasizes adaptation rather than avoidance. Complete digital withdrawal proves impractical given that economic participation, social connection, and civic engagement increasingly depend on digital access. Meier and Reinecke (2021) posit that digital health requires sustainable engagement strategies. These strategies should replenish, rather than deplete, personal well-being. Optimal digital health emerges from conscious choices about when, how, and why individuals engage with technology, acknowledging both unprecedented opportunities and novel challenges for human flourishing.

Digital health considerations increasingly intersect with marketing ecosystems as consumer journeys unfold across multiple digital touchpoints including social media platforms, mobile applications, e-commerce interfaces, and algorithm-driven recommendation systems. Brand-consumer relationships in digital spaces are mediated by algorithmic mechanisms that shape content exposure, personalization strategies, and engagement patterns, creating feedback loops between consumer behavior and platform design (Metzler & Garcia, 2023). Marketing practitioners face ethical imperatives to balance commercial objectives with consumer well-being, particularly when algorithmic management systems track behavioral data, optimize conversion funnels, and deploy persuasive design elements that may undermine user autonomy (Zhang et al., 2025). Consumer journey touchpoints—from initial awareness through consideration, purchase, and post-purchase engagement—now operate within algorithmic architectures that influence attention allocation, emotional responses, and decision-making processes. Understanding these dynamics proves essential for developing marketing strategies that enhance rather than deplete consumer psychological resources across global multicultural marketplaces.

1.2 Emotional Resilience in Digital Contexts

Emotional resilience represents the adaptive capacity to navigate digital stressors effectively. This construct involves bouncing back from negative online experiences, regulating emotions during digital interactions, and maintaining psychological equilibrium (Sun et al., 2022). Digital contexts present unique challenges that demand specialized resilience skills. Unlike traditional stressors that occur episodically, digital stressors operate continuously through persistent connectivity.

Emotional regulation in digital environments requires managing responses to continuous information streams shaped by algorithmic curation and social feedback mechanisms. Users encounter potentially distressing content, algorithmic echo chambers, social comparisons, and communication conflicts regularly, with algorithm awareness influencing both resistance and compliance behaviors toward platform engagement (Yuan et al., 2025). News feeds deliver global crises alongside mundane updates through algorithmically optimized content streams, creating emotional whiplash and information overload, while social comparison processes intensify through curated self-presentations highlighting others' achievements and life experiences. Resilient individuals employ cognitive reappraisal strategies to reframe digital experiences constructively, recognizing that online presentations represent selective, algorithm-amplified reality rather than comprehensive truth, and developing metacognitive awareness of how platform design shapes their emotional responses.

The speed of digital communication compounds emotional regulation challenges. Instantaneous messaging creates pressure for immediate responses before emotions settle, while asynchronous communication removes nonverbal cues that typically guide emotional understanding. Misinterpretations escalate quickly in text-based exchanges lacking tone and facial expression. Emotionally resilient users develop strategies for pausing before responding and seeking clarification when communications seem unclear.

Recovery from digital stressors represents another critical component of emotional resilience, including disengaging from overwhelming digital stimuli, algorithmic content streams, and restoring emotional balance through offline activities and restorative experiences. Recovery capacity predicts sustained well-being and psychological resilience in digitally intensive lifestyles, particularly in post-pandemic contexts where digital demands have intensified across work, social, and personal domains (Schäfer et al., 2024). Psychological detachment from digital demands allows emotional resources to replenish, requiring both physical disconnection from devices and mental disengagement from digital concerns, notifications, and the compulsive monitoring of online information streams.

Digital retreats, notification management, and designated offline periods facilitate recovery. Some individuals benefit from structured digital detox periods creating complete separation, while others find success with incremental boundary setting limiting digital engagement in specific contexts. Recovery patterns must align with individual needs, work requirements, and social obligations.

Adaptive capacity encompasses learning from negative digital experiences and adjusting future behaviors accordingly. Resilient consumers develop personalized strategies including setting boundaries, curating digital environments, and seeking social support (Kircaburun et al., 2020). They modify privacy settings, unfollow accounts triggering negative emotions, and selectively engage with platform features.

Digital resilience differs from general psychological resilience by requiring technological literacy, awareness of platform dynamics, and skills specific to online interaction management. Understanding how algorithms shape content exposure empowers users to interpret digital experiences critically. Building emotional resilience for digital contexts emerges as essential for maintaining life satisfaction as technology evolves and creates new challenges.

1.3 Overview of Chapter Structure and Key Contributions

This chapter offers several distinctive contributions to understanding digital health and consumer well-being. First, it presents an integrated theoretical model connecting digital health, emotional resilience, and life satisfaction. This model synthesizes perspectives from health psychology, consumer behavior, and digital media research.

Second, the chapter adopts a cross-cultural perspective on digital health phenomena. Global markets exhibit substantial variation in digital adoption patterns, cultural values, and regulatory environments. The analysis examines how these contextual factors shape relationships between digital engagement and well-being outcomes.

Third, the chapter addresses measurement challenges in assessing digital health constructs. It reviews existing instruments and proposes refined approaches for capturing multidimensional digital health indicators. Valid measurement proves essential for both research advancement and practical intervention development.

Fourth, the chapter evaluates evidence-based interventions for enhancing digital health and emotional resilience. It examines individual-level strategies, organizational initiatives, and policy approaches. The interventions section bridges theory and practice by identifying actionable recommendations.

The chapter proceeds systematically through conceptual foundations, empirical evidence, cultural considerations, and applied implications. It synthesizes recent research while identifying gaps requiring future investigation. The structure supports both academic readers seeking comprehensive understanding and practitioners seeking evidence-based guidance.

2. THEORETICAL FOUNDATIONS

2.1 Attention Restoration Theory: Foundations and Components

Attention Restoration Theory (ART) provides a critical framework for understanding cognitive functioning in contemporary digital environments. Kaplan (1995) originally developed ART to explain how natural environments restore depleted attentional resources. The theory distinguishes between two forms of attention that operate fundamentally differently. Kaplan and Berman (2010) characterize *directed attention* as the voluntary mental effort required to sustain cognitive focus. This form of attention underlies goal-directed behavior, selective focus, and inhibition of distractions. Involuntary attention operates through fascination with inherently engaging stimuli that require minimal cognitive effort. Natural environments elicit soft fascination—a gentle, effortless form of attentional engagement that captures attention modestly without depleting directed attention resources (Liu et al., 2024). Exposure to natural elements such as sunsets, flowing water, rustling leaves, and greenspace engages involuntary attention while allowing mental restoration and recovery from cognitive fatigue (McDonnell & Strayer, 2024). This gentle engagement permits reflection and mind-wandering in a less structured manner, ultimately facilitating recovery from directed attention depletion and mental exhaustion (Piedimonte et al., 2025).

Directed attention represents a finite resource that becomes exhausted through sustained use in contemporary digital and workplace environments. Cognitive fatigue manifests when directed attention depletes beyond sustainable levels, particularly in contexts involving algorithmic management systems and continuous digital connectivity (Zhang et al., 2025). Symptoms include difficulty concentrating, irritability, impulsiveness, reduced performance on tasks requiring executive function, and increased susceptibility to information overload and decision paralysis (Marsh et al., 2024). Modern digital workplaces demand continuous directed attention for extended periods across multiple concurrent responsibilities, screen-based tasks, and fragmented communication channels. Restorative experiences replenish depleted attentional capacity through four key components validated by recent empirical research. Being away involves psychological or physical distance from attention-demanding contexts and digital stimuli. Extent refers to the richness and coherence of the restorative environment. Fascination captures attention effortlessly without requiring directed effort, allowing cognitive resources to recover. Compatibility describes how well the environment matches individual inclinations and purposes (Liu et al., 2024).

Natural environments exemplify settings high in restorative potential that counteract digital and workplace cognitive demands. Parks, forests, and gardens provide opportunities for attention restoration that urban built environments and digital interfaces typically lack. Contemporary neuroscience research consistently demonstrates cognitive benefits following nature exposure, with measurable improvements in neural indices of executive attention (McDonnell & Strayer, 2024). Even brief contact with natural settings improves performance on attention-demanding tasks, reduces mental fatigue, and enhances psychological well-being in digitally intensive contexts (Büchi, 2024).

2.2 Digital Environments as Chronic Attention Demand

Digital technologies create fundamentally different attentional dynamics than those addressed in original ART formulations. Digital environments function as perpetual sources of directed attention demand rather than restoration opportunities. Notifications interrupt ongoing activities and fragment attention across multiple competing stimuli. Each notification requires cognitive evaluation, decision-making, and potential response (Mark et al., 2016). The frequency and unpredictability of notifications amplify their attentional cost. Users cannot predict when notifications will arrive, creating constant vigilance. This sustained monitoring state depletes directed attention even when users attempt to ignore notifications. Research indicates that merely having notifications enabled reduces cognitive performance compared to notification-free conditions (Stothart et al., 2015).

Multitasking represents another chronic attention demand inherent in digital environments, particularly in contemporary workplaces characterized by algorithmic management systems and platform-mediated communication. Digital platforms facilitate rapid switching between tasks, applications, and information streams driven by notification architectures and real-time connectivity expectations (Zhang et al., 2025). Users check email while participating in video meetings, browse social media while watching streaming content, and toggle between numerous browser tabs, creating patterns of fragmented attention and information overload that contribute to workplace stress and burnout (Marsh et al., 2024). Each task switch incurs switching costs that accumulate cognitive depletion and mental exhaustion. Attention residue persists from previous tasks and impairs performance on subsequent activities, reducing work quality and employee well-being in digitally intensive environments. Algorithmic feeds present continuously refreshing content designed to capture and retain attention through sophisticated engagement optimization. Social media platforms employ recommendation algorithms that create feedback loops between user behavior and content delivery, optimizing for engagement metrics while potentially undermining mental health and psychological well-being (Metzler & Garcia, 2023). Feeds provide endless scrolling experiences without natural stopping points, exploiting psychological vulnerabilities through variable reward schedules. Content curation algorithms learn user preferences and deliver increasingly targeted material, creating personalized information ecosystems. This algorithmic personalization enhances content relevance while intensifying attention capture, reducing user autonomy, and creating echo chambers that reinforce existing preferences and behaviors (Yuan et al., 2025).

The attentional architecture of digital platforms exploits psychological vulnerabilities through algorithmic design mechanisms that prioritize engagement over well-being. Variable reward schedules keep users checking for updates through intermittent reinforcement. Auto-playing videos minimize friction in continued consumption. Infinite scroll eliminates closure cues that would otherwise signal stopping points. These design patterns prioritize engagement duration over user well-being, creating tensions between platform profitability and user autonomy. Cognitive fatigue from digital engagement manifests distinctively from traditional directed attention depletion. Digital fatigue includes mental exhaustion, difficulty sustaining focus, impaired executive functioning, and workplace burnout. Users experience decision fatigue from constant micro-choices about where to direct attention amid competing information streams. The volume of available information exceeds processing capacity, creating chronic cognitive overload, stress, and diminished psychological well-being in digital workplace environments (Marsh et al., 2024).

Recovery from digital attention demands proves challenging because digital devices pervade most environments. Smartphones accompany users throughout daily activities, providing constant access and temptation. Work-from-home arrangements eliminate physical separation between professional and personal spaces. Digital devices in bedrooms disrupt sleep, preventing the restorative benefits of adequate rest. The ubiquity of digital technology limits opportunities for genuine being away experiences (Kushlev & Dunn, 2015).

2.3 Western Models of Resilience: Coping and Psychological Flexibility

Western psychological frameworks emphasize individual agency and control in resilience development. Coping theory conceptualizes resilience as successful adaptation to stress through cognitive and behavioral strategies. Problem-focused coping involves direct action to modify stressful situations. Emotion-focused coping addresses emotional responses to stressors through reappraisal and regulation techniques (Folkman & Moskowitz, 2004). Stress appraisal processes determine how individuals interpret potentially threatening situations. Primary appraisal evaluates whether a situation poses harm, threat, or challenge. Secondary appraisal assesses available coping resources and response options. Reappraisal involves revising initial evaluations based on new information or perspective shifts. Lazarus and Folkman (1984) demonstrate that cognitive appraisal drives both emotional responses and the selection of coping mechanisms.

Psychological flexibility represents another prominent Western resilience construct. Acceptance and Commitment Therapy (ACT) frameworks define psychological flexibility as the ability to contact the present moment while pursuing valued actions despite uncomfortable thoughts and feelings. Psychological flexibility involves six core processes: acceptance, cognitive defusion, present moment awareness, self-as-context, values clarification, and committed action (Hayes et al., 2006). Cognitive defusion techniques help individuals observe thoughts without being controlled by them. Rather than attempting to eliminate negative thoughts, defusion creates distance between the person and their cognitions. This distance allows individuals to choose responses aligned with values rather than reacting automatically to cognitive content. Defusion proves particularly relevant for digital contexts where intrusive thoughts about missing information create anxiety (Levin et al., 2012).

Western resilience models emphasize personal growth through adversity. Posttraumatic growth theory describes positive psychological changes resulting from struggles with challenging life circumstances. Growth domains include enhanced personal strength, closer relationships, greater appreciation for life, new possibilities, and spiritual development. Tedeschi and Calhoun (2004) posit that adversity can serve as a catalyst for growth rather than solely causing psychological damage.

Self-efficacy beliefs influence resilience by shaping individuals' confidence in their coping abilities. People with strong self-efficacy persevere longer in facing difficulties and recover more quickly from setbacks. Self-efficacy develops through mastery experiences, vicarious learning, social persuasion, and physiological state interpretation. Digital environments challenge self-efficacy when users feel unable to control their technology use despite intentions (Bandura, 1997). Emotion regulation capacity represents a critical component of Western resilience frameworks. Gross's (1998) process model distinguishes between antecedent-focused and response-focused regulation strategies. Antecedent-focused strategies modify situations before emotional responses fully develop. Response-focused strategies address emotions after they arise. Effective regulation requires flexibility in strategy selection based on contextual demands.

2.4 Eastern and Indian Perspectives: Equanimity and Balance

Eastern philosophical traditions offer complementary perspectives on resilience that emphasize equanimity and acceptance. Buddhist psychology conceptualizes suffering (dukkha) as inherent in existence, arising from attachment, aversion, and ignorance. Resilience derives from altering one's engagement with inevitable struggles rather than attempting to remove them, particularly relevant in managing digital stressors and algorithmic pressures (Schäfer et al., 2024). Equanimity (upeksha in Sanskrit) represents balanced mental composure maintained across changing circumstances—remaining centered amid pleasure and pain, success and failure, praise and criticism. This reflects engaged presence without clinging to preferred outcomes or rejecting unwanted experiences, essential for navigating curated social media content and online validation-seeking.Mindfulness practices cultivate present-moment awareness with acceptance and non-judgment. Vipassana meditation traditions train practitioners to observe thoughts, emotions, and sensations without reactive identification, creating space between stimulus and response. Mindfulness reduces rumination, worry, and emotional reactivity while enhancing cognitive flexibility, proving effective in digital resilience interventions post-pandemic (Sheng et al., 2025).

Yoga philosophy presents an integrated system addressing physical, mental, and spiritual dimensions. Pranayama (breath control) techniques regulate the autonomic nervous system, with specific breathing patterns activating parasympathetic responses that counter stress physiology. These practices offer accessible resilience tools applicable to digital workplace stress and information overload contexts (Mayiwar et al., 2025).

Vedantic philosophy distinguishes between unchanging witness consciousness (sakshi) and fluctuating mental contents, reducing over-identification with transient thoughts and emotions. Karma yoga presents action without attachment to results—engaging fully while releasing fixation on outcomes. Applied to digital contexts, this framework suggests purposeful technology use without compulsive checking or FOMO anxiety. Indian traditions emphasize experiential knowledge (anubhava) and community support (sangha) for sustained practice and individual development.

2.5 Synthesis: Culturally Grounded Digital Emotional Resilience

Integrating Western and Eastern perspectives creates a comprehensive framework for digital emotional resilience. This hybrid approach combines action-oriented coping strategies emphasized in Western psychology with acceptance and equanimity cultivated through Eastern practices. Neither tradition alone addresses the full complexity of digital age resilience demands, particularly in algorithmic environments and post-pandemic contexts (Schäfer et al., 2024).

Western contributions include structured problem-solving approaches for managing digital demands: setting boundaries, configuring notifications, and scheduling digital detox periods. Cognitive reappraisal techniques help individuals reframe digital experiences constructively, while psychological flexibility principles encourage value-aligned technology use despite FOMO discomfort. These approaches empower individuals to modify their digital environments and resist algorithmic manipulation (Yuan et al., 2025).

Eastern traditions contribute practices for internal state regulation that complement external behavior change. Mindfulness meditation develops metacognitive awareness about digital impulses before acting on them. Equanimity practices reduce emotional reactivity to social media content and online interactions. Yogic breathing techniques provide immediate stress management tools applicable during overwhelming digital experiences, particularly effective in workplace contexts experiencing information overload (Mayiwar et al., 2025).

The synthesis acknowledges cultural differences in individualism versus collectivism that shape resilience conceptualizations. Western models emphasize individual agency and self-reliance, while Eastern perspectives recognize interdependence and community roles in well-being. Digital resilience frameworks must accommodate both individual self-regulation and collective approaches to healthy technology use, particularly in multicultural global marketplaces (Tarnanidis et al., 2026). Culturally grounded digital emotional resilience recognizes that optimal practices vary across individuals and contexts. The integrated model encourages individuals to draw from diverse traditions in developing personalized resilience approaches, addressing multiple ecological levels simultaneously: individual practices, interpersonal norms, community interventions, and policy applications.

2.6 Integrated Conceptual Model

The conceptual model integrates theoretical foundations into a comprehensive framework explaining relationships between digital exposure, cognitive and emotional processes, resilience mechanisms, and life satisfaction outcomes. This model guides empirical research and practical interventions addressed in subsequent chapters.

Digital exposure encompasses multiple dimensions of technology engagement. Screen time quantifies duration spent with digital devices across work, leisure, and social activities. Notification frequency affects attentional interruption patterns, social comparison processes occur through exposure to curated self-presentations on social platforms, and algorithmic feed characteristics shape content consumption patterns and emotional experiences (Metzler & Garcia, 2023).

Cognitive effects emerge from sustained digital exposure as predicted by Attention Restoration Theory. Attention fatigue manifests through reduced capacity for sustained concentration and executive functioning, particularly in algorithmic management environments. Cognitive fragmentation results from rapid task-switching and interrupted work patterns, while information overload creates decision paralysis, processing difficulties, and workplace burnout (Marsh et al., 2024). These cognitive impacts mediate relationships between digital exposure and emotional outcomes. Emotional processes represent critical mediating mechanisms linking digital exposure to well-being outcomes. Emotional dysregulation includes difficulty managing negative affect triggered by algorithmic content streams and social comparison. Excessive worry about missing information creates persistent anxiety, while compulsive checking behaviors reflect attempts to reduce uncertainty discomfort shaped by platform design mechanisms (Metzler & Garcia, 2023). Conversely, emotional regulation capacity and algorithmic awareness enable adaptive responses to digital stressors.

Emotional resilience emerges through two primary pathways. Attention restoration practices include nature exposure, digital detox periods, and engagement with inherently restorative activities. Cultural practices encompass meditation, yoga, breathing exercises, and community rituals supporting well-being. These resilience mechanisms moderate the relationship between digital exposure and life satisfaction, with high resilience buffering negative impacts while enabling benefits (Schäfer et al., 2024). Life satisfaction outcomes represent the ultimate dependent variables. Purpose reflects sense of meaning and direction, autonomy captures ability to make self-determined choices, relationship quality encompasses depth and satisfaction with social connections, and general well-being includes positive affect and psychological flourishing.

The model includes moderating factors influencing relationships between variables. Cultural context shapes resilience processes through individualist versus collectivist orientations. Individual differences in personality, age, and digital literacy further moderate model relationships. Conscientiousness predicts more structured technology use, while neuroticism associates with greater vulnerability to digital stressors.

The integrated model emphasizes dynamic, reciprocal relationships rather than linear causation. Life satisfaction feeds back to influence subsequent digital exposure patterns. Individuals experiencing well-being may use technology more intentionally, while those struggling may increase digital consumption seeking relief. This comprehensive framework synthesizes attention restoration mechanisms, cultural resilience traditions, and consumer psychology perspectives, providing testable predictions about factors influencing digital well-being.

Figure 1. Integrated Conceptual Model of Digital Emotional Resilience and Life Satisfaction

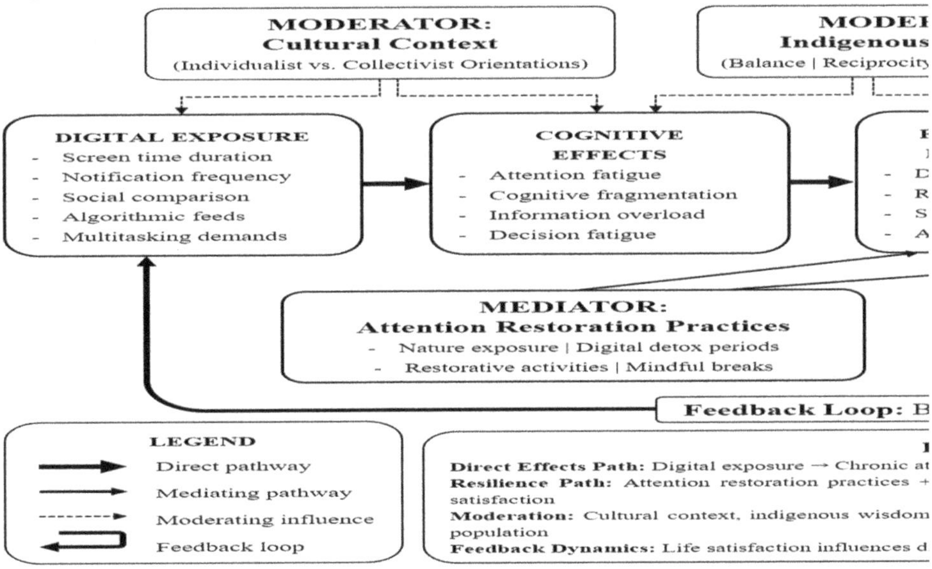

Note: This diagram illustrates the Integrated Conceptual Model of Digital Emotional Resilience and Life Satisfaction. It shows the relationships between digital exposure, cognitive effects, emotional processes, resilience mechanisms, and life satisfaction outcomes, along with mediating and moderating factors.

3. PATHWAYS FROM DIGITAL ENGAGEMENT TO EMOTIONAL RESILIENCE AND LIFE SATISFACTION

3.1 Mechanisms Linking Digital Exposure to Emotional States and Well-Being

Digital engagement affects emotional states and well-being through interconnected physiological, cognitive, and social mechanisms. Screen use disrupts sleep patterns through blue light exposure and sedentary behavior (Lissak, 2018). Screen exposure before bedtime suppresses melatonin production, delaying circadian rhythms. Poor sleep quality cascades into mood disturbances, reduced emotional regulation capacity, and diminished cognitive functioning. Cognitive mechanisms center on attention depletion and information overload. Constant task-switching fragments attention and impairs sustained concentration. Working memory becomes overloaded when multiple information streams demand simultaneous processing (Ophir et al., 2009). Cognitive fatigue accumulates as individuals navigate competing demands from email, messaging, social media, and work applications. This depletion manifests as irritability, reduced patience, and difficulty managing emotions.

Social comparison represents a potent mechanism linking digital engagement to emotional outcomes. Social media platforms showcase curated self-presentations that highlight achievements, experiences, and appearance. Users engage in upward comparisons with these idealized presentations. Such comparisons trigger feelings of inadequacy, envy, and diminished self-worth (Vogel et al., 2014). The frequency of comparison correlates with depressive symptoms and life dissatisfaction. Passive consumption intensifies these comparison effects. Fear of missing out creates another pathway to distress. Algorithmic feeds continuously display activities, events, and experiences others enjoy. Users develop anxiety about missing rewarding experiences available to peers. FOMO motivates compulsive checking behaviors that paradoxically increase rather than reduce anxiety (Przybylski et al., 2013).

Validation-seeking behaviors emerge when users depend on digital feedback for self-worth. Likes, comments, and shares provide intermittent reinforcement that shapes behavior. Self-esteem becomes contingent on external validation rather than internal standards, creating vulnerability to emotional fluctuations. Indirect pathways operate through displacement of beneficial activities. Time spent on digital devices replaces face-to-face interaction, physical activity, and restorative experiences. Twenge and Campbell (2018) argue that excessive digital consumption displaces behaviours essential for psychological health.

3.2 Attention Restoration as a Key Pathway

Attention restoration provides a critical pathway for recovering from digital demands. Kaplan's (1995) theory identifies environmental characteristics that facilitate restoration. Natural environments exemplify restorative settings through their capacity to engage involuntary attention gently. Parks, gardens, forests, and water features capture attention effortlessly without requiring directed effort. This soft fascination allows directed attention resources to replenish. Micro-breaks during digital work offer accessible restoration opportunities. Brief pauses every 20-30 minutes interrupt sustained attention demands. Effective micro-breaks involve shifting gaze to distant objects, stretching, or walking away from screens. The key involves complete disengagement from digital stimuli during break periods. Checking smartphones during breaks fails to provide restoration benefits.

Nature exposure represents a powerful restoration intervention with robust empirical support. Studies demonstrate cognitive performance improvements following nature walks compared to urban walks. Even viewing nature images or having window views of greenery provides measurable benefits (Li & Sullivan, 2016). Nature's restorative capacity stems from its ability to capture attention modestly while permitting reflection. The absence of digital notifications creates psychological distance from stressors. Mindfulness practices cultivate attention restoration through present-moment awareness. Focused attention meditation trains sustained attention on a single object like breath. Open monitoring meditation develops awareness of thoughts and sensations without reactive engagement. Both practices strengthen attentional control and reduce mind-wandering (Jha et al., 2015). Regular practice builds metacognitive awareness about attentional state.

Offline rhythms establish predictable patterns of digital engagement and restoration. Designating technology-free times creates guaranteed restoration periods. Evening digital curfews protect sleep by eliminating pre-bedtime screen exposure. Weekend digital sabbaticals provide extended recovery from accumulated weekly demands. These structured rhythms prevent chronic depletion by ensuring regular restoration. The restoration pathway operates as both prevention and intervention. Proactive restoration practices prevent attention fatigue from accumulating. Intervention applications involve intensive restoration following periods of excessive digital demands.

3.3 Emotional Regulation Strategies in Digital Contexts

Emotional regulation strategies help individuals manage the emotional challenges inherent in digital engagement. Cognitive reappraisal involves reinterpreting digital experiences to modify their emotional impact. Users reframe social media content as curated highlights rather than comprehensive reality. This perspective shift reduces the sting of upward comparisons. Reappraising notification urgency as constructed rather than inherent reduces response pressure (Gross, 2015). Acceptance-based strategies involve acknowledging negative emotions without attempting to suppress or avoid them. Users notice feelings of FOMO, inadequacy, or anxiety without reacting reflexively. Acceptance creates space between emotional experience and behavioral response. This gap enables choice rather than automatic checking or scrolling. Acceptance and Commitment Therapy principles apply effectively to digital contexts (Levin et al., 2017).

Self-compassion practices counteract the harsh self-criticism often triggered by digital experiences. Users treat themselves with kindness when experiencing digital-related distress. Self-compassion involves recognizing that struggles with technology are common human experiences. It replaces self-judgment with understanding and patience. Research demonstrates that self-compassion buffers negative effects of social media use on well-being (Yang, 2016). Boundary-setting represents a practical emotional regulation strategy addressing environmental factors. Users establish rules governing when, where, and how they engage with technology. Physical boundaries include device-free zones like bedrooms and dining areas. Temporal boundaries specify times when digital devices remain off or silenced. Social boundaries involve negotiated norms with family and colleagues about response expectations (Mattern et al., 2017).

Digital decluttering reduces emotional demands by simplifying the digital environment. Users unfollow accounts that consistently trigger negative emotions. They unsubscribe from unnecessary email lists and turn off non-essential notifications. App deletion removes temptation sources from immediate access. These environmental modifications reduce exposure to triggers rather than relying solely on willpower (Newport, 2019). Emotional regulation strategy selection depends on contextual factors. Some situations call for acceptance while others benefit from active problem-solving. Flexible deployment of diverse strategies characterizes effective emotional regulation. Users develop personalized toolkits drawing from multiple approaches. They experiment to identify which strategies work best for their specific challenges and contexts.

3.4 Role of Autonomy and Meaning

Autonomy in digital engagement involves aligning technology use with personal values and self-determined goals. Ryan and Deci (2000) posit that autonomy constitutes a fundamental human necessity for optimal functioning. Digital environments often undermine autonomy through design features that exploit psychological vulnerabilities. Infinite scroll, autoplay, and variable rewards hijack agency by making disengagement difficult. Users experience their behavior as externally controlled rather than self-directed. Values clarification helps individuals identify what matters most in their lives. Reflective exercises prompt consideration of how technology use supports or undermines core values. A person valuing family connection might recognize that smartphone use during family time contradicts this value. This awareness creates motivation for behavior change rooted in authentic priorities rather than external pressure (Deci & Ryan, 2012).

Intentional technology use flows from clear purpose rather than habit or impulse. Users ask themselves why they are reaching for devices before doing so. They distinguish between purposeful use aligned with goals and mindless scrolling filling empty time. Purposeful use includes activities like connecting with distant loved ones, learning new skills, or accomplishing work tasks. Mindless use provides temporary escape without advancing meaningful objectives. Meaning making involves interpreting digital experiences within broader life narratives. Users consider how their digital behaviors contribute to or detract from the life they want to create. Digital activities that support growth, connection, and contribution enhance meaning. Those that merely pass time without enrichment diminish it. This evaluative process guides adjustments toward more meaningful engagement patterns (Martela & Steger, 2016). Goal setting translates values and meaning into concrete behavioral targets. Specific, measurable goals provide direction for behavior change. A goal might specify reducing social media use to 30 minutes daily or scheduling device-free dinners three nights weekly. Implementation intentions link goals to contextual cues. Users plan exactly when and where they will engage in desired behaviors.

Autonomy support from social environments facilitates self-determined digital use. Family members and colleagues can create norms that encourage rather than undermine healthy boundaries. Organizational policies that respect non-work time enable employees to disconnect without career penalties. These external supports align with rather than contradict individual autonomy efforts (Derks et al., 2015). The autonomy pathway addresses motivation for resilience-building behaviors. When individuals connect digital changes to core values and meaningful goals, sustained behavior change becomes more likely. External mandates or fear-based motivations produce temporary compliance that fades. Autonomous motivation generates commitment that persists through challenges and setbacks.

3.5 Emotional Resilience as Mediator

Emotional resilience functions as a critical mediating variable between digital engagement and life satisfaction. Bajaj and Pande (2016) illustrate that resilience mechanisms determine why certain individuals flourish under high digital demands, whereas others experience distress even with limited exposure. The mediation model proposes that digital exposure affects life satisfaction indirectly through its impact on emotional resilience. Excessive or poorly managed digital engagement depletes resilience by exhausting attentional resources, disrupting sleep, and displacing restorative activities. Depleted resilience then impairs life satisfaction through reduced capacity to manage stressors and maintain positive functioning. Conversely, well-managed digital use paired with resilience practices maintains or enhances resilience capacity (Schäfer et al., 2024).

Partial mediation acknowledges that both direct and indirect pathways operate simultaneously. Digital engagement exerts direct effects on life satisfaction through mechanisms like sleep disruption while also operating indirectly through resilience. Statistical modeling tests whether the relationship between digital exposure and life satisfaction weakens when controlling for resilience, indicating that resilience explains part of this relationship (MacKinnon et al., 2007). Resilience components contribute differentially to mediation effects. Attention restoration primarily addresses cognitive pathways while emotional regulation targets affective processes. Both contribute to overall resilience that buffers against digital stressors. Comprehensive interventions targeting multiple resilience components likely produce stronger mediation effects than single-focus approaches.

Individual differences moderate the strength of mediation pathways. Personality traits like neuroticism may amplify vulnerability to resilience depletion from digital stressors. Age, gender, and cultural background also shape mediation processes. Understanding these moderators helps identify populations most likely to benefit from specific interventions. The practical implication involves targeting resilience as a leverage point for interventions. Rather than attempting to eliminate digital exposure, interventions can strengthen resilience to buffer its negative effects. This approach proves more realistic given the essential role of technology in modern life. Resilience mediation suggests that life satisfaction improvements may lag-behind behavior change. Building resilience takes time and consistent practice. Patience and persistence prove necessary as resilience capacity gradually strengthens.

Table 1. Pathways Linking Digital Engagement, Emotional Resilience, and Life Satisfaction

Digital Exposure Factor	Cognitive/Emotional Challenge	Resilience Mechanism (Intervention)	Expected Life Satisfaction Outcome
Screen-time overload	Attention fatigue, irritability, cognitive depletion	Attention restoration practices (scheduled breaks, nature exposure, mindfulness meditation)	Improved focus and concentration, reduced mental exhaustion, enhanced productivity
Social media comparison	Envy, low self-worth, inadequacy feelings, unstable mood	Self-compassion practices, values clarification, reframing cognitions	Healthier self-regard, stable self-worth, reduced social anxiety
Information overload	Anxiety, decision paralysis, overwhelm, processing difficulties	Mindfulness training, prioritization skills, boundary-setting protocols	Lower stress levels, greater mental clarity, improved decision quality
Algorithmic echo chambers	Narrow worldview, heightened reactivity, confirmation bias	Critical digital literacy, intentional diverse content curation, perspective-taking	Greater autonomy, balanced perspective, intellectual openness
24/7 connectivity	Role strain, work-life conflict, relationship tension, chronic stress	Digital boundaries, negotiated norms with others, communication agreements	Better work-life balance, relational satisfaction, reduced burnout
Notification interruptions	Fragmented attention, task-switching costs, reduced flow states	Notification management, batching communications, designated focus times	Enhanced task completion, deeper engagement, satisfaction with accomplishments
Passive consumption	Boredom, emptiness, time displacement, motivation loss	Intentional use planning, alternative activity scheduling, value-aligned goals	Increased purpose, meaningful time use, intrinsic motivation
Online conflict exposure	Vicarious trauma, emotional exhaustion, compassion fatigue	Selective disengagement, self-care routines, emotional boundaries	Emotional stability, preserved empathy, psychological protection

Note: The table grounds the proposed pathways in the theoretical work of Kaplan (1995) on attention, Ryan and Deci (2000) on autonomy, and Gross (2015) on emotion regulation. Each pathway represents a testable mediation model, where the resilience mechanisms buffer negative effects of digital exposure on life satisfaction outcomes.

4. CROSS-CULTURAL DYNAMICS OF DIGITAL HEALTH AND EMOTIONAL RESILIENCE

4.1 Individualist vs. Collectivist Orientations in Digital Engagement and Coping

Cultural orientations fundamentally shape how individuals experience and respond to digital challenges. Individualist cultures prioritize personal autonomy, independence, and self-expression, manifesting in digital behaviors emphasizing personal branding, self-disclosure, and individual achievement displays (Hofstede, 2001). Social media use centers on self-promotion and personal identity construction, with users curating profiles highlighting unique qualities and accomplishments.

Collectivist cultures emphasize interdependence, group harmony, and social obligations. Digital engagement serves relational maintenance and group cohesion more than self-expression. Social media facilitates fulfilling family duties and maintaining in-group connections (Kim et al., 2011). Posts often feature family activities, group celebrations, and collective achievements rather than individual showcasing. Coping strategies differ systematically across cultural orientations. Individualist approaches emphasize personal control, problem-focused coping, and self-reliance. Individuals facing digital stress seek personal solutions through boundary-setting, app deletion, or individual therapy, with responsibility for managing digital well-being resting primarily with the individual (Morling et al., 2002).

Collectivist coping involves seeking social support, maintaining harmony, and accommodating to circumstances. Individuals consult family members about digital challenges and seek collective solutions. Extended family involvement in decision-making extends to technology use patterns, with parental and elder guidance shaping youth digital engagement more substantially than in individualist contexts. Group norms establish acceptable technology use rather than purely individual preferences.

Emotional expression norms influence how digital stress manifests across cultures. Individualist cultures generally permit and encourage emotional expression, including negative emotions. Users freely share frustrations, anxieties, and distress online, facilitating recognition of digital-related problems. Collectivist cultures emphasize emotional restraint to preserve group harmony, with individuals suppressing distress expressions to avoid burdening others or disrupting relationships (Butler et al., 2007). The concept of face (*mianzi* in Chinese, *izzat* in Hindi/Urdu) shapes digital behavior in collectivist contexts. Face involves social standing, reputation, and dignity within one's community. Digital actions reflect on family and community, not merely individuals, creating strong motivation for careful impression management as social media missteps threaten collective face (Qi, 2011). Help-seeking patterns reflect cultural orientations. Individualist contexts normalize professional mental health support for digital-related distress through therapy, coaching, and self-help resources. Collectivist contexts prioritize informal support from family, friends, and community elders, with professional help-seeking potentially carrying stigma suggesting family inadequacy.

4.2 Family, Community, and Social Roles in Collectivist Digital Resilience

Family systems in collectivist societies provide both protective factors and unique stressors regarding digital engagement. Extended families sharing living spaces create natural limitations on private digital use. Family members monitor each other's technology engagement, providing informal regulation that prevents extreme isolation or excessive use through social accountability. However, this may also limit personal autonomy and create intergenerational conflicts (Mesch, 2006). Intergenerational relationships shape digital resilience through transmission of values and practices. Elders maintaining traditional practices model alternatives to digital immersion. Grandparents teaching yoga, cooking, or crafts provide restorative activities for youth, while family rituals around meals, prayer, and festivals create device-free connection opportunities. These traditions buffer against digital displacement of meaningful activities.

Community embeddedness creates social capital supporting digital resilience. Neighbors, religious congregations, and local associations provide face-to-face interaction and practical support. Community festivals, temple visits, and neighborhood gatherings offer regular offline engagement, reducing dependence on digital platforms for social needs. Strong community ties correlate with lower problematic technology use in collectivist contexts (Srite & Karahanna, 2006). Social role expectations influence digital behavior patterns distinctively in collectivist societies. Gender roles shape access to and use of technology, with traditional expectations potentially limiting women's independent digital engagement while granting men greater freedom. Age-based hierarchies establish elder authority over youth technology use.

Filial piety obligations create unique digital dynamics in Asian collectivist cultures. Adult children maintain frequent digital contact with aging parents to fulfill duty expectations. Cheng and Chan (2006) note that while digital tools facilitate remote caregiving, they can also exacerbate role strain when balanced against professional and personal responsibilities.

Workplace relationships in collectivist contexts emphasize harmony and hierarchy. Senior colleagues expect responsiveness reflecting respect and dedication, making individual boundary-setting difficult. Refusing after-hours work communication risks appearing uncommitted or disrespectful. Team members coordinate digital availability norms collectively rather than setting purely individual boundaries. Community-based interventions prove particularly effective in collectivist contexts. Group programs addressing digital wellness leverage existing social structures. Religious organizations hosting digital detox retreats align interventions with trusted institutions, while schools engaging parents and extended family in youth digital literacy programs acknowledge collective responsibility (Christopher et al., 2014).

4.3 Indian Contexts: Rural-Urban Contrasts and Youth Navigation

India presents remarkable diversity in digital adoption patterns reflecting geography, socioeconomic status, and generational factors. Urban centers like Mumbai, Delhi, and Bangalore exhibit high smartphone penetration and intensive social media use, with middle and upper-class urban youth facing challenges like Western contexts including screen time, social comparison, and information overload (Arora, 2019).

Rural India demonstrates different patterns shaped by infrastructure limitations and traditional lifestyles. Internet access remains inconsistent, with smartphones representing shared family resources rather than individual possessions. Digital engagement occurs in concentrated bursts rather than continuous connectivity, while agricultural rhythms and community activities provide natural breaks from technology. The digital divide creates disparate experiences. Urban privileged youth navigate abundance and choice overload, while rural and economically disadvantaged youth face access barriers and digital literacy gaps, compounding existing socioeconomic inequalities.

Indian youth demonstrate remarkable adaptability navigating emerging digital infrastructures. Rangaswamy and Cutrell (2012) observe that youth employ *jugaad* (frugal innovation) to navigate resource constraints through strategies like device sharing and data optimization. Language diversity shapes Indian digital experiences distinctively. English-dominant platforms create access barriers for regional language speakers, while the rise of vernacular content expands inclusion but increases family tensions when elders cannot navigate English-language devices.

Education system pressures intensify youth digital stress in urban India. Competitive examinations and career anxieties drive intensive online learning platform use, while educational technology companies market products promising competitive advantages (Deb et al., 2015). Traditional joint family structures persist even in urban contexts, creating unique digital dynamics. Privacy expectations differ from Western nuclear family norms, with shared devices limiting personal digital boundaries. However, constant family presence provides natural monitoring and support, with collective decision-making about technology purchases remaining common.

4.4 Indigenous and Indian Knowledge Systems as Resilience Resources

Yoga represents an ancient Indian system offering comprehensive digital resilience resources. *Asana* (physical postures) address sedentary behavior consequences from extended screen time. Regular practice improves posture, reduces musculoskeletal pain, and increases physical activity. *Pranayama* (breath control) regulates stress physiology activated by digital demands. Specific techniques like alternate nostril breathing balance autonomic nervous system activity (Streeter et al., 2012). *Dharana* (concentration) develops sustained attention capacity depleted by multitasking. *Dhyana* (meditation) cultivates present-moment awareness opposing digital distraction. Regular practice strengthens metacognitive awareness about attentional state and digital impulses.

Dharmic perspectives from Hindu, Buddhist, and Jain philosophies offer frameworks for understanding digital challenges. The concept of *maya* (illusion) applies to curated social media realities. Recognizing digital presentations as constructed rather than authentic reduces comparison distress. Teachings on attachment and detachment address compulsive technology use. Practicing *aparigraha* (non-possessiveness) counters consumer culture pressures intensified through digital marketing (Chapple, 2009). The principle of *dharma* (righteous duty) provides ethical guidelines for technology use. Users evaluate whether digital behaviors align with their duties toward self, family, and society. This framework emphasizes responsibility alongside rights. Digital engagement that neglects family duties or personal health violates dharma. This perspective motivates moderation through ethical rather than merely practical considerations (Menon, 2014).

Karma yoga philosophy presents action without attachment to outcomes. This approach addresses anxiety about digital metrics like likes, shares, and follower counts. Practitioners engage authentically without fixating on validation measures. The teaching that one controls effort but not results reduces performance anxiety in digital spaces. This detachment protects against self-worth dependence on external feedback (Bhagavad Gita, 2000). Ayurvedic principles of balance and rhythm inform healthy technology integration. The concepts of *dinacharya* (daily routine) and *ritucharya* (seasonal routine) emphasize regular patterns. Applying these principles to digital engagement creates sustainable rhythms. Morning and evening practices bookend the day with offline activities. Seasonal variations in technology use align with natural cycles (Lad, 2002).

Guru-shishya (teacher-student) relationships model in-person knowledge transmission. This tradition emphasizes embodied learning and relationship-based education. The value placed on direct human connection counters digital mediation of all relationships. Respect for elder wisdom encourages consulting experienced guides rather than relying solely on online information (Saraswathi, 1999).

4.5 Cultural Variability in Life Satisfaction and Well-Being Concepts

Western models of life satisfaction emphasize individual happiness, personal achievement, and subjective well-being, assessing whether people feel satisfied with their own lives. These frameworks assume a universal preference for positive affect and fulfillment, reflected in measures focused on personal happiness and satisfaction (Diener et al., 1985). In contrast, collectivist cultures conceptualize well-being in relational terms—through social harmony, role fulfillment, and family prosperity. Individual satisfaction is secondary to collective welfare; one may experience well-being through family success or social cohesion despite personal dissatisfaction. Western-developed measures often fail to capture these relational dimensions (Uchida et al., 2004).

Indian philosophical traditions further challenge hedonic assumptions. Well-being is associated with eudaimonic goals such as self-realization (*atma-bodha*) and liberation (*moksha*), while pleasure is viewed as transient. Enduring contentment arises from spiritual development and self-knowledge rather than external circumstances (Salagame, 2013). Relatedly, the concept of *sukha* denotes flourishing and inner ease, whereas *dukha* reflects fundamental dissatisfaction rooted in impermanence. Well-being thus involves transcending suffering through wisdom and practice, not maximizing pleasure.

Social well-being in collectivist settings also includes family honor, social reputation, and community standing. Digital behaviors that enhance or threaten these collective values can significantly affect well-being beyond individual distress. Cultural display rules further shape how well-being is expressed; modesty norms may suppress positive self-reports, creating measurement biases (Kitayama et al., 2000).

Generational change adds complexity, as younger cohorts balance individual aspirations with traditional obligations (Arnett, 2002). Finally, cross-cultural digital well-being research requires culturally sensitive methods—ensuring conceptual equivalence, incorporating qualitative insights, and engaging cultural insiders—to avoid imposing narrow frameworks and to enhance validity (van de Vijver & Leung, 2011).

5. MEASURING DIGITAL EMOTIONAL RESILIENCE AND LIFE SATISFACTION IN GLOBAL MARKETS

5.1 Rationale for Measurement

Measuring digital emotional resilience and life satisfaction serves several critical functions in contemporary global contexts. Accurate measurement helps identify which components of resilience require strengthening, enabling practitioners to design targeted and effective interventions. Without baseline assessment across key domains, intervention planning and evaluation remain imprecise. Standardized measurement also allows assessment of intervention effectiveness through pre–post comparisons and controlled studies. Policy development similarly relies on reliable population-level data. Governments and institutions addressing digital health challenges require evidence on the prevalence and severity of problems to inform regulation, education, and resource allocation. In workplaces, data on digital strain and recovery patterns support policies around connectivity expectations and employee well-being.

Measurement is also central to responsible digital design. As technology companies face growing pressure to prioritize user well-being, empirical tools are needed to test whether design features—such as notification controls or usage limits—enhance resilience and reduce harm. Evidence-based assessment enables systematic evaluation of design choices rather than reliance on intuition alone (Calvo & Peters, 2014). In global and culturally diverse markets, measurement tools must capture equivalent constructs across populations. Universal instruments risk imposing culturally specific assumptions, particularly Western models of well-being. Culturally adapted measures balance local relevance with cross-cultural comparability, strengthening both validity and generalizability (van de Vijver & Leung, 2011).

Scientific progress in digital health research further depends on standardized, psychometrically validated instruments. Shared measurement frameworks enable replication, comparison, and meta-analysis, supporting cumulative knowledge building (Hinkin, 1998). Finally, structured measurement benefits individuals by promoting self-awareness, tracking change over time, and supporting autonomous efforts to improve digital well-being.

5.2 Multidimensional Measurement Model

The proposed measurement framework encompasses five interconnected constructs representing key dimensions of digital emotional resilience and life satisfaction. This multidimensional approach acknowledges that no single indicator adequately captures the complexity of digital well-being. Comprehensive assessment requires examining attention, emotion, autonomy, resilience, and satisfaction domains simultaneously (Ryff, 1989).

Attention Quality

Attention quality reflects cognitive functioning essential for productive engagement and well-being. Sustained focus measures the ability to maintain concentration on chosen tasks without distraction. Users experiencing high attention quality complete work efficiently without frequent interruptions. Task completion rates provide behavioral indicators of attention capacity. Attentional fatigue represents the depletion of directed attention resources through sustained use. Individuals report difficulty in concentrating, increased distractibility, and mental exhaustion. Attention restoration opportunities replenish these depleted resources. Kaplan and Berman (2010) argue that assessment must evaluate both current attentional states and restorative capacity. This approach accounts for the significant temporal fluctuations inherent in cognitive functioning.

Emotional Regulation

Emotional regulation encompasses strategies for managing affect and maintaining psychological equilibrium. Affect balance compares the frequency and intensity of positive versus negative emotions. Individuals with strong regulation maintain relatively stable positive affect despite stressors. Recovery time measures how quickly individuals return to baseline after emotional disturbances (Gross & John, 2003). Regulation strategy repertoire reflects the diversity of approaches individuals employ. Adaptive regulation involves flexible strategy selection based on context. Assessment examines both strategy knowledge and actual implementation.

Digital Autonomy

Digital autonomy captures perceived control over technology use and boundary effectiveness. Individuals with high autonomy experience technology as serving their goals rather than controlling them, feeling capable of limiting use when desired and maintaining established limits despite temptation or external pressure. Autonomous motivation versus controlled motivation distinguishes self-determined from pressured technology use. Users may engage because they genuinely value activities or because they feel obligated. Value-aligned use supports well-being while obligated use creates resentment. The successful enforcement of boundaries serves as behavioural proof of autonomy. Ryan and Deci (2017) note that gaps between intended and actual usage highlight a lack of control.

Resilience Capacity

Resilience is the adaptive capacity to navigate digital stressors, characterized by the "bounce-back" ability to recover quickly from setbacks and the flexibility to deploy diverse coping strategies. Beyond mere recovery, this process often involves meaning making, where individuals transform adversity into opportunities for post-traumatic growth by deriving lessons from their experiences (Southwick et al., 2014). Effective resilience also relies on mobilizing social support and drawing upon personal values or spirituality to maintain psychological equilibrium. Social support mobilization reflects capacity to access and utilize interpersonal resources. Connor and Davidson (2003) identify spirituality and personal value systems as fundamental components of psychological resilience.

Life Satisfaction

Life satisfaction represents the ultimate outcome reflecting overall well-being and flourishing. Purpose involves experiencing meaning and direction in life. Social connection quality encompasses relationship depth, trust, and mutual support. Sense of progress reflects perceiving growth and advancement toward goals. Ryff and Keyes (1995) define balance as the harmonious integration of diverse life domains, such as work, health, and leisure. Domain-specific satisfaction complements global life satisfaction assessment. Cultural values shape which domains matter most for life satisfaction.

5.3 Methodological Approaches

Self-Report Scales

Self-report instruments provide accessible and efficient measurement suitable for large samples. Existing validated scales measure related constructs requiring adaptation for digital contexts. The Connor-Davidson Resilience Scale (CD-RISC) assesses general resilience capacity through items about coping and adaptation. Following the logic of Connor and Davidson (2003), specific iterations should directly reference the unique pressures of the digital environment. Ryff's (1989) Psychological Well-Being Scales operationalize eudaimonic well-being through six dimensions. Purpose in life, personal growth, autonomy, environmental mastery, positive relations, and self-acceptance align well with life satisfaction conceptualization. The Satisfaction with Life Scale (SWLS) provides global satisfaction assessment through five items. Its brevity facilitates repeated measurement (Diener et al., 1985).

Structural Equation Modeling

Structural Equation Modeling (SEM) enables testing the integrated conceptual model presented in Figure 1. This approach examines multiple relationships simultaneously rather than in isolation. Measurement models specify how observed indicators relate to latent constructs. Structural models test hypothesized pathways between constructs (Kline, 2015). Mediation analysis investigates whether resilience mechanisms explain relationships between digital exposure and life satisfaction. Statistical tests determine if indirect effects through mediators are significant. Moderation analysis examines whether cultural context or individual differences alter pathway strengths. Interaction terms test whether relationships vary across groups (Hayes, 2017).

Longitudinal SEM tracks changes over time and tests directional hypotheses. Cross-lagged panel models examine reciprocal relationships between variables. These designs provide stronger causal inference than cross-sectional approaches. Growth curve models characterize developmental trajectories across extended periods. Random intercepts capture individual differences in baseline levels (Little, 2013).

Cross-Cultural Adaptation and Validation

Cultural adaptation extends beyond simple translation to ensure conceptual equivalence. Translation-back-translation procedures verify meaning preservation across languages. Bilingual experts review translations for accuracy and naturalness. Cognitive interviews with target population members identify comprehension problems. Construct equivalence examination tests whether scales measure the same constructs across cultures. Configural invariance requires the same factor structure across groups. Metric invariance demands equivalent factor loadings. Scalar invariance necessitates equivalent item intercepts. Sequential testing determines the level of equivalence achieved (Vandenberg & Lance, 2000).

Culture-specific item development adds indicators relevant to contexts. Indian samples might include items about dharma, family duty, or spiritual practice. Indigenous samples could reference community rituals or traditional practices. These culturally specific indicators enrich understanding beyond universal frameworks (Cheung et al., 2011).

5.4 Integration of Quantitative and Qualitative Approaches

Mixed-methods research combines quantitative and qualitative strengths. Quantitative methods enable statistical analysis and generalization through standardized assessment. Qualitative methods capture contextual understanding and live experiences. Integration produces richer insights than either approach alone.

Narratives of digital burnout provide detailed accounts of how exhaustion develops over time. Individuals describe specific triggers, accumulation patterns, and tipping points, revealing mechanisms in natural contexts. Thematic analysis identifies common patterns across diverse narratives, while recovery narratives document helpful strategies and obstacles encountered.

Sequential mixed methods designs use one phase to inform the next. Initial qualitative interviews generate items for quantitative scale development, while survey results identify subgroups for in-depth follow-up. This iteration refines understanding through multiple cycles. Convergent designs collect both data types simultaneously for triangulation (Fetters et al., 2013).

Experience sampling methods combine quantitative repeated measurement with qualitative context capture. Participants complete brief smartphone surveys multiple times daily, providing quantitative ratings of affect, attention, and satisfaction alongside open-ended responses about activities and thoughts. This reveals within-person dynamics across situations (Csikszentmihalyi & Larson, 2014).

Participatory approaches involve community members in research design and interpretation, ensuring cultural appropriateness and practical relevance. This partnership produces actionable knowledge addressing real community needs (Israel et al., 2013).

Table 2. Proposed Measurement Framework for Digital Emotional Resilience and Life Satisfaction

Construct	Example Indicators	Possible Measures/Methods	Psychometric Considerations
Attention Quality	• Sustained focus duration • Task completion rates • Perceived cognitive clarity • Mental sharpness vs. fogginess • Distractibility frequency	• Experience-sampling of focus states • Attentional Fatigue Scale • Sustained Attention to Response Task (SART) • Self-report concentration items • Objective task performance metrics	• Test-retest reliability across time • Convergent validity with cognitive tests • Sensitivity to restoration interventions • Cultural equivalence in subjective clarity
Emotional Regulation	• Frequency of negative affect • Intensity of emotional reactions • Recovery time after distress • Strategy repertoire diversity • Affect balance ratios	• DERS subscales (awareness, clarity, acceptance) • PANAS positive/negative affect • Emotion Regulation Questionnaire (ERQ) • Daily affect diaries • Recovery time self-monitoring	• Internal consistency of subscales • Discriminant validity from general distress • Responsiveness to regulation training • Cross-cultural display rule considerations
Digital Autonomy	• Perceived control over usage • Boundary efficacy beliefs • Value-aligned use frequency • Discrepancy: intended vs. actual use • Self-determination in engagement	• Perceived autonomy scales adapted for digital contexts • Digital self-control items • Autonomous vs. controlled motivation items • Objective usage tracking (screen time) • Boundary implementation logs	• Convergent validity with actual usage data • Predictive validity for behavior change • Test-retest across implementation periods • Cultural autonomy conceptualizations
Resilience Capacity	• Coping flexibility across situations • Meaning-making from stress • Bounce-back ability/ recovery • Social support mobilization • Post-adversity growth	• CD-RISC (Connor-Davidson Resilience Scale) • Brief Resilience Scale • Narrative coding of coping strategies • Meaning in Life Questionnaire • Social support scales	• Factor structure validation • Concurrent validity with stress outcomes • Longitudinal stability vs. malleability • Indigenous resilience concept inclusion

continued on following page

Table 2. Continued

Construct	Example Indicators	Possible Measures/Methods	Psychometric Considerations
Life Satisfaction	• Sense of purpose/ meaning • Quality of social connections • Progress toward goals • Domain balance (work-life-health) • Environmental mastery	• Ryff PWB subscales (6 dimensions) • SWLS (Satisfaction with Life Scale) • Domain-specific satisfaction items • Purpose in Life Test • Relationship quality scales	• Structural validity of multidimensional model • Measurement invariance across cultures • Sensitivity to life changes • Eudaimonic vs. hedonic components
Digital Exposure (predictor)	• Screen time duration • Notification frequency • Social media intensity • Multitasking patterns • Passive vs. active use	• Objective tracking apps (Rescue Time, Moment) • Social Media Intensity Scale • Digital Multitasking Inventory • Usage logs and analytics • Self-report estimates	• Accuracy of self-report vs. objective • Device-specific vs. total exposure • Context-dependent measurement • Privacy and ethical considerations

Notes: Structural equation modeling tests mediation pathways from digital exposure through attention and emotion to resilience and life satisfaction, with cultural moderation. Longitudinal designs capture change trajectories and reciprocal influences. All measures require cross-cultural validation ensuring conceptual equivalence. Mixed methods combine quantitative scores with qualitative narratives for contextual depth.

Measurement Recommendations: Use multiple methods for triangulation, including self-report, objective measures, and qualitative data. Assess both momentary states and dispositional traits. Culturally adapt instruments while maintaining psychometric rigor. Balance comprehensiveness with participant burden. Establish population norms across diverse groups and develop digital platforms for efficient large-scale data collection.

6. BUILDING HUMAN-CENTERED DIGITAL ECOSYSTEMS: INTERVENTIONS AND FUTURE DIRECTIONS

6.1 Individual-Level Practices

Individual-level interventions empower users to cultivate digital emotional resilience through accessible practices. Mindfulness training provides foundational skills for managing digital demands, with brief daily meditation practices strengthening attention control and emotional regulation capacities (Schäfer et al., 2024).

Focused attention meditation develops sustained concentration despite distractions, while open monitoring meditation cultivates awareness of digital impulses before acting on them.

Attention restoration routines integrate restorative experiences into daily schedules. Morning nature walks before digital engagement prime attention resources. Micro-breaks every 30 minutes during screen work prevent cumulative fatigue. Evening wind-down routines excluding screens for 60-90 minutes before sleep protect circadian rhythms. Digital detox practices range from brief disconnections to extended sabbaticals. Weekly technology-free evenings create guaranteed offline time with family, while monthly 24-hour digital fasts provide intensive recovery experiences.

Emotion regulation skills specifically address digital contexts shaped by algorithmic mechanisms. Cognitive reappraisal techniques reframe social media content as curated highlights rather than comprehensive reality, while acceptance practices acknowledge FOMO feelings without reactive checking (Yuan et al., 2025). Self-compassion practices counter harsh self-judgment triggered by digital comparisons, helping users treat themselves kindly when experiencing inadequacy feelings. Implementation intentions translate general goals into specific action plans, specifying exactly when, where, and how individuals will engage in resilience practices.

6.2 Managerial Decision Frameworks and KPIs

Organizations require evidence-based frameworks and key performance indicators (KPIs) that balance commercial objectives with user well-being in digital environments. Traditional engagement metrics—such as time-on-site, click-through rates, and daily active users—fail to capture whether digital interactions enhance or diminish consumer psychological health and life satisfaction. Emerging well-being-centered KPIs include engagement quality indices that measure meaningful interactions relative to passive consumption, attention restoration ratios tracking restorative versus depleting digital experiences, and emotional balance scores assessing positive-to-negative affect during platform use.

Customer lifetime value (CLV) calculations must evolve beyond transactional revenue projections to incorporate well-being sustainability metrics, recognizing that depleted, burned-out consumers exhibit reduced long-term loyalty and advocacy (Mandania et al., 2025). Well-being return on investment (ROI) frameworks quantify how ethical design features—such as usage reminders, customizable notification controls, and digital detox support tools—impact both consumer satisfaction and business outcomes including retention rates, brand reputation, and reduced churn in competitive global markets.

Design heuristics for ethical platform development translate well-being principles into actionable guidelines for product teams and marketing strategists. Core heuristics include: (1) autonomy preservation—ensuring users maintain control over their engagement through transparent settings and easy opt-out mechanisms; (2) attention respect—minimizing exploitative design patterns like infinite scroll and auto-play that bypass conscious choice; (3) emotional safety—implementing content moderation and algorithmic fairness to reduce harm from social comparison and discriminatory targeting; and (4) cultural responsiveness—adapting platform features to diverse values across multicultural marketplaces, recognizing that individualist and collectivist orientations require differentiated approaches to privacy, sharing, and community engagement (Tarnanidis et al., 2026). Managerial decision frameworks must integrate cross-functional collaboration between marketing, user experience design, data science, and consumer psychology teams, establishing governance structures that audit algorithmic systems for well-being impacts alongside performance metrics (Ghasemaghaei & Kordzadeh, 2025).

6.3 Organizational-Level Strategies

Organizations shape digital experiences through design decisions, policies, and cultural norms. Ethical platform design prioritizes user well-being alongside engagement metrics through features supporting autonomy including accessible usage statistics, customizable notification controls, and prominent logout options. Design elements reducing addictive potential involve eliminating infinite scroll, removing autoplay defaults, and creating natural stopping points.

Workplace policies addressing digital overload protect employee well-being and productivity in post-pandemic contexts (Abidi et al., 2023). Right-to-disconnect legislation prohibits after-hours work communication expectations. Email-free time blocks during workdays enable deep focus periods. Meeting-free days reduce scheduling fragmentation and Zoom fatigue, while well-being programs incorporate digital health education and support. Leadership modeling proves critical for policy effectiveness—when executives demonstrate healthy boundaries, employees feel permission to do likewise. Physical workspace design influences digital engagement patterns through designated device-free zones, standing desks, and natural elements providing passive restoration.

6.4 Market and Policy Implications

The digital economy currently prioritizes engagement metrics that misalign with user welfare, creating market pressure for fundamental shifts toward well-being metrics. Platforms could measure user satisfaction, life balance maintenance, and purpose alignment through validated assessment tools integrated into platforms. Regulatory frameworks protect citizens from predatory digital design through attention protection legislation mandating transparency about persuasive techniques employed and age-appropriate design codes restricting manipulative features. Governance structures involving multiple stakeholders—technology companies, researchers, policymakers, and civil society organizations—collaborate on standards development with independent audits verifying ethical compliance.

6.5 Cross-Cultural Implementation and Future Directions

Intervention effectiveness depends on cultural appropriateness and local adaptation. Collectivist societies may respond better to group-based programs than individual therapy, while family-inclusive interventions acknowledge relational contexts shaping technology use (Sheng et al., 2025). Materials require translation into local languages with culturally relevant examples. Traditional practices provide indigenous resilience resources—yoga and meditation already embed within Indian cultural contexts, while community festivals offer established offline engagement opportunities.

Future research priorities include longitudinal studies tracking digital engagement and well-being across extended periods, integration with neuroscience approaches illuminating biological mechanisms, and intervention optimization identifying active ingredients and optimal delivery parameters. Emerging technologies including virtual reality and artificial intelligence present both challenges and opportunities requiring proactive research on algorithmic curation impacts on well-being (Metzler & Garcia, 2023).

6.6 Conclusion

Digital health and emotional resilience represent necessary foundations for unlocking life satisfaction in global digital markets. Emotional resilience emerges as the critical mediating factor explaining individual differences in digital well-being outcomes. Building human-centered digital ecosystems requires sustained commitment from multiple stakeholders: individuals cultivating resilience practices, organizations prioritizing ethical design, and policymakers establishing protective regulatory frameworks. By integrating evidence-based interventions and building ethical digital ecosystems that respect cultural diversity, global markets can support genuine human flourishing in the digital age.

REFERENCES

Abidi, N., Herradi, M. E., & Sakha, S. (2023). Digitalization and resilience during the COVID-19 pandemic. *Telecommunications Policy*, *47*(4), 102522. DOI: 10.1016/j.telpol.2023.102522 PMID: 37051116

Arnett, J. J. (2002). The psychology of globalization. *The American Psychologist*, *57*(10), 774–783. DOI: 10.1037/0003-066X.57.10.774 PMID: 12369500

Arora, P. (2019). *The next billion users: Digital life beyond the West*. Harvard University Press. DOI: 10.4159/9780674238879

Bajaj, B., & Pande, N. (2016). Mediating role of resilience in the impact of mindfulness on life satisfaction and affect as indices of subjective well-being. *Personality and Individual Differences*, *93*, 63–67. DOI: 10.1016/j.paid.2015.09.005

Bandura, A. (1997). Self-efficacy: The exercise of control. *The Freeman.*

Büchi, M. (2024). Digital well-being theory and research. *New Media & Society*, *26*(1), 172–189. DOI: 10.1177/14614448211056851

Butler, E. A., Lee, T. L., & Gross, J. J. (2007). Emotion regulation and culture: Are the social consequences of emotion suppression culture-specific? *Emotion (Washington, D.C.)*, *7*(1), 30–48. DOI: 10.1037/1528-3542.7.1.30 PMID: 17352561

Calvo, R. A., & Peters, D. (2014). *Positive computing: Technology for wellbeing and human potential*. MIT Press. DOI: 10.7551/mitpress/9764.001.0001

Chapple, C. K. (2009). *Yoga and the luminous: Patañjali's spiritual path to freedom*. State University of New York Press.

Cheng, S. T., & Chan, A. C. M. (2006). Filial piety and psychological well-being in well older Chinese. *The Journals of Gerontology. Series B, Psychological Sciences and Social Sciences*, *61*(5), 262–P269. DOI: 10.1093/geronb/61.5.P262 PMID: 16960229

Cheung, F. M., van de Vijver, F. J. R., & Leong, F. T. L. (2011). Toward a new approach to the study of personality in culture. *The American Psychologist*, *66*(7), 593–603. DOI: 10.1037/a0022389 PMID: 21261408

Christopher, J. C., Wendt, D. C., Marecek, J., & Goodman, D. M. (2014). Critical cultural awareness: Contributions to a globalizing psychology. *The American Psychologist*, *69*(7), 645–655. DOI: 10.1037/a0036851 PMID: 24841336

Connor, K. M., & Davidson, J. R. (2003). Development of a new resilience scale: The Connor-Davidson Resilience Scale (CD-RISC). *Depression and Anxiety*, *18*(2), 76–82. DOI: 10.1002/da.10113 PMID: 12964174

Csikszentmihalyi, M., & Larson, R. (2014). Validity and reliability of the experience-sampling method. In Csikszentmihalyi, M. (Ed.), *Flow and the foundations of positive psychology* (pp. 35–54). Springer., DOI: 10.1007/978-94-017-9088-8_3

Deb, S., Strodl, E., & Sun, J. (2015). Academic stress, parental pressure, anxiety and mental health among Indian high school students. *International Journal of Psychology and Behavioral Sciences*, *5*(1), 26–34.

Deci, E. L., & Ryan, R. M. (2012). Self-determination theory. In Van Lange, P. A. M., Kruglanski, A. W., & Higgins, E. T. (Eds.), *Handbook of theories of social psychology* (pp. 416–436). Sage., DOI: 10.4135/9781446249215.n21

Derks, D., van Duin, D., Tims, M., & Bakker, A. B. (2015). Smartphone use and work–home interference: The moderating role of social norms and employee work engagement. *Journal of Occupational and Organizational Psychology*, *88*(1), 155–177. DOI: 10.1111/joop.12083

Diener, E., Emmons, R. A., Larsen, R. J., & Griffin, S. (1985). The satisfaction with life scale. *Journal of Personality Assessment*, *49*(1), 71–75. DOI: 10.1207/s15327752jpa4901_13 PMID: 16367493

Fetters, M. D., Curry, L. A., & Creswell, J. W. (2013). Achieving integration in mixed methods designs: Principles and practices. *Health Services Research*, *48*(6 Pt 2), 2134–2156. DOI: 10.1111/1475-6773.12117 PMID: 24279835

Firth, J., Torous, J., Stubbs, B., Firth, J. A., Steiner, G. Z., Smith, L., Alvarez-Jimenez, M., Gleeson, J., Vancampfort, D., Armitage, C. J., & Sarris, J. (2019). The "online brain": How the Internet may be changing our cognition. *World Psychiatry; Official Journal of the World Psychiatric Association (WPA)*, *18*(2), 119–129. DOI: 10.1002/wps.20617 PMID: 31059635

Folkman, S., & Moskowitz, J. T. (2004). Coping: Pitfalls and promise. *Annual Review of Psychology*, *55*(1), 745–774. DOI: 10.1146/annurev.psych.55.090902.141456 PMID: 14744233

Ghasemaghaei, M., & Kordzadeh, N. (2025). Ethics in the Age of Algorithms: Unravelling the Impact of Algorithmic Unfairness on Data Analytics Recommendation Acceptance. *Information Systems Journal*, *35*(4), 1166–1197. DOI: 10.1111/isj.12572

Gross, J. J. (1998). The emerging field of emotion regulation: An integrative review. *Review of General Psychology*, *2*(3), 271–299. DOI: 10.1037/1089-2680.2.3.271

Gross, J. J. (2015). Emotion regulation: Current status and future prospects. *Psychological Inquiry*, *26*(1), 1–26. DOI: 10.1080/1047840X.2014.940781

Gross, J. J., & John, O. P. (2003). Individual differences in two emotion regulation processes: Implications for affect, relationships, and well-being. *Journal of Personality and Social Psychology*, *85*(2), 348–362. DOI: 10.1037/0022-3514.85.2.348 PMID: 12916575

Hayes, A. F. (2017). *Introduction to mediation, moderation, and conditional process analysis: A regression-based approach* (2nd ed.). Guilford Press.

Hayes, S. C., Luoma, J. B., Bond, F. W., Masuda, A., & Lillis, J. (2006). Acceptance and commitment therapy: Model, processes and outcomes. *Behaviour Research and Therapy*, *44*(1), 1–25. DOI: 10.1016/j.brat.2005.06.006 PMID: 16300724

Hinkin, T. R. (1998). A brief tutorial on the development of measures for use in survey questionnaires. *Organizational Research Methods*, *1*(1), 104–121. DOI: 10.1177/109442819800100106

Hofstede, G. (2001). *Culture's consequences: Comparing values, behaviors, institutions and organizations across nations* (2nd ed.). Sage.

Israel, B. A., Schulz, A. J., Parker, E. A., Becker, A. B., Allen, A. J., & Guzman, J. R. (2013). Critical issues in developing and following CBPR principles. In Israel, B. A., Eng, E., Schulz, A. J., & Parker, E. A. (Eds.), *Methods for community-based participatory research for health* (2nd ed., pp. 31–55). Jossey-Bass.

Jha, A. P., Morrison, A. B., Dainer-Best, J., Parker, S., Rostrup, N., & Stanley, E. A. (2015). Minds "at attention": Mindfulness training curbs attentional lapses in military cohorts. *PLoS One*, *10*(2), e0116889. DOI: 10.1371/journal.pone.0116889 PMID: 25671579

Kaplan, S. (1995). The restorative benefits of nature: Toward an integrative framework. *Journal of Environmental Psychology*, *15*(3), 169–182. DOI: 10.1016/0272-4944(95)90001-2

Kaplan, S., & Berman, M. G. (2010). Directed attention as a common resource for executive functioning and self-regulation. *Perspectives on Psychological Science : A Journal of the Association for Psychological Science*, *5*(1), 43–57. DOI: 10.1177/1745691609356784 PMID: 26162062

Kim, Y., Sohn, D., & Choi, S. M. (2011). Cultural difference in motivations for using social network sites: A comparative study of American and Korean college students. *Computers in Human Behavior*, *27*(1), 365–372. DOI: 10.1016/j.chb.2010.08.015

Kircaburun, K., Alhabash, S., Tosuntaş, Ş. B., & Griffiths, M. D. (2020). Uses and gratifications of problematic social media use among university students: A simultaneous examination of the Big Five of personality traits, social media platforms, and social media use motives. *International Journal of Mental Health and Addiction, 18*(3), 525–547. DOI: 10.1007/s11469-018-9940-6

Kitayama, S., Markus, H. R., & Kurokawa, M. (2000). Culture, emotion, and well-being: Good feelings in Japan and the United States. *Cognition & Emotion, 14*(1), 93–124. DOI: 10.1080/026999300379003

Kline, R. B. (2015). *Principles and practice of structural equation modeling* (4th ed.). Guilford Press.

Kushlev, K., & Dunn, E. W. (2015). Checking email less frequently reduces stress. *Computers in Human Behavior, 43*, 220–228. DOI: 10.1016/j.chb.2014.11.005

Lad, V. (2002). *Textbook of Ayurveda: Fundamental principles*. Ayurvedic Press.

Lazarus, R. S., & Folkman, S. (1984). *Stress, appraisal, and coping*. Springer.

Levin, M. E., Haeger, J. A., Pierce, B. G., & Twohig, M. P. (2017). Web-based acceptance and commitment therapy for mental health problems in college students: A randomized controlled trial. *Behavior Modification, 41*(1), 141–162. DOI: 10.1177/0145445516659645 PMID: 27440189

Levin, M. E., Hildebrandt, M. J., Lillis, J., & Hayes, S. C. (2012). The impact of treatment components suggested by the psychological flexibility model: A meta-analysis of laboratory-based component studies. *Behavior Therapy, 43*(4), 741–756. DOI: 10.1016/j.beth.2012.05.003 PMID: 23046777

Li, D., & Sullivan, W. C. (2016). Impact of views to school landscapes on recovery from stress and mental fatigue. *Landscape and Urban Planning, 148*, 149–158. DOI: 10.1016/j.landurbplan.2015.12.015

Lissak, G. (2018). Adverse physiological and psychological effects of screen time on children and adolescents: Literature review and case study. *Environmental Research, 164*, 149–157. DOI: 10.1016/j.envres.2018.01.015 PMID: 29499467

Little, T. D. (2013). *Longitudinal structural equation modeling*. Guilford Press.

Liu, Y., Zhang, J., Liu, C., & Yang, Y. (2024). A Review of Attention Restoration Theory: Implications for Designing Restorative Environments. *Sustainability (Basel), 16*(9), 3639. DOI: 10.3390/su16093639

MacKinnon, D. P., Fairchild, A. J., & Fritz, M. S. (2007). Mediation analysis. *Annual Review of Psychology, 58*(1), 593–614. DOI: 10.1146/annurev.psych.58.110405.085542 PMID: 16968208

Mandania, R., Cadogan, J., Liu, J., & Kazmi, N. (2025). Optimizing Promotional Campaigns to Maximize Customer Lifetime Value: A Dynamic Learning Approach. *Journal of Service Research, 0*(0), 10946705251365524. Advance online publication. DOI: 10.1177/10946705251365524

Mark, G., Iqbal, S. T., Czerwinski, M., Johns, P., & Sano, A. (2016). Email duration, batching and self-interruption: Patterns of email use on productivity and stress. *Proceedings of the 2016 CHI Conference on Human Factors in Computing Systems*, 1717–1728. https://doi.org/DOI: 10.1145/2858036.2858262

Marsh, E., Perez Vallejos, E., & Spence, A. (2024). Overloaded by information or worried about missing out on it: A quantitative study of stress, burnout, and mental health implications in the digital workplace. *SAGE Open, 14*(3), 21582440241268830. DOI: 10.1177/21582440241268830

Martela, F., & Steger, M. F. (2016). The three meanings of meaning in life: Distinguishing coherence, purpose, and significance. *The Journal of Positive Psychology, 11*(5), 531–545. DOI: 10.1080/17439760.2015.1137623

Mattern, J., Lansmann, S., & Hüllmann, J. A. (2017). Towards a self-regulation framework for digital workplaces. In *Proceedings of the 25th European Conference on Information Systems* (pp. 1641–1656).

Mayiwar, L., Asutay, E., Tinghög, G., Västfjäll, D., & Barrafrem, K. (2025). Determinants of digital well-being. *AI & Society, 40*(5), 3063–3073. DOI: 10.1007/s00146-024-02071-2

McDonnell, A. S., & Strayer, D. L. (2024). Immersion in nature enhances neural indices of executive attention. *Scientific Reports, 14*(1), 1845. DOI: 10.1038/s41598-024-52205-1 PMID: 38253734

Meier, A., & Reinecke, L. (2021). Computer-mediated communication, social media, and mental health: A conceptual and empirical meta-review. *Communication Research, 48*(8), 1182–1209. DOI: 10.1177/0093650220958224

Menon, A. (2014). *Everyday nationalism: Women of the Hindu right in India.* University of Pennsylvania Press.

Mesch, G. S. (2006). Family characteristics and intergenerational conflicts over the Internet. *Information Communication and Society, 9*(4), 473–495. DOI: 10.1080/13691180600858705

Metzler, H., & Garcia, D. (2023). Social Drivers and Algorithmic Mechanisms on Digital Media. *Perspectives on Psychological Science : A Journal of the Association for Psychological Science, 19*(5), 735–748. DOI: 10.1177/17456916231185057 PMID: 37466493

Morling, B., Kitayama, S., & Miyamoto, Y. (2002). Cultural practices emphasize influence in the United States and adjustment in Japan. *Personality & Social Psychology Bulletin, 28*(3), 311–323. DOI: 10.1177/0146167202286003

Newport, C. (2019). *Digital minimalism: Choosing a focused life in a noisy world.* Portfolio/Penguin.

Ophir, E., Nass, C., & Wagner, A. D. (2009). Cognitive control in media multitaskers. *Proceedings of the National Academy of Sciences of the United States of America, 106*(37), 15583–15587. DOI: 10.1073/pnas.0903620106 PMID: 19706386

Piedimonte, A., Lanzo, G., Campaci, F., Volpino, V., & Carlino, E. (2025). Spreading New Light on Attention Restoration Theory: An Environmental Posner Paradigm. *Brain Sciences, 15*(6), 578. DOI: 10.3390/brainsci15060578 PMID: 40563750

Przybylski, A. K., Murayama, K., DeHaan, C. R., & Gladwell, V. (2013). Motivational, emotional, and behavioral correlates of fear of missing out. *Computers in Human Behavior, 29*(4), 1841–1848. DOI: 10.1016/j.chb.2013.02.014

Qi, X. (2011). Face: A Chinese concept in a global sociology. *Journal of Sociology (Melbourne, Vic.), 47*(3), 279–295. DOI: 10.1177/1440783311407692

Rangaswamy, N., & Cutrell, E. (2012). Anthropology, development and ICTs: Slums, youth and the mobile Internet in urban India. In *Proceedings of the Fifth International Conference on Information and Communication Technologies and Development* (pp. 85–93). https://doi.org/DOI: 10.1145/2160673.2160685

Ryan, R. M., & Deci, E. L. (2000). Self-determination theory and the facilitation of intrinsic motivation, social development, and well-being. *The American Psychologist, 55*(1), 68–78. DOI: 10.1037/0003-066X.55.1.68 PMID: 11392867

Ryan, R. M., & Deci, E. L. (2017). *Self-determination theory: Basic psychological needs in motivation, development, and wellness*. Guilford Press., DOI: 10.1521/978.14625/28806

Ryff, C. D. (1989). Happiness is everything, or is it? Explorations on the meaning of psychological well-being. *Journal of Personality and Social Psychology, 57*(6), 1069–1081. DOI: 10.1037/0022-3514.57.6.1069

Ryff, C. D., & Keyes, C. L. M. (1995). The structure of psychological well-being revisited. *Journal of Personality and Social Psychology*, *69*(4), 719–727. DOI: 10.1037/0022-3514.69.4.719 PMID: 7473027

Salagame, K. K. K. (2013). Well-being from the perspective of Indian psychology. In David, S. A., Boniwell, I., & Conley Ayers, A. (Eds.), *The Oxford Handbook of Happiness* (pp. 371–383). Oxford University Press.

Saraswathi, T. S. (1999). *Culture, socialization, and human development: Theory, research, and applications in India*. Sage Publications.

Schäfer, S. K., von Boros, L., Schaubruch, L. M., Kunzler, A. M., Lindner, S., Koehler, F., Werner, T., Zappalà, F., Helmreich, I., Wessa, M., Lieb, K., & Tüscher, O. (2024). Digital interventions to promote psychological resilience: A systematic review and meta-analysis. *NPJ Digital Medicine*, *7*(1), 30. DOI: 10.1038/s41746-024-01017-8 PMID: 38332030

Sheng, J., Ng, D. T. K., Tian, P., & Zheng, Z. (2025). University students' resilience in post-pandemic period: A socio-ecological perspective. *Frontiers in Psychology*, *16*, 1574153. DOI: 10.3389/fpsyg.2025.1574153 PMID: 40417036

Southwick, S. M., Bonanno, G. A., Masten, A. S., Panter-Brick, C., & Yehuda, R. (2014). Resilience definitions, theory, and challenges: Interdisciplinary perspectives. *European Journal of Psychotraumatology*, *5*(1), 25338. DOI: 10.3402/ejpt.v5.25338 PMID: 25317257

Srite, M., & Karahanna, E. (2006). The role of espoused national cultural values in technology acceptance. *Management Information Systems Quarterly*, *30*(3), 679–704. DOI: 10.2307/25148745

Stothart, C., Mitchum, A., & Yehnert, C. (2015). The attentional cost of receiving a cell phone notification. *Journal of Experimental Psychology. Human Perception and Performance*, *41*(4), 893–897. DOI: 10.1037/xhp0000100 PMID: 26121498

Streeter, C. C., Gerbarg, P. L., Saper, R. B., Ciraulo, D. A., & Brown, R. P. (2012). Effects of yoga on the autonomic nervous system, gamma-aminobutyric-acid, and allostasis in epilepsy, depression, and post-traumatic stress disorder. *Medical Hypotheses*, *78*(5), 571–579. DOI: 10.1016/j.mehy.2012.01.021 PMID: 22365651

Sun, H., Yuan, C., Qian, Q., He, S., & Luo, Q. (2022). Digital resilience among individuals in school education settings: A concept analysis based on a scoping review. *Frontiers in Psychiatry*, *13*, 858515. Advance online publication. DOI: 10.3389/fpsyt.2022.858515 PMID: 35432032

Tarnanidis, T., Manda, V. K., Sousa, B. B., Vlachopoulou, M., & Papachristou, E. (2026). Marketing Complexity of Smart Consumer Products to Global Millennial Segments. In Tarnanidis, T., Sousa, B., Vlachopoulou, M., Papachristou, E., & Kittu Manda, V. (Eds.), *Diversity and Inclusion-Driven Marketing for Multicultural Marketplaces* (pp. 1–16). IGI Global Scientific Publishing., DOI: 10.4018/979-8-3373-2111-0.ch001

Tedeschi, R. G., & Calhoun, L. G. (2004). Posttraumatic growth: Conceptual foundations and empirical evidence. *Psychological Inquiry*, *15*(1), 1–18. DOI: 10.1207/s15327965pli1501_01

Twenge, J. M., & Campbell, W. K. (2018). Associations between screen time and lower psychological well-being among children and adolescents: Evidence from a population-based study. *Preventive Medicine Reports*, *12*, 271–283. DOI: 10.1016/j.pmedr.2018.10.003 PMID: 30406005

Uchida, Y., Norasakkunkit, V., & Kitayama, S. (2004). Cultural constructions of happiness: Theory and empirical evidence. *Journal of Happiness Studies*, *5*(3), 223–239. DOI: 10.1007/s10902-004-8785-9

van de Vijver, F. J., & Leung, K. (2011). Equivalence and bias: A review of concepts, models, and data analytic procedures. In D. Matsumoto & F. J. van de Vijver (Eds.), *Cross-cultural research methods in psychology* (pp. 17–45). Cambridge University Press.

Vandenberg, R. J., & Lance, C. E. (2000). A review and synthesis of the measurement invariance literature: Suggestions, practices, and recommendations for organizational research. *Organizational Research Methods*, *3*(1), 4–70. DOI: 10.1177/109442810031002

Vogel, E. A., Rose, J. P., Roberts, L. R., & Eckles, K. (2014). Social comparison, social media, and self-esteem. *Psychology of Popular Media Culture*, *3*(4), 206–222. DOI: 10.1037/ppm0000047

Yang, C. C. (2016). Instagram use, loneliness, and social comparison orientation: Interact and browse on social media, but don't compare. *Cyberpsychology, Behavior and Social Networking*, *19*(12), 703–708. DOI: 10.1089/cyber.2016.0201 PMID: 27855266

Yuan, Y., Shi, Y., Su, T., & Zhang, H. (2025). Resistance or compliance? The impact of algorithmic awareness on people's attitudes toward online information browsing. *Frontiers in Psychology*, *16*, 1563592. DOI: 10.3389/fpsyg.2025.1563592 PMID: 40823401

Zhang, M. M., Cooke, F. L., Ahlstrom, D., & McNeil, N. (2025). The Rise of Algorithmic Management and Implications for Work and Organisations. *New Technology, Work and Employment, 40*(3), 659–671. DOI: 10.1111/ntwe.12343

KEY TERMS AND DEFINITIONS

Algorithmic feeds: Continuously refreshing content streams on digital platforms that employ recommendation algorithms optimizing for engagement metrics rather than user well-being. These systems use machine learning to curate personalized content that maximizes time-on-site and clicks. For example, TikTok and Instagram feeds deliver endless scrolling experiences without natural stopping points. While enhancing content relevance, algorithmic feeds often create echo chambers and exploit psychological vulnerabilities through variable reward schedules.

Attentional fatigue: Acceptance and Commitment Therapy (ACT) technique helping individuals observe thoughts without being controlled by them, creating distance between person and cognitions. This metacognitive skill treats thoughts as mental events rather than literal truths requiring immediate action. For example, noticing "I'm having the thought I must check my phone" rather than automatically acting. Defusion enables value-aligned choices rather than reflexive responses to anxious cognitions or FOMO-related urges.

Digital autonomy: Perceived control over technology use and boundary effectiveness, experiencing technology as serving one's goals rather than controlling them. This encompasses both subjective agency in digital decisions and actual ability to maintain healthy boundaries. Individuals with high autonomy successfully limit social media to designated times and resist compulsive checking. Autonomy erodes when platform designs exploit cognitive biases or work demands constant availability despite personal intentions.

Domain-specific satisfaction: Assessment of satisfaction within life domains (work, relationships, leisure, health) that contribute differentially to overall well-being. This multidimensional approach recognizes different areas hold varying importance across individuals and cultures. One person may derive primary satisfaction from career achievements while another prioritizes family relationships. Measuring domain-specific satisfaction provides nuanced understanding beyond global life satisfaction scores.

Equanimity (upeksha): Balanced mental composure maintained across changing circumstances in Buddhist and yoga psychology, involving centered presence without clinging or rejecting. This quality enables remaining psychologically stable amid both pleasant and unpleasant experiences without reactive grasping. For example, maintaining inner calm when receiving praise or criticism on social media posts. Equanimity differs from indifference; it reflects engaged awareness without attachment to specific outcomes or emotional volatility.

Eudaimonic well-being: Well-being conceptualized through purpose, personal growth, autonomy, environmental mastery, positive relations, and self-acceptance rather than merely pleasure. This approach emphasizes meaning and self-realization over momentary happiness or hedonic gratification. For example, pursuing challenging work that provides fulfillment even when requiring effort and sacrifice. Eudaimonic well-being aligns with Aristotelian concepts of human flourishing through virtue and actualizing one's potential.

Filial piety: Cultural value emphasizing adult children's duty to aging parents, creating unique digital dynamics regarding communication frequency and caregiving obligations. This Confucian-rooted principle shapes technology use patterns in collectivist Asian cultures. Adult children maintain daily video calls or messaging with elderly parents to fulfill respect obligations. Digital tools facilitate remote caregiving while potentially intensifying role strain when balancing filial duties with work demands.

Hedonic well-being: Well-being conceptualized through maximization of pleasure and positive affect, contrasting with eudaimonic approaches emphasizing meaning and growth. This perspective prioritizes subjective happiness, enjoyment, and satisfaction of desires as primary wellness indicators. For example, seeking entertainment, comfort, and pleasurable experiences through leisure activities or consumption. Hedonic well-being focuses on feeling good in the moment rather than deeper purpose or self-development.

Information overload: Cognitive state where the volume of available information exceeds processing capacity, creating decision paralysis and chronic cognitive strain. Digital environments expose users to continuous streams of news, messages, notifications, and content beyond manageable limits. Workers receiving hundreds of daily emails have trouble prioritizing, delayed responses, and decision fatigue. Information overload impairs judgment quality, increases stress, and reduces productivity despite access to abundant data.

Resilience capacity: Adaptive ability to navigate digital stressors through coping flexibility, meaning-making, bounce-back ability, and social support mobilization. This multidimensional construct encompasses both recovering from setbacks and growing through adversity in digital contexts. Resilient individuals employ diverse strategies: cognitive reappraisal of social media comparisons, digital boundaries, and seeking support. Resilience capacity predicts sustained well-being despite exposure to algorithmic manipulation and information overload.

Right-to-disconnect: Legislation prohibiting after-hours work communication expectations to protect employee well-being and work-life boundaries. These laws, enacted in France (2017) and other countries, grant workers legal permission to ignore emails outside working hours. Employers cannot penalize employees who don't respond to non-emergency communications during personal time. Right-to-disconnect policies address chronic stress from constant availability expectations enabled by smartphones and remote work technologies.

Compilation of References

Abbasi, A. Z., Fayyaz, M. S., Abbasi, G. A., Rather, R. A., & Hussain, A. (2025). Deriving gamers' subjective well-being through satisfaction, cognitive, affective, and behavioral engagement: Symmetrical and asymmetrical approaches. *Acta Psychologica, 260*, 105632. DOI: 10.1016/j.actpsy.2025.105632

Abdul Majeed, A. (2025). The adoption of technology acceptance model in e-commerce with artificial intelligence as a mediator. SSRN Electronic Journal. https://doi.org/DOI: 10.2139/ssrn.5190191

Abdulwahab, B., & Kumar, T. P. K. (2025). Hyper-personalization and the privacy paradox: An opinion-based academic perspective. *Advances in Psychological Sciences and Applications, 1*(3), 120–129. DOI: 10.56741/apsa.v1i03.1373

Abidi, N., Herradi, M. E., & Sakha, S. (2023). Digitalization and resilience during the COVID-19 pandemic. *Telecommunications Policy, 47*(4), 102522. DOI: 10.1016/j.telpol.2023.102522 PMID: 37051116

Acemoglu, D., & Restrepo, P. (2020). The wrong kind of AI? Artificial intelligence and the future of labour demand. *Cambridge Journal of Regions, Economy and Society, 13*(1), 25–35. DOI: 10.1093/cjres/rsz022

Aderinto, A. A. (2025). Financial Risk Management and Corporate Performance of Selected Small-scale Firms in Nigeria. *Asian Journal of Advanced Research and Reports, 19*(4), 316–330. DOI: 10.9734/ajarr/2025/v19i4986

AERC—Ndung'u. N. S. (2021). A digital financial services revolution in Kenya: The M-Pesa case study. African Economic Research Consortium. https://aercafrica.org/old-website/wp-content/uploads/2021/03/AERC-MPesa-Case-Study.pdf

Agnihotri, A., & Rengaraj, S. (2025). Harnessing generative AI for transforming marketing strategies: Enhancing consumer engagement through precision and personalization. In *Proceedings of the 2025 5th International Conference on Pervasive Computing and Social Networking (ICPCSN)* (pp. xx–xx). IEEE. https://doi.org/ DOI: 10.1109/ICPCSN65854.2025.11035208

Agostini, A., Masiero, A. V., & Kanan, L. A. (2018). Assessment of well-being at work of information technology professionals. *International Journal of Humanities and Social Science*, *8*(6), 44–54. DOI: 10.30845/ijhss.v8n6a6

Ahmad, R., Mat Yusof, N. A., & Ramely, A. (2025). MALAYSIAN YOUTH PERCEPTIONS OF SOLUTIONS TO ENVIRONMENTAL ISSUES. *Journal of Event. Tourism and Hospitality Studies*, *5*, 20–32. DOI: 10.32890/jeth2025.5.2

Al Issa, H.-E., & Maheshwari, G. (2025). Shaping the future of education: A cluster analysis of generative AI's transformative impact. *Interactive Technology and Smart Education*. Advance online publication. DOI: 10.1108/ITSE-01-2025-0013

Alabi, B. A., Apata, A. O., Akindumila, O. I., Oloyede, O. J., Obasusi, B. A., Oladoja, N. A., & Ololade, I. A. (2025). Trace metal in soils of auto-mechanics workshops in Akure metropolis, Nigeria: Assessment of environmental quality. *International Journal of Environmental Science and Technology*, *22*(11), 10755–10768. DOI: 10.1007/s13762-025-06354-z

Allil, K. (2024). Integrating AI-driven marketing analytics techniques into the classroom: Pedagogical strategies for enhancing student engagement and future business success. *Journal of Marketing Analytics*, *12*(2), 142–168. DOI: 10.1057/s41270-023-00281-z

Almaiah, M. A., Al-Otaibi, S., Shishakly, R., Hassan, L., Lutfi, A., Alrawad, M., Qatawneh, M., & Alghanam, O. A. (2023). Investigating the role of perceived risk, perceived security and perceived trust on smart m-banking application using SEM. *Sustainability (Basel)*, *15*(13), 9908. DOI: 10.3390/su15139908

Almelhem, M., Buics, L., Süle, E., & Simoes, R. (2025). Industry 4.0 for sustainable reverse waste collection: A systematic literature review. *Journal of Transport and Supply Chain Management*, *19*, a1179. DOI: 10.4102/JTSCM.v19i0.1179

Alsanie, G., Unnisa, S. T., & Hamad, N. H. A. (2025). Transforming the Supply Chain Operations of Electric Vehicles' Batteries Using an Optimization Approach. *Sustainability (Basel)*, *18*(1), 367. DOI: 10.3390/su18010367

Amirkhizi, P. J.. (2025). "The Role of Human-Centered Design in Enhancing Trust and Satisfaction in E-Commerce within Industry 5.0," *2025 IEEE International Systems Conference (SysCon)*, Montreal, QC, Canada, pp. 1–8, DOI: 10.1109/SysCon64521.2025.11014837

Anton, A. (2025). Subjective well-being of public relations and communication professionals in the context of perceived organisational support. *Journal of Communication Management (London)*, *29*(3), 324–339. DOI: 10.1108/JCOM-03-2024-0047

Anwar, M. S., Yang, J., Frnda, J., Choi, A., Baghaei, N., & Ali, M. (2025). Metaverse and XR for cultural heritage education: Applications, standards, architecture, and technological insights for enhanced immersive experience. *Virtual Reality (Waltham Cross)*, *29*(2), 51. DOI: 10.1007/s10055-025-01126-z

Appadurai, A. (1996). *Modernity at large: Cultural dimensions of globalization.* University of Minnesota Press.

Arata, S., Sugiuchi, M., Yazawa, R., Funatsu, H., & Kawakubo, S. (2025). Effects of perceived office environment on the subjective well-being of workers: Insights from a structural equation modeling analysis. *Building and Environment*, *267*, 112180. DOI: 10.1016/j.buildenv.2024.112180

Argan, M., Gürbüz, B., Sivan, A., Argan, M. T., Dinç, H., & Bayazıt, E. (2025). Awe experience of leisure activity in the metaverse: Perceived value, satisfaction and intention. *World Leisure Journal*, *67*(3), 1–22. DOI: 10.1080/16078055.2025.2459933

Arnett, J. J. (2002). The psychology of globalization. *The American Psychologist*, *57*(10), 774–783. DOI: 10.1037/0003-066X.57.10.774 PMID: 12369500

Arora, P. (2019). *The next billion users: Digital life beyond the West.* Harvard University Press. DOI: 10.4159/9780674238879

Arslankara, V. B., Demir, A., Öztaş, Ö., & Usta, E. (2022). Digital well-being scale validity and reliability study. *Journal of Teacher Education and Lifelong Learning*, *4*(2), 263–274. DOI: 10.51535/tell.1206193

Asha, M., & Kumar, A. (2025). Employee Well-being in the Digital Age: A Study on Microsoft Teams Users. *The Nigerian Health Journal*, *25*(2), 649–663. DOI: 10.71637/TNHJ.V25I2.1060

Ashok, M., Madan, R., Joha, A., & Sivarajah, U. (2022). Ethical framework for artificial intelligence and digital technologies. *International Journal of Information Management*, *62*, 102433. DOI: 10.1016/j.ijinfomgt.2021.102433

Aslan, M., Sağtaş, S., & Özkaynar, K. (2025). Metaverse Perception Scale Development and Validation. *SAGE Open*, *15*(2), 21582440251329126. DOI: 10.1177/21582440251329126

Attia, M., Abdel-Fattah, M. A., & Khedr, A. E. (2022). A proposed multi criteria indexing and ranking model for documents and web pages on large scale data. *Journal of King Saud University. Computer and Information Sciences*, *34*(10), 8702–8715. DOI: 10.1016/j.jksuci.2021.10.009

Aulia, S. R., & Lin, W. S. (2024). Embracing the digital shift. *Asia Pacific Management Review*, *30*(3), 100339. DOI: 10.1016/j.apmrv.2024.12.003

Badra, R., Majhi, M., Panda, B. B., Behera, I. D., Das, A. P., & Bal, M. (2026). Petroleum Hydrocarbon Pollutants from Waste Engine Oil in Municipal Waste: Concern and Remediation Strategies. In Das, A. P., Sirisena, K., & Bhanja, D. (Eds.), *Sustainable Municipal Waste Management with a Zero Waste Approach* (pp. 497–519). Springer Nature Switzerland., DOI: 10.1007/978-3-032-05950-5_20

Bafadhal, A. S., Hanafiah, M. H., & Anuar, F. I. (2025). Human behaviour in virtual tourism: A systematic literature review from a digital humanities perspective. *Current Issues in Tourism*, •••, 1–39. DOI: 10.1080/13683500.2025.2534460

Bajaj, B., & Pande, N. (2016). Mediating role of resilience in the impact of mindfulness on life satisfaction and affect as indices of subjective well-being. *Personality and Individual Differences*, *93*, 63–67. DOI: 10.1016/j.paid.2015.09.005

Baker, R. S., & Hawn, A. (2022). Algorithmic Bias in Education. *International Journal of Artificial Intelligence in Education*, *32*(4), 1052–1092. DOI: 10.1007/s40593-021-00285-9

Bálint, M., Ferreira, L. M. D. F., Vilas-Boas Da Silva, J. M., & Möhring, M. M. (2026). Integrating external stakeholders for green innovation in third-party logistics: The mediating role of green absorptive capacity. *International Journal of Logistics Management*, *37*(7), 1–30. DOI: 10.1108/IJLM-05-2024-0307

Bandura, A. (1997). Self-efficacy: The exercise of control. *The Freeman.*

Barber, B. M., & Odean, T. (2001). Boys will be Boys. *The Quarterly Journal of Economics*, *116*(1), 261–292. DOI: 10.1162/003355301556400

Barberis, N. (2018). Psychology-based models of asset prices and trading volume. In *Handbook of behavioral economics: applications and foundations 1* (Vol. 1, pp. 79–175). North-Holland. DOI: 10.3386/w24723

Bartels, A. L., Peterson, S. J., & Reina, C. S. (2019). Understanding well-being at work: Development and validation of the eudaimonic workplace well-being scale. *PLoS One, 14*(4), e0215957. DOI: 10.1371/journal.pone.0215957 PMID: 31022285

Barth, L. L., Mostajeran, F., Riecke, B. E., & Kühn, S. (2025). Immersive videos of natural and urban environments can enhance awe and psychological well-being. *Frontiers in Virtual Reality, 6*, 1532991. Advance online publication. DOI: 10.3389/frvir.2025.1532991

Basuvaraj, M., & Rastogi, K. (2025). Illuminating the convergence of artificial intelligence (AI) and business intelligence (BI) in e-commerce and fintech in India. In *AI-powered business intelligence for modern organizations* (pp. 243–264). IGI Global., DOI: 10.4018/979-8-3693-1140-0.ch012

Batool, A., Zowghi, D., & Bano, M. (2024). AI governance: A systematic literature review. *AI and Ethics*. Advance online publication. DOI: 10.1007/s43681-024-00653-w

Bauer, R., Ruof, T., & Smeets, P. (2021). Get real! Individuals prefer more sustainable investments. *Review of Financial Studies, 34*(8), 3976–4043. DOI: 10.1093/rfs/hhab037

Baumeister, R. F. (2002). Yielding to temptation: Self-control failure, impulsive purchasing, and consumer behavior. *The Journal of Consumer Research, 28*(4), 670–676. DOI: 10.1086/338209

Baumeister, R. F., Bratslavsky, E., Muraven, M., & Tice, D. M. (1998). Ego depletion: Is the active self a limited resource? *Journal of Personality and Social Psychology, 74*(5), 1252–1265. DOI: 10.1037/0022-3514.74.5.1252 PMID: 9599441

Belk, R. W. (1988). Possessions and the extended self. *The Journal of Consumer Research, 15*(2), 139–168. DOI: 10.1086/209154

Belk, R. W. (2013). Extended self in the digital world. *The Journal of Consumer Research, 40*(3), 477–500. DOI: 10.1086/671052

Benartzi, S., & Thaler, R. H. (2013). Behavioral economics and the retirement savings crisis. *Science, 339*(6124), 1152–1153. DOI: 10.1126/science.1231320 PMID: 23471389

Beneito-Montagut, R., Begueria, A., & Cassián, N. (2023). The social connectedness of digital practices in later life: It's not just about learning, it's all about relationships. *The Sociological Review, 71*(3), 581–600. DOI: 10.1177/00380261221144154

Berg, F., Kölbel, J. F., & Rigobon, R. (2022). Aggregate confusion: The divergence of ESG ratings. *Review of Finance*, *26*(6), 1315–1344. DOI: 10.1093/rof/rfac033

Biagini, G. (2025). Towards an AI-Literate Future: A Systematic Literature Review Exploring Education, Ethics, and Applications. *International Journal of Artificial Intelligence in Education*, *35*(4), 2616–2666. DOI: 10.1007/s40593-025-00466-w

Biocca, F., Harms, C., & Burgoon, J. K. (2003). Toward a more robust theory of social presence. *Presence (Cambridge, Mass.)*, *12*(5), 456–480. DOI: 10.1162/105474603322761270

Bitra, S. K.Sai Kumar Bitra. (2025). The convergence of generative AI and hyper-personalization: Transforming customer experience at scale. *World Journal of Advanced Research and Reviews*, *26*(2), 669–678. DOI: 10.30574/wjarr.2025.26.2.1648

Blinda, K., Niebel, C., & Rammer, C. (2024). The impact of the EU GDPR on product innovation. *Industry and Innovation*, *31*(3), 311–351. DOI: 10.1080/13662716.2023.2271858

Boegman-Watt, S. J., & Carodenuto, S. (2026). Place, Process, People: Digital Placemaking across Global Supply Chains. *Geoforum*, *170*, 104530. DOI: 10.1016/j.geoforum.2025.104530

Boni, E. K. (2024). *Exploring perceived risk and digital ethics affecting consumer experiences and decision-making in smart retailing* (Doctoral dissertation, Brunel University London).

Borderless Access. (2025). Digital consumer behavior trend of 2025. https://borderlessaccess.com/blog/consumer-behavior-trends-2025/

Böttcher, T. P., Weking, J., Hein, A., Böhm, M., & Krcmar, H. (2022). Pathways to digital business models: The connection of sensing and seizing in business model innovation. *The Journal of Strategic Information Systems*, *31*(4), 101742. Advance online publication. DOI: 10.1016/j.jsis.2022.101742

Brickman, P., & Campbell, D. T. (1971). Hedonic relativism and planning the good society. In Appley, M. H. (Ed.), *Adaptation-level theory* (pp. 287–302). Academic Press.

Brüggen, E. C., Hogreve, J., Holmlund, M., Kabadayi, S., & Löfgren, M. (2017). Financial well-being: A conceptualization and research agenda. *Journal of Business Research*, *79*, 228–237. DOI: 10.1016/j.jbusres.2017.03.013

Bucci, I., Fani, V., & Bandinelli, R. (2024). Towards human-centric manufacturing: Exploring the role of human digital twins in Industry 5.0. *Sustainability (Basel)*, *17*(1), 129. DOI: 10.3390/su17010129

Buchi, M. (2024). Digital well-being theory and research. *New Media & Society*, *26*(1), 172–189. DOI: 10.1177/14614448211056851

Buchi, M., Just, N., & Latzer, M. (2016). Modeling the second-level digital divide: A five-country study of social differences in Internet use. *New Media & Society*, *18*(11), 2703–2722. DOI: 10.1177/1461444815604154

Buolamwini, J., & Gebru, T. (2018). Gender shades: Intersectional accuracy disparities in commercial gender classification. Proceedings of Machine Learning Research, 81, 1–15. https://proceedings.mlr.press/v81/buolamwini18a.html

Buragohain, D., Khichar, S., Deng, C., Meng, Y., & Chaudhary, S. (2025). Analyzing metaverse-based digital therapies, their effectiveness, and potential risks in mental healthcare. *Scientific Reports*, *15*(1), 17066. DOI: 10.1038/s41598-025-00916-4 PMID: 40379748

Bureau, C. F. P. (2015). *Financial well-being: The goal of financial education.*

Burr, C., Taddeo, M., & Floridi, L. (2020). The ethics of digital well-being: A thematic review. *Science and Engineering Ethics*, *26*(4), 2313–2343. DOI: 10.1007/s11948-020-00175-8 PMID: 31933119

Butler, E. A., Lee, T. L., & Gross, J. J. (2007). Emotion regulation and culture: Are the social consequences of emotion suppression culture-specific? *Emotion (Washington, D.C.)*, *7*(1), 30–48. DOI: 10.1037/1528-3542.7.1.30 PMID: 17352561

Buzeta, C., De Pelsmacker, P., & Dens, N. (2024). Branded content and motivations for social media use as drivers of brand outcomes on social media: A cross-cultural study. *. *International Journal of Advertising*, *43*(4), 637–671. Advance online publication. DOI: 10.1080/02650487.2023.2215079

Callaghan, C. (2025). *Rethinking growth and the future of work: The alignment economy as a general theory of human-centered AI*. SSRN working paper.

Calvo, R. A., & Peters, D. (2014). *Positive computing: Technology for wellbeing and human potential*. MIT Press. DOI: 10.7551/mitpress/9764.001.0001

Cao, S., & Li, H. (2023). A scoping review of digital well-being in early childhood: Definitions, measurements, contributors, and interventions. *International Journal of Environmental Research and Public Health*, *20*(4), 3510. DOI: 10.3390/ijerph20043510 PMID: 36834204

Carnegie Endowment for International Peace. (2024, October 3). Japan's aging society as a technological opportunity (K. Kushida). https://carnegieendowment.org/research/2024/10/japans-aging-society-as-a-technological-opportunity?lang=en

Casiddu, N., Burlando, F., & Chen, B. (2024). Human-de-centred design: Towards a (new) era of suffering. *Agathón | International Journal of Architecture. Art and Design, 16*, 242–249.

Chandra, S., Verma, S., Lim, W. M., Kumar, S., & Donthu, N. (2022). Personalization in personalized marketing: Trends and ways forward. *Psychology and Marketing, 39*(8), 1529–1562. DOI: 10.1002/mar.21670

Chang, A., Winquist, N. W., Wescott, A. B., Lattie, E. G., & Graham, A. K. (2021). Systematic review of digital and non-digital non-pharmacological interventions that target quality of life and psychological outcomes in adults with systemic lupus erythematosus. *Lupus, 30*(7), 1058–1077. DOI: 10.1177/09612033211005085 PMID: 33779388

Chan, M. (2018). Digital communications and psychological well-being across the life span: Examining the intervening roles of social capital and civic engagement. *Telematics and Informatics, 35*(6), 1744–1754. DOI: 10.1016/j.tele.2018.05.003

Chapple, C. K. (2009). *Yoga and the luminous: Patañjali's spiritual path to freedom.* State University of New York Press.

Chayko, M. (2014). Techno-social Life: The Internet, Digital Technology, and Social Connectedness. *Sociology Compass, 8*(7), 976–991. DOI: 10.1111/soc4.12190

Chen, B., Vansteenkiste, M., Beyers, W., Boone, L., Deci, E. L., Van der Kaap-Deeder, J., Duriez, B., Lens, W., Matos, L., Mouratidis, A., Ryan, R. M., Sheldon, K. M., Soenens, B., Van Petegem, S., & Verstuyf, J. (2015). Basic psychological need satisfaction, frustration, and strength across four cultures. *Motivation and Emotion, 39*(2), 216–236. DOI: 10.1007/s11031-014-9450-1

Cheng, S. T., & Chan, A. C. M. (2006). Filial piety and psychological well-being in well older Chinese. *The Journals of Gerontology. Series B, Psychological Sciences and Social Sciences, 61*(5), 262–P269. DOI: 10.1093/geronb/61.5.P262 PMID: 16960229

Cheng, Y.-M. (2025). AI-enabled service continuance: Roles of trust and privacy risk. *Journal of Computer Information Systems*, 1–16. Advance online publication. DOI: 10.1080/08874417.2025.2452544

Chen, S., Ebrahimi, O. V., & Cheng, C. (2025). New Perspective on Digital Well-Being by Distinguishing Digital Competency From Dependency: Network Approach. *Journal of Medical Internet Research, 27*, e70483. DOI: 10.2196/70483 PMID: 40132188

Chen, T., Samaranayake, P., Cen, X. Y., Qi, M., & Lan, Y.-C. (2022). The impact of online reviews on consumers' purchasing decisions: Evidence from an eye-tracking study. *Frontiers in Psychology, 13*, 865702. Advance online publication. DOI: 10.3389/fpsyg.2022.865702 PMID: 35756238

Cheshmehzangi, A. (2025). Cities as Living Systems: Circular Metabolisms, Climate Intelligence, and the Architecture of Regeneration. In A. Cheshmehzangi, *Generative AI-Powered Urban Digital Twins* (pp. 93–106). Springer Nature Singapore. DOI: 10.1007/978-981-95-4766-1_7

Cheung, F. M., van de Vijver, F. J. R., & Leong, F. T. L. (2011). Toward a new approach to the study of personality in culture. *The American Psychologist, 66*(7), 593–603. DOI: 10.1037/a0022389 PMID: 21261408

Chingan Thottathil, S., & Nandakumar, M. K. (2024). Integrating hedonic and eudaimonic perspectives of well-being. *Human Resource Development Review, 24*(2), 157–198. DOI: 10.1177/15344843241305650

Choi, D., Lee, H. K., & Kim, D. Y. (2023). Mood management through metaverse enhancing life satisfaction. *International Journal of Consumer Studies, 47*(4), 1533–1543.

Choi, J., Cho, H., Lee, S., Kim, J., & Park, E. C. (2018). Effect of the online game shutdown policy on internet use, internet addiction, and sleeping hours in Korean adolescents. *The Journal of Adolescent Health : Official Publication of the Society for Adolescent Medicine, 62*(5), 548–555. DOI: 10.1016/j.jadohealth.2017.11.291 PMID: 29434003

Choung, Y., Pak, T.-Y., & Chatterjee, S. (n.d.). *Digital Financial Literacy and Life Satisfaction: Evidence from South Korea.*

Christopher, J. C., Wendt, D. C., Marecek, J., & Goodman, D. M. (2014). Critical cultural awareness: Contributions to a globalizing psychology. *The American Psychologist, 69*(7), 645–655. DOI: 10.1037/a0036851 PMID: 24841336

Chrusciak, C. B., Szejka, A. L., & Junior, O. C. (2025). Integrating digital transformation with human-centric factors strategies to enhance organisational process performance: The HOPE model. *Journal of Industrial Information Integration, 44*, 100785. DOI: 10.1016/j.jii.2025.100785

Chughtai, A., Byrne, M., & Flood, B. (2015). Linking ethical leadership to employee well-being. *Journal of Business Ethics, 128*(3), 653–663. DOI: 10.1007/s10551-014-2126-7

Chu, M., Ma, H., Lee, C.-Y., Zhao, Z., Chen, T., Zhang, S., & Chiang, Y.-C. (2023). Effect of online and offline social network group clusters on life satisfaction across age groups. *Heliyon, 9*(5), e16176. DOI: 10.1016/j.heliyon.2023.e16176 PMID: 37229172

Cillo, P., & Rubera, G. (2025). Generative AI in innovation and marketing processes: A roadmap of research opportunities. *Journal of the Academy of Marketing Science, 53*(3), 684–701. DOI: 10.1007/s11747-024-01044-7

Connor, K. M., & Davidson, J. R. (2003). Development of a new resilience scale: The Connor-Davidson Resilience Scale (CD-RISC). *Depression and Anxiety, 18*(2), 76–82. DOI: 10.1002/da.10113 PMID: 12964174

Consiglio, I., & van Osselaer, S. M. J. (2022). The effects of consumption on self-esteem. *Current Opinion in Psychology, 46*, 101341. DOI: 10.1016/j.copsyc.2022.101341 PMID: 35436693

Cooke, F. L. (2024). Sustainability and human-centred human resource management. In *A research agenda for work and employment* (pp. 23–40). Edward Elgar Publishing. DOI: 10.4337/9781803929972.00007

Cropanzano, R., & Mitchell, M. S. (2005). Social exchange theory: An interdisciplinary review. *Journal of Management, 31*(6), 874–900. DOI: 10.1177/0149206305279602

Csikszentmihalyi, M., & Larson, R. (2014). Validity and reliability of the experience-sampling method. In Csikszentmihalyi, M. (Ed.), *Flow and the foundations of positive psychology* (pp. 35–54). Springer., DOI: 10.1007/978-94-017-9088-8_3

Cutolo, D., & Kenney, M. (2021). Platform-dependent entrepreneurs: Power asymmetries, risks, and strategies in the platform economy. *The Academy of Management Perspectives, 35*(4), 584–605. DOI: 10.5465/amp.2019.0103

Cyr, D., Head, M., Lim, E., & Stibe, A. (2018). Using the elaboration likelihood model to examine online persuasion through website design. *Information & Management, 55*(7), 807–821. DOI: 10.1016/j.im.2018.03.009

Czerw, A. (2019). Diagnosing well-being in work context. *Current Psychology, 38*(2), 331–346. DOI: 10.1007/s12144-017-9614-8

Daher, M. M., & Ziade, F. (2024). Technology, workforce, and the future of sustainable work. In *Navigating the intersection of business, sustainability and technology* (pp. 119–136). Springer Nature.

Dasgupta, A., Dutta, P., V, S., Kumar, P., Naveen, P. R., Gupta, H., & Singh Bisht, Y. (2025). Enhancing biodegradation of plastic wastes by adding used tire rubber: A sustainable solution for mitigating environmental pollution. *Waste Management & Research: The Journal for a Sustainable Circular Economy*, 0734242X251376880. DOI: 10.1177/0734242X251376880

DataReportal. (2025). Digital 2025: Oman. https://datareportal.com/reports/digital-2025-oman

Davis, F. D. (1989). Perceived usefulness, perceived ease of use, and user acceptance of information technology. *Management Information Systems Quarterly*, *13*(3), 319–340. DOI: 10.2307/249008

Davison, C. (n.d.-a). *Towards a theory of Digital Identity.*

Davison, C. (n.d.-b). *Towards a theory of Digital Identity.*

De Santis, A., & Fantinelli, S. (2024). Digital well-being as a new kind of adaptation to the new millennium needs: A state-of-the-art analysis. *Elementa*, *3*, 135–151.

Deb, S., Strodl, E., & Sun, J. (2015). Academic stress, parental pressure, anxiety and mental health among Indian high school students. *International Journal of Psychology and Behavioral Sciences*, *5*(1), 26–34.

Deci, E. L., & Ryan, R. M. (2000). The “what” and “why” of goal pursuits: Human needs and the self-determination of behavior. *Psychological Inquiry*, *11*(4), 227–268. DOI: 10.1207/S15327965PLI1104_01

Deci, E. L., & Ryan, R. M. (2012). Self-determination theory. In Van Lange, P. A. M., Kruglanski, A. W., & Higgins, E. T. (Eds.), *Handbook of theories of social psychology* (pp. 416–436). Sage., DOI: 10.4135/9781446249215.n21

Deloitte. (2025). 2025 connected consumer: Innovation with trust. https://www.deloitte.com/us/en/insights/industry/telecommunications/connectivity-mobile-trends-survey.html

Derks, D., van Duin, D., Tims, M., & Bakker, A. B. (2015). Smartphone use and work–home interference: The moderating role of social norms and employee work engagement. *Journal of Occupational and Organizational Psychology*, *88*(1), 155–177. DOI: 10.1111/joop.12083

Dhiman, N., & Kumar, A. (2023). What We Know and Don't Know About Consumer Happiness: Three-Decade Review, Synthesis, and Research Propositions. *Journal of Interactive Marketing*, *58*(2–3), 115–135. DOI: 10.1177/10949968221095548

Diderot, D. (2005). *Regrets on parting with my old dressing gown* In D. Goodman & K. E. Norberg (Eds.), *The portable Enlightenment reader* (pp. 417–420). penguin Classics. (Original) work (published 1769)

Diener, E. (1984). Subjective well-being. *Psychological Bulletin*, *95*(3), 542–575. DOI: 10.1037/0033-2909.95.3.542 PMID: 6399758

Diener, E., Emmons, R. A., Larsen, R. J., & Griffin, S. (1985). The Satisfaction With Life Scale. *Journal of Personality Assessment*, *49*(1), 71–75. DOI: 10.1207/s15327752jpa4901_13 PMID: 16367493

Diener, E., Lucas, R. E., & Scollon, C. N. (2006). Beyond the hedonic treadmill: Revising the adaptation theory of well-being. *The American Psychologist*, *61*(4), 305–314. DOI: 10.1037/0003-066X.61.4.305 PMID: 16719675

Diener, E., Oishi, S., & Lucas, R. E. (2003). Personality, culture, and subjective well-being: Emotional and cognitive evaluations of life. *Annual Review of Psychology*, *54*(1), 403–425. DOI: 10.1146/annurev.psych.54.101601.145056 PMID: 12172000

Diener, E., Oishi, S., & Tay, L. (2018). Advances in subjective well-being research. *Nature Human Behaviour*, *2*(4), 253–260. DOI: 10.1038/s41562-018-0307-6 PMID: 30936533

Diener, E., Suh, E. M., Lucas, R. E., & Smith, H. L. (1999). subjective well-being: Three decades of progress. *Psychological Bulletin*, *125*(2), 276–302. DOI: 10.1037/0033-2909.125.2.276

Dietrich, F., Arenz, A., & Reinecke, L. (2024). What constitutes experiences of autonomy in digital technology use? A (computational) scoping review through the lens of self-determination theory. *Interacting with Computers*. Advance online publication. DOI: 10.1093/iwc/iwae050

Duarte, P. (2025). Beyond incentives: Rethinking internal marketing drivers of commitment in the AI-transformed banking sector. *International Journal of Bank Marketing*, •••, 1–25.

Dubey, A., Kuriakose, S. M., Anand, S., Bhardwaj, N., & Sengupta, S. (2025). Virtual Social Immersive Multi-Sensory E-Commerce. *arXiv Preprint arXiv:2510.15894*. https://doi.org//arXiv.2510.15894DOI: 10.48550

Dulsrud, A., & Bygstad, B. (2022). Digital ecosystems as social institutions: Exploring the role of consumption through four research streams of digital ecosystems. *Consumption and Society*, *1*(1), 99–119. DOI: 10.1332/QUPH6141

Dwivedi, Y. K., Hughes, L., Wang, Y., Alalwan, A. A., Ahn, S. J. G., Balakrishnan, J., Barta, S., Belk, R., Buhalis, D., Dutot, V., Felix, R., Filieri, R., Flavián, C., Gustafsson, A., Hinsch, C., Hollensen, S., Jain, V., Kim, J., Krishen, A. S., & Wirtz, J. (2023). Metaverse marketing: How the metaverse will shape the future of consumer research and practice. *Psychology and Marketing*, *40*(4), 750–776. DOI: 10.1002/mar.21767

Dwivedi, Y. K., Ismagilova, E., Hughes, D. L., Carlson, J., Filieri, R., Jacobson, J., Jain, V., Karjaluoto, H., Kefi, H., Krishen, A. S., Kumar, V., Rahman, M. M., Raman, R., Rauschnabel, P. A., Rowley, J., Salo, J., Tran, G. A., & Wang, Y. (2021). Setting the future of digital and social media marketing research: Perspectives and research propositions. *International Journal of Information Management*, *59*, 102168. Advance online publication. DOI: 10.1016/j.ijinfomgt.2020.102168

Edmondson, A. C. (2018). *The fearless organization: Creating psychological safety in the workplace for learning, innovation, and growth*. John Wiley & Sons.

Ehrhardt, J. J., Saris, W. E., & Veenhoven, R. (2000). Stability of Life-satisfaction over Time. *Journal of Happiness Studies*, *1*(2), 177–205. DOI: 10.1023/A:1010084410679

Eisenmann, T., Parker, G., & Van Alstyne, M. (2011). Platform envelopment. *Strategic Management Journal*, *32*(12), 1270–1285. DOI: 10.1002/smj.935

Eroglu, S. A., Machleit, K. A., & Davis, L. M. (2003). Empirical testing of a model of online store atmospherics and shopper responses. *Psychology and Marketing*, *20*(2), 139–150. DOI: 10.1002/mar.10064

Ertürk, A., & Vurgun, L. (2015). Retention of IT professionals. *Journal of Business Research*, *68*(1), 34–46. DOI: 10.1016/j.jbusres.2014.05.010

European Commission. (2021). *2030 digital compass: The European way for the digital decade*. European Commission.

EY & NASSCOM. (2025). NASSCOM AI adoption index. https://www.ey.com/content/dam/ey-unified-site/ey-com/en-in/insights/ai/documents/ey-nasscom-ai-adoption-index.pdf

Fan, X., Li, H., & Jiang, X. (2026). How to retain users in the metaverse: Exert technological affordances through psychological ownership mechanism. *Technology in Society*, *84*, 103131. Advance online publication. DOI: 10.1016/j.techsoc.2025.103131

Fares, N., Islam, M. S., Jauhar, S. K., & Kucukaltan, B. (2025). Towards an International Digital Product Passport: The New Paradigm of a Worldwide Circular Economy. *Circular Economy and Sustainability*, *5*(6), 5475–5495. DOI: 10.1007/s43615-025-00690-5

Farmanesh, P., Saliba, C., Athari, S. A., Naaman, D., Hanna Al Geitany, S., & Abualrob, J. O. (2025). Bridging Sustainable Development: The Nexus of Business Safety, Health Management, and Corporate Social Sustainability—Do Affective Commitment and Emotional Intelligence Mediate? *Sustainability (Basel)*, *17*(7), 3080. DOI: 10.3390/su17073080

Farooqi, A., Das, D., Tripathi, M., Dutta, R., Goyal, N. K., & Sheikh, M. F. (2026). Navigating ethical frontiers in AI-driven geriatric care. In Stolakis, K., & Efthymiou, I. (Eds.), *AI for geriatric care in an aging society: Ethical, clinical, and policy challenges* (pp. 243–266). IGI Global Scientific Publishing., DOI: 10.4018/979-8-3373-5462-0.ch009

Farrell, J., & Klemperer, P. (2007). coordination and lock-in: Competition with switching costs and network effects. *Handbook of Industrial Organization, 3*, 1967–2072. DOI: 10.1016/S1573-448X(06)03031-7

Fatih, F. Z., Abbassy, S., & Hirawan, F. B. (2025). Transformative Paths to Economic Growth Through Circular Supply Chain Enablers and Environmental Initiatives—A Structural Equation Modeling Perspective. *Contemporary Management Research*, *21*(2), 99–125. DOI: 10.7903/cmr.24033

Ferrara, E. (2024). Fairness and bias in artificial intelligence: A brief survey of sources, impacts, and mitigation strategies. *Sci*, *6*(1), 3. Advance online publication. DOI: 10.3390/sci6010003

Festinger, L. (1954). A theory of social comparison processes. *Human Relations; Studies Towards the Integration of the Social Sciences*, *7*(2), 117–140. DOI: 10.1177/001872675400700202

Fetters, M. D., Curry, L. A., & Creswell, J. W. (2013). Achieving integration in mixed methods designs: Principles and practices. *Health Services Research*, *48*(6 Pt 2), 2134–2156. DOI: 10.1111/1475-6773.12117 PMID: 24279835

Firescu, V., & Filip, D. (2025). Human factors and ergonomics in sustainable manufacturing systems: A pathway to enhanced performance and wellbeing. *Machines (Basel)*, *13*(7), 595. DOI: 10.3390/machines13070595

Firth, J., Torous, J., Stubbs, B., Firth, J. A., Steiner, G. Z., Smith, L., Alvarez-Jimenez, M., Gleeson, J., Vancampfort, D., Armitage, C. J., & Sarris, J. (2019). The "online brain": How the Internet may be changing our cognition. *World Psychiatry; Official Journal of the World Psychiatric Association (WPA), 18*(2), 119–129. DOI: 10.1002/wps.20617 PMID: 31059635

Fisk, R. P., Gallan, A. S., Joubert, A. M., Beekhuyzen, J., Cheung, L., & Russell-Bennett, R. (2023). Healing the digital divide with digital inclusion: Enabling human capabilities. *Journal of Service Research, 26*(4), 542–559. DOI: 10.1177/10946705221140148

Fitzmaurice, J., & Comegys, C. (2006). Materialism and Social Consumption. *Journal of Marketing Theory and Practice, 14*(4), 287–299. DOI: 10.2753/MTP1069-6679140403

Flink, N. A., Black, H. G., & Dingus, R. (2025). Explore, Identify, and Align: Utilizing Generative AI as a Career Coach. *Marketing Education Review, 35*(2), 109–119. DOI: 10.1080/10528008.2024.2430266

Floridi, L. (2021). Translating principles into practices of digital ethics: Five risks of being unethical. In L. Floridi (Ed.), *Ethics, governance, and policies in artificial intelligence* (Philosophical Studies Series, Vol. 144, pp. 81–90). Springer. DOI: 10.1007/978-3-030-81907-1_6

Folkman, S., & Moskowitz, J. T. (2004). Coping: Pitfalls and promise. *Annual Review of Psychology, 55*(1), 745–774. DOI: 10.1146/annurev.psych.55.090902.141456 PMID: 14744233

Fournier, S. (1998). Consumers and their brands: Developing relationship theory in consumer research. *The Journal of Consumer Research, 24*(4), 343–373. DOI: 10.1086/209515

Friede, G., Busch, T., & Bassen, A. (2015). ESG and financial performance: Aggregated evidence from more than 2000 empirical studies. *Journal of Sustainable Finance & Investment, 5*(4), 210–233. DOI: 10.1080/20430795.2015.1118917

Fris, L., & Koster, N. (n.d.). *The understanding role of digital competence and social capital on contentment in life.*

Fusco Girard, L. (2024). The circular "human-centred" adaptive reuse of cultural heritage: Theoretical foundations. In *Adaptive reuse of cultural heritage: Circular business, financial and governance models* (pp. 15–69). Springer.

Gaggioli, A., Riva, G., Peters, D., & Calvo, R. A. (2017). Positive Technology, Computing, and Design: Shaping a Future in Which Technology Promotes Psychological Well-Being. In Jeon, M. (Ed.), *Emotions and Affect in Human Factors and Human-Computer Interaction* (pp. 477–502). Academic Press., https://doi.org/ https://doi.org/10.1016/B978-0-12-801851-4.00018-5 DOI: 10.1016/B978-0-12-801851-4.00018-5

Gagné, M., Parker, S. K., Griffin, M. A., Dunlop, P. D., Knight, C., Klonek, F. E., & Parent-Rocheleau, X. (2022). Understanding and shaping the future of work with self-determination theory. *Nature Reviews Psychology*, *1*(7), 378–392. DOI: 10.1038/s44159-022-00056-w PMID: 35574235

Gangadharan, S. P. (2017). The downside of digital inclusion: Expectations and experiences of privacy and surveillance among marginal Internet users. *New Media & Society*, *19*(4), 597–615. DOI: 10.1177/1461444815614053

Gao, Y., & Liu, H. (2023). Artificial intelligence-enabled personalization in interactive marketing: A customer journey perspective. *Journal of Research in Interactive Marketing*, *17*(5), 663–680. DOI: 10.1108/JRIM-01-2022-0023

Garcia, A. M. C., Alves, V. S. D. S., Cunha, L. R. A., Bianchini, V. K., Razzino, C. D. A., Bezerra, B. S., & De Brito, I.Jr. (2025). Approaches, Challenges, and Opportunities in Humanitarian Logistics Integrated with Reverse Logistics and Sustainability. *Logistics (Basel)*, *10*(1), 9. DOI: 10.3390/logistics10010009

Gathergood, J. (2012). Self-control, financial literacy and consumer over-indebtedness. *Journal of Economic Psychology*, *33*(3), 590–602. DOI: 10.1016/j.joep.2011.11.006

Gawande, N., & DoShi, P. (2025). Exploring Green Logistics: Impacts on Sustainability, Economic Efficiency, and Technological Innovation. In K. Patil, F. Moreira, & S. Dash (Eds.), *Proceedings of the International Conference on Sustainable Innovation with Artificial Intelligence and Machine Learning 2025 (ICSIAIML 2025)* (Vol. 200, pp. 925–941). Atlantis Press International BV. DOI: 10.2991/978-94-6463-948-3_64

Geetha, B. T., Yenugula, M., Randhawa, N., Purohit, P., Maney, K. L., & Venkteshwar, A. (2024). Advancement improving the acquisition of customer insights in digital marketing by utilising advanced artificial intelligence algorithms. In *Proceedings of the 2nd IEEE International Conference on Trends in Quantum Computing and Emerging Business Technologies (TQCEBT 2024)*. IEEE. https://doi.org/DOI: 10.1109/TQCEBT59414.2024.10545055

Gefen, D., Karahanna, E., & Straub, D. W. (2003). Trust and tam in online shopping: An integrated model 1. *Management Information Systems Quarterly*, *27*(1), 51–90. DOI: 10.2307/30036519

George, A. S. (2023). Preparing students for an AI-driven world: Rethinking curriculum and pedagogy in the age of artificial intelligence. *Partners Universal Innovative Research Publication*, *1*(2), 112–136. DOI: 10.5281/zenodo.10245675

Gerson, J., Plagnol, A. C., & Corr, P. J. (2016). Subjective well-being and social media use: Do personality traits moderate the impact of social comparison on Facebook? *Computers in Human Behavior*, *63*, 813–822. DOI: 10.1016/j.chb.2016.06.023

Ghasemaghaei, M., & Kordzadeh, N. (2025). Ethics in the Age of Algorithms: Unravelling the Impact of Algorithmic Unfairness on Data Analytics Recommendation Acceptance. *Information Systems Journal*, *35*(4), 1166–1197. DOI: 10.1111/isj.12572

Gillespie, T. (2014). The relevance of algorithms. In T. Gillespie, P. J. Boczkowski, & KA Foot (Eds.), *Media technologies: Essays on communication, materiality, and society* (pp. 167–194). The MIT Press. DOI: 10.7551/mitpress/9780262525374.003.0009

GizChina. (2024, July 22). From messaging to super pp: How WeChat dominates China's digital landscape. https://www.gizchina.com/news/from-messaging-to-super-app-how-wechat-dominates-chinas-digital-landscape

Gleiss, A., Degen, K., & Pousttchi, K. (2023). Identifying the patterns: Towards a systematic approach to digital platform regulation. *Journal of Information Technology*, *38*(2), 180–201. DOI: 10.1177/02683962221146803

Goyal, N. K., Goyal, N. K., Kumar, S., Dutta, R., Kothari, V., & Sinha, S. K. (2026). Empowering elderly care through artificial intelligence. In Stolakis, K., & Efthymiou, I. (Eds.), *AI for geriatric care in an aging society* (pp. 1–28). IGI Global Scientific Publishing., DOI: 10.4018/979-8-3373-5462-0.ch001

Goyal, N. K., Gulati, K., Avasthi, A., Kapoor, S. K., Keswani, B., & Gupta, S. (2026). Securing the imagination: Security and privacy challenges in generative AI systems. In Elbaghazaoui, B., Amnai, M., & Gherabi, N. (Eds.), *Generative AI-powered data architectures: From governance to autonomous analytics* (pp. 239–266). IGI Global Scientific Publishing., DOI: 10.4018/979-8-3373-5616-7.ch010

Granovetter, M. (1985). Economic action and social structure: The problem of embeddedness. *AJS; American Journal of Sociology*, *91*(3), 481–510. DOI: 10.1086/228311

Gray, J., Gerlitz, C., & Bounegru, L. (2018). Data infrastructure literacy *Big Data & Society, 5* (2). https://doi.org/(Original work (published 2018)DOI: 10.1177/2053951718786316

Grewal, D., Guha, A., Beccacece Satornino, C., & Becker, M. (2024). The Future of Marketing and Marketing Education. *Journal of Marketing Education, 47*(1), 61-77. https://doi.org/ (Original work published 2025)DOI: 10.1177/02734753241269838

Grewal, D., Satornino, C. B., Davenport, T., & Guha, A. (2025). How generative AI Is shaping the future of marketing. *Journal of the Academy of Marketing Science, 53*(3), 702–722. DOI: 10.1007/s11747-024-01064-3

Grönroos, C. (1994). From marketing mix to relationship marketing: Towards a paradigm shift in marketing. *Management Decision, 32*(2), 4–20. DOI: 10.1108/00251749410054774

Gross, J. J. (1998). The emerging field of emotion regulation: An integrative review. *Review of General Psychology, 2*(3), 271–299. DOI: 10.1037/1089-2680.2.3.271

Gross, J. J. (2015). Emotion regulation: Current status and future prospects. *Psychological Inquiry, 26*(1), 1–26. DOI: 10.1080/1047840X.2014.940781

Gross, J. J., & John, O. P. (2003). Individual differences in two emotion regulation processes: Implications for affect, relationships, and well-being. *Journal of Personality and Social Psychology, 85*(2), 348–362. DOI: 10.1037/0022-3514.85.2.348 PMID: 12916575

Guay, F. (2021). Applying Self-Determination Theory to Education: Regulations Types, Psychological Needs, and Autonomy Supporting Behaviors. *Canadian Journal of School Psychology, 37*(1), 75-92. https://doi.org/ (Original work published 2022)DOI: 10.1177/08295735211055355

Guest, D. E. (2017). Human resource management and employee well-being: Towards a new analytic framework. *Human Resource Management Journal, 27*(1), 22–38. DOI: 10.1111/1748-8583.12139

Guha, A. (2025). AI identity drift: Toward a new model for AI UX and governance (White paper). Phase 5 Consulting Group Inc. https://www.phase-5.com/hubfs/Phase5_AIidentity_whtppr_2025.pdf

Guo, J., Zhang, L., Wang, Y., & Li, H. (2025). Applying the S-O-R model to explore impulsive buying on social media influencers' s-commerce websites. *Heliyon*. Advance online publication. DOI: 10.1016/j.heliyon.2025.e40989

Guo, Y. (2022). Digital Trust and the Reconstruction of Trust in the Digital Society: An Integrated Model based on Trust Theory and Expectation Confirmation Theory. *Digital Government: Research and Practice, 3*(4), 1–19. DOI: 10.1145/3543860

Hadi, W., & AlShaikh-Hasan, M. N. (2025). AI-Driven Curriculum Transformation and Faculty Development in Developing Universities. In Al Maqousi, A., Almomani, A., Aldweesh, A., & Alauthman, M. (Eds.), *Revolutionizing Urban Development and Governance With Emerging Technologies* (pp. 289–322). IGI Global Scientific Publishing., DOI: 10.4018/979-8-3373-1375-7.ch010

Halaswamy, D., Tanmay, J., Raghavendra, A. N., & Vimaladevi, M. (2026). Impact of Green Supply Chain Management (GSCM) on consumer purchase intention in the Indian automobile industry. In K. Koppa, M. D. Shah, & S. S. Appadoo, *Empowering Inclusive Innovation* (1st ed., pp. 522–530). Routledge. DOI: 10.1201/9781003753445-61

Hale, S. A., Belisario, A., Mostafa, A. N., & Camargo, C. (2024). Analyzing misinformation claims during the 2022 Brazilian election on WhatsApp, Twitter, and Kwai. *International Journal of Public Opinion Research, 36*(3), edae032. Advance online publication. DOI: 10.1093/ijpor/edae032

Hamidah, D. N. A.. (2024). "User Interface Design of TUS Mart E-Commerce Website Using Design Thinking and Kansei Engineering," *Proc. ICIMCIS*, Jakarta, Indonesia, pp. 182–187, DOI: 10.1109/ICIMCIS63449.2024.10956865

Hanelt, A., Bohnsack, R., Marz, D., & Marante, C. A. (2021). A systematic review of the literature on digital transformation: Insights and implications for strategy and organizational change. *Journal of Management Studies, 58*(5), 1159–1197. DOI: 10.1111/joms.12639

Hanisch, M., Goldsby, C. M., Fabian, N. E., & Oehmichen, J. (2023). Digital governance: A conceptual framework and research agenda. *Journal of Business Research, 162*, 113777. DOI: 10.1016/j.jbusres.2023.113777

Hanna, R., Rohm, A., & Crittenden, V. L. (2011). We're all connected: The power of the social media ecosystem. *Business Horizons, 54*(3), 265–273. DOI: 10.1016/j.bushor.2011.01.007

Han, X., Yang, Y., Li, F., & Li, Y. (2022). Adding life to years: The influence of Internet use and appearance management on life satisfaction among the elderly. *Social Indicators Research, 160*(2), 585–600. DOI: 10.1007/s11205-020-02342-7

Harahap, E. P.. (2024). "User Interface Design's Impact on Customer Satisfaction and Loyalty in SaaS E-Commerce," *Proc. ICCIT*, Tangerang, Indonesia, pp. 1–6, DOI: 10.1109/ICCIT62134.2024.10701133

Hardcastle, K., Vorster, L., & Brown, D. M. (2025). Understanding customer responses to AI-driven personalized journeys: Impacts on the customer experience. *Journal of Advertising*, *54*(2), 176–195. DOI: 10.1080/00913367.2025.2460985

Harendsa, N. P., & Pulansari, F. (2025). Analysis of Finished Product Warehouse Activity Flow Using Lean Warehouse Method. [Information Technology Engineering Journals]. *ITE Journal*, *10*(1), 29–38. DOI: 10.24235/itej.v10i1.202

Hayes, A. F. (2017). *Introduction to mediation, moderation, and conditional process analysis: A regression-based approach* (2nd ed.). Guilford Press.

Hayes, S. C., Luoma, J. B., Bond, F. W., Masuda, A., & Lillis, J. (2006). Acceptance and commitment therapy: Model, processes and outcomes. *Behaviour Research and Therapy*, *44*(1), 1–25. DOI: 10.1016/j.brat.2005.06.006 PMID: 16300724

Helsper, E. J., & Eynon, R. (2013). Distinct skill pathways to digital engagement. *European Journal of Communication*, *28*(6), 696–713. DOI: 10.1177/0267323113499113

He, Y., Zhang, L., Zhang, C., & Zhou, Z. (2024). Hedonic adaptation in cultural consumption: Evidence from China Family Panel Studies. *Humanities & Social Sciences Communications*, *11*(1), 1688. DOI: 10.1057/s41599-024-04227-3

Hinkin, T. R. (1998). A brief tutorial on the development of measures for use in survey questionnaires. *Organizational Research Methods*, *1*(1), 104–121. DOI: 10.1177/109442819800100106

Hinks, T. (2024). Artificial Intelligence Perceptions and Life Satisfaction. *Journal of Happiness Studies*, *25*(1), 5. DOI: 10.1007/s10902-024-00727-w

Hmamed, H., Cherrafi, A., Garza-Reyes, J. A., & Hamani, N. (2026). Zero trust architecture for digital, sustainable, and resilient supply chains in the era of Industry 5.0/4.0. *Supply Chain Management*, *31*(2), 1–22. DOI: 10.1108/SCM-05-2025-0387

Hofstede, G. (1980). *Culture's consequences: International differences in work-related values*. Sage Publications., DOI: 10.1007/978-0-387-94806-4_13

Hofstede, G. (2001). *Culture's consequences: Comparing values, behaviors, institutions and organizations across nations* (2nd ed.). Sage Publications.

Hofstede, G. (2001). *Culture's Consequences: Comparing values, behaviors, institutions and organizations across Nations* (2nd ed.). Sage.

Hofstede, G. (2001). *Culture's consequences: Comparing values, behaviors, institutions, and organizations across nations* (2nd ed.). Sage.

Hofstede, G. (2011). Dimensionalizing cultures: The Hofstede model in context. *Online Readings in Psychology and Culture*, *2*(1), 8. DOI: 10.9707/2307-0919.1014

Hollebeek, L. D., Glynn, M. S., & Brodie, R. J. (2014). Consumer brand engagement in social media: Conceptualization, scale development and validation. *Journal of Interactive Marketing*, *28*(2), 149–165. DOI: 10.1016/j.intmar.2013.12.002

Hong, W., Liu, R.-D., Ding, Y., Zhen, R., Jiang, R., & Fu, X. (2020). Autonomy need dissatisfaction in daily life and problematic mobile phone use: The mediating roles of boredom proneness and mobile phone gaming. *International Journal of Environmental Research and Public Health*, *17*(15), 5305. DOI: 10.3390/ijerph17155305 PMID: 32717969

Huang, M.-H., & Rust, R. T. (2024). The Caring Machine: Feeling AI for Customer Care. *Journal of Marketing*, *88*(5), 1-23. https://doi.org/ (Original work published 2024)DOI: 10.1177/00222429231224748

Huang, M.-H., & Rust, R. T. (2021). A strategic framework for artificial intelligence in marketing. *Journal of the Academy of Marketing Science*, *49*(1), 30–50. DOI: 10.1007/s11747-020-00749-9

Huang, Y., & Miao, W. (2021). Re-domesticating social media when it becomes disruptive: Evidence from WeChat's Moments. *Mobile Media & Communication*, *9*(2), 177–194. DOI: 10.1177/2050157920940765

Iacus, S. M., & Porro, G. (2021). *Subjective well-being and social media*. Chapman and Hall/CRC., DOI: 10.1201/9780429401435

IJCRT. (2025). Privacy, dignity, and liberty: A critical examination of the Puttaswamy case. International Journal of Creative Research Thoughts. https://ijcrt.org/papers/IJCRT25A5528.pdf

Inmor, S., Na-Nan, K., Phanniphong, K., Jaturat, N., & Hirnšal, M. (2025). Unveiling the metaverse: The mediating role of social interaction in enhancing tourism experiences. *Journal of Open Innovation*, *11*(1), 100461. DOI: 10.1016/j.joitmc.2024.100461

International Monetary Fund. (2024, December 17). Oman: Selected issues—Embracing digitalization to accelerate Oman's economic transformation (IMF Country Report No. 25/14). https://www.elibrary.imf.org/downloadpdf/view/journals/002/2025/014/article-A004-en.pdf

International Telecommunication Union / U4SSC. (2025). A guide to digital well-being. https://www.itu.int/dms_pub/itu-t/opb/tut/T-TUT-SMARTCITY-2025-11-PDF-E.pdf

Iqbal, F., Afiat, A., Shoily, M. M., Turzo, S. S., & Arafat, M. S. (2025). AI-driven personalization in e-commerce: Evaluating the transformative effects on consumer behavior. *International Journal of Science and Research Archive, 16*(1), 264–273. DOI: 10.30574/ijsra.2025.16.1.2035

Ishii, K. (2017). Online communication with strong ties and subjective well-being in Japan. *Computers in Human Behavior, 66*, 129–137. DOI: 10.1016/j.chb.2016.09.033

Israel, B. A., Schulz, A. J., Parker, E. A., Becker, A. B., Allen, A. J., & Guzman, J. R. (2013). Critical issues in developing and following CBPR principles. In Israel, B. A., Eng, E., Schulz, A. J., & Parker, E. A. (Eds.), *Methods for community-based participatory research for health* (2nd ed., pp. 31–55). Jossey-Bass.

Issac, A. L. (2024). The human-centred workplace in Industry 4.0: Cultivating well-being and engagement. In *Smart cities and circular economy* (pp. 1–8). Emerald Publishing Limited. DOI: 10.1108/978-1-83797-957-820241001

Iyengar, S. S., & Lepper, M. R. (2000). When choice is demotivating: Can one desire too much of a good thing? *Journal of Personality and Social Psychology, 79*(6), 995–1006. DOI: 10.1037/0022-3514.79.6.995 PMID: 11138768

Jaakkola, E. (2020). Designing conceptual articles: Four approaches. *AMS Review, 10*(1), 18–26. DOI: 10.1007/s13162-020-00161-0

Jha, A. P., Morrison, A. B., Dainer-Best, J., Parker, S., Rostrup, N., & Stanley, E. A. (2015). Minds "at attention": Mindfulness training curbs attentional lapses in military cohorts. *PLoS One, 10*(2), e0116889. DOI: 10.1371/journal.pone.0116889 PMID: 25671579

Jia, Y., & Mvondo, G. F. N. (2025). Exploring the adverse effects of the metaverse on users' psychological well-being and Self-Esteem: A mixed-methods study. *Journal of Retailing and Consumer Services, 86*, 104321. DOI: 10.1016/j.jretconser.2025.104321

Jiayuan, Z., & Rogers, Z. S. (2025). *Consumer tradeoff preferences regarding logistics service and sustainability in last-mile delivery.*

Jo, H., & Lee, J. K. (2024). A comprehensive analysis of presence, seamlessness, and player responses in metaverse gaming. *Computers in Human Behavior, 159*, 108345. Advance online publication. DOI: 10.1016/j.chb.2024.108345

Joseph, J. (2025). The algorithmic self: How AI is reshaping human identity, introspection, and agency. *Frontiers in Psychology, 16*, 1645795. Advance online publication. DOI: 10.3389/fpsyg.2025.1645795 PMID: 40718563

Kahneman, D., & Tversky, A. (2013). Prospect theory: An analysis of decision under risk. In *Handbook of the fundamentals of financial decision making: Part I* (pp. 99-127).

Kahneman, D. (2011). *Thinking, fast and slow*. Farrar, Straus and Giroux.

Kaplan, S. (1995). The restorative benefits of nature: Toward an integrative framework. *Journal of Environmental Psychology*, *15*(3), 169–182. DOI: 10.1016/0272-4944(95)90001-2

Kaplan, S., & Berman, M. G. (2010). Directed attention as a common resource for executive functioning and self-regulation. *Perspectives on Psychological Science : A Journal of the Association for Psychological Science*, *5*(1), 43–57. DOI: 10.1177/1745691609356784 PMID: 26162062

Karimova, G. Z., Kim, Y. D., & Shirkhanbeik, A. (2025). Poietic symbiosis or algorithmic subjugation: Generative AI technology in marketing communications education. *Education and Information Technologies*, *30*(2), 2185–2209. DOI: 10.1007/s10639-024-12877-8

Katz, E., Blumler, J. G., & Gurevitch, M. (1973). Uses and gratifications research. *Public Opinion Quarterly*, *37*(4), 509–523. DOI: 10.1086/268109

Katz, E., Blumler, J. G., & Gurevitch, M. (1974). Utilization of mass communication by the individual. In Blumler, J. G., & Katz, E. (Eds.), *The uses of mass communications: Current perspectives on gratifications research* (pp. 19–32). Sage Publications.

Khamdamov, S. J., Shahbaz, M., Mamadiyarov, Z., Usmanov, A., Xonturayev, B., Rashidov, S., & Izzatillayev, A. (2025). The impact of AI and machine learning on e-commerce personalization. In *Proceedings of the 8th International Conference on Future Networks & Distributed Systems* (pp. 115–128). https://doi.org/DOI: 10.1145/3726122.3726142

Khandelwal, S., Sansare, V., & Bhatt, V. (2025). *Sustainable Futures: Empowering Change with Artificial Intelligence. 3*(12).

Khan, P., Shahid, M. S., & Majid, H. A. (2024). MEDIATING ROLE OF ONLINE SOCIAL CONNECTEDNESS IN SMARTPHONE ADDICTION AND ONLINE RELATIONSHIP AMONG YOUNG ADULTS. *Gomal University Journal of Research*, *40*(3), 327–336. DOI: 10.51380/gujr-40-03-05

Kim, D., Magane, R., Poitier, M., Kuang, J., Wang, A., Adderley, R., & Deveaux, L. (2025). Social media use, risk behavior engagement, and mental health among middle adolescents in the Caribbean. *BMC Public Health*, *25*(1), 2468. Advance online publication. DOI: 10.1186/s12889-025-23646-8 PMID: 40670957

Kim, J. J. H., Soh, J., Kadkol, S., Solomon, I., Yeh, H., Srivatsa, A. V., Nahass, G. R., Choi, J. Y., Lee, S., Nyugen, T., & Ajilore, O. (2025). AI Anxiety: A comprehensive analysis of psychological factors and interventions. *AI and Ethics*, *5*(4), 3993–4009. DOI: 10.1007/s43681-025-00686-9

Kim, S., & Tam, L. (2024). Unpacking publics' disengagement and information behaviors: Roles of psychological distance, feasibility and desirability in an environmental sustainability issue. *Public Relations Review*, *50*(4), 102491. DOI: 10.1016/j.pubrev.2024.102491

Kim, Y., Sohn, D., & Choi, S. M. (2011). Cultural difference in motivations for using social network sites: A comparative study of American and Korean college students. *Computers in Human Behavior*, *27*(1), 365–372. DOI: 10.1016/j.chb.2010.08.015

Kircaburun, K., Alhabash, S., Tosuntaş, Ş. B., & Griffiths, M. D. (2020). Uses and gratifications of problematic social media use among university students: A simultaneous examination of the Big Five of personality traits, social media platforms, and social media use motives. *International Journal of Mental Health and Addiction*, *18*(3), 525–547. DOI: 10.1007/s11469-018-9940-6

Kitayama, S., Markus, H. R., & Kurokawa, M. (2000). Culture, emotion, and well-being: Good feelings in Japan and the United States. *Cognition & Emotion*, *14*(1), 93–124. DOI: 10.1080/026999300379003

Kline, R. B. (2015). *Principles and practice of structural equation modeling* (4th ed.). Guilford Press.

Koc-Michalska, K., & Lilleker, D. (2017). Digital Politics: Mobilization, Engagement, and Participation. *Political Communication*, *34*(1), 1–5. DOI: 10.1080/10584609.2016.1243178

Kotler, P., Pfoertsch, W., Ancarani, F., & Ureta, I. (Eds.). (2024). *Humanism in marketing: Responsible leadership and the human-to-human approach*. Springer Nature. DOI: 10.1007/978-3-031-67155-5

Kourtesis, P. (2024). A comprehensive review of multimodal XR applications, risks, and ethical challenges in the metaverse. *Multimodal Technologies and Interaction*, *8*(11), 98. DOI: 10.3390/mti8110098

Kowalski, T. H., & Loretto, W. (2017). Well-being and HRM in the changing workplace. *International Journal of Human Resource Management*, *28*(16), 2229–2255. DOI: 10.1080/09585192.2017.1345205

Ko, Y. M., Lee, E. S., & Park, S. (2024). Prevalence and correlates of internet gaming disorder in Korea (National Mental Health Survey 2021). *Frontiers in Psychiatry*, *15*, 1442224. DOI: 10.3389/fpsyt.2024.1442224 PMID: 39473915

KPMG International. (2025). Trust, attitudes and use of artificial intelligence: A global study 2025. https://assets.kpmg.com/content/dam/kpmgsites/xx/pdf/2025/05/trust-attitudes-and-use-of-ai-global-report.pdf

Krishen, A. S., Berezan, O., Agarwal, S., Kachroo, P., & Raschke, R. (2021). The digital self and virtual satisfaction: A cross-cultural perspective. *Journal of Business Research*, *124*, 254–263. DOI: 10.1016/j.jbusres.2020.11.056

Kristiyanto, D. Y., Purnomo, H. D., Cesna, G. P., & Ani, N. (2025). The strategic role of orange technology in cultivating innovation and well-being. *IAIC Transactions on Sustainable Digital Innovation*, *7*(1), 27–37. DOI: 10.34306/itsdi.v7i1.707

Kubatko, O., Roubik, H., Kubatko, V., Odewole, O., Stepanenko, Y., Kovalov, B., & Kozmenko, S. (2022). Life satisfaction and digital transformation of society evidence from European economies. *International Journal of Global Environmental Issues*, *21*(2-4), 245–258. DOI: 10.1504/IJGENVI.2022.126203

Kuijer, L., & Laschke, M. (2024). Designing for a post-growth society through the eco-harmonist: A critical examination of the role of HCI and technology design. In *Proceedings of the 13th Nordic Conference on Human-Computer Interaction* (pp. 1–13). DOI: 10.1145/3679318.3685405

Kumar, D., & Suthar, N. (2024). Ethical and legal challenges of AI in marketing: An exploration of solutions. *Journal of Information. Communication and Ethics in Society*, *22*(1), 124–144. DOI: 10.1108/JICES-05-2023-0068

Kumari, M., & Goyal, N. K. (2026). Artificial intelligence in the cryptocurrency ecosystem: Crime mechanisms, detection strategies, and legal perspectives. In Lin, L. (Ed.), *Innovations in cryptocrime and financial fraud* (pp. 245–282). IGI Global Scientific Publishing., DOI: 10.4018/979-8-3373-0675-9.ch007

Kumari, M., Kumawat, R., Tripathi, M., Suganthi, K., Goyal, N. K., & Sheikh, M. F. (2026). Blockchain for transparency and traceability in supply chains. In Khan, M., Mehmood, T., & Rao, M. (Eds.), *Maximizing operational efficiency at the intersection of supply chain management and marketing* (pp. 35–64). IGI Global Scientific Publishing., DOI: 10.4018/979-8-3373-3109-6.ch002

Kushlev, K., & Dunn, E. W. (2015). Checking email less frequently reduces stress. *Computers in Human Behavior*, *43*, 220–228. DOI: 10.1016/j.chb.2014.11.005

Lad, V. (2002). *Textbook of Ayurveda: Fundamental principles*. Ayurvedic Press.

Laibson, D. (1997). Golden eggs and hyperbolic discounting. *The Quarterly Journal of Economics, 112*(2), 443–478. DOI: 10.1162/003355397555253

Lai, P. C., & Liew, E. J. Y. (2021). Towards a cashless society: The effects of perceived convenience and security on gamified mobile payment platform adoption. *AJIS. Australasian Journal of Information Systems, 25*, 1–25. DOI: 10.3127/ajis.v25i0.2809

Lazarus, R. S., & Folkman, S. (1984). *Stress, appraisal, and coping*. Springer.

Leng, S., Wang, Y., Zhou, Y., Feng, X., Lee, P. T. W., & Bai, R. (2026). The growing role of artificial intelligence in smart container ports: Its application and future research directions. *Journal of International Logistics and Trade, 24*(1), 1–35. DOI: 10.1108/JILT-11-2025-0105

Levin, M. E., Haeger, J. A., Pierce, B. G., & Twohig, M. P. (2017). Web-based acceptance and commitment therapy for mental health problems in college students: A randomized controlled trial. *Behavior Modification, 41*(1), 141–162. DOI: 10.1177/0145445516659645 PMID: 27440189

Levin, M. E., Hildebrandt, M. J., Lillis, J., & Hayes, S. C. (2012). The impact of treatment components suggested by the psychological flexibility model: A meta-analysis of laboratory-based component studies. *Behavior Therapy, 43*(4), 741–756. DOI: 10.1016/j.beth.2012.05.003 PMID: 23046777

Liadeli, G., Sotgiu, F., & Verlegh, P. (2023). A meta-analysis of the effects of brands' owned social media on social media engagement and sales. *Journal of Marketing, 87*(3), 406–427. DOI: 10.1177/00222429221123250

Licsandru, T. C., Mari, C., Kipnis, E., Galalae, C., Johnson, E., Cross, S. N. N., Cui, C. C., Kearney, S., Martín Ruiz, V., Vorster Larsen, L., & Yoruk, I. (2025). Integrating diversity, equity, and inclusion in management education: An empathy framework. *British Journal of Management*. Advance online publication. DOI: 10.1111/1467-8551.70008

Li, D., & Sullivan, W. C. (2016). Impact of views to school landscapes on recovery from stress and mental fatigue. *Landscape and Urban Planning, 148*, 149–158. DOI: 10.1016/j.landurbplan.2015.12.015

Li, J., Chen, W., & Liu, Z. (2025). Addiction, donut, or extended self: An interpretive analysis of nomophobia. *Well-Being Sciences Review, 1*(1), 31–47. DOI: 10.54844/wsr.2025.0905

Lima, R. T., Durão, A. F., de Guimarães, J. C. F., Perinotto, A. R. C., & da Silva, N. P. (2025). The digital extended self of influencers: A case study of a travel channel. *Tourism and Hospitality*, *6*(5), 262. DOI: 10.3390/tourhosp6050262

Limone, P., & Toto, G. A. (2022). Psychological and Emotional Effects of Digital Technology on Digitods (14–18 Years): A Systematic Review. *Frontiers in Psychology*, *13*, 938965. DOI: 10.3389/fpsyg.2022.938965 PMID: 35874342

Lim, P. C., Lim, Y. L., Rajah, R., & Zainal, H. (2025). Usability questionnaire for standalone or interactive mobile health applications: A systematic review. *BMC Digital Health*, *3*(1), 11. DOI: 10.1186/s44247-025-00150-y

Lin, Z., & Yaakop, M. R. (2024). Research on digital governance based on Web of Science—A bibliometric analysis. *Frontiers in Political Science*, *6*, 1403404. DOI: 10.3389/fpos.2024.1403404

Lissak, G. (2018). Adverse physiological and psychological effects of screen time on children and adolescents: Literature review and case study. *Environmental Research*, *164*, 149–157. DOI: 10.1016/j.envres.2018.01.015 PMID: 29499467

Lissitsa, S., & Chachashvili-Bolotin, S. (2016). Life satisfaction in the internet age – Changes in the past decade. *Computers in Human Behavior*, *54*, 197–206. https://doi.org/https://doi.org/10.1016/j.chb.2015.08.001. DOI: 10.1016/j.chb.2015.08.001

Little, T. D. (2013). *Longitudinal structural equation modeling*. Guilford Press.

Liu, X., Xu, Q., Feng, Z., Jian, Y. I., & Wang, Q.-C. (2026). Understanding subjective well-being in urban emergencies: The role of time use and personality traits. *Computational Urban Science*, *6*(1), 3. DOI: 10.1007/s43762-026-00236-x

Liu, Y., Zhang, J., Liu, C., & Yang, Y. (2024). A Review of Attention Restoration Theory: Implications for Designing Restorative Environments. *Sustainability (Basel)*, *16*(9), 3639. DOI: 10.3390/su16093639

Livingstone, S. (2004). Media Literacy and the Challenge of New Information and Communication Technologies. *Communication Review*, *7*(1), 3–14. DOI: 10.1080/10714420490280152

Lusardi, A., Hasler, A., & Yakoboski, P. J. (2021). Building up financial literacy and financial resilience. *Mind & Society*, *20*(2), 181–187. DOI: 10.1007/s11299-020-00246-0

Lusardi, A., & Mitchell, O. S. (2014). The economic importance of financial literacy: Theory and evidence. *Journal of Economic Literature*, *52*(1), 5–44. DOI: 10.1257/jel.52.1.5 PMID: 28579637

Lu, Z., Xiang, J., Li, S., Zhang, C., & Wu, C. (2025). Technology-based physical activities and adults' physical activity levels, mental health, life satisfaction, and happiness: A mixed methods study. *BMC Psychology*, *13*(1), 1199. DOI: 10.1186/s40359-025-03217-7 PMID: 41168901

Lythreatis, S., Singh, S. K., & El-Kassar, A.-N. (2022). The digital divide: A review and future research agenda. *Technological Forecasting and Social Change*, *175*, 121359. DOI: 10.1016/j.techfore.2021.121359

MacKinnon, D. P., Fairchild, A. J., & Fritz, M. S. (2007). Mediation analysis. *Annual Review of Psychology*, *58*(1), 593–614. DOI: 10.1146/annurev.psych.58.110405.085542 PMID: 16968208

Mampilly, A. J., & Manda, V. K. (2024). Driving Change: Securing Success through Digital Transformation. In *Modern Management Challenges: A Case Compendium (ss* (pp. 196–205). Excel India Publishers., DOI: 10.5281/zenodo.11910143

Manda, V. K., Bezawada, K., & Bhukya, M. (2025). Applications of Artificial Intelligence in Education: Implications for Pedagogy, Learning Outcomes, and Policy Development. In *Artificial Intelligence Implementation in Education Processes* (pp. 01–21). Deep Science Publishing. https://doi.org/DOI: 10.70593/978-81-984306-7-0_1

Mandania, R., Cadogan, J. W., Liu, J., & Kazmi, N. (2025). Optimizing promotional campaigns to maximize customer lifetime value: A dynamic learning approach. *Journal of Service Research*, *28*(1), 1–15. DOI: 10.1177/10946705251365524

Manda, V. K., & Madhu, B. (2025). Sharding as a Sustainability Blockchain Optimization Tool. In Dsilva, J. (Ed.), *Redefining Sustainability* (pp. 227–233). Springer Nature Switzerland., DOI: 10.1007/978-3-031-88380-4_21

Manda, V. K., Yadav, A., & Khaliq, L. N. (2024). Role of Payment Systems in Financial Well-Being: An Examination from India. In Malik, G., Bansal, R., Gupta, S., & Ansari, Y. (Eds.), *Emerging Perspectives on Financial Well-Being* (pp. 228–251). IGI Global Scientific Publishing., DOI: 10.4018/979-8-3693-1750-1.ch012

Mani, S., Tiwari, P., Ramchandani, S., Acharya, P. S., & Irudayaraj, V. D. (2025). From clicks to conversions: How AI shapes consumer trust, experience, and online buying behaviour. *Advances in Consumer Research. Association for Consumer Research (U. S.)*, *2*, 5028–5035.

Mark, G., Iqbal, S. T., Czerwinski, M., Johns, P., & Sano, A. (2016). Email duration, batching and self-interruption: Patterns of email use on productivity and stress. *Proceedings of the 2016 CHI Conference on Human Factors in Computing Systems*, 1717–1728. https://doi.org/DOI: 10.1145/2858036.2858262

Markus, H. R., & Kitayama, S. (1991). Culture and the self: Implications for cognition, emotion, and motivation. *Psychological Review*, *98*(2), 224–253. DOI: 10.1037/0033-295X.98.2.224

Marsh, E., Perez Vallejos, E., & Spence, A. (2024). Overloaded by information or worried about missing out on it: A quantitative study of stress, burnout, and mental health implications in the digital workplace. *SAGE Open*, *14*(3), 21582440241268830. DOI: 10.1177/21582440241268830

Martela, F., & Steger, M. F. (2016). The three meanings of meaning in life: Distinguishing coherence, purpose, and significance. *The Journal of Positive Psychology*, *11*(5), 531–545. DOI: 10.1080/17439760.2015.1137623

Marvella, W. G., & Taylor, S. A. (2025). "Factors Influencing E-Commerce Repurchase Intention: Customer Experience and E-Service Quality," *Proc. ICCIT*, Kota Cirebon, Indonesia, pp. 1–7, DOI: 10.1109/ICCIT65724.2025.11166807

Mathew, J., Nair, S., Gomes, R., Mulasi, A., & Yadav, P. (2023). Design and validation of the digital well-being scale. *Ricerche Di Pedagogia e Didattica. Journal of Theories and Research in Education*, *18*(1), 239–251. DOI: 10.6092/issn.1970-2221/16365

Mattern, J., Lansmann, S., & Hüllmann, J. A. (2017). Towards a self-regulation framework for digital workplaces. In *Proceedings of the 25th European Conference on Information Systems* (pp. 1641–1656).

Mattern, J., Tarafdar, M., Klein, S., & Schellhammer, S. (2024). Thriving in a bruising job. *Information Systems Journal*, *34*(6), 1902–1934. DOI: 10.1111/isj.12513

Matus, N., Rusu, C., Rusu, V., & Botella, F. (2025). Developing and Validating an Intercultural Student Experience Scale Using Structural Equation Modeling. *Sustainability (Basel)*, *17*(18), 8224. DOI: 10.3390/su17188224

Maulana, H. T., & Rosyidah, U. (2022). "User Experience Model using Concise User-Centered Design in Small and Medium Enterprise E-Commerce," 2022 International Seminar on Application for Technology of Information and Communication (iSemantic), Semarang, Indonesia, pp. 377–382, DOI: 10.1109/iSemantic55962.2022.9920381

Mayer, R. C., Davis, J. H., & Schoorman, F. D. (1995). An integrative model of organizational trust. *Academy of Management Review*, *20*(3), 709–734. DOI: 10.2307/258792

Mayiwar, L., Asutay, E., Tinghög, G., Västfjäll, D., & Barrafrem, K. (2025). Determinants of digital well-being. *AI & Society*, *40*(5), 3063–3073. DOI: 10.1007/s00146-024-02071-2

McCracken, G. (1988). *Culture and Consumption: New Approaches to the Symbolic Character of Consumer Goods and Activities*. IndianaUniversity Press.

McDonnell, A. S., & Strayer, D. L. (2024). Immersion in nature enhances neural indices of executive attention. *Scientific Reports*, *14*(1), 1845. DOI: 10.1038/s41598-024-52205-1 PMID: 38253734

Media Scope Group. (2025, April 4). WeChat ecosystem: An overview of China's digital super app. https://mediascope.group/wechat-ecosystem-an-overview-of-chinas-digital-super-app

Mehrabian, A., & Russell, J. A. (1974). *An approach to environmental psychology*. MIT Press.

Meier, A., & Reinecke, L. (2021). Computer-mediated communication, social media, and mental health: A conceptual and empirical meta-review. *Communication Research*, *48*(8), 1182–1209. DOI: 10.1177/0093650220958224

Meng, S., Kong, F., Dong, W., Zhang, Y., Yu, T., & Jin, X. (2023). Mobile social media use and life satisfaction among adolescents: A moderated mediation model. *Frontiers in Public Health*, *11*, 1117745. Advance online publication. DOI: 10.3389/fpubh.2023.1117745 PMID: 38094229

Meng, Z. (2025). Construal Theory: A Review and Future Prospects. *Journal of Society Innovation and Development*, *7*(1), 143–151. DOI: 10.63924/jsid.v7i1.212

Menon, A. (2014). *Everyday nationalism: Women of the Hindu right in India*. University of Pennsylvania Press.

Mesch, G. S. (2006). Family characteristics and intergenerational conflicts over the Internet. *Information Communication and Society*, *9*(4), 473–495. DOI: 10.1080/13691180600858705

Metzler, H., & Garcia, D. (2023). Social Drivers and Algorithmic Mechanisms on Digital Media. *Perspectives on Psychological Science : A Journal of the Association for Psychological Science*, *19*(5), 735–748. DOI: 10.1177/17456916231185057 PMID: 37466493

MIC (Japan). (2022). Promoting support for digital usage by the elderly (White Paper, Column 3). https://www.soumu.go.jp/johotsusintokei/whitepaper/eng/WP2022/chapter-4_c3.pdf

Minkov, M., & Hofstede, G. (2012). Hofstede's fifth dimension: New evidence from The World Values Survey. *Journal of Cross-Cultural Psychology*, *43*(1), 3–14. DOI: 10.1177/0022022110388567

Mirowska, A., & Bakici, T. (2024). Working in a bubble: Techno-isolation as an emerging techno-stressor in teleworkers. *Information Technology & People*, *37*(3), 1403–1422. DOI: 10.1108/ITP-09-2022-0657

Mishra, R., Tripathi, P., & Kumar, N. (2025). Human-centered infrastructure for sustainable smart cities in Industry 5.0. In *Building a human-centred infrastructure for sustainable Industry 5.0 in Asia* (pp. 301–319). Springer Nature Singapore. DOI: 10.1007/978-981-95-0417-6_13

Mittameedi, S. K., Dogra, V., & Sayal, A. (2025). Customer Experience in E-Commerce: A Systematic Review of Metrics, Models, and the Role of AI. *IEEE Access : Practical Innovations, Open Solutions*, *13*, 154422–154437. DOI: 10.1109/ACCESS.2025.3600729

Moodley, K., & Sookhdeo, L. (2025). The role of artificial intelligence personalisation in e-commerce: Customer purchase decisions in the retail sector. *South African Journal of Information Management*, *27*(1), a1926. DOI: 10.4102/sajim.v27i1.1926

Moqaddem, O. (2025). Investigating the impact of AI on personalization and customer engagement in intelligent marketing strategies. *European Journal of Management and Marketing Studies*, *10*(1). Advance online publication. DOI: 10.46827/ejmms.v10i1.1922

Morales Almeida, P., & Alemán Ramos, P. (2025). The Subjectivity of Subjective Well-Being. *SAGE Open*, *15*(1), 21582440251329860. DOI: 10.1177/21582440251329860

Morley, J., Elhalal, A., Garcia, F., Kinsey, L., Mökander, J., & Floridi, L. (2021). Ethics as a service: A pragmatic operationalisation of AI ethics. *Minds and Machines*, *31*(2), 239–256. DOI: 10.1007/s11023-021-09563-w PMID: 34720418

Morling, B., Kitayama, S., & Miyamoto, Y. (2002). Cultural practices emphasize influence in the United States and adjustment in Japan. *Personality & Social Psychology Bulletin*, *28*(3), 311–323. DOI: 10.1177/0146167202286003

Mortezapour, A., & Vitiello, G. (2025). Human-centered AI with focus on human–robot interaction. *arXiv preprint*.

Mrad, M., Itani, O. S., & Cui, C. C. (2025). Unlocking life satisfaction: The impact of self-image congruence on consumers' life satisfaction through brand love and brand addiction. *European Journal of Marketing*, *59*(8), 2054–2088. DOI: 10.1108/EJM-02-2024-0103

Muntinga, D. G., Moorman, M., & Smit, E. G. (2011). Introducing COBRAs: Exploring motivations for brand-related social media use. *International Journal of Advertising*, *30*(1), 13–46. DOI: 10.2501/IJA-30-1-013-046

Murray, D. (2024). Facial recognition and the end of human rights as we know them? *Netherlands Quarterly of Human Rights*, *42*(2), 179–189. DOI: 10.1177/09240519241253061

Narang, U., Sachdev, V., & Liu, R. (2025). When AI Wears Many Hats: The Role of Generative Artificial Intelligence in Marketing Education. *Journal of Public Policy & Marketing*, *44*(3), 473–489. DOI: 10.1177/07439156251328237

Nasar, M. R. A. (2025). "Evaluating Platform Usability in E-Commerce: Empirical Insights from User Interactions with Amazon's App and Website," 2025 3rd International Conference on Business Analytics for Technology and Security (ICBATS), Dubai, United Arab Emirates, pp. 1–7, DOI: 10.1109/ICBATS66542.2025.11258426

Nasir, V., Hosseini, A., Binfield, L., Hasani, N., Ghotb, S., Diederichs, V., & Hansen, E. (2025). Human-centric Industry 5.0 manufacturing: A multi-level framework from design to consumption within Society 5.0. *International Journal of Sustainable Engineering*, *18*(1), 2551000. DOI: 10.1080/19397038.2025.2551000

Natoli, R., Feeny, S., Li, J., & Zuhair, S. (2024). Aggregating the Human Development Index: A non-compensatory approach. *Social Indicators Research*, *172*(2), 499–515. DOI: 10.1007/s11205-024-03318-7

Netemeyer, R. G., Warmath, D., Fernandes, D., & Lynch, J. G.Jr. (2018). How am I doing? Perceived financial well-being, its potential antecedents, and its relation to overall well-being. *The Journal of Consumer Research*, *45*(1), 68–89. DOI: 10.1093/jcr/ucx109

Neufeld-Wall, M. E. (n.d.). *Being Real: Gen-Z.* Self-Presentation, and Authenticity on Social Media.

Newport, C. (2019). *Digital minimalism: Choosing a focused life in a noisy world.* Portfolio/Penguin.

Ngai, E. W. T., & Wu, Y. (2022). Machine learning in marketing: A literature review, conceptual framework, and research agenda. *Journal of Business Research*, *145*, 35–48. DOI: 10.1016/j.jbusres.2022.02.049

Nguyen, M. H., & Hargittai, E. (2024). Digital disconnection, digital inequality, and subjective well-being: A mobile experience sampling study. *Journal of Computer-Mediated Communication, 29*(1), zmad044. Advance online publication. DOI: 10.1093/jcmc/zmad044

Nieborg, D. B., & Poell, T. (2018). The platformization of cultural Production: Theorizing the contingent cultural commodity. *New Media & Society, 20*(11), 4275–4292. DOI: 10.1177/1461444818769694

Niemiec, C. P., & Ryan, R. M. (2009). Autonomy, competence, and relatedness in the classroom: Applying self-determination theory to educational practice: Applying self-determination theory to educational practice. *Theory and Research in Education, 7*(2), 133-144. https://doi.org/ (Original work published 2009)DOI: 10.1177/1477878509104318

Niemiec, C. P. (2024). Eudaimonic well-being. In *Encyclopedia of quality of life and well-being research* (pp. 2212–2214). Springer International Publishing.

Nissenbaum, H. (2010). *Privacy in context: Technology, policy, and the integrity of social life*. Stanford University Press.

Noble, S. U. (2018). *Algorithms of oppression: How search engines reinforce racism*. NYU Press. DOI: 10.18574/nyu/9781479833641.001.0001

OECD (2020), Financial Consumer Protection Policy Approaches in the Digital Age:Protecting consumer's assets, data and privacy

OECD. (2019). OECD recommendation on artificial intelligence. https://oecd.ai/en/dashboards/policy-areas/oecd-recommendation

OECD. (2020). *OECD digital economy outlook 2020*. OECD Publishing.

OECD. (2021). *ESG investing and climate transition: Market Practices, Issues and Policy Considerations*. OECD Publishing., DOI: 10.1787/a2fc6c39-

Oesterreich, T. D., Anton, E., Hettler, F. M., & Teuteberg, F. (2025). What drives individuals' trusting intention in digital platforms? An exploratory meta-analysis. *Management Review Quarterly, 75*(4), 3615–3667. DOI: 10.1007/s11301-024-00477-2

Office of the Surgeon General. (2023). Social media and youth mental health: The U.S. Surgeon General's advisory. U.S. Department of Health and Human Services. https://www.hhs.gov/sites/default/files/sg-youth-mental-health-social-media-advisory.pdf

Ophir, E., Nass, C., & Wagner, A. D. (2009). Cognitive control in media multitaskers. *Proceedings of the National Academy of Sciences of the United States of America*, *106*(37), 15583–15587. DOI: 10.1073/pnas.0903620106 PMID: 19706386

Orben, A. (2020). Teenagers, screens and social media: A narrative review of reviews and key studies. *Social Psychiatry and Psychiatric Epidemiology*, *55*(4), 407–414. DOI: 10.1007/s00127-019-01825-4 PMID: 31925481

Ouyang, Y., Cao, E., & Wu, P. (2025). Study on the psychological influence mechanism of consumer reviews of ceramic products on purchasing decisions in e-commerce platforms. *Environment and Social Psychology*, *10*(8). Advance online publication. DOI: 10.59429/esp.v10i8.3910

Oxford Human Rights Hub. (2024, April 5). The Indian Puttaswamy judgments: Privacy rights at stake in the pursuit of social security. https://ohrh.law.ox.ac.uk/the-indian-puttaswamy-judgments-privacy-rights-at-stake-in-the-pursuit-of-social-security/

Park, Y. W., & Ryosuke, S. (2025). CE Strategy in the Automotive Industry. In Y. W. Park & K. Tamaki, *Circular Economy Strategy for SDG Business Management* (pp. 47–62). Springer Nature Singapore. DOI: 10.1007/978-981-96-4194-9_3

Parker, G. G., Van Alstyne, M. W., & Choudary, S. P. (2016). *Platform revolution*. W. W. Norton.

Passalacqua, M., Pellerin, R., Magnani, F., Doyon-Poulin, P., Del-Aguila, L., Boasen, J., & Léger, P. M. (2025). Human-centred AI in Industry 5.0: A systematic review. *International Journal of Production Research*, *63*(7), 2638–2669. DOI: 10.1080/00207543.2024.2406021

Patel, U. R., Ghaffarianhoseini, A., GhaffarianHoseini, A., & Burgess, A. (2026). Towards a well-being-oriented framework for urban digital twins. *Cities (London, England)*, *169*, 106579. DOI: 10.1016/j.cities.2025.106579

Pavlov, N., & Almanza, L. C. M. (2026). Artificial Intelligence in the Professional Activity and Education of Marketing Specialists: A Survey of Students' Opinions. In Krastev, K. V., Rani, C., Ergunova, O., Kansra, P., & Kajla, T. (Eds.), (pp. 59–102). Advances in Computational Intelligence and Robotics. IGI Global Scientific Publishing., DOI: 10.4018/979-8-3373-8612-6.ch003

Peter, R., Roshith, V., Lawrence, S., Mona, A. E., Narayanan, K. B., & Yusaira, F. (2025). Gen AI–Gen Z: Understanding Gen Z's emotional responses and brand experiences with Gen AI-driven, hyper-personalized advertising. *Frontiers in Communication*, *10*, 1554551. Advance online publication. DOI: 10.3389/fcomm.2025.1554551

Pew Research Center. (2019). Americans and privacy: Concerned, confused and feeling lack of control over their personal information. https://www.pewresearch.org

Piedimonte, A., Lanzo, G., Campaci, F., Volpino, V., & Carlino, E. (2025). Spreading New Light on Attention Restoration Theory: An Environmental Posner Paradigm. *Brain Sciences*, *15*(6), 578. DOI: 10.3390/brainsci15060578 PMID: 40563750

Piper, D. L. A. (2025, January 16). Data protection laws in Germany. https://www.dlapiperdataprotection.com/index.html?t=law&c=DE Emirates Health Services. (2025). UAE Digital Government Strategy 2025 (dimensions). https://www.ehs.gov.ae/en/about-us/the-uae-digital-government-strategy-2025

Pisarska, A. M., Kryczka, A., & Castellone, D. (2025). Organizational Trust as a Driver of Eudaimonic and Digital Well-Being in IT Professionals: A Cross-Cultural Study. *Sustainability (Basel)*, *17*(11), 5124. DOI: 10.3390/su17115124

Prelec, D., & Loewenstein, G. (1998). The Rejection and The Black: Mental accounting of savings and debt. *Marketing Science*, *17*(1), 4–28. DOI: 10.1287/mksc.17.1.4

Priyadarsini, S., & Das, A. P. (2026). Lithium in waste water: Impacts on pollution and human health. In *Decarbonization of Wastewater Pollutants as a Sustainable Solution* (pp. 353–364). Elsevier., DOI: 10.1016/B978-0-443-33062-9.00010-2

Przybylski, A. K., Murayama, K., DeHaan, C. R., & Gladwell, V. (2013). Motivational, emotional, and behavioral correlates of fear of missing out. *Computers in Human Behavior*, *29*(4), 1841–1848. DOI: 10.1016/j.chb.2013.02.014

Przybylski, A. K., & Weinstein, N. (2017). A large-scale test of the Goldilocks hypothesis: Quantifying the relations between digital-screen use and the mental well-being of adolescents. *Psychological Science*, *28*(2), 204–215. DOI: 10.1177/0956797616678438 PMID: 28085574

Qandeel, M. (2024). Facial recognition technology: Regulations, rights and the rule of law. *Frontiers in Big Data*, *7*, 1354659. DOI: 10.3389/fdata.2024.1354659 PMID: 38895177

Qi, X. (2011). Face: A Chinese concept in a global sociology. *Journal of Sociology (Melbourne, Vic.)*, *47*(3), 279–295. DOI: 10.1177/1440783311407692

R. P. S. K. K. S., S. R. S., S. K., and A. P., (2024). "Optimizing User Satisfaction and Streamlining Operations in Online Retail Using CNN Algorithm," Proc. IITCEE, Bangalore, India, pp. 1–7, DOI: 10.1109/IITCEE59897.2024.10467533

Ragnedda, M., & Ruiu, M. L. (2020). *Digital capital: A Bourdieusian perspective on the digital divide*. Emerald Publishing Limited., DOI: 10.1108/9781839095504

Rahman, S. M., Carlson, J., Gudergan, S. P., Wetzels, M., & Grewal, D. (2022). Perceived omnichannel customer experience (OCX): Concept, measurement, and impact. *Journal of Retailing, 98*(4), 611–632. DOI: 10.1016/j.jretai.2022.03.003

Raj, A. B., & Goute, A. K. (2025). Internal branding and technostress among employees—The mediation role of employee wellbeing and moderating effects of digital internal communication. *Acta Psychologica, 255*, 104943. DOI: 10.1016/j.actpsy.2025.104943 PMID: 40185038

Raj, J. D., & Sathiyan, G. (2024). Enhancing Life Skill Progression and Psychological Well-being of Undergraduate Students through AI-driven Recommendation System. *Multidisciplinary Science Journal, 7*(2), 2025054. DOI: 10.31893/multiscience.2025054

Ramadhani, I. S., & Indradjati, P. N. (2023). Toward contemporary city branding in the digital era: Conceptualizing the acceptability of city branding on social media. *Open House International, 48*(4), 666–682. DOI: 10.1108/OHI-08-2022-0213

Raman, R., Kowalski, R., & Achuthan, K. (2025). Metaverse Technologies and Human Behavior: Insights into Engagement, Adoption, and Ethical Challenges. *Computers in Human Behavior Reports, 100712*, 100712. Advance online publication. DOI: 10.1016/j.chbr.2025.100712

Rangaswamy, N., & Cutrell, E. (2012). Anthropology, development and ICTs: Slums, youth and the mobile Internet in urban India. In *Proceedings of the Fifth International Conference on Information and Communication Technologies and Development* (pp. 85–93). https://doi.org/DOI: 10.1145/2160673.2160685

Richter, S., Giroux, M., Piven, I., Sima, H., & Dodd, P. (2025). A Constructivist Approach to Integrating AI in Marketing Education: Bridging Theory and Practice. *Journal of Marketing Education, 47*(2), 94–111. DOI: 10.1177/02734753241288876

Rietveld, J., & Schilling, M. A. (2021). Platform competition: A systematic and interdisciplinary review of the literature. *Journal of Management, 47*(6), 1528–1563. DOI: 10.1177/0149206320969791

Ritzer, G. (2015). *The McDonaldization of society* (8th ed.). Sage.

Rocheteau, M. X. T. (2026). Driving circular economy adoption in temporary organizations: Lessons from the humanitarian sector. *Journal of Organizational Change Management, 39*(1), 1–22. DOI: 10.1108/JOCM-03-2025-0258

Rodrigues, S. P., Gomes, L. D. C., Peres, F. A. P., Correa, R. G. D. F., & Baierle, I. C. (2025). A Framework for Leveraging Digital Technologies in Reverse Logistics Actions: A Systematic Literature Review. *Logistics (Basel)*, *9*(2), 54. DOI: 10.3390/logistics9020054

Roy, A.. (2025). "E-Commerce Enhancement Through Intelligent Customer Interaction: Integration of GPT-Powered Chatbot with Sentiment Analysis," *Proc. CVMI*, Rourkela, India, pp. 1–6, DOI: 10.1109/CVMI66673.2025.11337625

Roy, S. K., Singh, G., Sadeque, S., Harrigan, P., & Coussement, K. (2023). Customer engagement with digitalized interactive platforms in retailing. *Journal of Business Research*, *164*, 114001. Advance online publication. DOI: 10.1016/j.jbusres.2023.114001

Ruiz-Alba, J. L., Abou-Foul, M., Nazarian, A., & Foroudi, P. (2022). Digital platforms: Customer satisfaction, eWOM and the moderating role of perceived technological innovativeness. *Information Technology & People*, *35*(7), 2470–2499. DOI: 10.1108/ITP-07-2021-0572

Ruohonen, J., & Mickelsson, S. (2023). Reflections on the Data Governance Act. *Digital Society : Ethics, Socio-Legal and Governance of Digital Technology*, *2*(1), 25. Advance online publication. DOI: 10.1007/s44206-023-00041-7

Ryan Richard, M., & Deci, E. L. (2000). Self-determination theory and the facilitation of intrinsic motivation, social development, and well-being. *The American Psychologist*, *55*(1), 68–78. DOI: 10.1037/0003-066X.55.1.68 PMID: 11392867

Ryan, M., & Stah, B. C. (2021). Artificial intelligence ethics guidelines for developers and users: Clarifying their content and normative implications. *Journal of Information. Communication and Ethics in Society*, *19*(1), 61–86. DOI: 10.1108/JICES-12-2019-0138

Ryan, R. M., & Deci, E. L. (2000). Intrinsic and extrinsic motivations: Classic definitions and new directions. *Contemporary Educational Psychology*, *25*(1), 54–67. DOI: 10.1006/ceps.1999.1020 PMID: 10620381

Ryan, R. M., & Deci, E. L. (2017). *Self- determination theory: Basic psychological needs in motivation, development, and wellness.* The Guilford Press., DOI: 10.1521/978.14625/28806

Ryff, C. D. (1989). Happiness is everything, or is it? Explorations on the meaning of psychological well-being. *Journal of Personality and Social Psychology*, *57*(6), 1069–1081. DOI: 10.1037/0022-3514.57.6.1069

Ryff, C. D., & Keyes, C. L. M. (1995). The structure of psychological well-being revisited. *Journal of Personality and Social Psychology*, *69*(4), 719–727. DOI: 10.1037/0022-3514.69.4.719 PMID: 7473027

Ryff, C. D., & Singer, B. H. (2008). Know thyself and become what you are: A eudaimonic approach to psychological well-being. *Journal of Happiness Studies*, *9*(1), 13–39. DOI: 10.1007/s10902-006-9019-0

Sabatini, F., & Sarracino, F. (2017). Online Networks and Subjective Well-Being. *Kyklos*, *70*(3), 456–480. DOI: 10.1111/kykl.12145

Saha, A. (2025). Human-centred innovation in Society 5.0. In *Society 5.0: A transformation towards human-centered artificial intelligence* (p. 143). Springer. DOI: 10.1201/9781003643166-7

Salagame, K. K. K. (2013). Well-being from the perspective of Indian psychology. In David, S. A., Boniwell, I., & Conley Ayers, A. (Eds.), *The Oxford Handbook of Happiness* (pp. 371–383). Oxford University Press.

Salminen, J., Mustak, M., Sufyan, M., & Jansen, B. J. (2023). How can algorithms help in segmenting users and customers? A systematic review and research agenda for algorithmic customer segmentation. *Journal of Marketing Analytics*, *11*(4), 677–692. DOI: 10.1057/s41270-023-00235-5

Sanchez-Monedero, J., & Dencik, L. (2022). Data justice. *Internet Policy Review*, *11*(1). Advance online publication. DOI: 10.14763/2022.1.1615

Saraswathi, T. S. (1999). *Culture, socialization, and human development: Theory, research, and applications in India*. Sage Publications.

Sardashti, H., & Calantone, R. J. (2022). Does equity-based compensation motivate executives to build strong brands? *Journal of Marketing Management*, *38*(13–14), 1433–1460. DOI: 10.1080/0267257X.2022.2041068

Savardi, M., Signoroni, A., Benini, S., Vaccher, F., Alberti, M., Ciolli, P., Di Meo, N., Falcone, T., Ramanzin, M., Romano, B., Sozzi, F., & Farina, D. (2025). Upskilling or deskilling? Measurable role of an AI-supported training for radiology residents: A lesson from the pandemic. *Insights Into Imaging*, *16*(1), 23. DOI: 10.1186/s13244-024-01893-4

Savaş, B. Ç., Turan, M., & Asan, S. (2025). The relationship between digital burnout and academic procrastination and the mediating roles of life satisfaction and the fatigue in this relationship. *BMC Psychology*, *13*(1), 1223. DOI: 10.1186/s40359-025-03510-5 PMID: 41188990

Schäfer, S. K., von Boros, L., Schaubruch, L. M., Kunzler, A. M., Lindner, S., Koehler, F., Werner, T., Zappalà, F., Helmreich, I., Wessa, M., Lieb, K., & Tüscher, O. (2024). Digital interventions to promote psychological resilience: A systematic review and meta-analysis. *NPJ Digital Medicine*, *7*(1), 30. DOI: 10.1038/s41746-024-01017-8 PMID: 38332030

Scheibehenne, B., Greifeneder, R., & Todd, P. M. (2010). Can there ever be too many Options? A meta- analytic review of choice overload. *The Journal of Consumer Research*, *37*(3), 409–425. DOI: 10.1086/651235

Schlegelmilch, B. B., & Mills, A. J. (2025). Artificial Intelligence and the Future of Marketing Education. *Journal of Marketing Education*, *47*(2), 91–93. DOI: 10.1177/02734753251336956

Schneider, S., & Haried, P. (2024). Use of artificial Intelligence in higher education with particular reference to automated content generation, trust, and anxiety. *Journal of Business and Educational Leadership*, *14*(1), 4–21.

Schwartz, B. (2004). *The paradox of choice*. HarperCollins.

Schwartz, B. (2004). *The paradox of choice: Why more is less*. HarperCollins.

Schwartz, S. H. (1999). A theory of cultural values and some implications for work. *Applied Psychology = Psychologie Appliquée*, *48*(1), 23–47. DOI: 10.1111/j.1464-0597.1999.tb00047.x

Schwartz, S. H. (2004). Mapping and Interpreting Cultural Differences around the world. In Vinken, H., Soeters, J., & Ester, P. (Eds.), *Comparing Cultures, Dimensions of Culture in a Comparative Perspective, Leiden* (pp. 43–73). Brill. DOI: 10.1163/9789047412977_007

Schweidel, D. A., Bart, Y., Inman, J. J., Stephen, A. T., Libai, B., Andrews, M., Rosario, A. B., Chae, I., Chen, Z., Kupor, D., Longoni, C., & Thomaz, F. (2022). How consumer digital signals are reshaping the customer journey. *Journal of the Academy of Marketing Science*, *50*(6), 1257–1276. DOI: 10.1007/s11747-022-00839-w PMID: 35221393

Seligman, M. E. P. (2011). *Flourish: A visionary new understanding of happiness and well-being*. Free Press.

Shamim, N., Wei, M., Gupta, S., Verma, D. S., Abdollahi, S., & Shin, M. M. (2025). Metaverse for digital health solutions. *International Journal of Information Management*, *83*, 102869. DOI: 10.1016/j.ijinfomgt.2025.102869

Shao, Q. (2022). Does less working time improve life satisfaction? Evidence from European Social Survey. *Health Economics Review*, *12*(1), 50. DOI: 10.1186/s13561-022-00396-6 PMID: 36178635

Shao, Y., Liu, S., Chen, G., Ma, R., Wang, X., & Li, Q. (2025, November–December). FashionCook: A Visual Analytics System for Human–AI Collaboration in Fashion E-Commerce Design. *IEEE Computer Graphics and Applications*, *45*(6), 61–75. DOI: 10.1109/MCG.2025.3597849 PMID: 40864590

Shapiro, C., & Varian, H. R. (1999). *Information rules*. Harvard Business School Press.

Sharif, O. O., & Sudirman, I. D. (2024). "Investigating Trust Determinants in E-commerce Through User Experience and Delivery Satisfaction," 2024 9th International Conference on Information Technology and Digital Applications (ICITDA), Malaysia, pp. 1–6, DOI: 10.1109/ICITDA64560.2024.10809747

Sharma, N., Manda, V. K., Shivasharana, A., & Mohammed, M. (2025). Optimizing Reverse Logistics in Retail Sector. In Hlali, A. (Ed.), *Emerging Trends in Smart Logistics Technologies* (pp. 397–430). IGI Global Scientific Publishing., DOI: 10.4018/979-8-3373-2434-0.ch014

Sharma, P., Kumawat, R., Jain, G., Keswani, G., Goyal, N. K., & Sheikh, M. F. (2026). Machine learning-based intrusion detection systems for healthcare Internet of Things (HIoT). In Shieh, C., Goel, P., Horng, M., & Pandey, H. (Eds.), *Resilient healthcare Internet ofThings systems: Architectures, security, and trust* (pp. 185–214). IGI Global Scientific Publishing., DOI: 10.4018/979-8-3373-7610-3.ch007

Sharma, R. (2025). AI-enabled hyper-personalization strategies in India's evolving marketing landscape. EPRA International Journal of Economics. *Business and Management Studies*, *12*(6), 45–52.

Sheldon, K. M., & Lyubomirsky, S. (2012). The challenge of staying happier: Testing the hedonic adaptation Prevention model. *Personality & Social Psychology Bulletin*, *38*(5), 670–680. DOI: 10.1177/0146167212436400 PMID: 22361725

Sheng, J., Ng, D. T. K., Tian, P., & Zheng, Z. (2025). University students' resilience in post-pandemic period: A socio-ecological perspective. *Frontiers in Psychology*, *16*, 1574153. DOI: 10.3389/fpsyg.2025.1574153 PMID: 40417036

Short, J. A., Williams, E., & Christie, B. (1976). *The social psychology of telecommunications*. John Wiley & Sons.

Shukla, A., Mishra, P., & Singh, R. K. (2023). The road to learning "who am I" is digitized: A study on consumer self-discovery in the online world. *Journal of Consumer Behaviour*, *22*(3), 544–554. DOI: 10.1002/cb.2185

Singh, G., Roy, S. K., Apostolidis, C., Quaddus, M., & Sadeque, S. (2025). Identifying the metaverse value recipe (s) affecting customer engagement and well-being in retailing. *Technological Forecasting and Social Change*, *210*, 123870. DOI: 10.1016/j.techfore.2024.123870

Sirgy, M. J. (2012). *The psychology of quality of life: Hedonic well-being, life satisfaction, and eudaimonia* (Vol. 50). Springer science & business media. DOI: 10.1007/978-94-007-4405-9

Sivadas, E., Bruvold, N. T., & Nelson, M. R. (2008). A reduced version of the horizontal and vertical individualism and collectivism scale: A four-country assessment. *Journal of Business Research*, *61*(3), 201–210. DOI: 10.1016/j.jbusres.2007.06.016

Smits, M., Kim, C. M., Van Goor, H., & Ludden, G. D. (2022). From digital health to digital well-being: Systematic scoping review. *Journal of Medical Internet Research*, *24*(4), e33787. DOI: 10.2196/33787 PMID: 35377328

Sonnentag, S., Tay, L., & Nesher Shoshan, H. (2023). A review on health and well-being at work. *Personnel Psychology*, *76*(2), 473–510. DOI: 10.1111/peps.12572

Soren, A., & Ryff, C. D. (2023). Meaningful work, well-being, and health: Enacting a eudaimonic vision. *International Journal of Environmental Research and Public Health*, *20*(16), 6570. DOI: 10.3390/ijerph20166570 PMID: 37623156

Southwick, S. M., Bonanno, G. A., Masten, A. S., Panter-Brick, C., & Yehuda, R. (2014). Resilience definitions, theory, and challenges: Interdisciplinary perspectives. *European Journal of Psychotraumatology*, *5*(1), 25338. DOI: 10.3402/ejpt.v5.25338 PMID: 25317257

Srite, M., & Karahanna, E. (2006). The role of espoused national cultural values in technology acceptance. *Management Information Systems Quarterly*, *30*(3), 679–704. DOI: 10.2307/25148745

Srnicek, N. (2017). Platform capitalism. *Polity*.

Stănculescu, E., & Griffiths, M. D. (2024). The association between problematic internet use and hedonic and eudaimonic well-being: A latent profile analysis. *Technology in Society*, *78*, 102588. DOI: 10.1016/j.techsoc.2024.102588

Starke, C., Baleis, J., Keller, B., & Marcinkowski, F. (2022). Fairness perceptions of algorithmic decision-making: A systematic review of the empirical literature. *Big Data & Society*, *9*(2), 20539517221115189. Advance online publication. DOI: 10.1177/20539517221115189

Steckermeier, L. C. (2021). The Value of Autonomy for the Good Life. An Empirical Investigation of Autonomy and Life Satisfaction in Europe. *Social Indicators Research*, *154*(2), 693–723. DOI: 10.1007/s11205-020-02565-8

Steinert, S., & Dennis, M. J. (2022). Emotions and digital well-being: On social media's emotional affordances. *Philosophy & Technology*, *35*(2), 36. DOI: 10.1007/s13347-022-00530-6 PMID: 35450167

Stengg, W. (2024). *Digital policy in the EU: Towards a human-centred digital transformation*. Edward Elgar Publishing. DOI: 10.4337/9781035338641

Sterner, P., De Roover, K., & Goretzko, D. (2025). New developments in measurement invariance testing: An overview and comparison of EFA-based approaches. *Structural Equation Modeling*, *32*(1), 117–135. DOI: 10.1080/10705511.2024.2393647

Stothart, C., Mitchum, A., & Yehnert, C. (2015). The attentional cost of receiving a cell phone notification. *Journal of Experimental Psychology. Human Perception and Performance*, *41*(4), 893–897. DOI: 10.1037/xhp0000100 PMID: 26121498

Straub, D., Keil, M., & Brenner, W. (1997). Testing the technology acceptance model across cultures: A three country study. *Information & Management*, *33*(1), 1–11. DOI: 10.1016/S0378-7206(97)00026-8

Streeter, C. C., Gerbarg, P. L., Saper, R. B., Ciraulo, D. A., & Brown, R. P. (2012). Effects of yoga on the autonomic nervous system, gamma-aminobutyric-acid, and allostasis in epilepsy, depression, and post-traumatic stress disorder. *Medical Hypotheses*, *78*(5), 571–579. DOI: 10.1016/j.mehy.2012.01.021 PMID: 22365651

Sugosha, K. G., Andreswari, R., & Hardiyanti, M. (2021). "Design and Implementation of User Interface and User Experience in Online Sales Applications at Sugosha Pharmacy with User Centered Design Method," *2021 International Conference on Advanced Computer Science and Information Systems (ICACSIS)*, Depok, Indonesia, pp. 1–5, DOI: 10.1109/ICACSIS53237.2021.9631344

Sun, H., Yuan, C., Qian, Q., He, S., & Luo, Q. (2022). Digital resilience among individuals in school education settings: A concept analysis based on a scoping review. *Frontiers in Psychiatry*, *13*, 858515. Advance online publication. DOI: 10.3389/fpsyt.2022.858515 PMID: 35432032

Sunstein, C. R. (2016). *The ethics of influence: Government in the age of behavioral science*. Cambridge University Press. DOI: 10.1017/CBO9781316493021

Sunstein, C. R. (2019). *How change happens*. MIT Press. DOI: 10.7551/mit-press/11974.001.0001

Super, A. G. I. (2025, June 27). Hyper-personalization at scale: How AI is revolutionizing customer segmentation in 2025. https://superagi.com/hyper-personalization-at-scale-how-ai-is-revolutionizing-customer-segmentation-in-2025/

Szostak, M. (2025). Aesthetic insight into humanistic management and AI: Research perspectives. In *AI and humanistic management* (pp. 13–58). Springer. DOI: 10.4324/9781003654377-3

Tang, Y. M., Wong, J. K. N., & Ho, G. (2025). Exploring Consumer Acceptance of Metaverse Marketing for Branding Activities and the Pre-Purchase Stage. *Journal of Theoretical and Applied Electronic Commerce Research*, *20*(3), 159. DOI: 10.3390/jtaer20030159

Tao, M., Khan, J., Abbass, A., & Mehmood, K. (2025). Metaverse Characteristics: The Role of Consumer Experience Shaping Consumer Behavior in the Metaverse. *Journal of Theoretical and Applied Electronic Commerce Research*, *20*(3), 166. DOI: 10.3390/jtaer20030166

Tariq, M. U. (2026). Breaking the Glass Ceiling: Strategies for Closing the Gender Gap in the Modern Workplace. In Montaudon-Tomas, C., & Pinto-López, I. (Eds.), *Reducing the Gender Gap in the Workplace* (pp. 65–88). IGI Global Scientific Publishing., DOI: 10.4018/979-8-3693-9000-9.ch003

Tariq, M. U. (2026). Innovation and Agility-Adapting Business Strategies for Sustainable Growth in Dynamic Markets. In Ananthan, S., Kohli, A., Manickam, T., & Dhanabalan, T. (Eds.), *New Business Development Strategies for Achieving Sustainable Growth* (pp. 113–140). IGI Global Scientific Publishing., DOI: 10.4018/979-8-3373-2048-9.ch005

Tariq, M. U. (2026). The Semiotics of AI-Driven Consumer Experiences: Decoding Emotional Branding and the Experience Economy. In Piccolo, R., & Boero, M. (Eds.), *Emotional and Experiential Dimensions of Modern Marketing* (pp. 245–268). IGI Global Scientific Publishing., DOI: 10.4018/979-8-3373-7615-8.ch010

Tarnanidis, T. (Ed.). (2026). *AI-driven decision-making for diversity, equity, and inclusion in marketing*. IGI Global Scientific Publishing., DOI: 10.4018/979-8-3373-6731-6

Tarnanidis, T. K. (Ed.). (2024). *Reshaping Marketing Science in Wholesaling and Retailing*. IGI Global Scientific Publishing., DOI: 10.4018/979-8-3693-6145-0

Tarnanidis, T., Manda, V. K., Sousa, B. B., Vlachopoulou, M., & Papachristou, E. (2025). Marketing Complexity of Smart Consumer Products to Global Millennial Segments. In Tarnanidis, T., Sousa, B., Vlachopoulou, M., Papachristou, E., & Kittu Manda, V. (Eds.), *Diversity and Inclusion-Driven Marketing for Multicultural Marketplaces* (pp. 1–16). IGI Global Scientific Publishing., DOI: 10.4018/979-8-3373-2111-0.ch001

Tarnanidis, T., Owusu-Frimpong, N., Nwankwo, S., & Omar, M. (2015). Why We buy? Modeling consumer selection of referents. *Journal of Retailing and Consumer Services, 22*, 24–36. DOI: 10.1016/j.jretconser.2014.09.004

Tarnanidis, T., Sousa, B. B., Vlachopoulou, M., Papachristou, E., & Kittu Manda, V. (Eds.). (2026). *Diversity and inclusion-driven marketing for multicultural marketplaces*. IGI Global Scientific Publishing., DOI: 10.4018/979-8-3373-2111-0

Tarnanidis, T., & Vlachopoulou, M. (Eds.). (2025). *Cultural Sensitivity, Cross-Border Logistics, and E-Commerce in Global Marketing*. IGI Global Scientific Publishing., DOI: 10.4018/979-8-3373-0528-8

Taylor, A., tom Dieck, M. C., Jung, T., Cho, J., & Kwon, O. (2024). XR and mental wellbeing: State of the art and future research directions for the Metaverse. *Frontiers in Psychology, 15*, 1360260. DOI: 10.3389/fpsyg.2024.1360260 PMID: 38524293

Tedeschi, R. G., & Calhoun, L. G. (2004). Posttraumatic growth: Conceptual foundations and empirical evidence. *Psychological Inquiry, 15*(1), 1–18. DOI: 10.1207/s15327965pli1501_01

Teepapal, T. (2025). AI-driven personalization: Unraveling consumer perceptions in social media engagement. *Computers in Human Behavior, 165*, 108549. Advance online publication. DOI: 10.1016/j.chb.2024.108549

Thaler, R. H. (2016). *Misbehaving*. W. W. Norton.

Thaler, R. H., & Sunstein, C. R. (2008). *Nudge*. YaleUniversity Press.

Thaler, R. H., & Sunstein, C. R. (2009). *Nudge: Improving decisions about health, wealth, and happiness*. Penguin.

Ting, L., & Ahn, J. (2023). Understanding the roles of interaction and trust in formation of loyalty toward customer-to-customer (C2C) platforms. *Asia Pacific Journal of Marketing and Logistics, 35*(10), 2565–2581. DOI: 10.1108/APJML-12-2022-1072

Tokdemir, G. (2022). Software professionals during the COVID-19 pandemic in Turkey. *Journal of Systems and Software*, *188*, 111286. DOI: 10.1016/j.jss.2022.111286 PMID: 35250124

Trepte, S., Dienlin, T., & Reinecke, L. (2015). Influence of Social Support Received in Online and Offline Contexts on Satisfaction With Social Support and Satisfaction With Life: A Longitudinal Study. *Media Psychology*, *18*(1), 74–105. DOI: 10.1080/15213269.2013.838904

Triandis, H. C. (1995). *Individualism and collectivism.* Westview Press.

Triberti, S., Sapone, C., & Riva, G. (2025). Being there but where? Sense of presence theory for virtual reality applications. *Humanities & Social Sciences Communications*, *12*(1), 1–6. DOI: 10.1057/s41599-025-04380-3

Tsai, J. L. (2007). Ideal affect: Cultural causes and behavioral consequences. *Perspectives on Psychological Science : A Journal of the Association for Psychological Science*, *2*(3), 242–259. DOI: 10.1111/j.1745-6916.2007.00043.x PMID: 26151968

Tseng, E., Bellini, R., Lee, Y.-Y., Ramjit, A., Ristenpart, T., & Dell, N. (2024). Data Stewardship in Clinical Computer Security: Balancing Benefit and Burden in Participatory Systems. *Proceedings of the ACM on Human-Computer Interaction*, *8*(CSCW1), 1–29. DOI: 10.1145/3637316

Tsimnadis, K., Kyriakopoulos, G. L., Arabatzis, G., Leontopoulos, S., & Zervas, E. (2023). An Innovative and Alternative Waste Collection Recycling Program Based on Source Separation of Municipal Solid Wastes (MSW) and Operating with Mobile Green Points (MGPs). *Sustainability (Basel)*, *15*(4), 3106. DOI: 10.3390/su15043106

Tsouparopoulou, E., Symeonaki, M., Parsanoglou, D., & Kazani, A. (2025). European Youth and Digital Engagement: Attitudes, Skills, and Civic Participation. *Journal of Applied Youth Studies*, *8*(2), 219–247. DOI: 10.1007/s43151-025-00168-z

Tushar, S., Singh, A., Sutrave, Y., & Azhar, M. (2024). Circular Supply Chains: Digital Tools for Enhanced Traceability. In Ozen, E., Singh, A., Taneja, S., Rajaram, R., & Davim, J. P. (Eds.), (pp. 175–202). Advances in Finance, Accounting, and Economics. IGI Global., DOI: 10.4018/979-8-3373-0578-3.ch009

Tutar, H., Mutlu, H. T., & Streimikiene, D. (2025). Rethinking Sustainable Development: Multidimensional Comparisons Across Countries and Regions. *Sustainable Development (Bradford)*. Advance online publication. DOI: 10.1002/sd.70157

Tutor2u. (2023). *In business and economics, what is an Eco-System Lock In?* Access address: https://www.tutor2u.net/economics/reference/eco-system-lock-in-business-and-economics (18.01.2026).

Twenge, J. M., & Campbell, W. K. (2018). Associations between screen time and lower psychological well-being among children and adolescents: Evidence from a population-based study. *Preventive Medicine Reports*, *12*, 271–283. DOI: 10.1016/j.pmedr.2018.10.003 PMID: 30406005

Tyagi, S., Gupta, V., & Mehndiratta, V. (2024). Building Smart Campuses: Integrating AI in Higher Education. In Arya, R., Sharma, S. C., Verma, A. K., & Iyer, B. (Eds.), *Recent Trends in Artificial Intelligence Towards a Smart World: Applications in Industries and Sectors* (pp. 399–431). Springer Nature Singapore., DOI: 10.1007/978-981-97-6790-8_15

Uchida, Y., Norasakkunkit, V., & Kitayama, S. (2004). Cultural constructions of happiness: Theory and empirical evidence. *Journal of Happiness Studies*, *5*(3), 223–239. DOI: 10.1007/s10902-004-8785-9

Umair, A., Conboy, K., & Whelan, E. (2023). Examining technostress and its impact on worker well-being in the digital gig economy. *Internet Research*, *33*(7), 206–242. DOI: 10.1108/INTR-03-2022-0214

UNESCO. (2019). AI in education: Challenges and opportunities. United Nations Educational, Scientific and Cultural Organization. https://unesdoc.unesco.org

UNICEF. (2017). [Children in a digital world. UNICEF. https://www.unicef.org]. *The State of the World's Children*, *2017*, •••.

United Arab Emirates Government. (2025). UAE Digital Government Strategy 2025. https://u.ae/en/about-the-uae/strategies-initiatives-and-awards/strategies-plans-and-visions/government-services-and-digital-transformation/uae-national-digital-government-strategy USE/Metropolis. (n.d.). "I Will Centers"—Internet addiction prevention & intervention centers for children and youths (Seoul). https://use.metropolis.org/case-studies/seoul-i-will-centre

United Nations. (2015). *Transforming our world: The 2030 agenda for sustainable development*. United Nations.

Universiti Malaya, M. Adnan, H., Mavi, S. R., & Universiti Malaya. (. (2015). Facebook Satisfaction, Life Satisfaction: Malaysian Undergraduate Experience. *Jurnal Komunikasi. Malaysian Journal of Communication*, *31*(2), 649–671. DOI: 10.17576/JKMJC-2015-3102-37

Usakli, A., & Rasoolimanesh, S. M. (2023). Which SEM to use and what to report? A comparison of CB-SEM and PLS-SEM. In *Cutting edge research methods in hospitality and tourism* (pp. 5–28). Emerald Publishing Limited., DOI: 10.1108/978-1-80455-063-220231002

Uth, R., Niemitz, N., Valera, I., & Langer, M. (2026). Personalizing explanations in AI-based decisions: The effects of personalization and (mis)aligning with individual preferences. *Computers in Human Behavior*, *177*, 108854. DOI: 10.1016/j.chb.2025.108854

Uzun, K., & Arslan, G. (2025). Meaning in Life Across Life Stages: Pathways from Uncertainty to Subjective Well-being. *Applied Research in Quality of Life*, *20*(3), 1197–1220. DOI: 10.1007/s11482-025-10461-x

Van Boven, L., & Gilovich, T. (2003). To do or to have? That is the question. *Journal of Personality and Social Psychology*, *85*(6), 1193–1202. DOI: 10.1037/0022-3514.85.6.1193 PMID: 14674824

Van Dam, S., & Bakker, C. (2024). Between a Rock and a Hard Place. A Case Study on Simplifying the Reverse Logistics of Car Parts to Enable Remanufacturing. *Journal of Circular Economy*, *2*(2). Advance online publication. DOI: 10.55845/MWAX4474

Van De Casteele, M., Flamant, N., Morbée, S., Van Den Bogaard, D., & Vansteenkiste, M. (2026). Online and offline need fulfillment seeking: The relation between need crafting profiles, well-being, and social media use. *Computers in Human Behavior*, *175*, 108843. DOI: 10.1016/j.chb.2025.108843

van de Vijver, F. J., & Leung, K. (2011). Equivalence and bias: A review of concepts, models, and data analytic procedures. In D. Matsumoto & F. J. van de Vijver (Eds.), *Cross-cultural research methods in psychology* (pp. 17–45). Cambridge University Press.

Van De Voorde, K., Paauwe, J., & Van Veldhoven, M. (2012). Employee well-being and the HRM–organizational performance relationship. *International Journal of Management Reviews*, *14*(4), 391–407. DOI: 10.1111/j.1468-2370.2011.00322.x

Van Deursen, A. J., & Helsper, E. J. (2015). The third-level digital divide: Who benefits most from being online? In *Communication and information technologies annual* (Vol. 10, pp. 29–52). Emerald Group Publishing Limited., DOI: 10.1108/S2050-206020150000010002

Van Deursen, A. J., & Van Dijk, J. A. (2014). The digital divide shifts to differences in usage. *New Media & Society*, *16*(3), 507–526. DOI: 10.1177/1461444813487959

Van Dijk, J. A. & Van Deursen, A. J., (2014). *Digital Skills: Unlocking the information society*. Palgrave Macmillan., DOI: 10.1057/9781137437037

van Dijk, J. (2005). The deepening divide: Inequality in the information society. *Sage (Atlanta, Ga.)*. Advance online publication. DOI: 10.4135/9781452229812

Van Hove, L., & Dubus, A. (2019). M-Pesa and financial inclusion in Kenya: Of paying comes saving? *Sustainability (Basel), 11*(3), 568. DOI: 10.3390/su11030568

Vanden Abeele, M. M. (2021). Digital wellbeing as a dynamic construct. *Communication Theory, 31*(4), 932–955. DOI: 10.1093/ct/qtaa024

Vandenberg, R. J., & Lance, C. E. (2000). A review and synthesis of the measurement invariance literature: Suggestions, practices, and recommendations for organizational research. *Organizational Research Methods, 3*(1), 4–70. DOI: 10.1177/109442810031002

Venkatesh, V., Morris, M., Davis, G., & Davis, F. (2003). User acceptance of information technology: Toward a unified view. *Management Information Systems Quarterly, 27*(3), 425–478. DOI: 10.2307/30036540

Ventura, T., Majumdar, R., Nagler, J., & Tucker, J. A. (2024). Reducing exposure to misinformation: Evidence from WhatsApp in Brazil (2022 election). Center for Social Media and Politics (CSMaP), NYU. https://csmapnyu.org/research/reports-analysis/reducing-exposure-to-misinformation-evidence-from-whatsapp-in-brazil

Verhoef, P. C., Broekhuizen, T., Bart, Y., Bhattacharya, A., Dong, J. Q., Fabian, N., & Haenlein, M. (2021). Digital transformation: A multidisciplinary reflection and research agenda. *Journal of Business Research, 122*, 889–901. DOI: 10.1016/j.jbusres.2019.09.022

Verma, A., Singh, P., & Kumar, R. (2025). Navigating ethical ambiguities: The AI paradox among Indian college students. ResearchGate. https://doi.org/DOI: 10.13140/RG.2.2.12345.67890

Vijaya Kumar, V. K., & Suresh, S. (2025). Exploring Challenges and Enablers of Sustainable Supply Chains in Indian Automotive SMEs for Enhancing Long-Term Competitiveness. *JES. Journal of Engineering Sciences, 0*(0), 0–0. DOI: 10.21608/jesaun.2025.404637.1615

Villar-Guevara, M., García-Salirrosas, E. E., Gómez-Bayona, L., Villar, D., Pari-Apaza, M., & Fernández-Mallma, I. (2025). Changes in the Digital World: An Explanatory Analysis of the Key Factors Linked to Virtual Interactivity. *Administrative Sciences, 15*(7), 276. https://doi.org/Changes%2520in%2520the%2520digital%2520world:%2520Virtual%2520interactivity%2520and%2520sequential%2520mediation%2520mechanisms. DOI: 10.3390/admsci15070276

Vogel, E. A., Rose, J. P., Roberts, L. R., & Eckles, K. (2014). Social comparison, social media, and self-esteem. *Psychology of Popular Media Culture, 3*(4), 206–222. DOI: 10.1037/ppm0000047

Vohs, K. D., Baumeister, R. F., Schmeichel, B. J., Twenge, J. M., Nelson, N. M., & Tice, D. M. (2018). Making choices impairs subsequent self-control: A limited-resource account of decision making, self-regulation, and active initiative. In *Self-regulation and self-control* (pp. 45–77). Routledge., DOI: 10.4324/9781315175775-2

Voukelatou, V., Gabrielli, L., Miliou, I., Cresci, S., Sharma, R., Tesconi, M., & Pappalardo, L. (2021). Measuring objective and subjective well-being: Dimensions and data sources. *International Journal of Data Science and Analytics*, *11*(4), 279–309. DOI: 10.1007/s41060-020-00224-2

Wang, C. K. J., Liu, W. C., Kee, Y. H., & Chian, L. K. (2019). Competence, autonomy, and relatedness in the classroom: Understanding students’ motivational processes using the self-determination theory. *Heliyon*, *5*(7), e01983. Advance online publication. DOI: 10.1016/j.heliyon.2019.e01983 PMID: 31372524

Wang, X., Li, Y., & Zhang, J. (2025). Understanding the influence of personalized recommendation on purchase intentions from a self-determination perspective: Contingent upon product categories. *Journal of Theoretical and Applied Electronic Commerce Research*, *20*(1), 32. Advance online publication. DOI: 10.3390/jtaer20010032

Wei, B., Zhao, C., & Luo, M. (2024). Online markets, offline happiness: E-commerce development and subjective well-being in rural China. *China Economic Review*, *87*, 102247. DOI: 10.1016/j.chieco.2024.102247

Westerman, D., Spence, P. R., & Van Der Heide, B. (2013). Social media as information source: Recency of updates and credibility of information. *Journal of Computer-Mediated Communication*, *19*(2), 171–183. DOI: 10.1111/jcc4.12041

Wibowo, A., Chen, S.-C., & Sallam, M. A. (2024). Artificial intelligence features and expectation confirmation theory in digital banking apps: Gen Y and Z perspective. *Journal of Theoretical and Applied Electronic Commerce Research*, *19*(3), 1954–1977. DOI: 10.3390/jtaer19030094

Widiatmo, G. (2024). "The Future of E-commerce: Creating Immersive Experiences in Live Streaming Commerce to Drive Consumers' Impulse Buying," *Proc. ECTI-CON*, Khon Kaen, Thailand, pp. 1–6, DOI: 10.1109/ECTI-CON60892.2024.10594963

Widjaja, G., Nagabhooshanam, N., Prasad, K. D. V., Hassan Shari, F. H., Valavan, A. T., Sridhar, A. P., & Ambika, K. S. B. (2024). Machine learning-driven model for identifying depression via social network information. *Journal of Environmental Protection and Ecology*, *25*(5), 1627–1637. https://scibulcom.net/en/article/06EER86UphR8ttSUSTvW

Wijaya, L.. (2025). "E-Commerce Uncovered: Exploring Key Drivers of Consumer Impulse Buying Behavior," *Proc. ICWR*, Tehran, Iran, pp. 294–298, DOI: 10.1109/ICWR65219.2025.11006215

Wood, M. A., Bukowski, W. M., & Lis, E. (2016). The digital self: How social media serves as a setting that shapes youth's emotional experiences. *Adolescent Research Review, 1*(2), 163–173. DOI: 10.1007/s40894-015-0014-8

Wu, C. C., Huang, D. H., Huang, K. C., & Liu, Y. C. (2025). Modelling social media engagement and life satisfaction among older Taiwanese adults: The roles of technology anxiety, attitudes, and psychological well-being using PLS-SEM. *Educational Gerontology*, •••, 1–23. DOI: 10.1080/03601277.2025.2575351

Xiao, J. J., & O'Neill, B. (2016). Consumer financial education and financial capability. *International Journal of Consumer Studies, 40*(6), 712–721. DOI: 10.1111/ijcs.12285

Xu, Y., & Chen, L. (2025). University students' metaverse attachment and its predictors: Escaping from reality. *Frontiers in Psychology, 16*, 1594256. DOI: 10.3389/fpsyg.2025.1594256 PMID: 41064179

Yang, C. C. (2016). Instagram use, loneliness, and social comparison orientation: Interact and browse on social media, but don't compare. *Cyberpsychology, Behavior and Social Networking, 19*(12), 703–708. DOI: 10.1089/cyber.2016.0201 PMID: 27855266

Yang, H. (2020). Do SNSs really make us happy? The effects of writing and reading via SNSs on subjective well-being. *Telematics and Informatics, 50*, 101384. DOI: 10.1016/j.tele.2020.101384

Yang, J., Soltan, A. A. S., Eyre, D. W., & Clifton, D. A. (2023). Algorithmic fairness and bias mitigation for clinical machine learning with deep reinforcement learning. *Nature Machine Intelligence, 5*(8), 884–894. DOI: 10.1038/s42256-023-00697-3 PMID: 37615031

Yen, H.-Y., Hsu, H., & Huang, W.-H. (2024). Virtual reality natural experiences for mental health: Comparing the effects between different immersion levels. *Virtual Reality (Waltham Cross), 28*(1), 52. DOI: 10.1007/s10055-024-00958-5

Yesim, O., & Yavaş, V. (2023). A Study On Critical Factors Of Digitalization In Reverse Logistics. *Beykent Üniversitesi Fen ve Mühendislik Bilimleri Dergisi, 16*(1), 1–6. DOI: 10.20854/bujse.1211274

Yeung, K. (2017). ' Hypernudge ': Big data as a mode of regulation by design. *Information Communication and Society*, *20*(1), 118–136. DOI: 10.1080/1369118X.2016.1186713

Yip, C., Dong, Z. Y., Tao, Y., & Lai, S. (2025). Towards sustainable human-centred smart cities: Design framework and case studies for Hong Kong and Riyadh. *IET Smart Cities*, *7*(1), e70010. DOI: 10.1049/smc2.70010

Youssef, E., Medhat, M., Abdellatif, S., & Babiker Yousif, N. (2024). Analyzing the impact of Metaverse technology on social development: A field study on generation Z in the United Arab Emirates. *Social Sciences (Basel, Switzerland)*, *13*(9), 446. DOI: 10.3390/socsci13090446

Yu, A., Lee, G., Liu, Y., Zhang, M., Jung, S., Park, J., Rhee, J., & Cho, K. (2025). Development and Evaluation of an Immersive Metaverse-Based Meditation System for Psychological Well-Being Using LLM-Driven Scenario Generation. *Systems*, *13*(9), 798. DOI: 10.3390/systems13090798

Yuan, Y., Shi, Y., Su, T., & Zhang, H. (2025). Resistance or compliance? The impact of algorithmic awareness on people's attitudes toward online information browsing. *Frontiers in Psychology*, *16*, 1563592. DOI: 10.3389/fpsyg.2025.1563592 PMID: 40823401

Yue, Y., Liu, D., & Hao, J. (2025). From Gaming to Well-Being: Analyzing the Impact of Social Engagement in Online Games on Silver Gamer's Well-Being. *International Journal of Human-Computer Interaction*, •••, 1–17. DOI: 10.1080/10447318.2025.2546659

Yu, J. H., Chauhan, D., Iqbal, R. A., & Yeoh, E. (2025). Mapping academic perspectives on AI in education: Trends, challenges, and sentiments in educational research (2018–2024). *Educational Technology Research and Development*, *73*(1), 199–227. DOI: 10.1007/s11423-024-10425-2

Zeshan, M., Morelli, M., Rasool, S., Centobelli, P., & Cerchione, R. (2025). Empowering sustainable workplaces: A perspective on employee well-being in the light of the job demand resource model. *Sustainable Development (Bradford)*, *33*(2), 1861–1878. DOI: 10.1002/sd.3179

Zhang, L., & Fröhling, M. (2025). Integration of blockchain and life cycle assessment: A systematic literature review. *The International Journal of Life Cycle Assessment*, *30*(1), 1–19. DOI: 10.1007/s11367-024-02371-1

Zhang, L., Yin, Y., Liu, L., & Yan, S. (2025). Exploring the effects of AR presence and personal norms on museum visitor pro-environmental behaviour intentions. *Scientific Reports*, *15*(1), 25633. Advance online publication. DOI: 10.1038/s41598-025-11119-2 PMID: 40664893

Zhang, M. M., Cooke, F. L., Ahlstrom, D., & McNeil, N. (2025). The Rise of Algorithmic Management and Implications for Work and Organisations. *New Technology, Work and Employment*, *40*(3), 659–671. DOI: 10.1111/ntwe.12343

Zhang, X., Yu, J., Yan, W., Wang, Y., & Subramanian, N. (2023). A Comprehensive Review of Reverse Logistics in the Automotive Industry. *IEEE Access : Practical Innovations, Open Solutions*, *11*, 47112–47128. DOI: 10.1109/ACCESS.2023.3273591

Zhang, Y., Cao, B., Wang, Y., Peng, T., & Wang, X. (2020). When Public Health research meets social media: Knowledge Mapping from 2000 to 2018. *Journal of Medical Internet Research*, *22*(8), e17582. DOI: 10.2196/17582 PMID: 32788156

Zheng, H., & Ma, W. (2021). Click it and buy happiness: Does online shopping improve subjective well-being of rural residents in China? *Applied Economics*, *53*(36), 4192–4206. DOI: 10.1080/00036846.2021.1897513

Zhuo, X., Sun, Y., & Zhou, S. (2025). Impact of Consumers Traceability Awareness on Blockchain Adoption in Supply Chains. *IEEE Transactions on Engineering Management*, *72*, 1140–1153. DOI: 10.1109/TEM.2025.3552437

Zhu, Y., & Wan Hussain, W. M. H. (2025). Artificial intelligence (AI) awareness (2019–2025): A systematic literature review using the SPAR-4-SLR protocol. *Social Sciences & Humanities Open*, *12*(Suppl. C), 101870. Advance online publication. DOI: 10.1016/j.ssaho.2025.101870

Zittrain, J. (2008). *The future of the Internet— and how to stop it*. Yale University Press.

About the Contributors

Theodore Tarnanidis is a professiorial research fellow & marketing scholar, adjunct professor at the International Hellenic University and researcher in Applications of D.Sc. and MCDA. Theodore has six years experience as a marketing and decision making practitioner. He made his post-doc research in the area of sustainable entrepreneurship from the University of Macedonia. He obtained a Ph.D. from the University of London Met., UK. He received his M.B.A from Liverpool University, UK and is a graduate from the University of Macedonia (Business Administration) and Alexander Technological Educational Institute (Marketing). His research focuses on International Marketing, Multi-cultural Marketing, Business Marketing, Consumer science, Marketing Management, Methodology, Advanced Quantitative Methods, Decision Science, Multiple-Criteria Decision Analysis, Management of Education, Sustainable Entrepreneurship. His work has been published in various internationally renowned scientific conferences (Academy of Marketing, European Marketing Academy, PROMETHEE Days, Hellenic Operational Research) and in the Journal of Business Ethics, World Review of Entrepreneurship, Management and Sustainable Development, Journal of Retailing and Consumer Services, Current Issues in Tourism, Marketing Science & Inspirations, European Journal of Educational Management, Management Science Letters, Administrative Sciences and other journals.

Vijaya Kittu Manda has nearly 13+ years of experience in capital markets, financial planning, and investing. He is a Researcher at PBMEIT. He is an Advocate, a technocrat, an academician, a book writer, and a stock market enthusiast. He has 12 University Postgraduate Degrees in various disciplines, ranging from Arts and Humanities, Business Management to Economy, and Computer Science to Psychology. He is a Ph.D. in Management (Finance). His thesis was on Mutual Funds and their Market Competition. His thesis won the prestigious NSE-IEA Best Thesis Award in 2023. He is currently pursuing his second Ph.D. in Computer Science with focus on Blockchain. He contributed over 750 articles to various magazines. He is the Chief Editor for a Management Book Series, is a Peer Review, is a Certified Peer Review Supervisor, is a Session Chair and an Advisor for various academic and industrial conferences. He writes Research Papers and Case Studies, Book Chapters, and sits on Editorial Boards of various publishers. He is a guest speaker for colleges and universities. He serves as the host of a research talk show, PBMEIT Expert Insights, and of mentorship programs under the names Art of Researching, Research Mornings, and Research Evenings.

***

Shivasharana is an Associate Professor at the REVA Business School, REVA University. He has altogether 35 years of experience that includes both Industry and Teaching. In the field of Academics (Teaching), he has worked in various capacities as a Lecturer, Sr. Lecturer, Reader, Assistant Professor, and Head of the Department. He is a Doctorate in the field of Management (Specialized in Operations and Systems). He has taught various subjects and in continuation too. He has published/presented papers at national and international conferences. He is a self-directed, action-oriented professional with over 25 years of experience in education. His educational qualifications are M.Sc. (Mathematics'), MBA (Operations and Systems'), M.Phil. (Management), PGCCA (Computers), Masters in Induction Programming, and Ph.D. (Logistics and Supply Chain Management).

Duggirala Aravind is currently associated with the Department of Aviation, ASET College of Science and Technology, Chennai, India. He previously completed his Bachelor's degree in Electrical and Electronics Engineering at MITS University. His research interests include aviation operations, renewable energy technologies in air transport, Artificial Intelligence, Logistics and Business management. (aravindaset.edu@gmail.com).

Prerna is an Assistant Professor in the School of Commerce and Business Management at Geeta University, Panipat, India. She is UGC-NET qualified and holds a Master's degree in Commerce from Kurukshetra University. With experience in teaching, academic administration, and curriculum coordination, her areas of interest include digital marketing, financial inclusion, rural and sustainable development, and the application of emerging technologies in business and management. She has published research papers in UGC- and WoS-indexed journals and contributed book chapters on contemporary management themes. She is also the holder of Indian and UK design patents and actively participates in national and international conferences and faculty development programs.

Ipek Deveci Kocakoç received her PhD in Econometrics with a major in Industrial Engineering from Dokuz Eylul University, Turkey. Her recent research interests include Data Science, Artificial Intelligence, Scientific Programming and Quantitative methods. She is currently a full time professor at Econometrics Department of Dokuz Eylul University. ORCID: 0000-0001-9155-8269

Suresh G M.Com., NET., M.B.A (FM)., NET., M.A (Eco)., PGDIB., PGDCG., (Ph.D)., working as an Assistant Professor in the Department of Management Science - BBA at Sri Ramakrishna College of Arts & Science (Autonomous), Coimbatore, Tamil Nadu, India. He has qualified the UGC-National Eligibility Test in Commerce twice in June 2019 & December 2019 and Management in June 2023. He is having an experience of 5 years in dedicated teaching at UG and PG level in both Commerce as well as in Management streams. His area of specialization is Accounting and Finance. He published numerous articles in UGC care listed journals & Scopus journals and presented various papers in International and National Conferences. He published two books as author, one book as an editor and published several book chapters.

Deeksha Gupta Ganguly is an accomplished academician with over 14 years of experience spanning academia and industry. She is currently associated with the School of Business and Management, Christ University, Delhi NCR Campus, India. Her professional journey has been shaped by a strong commitment to teaching, research, and institutional development. She has mentored MBA and BBA students in the areas of Human Resource Management, Organizational Behavior, and Management Principles. Dr. Ganguly has actively coordinated academic events, conferences, fests, and alumni meets, fostering strong collaborations with industry leaders and guest speakers. Her research contributions include Scopus-indexed publications and the authorship of a book on Organizational Behaviour. Dedicated to lifelong learning, she regularly participates in Faculty Development Programs and workshops on digital tools, data analytics, and research methods. Before joining Christ University, Dr. Ganguly gained valuable industry experience in business development, marketing, and corporate relations, which continues to enrich her teaching and research perspectives.

Deepak Gupta is a distinguished academician with over 20 years of teaching experience and expertise in Computer Science and Engineering. He holds a Ph.D. in Computer Engineering and has an extensive research portfolio, including many international journal papers, multiple conference proceedings, and several books. His research interests span machine learning, artificial intelligence, and data mining. Currently, Dr. Gupta serves as an Associate Professor and Head of Department of

CSE (Emerging Branches) at ITM Gwalior, MP, India. He has also contributed significantly to the field through patents and copyrights and actively engages as a reviewer, conference chair and editor.

J. Vidhya, an accomplished Assistant Professor with 15 years of academic and 4 years of industry experience, is a university rank holder and gold medalist. Specializing in logistics, IBM, marketing, and entrepreneurship, she has published one Scopus-indexed article in the Q2 journal, three book chapters (Scopus-indexed), four UGC CARE indexed papers, and one in Springer Nature-partnered international journal. She has received six Best Research Paper awards at International conferences. She has received six excellence awards, including Best Mentor (NPTEL) and Best Teacher. As a dedicated scholar, she is a reviewer for two international journals and a co-editor of a book published by IIP. She holds a Master's, M.Phil, and NET qualification, and is pursuing a Ph.D. in digital marketing at Loyola Institute of Business Administration.

M. Mohanraj is an Assistant Professor in the Department of Management Studies at K.S. Rangasamy College of Technology (Autonomous), located in Tiruchengode, Namakkal District, Tamil Nadu. With a strong academic and professional background, Dr. Mohanraj specializes in fostering management expertise among students. His dedication to education and research contributes to the institution's reputation for excellence in management studies.

Manoj Mallick is an Assistant Professor of Psychology with over three decades of teaching and research experience since 1991. His academic interests span positive psychology, mental health, the Indian Knowledge System (IKS), criminal psychology, ethnic diversity, and gender equity. He has also contributed significantly to scholarship in psychological measurement theory, neurodiversity, and institutional accountability, reflecting his commitment to methodological rigor and inclusive practice. His recent publications in leading journals have examined locus of control and psychological well-being among youth in specific socio-cultural contexts, emphasizing the intersection of individual agency and structural determinants. Building on this foundation, his current research explores psychosocial learner support in under-resourced settings, systemic models of school-based counselling, and task-shifting interventions for community mental health. His broader intellectual pursuits include rural women's empowerment through digital micro-enterprises, intersectionality in education and work, resilience in cancer care, psychological safety and emotional intelligence in organizational contexts, socio-psychological implications of Green AI, algorithmic justice and workplace dignity, and the dynamics of cognitive dissonance in decision-making.

He actively participates in national seminars, faculty development programs, and interdisciplinary collaborations across India, advancing scholarship that integrates cultural relevance, ethical clarity, and social impact.

Dhadurya Naik M has worked as Assistant Professor in the Department of Business Administration at Prasad V Potluri Siddhartha Institute of Technology, has also served as Associate NCC Officer with Lieutenant Rank (IT) since 2013, has been teaching for more than a decade, with MBA, MA (Economics), UGC NET (Management)and Ph.d. qualifications. Dr. Naik has published one Scopus, two UGC, seven peer reviewed journals and 14 other national and international journals, has also participated in more than 20 national and international conferences, and has attended 17 faculty development programme and workshops. He has won the best Best NCC Officer Award three times.

Pinar Ozkan, Ph.D., is an Associate Professor of Marketing in the Department of Business Administration at Dokuz Eylul University. She earned her doctoral degree from the same institution. Her academic research focuses on relationship marketing, key account management, consumer behavior, and service marketing. She has numerous peer-reviewed scientific publications in these fields at both national and international levels.

E.Eswara Reddy presently working as Professor in the School of Economics and Comemerce CMR University Bangalore.He has done his M.Com from SV University and MBA frm IGNOU and Ph.D in Commerce from SK University anantapur in 1996. He has completed 29 years of edperience in teaching research and administration in the filed of commerce and manaement

Patil Jaya Lakshmi Reddy is presently serving as an Assistant Professor in the School of Management at CMR University, Bangalore. She obtained her LL.M. from Annamalai University and completed her MBA from Vinayaka University in the year 2011. She possesses over seven years of professional experience encompassing both teaching and administrative responsibilities in the domains of Engineering and Management education.

Amrik Singh is working as Professor and HOD in the School of Hotel Management and Tourism at Lovely Professional University, Punjab, India. He obtained his Ph.D. degree in Hotel Management from Kurukshetra University, Haryana, India. He has published 115 Scopus-indexed publications. He has published 12 patents, and 01 patent has been granted in the inter-disciplinary domain. Dr. Amrik Singh participated and acted as a resource person in various national and international conferences, seminars, research workshops, and industry talks. He has published 20 books with IGI Global Publication, Emerald Publication, Bentham Publication, Nova Publication etc., on trending areas such as Food waste, Artificial Intelligence, Mountain Tourism, Virtual tourism, Healthcare Tourism, Guest behavior in tourism and hospitality. His area of research interest are Accommodation management, sustainability, Green practices, Human Resource Management in Hospitality, Artificial Intelligence, AR VR in hospitality, Hotel pricing, Employee Disability, Work life balance, women empowerment etc. He is currently guiding 8 Ph.D. scholars, and 5 Ph.D. scholars have been awarded Ph.D.

Bruno Sousa is an Professor Coordinator of Marketing at Polytechnic University of Cávado and Ave (IPCA), Portugal and holds a PhD in Marketing and Strategy in Universidade do Minho, Portugal. Bruno Sousa is also Head of Masters Program - Tourism Management and Tourism Marketing (IPCA); CiTUR – Center for Tourism Research, Development and Innovation and UNIAG research member. Bruno Sousa teaching fields include marketing, strategy and tourism. Bruno Sousa research areas include brand management and consumer behavior, strategy implementation, niche marketing, niche tourism and brand attachment. He has published in the Journal of Enterprising Communities, Tourism Management Perspectives, Current Issues in Tourism, Journal of Organizational Change Management, World Review of Entrepreneurship, Management and Sust. Development, among others. Email: bsousa@ipca.pt,

N.V. Suresh, renowned academician from Chennai, Tamil Nadu. He completed his schooling in Chennai. He obtained his BA degree (2012) from D.G.Vaishnav College, Madras University. He joined the Bharathiar University received an MBA degree and PGDM. He Awarded Ph.D. in Management from University of Madras. Dr.N.V.Suresh joined then IIKM in June 2014 as an Assistant Professor (2014 to 2016). He moved to Remo International College in June, 2019 as an Assistant Professor and rose through the ranks to the position of Head of the Department in Aug 2020 to July 2021 then Shifted to Working Academy of Maritime Education and Training (Deemed to be University) Presently Working as Associate Professor and Vice-Principal in ASET College of Science and Technology from March 2022 to Till Date. He is the Visiting Faculty for Institute of Distance Education, University of Madras, Tamil Nadu Open University, Anna University and Directorate of Online Education SRM University for MBA from 2015 to till date. Dr.N.V. Suresh has carried out all his research work entirely in India and has published 30 research papers in international journals.

Muhammad Usman Tariq is a strategic higher education leader and scholar with more than 17 years of international experience across academia, research, and industry. He holds dual doctorates, a PhD in Artificial Intelligence and a Doctorate in Business Administration and has published extensively as the author of research articles, case studies, book chapters, and academic texts. His contributions also include several patents, reflecting his applied research in technology, business, and education. He is the Founder and CEO of TheCaseHQ.com, a global hub for professional certification programmes, narrative and video case studies, and digital learning innovation. In addition, he serves as President of the Gulf Higher Education Network (Gulf HE), an initiative dedicated to advancing academic practice, faculty development, and institutional collaboration across the region. He is a Principal Fellow of Advance HE (UK), Chartered Fellow of the CIPD (UK), Senior Fellow of SEDA (UK), and a Senior Member of IEEE, reflecting his standing as both an academic innovator and a global professional leader.

Index

A

C

D

E

F

G

H

I

L

M

O

P

Q

R

S

T

U

W

Y

www.ingramcontent.com/pod-product-compliance
Lightning Source LLC
LaVergne TN
LVHW061532290926
849162LV00004B/767
* 9 7 9 8 3 3 7 3 8 3 5 7 6 *